Education and Communication for Development

Second Edition

OP Dahama
OP Bhatnagar

Oxford & IBH Publishing Co. Pvt. Ltd.
New Delhi
(*A Unit of* CBS Publishers & Distributors Pvt Ltd)

CBS Publishers & Distributors Pvt Ltd

New Delhi • Bengaluru • Chennai • Kochi • Kolkata • Lucknow • Mumbai
Hyderabad • Jharkhand • Nagpur • Patna • Pune • Uttarakhand

Education and Communication for Development
Second Edition

ISBN-13: 978-81-204-0030-6
ISBN-10: 81-204-0030-5

Reprint: 2017, 2019, 2020, 2022 **2024**

OXFORD & IBH
New Delhi
(*A Unit of* CBS Publishers & Distributors Pvt Ltd)

Published by Satish Kumar Jain and produced by Varun Jain for
CBS Publishers & Distributors Pvt Ltd
4819/XI Prahlad Street, 24 Ansari Road, Daryaganj, New Delhi 110 002, India
Ph: 011-23289259, 23266861, 23266867   Website: www.cbspd.com
Fax: 011-23243014   e-mail: delhi@cbspd.com;
                                          cbspubs@airtelmail.in.

Corporate Office: 204 FIE, Industrial Area, Patparganj, Delhi 110 092, India
Ph: 011-4934 4934   Fax: 011-4934 4935   e-mail: publishing@cbspd.com;
                                             publicity@cbspd.com

Branches

- **Bengaluru:** Seema House 2975, 17th Cross, KR Road, Banasankari 2nd Stage, Bengaluru 560 070, Karnataka, India
  Ph: +91-80-26771678/79   Fax: +91-80-26771680   e-mail: bangalore@cbspd.com
- **Chennai:** 7, Subbaraya Street, Shenoy Nagar, Chennai 600 030, Tamil Nadu, India
  Ph: +91-44-26680620, 26681266   Fax: +91-44-42032115   e-mail: chennai@cbspd.com
- **Kochi:** 42/1325, 1326, Power House Road, Opp KSEB, Power House, Ernakulum Kochi 682 018, Kerala, India
  Ph: +91-484-4059061-65,67   Fax: +91-484-4059065   e-mail: kochi@cbspd.com
- **Kolkata:** 147, Hind Ceramics Compound, 1st Floor, Nilgunj Road, Belghoria, Kolkata-700056, West Bengal, India
  Ph: +91-9096713055/7798394118, 9836841399   e-mail: kolkata@cbspd.com
- **Lucknow:** Basement, Khushnuma Complex, 7 Meerabai Marg (Behind Jawahar Bhawan),Lucknow-226001, UP, India
  Ph: +0522-4000032   e-mail: tiwari.lucknow@cbspd.com
- **Mumbai:** PWD Shed, Gala no 25/26, Ramchandra Bhatt Marg, Next to JJ Hospital Gate no. 2, Opp. Union Bank of India, Noorbaug, Mumbai-400009, Maharashtra, India
  Ph: 022-66661880/89   e-mail: mumbai@cbspd.com

Representatives

• Hyderabad	0-9885175004	• Jharkhand	0-9811541605	• Nagpur	0-9421945513
• Patna	0-9334159340	• Pune	0-9623451994	• Uttarakhand	0-9716462459

Printed at Chaman Enterprises, Daryaganj, New Delhi, India

PREFACE TO THE SECOND EDITION

The concept and philosophy, discipline and profession and theory and practices in the field of Extension Education have gone into a revolutionary changes in the last decade, almost all over the world. However, on the backdrop of these senario of changes and developmental transformation there is a continuously growing demand and dialogue to further improve, design and expand the goals and means of extension—specially in the developing world.

As a result of the need to expand by various technological sectors such as Industrial, Health, Family Welfare and Nutrition, the discipline has become 'technology-neutral'. This means that the professional engaged in Extension Educational task are using the same model (with slight variation) in transforming the technology from their sources of origin to ultimate utilisation. This has created a demand of large number of trained professionals in Extension everywhere—Research establishments, Inputs and Credit supplying institutions and various other services and supporting organisations.

The above situation has created a pressing need of research-based, field and farmers-problem-oriented and multi-disciplinary approach literature, both as reference and field-guide preferably in a single volume. As a result of this, the book *Education and Communication for Development* is in demand cross-culturally and has acquired its place in several technological sectors. Policy makers, planners, scholars and academicians, and field level executors of the development programmes in general and transfer technology in particular have benefited from this book equally.

In the Second Edition two new Chapters have been added and some matter up dated.

The author invites suggestions for improvement and guidance for future revisions.

O.P. BHATNAGAR

FOREWORD

Newer technologies for increasing agricultural production are now becoming available at a much faster rate. But the mechanism for transferring them to the uneducated and small producers in an effective manner does not exist. There is an urgent need for a communication network at the service of the poor farmers in our country like the global communication network which makes the latest findings available without delay to research workers in any particular field. It is not only knowledge that is needed, but an approach which will be able to supply the right knowledge and tools to the right people and at the right time. It is estimated that not more than 15-20. per cent of the available technology reaches our Indian farmers, as against 80-85 per cent in some of the developed countries, though the agricultural universities are attempting this transfer through a number of programmes like the National Demonstrations, Agricultural Operational Research Projects, Krishi Vigyan Kendras and Lab to Land Programme initiated by the ICAR. One of the important lacunae in this field seems to be the lack of socio- econmic research needed to tap economically feasible and socially acceptable technologies. Hence the need is to devise means to remove all bottlenecks in this regard so that knowledge and experience obtained is fully utilised. An insight into the behavioural pattern of the small landowner and landless labour to the newer technologies becomes necessary, if the transfer of technology is to reach optimum levels. Hence this book *Education and Communication for Development*, which is concerned with the deliberate attempts people make to change the attitudes and behaviours of those around them, is very opportune. It follows a behavioural approach and includes conclusions from scientific research in psychology, social psychology, sociology, education, communication and the administration with particular reference to rural development. The Rural Development experiences which are unique and extremely complex in India are available as research publications and reports. Late Dr. O.P. Dahama and Dr. O.P. Bhatnagar have compiled the available material on the subject of Education and Communication in the form of this book, which I think, would be of use to college teachers and trainers of field workers alike.

Indian Council of Agricultural Research,
Krishi Bhawan, New Delhi 110001
(India)

Dr. O.P. GAUTAM
Director-General, ICAR
and Secretary, Department
of Agriculture, Research
and Education

PREFACE TO THE FIRST EDITION

This book is directed to the students and staff of the universities and also to the professional workers in the field who have a genuine career interest in the task of 'Development', whether it relates to an individual, group or community. It has been fully demonstrated that the task of development is a stupendous and baffeling one, yet it has to be accelerated and achieved at a much faster rate. Proper utilisation of available resources depends upon the abilities, capabilities and potentialities of a person to create congenial learning-situation through the gateway of multidisciplinary and interdisciplinary team work. The present work is not the sole effort of the authors but is a compilation of research findings of a large number of academicians, research workers and change agents including students and rural people. The book follows a behavioural approach. Most of the material is derived from scientific research in the field of sociology, psychology, social psychology, education, communication, public administration and the related fields.

The first draft of this volume was prepared in early 1960s and since then the process of accumulation of more work in the related fields and knitting them together continued, resulting in its present form. What is lost during this period is a precious soul, the senior author of the book Dr. O.P. Dahama. This book will keep him alive among the professionals and admirors who loved him so much.

The author is extremely grateful to Dr. O.P. Gautam, Director-General, Indian Council of Agricultural Research and Secretary, Department of Agricultural Education and Research for writing the Foreword to this book. He has been the main spirit behind the revolution of rural education in the country, hence this book is rightly dedicated to him. Our special thanks are due to the National Book Trust for giving subsidy for this book and also to Oxford & IBH Publishing Company for accepting this for publication. Heartiest thanks to all the authors whose works has been incorporated in this book. Respected Mrs. Indra Dahama always remained a great motivational force to the author to the last three decades. She deserves rich tributes and regards, indeed.

Lastly, my wife Mrs. Saroj Bhatnagar and the members of my family, who provided the needed atmosphere to complete this work deserves special appreciation and compliments. Thanks are also due to Dr. C. Prasad, Assistant Director-General, ICAR, Dr. A.P. Saxena, Senior Scientist, ICAR and Mr. V. Kumar Administrative Officer, UNDP for their help and cooperation. Mr. Sunder Shyam who typed the manuscript and took a lot of interest in it needs special mention and thanks.

This book is now in the hands of the users. Critical comments from the users on material presented will go a long way in improving the future editions of this book.

New Delhi

O.P. BHATNAGAR

CONTENTS

Preface to the Second Edition   *iii*
Foreword   *v*
Preface to the First Edition   *vii*

PART I
CONCEPT AND TYPES OF EDUCATION

1. Concept and Types of Education   **3**

What is Education? 3; Behaviour, 4; The Need of Education, 4; Types of Education, 5; Formal Education, 6; Non-formal, 6; Extension Education. 6

2. Non-formal Education   **7**

For Whom is it Intended? 8; For Whom First? 8; Where, When, How and for How Long? 8; What is its Content? 8; What are the Learning Processes? 9; Where Does it Lead to? 9; Main Schemes of Non-formal Education, 10; Non-formal Education for Non-school-Going-Children in the Age Group 6-14, 10; Non-formal Education Programme for Young People in the Age Group 15-25, 12; Functional Development Programme Linked with Development Schemes, 15

3. Extension Education   **19**

Concepts of Extension Education, 19; Philosophy of Extension Education, 21; Principles of Extension Education, 23; Extension Education—A Developed Discipline, 27; Conditions Fostering the Rise of the Discipline, 29; Aims of Extension Education Discipline, 30; Professional Growth of the Discipline, 31; Extension Education and its Relationship with Other Social Sciences, 33; Extension Education—An Applied Behavioural Sciences, 33; Relationship with other Social Sciences, 34; Symbiosis with other Social Disciplines and Practices, 35; Sources and Contribution from Various Disciplines, 36; Conclusion, 37

4. History of Extension Activities   **38**

Extension Activities in India—Early Attempts, 38; Attempts in the Pre-British Period, 38; Efforts by British Government, 38; Work at Shantiniketan, 39; Gurgaon Experiment, 39; Servants of India Society, Poona, 39; Sir Daniel Hamilton's Scheme for Rural Reconstruction, 40; Rural Reconstruction Work by Christian Missions, 40; Marthandam, 40; Gandhian Constructive Programme, 41; Etawah Pilot Project, 42; Andhra Sewa Sangh, Pohri (Gwalior), 43; I.V.S. (Indian Village Service), 43; Sarvodaya Programme, 43; Firka Development Scheme of Madras State, 43; Nibkheri Experiment, 44; Extension Need of Intensive Efforts at National Level, 45; The Programme Was Not New, 45; Organisation upto 1958, 45; Organisation between 1958-65, 46; Intensive Agricultural District Programme, 46; I.A.D.P. versus General Community Development, 47; A Case Study of Raipur I.A.D.P., 48; Extension in Madhya Pradesh—A Case Study, 49; State Agriculture Department and Cattle Improvement, 52; Extension Service by Jawaharlal Nehru Agricultural University, Jabalpur, 52; Extension Abroad, 56; U.S.A., 56; Cooperative Extension Service, 57; Organisation of Extension Work, 57; Organisation Set-up, 60; Israel, 64; Training and Guidance in New Settlements, 64; Working of the Publications Division, 65; Audio-Visual Aid Section, 66; Auxiliary Farms, 66; Taiwan, 68; J.C.R.R., 69; Natural Resources of Taiwan, 69; Multiple Cropping, 69; China, 70; History of Extension, 70; Efforts by Colleges and Universities, 70; National Extension Service, 70; The Peoples Republic of China, 71; Japan, 71; History, 71; Philippines, 73; Republic of Korea, 73; Nepal, 74; Planning, 74; Burma, 74; Ceylon, 75; Pakistan, 75; Aid and Objectives of V-AID, 76; Argentina, 76; Jamica, 78; Greece, 79

5. Role of Teacher, Subject-Matter Specialist and Extension Worker   **80**

Role of Teachers of Agricultural Universities, 80; Role Expectations/ Role Performance Instrument for Teachers of Agricultural Universities, 81; Attributes of a Good Teacher, 82; Role of Subject-Matter Specialist, 84; Training Needs, 85; Problems of Subject-Matter Specialists, 86; Role of Extension Worker, 88; Qualities of an Extension Worker, 90; The Extension Worker as a Communicator, 92

6. Role of Extension Education in Development   **95**

Development Aspects of Extension, 96; Agricultural Extension, 96; Home Science Extension, 97; Uniqueness of the Extension Programme in India, 99; Objectives Behind Extension Education Progromme, 99; Broad Objectives, 99; Specific Objectives, 100; Financing, 100; Extension as a Programme and Process, 100; Field Covered by Extension,

101; Characteristics of Extension, 102; Role of Agricultural Extension in Developing Countries, 102

PART II
EDUCATIONAL PSYCHOLOGY AS APPLIED TO DEVELOPMENT

7. Educational Psychology: Concept and History   **107**

Concept of Psychology, 107; Branches of Psychology, 109; Education and Educational Psychology, 111; General Psychology and Educational Psychology, 111; Historical Development, 112; Nature of Psychology, 113; Methods of Getting Information in Psychology, 113; Scope of Psychology, 114; Educational Psychology as Applied to Education, 115; Objectives and Contributions of Psychology, 116; Aims of Educational Psychology, 117

8. Intelligence   **119**

Nature of Intelligence, 120; Factors Affecting Intelligence, 121; Measurement of Intelligence, 124; Characteristics of a Good Measuring Instrument, 124; Classification of Psychological Tests, 124; Intelligence Tests, 124: Aptitudes Testing, 127

9. Emotions   **129**

What is Emotion? 129; Instinct, 130; Theories of Emotions, 130; Physiological Changes During Emotional States, 132; Expression of Emotions, 132; Emotional Control, 132; Training in Emotional Control, 133; Dealing with Children, 133; Emotional Adjustments in Adults, 134; Emotional Problems of Old Age, 135; A Few Roles for Emotional Control, 135; Importance of the Study in Extension Education, 135

10. Motivation   **137**

Needs which Motivate, 137; Organic Needs or Appetites, 137; Wants, 138; Emotions as Motives, 138; Feelings and Attitudes as Motives, 138; Social Motives, 138; Problems of Adjustment, 139; Types of Adjustment, 139; Common Methods of Adjusting to Frustration, 139; Influencing Other People, 141; Suggestion, 141; Conditions, 141; Techniques of Influencing Others, 142; Effective Speaking, 143; Motivation in Extension, 143; Importance in Extension, 143; Drives, 144; Value Aspects of Motivation, 144, Motivating the Village People, 145; Award and Their Effects in Motivating People in Extension Work, 145; Basic Elements We Need to Know to Motivate the Villagers, 146; Motivating Extension Workers, 147; Research in Motivation, 147; Techniques of Motivation, 148

11. Principles of Teaching and Learning ... 150

Learning, 150; The Learning Process, 150; The Learning Experiences, 150; Laws of Learning, 151; Principles of Learning, 151; Teaching, 152; Teaching Process, 152; Principles for Consideration in Selection of Teaching Methods, 153; Types of Teaching Methods, 153; Teaching how to Acquire Knowledge by Problem Solving, 153; Teaching Manual Skills, 154; Developing Desirable Attitudes for Working with Villagers, 154; Reviewing the Teaching—Learning Process, 155; Types of Tests, 155; Teacher Evaluation, 156; Guidelines for the Teacher, 158; Principles of Teaching, 158; Qualities of a Good Teacher, 151; Suggestions, 159; Essentials of a Teaching Plan, 160; Considerations in Developing Educational Objectives, 160; Learning Experiences, 161; The Teacher, 161

12. The Psychology of Learning ... 163

Theories of Learning, 163; Factors Affecting Learning, 163; Factors which are Within the Control of Learning, 163; Factors to be Taken into Consideration by the Teachers or Extension Workers in Teaching the Learners/Farmers, Housewives, 164; Types of Learning, 165; Conditioning, 165; Verbal Learning, 165; Motor Learning, 165; Perceptual Learning 166; Attitude Learning, 166; Problem Solving, 166; Measuring Learning, 166; Forgetting and Recall, 167; Transfer of Learning, 167; Group Psychology and its Effects on Learning, 168; Principles of Group Dynamics, 168; Problem Solving 169; Adult Learning in Extension, 169; The Power of Adults to Learn, 170; Learning and Goal Formation, 171; The Role of Attitudes, 171; Psychological Factors in Adult Learning, 172; Rapport and Empathy, 172; The Four Basic Wishes, 173; Emotionality and Rationality, 175; Suggestibility and Suspeciousness, 176; Imitativeness and Assertiveness, 176; Group Loyalty and Individualism, 176; Adherence to Tradition and Changeability, 177; Creativity and Pragmatism, 177; Artistry and Devotion to Forms, 178; Religiousness and Scepticism, 178, Relating Negative Traits 179.

13. Other Psychological Concepts ... 182

Development of an Individual, 183; What Determines Human Development? 183; Environment and Maturation After Learning 183; How Psycho-Social Development Stages are Related to Development Tasks? 183; The Senses Provided to the Human Beings, 184; Attention and Perception, 185; Perception, 185; Attention, 185; Factors Determining What We perceive, 186; Cutaneous Senses, 186, The Senses of Taste, 186; Sense of Smell, 187; Thinking, 187; Definition, 187; Mechanics of Thinking, 187; Kinds of Thinking, 187; Avoiding Cloudy

Thinking, 187; Common Pitfalls in Thinking 188; Communication and Group Process, 188; Information Theory, 188; Importance of Feedback in Communication, 188; Group Dynamics, 188; Effective Leadership, 189; Ways of Avoiding the Pitfalls, 189; Education for Democracy, 189; Propaganda, 190; Problems in Group Living, 190; Problems and Causes of Success or Failure of Marriages, 190; Problems of Illegal Behaviour, 191; Crime Prevention, 191; Racial Antogonism, 192; Characteristics of Leaders, 193; Use of Competitions and Co operation in Educational Work, 193, Planning for Effective Competition, 193; How to Improve Group Activity, 193; Rural Psychology and Personality, 193; Factors Determining the Rural Mind, 194; Natural Opposition to Change, 194; Agriculture and Religion, 194; Standing Habits, 195; Conflicts, 195; Basic Principles in Rural Psychology, 195; Personality, 196; Meaning of Personality, 196; Analysis of Personality, 197; Personality Traits, 197; The Process of Self-development, 199; What is 'Self'? 200; Theories of Personality, 200; Teaching Farmers, 201; Durable Conditions for Teaching Farmers, 202: Psychological Barriers, 203; Perception, 204; Communication, 204 Demonstration Dangers, 204; Learning Problems, 204

PART III
RURAL SOCIOLOGY AND PLANNED SOCIAL CHANGE

14. Rural Sociology—Subject-Matter and Importance 207

Definition and Meaning of Rural Sociology, 207: Sociology, 207; Rural Sociology, 207; Nature of Rural Sociology, 207; Rural Sociology as a Science, 209; Limitations, 210; Scope of Rural Sociology, 210: Elements of Rural Sociology, 211; Scope of Rural Sociology in India, 211; Origin and Development of Rural Sociology, 211; Rural Sociology in India, 212; Importance of the Study of Rural Sociology, 213; Science of Human Relationship 213; Importance in Development Programme, 215

15. Important Sociological Concepts 216

Place of Culture in Rural Society, 216; Definition of Culture, 216; Nature and Analysis of Culture, 217; Content of Culture, 217; Functions of Culture, 217; Culture Norms, 218; Mores, 218; Folkways, 218; Laws, 218; Institutions, 219; Conformity to and Deviation from Norms, 219; Culture Patterns, 220; Culture Heritage, 220; Culture History, 221; Culture Diffusion, 221; Cultural Lag, 221; Marginal Man, 222; Ways in which Culture Is Involved in Group Life, 222, Social Action, 222; Elements of Social Action, 222; Social Values, 224; Formation of Social Values, 224; Social Values in Relation to Farming, 227;

Social Control, 228; Agents of Social Control, 228; Rural and
Urban Life, 229; Characteristics of Rural Society, 230; Characteristics of Urban Life, 232; Contrast Between Rural and Urban Life, 232

16. Village Patterns and Modes of Living   **234**

Origin of Villages, 234; Emergence of Villages, 234; First Method, 234;
Second Method, 234; Types of Villages, 235; First Criterion, 235;
Second Criterion, 235; Third Criterion, 236; Fourth Criterion, 236;
Pattern of Settlement, 237; Village Settlement 237; Scattered Settlement, 238; Cross-road Settlement, 238; Line Settlement, 239; Circular Settlement, 241; Regional Settlement, 241; Village Types on Land-ownership Basis, 243; Landlord Villages, 243; Peasant Proprietor's
Villages, 243; Cooperative Villages, 243; Collective Villages, 244;
Other Specialities, 246; What Facilitated the Establishment of
Kibbutzim in Israel, 247; Semi-Collective Village, 248

17. Village Life and Rural Social Institutions in India   **250**

Village Life in India, 250; Concept of Community Life, 250; Structure of Rural Society, 250; Family Life, 251; Family as a Functional
Unit, 251; Family as an Association, 251; Other Forms of Family,
251; The Characteristics of Patriarchial Rural Joint Family, 252;
The Joint Family System, 253; Muslim Family System, 254; Racial
Element, 254: Caste System, 254: Status Groups, 255; Social Distance, 255; Functional Basis, 256; How the Caste System Preserved
and Developed Hindu Society, 256; Rural Social Institutions in
India, 227; Customs, 257; Religion, 258; Major Religions in India,
259; Festivals, 260; Marriage, 262; Rural Act, 266

18. Social Welfare and Welfare Organisation   **271**

Concept of Social Welfare, 271; Theories of the Philanhropic Group,
272; Theories of the Reformist Group, 272; Philosophy of Sarvodaya,
273; Bhoodan, 273; Gramdan, 274; Welfare State, 275; What Are
Fundamental Human Rights? 275; How far India is a Welfare State?
276; Welfare Organisation, 277; Early Welfare Organisations, 277;
Recent Welfare Organisations, 279; International Welfare Organisations Working in India, 281; Aids from the U. S. A., 283; Amenities
and Services for Rural Development, 284; Education, 284; General
Education, 284; Technical Education, 286; Social Education, 286;
Rural Education, 286; Audio-Visual Education, 287; Education of the
Handicapped, 287; Medical Education and Training, 287: Health and
Medical Facilities, 287; Nutrition, 287; Primary Health Centres at
the Block Level, 288; Family Planning/Family Welfare, 288; Water

Supply and Sanitation, 288; Recreation and Utilisation of Leisure, 288.

19. Social Organisation, Disorganisation and Changes in Rural Organisations   291

Social Organisation, 291; Definition; 291; Relationship of Social Organisation with Social Culture, 291; The Status and the Role, 292; Social Process in a Dynamic Society, 293; Social Change in Dynamic Society, 293; Social Control in Dynamic Society, 294; Normality of Social Organisation, 295; Consensus of Social Organisation 296; Social Disorganisation in India, 296; Types of Social Disorganisation, 297; Individual Disorganisation, 297; Family Disorganisation, 299; Community Disorganisation, 300; Changes in Rural Social Organisations in India, 301; Family Life, 302; Caste System, 302; Religion, 303; Marriage, 304; Panchayats, 304; Education, 304; Occupational Mobility, 305; Youth Organisation, 305; Women Organisation, 305; Impact of Development Programmes on Social Organisation, 306; Impact of Transport Facilities, 306; Impact of Community Development, 306; Suggestions 307

20. Planned Social Change   308

Processes of Planned Change, 308; Stimuli Forcing Human Beings to Change, 308: Problem Solving Efforts of Different Strata of Society Compel Change, 309; Notion of Planned Change, 310; Theories of Social and Cultural Change, 310; Contemporary Schools of Thought on the Types or Theories of Social and Cultural Change, 311; Social Behaviouristic Theory of Social and Cultural Change, 311; The Approach of the Change Agent Towards Planned Change, 311; Diagnostic Orientations, 312; Motivations for Change, 312; Resistance to Change, 313; Role of the Change Agents, 313; Methods of Initiating Towards Change, 314; Initiation of Change Sequence, 314; Working Towards Ensuring Change, 315; Working Towards Change, 315: Transfer of Change, 316; Stabilisation of Change, 316; Training the Change Agent, 316; Agricultural Technology and Rural Social Change, 317; Effects of Technology, 318; Innovations in Indian Agriculture, 320; Extension Activities of Agricultural Colleges/Universities and Their Role in Acceleration of Acceptance of Innovation, 322; Impact of Technology on Rural Society, 323 Sources of Information and Their Effectiveness in Adoption of Technology, 325 :Channels of Communications Used by Extension Officers, 325; Influence of Socio-economic Characteristics on the Utilisation of Sources of Information, 326

21. Group Mobilisation and Leadership Development   327

Definition of Group, 327; Occasions for Group Association, 327;

Nature of the Group, 328; Types of Groups, 328; Groups in the Rural Community and Methods of Approach to Them, 329; Group Dynamics, 331; Principles of Working with Groups and Their Mobilisation, 331; Leadership for Development, 331; Concepts Defined, 332; Theories of Leadership, 333; Some Principles of Democratic Leadership, 333; Functions of a Leader, 334; Determinants of Effectiveness in Leadership Functions (Ten 'A's), 335; Factors Determining Effectiveness of a Leader, 335; The Bases of Power for Leadership, 335; Pattern of Farm Leadership, 336; Characteristic of Farm Leaders, 336; Homophily-Heterophily between Leaders, 336; Role of Farm Leaders, 337

22. **Problems of Scheduled Castes, Tribes and Other Backward Classes and India's Approach to it**   339

Social Problems, 340; Economic Problems, 341; Medical and Public Health Problems, 341; Problem of Housing, 342; Problems of Tribes 342; Economic Problems, 342; Communication, 343; Health and Sanitation, 343; Education, 343; Problems of Drink, 343; Solution of the Problems, 343; The Social Service Approach, 344; Political Approach, 344; Religious Approach, 344; Anthropological Approach, 344; State Approach to Tribals, 344

PART IV
COMMUNICATION AND AUDIO-VISUALS FOR DEVELOPMENT

23. **Concept and Functions of Communication**   347

Definitions and Meaning, 347; Communication Can Occur Even Without Uttering Words, 348; Communication—A Two-way Process, 349; Communication Has Many Varieties, 349; Communication Process, 349; Elements, 349; Communication—Complex and Mostly Indirect, 349, Importance of Communication in Extension Work, 349; Communication Models, 350; Other Models of Communication Process, 351; Scope of Communication, 352; Functions of Communication, 353; The Information Function, 353; Command or Instructive Functions, 354; Influence of Persuasive Functions, 354; Integrative Functions, 355; Dimension of Purpose, 355; Conclusion, 356

24. **Communication Channels**   357

Definition, 357; Dimension of Channel, 357; Classification of Channels, 357; The Nature of Channels, 358; Selection of Communication Channels, 360

25. Communicator-Communicattee Relationships   362

Orientation, 362; Empathy, 363; Feedback, 364; Physical Interdependence, 364; Credibility, 364; Interaction, 364; Homophily-Heterophily, 365

26. Feedback in Communication   366

The Feedback Process, 366; Feedback as Resource Orientation, 367; Role of Feedback in Extension Education, 367; Feedback in Communication of Information, 368; Effect of Feedback in Communication of Information, 369

27. Organisational Communication in Agricultural Development   370

Understanding Organisational Communication, 372; Types of Orgasational Communication, 373; Cross-Communication, 373; Downward Communication, 373; Upward Communication, 374; A Few Basic Tips, 375; Some Recent Studies, 376; Conclusion, 378

28. Communication Planners: Role and Training   379

Meaning and Scope of Communication and Communication Planning, 379; Sources of Communication and Resistance, 380; Elements in the Planning Process, 381; Future Role of the Communication Planner, 381; Communication in Support of Development, 381; Extension or Organised Face-to-Face Communication, 381; Technological Options and Prolems of Planning for Future Change, 382; Role and Task of the Communication Planner, 383; Objectives, 384; Approach to Objectives, 384; Qualities of a Communication Planner, 385; Functions, 385; Levels of Planning, 385; Training Strategies and Options, 386

29. Problems in Communication   389

Main Problems in Communication, 389; According to Phases of Communication, 390; According to Various Types of Problems, 391; According to Nature of Problems, 392

30. Interpersonal Communication and the Mass Media in Developing Societies   393

Developmental Issues of Cnmmunication, 393; Integration with Key Sectors of Development, 393; Promotion of False Sense of Optimism, 394; Supportive Role of Media, 394; Communication in Developing Countries, 394: Mass Media are Class Media, 395; Absence of Fit, 396; Impersonal Network, 396

31. Communication Approaches and Audio-Visual Aids 398

Communication and Extension Approaches, 398; Advantages, 399; Group Approach, 399; Mass Approach, 399; Motivating Our Audience, 399; Individuals, 399; Groups, 400; Communication and Extension Methods, 401; Difference in Methods of Extension and Formal Education, 402; How People Can Learn? 403; Methods of Extension Teaching, 404; Personal Group and Mass Approach, 404; How to Select Teaching Tools, 405; Direct Contact, 406; Demonstration, 406; Phase of Demonstrations, 408; Important Tips of Conducting a Good Demonstration, 409

32. Visual Aids 413

Visuals in Information and Communication, 413; Choice of Visuals, 413; Planning for Use of Visuals, 414; Selecting a Theme for Visuals, 414; Layout and Design of Visual Aids, 415; Visual Aids—Non-Projected, 415; Teaching Aids, 416; Display Visuals, 416; Posters, 416; Diagrams, 417; Flip Chart, 422; Flash Cards, 423; Felt-boards, Flannel Graphs or Khaddargraphs, 424; Chalk Board, 424; Bulletin Board, 425; Exhibitions, 426; Visual Aids—Projected, 427; Projectors, 428; Threading the Film, 433; Cameras, 438; Automatic Picture Taking, 440; Handling the Movie Camera, 441; Angle of Filming, 441; Length of Scenes, 441; Editing the Film, 441; Three Dimensional Pictures, 441

33. Audio-Aids Recording 443

Disc Recording, 443; Wire Recording, 444; Tape Recording, 444; How to Operate a Tape Recorder, 445; Useful Hints for the Operator, 446; Uses of a Tape Recorder, 448; Ten Features to Look for in a Tape Recorder, 449; Public Address Equipment, 450; Operating the Public Address Equipment, 451; Radio, 451; Handling a Radio Set, 452; Power for Radios, 452; Installing a Radio, 452; Operating a Radio, 452: Nature of the Medium, 453; Use, 453

34. Other Teaching Aids 455

Puppets, 455; Drama, 456; Folk Songs and Folk Dances, 457; Use of Talks, Meetings, Conferences, Tours, Campaigns, Camps, etc., for Extension, 457; Talks, 457; Meetings, 461; Conferences, 463; Tours, 465; Campaigns, 466; Village Camps, 467; Journalism in Extension Work, 472; Scope 473, Functions of Journalism, 473

35. Communication Through Written Words 475

Need for News to Our Client System, 476; Writing for Newspapers,

477; Feature Stories, 478; Practical Examples, 478; Leaflet, Pamphlet and Bulletins, 480; Circular Letters, 480; Writing for a Radio Talk, 481

36. Communication Through Satellite   483

Evolution of Satellite Communication, 483; Indian Space Research Organisation, 483; Aryabhata, 483; Bhaskara, 483; Rohini, 483; Space Application Centre, 484; Satellite Instructional Television Experiment, 484; Satellite Telecommunication and Experiments Project, 484; Indian National Satellite 484, Software for the Satellite Communication, 485

PART V
PROGRAMME PLANNING AND FIVE-YEAR PLANS

37. Programme Planning   489

Meaning and Principles of Programme Planning, 489; Extension Programme, 489; Components of Programme Planning, 490; Principles of Programme Planning as Applied to Extension Programme, 490; Basic Principles Used in Educational Planning, 491; Abilities Needed by Planners, 492; Programmes Projection, 494; Objectives of Programme Projection, 494; Programme Planning and Programme Projection, 494

38. Developing a Plan of Work   495

Definition and Analysis of the Concept, 495; Why Have A Plan of Work—Importance and Scope in Extension, 496; Plan of Work—A Format or A Model, 496; Elements of the Plan of Work, 497; Prerequisites for Developing a Plan of Work, 498; Farm and Village Agricultural Production Plans, 499; Farm Planning, 499; Village Agricultural Production Plan, 503; Guidelines for Developing a Written Annual Plan of Work, 504; Selecting Methods and Structuring Learning Experiences, 505; Criteria for Judging the Plan of Work, 512

39. A Plan for Improved Procedures of Programme Development in India   515

Steps, 515; Who is to Build the Extension Programme? 516; Constituting A Programme Building Committee, 518, Stepping up Objectives, 519; Plan for Carrying out the Programme, 519; Problem Regarding Fixing of the Targets, 520; Coordination of Various Servi-

ces in Community Development and Extension, 525; Important
Aspects of Coordination, 525; How a National Programme is Deve-
loped, 527; National Plans in India, 529; Basic Plans in India, 529;
National Planning Committee, 530; Government Planning in India,
530; The Planning Machinery and Method of Making Plans, 530;
Planning Commission, 531; Planning Machinery, 532; Five-Year and
Annual Plans, 533; Fifth Five-Year Plan, 534; Objectives of Different
Plans, 536; Strategy of the Plans, 537; Achievements During Plans,
537; Weaknesses in Our Planned Programme, 539; Suggestions, 540;

PART VI
DEVELOPMENT PROGRAMMES

40. **Community Development Programme**   543

The Problem, 545; The Community, 546; Development, 546; Com-
munity Work, 546; Self-Determination, 546; Community Pace, 547;
Growth in Community Capacity, 548; The Will to Change, 548;
Major Divisions of Community Works, 548; Analysis of the Term—
Community Development, 550; Essential Elements of Community
Development, 551; Faiths Behind Community Development, 552;
Objectives of the Community Development Programme, 552; Philo-
sophy Behind Community Development Programme, 553; Approach
to Rural Development in a Democratic Society, 553; Types of Com-
munity Development Programmes, 555; Integrative Type, 555;
Adaptive Type, 556; Project Type, 557; Principles of Community
Development and Community Organisation, 558; Community
Development Processes, 560; Extension Education, 560; Community
Organisation, 560; Establishing Rapport in the Community, 561;
Appraising the situation—Identifying Problems and Needs, 561;
Planning the Programme and Projects, 562; Selecting Initial Projects
and Long-run Projects, 562; Securing Participation of the People and
Involving Them, 562; Developing Effective Communication Channels,
563; Developing and use of Organisation Channels, 567; Developing
Adequate Community Leadership, 578; Scope of Community Deve-
lopment, 581; Speciality of Farming Occupation, 582; Limitations,
583; Weakness in the Community Development Programme and
Suggestions for Improvement, 584; Abolition and Revival of Posts of
BDOs in Madhya Pradesh, 590; The Challenges to the Scientists,
590; Expert Views on the Weakness of the Community Development
Programme, 592; Similarities and Dissimilarities Between C.D. and
Extension Education, 593; Objectives, 593; Processes, 594; Form, 594;
Cultural Factors in Community Development, 595; How the Know-
ledge of These Factors Affects Community Development Work, 595;
Role of the Community Development Worker, 598; Role as a Guide,

598; Role as an Enabler, 600; Role as an Expert, 602; Role as a Therapist, 602; Difference Between an Extension Worker and a Community Development Worker, 603

41. Case Studies of Community Development Programmes of Different Countries   604

C.D. in India: Progress and Prospects, 604; Programme Pattern, 604; Finance, 606; Expenditure Under the Plans, 606; Policy, 606; Advisory Body, 606; Organisation, 606; Community Development in the Philippines, 607; Set-up and Working, 607; Community Development in Egypt, 607; Community Development in Iran, 608; Community Development in Formosa, 608; Community Development in Peurto-Rico, 609; Community Development in Pakistan, 609; Community Development in Thailand, 610; Community Development in Thaiwan, 611; Impact of Community Development Programme on Rural Life in India, 612; Awareness of Community Development Programme, 612; Adoption of Improved Practices, 612; Communication with the Outside World, 613; Institutional Development, 614; Leadership Development, 615

42. Other Rural Development Programmes in India   616

Agricultural Development Programmes, 616; Intensive Agricultural District Programme, 616; High Yielding Varieties Programme, 616; Drought Prone Areas Programme, 617; Whole Village Development Programme, 617; Sectoral Development Programme, 618; Tribal Development Block, 618; Pilot Project for Tribal Development, 618; Hill Areas Development Programmes, 618; Animal Husbandry, 618; Cattle and Dairy Development, 618; Sheep Development, 619; Poultry Development, 619; Piggery Development, 620; Fisheries Development, 620; Integrated Rural Development Programme, 620; Criteria for Selection of District, 620; The Guidelines for Action, 621; The Planning Phase, 621; Providing an Operational Base, 622; Task Adoption at Planning Phase, 623; Programme Implementation, Coordination and Monitoring, 623; Self-replicating Model of Rural Development, 624; District Rural Development Agency (DRDA), 625; Council for Advancement of Rural Technology (CART), 627; National Agricultural Research and Extension Projects, 629; National Agricultural Research Project (NARP) 629; National Agricultural Extension Project (NAEP), 630

PART VII
EXTENSION, ADMINISTRATION AND TRAINING

43. Administration   635

Administration: Trends, 635; Public Administration, 636; Concepts in

Public Administration, 636; Public and Private Administration, 637;
Nature of Public Administration, 637; Characteristics of Public
Administration as a Social Science, 638; Purposes of Public Adminis-
tration, 638; Scope of Public Administration, 639; Functions of Public
Administration, 640

44. Administration and Organisation   **641**

Meaning of Organisation, 641; Organisation of Organisation, 641;
Concepts of Organisation, 642; Formal and Informal Organisations,
642; Units of Organisation, 642; The Hierarchy, 645; Span of Control,
646; Delegation of Authority, 646; Integration vs Disintegration, 648;
Centralisation vs Decentralisation, 649; Coordination, 651; Administrative Control, 654; Factors Influencing Coordination, 655; Building
an Organisation, 655; Organisation of the Development Department,
656; Problems of Public Administration, 657; Basis of Organisation,
657

45. Personnel Administration   **659**

Definition, 659; Problems of Personnel Administration, 659; Recruitment of Extension Workers, 659; Types of Requirement, 640; Selection, 661; Classification of Positions, 663; Maintenance of Efficiency
and Morale, 664; Development of Code of Ethics, 671; Principles to
be Included in Code of Ethics, 672; Supervision, 672; Administrative
Areas and Field Services, 679; The Headqurters and Field Services,
679; General and Administrative Areas, 680; Factors Determining the
Formation of Government Areas, 680; Criteria of the Suitability of
Governmental and Administrative Areas, 681; Field Organisation,
681; Various Patterns of Field Organisation, 681; Reasons for the
Growth of Field Organisation, 682

46. Training Principles and Practices   **684**

Meaning of Training, 684; Education Versus Training, 685; Impor-
tance of Training, 685; Need for Training, 686; Types of Training for
Extension Workers, 687; Training Process, 688; Principles of Exten-
sion Training, 689; Nature of Training, 690; Problem and Prospects
of Training, 698; Training of Villagers and Professionals in Technical
Things, 692; Training of the Farmers, 692; Training for Farmers'
Sons, 692; Ministry of Agriculture and Irrigation, 693; Directorate of
Extension (Department of Agriculture), 693; Indian Council of
Agricultural Research, 695; Krishi Vigyan Kendra, 695; Training
Programmes, 696; Organisation Aspects, 696; Staff Development
Programme, 698; Trainers' Training Centres, 698; Organisation
Aspects, 698; Department of Rural Development, 699; Ministry of

Education and Social Welfare, 699; Department of Education—Youth Services Wing, 699; Nehru Yuvak Kendras, 700; National Service Scheme, 700; Department of Social Welfare, 700; Ministry of Labour, 701; Constraints on Development of Rural Youth Programmes, 701; Mobilisation of Rural Youth in Agricultural Production and Other Development Programmes, 702; Workshop Wings, 703; Khadi Gram Udyog Bhavan, 703; Auxiliary Courses, 703; Developing Course Syllabus, Course Objectives and Lesson Plans, 703; Course Syllabus, 703; Factors for Consideration in Planning a Course of Study, 704; Instructions Regarding Examinations and Tests, 704; Other Instructions, 704; Steps in Selecting Course Content, 705; Characteristics of Good Teaching Objectives, 705; Considerations for Deciding Objectives, 706; Preparing Lesson Plans, 706; Essentials of a Teaching Plan, 706

47. **Training and Visit System (T&V)**   **709**

Objectives of the Training and Visit System, 709; Basic Assumptions 710; Monitoring and Evaluation 711; Organisational Structure, 711

Abbreviations and Titles of Development Programmes in India   *713*
Appendix A   *720*
Appendix B   *722*
Bibliography   *725*
Author Index   *731*
Subject Index   *733*

PART I

CONCEPT AND TYPES OF EDUCATION

CHAPTER 1

CONCEPT AND TYPES OF EDUCATION

The general notion of education a few thousand years ago was that of someone assigning lessons to a group of young people and punishing them for their mistakes. But now with the introduction of several communication media in transferring the sophisticated knowledge into simple and understandable form and with substantial changes in the educational norms as well as the norms of the teachers, the system of education is moving towards a speedy evolution.

WHAT IS EDUCATION ?

Education is the process of bringing desirable change into the behaviour of human beings. It can also be defined as the process of imparting or acquiring knowledge and habits through instruction or study. When learning is progressing towards goals that have been established in accordance with a philosophy which has been defined for, and is understood by the learner, it is called 'Education'.

If education is to be effective it should result in changes in all the behavioural components (Fig. 1.1).

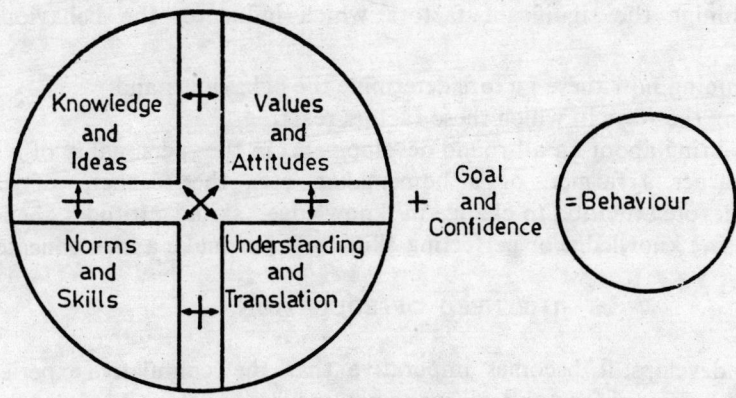

Fig. 1.1. Behavioural components

The behavioural changes must be directed towards a desirable end. They should be acceptable socially, culturally and economically, and result in a change in knowledge, skill, attitude and understanding. Thus, in education, the greatest emphasis should be placed on the behavioural component of an individual.

Behaviour

The behaviour of an individual, in a broad sense, refers to anything the individual does. This is goal-oriented, it includes the goals one selects and the means one chooses to achieve these goals and, as such, it is action-oriented.

Parsons and Shils (1965) proposed a theory of action which could serve as a conceptual model for the analysis of human behaviour. They say that:

(i) Behaviour is oriented to the attainment of ends or goals or other anticipated state of affairs;

(ii) It takes place in a situation;

(iii) It is normatively regulated; and

(iv) It involves expenditure of energy or effort or motivation.

According to Leagans (1961), behaviour refers to what an individual knows (knowledge), what he can do (skills—mental and physical), what he thinks (attitudes) and what he actually does (action).

Behaviour is, therefore, a function of the person in interaction with the situation. The factors motivating behaviour either in the person or situation, are:

(i) An environmental determinant;

(ii) The internal urge, wish, feeling, emotion, drive, instinct, need, want, desire, demand, purpose, interest, aspiration or motive which gives rise to the action; and

(iii) The incentive or goal which attracts or repels an organism.

When the relationship between environmental and behavioural components are not identifiable, some hypothetically intervening variable is postulated to account for the behaviour. Thus, individual variations do exist in the learner's behaviour. His behaviour is extremely difficult to predict.

In the experimental analysis of human behaviour, three fundamental problems arise:

(1) Determining the significant factors which influence the behaviour under investigation;

(2) Determining how these factors determine the behaviour; and

(3) Deciding the ways in which these factors react.

In order to bring about an all-round development in the personality of a student, a trainee or learner, a farmer, or a homemaker, etc., the teacher, or extension worker must devote attention to change in knowledge, skills, attitudes, beliefs, etc. Merely increasing knowledge or perfecting skills will not make a man educated.

THE NEED OF EDUCATION

As society develops, it becomes imperative that the cumulative experience and the knowledge necessary for political, economic, social and other development should be passed on to new generations, or to the people who need this knowledge. The accepted customs, norms, values, skills, which are required to be preserved need to be passed on to successive generations. It is the need for education that gradually gave rise to a philosophy of education.

Education as a learning experience has several facets. Before these facets are examined, the basic proposition that education is a learning experience needs some examination. Education comprises instruction, teaching, information gathering, knowledge gathering and transmittance, study and reflection, discussion, demonstration and the formulation of pilot programmes. What is common to these several forms of education in which one individual confronts another or several others, or in which an individual is placed face to face with a book, film, museum or experiment, is that they are means of acquiring knowledge and/or information. In these various forms, it is possible to distinguish between the bits and pieces of knowledge and information acquired, and the process of acquiring them. The former is intellectual baggage and the latter is what is termed the learning process.

Learning has several objectives. At the highest and most idealistic plane, learning entails becoming a whole and complete man, physically, mentally and spiritually; learning how to create a pathway to knowledge which continues to evolve throughout the course of one's life is yet another grand objective. Defending oneself against exploitation by the dominant classes, understanding the conflicts in and between societies and the utilising of collective action by those who are powerless and hungry are the other facets of the new education.

Learning also has a more specific, and relevant objective, namely, To Do, By Doing, and For Doing. Learning To Do refers to two interrelated activities, learning and doing. They comprise: (a) the formation of new ideas or new combinations of existing ideas, which we call learning; and (b) purposeful activity, leading from one overriding purpose to another, which may be called doing. These activities are interrelated for the union of learning with doing results in the socialisation of the ideas and the purposes of the activity. Learning To Do, unlike learning *per se* cannot be self-centred, and, unlike doing along, cannot be wasteful or self-serving.

Learning To Do permeates all forms and types of education. In adult education as well as in all out-of-school and out-of-college education, the work situation through which learning is acquired is there at hand.

The main task is to design the curriculum around the concepts and resultant skills that conform to the various forms of work. This is a hard exercise because it is innovative, individual and informal. It is innovative because there are no prior models that can be copied or adopted. It is individual because the learning programme for each new case will be different from the others. It is informal because it does not have the pomp and paraphernalia surrounding formal degrees and diplomas and their false promises of attractive employment and rewarding remuneration.

TYPES OF EDUCATION

With the development of society, education has taken many shapes, such as: (a) Child Education, (b) Adult Education, (c) Technical Education, (d) Education in the Humanities and Social Sciences, (e) Education in the Arts and Crafts, (f) Health Education, (g) Physical Education, and several others. The other broad classification of education could be: (1) Formal Education, (2) Non-formal Education, and (3) Extension Education, which will be discussed in succeeding parts of the book.

Formal education

Formal Education is basically an institutional activity, uniform and subject-oriented, full-time, sequential, hierarchically structured, leading to certificates, degrees and diplomas.

Non-formal

Non-formal Education, is *not formal*, which means:
It is flexible.
It is life, environment and learner-oriented.
It is diversified in content and method.
It is non-authoritarian.
It is built on learner-participation.
It mobilises local resources.
It enriches human and environmental potential.

Extension education

This new term Extension Education combines both adult education and informal education. It is concerned with educating adults, i.e., farmers or homemakers, not in the letters and alphabet, grammar or language, but in the techniques of raising better crops, better animals, better fruit trees, managing the home in a more efficient way, rearing children scientifically, taking care of the nutrition of the family, etc.

The areas of our concern can be defined thus:

(a) Agricultural Extension—extending knowledge to the agriculturists;

(b) Veterinary and Animal Husbandry Extension—extending knowledge about breeding, managing, feeding and care of animals, and birds, etc;

(c) Agricultural Engineering Extension—extending knowledge about agricultural machinery such as tractors and pumps, the levelling of land, water use, soil conservation, etc;

(d) Home Science Extension—extending technical knowledge to farm wives, or ladies in urban and rural areas on food. child care, home decoration, kitchen gardening;

(e) Industry Extension—extending knowledge on the managing and running of industries.

Similarly it can be sanitation and health extension, or any area which seeks to extend technical and scientific knowledge to a client system or the audience or the people who are to be educated along the lines of the innovations developed in the respective technological disciplines.

CHAPTER 2

NON-FORMAL EDUCATION

Mere reliance on Formal Education cannot cover all the educational needs in India, and it is disproportionate both to the growing quantitative requirements and to the increasing demands for greater relevance of education. Therefore, the Central Advisory Board of Education endorsed this proposal and made the following recommendations:

(1) The exclusive emphasis on the formal system of education should be given up and a large element of Non-formal education should be introduced within the system. Multiple-entry and programmes of part-time education have to be adopted in a big way. At the secondary and university stages, part-time and correspondence education should be developed and all encouragement given for programmes of self-study.

(2) Programmes of adult education are of great significance for the success of the programme of universalisation of elementary education, as well as for securing the intelligent participation of the people in all programmes of National Development. They should, therefore, be developed on a priority basis. In particular, the Board recommends that the Functional Literacy Programme which represents the single largest on-going effort of intensive Non-formal Education linked to a developmental activity, should be strengthened and expanded; and that similar functional literacy programmes should be developed in relation to other developmental schemes appropriate to rural and urban situations. The Board further recommends that adult education programmes should form an in-built part of every developmental activity whether in the rural or urban, public or private sector, and that every Central and State Ministry/Department should make appropriate provision in the respective schemes.

(3) Adequate financial allocations should be made in the State Plans for non-formal education for the age group 15-25 on the basis of well-defined norms set up by the State Governments (Broad guidelines on the subject may be given by the Government of India).

(4) The programme should be flexible, diversified and functionally related to the needs and interests of youth and should equip them for participation in developmental activities.

(5) During the year 1974-75, all efforts were made to begin the programme in.

(a) one district in each State with Central assistance, and (b) at least one additional district with State funds.

(6) By the end of the Fifth Plan efforts were made to cover at least six to seven million illiterates in this age group.

For whom is it intended?

Non-formal education is intended for all age groups and sections of society—children, youth and adults; working men and women; the unemployed and those with leisure; the illiterate, semi-literate, literate or educated; urban or rural people. This means that all categories of people if and when they need, if and when they want—should be in a position to have access to non-formal opportunities for learning. Those who are in formal education or who have benefited from it, may also need non-formal education for personal fulfilment, professional growth, or deeper understanding.

For whom first?

First priority is now being given to those who have been neglected for a long time, the group of out-of-school youth for whom practically no learning facilities are available, but whose potential for the country's development is most precious and vital.

The emphasis in the Fifth Five Year Plan, therefore, is on providing non-formal education opportunities to youth in the 15-25 age group. Of the 90 million youth in this age-span, nearly 50 million are illiterate and another 20 million are semi-literate; a large proportion of them live in rural areas under deprived and under-privileged circumstances.

This programme is now being started in one district of each of the 24 States/Union Territories with Central Government funds. State Governments are also starting the same kind of programme in one or more districts with their own funds.

Where, when, how and for how long?

Non-formal Education Programmes can be organised wherever it is most convenient to learners.

The classes could be held whenever possible—in the mornings, afternoons, late evenings or on holidays. The courses could be continuous, extending over a long period with a shorter duration each day, or for a shorter term with longer hours each day, or as a recurrent course spread out over two or three summers or at convenient intervals. The exact timings and the length of the classes should be governed by the environmental conditions as well as the learners' work and occupational schedule, also important is the interest, need and will of the learners. The duration of classes may be prolonged or cut short as required.

What is its content?

By its very nature, the content of the Non-formal Education Programme is related to the specific social, cultural, economic and environmental needs of each learner group.

This means that the curriculum is flexible, diversified and responsive to contemporary national problems, current community issues and prevailing learner concerns In any case, it should present a fair balance of major national, community and individual goals and interests.

As it is inter-disciplinary and since it is made up of several elements according to the environmental and learner requirements, no person can handle the programme single-handed. The programme, therefore, envisages the mobilisation of resources and persons drawn from various disciplines, as well as the use of multi-media. Instructors would include employed and unemployed educated youth, skilled workers and technicians, educated and progressive farmers, social workers, retired persons, educated housewives, university, college and school teachers and students, personnel from teacher training colleges, craftsmen and artisans.

What are the learning processes?

Learning in a Non-formal Education Programme takes place through:

Democratic discussion and dialogue

Critical analyses of factors in the environment

Self-analysis and reflection leading to understanding

Autonomous selection of information and cognizance

Acquiring of new communication potential such as reading, writing and calculating capabilities

Action programmes and community activities

Training in practical skills

Sharing experiences

Relating education to life, social and work experiences.

In short, it should be an exciting, revealing and profitable experience. Non-formal education should not be:

Authoritarian and imposed

Abstract and theoretical

Mechanical and routine

Unrelated to the concerns and interests of learners.

Where does it lead to?

Non-formal education processes and programmes should, in the long run, lead to:

Creating an awareness, in individuals and society, of the prevailing environmental situations and the need for and direction of change.

Cultivating a rational, objective and scientific temper.

Enriching human potential and thereby increasing community resources, and promoting individual and group creativity.

Increasing the functional relevance of learning both to the learners and to the community.

Achieving a greater degree of individual, social, cultural and economic development through democratic action and active participation.

Building a learning environment in which every individual shall have equal opportunity for continuing self-learning.

A better sharing of opportunities and social wealth and particularly, a more equitable and just distribution of knowledge among various sections of society.

Who can help?

The answer to this is that everyone can help.

Legislators *by* political action;

Administrators *by* planning and implementation;

Developmental agencies *by* integrating education with development;

Industry and business *by* offering physical and material facilities;

Professional bodies *by* exploration of new methodologies;

Institutions for formal education *by* opening their doors to the non-formal education of the community;

Mass media *by* giving motivational and follow-up support;

Educated men and women *by* donating their time and labour;

Teachers and students *by* teaching, mobilising resources, organising classes, guiding and assisting the learners; and

Educational institutions and specialists *by* preparing teaching/learning materials.

MAIN SCHEMES OF NON-FORMAL EDUCATION

The Fifth Five Year Plan's educational strategy was built on the assumption that formal and non-formal education should be correlated and integrated. Since in a country like India with its enormous educational needs, formal education through full-time and institutional education alone cannot be sufficient for the achievement of major educational objectives. However, non-formal education should not follow the same pattern and methods as the formal systems but should adopt new flexibilities and adaptations to real learning needs. It must be developed for all categories of learners and at all levels of education. The main emphasis will be laid on the following programmes:

(1) Non-formal education for non-school going children in the age group 6-14;

(2) Non-formal education for youth in the 15-25 age group;

(3) Functional literacy linked with development schemes.

(1) Non-formal education for Non-school-going children in the age group 6-14

Part-time programme and multiple point entry

The universalisation of primary education is certainly one of the major, if not the major, national goals in the whole educational sphere.

Indian primary education, both for the 6-11 and for the 11-14 age groups, has its bright sides and shadows:

(a) Although the enrolment in elementary education rose between 1950 and 1973, from 22.3 million to 78.8 million, there are many millions of children still to be enrolled in primary schools;

(b) Although a very large percentage of children start elementary education, a considerable number of drop-outs, even at a rather early stage, is decreasing the positive effects of primary schooling; and

(c) Although the network of primary schools has practically covered all areas, there are millions of children who for various reasons (mainly socio-economic, but educational as well) are missing elementary education.

In spite of the availability many children are not enrolled in primary schools for reasons like the necessity to work (numerous children are not only working at home or on the family farm, but are also employed in handicrafts, industries, shops etc.) or (particularly in the case of girls) the need to take care of younger children inpove s ty-stricken families.

Many other children are not enrolled or leave school at an early stage because there are prejudices against formal schooling. Many pupils, as well as their parents, have the feeling that the existing curriculum is neither relevant to their needs, nor suitable to their interests, and, in addition, the ways of formal education are often unattractive and even loathsome to them. Parents, particularly in families where the children are the first generation of learners, often cannot perform their educational and motivational roles.

Therefore, universalisation of primary education necessitates economic measures, social promotion, improvement of the existing school education, parents' education and the search for new educational alternatives in order to attract non-school-goers and early school-leavers. Here we are concerned only with the last aspect.

Basic objectives

The basic objective is to offer elementary education to children who cannot afford it under existing circumstances and modalities, particularly through: (1) Part-time instruction for children who cannot follow full-time programmes; (2) The possibility of multiple entry into primary schools at later stages (at the age of 9, 11 or even 14); (3) Remedial programmes for so-called drop-outs. There are already interesting experiences in this respect ("Three-hour Schools", or evening classes for "Working Children", or schools functioning as "Community Centres", etc.) which should be studied, popularised and utilised on a large scale.

Beneficiaries

Different categories of children and youngsters may benefit from these different programmes and facilities:

(a) Children in the age group 6-11 who are not in a position to follow full-time, regular primary school instruction;

(b) Children in the age group 6-11 who have left primary education after a few years of schooling;

(c) Illiterate children in the age group 11-14, who have not had the chance to be enrolled in the primary schools, or have left them after one or two years only; and

(d) Literate children in the age group 11-14 who for various reasons, after having completed class V, are not continuing their education through the formal system.

The educational needs of these children may vary. Some may be interested in returning to educational institutions and continuing their regular education, others may be more inclined towards receiving some basic additional knowledge and know-how, as well as acquiring a broad understanding of different aspects of work life so as to prepare for it. Various methods of non-formal education for children in these age groups should be devised, so as to meet the educational needs of all these categories.

Programmes

The programme for the beneficiaries in the 6-14 age group cannot be uniform as there is diversification of interest and concern in the group. They should be adapted both to the different children's groups and to the varying environments. There are, in reality, two main categories of programmes:

(1) Part-time primary education, meant to enable out-of-school children to join the main stream of formal education. These programmes will practically follow the same curriculum as in regular schools, with a shorter duration due to the children's age, maturity and experiences; and

(2) Non-formal education, meant to cover the various educational needs of non-school going children or "drop-outs". These programmes will need to be differentiated, based on conditions prevailing in various environments and oriented to help children improve their work, earnings, health, family life, understanding of the natural and social surroundings, etc. These programmes should be of various durations, using different learning and instructional materials and methods.

Instructional materials

A portion of the learning and teaching materials can be the usual textbooks and other aids utilised in formal primary education. But, the need will gradually arise for new types of didactic materials as the content of learning for this age group has to be enlarged and made more practical, and also adapted more to the psychological and mental traits of working children, drop-outs, etc.

Agencies

Community support will come through the provision of learning facilities as well as through the adaptation of the programme to community needs. The agencies will be the same as for formal education: primary and middle schools, primary school teachers and existing supervisory machinery at the State and District levels.

(2) Non-formal education programme for young people in the age group 15-25

This scheme is of paramount importance and had a priority role in the Fifth Five Year Plan period. Its implementation should be the joint effort of the Central Government, State Governments and voluntary organisations.

The problem

The largest portion of the youth in the 15-25 age group which is illiterate or semi-literate have either not got involved in the primary schools at all, or have left primary school at an early stage. The members of this group play a very important role in society. They are often engaged in economically productive occupations and not only render socially useful services, but are involved in many community activities as well. Most young people get married and make a home and start a family in this age span and they are thus in the most dynamic stage, imbibed with both the potential and the thirst for learning.

Past experience has shown that a programme which is based purely on, and limited to, literacy does not attract and hold the attention of the illiterate. Past experience has also shown that, particularly in rural areas, out-of-school educational activities should not be developed in isolation, but in close correlation with family and community life, as well as with various development programmes. It is, therefore, essential to relate the educational content to the needs, interests and environment of the persons for whom it is intended to make it as functionally relevant as possible and also to link such a programme to the other social and economic in puts in a rural or urban community. It should form the "Educational Component" in schemes such as food production, water supply, agrarian reform, resettlements, employment programmes, generation of self-employment, family planning, small scale industry, sanitation, various minimum needs programmes, etc. This will be a departure from the previous literacy courses, in the sense that it will be a composite programme of non-formal education, including literacy.

Motivation and encouragement

Motivation should be intrinsic, based on the internal and practical needs of young people. This is why: (a) programmes should be diversified, in order to correspond, as much as possible, to the different environments, interests and needs of various categories of boys and girls; (b) starting from a general framework and proto-type learning material, adaptation of the curriculum should be founded on a survey of each environment.

This type of non-formal educational programme needs a lot of encouragement, both before (political and moral support, psychological preparation, etc.), and during the implementation of the programme (use of attractive methods, cultural and outdoor activities, excursions, etc.). The learners involved in non-formal educational programmes should get some priority treatment such as employment, job promotion, credit facilities, fertiliser distribution, new seed varieties, etc.

There is another type of motivation which is certainly advisable. This is the opportunity to be provided to non-formal learners (the best of them) to gain admission (on the basis of a test or other examination) to formal education or higher types of vocational, professional, non-formal, training facilities. For the time being, in the Indian system, the interlink between the formal and non-formal is practically non-existent and at best marginal. A lot of improvement and innovation has to be done in this respect.

Agencies

In the implementation of this programme there is a role for a variety of institutions and agencies—schools. vocational institutions of all categories, Nehru Yuvak Kendras, Youth Clubs, Agricultural Training Centres, Industrial Training Institutes, Institutions for Health Education, Family Planning Centres, various voluntary organisations, Village Literacy Centres, Farmers' Functional Literacy Project Centres, local skill training facilities, social service schemes, libraries, local non-governmental schemes for rural development or social welfare, and many other "potential" institutions and individuals whose contribution to such a vast and multifaceted programme is essential.

Contents

It is evident that the content of the programme has to be complex:

(a) It has enabled the participants to get the basic understanding of the social and environmental structure around them, based on an elementary scientific knowledge and mode of thinking;

(b) It must encourage a positive set of attitudes towards themselves, their fellow-men, and their society;

(c) Equally, it should enable them to participate in the local economy through employment or self-employment, and also improve their way of living; and

(d) Finally, it has to equip them mentally and functionally to raise a family and run a household.

The emphasis of the learning-teaching process is not so much on accumulation of knowledge or skills, but more on aptitudes and attitudes for problem-solving, and for active participation in the surrounding environment.

Curriculum

The curriculum will contain:

(a) Information and knowledge about the living environment and the development process in the country;

(b) Basic knowledge for understanding various social, economic, scientific and technological changes in the midst of which the youth has to live and work, and to which he has to adjust in terms of knowledge and skill, in order to play a fully contributory role;

(c) Elementary principles of health and hygiene, child care and nutrition;

(d) Basic skills in reading writing and arithmetic, correlated with attitudinal changes and aptitudinal promotion; and

(e) Introductory occupational/vocational skill programmes to prepare him for employment and self-employment.

The learner should be brought up to a level where a habit of continuing education or self-education could start.

Methods

The basic principles for methods used in the scheme are:

(a) That the educational process should be a dialogue about problems stemming from life;

(b) That the methods should be active, in order to involve the learner as a true participant;

(c) That such methods should be attractive to young people;

(d) That the methods should be based on facilities existing predominantly in the local environment; and

(e) That in communicating the programme, the method should be largely audio-visual media based.

Types of programmes—extensive vs. *intensive*

With as large a target as six million to be reached in a period of five years, it is essential to mount a programme on as wide a base as possible, covering all the districts in the country. Although this means an extensive effort and coverage, the programme is more of an intensive nature, from the standpoint of its educational objectives, its broad curriculum and the methods to be used.

Incentives to student volunteers

Student volunteers who participate in the non-formal education programme could be awarded certificates of honour on the successful completion of their assignments. A certificate required to be provided by the village school headmaster to the effect that during the given period, the student volunteer appointed for the purpose has discharged his functions and imparted the non-formal education programme to the given number of students.

Follow-up

Follow-up is very important for the continued success of the programme of non-formal education. The responsibility in regard to the follow-up action may be taken up by the local school, or through a mobile library service, or through other available agencies. An intensive programme may be launched with the assistance of the local school teacher, who may be given a suitable honorarium for the purpose. An adequate follow-up programme will have to be devised and tested. It should include the production of literature, local journals, discussion forums, various community activities, etc., in order to maintain the literacy skill reached and to prevent relapse into illiteracy. This follow-up action will apply to all the three patterns.

(3) Functional Literacy Programme linked with Development Schemes

The Farmers' Functional Literacy Programme is the biggest on-going country-wide programme of out-of-school adult education. It is in reality a complex non-formal education system at its initial stage. Its implementation is the responsibility of the Central Government, and the scheme is classified as a Central Sector Programme.

The problem

There are many development schemes and projects in the country whose efficient implementation is hampered by the low level of educational attainments. This is particularly true of the enormous scheme of High Yield Crop Varieties, since the modernisation of agricultural practices has to be accompanied and supported by a programme of man-power development.

The farmers' training and functional literacy programme, an inter-ministerial project implemented jointly by the Ministries of Agriculture, Education, and Information and Broadcasting, is an attempt to get a qualified answer to this fundamental challenge. The basic idea behind the project is that there is a direct correlation between the physical and human ingredients in agriculture, between agricultural inputs and the upgrading of human resources. In other words, this is an integrated approach to a comprehensive rural development programme, to the "Green Revolution". The main goal of the scheme is to support and strengthen one of the basic national objectives; self-sufficiency in food, increase in crop production and growth of agricultural productivity. It is an attempt, and the first one on such a scale, to place educational activities in direct relation to one of the major development purposes.

The functional literacy component was not only viewed in correlation with other developmental objectives but from the very beginning was conceived as, more than a literacy programme, a method of training for development purposes, a comprehensive non-formal educational programme and an opening to continuing education.

Expansion of the approach

The basic approach will be expanded during the Fifth Five Year Plan in three directions:

(a) The number of districts where the Functional Literacy Programme is functioning in relation to the HYCV Schemes will be increased;

(b) The number of farmers involved in functional literacy courses will be increased in each of the districts, particularly those from the poorer sections of the rural population for whom this development scheme is intended, but who do not benefit from it adequately; and

(c) The functional literacy component will be included in several other development schemes—such as dryland farming, water supply schemes, small and marginal farmers' programmes, programmes of industrial development, public enterprises family planning programmes, sanitation, child care, cultural development, civic participation, etc.

Planning

The first aspect of the programme planning concerns the expansion of the farmers' functional literacy to additional HYV Districts in coordination with programmes of the Ministry of Agriculture. Based on plans for agricultural development and modernisation, the selection of districts, as well as the selection of village centres in each district will be made, by an interministerial group, in close consultation with State authorities.

The second aspect of the programme planning consists of the identification of environmental needs and problems in each district as well as of the main trends and problems encountered in rural and agricultural development. Based on these findings, the programme content and learning material (prepared by the Directorate of Adult Education) may be adapted, modified and complemented. For this purpose, an inter-disciplinary and interdepartmental group has to be established in every district.

The third aspect of the programme planning concerns the development of functional literacy programmes linked with social and economic development purposes other than HYV, such as those mentioned earlier. The most important and difficult task consists in selecting well-suited development schemes for this purpose, and building an educational "component" around them. In other words, there will be a certain number of non-formal educational programmes, diversified in their nature, based on and linked with environmental needs, developed round the interests of potential clientele groups, differentiated in content and methods, and selective in approach. Proposals for these types of programmes will have to be initiated by State authorities and/or voluntary organisations.

Type of Programme—Intensive/Selective

Bearing in mind the general objectives of the programme, it has to be both intensive and selective. Having overcome the mere goals of literacy skills the programme has to be intensive regarding its educational pattern, methods and results, and selective regarding the environments and areas chosen for operational work, clientele to be served and messages and content to be acquired.

Duration and timing

The duration of the programme for each group of learners would be eight to nine months, divided in two or three programme cycles.

The timing of the programme, i.e., beginning and closure, need not be uniform, but rather linked closely with the "cycles" of the development programme itself, the production cycle in a factory, the agricultural calendar in rural areas, etc.

Content and curriculum

The content and curriculum have been well formulated at the beginning of the programme, and have been constantly revised and improved.

The emphasis will now be placed on:

(1) A better implementation of the curriculum; and

(2) Closer adaptation to local needs, environmental circumstances and learners' abilities.

Learning materials

The learning material for the programme (linked with the utilisation of seeds of high yield crops) has been prepared and issued in Hindi (revised already four times), and adapted and translated into Assamese, Bengali, Gujarati, Kannada, Marathi, Oriya, Punjabi, Tamil and Telegu.

Thirty-two booklets, on different subjects linked with the "Green Revolution", have been produced in six languages.

The main tasks during the Fifth Plan period are the following:

(1) Enriching learning materials for functional literacy groups (providing a complete set consisting of at least eight items: primer, reading booklets, content sheets, newsletter, charts, other visuals, film strips for learners and teachers' guide for the group leader);

(2) Up-dating reading materials (by organising, in as many districts as possible, the production and circulation of a monthly newsletter, or local newspaper, or a page in an existing newspaper with news, lectures, texts, answers to farmers' queries, etc.); and

(3) Diversifying learning materials according to the variety of programmes and clientele, but basing them on the same methodological approach as for HYVP.

Methods

There is already a basic understanding of learning methods to be used in Farmers' Functional Literacy Programme.

Nevertheless, there are three additional points which need to be emphasised:

(a) The learners are neither sufficiently involved as active participants, nor has there been a real dialogue and a common search for solutions established on a sufficiently large scale;

(b) Practical agricultural work is not yet generally included in the curriculum. Village centres for functional literacy are rarely equipped with seeds, fertilisers, tools, etc., to serve as learning equipment which will aid in increasing the know-how of learners; and

(c) Different activities organised by agricultural departments or farmers training centres, such as national demonstrations, agricultural extension work, dissemination of agricultural information through printing or broadcasting, etc., are seldom integrated with the teaching process in functional literacy centres.

Administration and coordination

The programme has to be implemented through machinery whose main "wheels" are:

(1) The respective unit in the Union Ministry of Education, for planning the general lines of the scheme, for the allocation of financial resources, for basic supervision and general guidance;

(2) One unit in the Directorate of Adult Education for technical and professional guidance and coordination;

(3) An officer of a small unit for non-formal education and functional literacy at the State level, in the Department of Education;

(4) A full-time project officer in each district who will be responsible for the two programmes (non-formal education for young people in the 15-25 age group and the functional literacy programme linked with development schemes);

(5) A professional, full-time, supervisory machinery in every district; and

(6) Coordinating committees at the central, state and district or local levels.

CHAPTER 3

EXTENSION EDUCATION

A dynamic and flexible type of education is one which serves the people wherever they are, whatever they are. It assists in the development of the individual as well as all categories of the constituents of society. These characteristics and qualifications are well suited to the discipline of Extension Education.

Lewis Jones says: "Invention of Extension Teaching was so original, so far in advance of conventional educational practice, that it has been little understood or even noticed by the main body of education."

Sohal has remarked: "On account of its simple but generic nature, extension education is taken for granted to be thoroughly and completely understood in its entirety by each and every person concerned directly or indirectly with it. But whereas it can be admitted that one or a few aspects of this subject can be expected to be known extensively, yet there are only a few individuals with professional insight into the subject who really know all of its varied facets."

Concepts of extension education

There are as many definitions as those who define. Shukla[1] (1972) collected and studied several prevailing concepts of extension education using psycho-physical methods to find out the comparative attitudinal positions for these concepts. The findings of his study are given as follows:

Rank Order of the Concept	Concept

I Extension education is an applied science consisting of contents derived from researches, accumulated field experiences and relevant principles drawn from the behavioural sciences, synthesised with useful technology, in a body of philosophy, principles, contents and methods focussed on the problems of out of school education for adults and youths (Leagans, J.P.).

[1]Shukla, A.N. (1972) "The Concept of Extension Education: A Study in Psycho-physical Methods," *Studies in Extension Education*. (Ed.). PRR Sinha. NLCO, Hyderabad.

Rank Order of the Concept	Concept

II Extension is an education and its purpose is to change the attitude and practices of the people with whom the work is done. (Ensminger. D.)

III Extension education is defined as an educational process to provide knowledge to the rural people about the improved practices in a convincing manner and to help them to take decisions within their specific local conditions. (Dahama, O.P.).

IV Agricultural extension is concerned with agricultural education aimed at assisting rural people to bring about continuous improvement in their physical, economic and social well being, through individual and cooperative efforts. It makes available to the villages, scientific and other factual information and training and guidance for the solution of problems of agriculture and rural life.

V Extension education is the act of putting across to the people, in an understandable manner, new ideas and improved technology of practical utility and to enable them to put them into practice so as to improve their general standard of living through their own realisation and efforts.

VI Extension education is a science which deals with various strategies of change in the behavioural patterns of human beings through technological and scientific innovations for the improvement of their standard of living.

VII Extension is a continuous process designed to make the rural people aware of their problems and indicating to them the ways and means by which they can solve them. It involves not only educating rural people in determining their problems and methods of solving them but also inspiring them towards positive action in achieving them.

VIII Agricultural extension is a bridge that fills the gap between agricultural research stations on the one hand and the farming population on the other by establishing a suitable teaching organisation at various levels of administration.

IX Extension education is an applied behavioural science, the knowledge of which is to be applied for desirable change in the behavioural complex of the people.

X Extension is defined primarily as an educational process aiming at the development of individuals; through this process the villagers are helped to become discontented with the present conditions and are helped by extension workers to improve their conditions of living.

XI Extension is to teach a person how to think, not what to think, and to teach people to determine accurately their own needs to find solution to their own problems and to help them acquire knowledge and develop convictions in that direction.

XII Extension is an out-of-school system of education in which adults and young people learn by doing. It is a partnership between Government, the Land Grant Colleges and the People, which provides services and education designed to meet the needs of the people.

XIII Extension or agricultural extension is a method, or a series of methods, by which the technical know-how of science is carried to and included in the practices of the cultivators.

Rank Order of the Concept	Concept

XIV Extension education is the education of the people as to what more to want as well as how to work out ways of satisfying them. Informing people not to remain content with their present lot and inspiring them to work vigorously towards fulfilment of their self-created, increased wants or desires.

XV Extension is the education of the rural adults outside the school in matters of their choice and interest. It is education for freedom, which seeks to help persons to use the liberty of action with which democratic society is constructed.

From the above definitions, the following basic questions have emerged:
1. What category of science is it?
2. What is its subject matter?
3. What is its relationship with technology and the other sciences?
4. Who are the clients of this discipline?
5. What are its methods, contents, principles and philosophies?

Precise, valid and objective answers to the above questions have been attempted in the succeeding part of this chapter. However, the following definition, which covers the various components will give an answer to the questions raised above.

"Extension education is a Behavioural Science following a continuous, persuasive and discriminating educational process. It aims at affecting the behavioural components of people in a desirable direction, through conviction, communication and diffusion, by its proven methods, principles and philosophies resulting in learning-involvement of both client and change-agent systems."

Philosophy of extension education

Philosophy, in the original and wider sense, is the pursuit of wisdom, or knowledge of things and their causes, both theoretical and practical. It is also defined as moral wisdom. Philosophy is an attempt to answer ultimate questions critically after investigating all. that makes such questions puzzling and after realising the vagueness and confusion·that underlie our ordinary ideas.

The philosophy of extension education has been described and interpreted in different ways by different authors and a clear picture cannot be drawn due to the very complexity of its nature. All one can do is try to gain a comprehensive idea by examining the view points of various authors.

Kelsey and Hearne (1955) state that the philosophy of extension work is based on the importance of the individual in the promotion of progress for rural people and for the nation. Extension educators work with the people to help them to develop themselves and achieve superior personal well-being. Together they establish specific objectives, expressed in terms of everyday life, which lead them in the direction of overall objectives. Some will make progress in one direction while others will do so in another direction. Progress varies with individual needs, interests and abilities. Through this process the whole community improves, as a result of cooperative participation and leadership development.

According to Ensminger (1962), the philosophy of extension can be expressed in the following lines:

(1) It is an educational process. Extension is changing the attitudes, knowledge and skills of the people;

(2) Extension is working with men and women, young people, boys and girls to answer their needs and their wants. Extension is teaching people what to want and ways to satisfy their wants.

(3) Extension is "helping people to help themselves";

(4) Extension is "learning by doing" and "seeing is believing";

(5) Extension is development of individuals, their leaders, their society and their world as a whole;

(6) Extension is working together to expand the welfare and happiness of people;

(7) Extension is working in harmony with the culture of the people;

(8) Extension is a living relationship, respect and trust for each other;

(9) Extension is a two-way channel; and

(10) Extension is a continuous, educational process.

Dahama (1965) gives the following points as the "Philosophy of Extension".

(a) Self-help;

(b) People are the greatest resources;

(c) It is a cooperative effort;

(d) It has its foundation in democracy;

(e) It involves a two-way channel of knowledge and experience;

(f) It is based on creating interest by seeing and doing;

(g) Voluntary, cooperative participation in programmes;

(h) Persuasion and education of the people;

(i) The programme is based on the attitudes and values of the people; and

(j) It is a never-ending process.

Mildred Horton has described four principles which make the philosophy of extension education. They are:

(1) The individual is supreme in a democracy.

(2) The home is the fundamental unit in a civilisation.

(3) The family is the first training group of the human race.

(4) The foundation of any permanent civilisation must rest on the partnership of man and land.

Shukla, while supporting the philosophy of Horton, emphasised—"Extension programme revolves around the individual, the cultivator, and we have to bring change in his attitude, knowledge, skill, understanding, capacity and ability through persuasion by educational means."

Rudramurthy (1966) has linked the philosophy of extension work with the Vedas, the Upanishads, the Gita as well as the orthodox and unorthodox schools of philosophy. This is based on the concept of man and the values which are worthy of human pursuit.

Bhatnagar (1971) perceives extension to be the activities of the State Governments (with, or without, the help of Central Government, or other agencies) which provide the farmers with technical know-how as a guide to improved methods, in order to bring desirable changes in their behaviour with the aim of attaining higher production.

In this sense, the extension activities relate closely to the activities in research and education.

Principles of extension education

Understanding of principles

Before taking up the discussion of the Principles of Extension it will be worthwhile to examine what is meant by the word "principle". "A principle is a statement of policy to guide decision and action in a consistent manner" (Mathews).

Its meaning will be clear when we try to understand the sequence of generalisation. When something is put forth as a point of view, or an assumption, and its proof is not known, it is called a hypothesis. When a hypothesis is put to a test and the point of view, or the assumption, turn out to be acceptable, it is called a theory. When a theory is put to several rigorous tests, under different settings, by different individuals and the findings are found to be in substantial agreement, then it is given the name of a principle. Thus, a principle is a universal truth that has been observed and found to be true under varying conditions and circumstances. A principle is a fundamental truth and a settled rule of action.

Importance of principles in extension work

It is usually believed that the knowledge of the principles is of no value to an extension worker. These principles are considered to be of academic interest for the students taking advance courses in extension. Leagans, however, holds out clearly on the need for a sound knowledge of the principles for the extension workers. He points out that without this knowledge extension workers either keep on labouring under some handicaps, or make grave mistakes, particularly in the initial stages. Further, if an extension worker aspires to become an administrator or a supervisor, it will be all the more necessary for him to possess a sound knowledge of the principles of extension.

Relative sequence of extension principles

The principles of extension are relative and not necessarily fixed in importance or sequence. Generally, however, it is also true that all the principles are important. It may also be relevant to point out that it is never possible to prepare a complete and final list of the extension principles. The principles discussed below are those which are either fundamental in nature or widely accepted in literature on the subject.

(1) Principles of interest and needs

To be effective, extension work must begin with the interests and needs of the people. Many times the interests of the rural people are not the interests of the extension worker. Even though he sees the needs of the people better than they do themselves, he must begin with the interests and needs as they (the people) see them.

In this way only can the extension agency mould the needs and interests of the people into realistic needs. Needs that can satisfy the individuals, groups, community and national interests, needs that can be fulfilled with the available resources, and the needs that should be fulfilled first.

(2) *Grass-roots principle of organisation*

For extension work to be effective and real, it has to be a synthesis of democracy obtained at the level of the family and more particularly at the village level. Things must spring from below and spread like grass.

At the same time, modern science calls for an advanced stage of organisation and a wiser coordination of thinking and action than is feasible in a single family or a single village. A higher level of living means wider specialisation in a village. This calls for the corresponding organisation of different professions and avocations. These will have to be woven together at the level of the enlarged family at the village community level. The Panchayats, as social institutions, have also to be established at the Block and the District levels. Thus, the establishment of the three-tier system namely, Village-Panchayat, Block-Samiti and Zila-Parishad, followed by State Legislatures and Parliament satisfies the grass-roots principle of organisation in the extension.

(3) *Principle of cultural differences*

In order to make extension programmes effective, the approach and procedure must be suited to the culture of the people who are taught. Different culture require different approaches. A blue-print of work designed for one part of the globe cannot be applied effectively to another part, mainly because of the cultural differences. These differences can be perceived in the way of life of the people, their attitudes, values, loyalties, habits and customs.

(4) *Principle of cultural change*

Because changed ways must be learnt and because all learning must be grafted on what is already known, it is obvious that the change agent who works personally with the villagers must know what the villagers know and what they think. With this in mind and with an attitude of mutual respect and receptiveness, the worker must seek to discover and understand the limitations, the taboos and the cultural values related to each phase of his programme, before it is introduced, in order that an acceptable approach may be selected.

This principle can be summed up in the words of Earl Moncur:

"As each culture is unique and each particular situation within which a change is occurring, or is to be made, is unique, it is not possible to lay down prescription for what to identify and to describe the process which occurs so that each particular individual or team charged with responsibility for planning, execution or adjusting to some type of change, may be able to act in terms of the process."

(5) *Principle of cooperation and participation*

In an attempt to involve a great number of persons in achieving desired common ends, there seems to be no acceptable alternative but to let them choose the ends, and then aiding them to organise their self-help efforts successfully to do the things they want to do Most members of the village community will willingly cooperate in carrying out a project which they helped to decide to undertake. It has been the experience of many countries that people become dynamic if they are permitted to take decisions concerning their own affairs, exercise responsibility for, and are helped to carry out projects in their own villages.

The participation of the people is of fundamental importance for the success of any educational endeavour. People must share in the development of a programme and must feel that it is their own programme.

(6) *Principle of applied science and democratic approach*

Applied agricultural science is not a one-way process. The problems of the people are taken to the scientists who do the experimentation necessary to find out the solutions. The extension worker translates the scientific findings of the laboratories in such a way that the farm families can voluntarily adopt them to satisfy their own needs.

However, extension work is democratic both in philosophy and procedure. It aims to operate through discussion and suggestion. Facts about a situation are shared with the people. All possible alternative solution are placed before the participants, and their merits are highlighted through mutual discussions. Ultimately, the people are left free to decide their line of action, the methods to be adopted in the local situation with their own resources and available government assistance.

(7) *Principle of learning by doing*

In extension work, farmers should be encouraged to learn new things by doing and by direct participation. As Dr. Newman (1889) said—"Farmers, like other people, hesitate to believe and set on theories, or even facts, until they see with their own eyes the proof of them in material form. We must, in some way, bring this work to their personal attention. We must carry it home to them."

The motive for improvement must come from the people, and they must practice the new ideas by actually doing them. It is learning by doing, which is most effective in changing people's behaviour and developing the confidence to use the new methods in future.

(8) *Principle of trained specialists*

It is very difficult for a multi-purpose extension worker to keep himself abreast with all the latest findings of research in all the branches of science he has to deal with in his day-to-day activity. Trained specialists have to be provided, who keep themselves in touch with their respective research institutes on the one hand, and extend to the extension worker, meaningful terms, the latest scientific developments, which have scope for adoption in particular areas.

(9) *Adaptability principle in the use of extension teaching methods*

No single extension teaching method is effective under all situations. Reading material is for those who can read, radio-programmes for those who have radios, meetings for those who can attend, demonstrations of recommended practices are for those who can come to the farms where the demonstrations of recommended practices are laid. Farm and home visits are, by far, the most valuable, but they take up considerable time. New situations also arise where a special combination of method is necessary.

Extension agents have found that they need a large number of teaching methods out of which they can select and revise the one effective for the purpose and best suited to the culture of the people. At times, new methods must be devised to meet new situations and changing conditions.

Further, the use of teaching methods must have flexibility to be adopted to the members of a community who differ in age, education, economic status, sex and proneness to change, etc.

(10) *Principle of leadership*

A good rule in extension work is "Never do anything yourself that you can get someone to do for you." This calls for the development of local voluntary leadership.

The involvement of leaders in extension programmes is the one single factor that determines the success or failure of those programmes. Local leaders are the guardians of local thought and action and can be trained and developed to best serve as interpreters of new ideas to the villagers.

There is no dearth of local leaders. All communities have leaders or potential leaders; it is a question of searching them out and creating an environment which will permit and encourage their development and performance.

In the promotion of change however, it is neither right nor wise to disregard old organised groups and leaders. Old leaders, it they are trusted can open—as well as close— the gates to new types of community action. If such leaders are converted to new functions, the multiplication of new things to be done will almost certainly lead or drive them to share the role of leadership with others.

(11) *Whole family principle*

The family is the unit of any society. All the members of the family have to be developed equally by involving all of them. This is because of the following reasons.

    (a) The Extension programme effects all members of the family.

    (b) The family members have great influence in decision-making.

    (c) It creates mutual understanding.

    (d) It aids in money management.

    (e) It balances farm and family needs.

    (f) It educates the younger members.

    (g) It provides an activity outlet for all.

    (h) It unifies related aspects, such as the social, economic and cultural, of the family.

    (i) It assures family service to the community and society.

It is not difficult to adopt this type of approach in extension programmes. There is much work in the field for the men and at home for the women. The 4-H clubs play a remarkable role in this regard so far as young boys and girls are concerned. A comparative study has shown that the young 4-H club members have greater confidence in scientific information than the non-members.

(12) *Principles of satisfaction*

Satisfaction of the people is very essential in extension work. Unless the people are satisfied with the end product of any programme, it is not going to be able to run. In democratic societies people cannot be made to move like machines. They must continue to act out of their own conviction and that is possible only when they derive full satisfaction through adoption of innovations well suited to their needs and resources.

Difference between formal education and extension education

Formal Education	Extension Education
1. Formal education starts from a theoretical or conceptual framework and leads to practical or actual field work.	Extension education is practical, field and farmer's problem-oriented, thus it starts from a practical and develops into a theoretical or basic understanding.
2. In this type of education there is a fixed or pre-decided curriculum.	In extension education there is no fixed curriculum. It has also possible flexibilities depending on the needs of the learners.
3. The audience in this type of education is homogeneous with common goals.	The audience is heterogeneous and have diversified goals.
4. Teaching is vertical and curriculum-centred.	Teaching is horizontal and mostly need-based and problem-oriented.
5. Strict adherence to institutional norms and no free choice for the learners.	Freedom and choice of subject matter left to the learners.
6. This education is of a specialised nature, i.e., class-oriented, subject-centred and degree-oriented.	Informal, with some elements of formal education in class teaching, but not degree oriented.
7. Learners are taught directly by the teachers.	Local teachers are used for training and dissemination of knowledge.

EXTENSION EDUCATION—A DEVELOPED DISCIPLINE

A widely accepted and well recognised view regarding Extension is "Extension is education and its aim is to bring the desirable changes in human behaviour." Whether one wishes to understand or improve human behaviour, it is necessary to know a great deal about the nature of Extension Education as a developed discipline. The distinguishing characteristics are:

(1) *Emphasis on theoretically significant empirical research*

Until the beginning of the new era of scientific and empirical application to extension education, those who were curious about the nature of extension education relied primarily upon their personal experience and historical record to provide answers to their questions. Not being burdened by the necessity of accounting for carefully gathered empirical data, writers in this speculative era devoted their energy to the creation of a comprehensive theoretical treatment of extension education.

By the second half of this century an empirical rebellion had begun in the social sciences. Instead of being content with speculation about nature of human behaviour, a few people began to seek out facts in an attempt to distinguish between objective data and subjective impressions. Although, initially rather simple questions guided this research, a fundamentally new criterion for evaluating new knowledge about human behaviour in the field of extension education was established in the late 1950's. Extension education began to emerge as an identifiable field, the empirical rebellion was moving the lines of social psychology and sociology. Thus, at the outset, the extension education discipline, closely related to psychology and sociology, could employ the research methods characteristic of an empirical science. In fact extension education is to be distinguished from the earlier intellectual endeavours in the social sciences primarily by its basic reliance on careful observation, quantification, measurement and experimentation. But one should not identify extension education too closely with extreme empiricism.

(2) Interest in the behavioural aspect of inter-dependence of phenomena

Although the phrase, "Extension Education" specifies extension as the objective of study, it also focuses attention more sharply on the "education" aspect of human life. The student of the extension education discipline is not satisfied with just a description of the properties of extension, or events associated with it, nor he is content with a classification of human groups and form of associations only. He wants to know how the phenomena he observes depend on one another, and what new phenomena might result from the creation of conditions never before observed. In short. he seeks to discover general principles concerning what conditions produce what effects. This search leads us to the reality of the interdependence of phenomena and reveals the fact about our success in applying the inter-disciplinary approach.

(3) Inter-disciplinary relevance

It is important to recognise that the studies and researches in the extension education have not been associated exclusively with any one of the social science disciplines. Various scientists from different fields helped further the cause of the growth of the discipline of extension education. Rural sociologists have, of course, devoted great energy to bringing out the factors of human life related to extension education behaviour. Psychologists have directed their attention to the study of individuals in group functioning by studying the attitudes behaviour and personality characteristics. Anthropologists, while investigating many facts as sociologists and psychologists, have contributed data on groups living under conditions quite different from those of modern industrial society. Political scientists have extended their traditional interest in large institutions to include studies of the functions of administrative, political and related aspects in rural areas. Economists have come close increasingly to collect and analyse data, so as to guide in decision-making regarding expenditure of savings at the farm and family levels, and also to make predictions about the economic consequences of methods and practices used or advocated. Group dynamics, communications, social psychology education and home science disciplines have significantly contributed and continue to contribute to the growth of extension education as a discipline.

Potential applicability of findings to social practice

Everyone, who feels the responsibility of strengthening the efforts of extension educators, must view his action in the light of the total programmes and practices under the extension education discipline. The professionalisation of the discipline has brought about a conscious desire to improve standards and establish the requirements for proper training. The major universities now have professional courses and divisions to provide such training at the highest level. It should not be surprising, therefore, to find that courses in extension education are becoming more and more common in professional schools, that people trained in extension education are being employed by agencies concerned with professional practices; and that extension education research is often carried out in connection with the work of such agencies. This has great potentialities.

Thus in short, it is proposed that extension education should be defined as a discipline, dedicated to advancing knowledge about the effect of the extension education approach in bringing about desirable change in human behaviour, and the laws of governing their development and their interrelations, etc.

Conditions fostering the rise of discipline

Extension education as a discipline has its historical roots in the USA, where people made a significant contribution to both research and theory in extension education. They also established the first organisation devoted explicitly to research in extension education.

The time and place of the rise of Extension Education were, of course, not accidental. The American Society of "Cooperative Extension Service" provided the kind of conditions required for the emergence of such an intellectual movement. Over the years, since that time only certain countries have afforded a favourable environment for its growth. Today, extension education has taken firm root in both the USA and in India. Three major conditions seem to have been necessary for its rise and subsequent growth (Fig. 3.1):

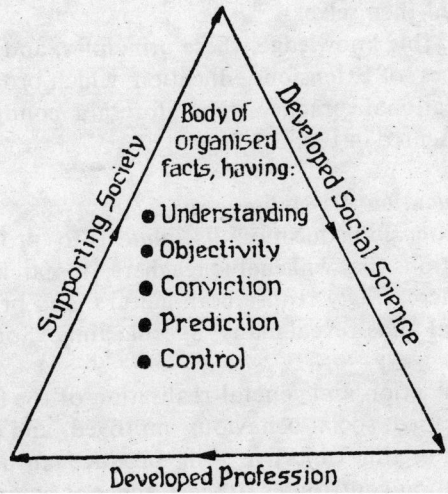

Fig. 3.1. Conditions for rise of discipline.

(a) A supporting society;

(b) Developed profession; and

(c) Developed social science.

The publication of "The Journal of Cooperative Extension Service" in the USA, and "The Indian Journal of Extension Education" in India, revolutionised thinking and led to the organising of the development of professionals in India and the USA The incentive to work for the growth of this discipline was no longer seen as simple and unitary but rather as infinitely varied, complex and dynamic. The new view opened the way for, and demanded, more research and new conceptualisations to handle the problems.

The controlled observations on social interaction, which was initially developed to provide objective and quantitative data concerning behaviour, subsequently has been used extensively in researches in extension education.

With the coming up of Agricultural Universities and Extension Education Institutes in India, the growth of this discipline was carried forward at a faster rate. Student researches and staff research projects opened new vistas in the development of the discipline.

Thus, it may be suggested that extension education has become an academic discipline and a field of study, as it fulfils Skinners' Criteria with the following achievements:

(a) The focus of extension education on human organisation has resulted from observation and investigation.

(b) It is a body of facts or information that has resulted from observation and investigation.

(c) This body of knowledge can be summarised, or generalised into principles or theories.

(d) Extension education uses social research methodology and statistics by which investigations are made, information is discovered, hypotheses are tested and theories are derived.

(e) This use of methodology is useful in arriving at the solution of educational problems, as they present themselves.

(f) This information, this knowledge, these principles, and the methodology used, constitutes the substances of extension education which provides a base for educational theory and educational practice. The aforesaid conditions fostering the rise of the discipline are presented in Fig. 3.1.

Aims of Extension Education Discipline

The general aim of extension education discipline is to provide a body of organised facts and generalisations that will enable teachers, researchers, extension workers and administrators to increasingly realise both cultural and professional objectives.

An analysis of general aims reveal many specific aims. Some of the most important are listed below:

(1) To develop a conviction and general realisation of the fact that growth can be promoted, learning acquired, social behaviour improved, and personality adjustments effected. The realisation of this objective will produce an increasing appreciation of what extension education contributes to the teacher or extension educators.

(2) To assist in defining and setting up extension educational objectives and standards in terms of desirable behaviour for bringing them about.

(3) To aid in developing an impartial but sympathetic attitude towards clientele, so that their behaviour will be regarded objectively.

(4) To assist in achieving a better understanding of the nature and importance of human relationships and the methods of developing these in clientele as well as such modes of functioning as getting along with others, participation in group efforts and cooperation.

(5) To provide a body of facts and principles that can be used as problem-oriented and project-directed solutions.

(6) To aid in affording the extension educators a better perspective for finding both the results of his own efforts and the practices of others.

(7) To furnish the teachers with the necessary facts and techniques for analysing behaviour—both his own and that of others—to the end that normal adjustment may be facilitated and growth effected.

(8) To assist in defining, maintaining and combining progressive extension methods, procedures and techniques for the dissemination of sophisticated technologies in a simple and understandable form.

Professional growth of the discipline

We possess a strong conviction that as a promoter of rapid development and, what Sinha terms, 'a complex of many disciplines'; the fundamental purpose of extension education is to provide an educational experience for the people with whom we are privileged to work. This is set down by Clark (1976) and Singh (1967) as a professional responsibility. It follows that teaching becomes the major profession. In other words, extension education, as a branch of instruction or education, or a department of knowledge, is solely responsible for teaching its clientele. Such educational tasks are the task for professionals. This raises the need for the clarification of the concept of profession.

(1) *Criteria for a profession*

Webster defines a profession thus: "A calling in which one professes to have acquired some special knowledge used by way of either instructing, guiding or advising others or of serving them in some act."

The famous English economist Tawney, gave a comprehensive difinition of profession: "It is a body of men who carry on their work in accordance with rules designed to enforce certain standards both, for the better protection of its members, and for the better service of the public".

A well recognised fact is that the educational task of extension is a task for professionals. Let us examine how this claim best fits in with the criteria evolved by Clark and Singh. These are:

(a) Members fulfil established requirements of personal and academic qualifications for admission into the profession.

(b) Its members adhere to a high standard of ethical conduct.

(c) They exhibit self-discipline and self-direction.

(d) The group attains self-fulfilment through public service.

(e) Members attain professional growth through continual research teaching and extension.

(f) It has a rapidly growing body of knowledge with both tools and techniques well developed.

(g) Periodic evaluation of an objective nature in an attempt to improve self-efforts and the efforts of others.

(h) Its members organise associations through which they act collectively to maintain and improve the service.

The authors of these criteria have very rightly claimed extension education to be a profession. Prasad says: "In fact, extension education with its applied value has grown into a profession". At another place he warns the professionals that they have: "an obligation to see that it rapidly and systematically grows and does more good to the public. Profession is made by people who dare, and we have to dare if we want to thrive professionally".

In fact, because of the very nature of extension education, its discipline and profession have nearly the same connotations.

In the beginning, the mushroom growth of extension education in the form of institutions and organisations, a highly heterogeneous group of professionals and the teaching of the discipline by unskilled and untrained staff hampered the professional growth of the discipline in India. But the untiring efforts, zeal and enthusiasm of the academicians of the discipline who demonstrated through their studies and researches and virtually 'educated the educated masses', were able to bring the discipline on a par with other well recognised ones.

(2) Recent breakthrough

Recent breakthrough in revolutionising and developing the professional leadership in the extension education discipline begin with:

(a) Establishing of the Indian Society of Extension Education on 22nd June 1964 and publication of the World's Second Journal of Extension Education.

(b) The opening and developing of a chain of agricultural universities in various states.

(c) The integration of resident teaching, research and extension in and about agricultural universities.

(d) The organising of a production unit and farm advisory services, with a team of subject-matter specialists in the integrated unit department, by the divisions of agricultural extension.

(e) Post-graduate teaching leading to doctoral programmes in such universities served as the breeding ground of highly skilled, field-oriented and sufficiently disciplined professionals.

(f) The rapidly growing body of knowledge with appropriate kinds of techniques.

(g) The continual process of evaluation, self-checking and self-directing.

(h) Lastly, the matching efficiency of the discipline to bridge the gap between morning invention of sophisticated technology and the evening diffusion of such innovation.

A Lacuna: But a lacuna of a very serious nature does exist. It has been found that some members, as teachers in the discipline, do not fulfil the established requirements of temperamental, personal and academic qualifications for admission into the profession. Barring this, we can easily claim that extension education, both as a discipline as well as a profession, are developing fast and providing a desirable leadership.

EXTENSION EDUCATION AND ITS RELATIONSHIP WITH OTHER SOCIAL SCIENCES

Extension Education—an Applied Behavioural Science

In the earlier part of this chapter it was firmly established that extension education is a discipline. This rising discipline has all the three ideals of science that is, understanding, prediction and control. It has been amply illustrated that extension education is a social science, different from Natural Science and Biological Science. Halayya has classified all the sciences in three groups:

(a) The physical sciences;
(b) The biological sciences; and
(c) The social sciences.

He has further classified the social sciences into following three levels:

(a) The purely social sciences;
(b) The semi-social sciences; and
(c) The sciences with social implications.

Accordingly, the place of extension education is in the category of semi-social sciences. Because the pure social sciences continue to be the concern of the intellectual aristocracy, the sciences with social implications are still standing at the gateway of the social science category.

Guilford has given a very interesting diagrammatic structure of the sciences, which depicts all the sciences as forming a solid structure, with a broad foundation, two columns, a capstone or a superstructure. To this the authors have added extension education as an arch at the top (Fig. 3.2).

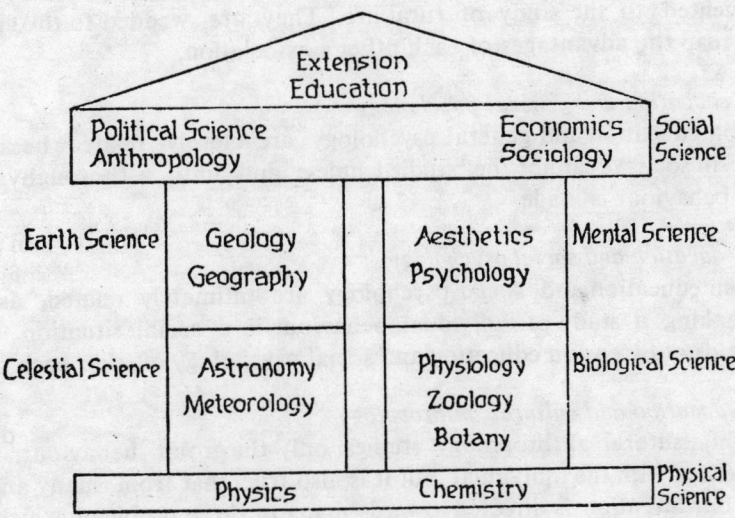

Fig. 3.2. Place of extension education in structure of sciences.

At the base are Physics and Chemistry which are regarded as the foundation of all the other sciences. The column at the left represents those physical sciences that study the universe and, in particular, the earth as the home of man (sciences of the environment). The column at the right represents a very logical sequence from the lowest living forms to the highest, leading step-by-step from the physical sciences to the social sciences (sciences of life). In the same column, along with the psychology, Aesthetics is also listed (Mental Science). The social sciences rest on both the columns of our symbolic structure. Anthropology, Economics, Political Science, Sociology and Extension Education have been grouped together as the social sciences (Social Sciences).

Among all the social sciences only extension education deals primarily with the *whole individual*.

Relationship with other social sciences

The student having a career interest in extension education is interested in acquiring knowledge about the various other disciplines, especially the social sciences and their inter-relationship with Extension Education. Let us examine this:

Extension education and sociology

Extension education and Sociology both study groups from nearly the same angle. The immediate purpose of sociology is to study the structure, function and organisation of the groups, while that of extension education is to study human behaviour in groups and also individual life, and how desirable changes can be introduced into them. But it is clear that neither extension education nor sociology can achieve this goal unless and until they seek the help of each other.

Extension education and rural sociology

Extension education and rural sociology are extremely close to each other. At this stage it is very difficult to distinguish between them, because both sciences are greatly oriented to the study of rural life. They are wedded to the cause of each other and reap the advantages of each other's association.

Extension education and general psychology

Extension education and general psychology are closely related because human behaviour in society cannot be studied unless and until a thorough study of the individual behaviour is made.

Extension education and social psychology

Extension education and social psychology are ultimately related, as both join hands in making a study of individual behaviour in a social situation. This shows that the fields of extension education and social psychology overlap each other.

Extension education and cultural anthropology

No doubt, cultural anthropology studies only the group behaviour. It is most often concerned with the individual but it is also true that from many anthropological studies our attention is directed towards many of those problems which extension education has to face.

Extension education and ethics

The ethical norms are framed in relation to the society. How these norms affect the individual behaviour is of great interest in extension education.

Extension education and economics

Again, the two sciences of extension education and economics work closely together with reference to economic conditions prevailing in a particular group, or a particular individual. Many of the problems of economics are the problems of extension education.

Extension education and political science

In spite of the fact that many of the problems of political science and extension education are common in the fields of individual and group behaviour and in institutions of administration it should be remembered that both the subjects are not identical but help in each others growth.

Extension education and abnormal psychology

The study of Abnormal Psychology is helpful in understanding the anti-social behaviour of people. Extension education gets help in understanding those abnormalities of individual behaviour which have social, economic or political origin.

Extension education and home science

Home science, the science of home, also deals with education through which desirable changes are brought about in family living. Extension education, which works with almost every institution and all individuals who come from these families or home fronts, has a very happy relationship with the Home Science discipline. Yet in certain countries like India, because of cultural and other reasons, the Home Science wings could not help extension education to the desirable extent.

Symbiosis with other social disciplines and practices

The secret of how to get along with others, and how to direct or influence their behaviour, depends upon the knowledge of extension education. The various fields of modern life in which knowledge and application of extension education is important will be viewed briefly:

(a) *Education:* Some fields attempt to change individuals for the better to make them more effective and happy. The educational field is the birth place of extension education, but the mother field derives a lot from the various extension methods and the available resources in planning and executing the educational programme so as to be more realistic and field-oriented.

(b) *Social Work:* Social work exerts its efforts both on the environment and the individual in his endeavours. Extension education helps social workers to plan socially-oriented, educational activities.

(c) *Medicine, Law and the Police:* Medicine, law and the police deal with human nature and its mental aspects as affected by socio-biological factors. As a preventive measure and as a cure of all, the above fields take the help of principles, practices and methods extension education.

(d) *Business, Banks and Industry:* A large number of disciplined extension educators are absorbed by the public and private sectors, in business, banks and industries. Extension educators, through their knowledge and training, know the technique of attracting customers and are proving efficient salesmen. They can work satisfactorily in any difficult situation.

(e) *Journalism and Public Service:* Journalism and extension education have a common aim, to disseminate information from the source of origin to the ultimate users. They are benefited by each other's efforts in providing the best service to the public.

(f) *Family planning:* Much earlier in foreign countries, but at a late stage in India, the programme of family planning and extension education are associated with each other. There exists a great demand for extension educators to help and boost up the Family Planning Programme.

(g) *Administration:* Administration, according to Newman, is the "guidance, leadership and control of the efforts of a group of individuals towards some common goal". In a democratic country the role of "executive" is changing to "extension" in the administration of human affairs. Administrators trained in extension education prove better than those who do not have this background.

Sources and contributions from various disciplines

In order to understand and appreciate the contributions received and utilised by the extension education discipline from various sources, it is imperative to go deep into this aspect.

It is well known that people coming to extension education from different disciplines bring with them the special vocabularies of these disciplines and certain assumptions, theories and principles about the relative importance of various aspects of human life. Thus a sociologist and a rural sociologist may emphasise, in studying human behaviour, their laws for the development of society. An anthropologist may stress the importance of culture, a psychologist may maintain that cognitive, effective and behavioural aspects are of greater significance; a psychoanalyst and social psychologist may be deeply interested in group psychotherapy and proving the effectiveness of interactions upon the individual's thoughts, feelings, conditions and habits. An economist may believe, by nature, that in extension education the dominant determinants are economic resources and technological skills.

Still there exist a number of disciplines such as Political Science, Ethics, Home Economics and other social sciences which rightly claim that their point of view need to be injected into the theoretical orientation and methodology so as to enrich the discipline of extension education.

Biological and natural scientists also have a significant contribution to make, and they rightly serve as the reservoir for the subject-matter concerned with the growth and successes of the discipline.

The various circumstances surrounding the conduct of teaching, research and extension in the discipline of extension education generate a diversity of terminologies, and a variety of conceptions, as to what the important determinants of human behaviour are. Many of the more obvious disparities in terminology, deriving from the special languages brought to the discipline, will undoubtedly be eliminated as research techniques become more standardised, and as people from different disciplines become accustomed to communicating with each other about the same research material.

Conclusion

Extension education has a long and distinguished history as a discipline, profession and an applied behavioural science. It has achieved great respect and confidence in the entire rural community. It has successfully helped the field workers and academicians in the growth of various disciplines, as well as in programmes of activities related to human improvement. Yet, recently, the extension educational activities, methods, resources, organisations and institutions have been called into question. While such questions are being raised, extension education is also being asked to expend still greater efforts in almost every activity occurring in, or related to, the agricultural community and certain parts of urban life.

Extension education is needed not just as an extension, it is an intimate part of an entity, a force much greater than itself. This force is of a very dynamic nature and that is why it has established a deep-rooted and happy relationship with the majority of the biological and social sciences. It is an excellent example of the application of an inter-disciplinary approach and social research techniques.

Inkeles very aptly emphasised: "Any attempt to set limits to a field of intellectual endeavour is inherently futile. The danger is really not too great if we keep in mind that any boundaries we establish are an aid to understanding. They should serve as a loose cloak to delimit from and not as a rigid suit of armory which is endlessly constraining no matter how useful for fighting off those from other disciplines making claims to the same territory".

All sciences freely borrow and incorporate ideas from other fields. Extension educators are often criticised for their use of jargon, their apparent predilection to develop new words while, at the same time, giving new and often strange meanings to old and familiar terms. The charges are rarely justified and this itself speaks for systematised knowledge, scientific communication and stability of the discipline of extension education.

CHAPTER 4

HISTORY OF EXTENSION ACTIVITIES

EXTENSION ACTIVITIES IN INDIA—EARLY ATTEMPTS

Attempts in the pre-British period

Because the villagers were self-contained, self-sufficient and self-governed units, there was little need for social welfare. The social system provided these in times of need. This was disturbed by the invasions of foreigners and Mughal rule when people felt the need for rural reconstruction work. The Panchayat system provided some of these facilities but the development of centralised seats of the government made these unimportant.

Efforts by British Government

Till the last quarter of the 19th century, nothing was done by these foreign rulers. But the series of famines, from 1875 to 1901, numbering 18 out of a total of 33 during the whole 19th century, forced the Government to appoint some Commissions. They recommended rural development work. There followed certain acts like: Land Improvement Loans Act, and Agricultural Loans Act of 1888, Cooperative Act of 1904 and then the amendment in the Cooperative Act in 1912, establishment of Development Departments like Agriculture, Animal Husbandry and Veterinary, Irrigation, etc. Some irrigation projects were also taken up to control famines. In 1935, the rural development work was transferred as a provincial subject and as a result of this, several provinces established their Rural Construction Departments or Village Uplift Boards. These Departments started some rural development activities and obtained funds from the Central Government for this work.

But these Development Departments could not take up any comprehensive programme. Their activities were not based on detailed studies of programme planning, or the needs and resources of the people. It never emphasised the people's participation, cooperation and involvement. It never tried to create confidence in the people through an educational approach but mostly the work remained that of a supply agency and the approach of the extension agents was the approach of bosses and not guides, or teachers.

EXTENSION BY VARIOUS AGENCIES AND ORGANISATIONS BEFORE 1952

Work at Shantiniketan

In 1908, Shri Rabindra Nath Tagore, under his scheme of rural development work, started youth organisations in the villages in the Kaligram Pargana of his Zamindari. He tried to create a class of functionary workers who could learn to identify themselves with the people. In 1921, he established a Rural Reconstruction Institute at Shantiniketan. A group of eight villages was the centre of the programme. The activities of the institute were development of agriculture, cooperatives, industries and education through village organisations.

Objectives of the Programme: (a) To create a real interest in people for rural welfare work; (b) to study rural problems and to translate conclusions into action; (c) to help villagers develop their resources, and (d) to improve village sanitation.

These objectives were desired to be achieved by: (a) creating a spirit of self-help, (b) developing village leadership, (c) organising village scouts called Brati Balika, (d) establishing training centres for handicrafts, and (e) establishing a demonstration centre at Shantiniketan.

Under its agricultural programme, the institute conducted demonstrations on farmers' holdings on improved practices; established a dairy to supply pure milk and better animals to the farmers for breeding; and established a poultry farm for the same purpose. The students and workers from the institute trained weavers, organised their cooperatives and provided facilities for training in tanning, pottery, embroidery, tailoring, etc. The institute now have a library which has a mobile unit for villagers, runs night schools, arranges film shows, meetings, etc. in the villages.

The institute could not get much help from the government and it could not conduct research work, so its work remained limited to the eight villages only. It has now been recognised as an important centre.

Gurgaon experiment

Rural uplift movement on a mass scale was first started by Mr. F. L. Brayne, Deputy Commissioner in the Gurgaon district of the Punjab, adjacent to Delhi. Under his programme, a village guide was posted in each village who was to act as a channel through which the advice of experts in various departments could be passed on to the villagers. The programme of introducing improved seeds, implements, improved methods of cultivation, etc., was started throughout the district. As these village guides were not technical men, very little of permanent value was achieved.

The work again gathered momentum after 1933, when Mr. Brayne was appointed Commissioner of Rural Reconstruction in the Punjab. In 1935-36, the Govt. of India granted Rs. 1 crore for distribution in various provinces for rural reconstruction work which acted as a stimulus. After that the work in the Punjab was transferred to the Cooperative Department and better living societies were organised to take up this work in villages.

Servants of India Society, Poona

At Mayapur village, in Madras, this organisation started a centre to impart training in agriculture and cottage industries to village boys and girls. It also started centres in U.P. and M.P. and published booklets on subjects like basic education, labour problems, indebtedness, etc.

Sir Daniel Hamilton's Scheme of Rural Reconstruction

In 1903, Sir Daniel Hamilton formed a scheme to create model villages, in an area in Sunderban (Bengal), based on cooperative principles. He organised one village of this type and set up one Cooperative Credit Society which functioned upto 1916. In 1924, he organised a Central Cooperative Bank and Cooperative Marketing Society and established a Rural Reconstruction Institute in 1934. The Institute provided training facilities in cottage and subsidiary industries.

Rural Reconstruction Work by Christian Missions

The activities of these Missions can be accounted under three heads: (1) Education, (2) Medical Service, and (3) Rural Reconstruction.

(1) *Education:* The aim of their education system has been to impart education which is in harmony with the rural environment and site. Their system has in view character-building, the raising of the standard of general intelligence, spread of literacy, recreation, cultural activities and instruction in subsidiary and constructive employment. The educational institutions run by these Missions, number about 2000 elementary schools, 325 high schools, and 38 colleges. In order to impart both theoretical and practical training to the students and to equip them for life, Central Institutes, attached to Rural Reconstruction Centres, have also been established.

Even the colleges, though situated in urban areas and imparting higher education, have not failed to take interest in village welfare work. The Christian College, Lahore (now in Pakistan), had a well-defined Department of Rural Life Research and Extension. Allahabad Agricultural Institute, typical of its type in India, has started a training centre for extension workers in its Agricultural Economics section. There is a separate Block attached to it for the extension work. The Christian College, Nagpur, has organised a rural extension service in order to relate the college to the life of the rural community.

(2) *Medical:* There are Mission Hospitals spread throughout the country which have become effective centres for imparting training in medicine, nursing, compounding and midwifery and many students, after receiving training in these institutions, have established themselves in villages to carry on their work.

(3) *Rural Reconstruction:* Several agricultural demonstration centres at Marthandam, Ramnathpuram, Patanchery, and the other Y.M.C.A. and Y.W.C.A. institutions have been doing useful work in rural areas.

Marthandam

It was set up under the auspices of Y.M.C.A. (Young Men's Christian Association) in Travancore. It was intended to symbolise the three-fold development of spirit, mind and body and evolved a five-sided programme, representing a development, not only spiritual, mental and physical, but also economic and social. The pioneer in this work was Dr. Spencer Hatch, an American agricultural expert. The essential technique of the centre was 'self-help with intimate expert counsel'. From the demonstration centre at Marthandam, about hundred villages were covered through Y.M.C.A. centres in villages. The extension secretary supervised the work.

Marthandam was in a strategic position to serve the villages. It kept prize bulls and goats, model bee-hives, demonstration plots for improving grain and vegetable seeds, poultry runs with prize laying-hens, a weaving shed, etc. Inside the centre, there was equipment like honey-extractors, health charts and the items needed for other cottage vocations. At the Centre, cottage vocations were taught and agricultural implements tested.

The emphasis throughout was on self-help and cooperation. The most successful projects was the Egg-Selling Club. By 1939, the egg-selling cooperative society became a self-governing body. Another co-operative society was the Honey Club, where the villagers were taught the use of modern bee-hives and extracted honey scientifically. The honey brought by the villagers was cured and marketed cooperatively. There were Bull Clubs, Weavers' Clubs, etc. The Centre had extensive social activities which could meet the mental, physical and spiritual needs of the villagers. It arranged exhibitions, lectures and had a wide range of health programmes.

Gandhian Constructive Programme

People know Gandhiji not only as a Mahatma, or a political agitator, but also as a social and economic reformer. He made people knew that India lives in village and that the common man's uplift is the uplift of the country. He wrote:[1] "*If the village perishes India will perish too. India will be no more India, her own mission in the world will be lost*".

Regarding development work in the country, he emphasised that, the "*Salvation of India lies in Cottages*". The key-words of his Economy are: (i) Decentralised production and equal distribution of wealth, (ii) self-sufficiency of Indian villages; equal distribution of wealth brought about not by the cruel process of extermination but through the hearts of the owners by persuasion and appeal to the better sense of man. He laid emphasis on the self-sufficiency of Indian villages as (a) he wanted to eradicate the class of middlemen exploiters so that the former could get the full price for his produce, (b) he wanted that the tiller should be able to consume his own products like fruits, milk, vegetables, etc.

For the emancipation of villagers he formulated an 18-point programme, which included the promotion of village industries basic and adult education, rural sanitation, uplift of backward tribes, uplift of women, education in public health and hygiene, propagation of national language, love for the mother-tongue, economic equality, organisation of *Kissans*, labour and students, and so on.

He sought to make the villagers self-sufficient and to develop in them that moral stamina which was essential to stand up against oppression and injustice.

The important institutions, which were organised to foster his ideas, were:

All-India Spinners Association, All-India Village Industries Association, *Go-Seva Sangh*, *Khadi Vidyalaya* at Sewagram, *Gandhi Ashram* at Tiruchungodi, *Gandhi Niketan*

[1]*The Harijan*, July 1936.

at Kallupatti, *Gandhi Gram* at Dindigal, *Gandhi Sewa Sadan* at Porur (Malawar), *Kasturba Ashram* in Trichur, etc.

Truely speaking, the Gandhian constructive programme was a movement of the people, by the people and for the people. His small works became big organisations and institutions, and the simple ideas of that time became philosophies. His emphasis on Khadi became the Charkha movement and then, the All-India Khadi and Village Industries Board. His thought, against untouchability and the caste system, resulted in the organisation of Harijan Sewak Sangh. Similar mention may be made of Hindustani Prachar Sangh, Sarvodaya, Bhudan Movement, etc. He created leaders like Vinoba, Nehru, Jayaprakash Narayan, Mira Ben, etc., who came from common stock, but got inspiration from Gandhiji. The Satyagrah Ashram at Sabarmati, and later Sewagram in Wardha, became not only places of training but of pilgrimage.

All those engaged in the constructive programme developed, in large or smaller measure, a missionary zeal, and, at whatever point they worked, they felt the inspiration that their work was needed in a great programme for their country's reconstruction. They were soldiers of the Grand Army of the Father of Nation; they were builders of a new society and torchbearers of a new civilisation in this great country which, due to their efforts, has again been recognised as an important country. That was the spirit and vision behind his constructive programme.

Etawah Pilot Project

The idea of starting this project was conceived and born in 1947. It was put into action with headquarters at Mahewa village about 17 miles from Etawah (U.P.), in September, 1948. First, 64 villages, which were then increased to 97, were covered under it. Lt. Col. Albert Mayer of USA, who came to India with the American forces in 1944, was the originator of the Project. He started it with the aim of introducing intensive work on the rural reconstruction front.

The Government of U.P. helped him in setting up machinery at the district level and with extra staff for the Project. The Point-4 Programme of America also provided finances.

The main objectives of this project were to see what degree of production and social improvement, initiative and cooperation could be obtained from an average area.

A review of the experiment showed that it had a widespread effect on educating the villagers and broadening their mental horizons. The experiment proved not only that the material was mouldable, but that the saying that the villager is ignorant, conservative and incapable of improvement, was an outmoded one.

The rural problem under the project was tackled by: (a) efforts to broaden the mental horizon of the villager so that he might accept new and tested ideas which might then become self-generating and self-perpetuating. (b) dealing with the villager's land, his tools, and his surroundings. The method of approach was educative and persuasive rather than coercive. For this it was essential that the extension workers live in the villages prove themselves to be friends of the villagers and win their confidence.

The Pilot Programme included introduction of improved agricultural and animal husbandry practices, public health education, literacy campaigns, improvement of cottage industries, training in repairing and evolving simple agricultural implements, in short a general awakening of all-round village-uplift activity so that the Panchayats get on a sounder footing.

The most effective achievement was that the entire area was under improved wheat crops. The area under vegetables was extended and diseases like Rinderpest and Haemorrhagic Septicaemia controlled. The other programmes taken on were the construction of roads, soak pits, adoption of improved agricultural practices, etc. All these resulted in improving the economic conditions of the villagers.

Adarsh Sewa Sangh, Pohri (Gwalior)

This plan of rural reconstruction was put into operation in 232 villages, falling in the Jagirdari of Col. Shitole. It aimed at increasing the per capita income of villagers. In each village, a Village Reconstruction Society was formed and the important items of work were compost making, deep ploughing, improved breeding and management of cattle, etc. The Sangh published a monthly journal "*Rural India*" which was devoted to Planning and Community Projects.

I.V.S. (Indian Village Service)

Its founder was Mr. Arther T. Mosher of New York, and Shri B.N. Gupta who established it in 1945. The objectives of this organisation were to assist village people to realise the best in their own villages by developing individuals, volunteer leaders and local agencies, and enabling them to be effective in helping themselves and others. The object was to assist the Government in developing villages.

For the realisation of the above objectives, the organisation adopted techniques like, personal contacts, informal group discussions, use of volunteers, demonstrations, use and production of visual aids, exhibitions, tours and trips, dramas, books and periodicals, etc. It was financially supported by contributions and donations. The organisation had branches in Lucknow and Etah (U.P.) and was affiliated to the Presbyterian Church in the USA Residents of 15 villages were the beneficiaries of this organisation.

Sarvodaya Programme[2]

It was a Gandhian concept and evoked great enthusiasm in Bombay State. The main features were simplicity, non-violence, sanctity of labour and reconstruction of human values. It aimed at raising the standard of living, scientific development of agriculture, promotion of cottage industries, spread of literacy, medical and health facilities and the development of Village Panchayat.

Firka Development Scheme of Madras State

It was Government-sponsored and aimed at the attainment of the Gandhian ideal of Gram Swaraj by bringing about not only educational, economic, sanitary and other improvements in villages, but also by making the people self-confident. The scheme was launched in the last quarter of 1946 in 34 Firkas throughout the State, and on April 1, 1950, it was extended to another 50 additional Firkas, at the rate of two

[2]Rambhai, B: *The Silent Revolution*, Jiwan Prakashan, Chawri Bazar, Delhi, India, 1958.

Firkas for each district. The selection of the Firkas was based on considerations of the general backwardness of the area and the possibilities for initiating the production of handloom cloth and other cottage industries.

The scheme, which aimed at attacking the rural problems as a whole, as well as in parts, consisted of short-term plans for the development of rural communications, water supply, formation of Panchayats, organisation of cooperatives and programmes for sanitation, as also long-term plans to make the area self-sufficient through agricultural, irrigational and livestock improvements, and the development of Khadi (hand-made cloth) and other Cottage Industries.

The Collector, who was primarily responsible for the successful working of the scheme in the district, was assisted by a rural welfare officer of the rank of Naib Tehsildar, who was put incharge of 2-3 selected Firkas. Each Firka was divided into 5 to 10 groups of villages which were put in the charge of Gram Sewaks[3] who were of the rank of Revenue Inspectors. Each Firka or group of Firkas was provided with special staff like agricultural fieldmen, administrative officers, Mistries[4], P.W.D. Supervisors and minor irrigation overseers. To associate the people with the implementation of the programme, Development Committees, consisting of officials and non-officials, were constituted in each Firka. At the State level, there was a State Rural Welfare Board comprising the heads of the Departments and influential and constructive social workers. It was this Board that drew up the comprehensive plan of Firka Development in October, 1947.

In order to effectively stimulate healthy competition between the official and non-official agencies, the Government of Madras decided to entrust the development schemes to non-official agencies engaged in doing constructive work. Five non-official agencies were actually selected and paid grants for doing Firka development of:

(1) Rural Reconstruction,
(2) Drinking water facilities,
(3) Sanitation,
(4) Agriculture, and
(5) Khadi and other village industries.

It was later realised that these efforts were restricted in scope and lacked coordination. They proved ineffective owing largely to lack of direction, support and encouragement from the central authority.

Nilokheri Experiment

It was originally started to rehabilitate 7000 displaced persons from Pakistan and later integrated with the 100 surrounding villages into what came to be a rural-cum-urban township. It was built round the vocational training centre that was transferred from Kurukshetra, in July, 1948 to the 1100 acres of swampy land on the Delhi-Ambala highway. The central figure of this Project was Shri S.K. Dey, later Union Minister for Community Development and Cooperatives upto 1965. The scheme called "Mazdoor Manzil" aimed at self-sufficiency for the rural-cum-urban

---

[3]Gram Sewak is village level worker.
[4]Mistry is a word used for mechanic.

township in all the essential requirements of life. The colony had school, an agricultural farm, polytechnic training centre, dairy, poultry farm, piggery farm, horticulture garden, printing press, garment factory, engineering workshop, soap factory, etc.

EXTENSION NEED OF INTENSIVE EFFORTS AT NATIONAL LEVEL

The policy of the British rulers was such that it resulted in the exploitation of India to enrich their own industries in Britain. This exploitation continued until India attained Independence, when there prevailed the problems of widespread poverty, ignorance, disease, etc. The Partition of India further increased these problems. The first year of our Independence faced with many extraordinary problems of floods and droughts. Then there was the problem of rehabilitating 9 million refugees from the Pakistan area. Our per capita income during this period was only Rs. 225 ($ 34) and 86% of our people were illiterates, the percentage in villages being 92%.

In 1949, the Constitution of India pledged to the people: social, economic and political justice, liberty of thought, belief, faith and worship, equality of status and opportunity and to promote among them all fraternity, assuring the dignity of the individual and the unity of the nation. The main aim was to create a welfare state. This created the need for community development. In 1951, India prepared its First Five Year Plan. As a part of total planning came the Scheme of Community Development Projects on October 2, 1952, the birthday of Mahatma Gandhi, the great leader who helped India achieve political independence.

The programme was not new

The Community Development Programme was a novel idea. The beginning was made in 55 selected projects. In 1952, each such project covered an area of about 500 sq miles, with 300 villages and a population of about 0.2 million. In 1953, the C.D. programme was extended to additional areas with a plan to cover the entire rural area of the country. Under this new scheme, new blocks of about 100-150 villages, covering an area of about 150-200 miles and a population of 60 to 70 thousand people were created. Each block was divided into Village Level Workers' circles.

Organisation upto 1958

Under this new approach, in 1953, a Central Office under the administrator for C.D., which later on became the Ministry for C.D. and Panchayati Raj and Cooperatives, was created. Shri S.K. Dey, who formerly worked as Project In-charge at Nilokheri, was appointed to it. In each State, a post of Development Commissioner was created to coordinate the activities of the various Development Departments like Agriculture and Animal Husbandry, Health, Education, P.W.D., etc. At the district level, the Collector was given the job of coordinating the activities of various District Development Officers. At the Block level, a team of various subject-matter specialists in Agriculture, Animal Husbandry, Cooperatives, Cottage Industries, Health, Social Education, and Panchayats was created. For using their technical advice was the village level worker who was a first-aid man trained for the job. Formerly, s training was for six months, then it was raised to one year, then to 1½ years and after 1958 to two years. The specialists were employees of various subject-matter Departments of the State. A post of Block Development Officer for each Block was created under the Development Department. The VLW was also an employee of the Development Department.

Organisation between 1958-65

Stages of the Programme: From April, 1958, the programme had three phases: (1) Pre-Extension Phase which was for 1 year, confined to agricultural development with a budget of Rs. 18,000. (2) Stage I: This was for intensive development for five years with a provision of Rs. 1.2 million. (3) Stage II. For another five years with an allocation of Rs. 0.5 millions. After the completion of Stage II, the Block was supposed to become the permanent unit of planning and development and an established channel for developmental expenditure. Where this was not achieved to any substantial extent, the State Government provides Post Stage II Blocks with a minimum outlay of Rs. 0.1 million a year.

The second major change was democratic decentralisation through Panchayati Raj as recommended by the Committee on Plan Projects.

Coverage. On January 1, 1965 there were 18 Pre-Extension Stage Blocks, 270 Stage I, and 2511 Stage II and Post Stage II Blocks thus totalling 5238 Blocks covering a population of 40.46 crores, living in 6.7 lakh villages. Andhra Pradesh had 445 of all types of Blocks, Assam 160, Bihar 575, Gujarat 224, Jammu & Kashmir 52, Kerala 142, Madhya Pradesh 416, Madras 375, Maharashtra 425, Mysore 268, Orissa 307, Punjab 221, Rajasthan 232, West Bengal 341, Himachal Pradesh 38 and Delhi 5.

INTENSIVE AGRICULTURAL DISTRICT PROGRAMME

The Intensive Agricultural District Programme was popularly known as a package programme. This name was given because of the collective and simultaneous application of all improved practices. These practices were improved seeds, irrigation, fertilisers, plant protection, implements, credit etc.

How this programme came to be: The agricultural production team comprised a group of experts, sponsored by the Ford Foundation in 1954, who were to study the agricultural problems of India and suggest ways and means to achieve self-sufficiency in food. This team, in its report, suggested intensified development efforts in selected areas so that rapid increase in production could be made.

Where started: The programme was started in July 1960 in 7 selected districts in various States. These were: (1) West Godavari (A.P.), Shahabad (Bihar), Tanjore (Madras), Raipur (M.P.), Ludhiana (Punjab), Pali (Rajasthan) and Aligarh (U.P.). The selection of the places was made on the basis of their high potentiality for increasing the yield in a shorter time. They were assured of irrigation facilities, were exposed to a minimum of natural hazards and did not have a drainage problem or soil conservation problem. They had well developed Panchayats and Cooperatives.

Extended to other places

Upto June 1963, the programme covered 120 blocks of those districts 45% of the villages and 30% of the total cultivated area in the seven districts. In many States, the programme had not been extended to other districts. The newly covered districts were Surat in Gujarat, Alleppey and Palghat in Kerala, Mandya in Mysore, Sambelpur in Orissa, Burdwan in West Bengal, Bhandra in Maharashtra, six blocks in Jammu & Kashmir, Cachar in Assam and two districts in M.P. (Balaghat and Narsinghpur).

Financing

About Rs. 9 crores for the farmers of the first seven districts and Rs. 8.5 crores for other districts were estimated to have been spent. This was shared by the Central Government, State Government and Ford Foundation. This was supposed to provide facilities for additional staff, implement workshops, soil testing laboratories, information units, training of workers etc.

Objectives

The short-term objective was, by providing the wherewithal for production, to aim at augmenting production to the extent of 50-60% in the districts covered by the programme, simultaneously developing good livestock and poultry. The long-term objective was to evolve a dynamic pattern of productivity which could be extended to other places and help the rural economy grow on its own strength and resources.

I.A.D.P. versus General Community Development

(1) I.A.D.P. made intensive efforts to make use of improved seeds and fertilisers in the entire cultivated area and to encourage adoption of improved farming techniques and agricultural implements. (2) The cultivators were provided with all supplies and services at the appropriate time and in adequate quantities. (3) Under the General Community Development Programme, credit was offered only to credit-worthy farmers, while in I.A.D.P. districts all farmers, who had production plans and participated in the programme, were offered this facility. (4) Marketing and storage facilities were developed within bullock-cart distances. (5) Technical assistance was provided in preparing production plans.

Farm production plans

The process of change from traditional farming to scientific farming, from subsistence to commercial farming, from extensive to intensive and from low income to high income enterprises warranted a phased development of farm planning. The I.A.D.P. envisaged three stages in this process.

(1) First phase: This consists of implementing simple but scientifically prepared farm production plans which involve the use of a package of improved and tested agricultural practices on important crops.

(2) Second phase: It comprises further elaboration of the process and its application to all crops raised on a farm.

(3) Third phase: It envisages long-term planning and the most economic utilisation of the farm resources so as to earn the maximum net income. This involves further research in farm management.

Demonstrations

Demonstrations on improved practices of important crops were conducted on farmers' holdings to show how new techniques were applied to crops, and to indicate levels to which the production could be stepped up, if all the recommended practices were adopted simultaneously, the economics of improved techniques was worked out in order to show the net profits and to stimulate others. The measures under this programme included (1) Advance arrangement for timely supply of seeds, fertilisers, pesticides, implements, spraying and dusting equipment and other requirements. (2) Wide publicity so that a greater number of farmers could see the methods and results at various stages. (3) In addition' demonstrations were arranged in every crop season to display the use of improved implements, plant protection equipment, etc., and to show the visible effects of new things and practices. (4) The schedule of practices for each crop and each tract was prepared for the I.A.D.P. district jointly by the research and extension staff, based on the results of trials conducted previously and also on the experiences of progressive farmers. One VLW was in charge of 4-5 composite demonstrations in each crop season.

Supply of credit

The increase in the area under improved practices called for additional credit to the farmers. The package programme strived to meet the requirements of credit for productive purposes. For this, cooperative societies were organised in these districts. To enable the primary cooperative societies to play their role effectively, the Cooperative Banks were strengthened and the rules regarding the sanction and disbursement of loans were simplified.

Cooperative marketing and storage facilities

In addition to credit facilities, efforts were also made to organise cooperative marketing and storage facilities.

For the certification of quality seeds, seed testing laboratories were set up in each such district. Agricultural implement workshops costing about five lakhs of rupees were established in every district. These had tested and developed prototype implements and also trained village artisans for their repair and upkeep. These workshops developed implements, manufactured prototypes, serviced implements and vehicles and trained artisans and farmers' sons. Such workshops had been set up in each such district. Other services included plant protection, soil testing, water use and management.

A case study of Raipur I.A.D.P.

The programme started from June 1961 with 16 blocks, which had covered 24 blocks. These blocks comprised 2947 villages and a population of 1.192 millions. The total cultivated area under the programme was 1.478 million acres.

Objectives

(1) To prepare the farm plans of farmers for loans in kind and cash,
(2) To supply the chemical fertilisers, improved seeds, insecticides and pesticide.

(3) To bring the cultivated area under package programmes like a, b, c, d packages.

(a) Improved Biasi (paddy cultivation) with 20N+20P, 5 gm agrosan, 20 kg BHC, loans of Rs. 100 per acre.

(b) Japanese Method: 60N+60P, 5 gm agrosan, 20 kg BHC, loans of Rs. 150 per acre.

(c) Wheat: 10N+10P+5 gm agrosan, 20 kg BHC, loans of Rs. 50 per acre.

(d) Groundnut: 10N+10P+10K, loans of Rs. 50 per acre.

(4) Organising cooperative societies and encouraging members to obtain loans.

(5) To conduct demonstrations of improved agricultural practices on farmers' holdings.

(6) Crop-cutting experiments were conducted to know the average yield of the crop.

(7) Introduction of improved implements for paddy cultivation.

(8) To bring the area under soil conservation activities.

(9) To collect soil samples and analyse the soil before sowing and applying the fertilisers.

(10) To lay out input and output demonstrations on cultivator's plots.

(11) To take plant protection measures.

(12) To improve cattle by better breeding and feeding programmes and introduce fish farming.

Organisation

The Headquarters of the Package Programme was located at Raipur. The officer in-charge of the programme was called Package Officer. He was to work in coopera-tion with the Collector of the district and other subject-matter specialists at the district level (see chart given on p. 50).

EXTENSION IN MADHYA PRADESH—A CASE STUDY

Madhya Pradesh is the largest State of India. It has about 40 million hectares of land and about 37 million people. Out of the total area, only about 18.7 million hectares are cropped in a year, thus giving about 0.58 hectares per head of population, which places this State second to Rajasthan State which is mostly a desert area. About 1/3rd of the land of the State is covered by forests in this respect it occupies the first position in India. About 7 million hectares of cultivable area in the State is still lying uncultivated. The State receives about 45 inches of rainfall in a year, which is not being properly utilised because it occurs mostly during a three month period. This requires training in water management. The levelling of the cultivable waste land requires training to farmers in land levelling. Only 7 per cent of the cultivated area has some irrigation facilities and in 93 per cent dry farming methods have to be used. The average yield of important crops like paddy, wheat, maize, sorghum, peanuts, etc., are below 5-6 quintals per hectare. This requires training the farmers in the use of high yielding varieties, cultural practices such as the use of fertilisers, placement of seed, sowing distances, cropping pattern, sequences or crop rotations and package of practices, as advocated by the research workers and the extension workers of the

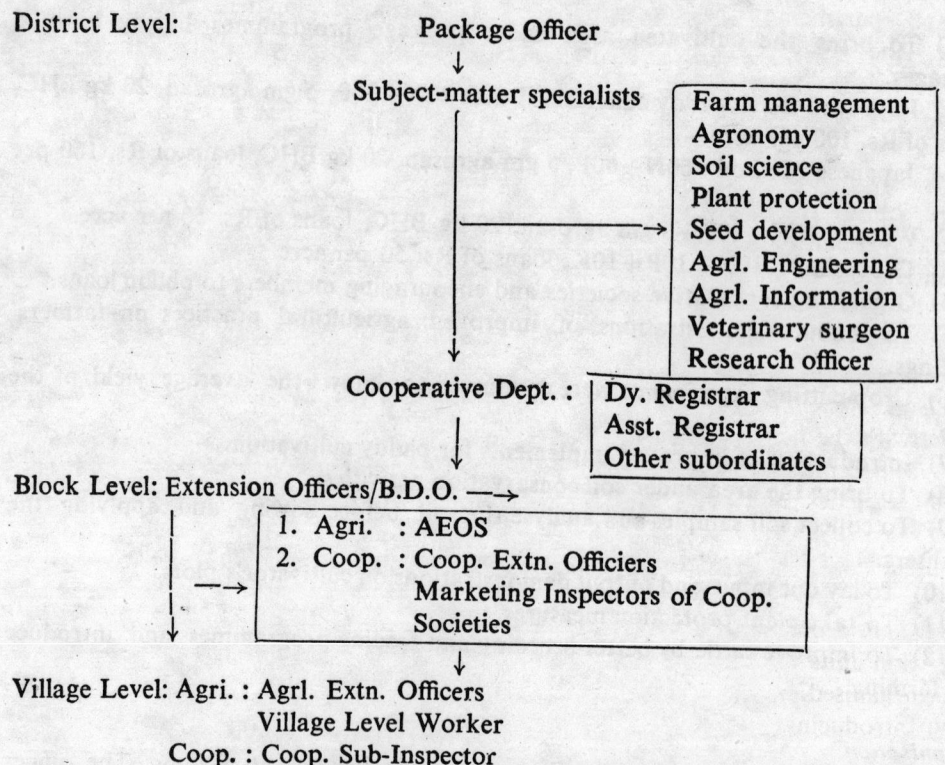

District Level: Package Officer
                                        ↓
                    Subject-matter specialists

| Farm management |
| Agronomy |
| Soil science |
| Plant protection |
| Seed development |
| Agrl. Engineering |
| Agrl. Information |
| Veterinary surgeon |
| Research officer |

Cooperative Dept. :

| Dy. Registrar |
| Asst. Registrar |
| Other subordinatcs |

Block Level: Extension Officers/B.D.O. ⟶

| 1. Agri. : AEOS |
| 2. Coop. : Coop. Extn. Officiers |
| Marketing Inspectors of Coop. |
| Societies |

Village Level: Agri. : Agrl. Extn. Officers
                       Village Level Worker
              Coop. : Coop. Sub-Inspector
                      Samiti Sewak

Agricultural University and the State Department of Agriculture. The State has in some respects, very rich resources, but it lags behind in the use of technology in agriculture. This is because its communication channels or flow of technology are not so well developed and the audience, i.e., the farmers are mostly illiterate which include 22 per cent population of tribals in some areas.

State agriculture department

The Headquarters of the Department are at Bhopal in T.T. Nagar. The Head of the office is the Director of Agriculture assisted by the Additional Director. They have some Joint Directors to share their work in Soil Conservation, Farm Machinery, Horticulture, etc. The State is divided into seven Divisions called Commissionaries, namely—Bhopal, Jabalpur, Raipur, Rewa, Gwalior, Indore, and Bilaspur. Each of these Divisions is headed by a Joint Director. In each Division there are Deputy Directors or District Agricultural Officers. Each district is divided in Blocks (about 10-15)—each block is again sub-divided into the Village Level Worker's Circles. Each such circle has about 10 villages, depending on the population. At each Block Head-quarters there is a Block Development Assistant. Administratively he is under the Sub-Divisional Officer of the Revenue Department. But for his help there is one Agricultural Extension Officer, and some other Extension Officers in cottage or other industries, cooperatives, animal husbandιy and veterinary, etc. They belong to the Subject-matter Departments of the State but work under the Development Assistant of the Block. The village level worker is under the Agriculture Department. He has education up to matriculation, with some special training for two years in agriculture and other areas so that he acts as a *first aid man* at village level. He is the key man. There may be a lady village level worker for helping village women in home science work.

The job of the extension staff of the State Agriculture Department is divided as: General Agricultural Development including introduction of high yielding varieties, demonstration of improved practices, plant production, storage, use and demonstration of machinery; soil conservation; management and supervision of Government farms maintained for multiplication of improved seeds; helping farmers in getting the finances and credit from banks and other financing agencies and starting Intensive Area Development Programmes as in Raipur district called the IADP Block or Package district with the help of the Ford Foundation, etc.

(1) *Under the general agricultural development:* (a) they conduct trials of high yielding varieties; (b) recommend dry farming practices like:

  (i) Urea spray on crops 5 to 20 per cent concentration.

 (ii) Demonstrate the use of various cultures in pulses, it costs about Rs. 3 per acre.

(iii) Recommend water harvesting methods, of course not so popular now.

(iv) Plant protection to spray and dusting. For this purpose there are plant protection units with each Joint Director in each division. Even aerial spray have been organised.

 (v) Introducing soybean on farmers' holdings through intensive work, as in Tikamgarh and Jabalpur, in collaboration with the Agricultural University.

(vi) Demonstrating the utility of growing oil seed crops like sesamum, peanuts.

(2) *Irrigation development:* For major schemes projects like Barghi, Bansagar and Beegh Ghat were set up. Great emphasis was placed on minor projects like (a) well-digging schemes. For the expenses on digging wells, installing pumping sets, etc., loans were given to farmers through cooperative and commercial banks. The agricultural Reorganisation Corporation helped in this work in Sagar, Rewa, Khargon, Gwalior, Tikamgarh and Sindhi districts. About 10,000 wells were then dug under this scheme. Up to September, 1970, 709 tube wells had been completed. Up to September end 53,469 water pumps were provided electricity.

Collecting water in tanks, utilising small rivulets, etc., were other schemes for developing irrigation.

(3) *Marginal holding development scheme:* In this State about 37 per cent farm holdings are less than two acres. So to help such farmers in the districts of Durg, Raisen and Sehore this scheme was started. Farmers were helped to get loans from various sources. Some small industries were also started to help remove unemployment.

(4) *Small farmers development agency:* To help farmers having holdings of less than 10 acres this scheme was started in four districts—Chhindwara, Bilaspur, Ratlam and Ujjain. About 130 thousand farmers were benefited by it. An amount of Rs. 16.6 million was provided.

Dairy development and cattle improvement

Just like the agriculture department there is a parellel animal husbandry and veterinary department at all levels in the State. Their main work is to provide: (1) Veterinary service hospitals. (2) Key village scheme centres which provide service in artificial insemination, castration of scrub bulls. (3) Running of Gosadans where useless and unproductive animals are maintained in forest areas, so that they may not breed further. (4) The Small Farmers Development Agency provides money upto Rs. 5000 for the purchase of milch animals and Rs. 3000 per family for poultry house and day old chicks. (5) Milk supply scheme. To help urban people in getting good milk, such schemes are operating in different cities in the State. The farmers got loans for purchase of milch animals, etc. Now the State has the M.P. Dairy Development Corporation.

Extension service of Jawaharlal Nehru Agricultural University, Jabalpur

The Headquarters of the University is at Jabalpur and it has six agricultural colleges at Jabalpur, Sehore, Raipur, Rewa, Indore, Gwalior; two veterinary colleges at Jabalpur and Mhow (near Indore); and, one agricultural engineering college at Jabalpur. This University is working on the Land Grant College pattern of the USA and has adopted the Trimester System. It is working in collaboration with the University of Illinois, USA.

It has a Director of Extension and a Head of Department of Extension Education and Rural Sociology at the Headquarters. There are some whole-time subject matter specialists in plant protection, horticulture, animal husbandry and home science. At each agricultural college there is a team of subject matter specialists drawn from various disciplines, namely, agronomy, soil science, horticulture, plant pathology, entomology, agricultural economics, plant breeding, botany, dairy and veterinary science and agricultural engineering. Their controlling officer is the Associate Dean of the college and the Coordinator is the Head of the Section of Extension Education. There is one lady extension teacher at each college and also at the Pawarkhera, wheat research station of the University.

I. *Objectives of the extension service of JNKVV (Jawaharlal Nehru*
  Krishi Vishwa Vidyalaya)

(a) To keep the extension personnel of the State Department of Agriculture, Veterinary Science and Animal Husbandry abreast of the latest technology in their respective fields. For it in-service courses, seminars, etc., were conducted and research stations maintained in the University in different regions.

(b) To communicate to the farmers useful and practical information on agriculture, veterinary, animal husbandry, and home science; to maximise production from land and animals by adoption of technology.

(c) To educate the farm wives in home science and agriculture.

(d) To promote welfare and development of youth—boys and girls in rural areas, who will be the future farmers to adopt technology.

(e) To work with farmers organisations with a view to developing leadership, initiative and participation on the part of the farming community.

(f) To coordinate research and extension education activities within the University on the one hand, and, with the State Department of Agriculture and Animal Husbandry on the other.

II. *Functions*

To achieve the above objectives their functions are:

(a) Farm advisory service;

(b) Training of workers and farmers;

(c) To collect information and process it at the communication centre and communicate it;

(d) To work with farm organisations; and

(e) Coordination.

III. *Activities*

(A) *Farm advisory service*

(1) *Working with adopted farmers:* The farm advisory service first works with selected farmers, and after two or three years shifts to a whole-holding programme, and then by adopting more and more farmers every year takes up the whole village. The approach is through organising film shows, exhibitions, talks from the SMS. The undergraduate and postgraduate students are also involved in demonstrating the practices and organising the work as part of their training.

(2) *Demonstrations:* (a) National Demonstrations. This is an All-India Scheme for which the Indian Council of Agricultural Research provides the money and the Agricultural Universities operate the scheme. These include demonstrations in dry farming and irrigated farming. Size of the plot has to be about one acre, and an amount of Rs. 550 per year (200 for *kharif*, 200 for *rabi* and 100 for summer crop and Rs. 50 for Board, etc.,) is provided by the ICAR. The package of practices, seed variety, etc., is decided by the Directorate of Extension and the SMS locally. (b) Maximisation Demonstrations. These are conducted by the SMS and students to show to the farmers the yield potential possible under their conditions by using the recommended package or practices. A little finance for fertilisers or plant protection is provided in the initial stage.

(3) *Farmers' days and field days:* To show the farmers the results of the latest technology through these demonstrations, and also the work being done at college farms and research plots, such days are organised at important stages of crops so that differences may be seen. Exhibitions of specimens and of other things of interest are also arranged to educate the visitors in the new techniques.

(4) *Farm women's programme:* The lady extension teachers work with farm women on projects like: kitchen gardening, use of plant protection material, use of fertilisers in kitchen gardens, control of household pests, home making, nutrition, sowing, knitting, child care, health and hygiene, fruit preservation, making of jellies and jams, pickles, etc. The extension education department of the University admits girl candidates with bachelors degrees in home science, these girls take up some home science projects and theses work in the surrounding areas and help the lady extension teachers in their project.

(5) *Youth work:* On the lines of 4-H clubs of the USA, the Bal Vikas Mandal Youth Clubs have been organised. Their projects are raising calves,

poultry birds, kitchen gardening, sowing, knitting, etc. Their pledge and emblem have also been decided on the lines of 4-H clubs. The students of undergraduate and postgraduate classes of the college, also work with these clubs as part of their practical work.

(6) *Poultry project:* The University finances some poultry farmers for two years under a scheme of developing poultry in the villages. Now the SMS at veterinary college Mhow, the SMS at Jabalpur and the SMS at regional agricultural colleges and research centres help in its development. The students with B.V. Sc. degree who join M. Sc. Extension Education at Jabalpur in the Department of Extension Education also take up survey, development and research on poultry units.

(7) *Popularising soybeans:* Because soybean has been introduced in this State very recently and people did not know much about its cultivation and consumption, about 30 demonstrations on this crop were laid out in different areas of the State. The Directorate of Extension and the Director of Research have brought out some publications on this crop and its use.

(B) *Training of Workers and Farmers*

The extension directorate and the department of extension education of the University, in collaboration with the State agriculture and animal husbandry department conducts training of the State staff, farmers and farm women and other interested parties as follows:

(1) *Working out package of practices for high yielding varieties:* Twice a year a workshop of the research staff of the University, the subject matter specialist and the staff of the State Agricultural Department and some progressive farmers is organised. Two bulletins—Package of practices for *kharif* (rainy season crops) and *rabi* (winter crops) in M.P. are being printed in Hindi. A separate publication on plant-protection "Guide Lines for Plant Protection Workers" has been printed. Other similar publications are Legume Inoculation, Organic Manures, Green Manures and their Long Term Effects, and Weed Control in M.P.

(2) *Plant protection seminar:* Once in a year a plant protection seminar of the plant protection workers at the State, divisional and district-levels is held. Manufacturers and distributors of insecticides and plant protection equipment are also invited to participate in this workshop.

(3) *Training-cum-workshop for animal husbandry staff*

(4) *Senior army officers' training programme*

(5) *Training in irrigation water use and management:* The experts from agricultural engineering college, Jabalpur, and the experts from the State department are available for this training.

(6) *Orientation of I.A.S.* (trainees for Indian Administrative Service) *Probationers.*

(7) *Apprenticeship training scheme for agricultural graduates:* Graduates in Agriculture are provided the facility of staying and working with progressive farmers for a period of one year. The University pays a stipend of Rs. 225 to them each month. The farmer provides other facilities.

(8) *Information workshop:* A workshop for the information officers of the State Department of Agriculture working at divisional level is organised. The duration is one week. Experts in communication from the University helps in this programme.

A communication centre for such facilities exists at Jabalpur. It produces teaching aids and other communication media.

(9) *Communication seminars:* To train the staff of the University and its constituent colleges, seminars are organised. The staff of the State Agriculture and Veterinary Departments also participates.

(10) *Ad hoc training programme:* Specialised training for farmers and workers in the cultivation of high yielding varieties of soybeans; management of poultry; fruit and vegetable preservation; management of large livestock farms, etc. is arranged from time to time.

(C) *Information Service*

(1) *Radio programmes:* The Indore-Bhopal station of All-India Radio runs a weekly radio programme, on every Sunday at 7 P.M., deals with the seasonal problems of farmers. This is a special feature prepared by the senior officials and specialists of the Vishwa Vidyalaya.

(2) *Arrangement of agricultural exhibitions, flower and vegetable shows.*

(3) *Publications.*

(4) *Organising trips to colleges for farmers from various parts of the State.*

(D) *Working with Farm Organisations*

The University helps organisations like the Progressive Farmers Association of M.P., Ali-India Farmers Forum, Krishak Samaj and other such organisations to become effective channels for developing agriculture. The 23rd session of All-India (Bharat) Krishak Samaj session was held at Jabalpur from 14th to 16th March, 1970.

(E) *Coordination*

There is an extension education council in the University and State-level coordination committee to deal with coordination within the University and between the State agricultural and animal husbandry departments and the University. Ad hoc meetings of the heads of the departments in the University are also held.

(F) *Communication Centre*

A communication centre has been established at Jabalpur. The centre has a media production section which prepares posters, slides, transparencies, charts, graphs, maps, etc., for the use of extension workers. This section also produces display material for exhibition.

The radio section of the communication centre plans, organises and executes radio features, talks, discussions, interviews and warning capsules for the benefit of the farmers and the extension workers. One programme is regularly broadcast on every Monday from all the stations of All-India Radio in Madhya Pradesh.

The communication centre also publishes a magazine 'Krishi Vishwa', in Hindi, for the benefit of the farmers and extension workers. In addition to the magazine, the centre publishes folders, bulletins, leaflets, etc. A circular letter to acquaint the extension workers of agriculture and veterinary departments with the latest research findings is also published every month.

(G) *Correspondence course for farmers*

A correspondence course for young *bona fide* farmers has been started. The main objective of the correspondence course is to acquaint interested young farmers with scientific knowledge in agriculture. The syllabus of the course consists of 25 lesson plans which are mailed to the farmers. After every fortnight, the performance of the participating farmers is judged on the basis of periodical evaluation and tests.

(H) *Training of students under village conditions*

Students enrolled in the Vishwa Vidyalaya need to develop competence, in solving problems of village people. It is, therefore, necessary to expose them to the village conditions wherein they can actively participate and become acquainted with village problems. A compulsory course, both at undergraduate and postgraduate levels, has been introduced for the students of all the three faculties. The students are required to work on various projects in adopted villages for six hours a week.

EXTENSION ABROAD

The Extension and C.D. programme of India has uniqueness and some originality and is one of the major experiments of the 20th century in the world. But, the rate of progress has been very low. The growth rate in Japan, Israel, Taiwan and the USA has been very high. For this purpose it is necessary that we study the extension service and their role in the development of these countries.

USA

About 170 years ago nearly 75 per cent of the population of the USA depended on agriculture, as is the situation at present in India. Their farmers also used animals for farm power and their tools and implements were as primitive as our farmers still use in India. The Farmers' Museum at Cooper's Town in New York State has all these machines and appliances to prove how technology and extension service changed the face of the USA.

In the USA between 1910 to 1955 the number of tractors increased from 1000 to 4.4 million and horse-power decreased from 24.2 million to 5 million during the same period. This decrease in the number of horses as farm power, as it was uneconomic, helped the farmer to complete the operations in time, and this resulted in the increased output per man hour. One bushel (about 34 kg) of maize, which took 100 minutes to produce in 1910, now takes only eight minutes. This means that the efficiency of a farmer, due to mechanisation, has increased by 12 times. The investment on farms in machinery, livestock, etc. which was only 2700 dollars is at present over 27,000 dollars i.e., an increase by ten times.

The increase in the output from farms raised the standard of living of the farmers. They purchased farm machines, household appliances like refrigerators, vehicles for transport, etc., and this gave rise to industrialisation. When the industries gave profitable employment their purchasing power per hour of work increased.

When the work in industries became profitable the surplus farm population started shifting from farming to other occupations. From 1800 to 1850, the decline in farm

Table 4.1.
An hours's wages of a worker bought

	1910	1970
Oranges	4	48
Eggs	8	48
Milk (in litres)	2	12
Bread	4	15

population was 2 per cent per decade and 6 per cent per decade from 1850-1875. This brought the farm population to only 50 per cent of the total of the USA. By 1920 the figure came down to only 25 per cent depending on farming. During 1950 to 1970 there has been a great fall (from 1950 to 1958 at 4 per cent per year), and it has come down to only 7 per cent depending on agriculture. The size of holdings increased as people sold their farms and shifted to industries and other occupations.

The economic size of holdings, the use of machinery in place of bullocks, farm investment, balancing in farming and adjustments in crop patterns and the technology provided to the farmers by their extension agency, etc., has brought about a rise in their standard of living. In 1940 only 33 per cent of the farm households had electricity, 18 per cent had piped running water and 15 per cent mechanical refrigerators, in 1970 every farmer had these things and also television and telephones.

One farmer in the USA, who could produce food for only 5 persons in 1850, produces now for 35 persons, 14 of the USA and 21 of other countries.

Much of the credit for improved technology, and its adoption by the farmers at such a rapid pace goes to the land grant colleges and the integrated service-cooperative extension service. The Universities provide solutions to the problems of the farmers and the integrated approach of Local, State and Federal Governments with the staff of the agricultural universities has helped to minimise the gap between the best known technology and the technology actually used by the farmers.

Cooperative Extension Service

In the USA, the extension service is called the cooperative extension and home economics service. It has the word cooperation because it ties together the local people or County Government, the State through its college of agriculture (land grant college) and the Federal Government through a special unit in the U.S. department of agriculture. The cooperative extension service is a branch of the Land Grant Institution. The levels at which the government may give authority and funds to the various parts of the service, is as in Table 4.2.

Organisation of Extension Work

The organisation differs from State to State. In some States there may be more staff for one particular branch while in others the agricultural agent may also take up the 4-H Club work and so on. The number of counties[1] may also vary on the size

---

[1]County: A big areager than a 'Tehsil' in India.

Table 4.2

Federal Congress	U.S. Department of Agriculture, Secretary, Director of Extension (One of many Divisions in the Department)

State
Legislature
	Land Grant Institution, President of the Governing Board, College of Agriculture. Research, Teaching and Cooperative Extension Service
	    (a) Director of Extension
	    (b) Supervisors and Specialists
	Other Colleges like Home, Eco., Vet., Mechanics, etc.

County Government	County Sponsoring Organisation, County Extension Service, County Extension Agents

and intensity of work in the State. The State of Missouri has 114, N.Y. 56 counties while Texas has 253 counties. As an example, we give the organisation in State of New York.

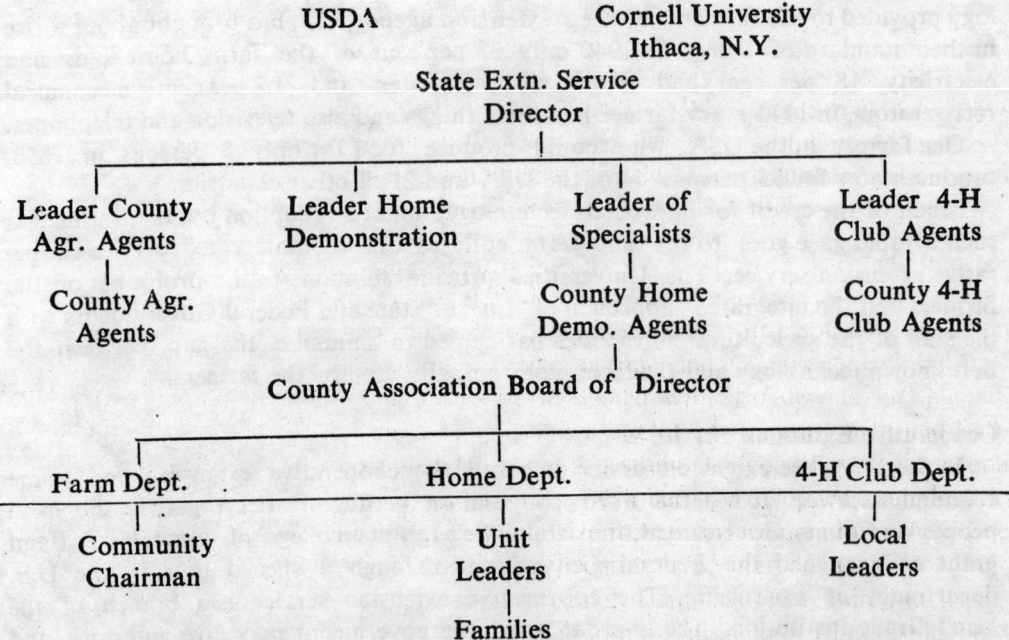

Organisation at Tompkin County: In Tompkin County, Ithaca, N.Y. State, there is one executive committee, elected from amongst the people of the county, consisting of ten persons—one President and nine members. They meet at least once a month. The important jobs of this Committee are the appointing or firing of an agent, control of finances, etc. It has Community Committees which have their separate programmes. They have combined meetings when needed and discuss general problems. The Chairman of each of the three Executive Committees namely, the Agriculture, Home Demonstration and 4-H Clubs make a Central Committee. In other States, the terminology in use may be different. In Illinois State, the County Agent is called an Advisor. Similarly, the word Chairman may be used in place of President in some States.

New York State has two State colleges of agriculture doing cooperative extension work, but the Director of extension is one. Subject to the authority of the Deans of colleges of agriculture and home economics. the Director of extension has over-all administration of the extension programme of both colleges. He is appointed to represent both the State and the Federal Governments in handling this responsibility. He is assisted by several administrative specialists and State leaders. All fiscal records are handled by the Director of finance of the State colleges of agriculture.

There are three State leaders for each type of agent in the counties, i.e. State leader of county agricultural agents, State leader for home demonstration agents, and State 4-H club leader. Each of these leaders has four or five assistants whose work is often assigned on a regional or district basis. The assistants also have certain Statewide responsibilities in the division of labour that is required in relationships and subject-matter—the woman dealing with home economics and the recruitment of women agents and the men having similar responsibilities in agriculture. They make their headquarters at the colleges and not in the field, as district agents do in many States. They are supervisors of agents and work on relations, programme building, selection and training, and maintenance of personnel in the counties.

All specialists are attached to their respective subject-matter departments and are responsible to the head of the department for the technical matter they teach. In the college of agriculture, all extension specialists are scheduled through the extension specialists scheduling office, and, in this respect, are also responsible to the Director of extension. In the college of home economics the specialists arrange their own schedules with the counties, working closely with the State leaders who supervise the Counties. Specialists in 4-H club work are employed by each college according to the various needs.

The activities like editorial, news, radio, visual aids, motion pictures, photography are handled by the department of extension teaching and information. This department is also responsible for all publications, such as bulletins, and their distribution to counties, to individuals and for correspondence courses. Undergradute training of prospective extension workers is done through this department, by credit courses in the college of agriculture.

How the county office serves the farmers? In each village, there are community leaders who have literature and are well-informed farmers. The farmer who needs some information, may call on the telephone, or he may see the county agent, or may inform him by phone or letter. The county agent manages to supply him the necessary guidance or may even call at his farm or home. If the farmer needs very technical advise, the county agent arranges this through the experts from the Research Station or University.

County agents: The county agent is generally an undergraduate of an agricultural college with special training, experience, ability to express ideas well, and able to advise farmers and cattle-breeders. Whenever there is a vacancy, the county committee requests the State Office to suggest a few names of persons for the post. The selection and removal of a person is entirely in the hands of the Local Committee.

Care is taken that the person should not be a resident of the same county and that his near relatives and wife are not employed in the same county office. Their salary is also decided by the local committee. It generally varies from $ 4000 to $ 7000 a year with facilities like a car for transport.

Local leaders. The county agent prepares a list of local leaders through election. These leaders play a very important role. They are unpaid and are supposed to be leading farmers or home-makers. They hold meetings in their communities and serve in county as regards 4-H club work, home demonstration work or farm demonstrations, etc.

Home economic agents: In each county office, there is one lady home agent exclusively responsible for extension work among women. At some places, there may be separate agents for rural and urban work or even separate agents for white and coloured Americans. About 5000 trained agents assisted by about 0.7 million volunteer local leady leaders, are carrying out work through about 70,000 clubs with a local membership of about 2 million women. This service helps the women in solving their farm and home problems.

4-H clubs: This is an organisation of boys and girls from 10 to 20 years of age with a definite programme of farm and home development and personal and social development. It is a part of the national agricultural extension system. One 4-H club agent or at some places two separate agents for boys and girls organise the clubs and look after the projects of individual and clubs. It has been given the name 4-H club because the club members are expected to have four Hs, the first H stands for HEAD, second for HEART, third for HANDS and the fourth H for HEALTH.

Organisation set-up

The organisation has three sets of principles; (1) Creed, (2) Pledge and (3) the Motto.

(1) *The National 4-H Club Creed*

(a) I believe in the 4-H Club work for the opportunity it gives to me to become a useful citizen.

(b) I believe in the training of my HEAD for the power it gives me to think to plan and to reason.

(c) I believe in the training of my HEART for the nobleness it gives me to become kind, sympathetic and true.

(d) I believe in the training of my HANDS for the dignity it gives me to be helpful and skilful.

(e) I believe in the training of my HEALTH for the strength it gives me to enjoy my life, to resist disease and to work efficiently, and

(f) I believe in my Country, my State and my Community and in my responsibility for their development.

In all these things, I believe and I am willing to dedicate efforts towards their fulfilment.

(2) *The 4-H Club Pledge*

Each member has to take a pledge before an authorised person.

I Pledge
My head to clear thinking,
My heart to greater loyalty,
My hands to larger service,
My health to better living for,
My club, my community and my country,

(3) *The 4-H Club Motto*
"To make the better best".
Objectives of 4-H Club: The 4-H Club Youth Organisation has eight distinctive educational objectives which are as follows:

(1) To help rural boys and girls to develop desirable ideals and standards for farming, home-making, community life and citizenship and a sense of responsibility for their attainments.

(2) To offer rural boys and girls technical instruction in farming and home-making so that they may acquire skill and understanding, and a clear vision of agriculture as a basic industry and of home-making as a worthy occupation.

(3) To provide rural boys and girls an opportunity "to learn by doing" through conducting certain farm and home enterprises and by demonstrating to others what they have learned.

(4) To instill in the minds of rural young people an intelligent understanding and appreciation of nature and of the environment in which they live.

(5) To teach rural boys and girls the value of research and to develop in them a scientific attitude towards the problems of farm and home.

(6) To train boys and girls in cooperative action with the idea that they may increase their accomplishments and, through associated efforts, assist better in solving rural problems.

(7) To develop in rural boys and girls habits of healthful living, to provide them with information and direction in the intelligent use of their leisure and to encourage them to continue to learn, in order that they may live worthier and richer lives.

(8) To teach and to demonstrate to the rural boys and girls methods designed to improve practices in agriculture and home-making with the object that farm incomes may be increased, standards of living improved and the amenities and life satisfaction enhanced.

Programme of work: The programme of work consists of:
(1) Farm and home project wq
(2) Health improvement.
(3) Club activities—every-day courtesies, first aid, prevention of accidents, etc.
(4) Recreation—such as singing, games, play, etc.
(5) Parliamentary procedure, in order that they may conduct good business meetings.

The agricultural projects include raising of livestock, dairy animals, poultry, vegetables and fruits, soil conservation, agricultural engineering, handicrafts, etc. Similarly, in home-making, the items are food preservation, preparation of garments, etc. The county and State and federal offices arrange to hold annual competitions at various levels. The winners of county competitions at the annual county fair are sent to compete at State fairs and similarly, the winners of State competitions are given chance to compete in national fair. It is very interesting to see the young boys and girls preparing their exhibits, for competition and presenting them to the Judges. The winners are given badges of different colours according to the place of their standing in the competition.

Financing of the organisation: For its financing no fee is levied but collected from sources like the provisions made by parents, sale of articles prepared by some members while learning, donations, running tea stalls or cafeterias at county or State fairs, etc. At the Stockton county fair in Kansas State, where author stayed for a couple of days, August 1960, the 4-H Club cafereria was being run very nicely by the members.

National 4-H Club Foundation: It is a non-official organisation serving the 4-H club through a variety of activities. Its Board of Trustees selected from the cooperative extension service and the land grant colleges and Universities, comprises eight members. It is financed by the 4-H builder's council, a citizenship group, comprising leaders of the business community, which seeks to develop continued support for work of the foundation. Additional support is received from concerns like the Ford Foundation, American Express Co., etc.

Other Youth Organisations in the USA

Other youth organisations are: (1) Future Farmers of America (F.F.A.). (2) Future Home-Makers of America. High School girls studing Home Economics are eligible to become its members (F.H.A.). (3) The Farmers Union, Farmers' Bureau and National Grange have their own Youth Organisations.

These are all organised on the lines of 4-H Clubs and the members compete with other youths. The county office help them in the same way as 4-H Clubs.

Farmer's Organisation: The farmers of the County are organised into various State and National Organisations for the development of their farming programmes.

Federal Farm Bureau: All the State Farm Bureaus were integrated into it in 1920. It assists in formulating the National Agricultural Policy on the legislation regarding farming. It also watches over the policies of the Department of Agriculture. It has its State branches and runs the Cooperative Marketing Societies of the farmers as well as handles Agricultural Insurance.

National Grange: Organised in 1867, it is one of the oldest farmers' organisations. It is a family organisation and adults, women and children all can become its members. It arranges for special talks on farm and home problems, takes the results from agricultural research stations to farmers holdings, helps the agricultural colleges and the research institutes, arranges for farm loans, helps in checking soil erosion, organises agricultural exhibitions and helps in improving the recreational centres, etc.

National Farmers' Union: It is organised on the lines of the National Grange.

Home Demonstration Clubs: These are organised by enrolling 12 to 25 home-makers or ladies to make a local club. They elect their office-bearers and arrange for lectures from outside experts and for training, etc. These small clubs are organised into State Organisations and from State and National Federations. They help in improving the home conditions, kitchen gardening preserving food, recreation, etc.

Other Farm Services in the USA

Besides the agricultural extension service, the following services play an important part in the overall development of farm people of the States.

(1) The farm credit association.
(2) The farmers' home administration.
(3) Rural electrification board.
(4) The forest service.
(5) The soil conservation service.
(6) The production and marketing administration.
(7) The commodity credit corporation.
(8) The federal crop insurance corporation.
(9) The commodity exchange authority.

Development of American Agriculture and the Cooperative Extension Service

If we go through the history of the development of extension service in the USA, we find that the professional people who became involved in this educational work also "Learned by doing". There were no pre-trained personnel. The individuals who found the ways to get the job done became leaders, but there was a great area of trial and error and experimentation. The important events can be given as follows:

1785—For the first time in 1785, a society for promoting agriculture was organised in Philadelphia to disseminate agricultural information through publications, newspapers, articles and lectures, and to foster local organisations.

1796—In this year, the First President of the U.S., George Washington, suggested to the Congress the establishment of a National Board of Agriculture.

1811—The Berkshire Agricultural Society (Massachusetts) organised agricultural fairs, sale of farm products, competitive exhibits, programmes in agricultural education. Mr. Elkana H. Watson founded it.

1852—The U.S. Agriculture Society was founded with representatives of 23 different States.

1854—Farmers' Institutes started by the Massachusetts State Board of Agriculture. During the next 50 years, these institutes became the principal means of providing rural people with agricultural information.

1862—The Morrill Act established Land Grant Colleges. As the Congress granted an endowment in terms of federal land and a grant of 5,000 dollars per year, these colleges were known as Land Grant Colleges. Some of these colleges have now become full-fledged Universities. The main object with which these colleges were established was to acquire and diffuse among the people of the United States, useful information on agriculture. Later on, experimental farms were started on the college campuses. It was thought that class-room teaching alone was not sufficient for bringing rapid change in agriculture so they employed top publicity men, arranged for lectures in villages and these professionals took tours to various places where they were invited by the farmers.

1867—The Grange Organisation was formed.

1884—Bureau of Animal Husbandary was orgainsed.

1887—The Hatch Act established experiment stations.

1900—13 Clubs to work with rural boys and girls were developed in many States.

1902—A National Farmers' Union was organised.

1903—Teaching by demonstration started by Seaman Knapp and community Demonstration Farms were established in Texas.

1904—Farm demonstration on cotton boll weevil control started in Texas and 24 special agent were engaged to help Dr. Knapp.

1906—First county agent appointed in Texas. Knapp further expanded the extension organisation and was successful in getting about 157 associates to undertake the extension work. By 1914, about 700 counties were able to have county agents.

1914—Smith Lever Act coordinated extension work nationally.

1917—Smith Hughes Vocational Education Act.

1920—American Farm Bureau Federation organised.

1923—Agricultural Credit Act.

1935—Soil Conservation Service Established.

1953—Congress amended Smith Lever Act.

1955—Extension Law (Public Law 360)—Rural Development Act—provided appropriation for cooperative extension to give "assistance and counselling to local groups in appraising resources for capability of improvement in agriculture, or introduction of industry designed to supplement farm income", and do this in cooperation with other agencies and groups.

Balanced Farming under the State Extension Programme

In some States, the agriculture extension service provides aid to farmers in planning a balanced farming system and putting it into operation. It involves planned farming in which each farm family can analyse the resources available, and develop a system for more profitable farms and better family-living. Under this programme, a plan is set out by each individual family with the help of its county extension agent. Every item in farm improvement is scheduled. Resources such as land, labour and capital determine the extent of the plan. Several alternative plans are considered before selecting one which seems most suitable. Every farm is supplied with a balanced farming work-book. In this book, records are maintained for checking the profitableness of each system and item. The system adapts to any farm regardless of its size and type.

ISRAEL[1]

The agency responsible for the agriculture extension service is the "Joint Centre for Agricultural Extension", run jointly by the Government (Ministry of Agriculture) and the Settlement Department of the Jewish Agency. The representative of the Government works as the head of the extension service. The main sections of the Centre are: (a) Training or guidance section in new settlements, (b) Publicatios Division, (c) Audio-Visual Aids, (d) Home Economics, and (e) Auxiliary farms.

(a) Training and guidance in the new settlements

As there has been much immigration after 1948 and as the country had very few

[1]Based on 'An Agro-Economic Survey of Israel' by the Author (Dahama) under UNESCO Plan in 1956.

agricultural graduates, the Centre decided to meet the situation in the following ways: (1) By engaging volunteer farmers to act as instructors in the new villages; (2) by training the new instructors; and (3) by providing facilities for in-service training.

(1) *Volunteer Farmers:* The movement of taking young people from well-settled villages who, with their families, settled in the new villages and worked as instructors, solved the problem, partially.

(2) *Training of New Instructors:* Arrangements were made at the Rupin agricultural college in which departmental instructors and even new persons, were trained to act as instructors in the new settlements.

With the cooperation of U. S. O. M. (United States Operation Mission), one training centre for training farm managers and branch managers at Ibim farm has been started. The aim of the course of farm management is to make the trained understand techniques of economic production. The trainees for the farm managers course have to study for four months devoting three days a week to practical work and three days to lectures on six subjects, including vegetables, industrial crops, orange groves, irrigation, mechanisation and farm management.

(3) *In-service Training of Instructors:* Every instructor has to get this training in order to refresh his knowledge and to get more basic knowledge. It is of 14 to 18 days duration. Some days are devoted to training and others to demonstration work.

Courses in writing: There is an agricultural institute for it, where lectures are prepared and sent to the instructors. The instructors are given question papers to be answered with the help of the postal lectures. An instructor can subscribe to this course, when he passes it. Seventy-five per cent of the expenditure incurred on the course is repaid by the Government. There is one library for this purpose at the agricultural research institute, Rehovot.

(b) Working of the publications division

This section publishes four types of publications: "leaflets" for the new settlers; "bulletins" for the old settlers; and advanced publications like "Farming Instructors News Sheet" (Alon Lamadrich Hachaklai); and advanced publications.

The leaflet is meant for the new settlers, wno are not expected to know anything of agriculture. It is short, concise and in simple Hebrew language. The sentences are very small, paragraphs are short and it has many coloured pictures. Such publications have been on corn, peas, manures. goats, onion, horse, tobacco, peanuts, potato, pastures, etc.

The bulletins are meant for old settlers and are sort of books giving more detailed information.

Farming Instructors' news sheet: It is a monthly publication and its intention is to give the village instructor some instructions in his day to day work as well as seasonal news.

Advanced publication are more complete studies on the subject with a research background.

(c) Audio-visual aid section

The U. S. O. M. under the point four plan has supplied equipment for the pre paring the recorded talks and coloured slides. They have special visual cars and with the cooperation of the General Information Bureau of Israel, they go to the villages. The slides and talks cover topics like preparation of compost, grading of vegetables, etc., and due consideration is given to variation in climate, irrigation, types of soil, cultural methods, etc. Different lectures are prepared for different regions.

Other activities

(1) *Evening Discussions with Farmers:* The instructor gives the villagers talks in evening which are recorded. These talks, to make them more impressive, are some-times aided by slides or pictures on agriculture. The farmers ask questions. Persons specialised in the particular subjects are often invited to give talks in the villages.

(2) *Demonstration Plots in the Villages:* Three or four plots of the farmers are selected for demonstration, under the village conditions in each village, where the farmers carry on operations according to the guidance of the experts. The cost is met by the Joint Centre.

(3) *Organising Village Exhibitions*

(4) *Contests and Awards of Prizes*

(5) *Agricultural Excursions*: The farmers of a settlement are taken to well-developed settlements. It gives an idea about the drawbacks in their own system

(d) Home economics section

This section is for the purpose of training the women to take care of home, family, child, cooking, etc. There is one Advisory Council consisting of representatives from the Ministry of Agriculture, the Jewish Agency, the W.I.Z.O. and the National Organisations of the different types of settlements. The council decides programme for the villages. It has extensison workers in home economics who are professionals but volunteers from the old settlements.

For training the instructors, in-service courses and study days are arranged where training is given in utilising the surplus vegetables by making tomato sauce, tomato juice, and preservation of fruits. After learning it, the instructors demonstrate it in the villages where they work.

They prepare model houses to show how a woman can make her house a nice one without much cost. The women from villages are brought and shown the utility of material, like citrus boxes, making of curtains from *talpatti*, and how to make beds, clean utensils, and prepare food, etc.

Recorded lectures, slides, charts, maps and pictures showing the use of tomatoes, kitchen gardening, care of babies, preparation of family budgets, vitamins in vegetables and fruits, balanced diet, hygiene, etc., are arranged.

(e) Auxiliary farms

Under this scheme, non-agriculturists or persons having some area in their compounds, are persuaded to grow vegetables and fruits, maintain some poultry, etc. It has five objectives behind it:

(1) *National Education:* As many of the immigrants who come to Israel are not

agriculturists hence in order to create a just contact between these families (especially among their children and women) and to awaken in them love and care for the soil, this system was introduced. This is called the national educational objective because, after the working hours, the inhabitants of small towns or of housing estates work on the plots by the side of their houses and thus become agriculture minded.

(2) *Economic:* It gives them livelihood, partial employment and ensures a varied supply of fresh agricultural produce in all seasons, and thus reduces the household expenses on these items. If there is a surplus, the family can sell it.

(3) *Health.* It brings the urban workers, the artisans, factory workers, clerks, or any type of such indoor workers out into the fresh air and enables them to exercise for at least one hour a day.

(4) *Aesthetic.* Changes the landscape by covering it with flowers, fruits, vegetables and gives it an attractive appearance.

(5) *Training for agricultural settlement:* It has been experienced that many immigrants who formerly did not like to accept agriculture as their occupation and had no interest in agriculture, after receiving training by working on their auxiliary farms, resolved to settle in villages as farmers.

Planning of auxiliary farms

Under this the area is one-third to half acre, varying according to the size of the family, the health of the members, and the inclination towards work. It should be protected from theft and stray cattle and should be situated near the house. As many branches as can be conveniently handled like vegetable, poultry, raising of fruits and crops, can be organised. Water arrangement is necessary.

The Government provides loans varying from IL 125 to IL 425, according to the size of the farm.

To provide agricultural extension service to the auxiliary farms, instructors are employed. The experience shows that the women instructors are more successful, and so 90 per cent of the instructors are women.

The programme of agricultural schools includes a special subject, "Instruction on Auxiliary Farms". All the students in the elementary schools are given training in elementary practical agricultural work and in their spare time, they do the work of their own farms. It has been noticed that the majority of the auxiliary farms are being run by boys of 10 to 14 years of age. The average annual net income per farm amounted to IL 579 (IL 1037-IL 458=IL 579) in 1955-56 in 18 years.

A comparative study

Extension service improved agriculture and gave a higher standard of living to the people of Israel, which has very poor natural resources. This is because its people accepted scientific ways of farming (Table 4.3). This country became independent in 1948, i.e., one year after India, and their population has increased from 5 lakhs in 1948 to 20 lakhs in 1966, i.e., 400 per cent increase in 18 years.

Exports

Exports of agricultural products amounted to 1/3 of their total of goods worth

Table 4.3
A Comparative study of farming in India and Israel

	In Israel		In India
	Average	In best villages	
Area in sq miles	7872		Jabalpur Narsingpur District 7491
Population in 66 (Lakhs)		20	20.5
Rainfall in inches (annual)		20 (2/3 desert)	56 Jabalpur
Temperature in F		40-110 F	46-106''
Milk production in litre			
per milch cow	5840	7320	150 India
per sheep	300	400	20
Eggs per laiyng hen	210	250	70
Citrus fruit per capita	10 mds.	—	—
Cotton (Lint)	13 mds.	23 mds.	1 md. M.P.
Groundnut	32 mds.	—	6½ mds.
Wheat	38 mds.	74 mds.	6 mds.
Jowar (Unirrigated)	25 mds.	60 mds.	6½mds.
Irrigated	76 mds.	120 mds.	

$ 391 in 1965. These included citrus 7 million dollars, other foodstuffs 32.3 million dollars. Agricultural products 13.5 million dollars, per capita exports from such a small country amount to Rs. 1,500 per capita of population per year which is about five times the average income per capita in India.

TAIWAN

Taiwan has about 14,000 sq miles of area and a population of 12 million, which gives it a density of 860 persons per sq miles. This is more than 2½ times that of India. The rapid progress made by this country since 1948 gives an illustration at how an underdeveloped country can make strides in agricultural production through entensive extension efforts and planning.

Here extension work is undertaken by the farmers' associations. An agreement was signed in 1957 by the Provincial Department of Agriculture and Forestry (PDAF), the Provincial Farmers' Association (PFA), and the Chinese American Joint Commission on Rural Reconstruction (JCRR). It specified that a unified system of extension was to be carried out by P.F.A.; under the sponsorship of P.D.A.F. and with financial and technical assistance from J.C.R.R.

The farmers' associations in Taiwan are organised on three levels: provincial, country, (HSIEN) (22) and township (317). About 85 per cent of the farm families on the Island belongs to these associations. Each association serves on the average 2,500 farms or 15,000 farm population. Agricultural extension is financed by associations with subsidies from government agencies and JCRR. Since extension supplies like seeds, fertilisers implement, etc., are provided by the associations, extension work is mainly educational. Up to the end of 1959, 3,500 4-H Clubs with 40,000 members, and 1,230 Farmers' Discussion Groups, 420 Home Improvement Clubs, had been organised.

At the State level, there is an advisory committee composed of representatives from various Government agencies, training institutes and private bodies with the Commissioner of PDAF as Chairman and the General Manager of PFA as Secretary. Pre-service and in-service training of Extension personnel is given great emphasis.

J.C.R.R.

The joint commission on rural reconstruction created by the Government of the Republic of China and the U.S.A. in 1948, is mainly responsible for this rapid growth. The development of agriculture has been the main focus of JCRR activities, but it also operates in such related fields as marketing and rural public health. Though the agricultural 4-year plans are drafted at the Centre, they are revised in consultation with Farmers' Associations and local Governments. The typical pattern is period of study followed by an action programme managed by the JCRR or the Central Government, then the farmers take over full or partial management. The Rat Control Programme for example, was studied for 3 years (1950-52), launched in 1953, managed from the Centre until 1959, and is now managed locally. Other examples are programmes of renewing rice seed, nursery improvement, introduction of machinery and implements, all of which are partially managed by farmers. All public health including family planning is conducted in partnership with local institutions. The prime burden of extension work has been assumed by the farmers themselves. Extension agents are hired by the Farmers' Association, which bears 2/3 of its cost, the rest is paid by the Government and the JCRR. The extensive farmers' cooperatives employ about 13,000 persons, many of them trained by the JCRR.

The lesson of Taiwan and JCRR is that agriculture is capable of rapid growth, but only if all the necessary factors are present. This underlines the importance of governments of underdeveloped countries and aid-giving nations alike, investing in the physical and human infrastructure that made Taiwan's success possible.

Natural resources of Taiwan

The climate is sub-tropical. The Island is mountanous with less than 1/3rd area arable. Of the 9 lakh hactares of cultivated land, 5.4 lakhs are paddy fields and the remaining are dry lands. The yearly rainfall is between 80-100 inches. Most of the lands are sloping and much water can not be retained.

Multiple cropping

It is common for the farmers to obtain four crops in a year, from the same plot, two of rice and one cash crop, harvested before each transplanting of rice seedlings. Tobacco, rape seed flax, maize, jute, sweet potato, peas, melon, sorghum, soybean and a number of vegetables are raised.

Sugar and rice were the predominant products in 1952, making up 81 per cent of the total production. Products for export now include bananas, canned vegetables, and fresh preserved fruits. Cash crops accounted for 76 per cent of the total value of agricultural exports in 1968.

If we take 1911-15 as the base year, the index number of crop production has gone up to 396 in total agricultural production in 1961-65. In crops, this figure was 386, and in livestock, 386 (1911-15=100). From 1951-55 to 1961-65 the annual growth rate of crop production has been three times faster than the annual growth rate in land area. During this period the annual growth rate of crop production per cultivated hectare was 3.5 per cent.

CHINA

History of extension

The first attempt was made by the National Committee of the Chinese Y.M.C.A. Around 1915, it sponsored a popular lecture tour on afforestation. The programme was conducted for nearly two years. In 1918, Dr. John H. Raisner, the Dean of the Agriculture College of the University of Nanking introduced the extension system to improve cotton production in China. A cotton specialist from U.S.A. was invited to conduct this work.

Mr. Y.C. James Yen took up a campaign to eliminate illiteracy. As a priority the first programme was literacy, the second Agriculture and Economic Reconstruction, the third was Rural Health and the last was Citizenship Education.

The second private group was the Lt. Chun Christian Rural Service Union. It took up a programme of tackling rural problems by the combined efforts of the Christian Church and the local Government.

Efforts by colleges and universities

The College of Agriculture of the National S. Eastern University took up work on cotton. A number of research stations were established in different cotton-producing provinces. Next was the Nanking Agriculture College in 1924 where a division of extension was established. In church-related institutions, training in agriculture extension was also started. Lingnan University of Canton did outstanding research in seed selection, fruit culture, soil analysis, insect control, crop rotation and home economics. Fukien Christian University in Foochow Fukien Province pioneered in 1934 the organisation of a Rural Service Centre.

National extension service

In 1924, a national committee of agriculture extension service was organised. The Ministry of Agriculture and Forestry was the central agency responsible for the planning and administration and operating it on national level. There were three important bodies for scientific research.

In 1943, the Chinese Agriculture Association drafted a preliminary outline for post-war agriculture reconstruction in China. It recommended the creation of nine Bureaus in the Ministry of Agriculture, one of which the Central Extension Office, was to serve as the general headquarters of all agriculture extension activities in the country. It had four divisions:

(1) *Agricultural cooperation:* Covering agricultural production, processing, marketing, distribution and farm insurance.

(2) *Land use:* It dealt with planning and development, farm implements and irrigation.

(3) *Information division:* For disseminating information on improved practices

and ways of living.

(4) *Coordination and Assistance:* It had travelling demonstration teams, each composed of subject-matter specialists, who kept close contact with different extension offices throughout the country.

The People's Republic of China

It was proclaimed independent in 1949 and began extension work as under:

China's First Five-Year Plan (1953-57). It aimed at laying a preliminary foundation for agriculture as a socialist enterprise. Agricultural production was to be raised by 23 per cent during the period and half of the 120 million peasant householders were to be incorporated into producer's cooperatives. Grain output was to be increased by 18 per cent, cotton 25 per cent and soybeans 18 per cent. Livestock was to be increased by—cattle 30 per cent, horse 36 per cent, dogs 54 per cent, sheep and goats 83 per cent.

Second Five-Year Plan: In September, 1956, the 8th Congress of the Communist Party of China adopted a directive for the development of the national economy in the period of 1958-62, which was considered as a Second Plan of China.

JAPAN

History

As early as 1870, the liberated farmers organised discussion meetings and invited lecturers. In 1881, the farmers' discussion meeting was held at the national level in Tokyo. In 1885, the Bureau of Agriculture started itinerant farm instruction. The first experimental farm was set up in 1886. During World War II, the Farmers' Association, Stock Raising Association, Sericulture Association and the like, were all united into the Imperial Agricultural Association. The post-war situation favoured a new system which started in 1948 when the U.S. system was adopted with little change. The organisational chart can be seen as on the next page.[1]

Local. The farm advisors and home advisors are local government officers. They are paid half by local and half by national funds. The subject-matter specialists are also local government officers but are paid from the national budget in the form of grants-in-aid. They belong to one of the 23 special fields like rice, soil, livestock, etc.

They are the link between the farmers, farm advisors and the experimental stations.

Prefectural level. They administer their local work.

National level. The Extension Division in the Ministry of Agriculture and Forestry has 3 sections: (1) Extension, (2) Extension Education, and (3) Home Improvement Bureau. The extension division takes charge of affairs such as the qualifying examinations for subject-matter specialists, production of slides and films, radio programmes and evaluation of the local work. The main task of the extension education section is pre-service and in-service training and also rural youth programmes. The home improvement section covers food, clothing and home management problems.

[1] Term Paper in class RE 227 April, 1960 read by Akira Hosokawa, page 4a, Cornell University, Ithaca (N.Y.), U.S.A.

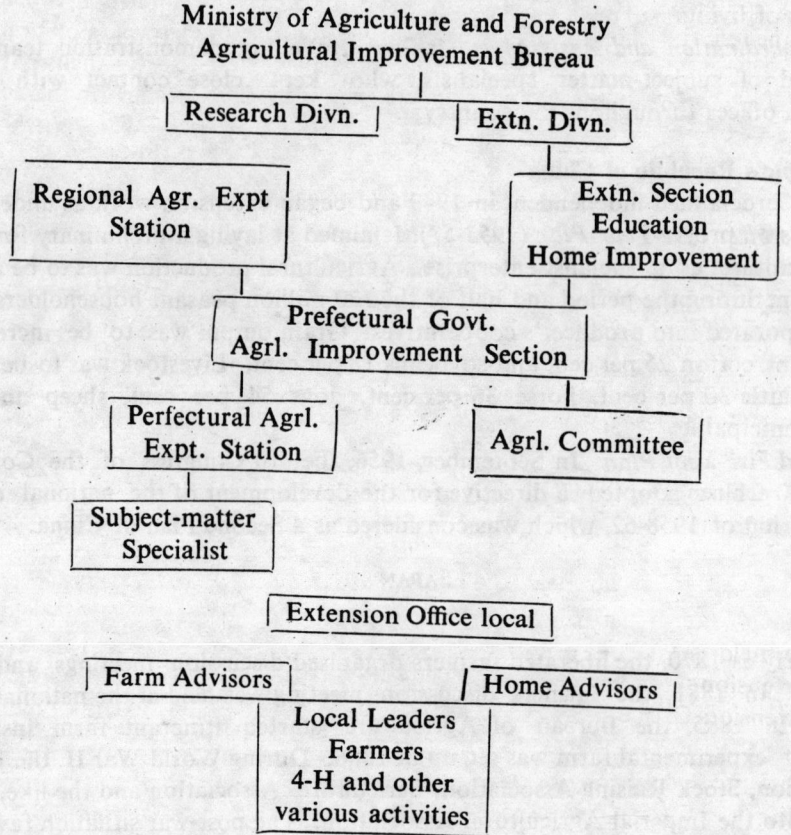

Advisory and Cooperative Organisation by farmers

Prefectural regulations make provisions for the extension to work with the prefectural agricultural committee in order to reflect farmers' needs in the extension programme. The committee expresses its opinions at the Governer's request.

The village local leaders are selected to be the promoters of the extension work.

Main features of extension in Japan

Due to the high rate of literacy, extension teaching is readily accepted by the farmers.

Close cooperation between research and extension at all levels of administration helps to make the work of both more meaningful and useful.

Farm advisors, are stationed in groups of 7 to 9 people, in each of the local offices. Each person serves on an average, about 600 farm households in a rather compact area. This permits a close contact between the farm advisors and the villagers. By working together as a team, they can discuss problems of common concern and receive inspiration and help from each other.

Rural boys and girls, after completion of their nine years' compulsory education, may enter one of the 54 youth training farms for one or two years of practical training in farm and home work. After graduation, they go back to their parents' farms, and may become youth club leaders, and, in time, leaders in their home committees.

PHILIPPINES

The extension programme in this country has a very prominent place in the Asian and Far-East countries. It is given the authority to consolidate, coordinate and expand agricultural extension work in the country. It is organised on national, provincial and municipal levels. The central office has seven divisions for administration, public relations, evaluation and training, specialists' services, agricultural programme, and rural club programme.

At the municipal level, there are about 850 agriculturists and 230 home demonstrators to work in about 22,000 villages (Barrios). About 50 per cent of the agriculturists and 10 per cent of home demonstrators are graduates of agricultural vocational schools and the remainder are all agricultural college graduates.

In-service training is given more emphasis. All regional and provincial extension workers are given 3-5 days in-service training four times a year at the regional offices. The municipal workers are given similar training at the provincial offices. In addition, each of the field staff is given 6 weeks of intensive training every five years in the summer. Extension work is mostly carried out through local organisations, e.g., Farmers' Extension Clubs for farmers, Rural Improvement Clubs for the women, and 4-H Clubs for the rural youth.[1]

REPUBLIC OF KOREA

The present agricultural extension service in this country was established in 1957, after the promulgation of the agriculture extension law. In June 1957, under the Ministry of Agriculture and Forestry, a National Institute of Agriculture was created by transforming the former Agricultural Technical Institute of Suwon. The institute of agriculture consists of two bureaus namely: Bureau of Agricultural Research and Bureau of Agricultural Extension, thus bringing both under one administration. Similarly, nine provincial institutes of agriculture were also established.

The extension work covers all fields like farm improvement, home demonstration, youth training, etc., and is concerned with all branches of farming. It is organised on national, provincial and county levels. In 1959, 937 people were employed for extension work—189 subject-matter specialists and 713 county agents and their assistants. In 1959, there were 3,730 4-H Clubs with a membership of 142,600 boys and girls.

Increasing attention is being given to training of extension personnel. In-service training facilities are provided to the staff at each level.[2]

[1] Sison O F. (Mrs.) Asstt. Prof. U.P. College of Ag. Philippines used as Resource person, 1960.
[2] Choi Sun Jung, Director Training Centre for Community Development in Republic of Korea Resource person. Visited Cornell University class RS 218 in Spring 1960, Ithaca, N.Y.

NEPAL[1]

Nepal, a country covering an area of 56,000 sq miles, lies between India and Tibet. It has a population of about 9 million. The annual rainfall is about 60″ varying between 50-100 inches. Being a hilly tract, it has transportation difficulties. About 95 per cent of the population lives on agriculture, and it was done by hand and in a traditional way. Important crops are paddy covering 6.6 million acres, maize and millets 2.9 million acres, wheat 0.77 million acres and then come potatoes, oil seeds, tobacco, jute, etc. Customs and traditions, etc., are just like in India.

Planning

First Five-Year Plan of the country was launched in 1956 with a total outlay of 33 crores of rupees for five years. Second Plan in 1961 and now they have entered their Fifth Five-Year Plan.

Village Development Programme

It was started in 1952 with the aid of the Government of U.S.A. through an agreement signed in 1951. Its organisation is on the Indian lines.

It has three levels of administration—National, District and Village. They have formed development blocks each covering approximately 100 villages and 66,000 people. The objectives and philosophy of the organisation is just the same as that of India. Until now, there are 36 blocks convering about two-fifth of the country. About 25 more were added. The programme is aided by the U.S. Government, India and His Majesty's government of Nepal. The country is divided into 3 divisions— Eastern, Western and Central. There are 3 section officers one in charge of each division including 10-12 districts and 10-15 blocks. At the block level, Block Development Officers are assisted by assistant B.D.O.'s. Besides, there are technical specialists and workers. In each block, there are 10-15 Village Development Workers (V.D.W.'s). There is a separate Development Department headed by a Director at the national level. The main programme consists of free demonstrations of improved methods of cultivation, subsidised services and loan services. There are three training centres for training V.D.W.'s and one for lady V.D.W.'s. These are just like India's training centres. Senior specialists are graduates in their branches. The B.D.O. is the coordinating person.

BURMA

Agricultural extension work in this country was started in 1927. It is now organised on national, divisional, district, township and village levels. Out of a total of 1,262 extension people, 1,113 work at the village level.

Farmers are organised into agricultural improvement societies, one for every five villages, served by a field assistant, who acts as the secretary of the society. At present there are about 700 such societies. These societies meet once a month and help to carry out field demonstrations, agricultural shows, contests and educational programmes. They also help in seed multiplication and distribution.[2]

[1]Resource person Mr. P. Basnyat of class 227 RE 1960, Cornell University Ithaca, N.Y., Asstt. Director, Nepal.
[2]Bill Gamble—class discussion RE 227 SPR. 1960, Cornell University, Ithaca (N.Y.), U.S.A.

Increasing attention is being given to farmers' training. In 1958 about 158 such classes were conducted in which 4,775 farmers were trained. Extension Officers from district level and above are agricultural graduates from college. The agricultural college did not provide courses in extension education up to 1960. Training centres for the training of agricultural assistants are working in full swing training extension workers. The State Agriculture Institute also provides three week in-service training.

There were no subject-matter specialists and no work was being done in home demonstration and for rural youth in 1960.[1]

CEYLON[2]

Since 1957, the Department of Agriculture has been reorganised and now extension service has been very much strengthened. A Deputy Director of Agriculture is now in-charge of extension and extension supplies. The country is divided into 21 districts and one district extension officer has been provided for this work. The district is further sub-divided into a number of revenue divisions. The plan is to establish one extension centre in each of the divisions where villagers can obtain information about their farm problems. Up to November, 1958, 53 such centres had been established. The subject-matter specialists take a two years' diploma course in Agriculture, and they are assisted by 1,500 food production overseers and field demonstrators who work at the village level. About 16 training centres are providing one year training course to these village level workers. Extension service of the country lays more emphasis on paddy cultivation. For every 250 acres of paddy-land, a Village Development Committee is organised, and one overseer is provided to look after every four such committees.

Recently, multi-purpose cooperative societies have been organised throughout the country—one for each village. Young Farmers' Clubs numbering about 1000, with a membership of boys and girls of over 20,000, have also been organised. Home demonstration work is still on a limited scale.

PAKISTAN

The Rural Community Development Programme in Pakistan is called the Village Aid Programme. The letters A, I and D in the title, although pronounced "Aid", are an abbreviation for part of the full title—Village Agricultural and Industrial Development, or more simply, "V-AID". This programme was initiated in June, 1952; training of first V-AID workers (VAW's) began in July, 1953. The first development area of 150 villages was opened in February 1954; and by September, 1957, fifty-nine development areas were in operation in all parts of Pakistan, encompassing approximately 10,000 villages having 6 million people.[3]

---

[1]Present Status of Agri. Extn. Development in Asia and the Far-East, F.A.O. Office, Bangkok, March, 1960.

[2]Ibid.

[3]Green, J.W.: "Rural Community Development in Pakistan—The Village Aid Programme," Chief V—AID Advisor, USOM to Pakistan. Mimeo—discussed in class 218, R.S. Spring 1960 in which he was a Professor (Cornell University, Ithaca, New York).

Aid and Objectives of V-AID[1]

The aim of V-AID programme is to assist villagers, both individually and collectively, plan and implement self-help programmes designed to eliminate or reduce their common problems, and to reach the agreed goals. The types of assistance rendered by the VAW's to the villagers are designed to give them the confidence and ability to act through organised effort, with a minimum of outside help. V-AID changes the concept of governmental assistance, from unilateral government planning and super-imposition of programmes upon the villagers—in a word, doing things for villagers—to one of *supplementing* the organised efforts of the villagers in planning and implementing their own programmes.

Organisation

The V-AID is administered jointly by the Central and Provincial Governments with the guidance and assistance of Advisory Committees at all levels. A separate Ministry of National Reconstruction has been established at the Centre since 1959.[2] In the States, the Provincial V-AID Administrator and his staff are a part of the development planning, administered by Development Commissioner who is charged with the coordination of all developmental work in the province. The V—AID Administration of West Pakistan is located in the Departments of Social Welfare and Local Government.

In East Pakistan,[3] the extension service was organised on provincial circle, district, sub-divisional, *Thana* and union levels. The agricultural stores were established at the *Thana* level for distribution of seeds, manures and fertilisers, etc. Union Agricultural Assistants were village level workers.

The basic unit of village aid is the development area, which is usually composed of 150 villages with a population of roughly 0.1 million. In West Pakistan, 30 men VAW's are placed in each area, giving an average of five villages per worker. In East Pakistan, the number allocated was twenty. The number of women extension workers was very small.

The Youth Organisation in Pakistan, is called "Chand Tara Club".

At present training for VAW's is carried out at 11 centres. The organisation is on Indian lines. The main emphasis is on agricultural development through fertiliser demonstration, use of improved seeds, and improved techniques in cultivation. The country is going ahead with Five-Year Plans as in India.

ARGENTINA

The extension service in this country has its origin in the service of regional agronomists, created by the Ministry of Agriculture in 1920. The function of these agronomists, who were agricultural graduates in agronomy, was to act as technical advisors to farmers. In 1957, the National Institute of Agricultural Technology (N.I.A.T.) was established. The essential characteristics of this Institute are: coordination between extension and research; administrative and economic autonomy,

[1]Ibid.

[2]Md. Mehmud, Sheikh of Pakistan Government Advisor, Plant Protection, Cornell Class RE 227, 1960, Fall.

[3]In December 1971, East Pakistan became the Democratic Republic of Bangla Desh.

which accelerates and guarantees availability of budget; and, decentralisation, which avoids a sterile bureaucratic organisation.

The N.I.A.T. was organised on four levels—National, Regional, Sub-regional and Local.

National level: There are three bodies at this level: (a) National Advisory Commission, which advises the Ministry of Agriculture, (b) Board of Directors—formed of seven members appointed by National Executive Power, (c) General Direction of Executive Body, integrated by a General Director and three Assistant Directors—one each for extension and promotion, agricultural research and livestock research. The main functions of these bodies are, to formulate objectives and general plans of work, to advise the board of directors, to coordinate technical and administrative work and to executive other functions. The Assistant Director of Agriculture has one advisor for 4-H Clubs and Home Economics.

Regional level: At this level are: (a) The National Agricultural Research Centre (NARC), (b) The Regional Centres numbering seven. These centres organise and coordinate regional agricultural research, and extension programmes of agricultural experimental stations.

The Directors of the National Agriculture Research Centre and the Directors of the Regional Centres coordinate the work of the institutes and the experimental stations according to the instructions of the Board of Directors.

Sub-regional level: There are several experimental stations in each regional centre, each headed by a director with one assistant in extension and one in research. There is an advisory committee for each experimental station formed by representatives of local rural organisations, banks, educational institutions, independent farmers and other local entities.

Local level: The extension agencies are located within the area of influence of each experimental station. The extension agencies report to the director of the experimental station who is responsible for extension work, but he delegates part of the responsibility to his extension assistant. Each extension agency has its area of influence composed of 2.6 counties *Partidos* with a total of 2000-5000 farms. For extension work, there is usually a Chief of Agency with one or two agriculture assistants, one 4-H Club Assistant and one Home Economics Assistant.

Integration, Autonomy and Decentralisation: The integration and close contact between extension and research achieved because the unit of work is the experimental station, where extension and research people get together to discuss common problems. The administrative and economic autonomy and executive decentralisation is reflected in the regional centres, experimental stations and extension agencies which have broad scope to solve directly their technical and administrative problems. The N.I.A.T. is also decentralised organisation by law, since not more than 5 per cent of the budget can be used in personnel expenditure by the Central Administration.[1]

In Mexico, which is one of the Latin American countries, there is superiority and

---

[1]Adopted from Programme Building in the Balcarce Extension Agency—Argentina Term Paper read in RE 227 class in Spring 1960 by C.A. Vismara, Cornell University, Ithaca, New York, U.S.A.

subordination and lack of local responsibilities for welfare work. The size of famiiles is large.

The Church is the most important formal, social organisation and the Catholic church is powerful. Here the changes in agriculture are going very slowly and have proximity to the type of work done in the U.S.A., because most of the workers of this country have worked with Americans. There is a great need for agricultural extension. The farmers use very little farm equipment and research results.

There are veterinarians and regional agriculturists, employed in the Government Department of Agriculture, who serve in a prescribed area. Agronomists are attached to local experimental stations who instruct farmers individually or in groups. The Government has provided specialists in various branches, and campaigns for work are organised.

In schools, the students have been organised in clubs and are given practical instructions by their teachers and government officials. They carry this knowledge to the villagers under their extension programme. The Ministry of Education has its own vocational agricultural programme and agricultural schools organise "farmers' weeks" in which agricultural methods, use of machinery, planting of trees, etc., are demonstrated.

The Federal Department of Education has 25 Rural Educational Missions, where 12 villages, forming one centrally located office, are controlled. After three years the office of the mission moves to another centre. Each mission includes one director, one agriculturist (who is an agricultural graduate), a nurse, a social worker, a recreation specialist, musician, carpenter, and two or more teachers of trade or crafts. The mission attempts to orient its programme to the needs of the people through a committee of Economic and Social Action.

Associations like National Federation of Coffee Growers, the Stockmen Association, etc., are doing private extension work in their own fields. Bank also have developed experimental stations and have their own extension programme.

Demonstration farms and ranches have been opened to guide farmers in the technique of crop raising and cattle breeding. 4-H Clubs, on the lines of there in the U.S.A., are being organised. A separate home economics section has been established for women.

JAMAICA[1]

Jamaica is the largest of the Islands of the former British West Indies.

It is situated in the Carribean Sea, commanding the gateway to the Panama Canal and lies 18° North of the Equator, and the eastern side of South America. It is 4,400 sq miles in extent. Size of holdings varies from 1 to 5 acres. Many companies own large estates and there are absentee proprietors. Population is about 1.75 millions.

In 1955, a new government was elected and a farm development scheme was started. It provides for generous incentives to insure participation of farmers. It provides for self-help and cash grants to approved applicants. Loans are also made proportionately as the work advances.

[1]Mr. R.M. Hanson: class RB 227 Fall 1960 worked as Resource person—Cornell University, Ithaca.

Organisations of Extension Service. A standing committee has been created at the highest level composed of Chief Executive Officers of the five agencies—Ministry of Agriculture and Land, Jamaica Social Welfare Commission, Jamaica Agricultural Society, Agricultural Loan Societies Board and 4-H Organisations. The principal organiser being Assistant Secretaries of the Ministry of Agricultural and Lands and Housing Social Welfare Organisation.

Then comes the divisional level having four Senior Agricultural Officers, and four Senior Branch Officers.

Below it there is Parish level having Parish Officers, Assistant Parish Officers. At the area level, there are field assistants, village instructors, and project officers.

The Island is divided into four divisions.

The community development work is taken up separately. There is one school of agriculture offering a three years' diploma course for extension workers.

GREECE

In Greece only 22 per cent of the surface area is suitable for cultivation. There is much pressure of population on the land, and the land per head of population is only 1.1 acres. Extensive farming, stress on the production of wheat and corn, with some nomadic herding of sheep and goats prevails there.

The extension service stresses home welfare and includes health programmes, recreational features, as well as improved agricultural practices. The Government agencies are taking up agricultural extension programmes through distribution of seeds protecting crops from pests, organisation of marketing in tobacco and table grapes, use of machinery, etc.

In the Ministry of Agriculture there is a Bureau of plant and animal industry for the control of animal research, organisation and operation of animal stations. In each Bureau, senior officers are provided for the extension training work. Pre-service training and in-service training for extension workers is arranged.

County agents with assistants in branches of animal husbandry horticulture, veterinary, etc., have been provided. The area covered by one county is equal to the area in the U.S.A. The county agent travels on horseback, or on foot. He is a well-qualified person. He visits and delivers lectures and talks to the farmers in the county.

CHAPTER 5

ROLE OF TEACHER, SUBJECT-MATTER SPECIALIST AND EXTENSION WORKER

India is predominantly an agricultural country and it is through effective agricultural education, useful research, as well as solution-oriented extension education, that a direct attack can be made on problems affecting the welfare of the people. This can be done by the integrated efforts of teachers, research workers and extension educators to transmit, create and communicate sophisticated agricultural technology into a simple and understandable form. Since 1960, with the continuous growth of Agricultural Universities (at present 21 in number) all possible efforts are being made in this direction. Each individual employee in the teaching cadre is responsible for performing at least two tasks, or, in certain cases, all the three functions of teaching, research and extension education.

ROLE OF TEACHERS OF AGRICULTURAL UNIVERSITIES

The definition of a teacher of an Agricultural University, as stated in the Acts and Statutes, indicates that the professional roles to be performed by a teacher are: teaching, research and extension education.

Recent studies by Indian Researchers (Dahama, 1960; Mishra, 1964; Jalihal, 1970; Bhatnagar, 1971) have emphasised the importance of identifying, defining and enlisting the roles of various persons occupying positions in the Agricultural Universities. Therefore, statements regarding the role of a teacher, a research worker and an extension educator constitutes a universe of interests in the forgoing discussions.

Efforts were also made to analyse the intricate problems of high expectations, low performance and the training needs, for effective and orderly role-performance of different functionaries, on a very sensitive role-expectations-performance instrument developed for the purpose. However, rarely were the areas of role-behaviours of teachers in these Universities explored. This could not be done because of the non-availablility of a precise instrument to measure the role-expectations-performance of the teachers working in these Agricultural Universities. Therefore, an effort was made to develop the same with the help of available scaling techniques. This led to the formation of a Role-Expectation-Performance Instrument given below.

**ROLE-EXPECTATIONS/ROLE-PERFORMANCE INSTRUMENT
FOR TEACHERS OF AGRICULTURAL UNIVERSITIES**

Role as teacher

1. Interest in the overall welfare of the students.
2. Possessing skill in using teaching aids.
3. Using as many teaching aids as possible.
4. Keeping personal contact with every student in the class.
5. Maintaining a democratic atmosphere in the class.
6. Behaving freely with students.
7. Developing a syllabus.
8. Evaluating the question papers within reasonable time.
9. Evaluating the progress of the student continuously.
10. Evaluating one's own progress in teaching.

Role as research worker

11. Having the insight and imagination necessary for anticipating and predicting probable actions and reactions.
12. Encouraging and training young workers.
13. Having sufficient time in hand to devote to research.
14. Discussing the Project freely with subordinates.
15. Not being scared by criticism.
16. Working on field-oriented problems.
17. Publishing papers on research undertakings.
18. Establishing contact with professional societies.
19. Taking part in various discussions on one's own subject matter.
20. Working on fundamental problems.

Role as extension worker

21. Keeping oneself well informed about the latest developments in the various disciplines of interest.
22. Establishing rapport with the clientele very easily.
23. Possessing skill in preparing extension teaching aids.
24. Knowing the social beliefs of the people.
25. Evaluating one's own progress from time to time.
26. Remaining motivated in odd situations.
27. Accepting failure sportingly.
28. Being able to recognise the felt needs of the people.
29. Knowing the principles of Extension Education.
30. Corresponding with the local leaders.

In order to perform the above roles, there are certain basic attributes needed in a teacher to make him effective and useful in the new system of agricultural education.

Attributes of a good teacher

(1) *Knowledge and understanding of his subject*

Only a true student, a sincere scholar of a subject, can be a good or even an acceptable teacher. This calls for complete dedication to the everlasting search for more and more information about the subject taught and, in addition, more understanding of it. It is absolutely essential that the teacher be "current" on his subject, since he just cannot lecture from notes that are even a year old. The great Indian philosopher, Rabindranath Tagore, put it quite aptly, "A teacher can never truly teach unless he is still learning himself. A lamp can never light another lamp unless it continues to burn its own flame. The teacher who has come to the end of his subject, who has no living traffic with his knowledge but merely repeats his lessons to his students, can only load their minds; he cannot quicken them. Truth not only must inform but must inspire. If the inspiration dies out and the information only accumulates, then truth looses its infinity."

(2) *Enthusiasm about his subject*

A good teacher likes the subject he teaches and he is enthusiastic about explaining it to anyone who wishes to learn about it. Usually, his enthusiesm is contagious. Of course, a good teacher likes to teach and he feels that his is the most important job in the world.

(3) *Interest in students*

The good teacher likes students and he likes to see them learn. He takes time in class and out of class, to explain the aspects of his subject which may be difficult for certain individual students to comprehend. He has patience with students and does not derate them when they have difficulty in learning. He knows that learning proceeds at varying rates among students, and at varying rates within the individual student, depending upon the topic.

(4) *A knowledge of teaching skills*

There are a number of techniques and arts and skills which contribute to good teaching. For example, the good teacher has clarity of expression and students are not left in doubt as to the meaning of what has been said. Such a teacher speaks clearly and forcefully enough to be heard and understood. He speaks to the class and not to the blackboard and maps. His grammar must be exemplary and he should use language which encourages learning. The teacher should be alert enough to observe whether he is teaching the subject at a level too far advanced for the understanding of the students. He must "pitch it" at their height. The instructor must be alert and perceptive so as to observe dishonesty, undue absences from class, time wasting in the laboratory, or inattention. He must be fair and display no favouritism. His examinations will be composed of questions and problems which are clearly stated and representative of the material he has stressed in the lectures, in the laboratories, and in reading assignments. He also studies the use of a number of techniques for teaching, such as, the less formal seminar approach, the auto-tutorial laboratory, the use of visuals of all types and the reinforcement and enrichment of learning possible through the use of study circles equipped with sound tapes, films, and slides.

He should admit that there is something of Educational Psychology and from that we do need to know what motivates students to want to learn. He will appreciate the need for studying measurement of student learning.

(5) *Broad interests and an engaging personality*

The most effective teacher is often a broad-gauged individual who is not provincial or narrow in his experiences and in his interests. He is well read and knows the relationship of his specific discipline to the needs of society. Usually, he is personable and likeable, with a fine sense of humour and is pleasing and congenial.

(6) *Demanding*

A thorough teacher demands that each student put forth his best effort. Such a teacher is not satisfied with poor performance on the part of the student, or on his own part. He drives himself without mercy to improve his own teaching. No lecture, discussion, or examination ever satisfies him. He continually evaluates his own teaching and seeks to learn what his students and his superiors think of his work.

(7) *Encourages and motivates*

Every learner needs encouragement. A compliment on a term paper or examination paper, when sufficiently earned, stimulates a student. Sarcastic, or cutting comments tend to discourage, as do unfair and unnecessarily severe cuts in grading. The teacher needs to comprehend that students and teachers are not adversaries but cooperators in an educational experience.

We think a college encourages good teaching when it provides the best possible facilities within the financial limitations of the institution, and when it makes certain that the teacher has time and it requires advance preparation.

Good teaching is most likely to result when it is properly rewarded. This reward can come about in a number of ways. The most practical acknowledgement of good teaching is via promotion and pay increase. Another more subtle reward is the development of the esteem of students and faculty alike. The high regard of former students and the excellence of the ratings given by present students—these are also rewards.

The longer we are in the teaching game, the more we may begin to suspect that teaching effectiveness does not necessarily tend to improve materially with experience. It seems likely that any increase in skills and professional competence resulting from maturity and experience tends to be offset by a loss of enthusiasm. There is often an increased preoccupation by the teacher with other tasks, or interests, that accumulate like barnacles as the faculty member continues his service to his institution. A formerly outstanding instructor may not fully realise how much he has been neglecting his teaching task until he is shocked by something, such as a published teacher-rating report. It takes time, lots of it, to prepare for a 50-minute lecture and our blessing falls on those professors who put their prime duty first.

Ultimately, the job of the teacher and the final goal of the entire educational system is, as John Gardner put it, ". . . to shift to the individual the burden of pursuing his own education". We, as teachers can assist this process by the kind of teaching we provide—not all spoon-feeding.

ROLE OF SUBJECT-MATTER SPECIALIST

The great concern of the Extension Education Discipline is to bring to the farmers and farm families knowledge of scientific methods developed in colleges of agriculture and research institutes. This task is now better performed by the teams of Subject-Matter Specialists (SMS) drawn from disciplines of Agriculture, Veterinary and Home Science and directly working under the leadership of the Director of Extension Services of the Universities. Such subject-matter specialists teams are also functioning in some states. The roles of these subject-matter specialists are of varied nature. In the wake of Agriculture technologies changing almost daily, these roles acquire special significance. Bhatnagar (1971) developed the following role expectation—Performance scale for assessing the roles of the subject-matter specialists.

Programme planning and execution roles
1. Involving himself in fixing the objectives (targets) in his area.
2. Knowledge about the agricultural production programme of his area.
3. Knowledge about steps and approaches to be adopted in programme planning.
4. Deciding the most suitable methods and techniques to be used in training people for each step in the programme.
5. Keeping ahead of the organisation supplied with technical information.
6. Be knowledgeable about use of results revealed by evaluation and field-studies.
7. Familiarity with what has been done in the past in his subject-matter area.
8. Acquainting himself with how it has been done in the past in his field of specialisation.
9. Taking extra care of special programmes as they develop.
10. Be knowledgeable about how to interpret the collected information.

Direct teaching and training roles
1. Delivering well prepared and useful lectures for Extension Workers.
2. Conducting Demonstrations,
3. Translating complex scientific knowledge into simple and understandable form.
4. Organising workshops.
5. Delivering Radio talks.
6. Organising field-trips of farmers to experimental fields.
7. Involvement in direct teaching of interest groups.
8. Serving as a resourceful person in highly complex problem-solving areas.

Subject-matter authority roles
1. Have thorough knowledge in his area of specialisation.
2. Considered a most authentic source of information at his level.
3. Serving as a liaison with research.
4. Selecting, interpreting and making available solutions to specific problems.
5. Having knowledge of trends.

6. Visiting demonstrations conducted in his area to provide guidance.
7. Availing of the opportunity for higher study and/or training.
8. Possessing a broad knowledge of the entire Extension programme and the role played by his subject of specialisation.

Relationship roles

1. Knowing that good relationships always pay in dealing with individuals and groups.
2. Maintaining a good relationship with extension workers.
3. Cooperating at all levels in developing "Package-Programmes."
4. Achieving team-spirit through coordination.
5. Appreciating the work of other specialists.
6. Understanding and practising the concept of integration of Teaching, Research and Extension.
7. Understanding and application of principles of extension in bringing about desirable changes in human behaviour.
8. Maintaining close relations with subject-matter departments and research stations.

With the above instrument in hand, the training needs of the subject-matter specialist were studied on the given items. The results are summarised as follows.

Training needs

To make the dissemination of information possible at the quickest speed, more sophisticated educational tools and techniques are being evolved and made available to these specialists and simultaneously more positions of subject-matter specialists are coming up to solve the problems of the farmers. However, sometimes subject-matter specialists do not have suitable answers to the growing problems of the farmers. Hence, there is also a need for training of S.M.S. from time to time. A recent study has revealed the immediate need for training of subject-matter specialists in the following areas:

(A) *Direct teaching and training roles*
 (1) Organising workshops.
 (2) Delivering radio talks.
 (3) Serving as a resource person in highly complex, problem-solving areas.
 (4) Translating complex scientific knowledge into simple and understandable form.
 (5) Involvement in direct teaching of interest groups.

(B) *Relationship roles*
 (1) Understanding and application of principles of extension in bringing about desirable changes in human behaviour.
 (2) Understanding and practising the concept of integration of Teaching, Research and Extension.
 (3) Appreciating other specialists' work.
 (4) Achieving team spirit through coordination.
 (5) Cooperating at all levels in developing package programmes.

Therefore, the training programme of the subject-matter-specialists may be planned on the various agreed upon role-items. The detailed outline on each role may further be worked out so as to equip them to meet the requirement of their satisfactory role-behaviour.

These functionaries, working both in Agricultural Universities and State Departments of Agriculture, are also facing certain problems in their orderly role performance.

Problems of subject-matter specialists

Mounder (1954) pointed out that for efficient performance, subject-matter specialists require suitable means of transport to enable them to move freely among those whom they are expected to reach. Gray (1956) gives a vivid description of problems of subject-matter specialists in the following words:

"The Agricultural Specialists in New York State, because ne has a car and good State roads to drive it on and because he can pick up the phone and call any extension Worker in the State in a few minutes, may be able to communicate fairly well with extension workers over a large part of the State, or even all of it. On the other hand, the same kind of specialist in Asia, because he would have to ride a slow train, or bus from one area to another and then finally walk or cycle 5 to 10 miles to see or talk to extension workers, could only stay in contact with extension workers over a small part of the State."

Brown and Deekens (1958) in their study revealed that the barriers most often mentioned by subject-matter specialists, in performing their roles are; lack of resources, inadequate researches, inadequate communications and interpersonal relationships.

Shearer (1961) indicated that sometimes 'alter' groups can become barriers to the subject-matter specialists position but such barriers only become challenges to his ingenuity. Further elaborating the point, he said that barriers to an effective subject-matter specialists programme may include: (1) lack of understanding of the mission of Cooperative Extension, the Planning Process and Group Dynamics, Social action, etc.; (2) The divergent demand of 'alter' groups; and (3) the Philosophy of the specialist himself.

The Expert Committee on Assessment and Evaluation (1960-1968) very aptly demanded special attention to develop a close, working relationship between the subject-matter specialists in the University and the Department of Agriculture. The Commitee observed:

"In order to keep the Agricultural Universities extension education and research programe attuned to the needs of agricultural modernisation, it is essential that the University subject-matter specialists also have access to the field problems. This can be-achieved in several ways, one of which would be to post some of the University subject-matter specialists in the Intensive Agricultural Districts to work with the district specialists and to forge links at the District level. The liaison between the University and extension can be further strengthened by the working together of the subject-matter specialists from the University and Agricultural Department on some selected projects such as Adaptive Research Field Trials. It is also recommended that both types of subject-matter specialists, should join hands in bringing out joint publications on extension recommendations in the local languages. The VLWs should be the main focus of such publications. A study was designed to investigate the problems of the subject-matter specialists, working both in the Department of Agriculture and Agricultural Universities. The findings of the study revealed the various problems that were faced by both the categories of subject-matter specialists." These are presented in Table 5.1.

Table 5.1
Problems Faced by subject-matter specialists in performing their roles

Problems	S. M. S. (U) (N=90)			S. M. S. (D) (N=65)		
	No.	%	Rank Order	No.	%	Rank Order
1. Interpersonal relationship	32	35.5	VII	27	41.5	VI
2. Inadequate field and farmers problem-oriented researches	64	71.5	V	52	80.0	I
3. Lack of transport facilities	78	86.6	II	50	76.9	II
4. Lack of resources and inputs with the farmers	76	84.4	III	45	69.2	III
5. Lack of motivation amongst the farmers	66	73.3	IV	32	49.2	V
6. Lack of incentives and recognition to S.M.S.	83	92.2	I	42	64.6	IV
7. Lack of leadership in S.M.S. team.	45	50.0	VI	32	49.2	V
8. Lack of training facilities to S.M.S. especially in extension education and use of audio visual aids.	29	32.2	VIII	16	29.2	VIII
9. Specialists being used as generalists	18	20.0	IX	27	41.5	VI
10. Paucity of funds for extension work	18	20.0	IX	10	15.3	IX
11. Emphasis on table work (office routine)	14	15.5	X	22	33.8	VII
12. Political interference	6	6.6	XI	16	29.2	VIII

S. M. S. (U) = Subject-Matter Specialist (University).
S. M. S. (D) = Subject-Matter Specialist (Department)

The S.M.S. while indicating the problems they were facing in their day-to-day working, also suggested certain measures which could help to remove these handicaps. These are summarised below:

The first problem of the S.M.S. was 'Interpersonal Relationships' which, in their view could be improved by providing telephone facilities, training in interpersonal communication, group dynamics, and selection of coordinators from the extension education discipline. "Inadequate field and farmers' problem-oriented researches" were the other great lacuna. The suggestions offered were the maintaining of closer coordination between Research and Extension; the opening of additional Regional Research Centres for the study of local problems; continued closer study of local problems by the S.M.S. and the communicating of these to the Research Centre; and, the taking up of research on these problems by themselves and the testing of them on farms or plots provided for the purpose.

The S.M.S. made strong reference to the 'lack of means of quick transport'. 'Inadequate provision for Travelling Allowance and also Dearness Allowance' acted as barriers. They suggested that loan facilities for purchasing their own conveyance, special remuneration and additional T. A. and D. A. facilities be extended to them.

They also indicated that required inputs, price support, and motivation were also not available to the farmers, proper recognition of their efforts and leadership of the S.M.S. themselves were lacking. Promotion of S.M.S. to proper cadre, institutions of awards and rewards, proper residential facilities, opportunities for higher studies and devising an evaluation procedure for their work were the suggestions offered to overcome the above barriers.

Proper leadership by selecting the coordinator of the S.M.S. Team from the extension education discipline would also be helpful. The S.M.S. also pointed out that granting recognition to the Agricultural Department as a Technical Department; minimisation of table work; arranging of periodical workshops, seminars, discussions; regular training in the handling of audio-visual aids and the other media of communications; orientations at University, National and International levels; providing well-equipped libraries, laboratories and other needed facilities were some of the measures that could be taken. They strongly felt that the team of S.M.S. may be further strengthened and can be extended to the district levels. All these suggestions, if implemented, can result in orderly role-behaviour from the S.M.S.

It is evident from the Table that both the categories of S.M.S. have some identical problems viz., lack of transport facilities (II), resources and inputs with the farmers (III), training facilities to S.M.S. especially in Extension Education and use of audio-visual aids (VIII), and paucity of funds for extension work (IX).

They have also pointed out some more problems such as: interpersonal relationship, lack of motivation amongst the farmers, lack of leadership to S.M.S. team and political interference. However, the S.M.S. (U) ranked the problem of lack of incentives and recognition to S.M.S. as I. The S.M.S. (D) have ranked it as IV. The S.M.S. (D) have ranked the inadequate field and farmers problem-oriented researches as I and the S.M.S.(U) it as V.

It is an interesting revelation that the S.M.S. (U) are very ambitious and rate themselves as being able to take high jumps first and foremost. It also denotes that probably the positions, or promotions, offered to them are not as many as they would desire to have. On the other hand, the S.M.S. (D) very aptly feel that field and farmers, problem-oriented researches are not adequate. This feeling, in some intensity, is noted by S.M.S. (U) also. This finding is an indicator that the problems faced by the S.M.S. (D) in their day-to-day work are rarely communicated to the research stations. This suggests the need for greater liaison between research and extension vis-a-vis the University and the Department.

The S.M.S. (D) have ranked higher (VI) and S.M.S. (U) also perceived (IX) the problem of 'Specialists being used as generalists' and 'emphasis on table work' (IV-IX. VII-X). This reveals that the S.M.S. (D) work in many directions including propagation of crop, planning the programme, conducting demonstrations, and are responsible for supplies and services. In addition to this, they are heavily loaded with their office work. The S.M.S. (U) also feel that their specialisation is not being properly utilised.

ROLE OF EXTENSION WORKER

Under this, term, "Extension Worker", in a wider sense, we include all persons working in the Extension field. We can very safely take into account the agencies like Village Level Workers, the Extension Officers and Block Development Officers, or any Extension Specialist or Home Economist. Extension work is mostly determined by the efforts of these agencies. The nature of work in the case of both these agencies is different, due to working at different levels, while the aim is ultimately the same, i.e., the development of the rural community from all aspects.

The extension worker plays an important and necessary role in the extension field. Extension work is not limited to the rural areas alone, but extends to urban side as well, although more emphasis is laid on the development of Rural Sector. Even in one Sector, the nature of work is multipurpose. The extension worker is bound to touch upon all aspects of rural life. He should have a comprehensive understanding of the village people and their problems. He should participate in sorrows and joys of the villagers and must develop a close contact with the village people. He is to win the willing and enthusiastic cooperation of the people and the work is to start with the local felt needs. No doubt, work is carried out at different levels by the various agencies working in the Extension sphere. The nature of the work may differ, but the goal is the same. The work at the lowermost level carried out in the village by V.L.W's is the foundation of rural uplift, for it is they who are in direct touch with village people.

The extension worker is to choose his own way of living in such a manner as to adjust himself to the society existing around him. He is to respect the villagers' customs, traditions and ways of life and create in them the spirit for real achievement. He is not to be above performing the lowest manual work in the village or taking an order. He must be a friend to the villagers and help them in all situations and even in awkward circumstances.

Keeping in view the multi-purpose nature of his work, the extension worker's activities and role in the various aspects of village life may be described as follows:

(1) He has to acquaint himself with all the families in the village and learn their problems, needs and capabilities. For this, he must survey the entire village, its people and their resources. He "helps people who help themselves" by being willing to learn from the people, willing to "show how to do" through actual participation, by working with all classes, castes and creeds, by getting village people to participate in developing a programme, working on the programme and in taking credit for the programme. He helps them by recognising that planning with the people is a continuous and important part of extension work.

(2) He should use as many methods of extension as are necessary, because experience has shown that extension workers who use more methods of extension are more successful. The use of all practical methods of teaching requires serious and careful planning.

(3) He should give the villagers every chance to work in co-operative group action. The villagers should be encouraged to have discussions because as a village discussion group grows and gains confidence it will naturally seek to become a village extension group. The extension worker must, in the beginning, give leadership to the group.

(4) He has to improve the village life and surroundings and create the conditions for farmers to become active members of our republic, socially, economically and politically. He is also responsible for making the villagers feel that he is a real partner

in village affairs and should make his help and cooperation needed and valued in every village activity. The field of the extension worker is very wide. He has to carry the teachings, recent research findings and discoveries from the institutions, experimental and research stations in the country, or elsewhere, to the villages to help the farmers in their business of farming, cattle-raising and home management. He is the man to raise the levels of living of the villagers and provide a more stable base for economic and mental security, other than the directive of increasing the yield, and improvement of personal and village wealth.

(5) He has to bring to our rural masses the basic knowledge of improved methods of Agriculture, Animal Husbandry, Home Management, etc., which will enable them to increase their agricultural production per acre, per animal and also improve their standard of living.

(6) He has to help villagers in crop and livestock raising so that their income is increased.

(7) He has to help the rural masses to appreciate the opportunities, duties and privileges of living in an organised way in the villages.

(8) He has to raise the whole standard of rural life by promoting social, cultural and intellectual activities in the villages.

(9) He has to bring to the rural people the knowledge of conditions prevailing in the progressive countries.

(10) He has to make the villagers intelligent, self-reliant and independent citizens who will love their homes and their country.

(11) He has to take the problems of the villagers to scientific institutions for the solution.

(12) He has to change the attitudes, knowledge and skill of the villagers.

(13) He has to bring about a psychological change in the minds of the village people to prepare them to adopt new ways of life.

Qualities of an extension worker

To play his role successfully, the extension worker, in a country like India, has to have the following qualities:

He must have a rural background, as far as possible coming from a cultivator's family. He must have some experience of working with village people successfully. We mention here that he must be a villager because the majority of extension workers coming from urban areas have difficulty in adjusting themselves to the villages.

(2) He should be acquainted with the nature of problems and the cultural background, otherwise there are chances that the farmers may not like him and he may be faced with failure in playing his role.

(3) He must have adjustability in village circumstances.

(4) He must have a thorough knowledge of the subjects with which he is concerned and be able to give correct replies to any questions asked by the villagers. In case he does not have the answer, he should be resourceful enough to find it out and convey it to them.

(5) He must be honest, sincere and hard-working and have a high general intelligence.

(6) He should have self-confidence and good judgement.

(7) He should be sympathetic to and share in the joys and sorrows of the villagers.

(8) He should be a sincere worker and not a show-off.

(9) He should have the firm determination to achieve his goal and direct all his efforts in that direction.

(10) He should always search out new methods for early and easier achievement of his targets.

(11) He should be prompt and able to influence the villagers in a positive way.

(12) He should have a burning enthusiasm to speed up change and progress by his activity.

(13) He should have the vision to frame future plans and programmes for the development of the village.

(14) He should be resourceful enough to satisfy the village needs by obtaining the assistance of the various Development Departments and Agencies responsible for village development.

(15) He should be courageous, hard-working and seek cooperation in meeting a difficult situation.

(16) He should be humble, polite, and friendly towards the villager. He should have a cool temperament.

(17) He should have a selfless nature.

(18) He should listen to others, respect their opinions and think over their problems and suggestions carefully.

(19) He should hold the ideal of "simple living and high thinking". His attitude should be that of service and helpfulness.

(20) He should be able to guide the villagers and work through their leaders.

(21) He should be well acquainted with the ways and means of teaching according to new methods and also be able to make use of audio-visual aids.

(22) While talking to villagers, he should let others do most of the talking and enter into conversation only when others seem willing to hear him. He should be friendly and speak slowly, taking care to be accurate in his statements.

(23) He should always be in search of new ideas and techniques. He should read the available literature and approach the subject specialists, research workers and others to acquaint himself with up-to-date ideas and new ways of solving the villagers' problems.

(24) He should search for the kind of organisation that:

    (a) Encourages growth of leadership ability;

    (b) Promotes the sense of community; and

    (c) He must accept a role of humbleness and be prepared to seek his triumphs in the lives of others. He is a cultivator of the art of applied patience. His motto should be "Suggest, wait and act" when the group is ready.

What he should not do? We list below a few 'Do Nots' which may help the extension workers. These are:

(1) Don't become impatient. Do not give up, if matters move slowly.

(2) Don't press. Offer a suggestion, raise a question, but don't press. If no one finds the idea challenging, let it rest for a time.

(3) Don't argue. Differ with people, yet state the points on which you differ as clearly and cheerfully as possible. Point out that all people have ideas of their own. Avoid a defence of your own position.

(4) Don't become worried and harassed. Community Development work is time-consuming, it puts pressure upon any who takes up the responsibility. People may call for your attention at any hour of the day and any day of the week, which can be wearisome. This unhappy state can be avoided by the efficient organisation of your time and the courage to say an occasional "no".

(5) Don't lose your sense of humour. It happens when one is over worked and worried.

(6) Don't interrupt. Let people finish even if their efforts be halting.

(7) Don't keep to the centre of the stage. Let the other fellows shine. Your success lies in the growth of a leader who develops as a result of your influence.

(8) Don't be too startled when praised. Everyone enjoys, praise or flattery, and you may even deserve it.

(9) Don't be unhappy when criticised. Try to correct your own inaptitude. No man is perfect and there may be some suggestions for improvement.

(10) Don't defend yourself if attacked. Let the attack come. Be interested and concerned, not defensive or alarmed.

(11) Don't be noble. If you are a saint, let this fact be discovered after you are dead. During life sainthood can be a serious handicap.

(12) Don't become alarmed when people lose maturity. Regression to childish behaviour is common to all humanity. The childishness will probably pass if not taken too seriously. Even Community Educators have their moments when maturity slips.

(13) Don't be dubious and clever. Be as direct and forthright as possible.

(14) Don't be partisan.

(15) Don't educate people by instructing them.

(16) Don't wait for disputes to come to you.

(17) Don't lose the ability to marvel at the way things work out.

The extension worker as a communicator

The overriding challenge to extension workers is to have ideas useful to an audience, to make their meaning clear, to get them accepted and to motivate people to adopt and practise them. The extension educator accepts both a grave and an exciting responsibility, grave in the sense that the welfare of people, often their very lives, depend upon his skill in conceiving and executing effective rural development programmes. Exciting in that he is a part of a great educational movement to help the masses of rural people improve their social and economic status.

To a large degree, the success of an extension worker is determined by his ability to communicate good ideas to others. In order to work effectively in the field of extension education for community development, it should be clear that the central challenge is to help village people put useful knowledge to work for them. This requires effective communication.

As a good communicator the extension worker should possess the following qualities:

(1) He should know his objectives, audience, message, channels, how to treat his message and his professional abilities and limitations.

(2) He should be interested in the welfare of his audience, his message and how it can help people, the results of communication and their evaluation, the communication process, communication channels, and how to improve his communication skills.

(3) He prepares for himself a plan for communication, communication materials and equipment and a plan for evaluation of results.

(4) He has skill in selecting messages, treating messages, expressing messages, selection and use of channels, understanding his audience and collecting evidence of results.

The above are well tested ways that can help to ensure an acceptable degree of success to a communicator engaged in extension education.

Keeping in view the multipurpose nature of his work, the activities and role of the extension worker in many aspects of village life may be described as follows:

(1) He has to acquaint himself with all the families in village and learn their problems, needs and capabilities.

(2) He has to survey the entire village, its people and their resources.

(3) He "helps people help themselves" by being willing to learn from the people, willing to "show how to do" through actual participation, by working with all classes, castes and creeds and having village people share in developing a programme, in working on the programme and in getting credit for the programme. He helps them by recognising that planning with the people is a continuous and important part of extension work.

(4) He should use as many methods of extension as are necessary, for experience has shown that extension workers who use more methods of extension are more successful. The use of all practical methods of teaching requires much serious and careful planning.

(5) He should give the villagers every chance to work in cooperative group action. The villagers should be encouraged to have discussions, because as a village discussion group grows and gains confidence, it will naturally seek to become a village extension group. The extension worker in the beginning must give leadership to the group.

(6) The ultimate aim of the extension worker is not only to help the rural people in increasing their efficiency and income but to improve the village life and surroundings and guide the farmers to becoming active members of our republic in its social, economical and political life. He is also responsible for making the villagers feel that he is a real partner in all village affairs and should make his help and cooperation needed and valued in every village activity.

(7) The field of the extension worker is very wide. He has to carry the teachings, recent research finding and discoveries of the institutions, experimental and research stations and from any part of the world to the villagers, to help the farmers in their business of farming and to improve their living conditions. He is the man to raise the levels of living of the villagers and provide a more stable base for economic and mental security other than the directive of increasing yields and improvement of personal and village wealth.

The extension worker (communicator), to communicate effectively, must understand the factors affecting his communication behaviour, the people with whom he works, those people's problems, the source of help towards solution of these problems the procedures for securing the help, the methods of utilising the help by practical application to the problems, and the evaluation by each farmer of his success in solving his problems. Not only must the extension worker understand all these aspects for his job, but he must be able to follow it through to the final stage with any given farmer or group of farmers.

CHAPTER 6

ROLE OF EXTENSION EDUCATION IN DEVELOPMENT

Extension education centres around three units: (a) Farmers or rural people or clients; (b) Innovations or discoveries or inventions; and (c) Extension workers or educators or specialists in extension services.

These are presented in detail as follows:

(a) *What extension education does for the people (farmers and clients)*
 (1) It imparts education leading to behavioural changes in the desired direction.
 (2) It is a process of informing people.
 (3) It motivates people to adopt innovations.
 (4) It suggests alternative fields for the needs and resources of the people.
 (5) It involves the active participation of the people.
 (6) It improves the decision-making ability of the people.
 (7) It brings permanent improvement in the conditions of the people.
 (8) It develops people's own programme.
 (9) It creates a congenial learning situation.
 (10) It builds confidence through action and conviction.

(b) *How extension education treats innovations*
 (1) Through field-trials and evaluations.
 (2) Through adoption, communication and diffusion.
 (3) Through overcoming problems of adjustment in different categories of people.
 (4) Through strategic combinations of workable technologies.
 (5) Through providing the facts and figures for consideration of consequences.

(c) *What extension education does for extension workers*
 (1) It establishes job-performance.
 (2) It helps in achieving team-spirit.
 (3) It assists in making workers organisation minded.
 (4) It trains the personnel as an in-built and continuous process.

(5) It develops the morale of the workers and makes them highly professional in the above roles.

(d) *What extension education does in general*

(1) It develops, strengthens and organises the groups, institutions and people to achieve their objectives.

(2) It develops leadership in local and professional situations.

(3) It acquaints the planners, policy makers and administrators with local conditions and the latest technologies suited to it.

(4) It provides sufficient data for developing plans and for coordination of activities.

(5) It gives direction and a package of educational practices for adoption and diffusion and also provides a communication media mix for innovations and evaluations.

DEVELOPMENT ASPECTS OF EXTENSION

The technological development of education can be related to various fields of Extension like Agriculture and Home Science.

(A) Agricultural extension

Agricultural extension is concerned with agricultural education assisting farmers to bring about continuous improvement in their physical, economic and social well being through their individual and cooperative efforts. It makes available to the farming community the scientific and other factual information the training and guidance for the solution of the problems in agriculture including Animal Husbandry, Gardening, Agricultural Engineering, etc.

If we want to adopt the above definition in various fields, we may attempt that with Agricultural Extension/Home Science Extension/Veterinary and Animal Husbandry/Medical Extension. This Extension is a method, or series of methods, by which the technical know-how of science in Agriculture/Home making etc., is carried to and included in the practices of farmers/home makers/animal breeders etc. who need this knowledge. In this way:

(1) Extension education is education (Formal as well as Informal) aiming at assisting people (rural as well as urban) to bring about continuous improvement in their physical, economic and social well-being through their individual and cooperative effort. It makes available to the client system (farmers/home makers etc.) scientific and other factual information, training and guidance for the solution of their problems in Agriculture/Home making/Nutrition/Sanitation etc.

(2) Extension education is a two-way process whereby the problems of the client system (farmers, home makers etc.) are brought by the change agents (extension workers, subject matter specialists of the Agricultural Universities, etc.) for solution to the Agricultural Universities/Research Stations/Home Science Colleges/ Veterinary Colleges/Medical Colleges etc., and the results are taken back to the client system in an acceptable form.

(B) Home science extension

What is Home Science ?

Preparing young girls for their future homemaking responsibilities has been in the past, and is still to some extent, the function of the mother and grandmothers in the family. During the last few decades, the concept of homemaking has undergone a considerable change. The homemaking knowledge of the older generation is very limited and has little relevance to the present day needs of homemaking. Besides many a modern housewife is physically too far away from her relatives to derive the benefit of their knowledge. Decision making, for example, in a very limited sense, was a dimension of the olden day's housewife's role. Life was steady and free of changes so that all that the young bride had to do was to conform to the established traditions of the joint family. Today, the young housewife cannot escape decision making. She is faced with the problem of selecting the 'right' foods, fabrics equipment, housekeeping methods, child-rearing methods, etc., from the large variety which the modern advances of science, technology and means of communication have rendered available to her. The decision must be hers.

Further, the present drive of formal education for women in schools and universities also necessitates them to spend a larger part of their day outside the home, which means that they have little or no time to spend with their mothers and grandmothers. And yet, homemaking continues to be an important function of every woman.

As such the need for agencies outside the home, which would assist in the task of educating women for homemaking, began to be felt around 1930 in this country. Since then many institutions, one by one, began offering courses in different aspects of homemaking. The concept, nature and scope of the subject have, in the last 40 years, undergone a tremendous change. The contents and duration for which the courses are offered still vary from University to University. But today, home science is largely conceived of as "...... a field of knowledge and service primarily concerned with strengthening family life through:

(a) Educating the individual for family living;

(b) Improving the services and goods used by families;

(c) Conducting research to discover the changing needs of individuals and families and the means of satisfying these needs; and

(d) Furthering community, national and world conditions favourable to family living."[1]

Generally the aspects of family life such as the following are of concern to the discipline:

(a) Family relationships and child development;

(b) Consumption and other aspects of personal and family living;

(c) Nutritional needs and the selection, preservation, preparation and use of food;

(d) Design, selection, construction and care of clothing, and its psychological significance;

[1]Dorothy D. Scott et. al., "What is Home Economics?" Journal of Home Economics, (October 1959), 680.

(e) Textiles for clothing and for the home;

(f) Housing for the family and equipment and furnishings for the household;

(g) Art as integral part of everyday life; and

(h) Management in the use of resources, so that values and goals of the individual, the family, or of society may be attained.[1]

A typical degree programme in the subject of home science consists of a number of elementary courses in the physical, biological and social sciences, as well as the arts, followed by a variety of courses in each of the following areas:

(a) Child and Family Development.

(b) Food and Nutrition.

(c) Clothing and Textiles.

(d) Housing and Home Management.

Apart from the knowledge drawn from the fundamental arts and sciences, home science also has to have its own research:

(a) To discover the changing needs of individuals and families and the means of satisfying these needs; and

(b) In improving the services and goods used by families.

Home science extension and its scope

Agricultural education has been the most important concern of extension ever since its commencement in 1952. About three years later i.e., 1955 a specific provision was made in the community development programme for the activities of women also. Homemaking being the important function of rural women by tradition, it is quite natural that the planners of the women's programme thought it fit to provide for educational activities which would increase their competence as home makers.

Role of home science extension in rural development

While developing an extension programme, the extension worker has two responsibilities. First, to guide his/her clients in satisfying their felt needs; and secondly to contribute, through the clients, in achieving the national goals. In the process of programme planning, which itself is an educational process, the extension worker must help his/her clients in developing an awareness of the national problems and objectives. When they set priorities for their day-to-day problems, to be solved with extension's help, they should be helped to see the importance of selecting those with the dual advantage of realising both their personal goals as well as the national goals. Some of the present day problems of our country, the strategy of solving which falls, at least in part, within the scope of home science extension, which include the following:

(a) Food and water shortage;

(b) Poor health and nutrition;

(c) Over population;

(d) Environmental pollution;

(e) Poverty;

[1]Ibid.

(f) Lack of understanding and/or practice of democracy; and

(g) Low work-efficiency on the part of all elements of our population, etc.

Home science extension has a definite role to play in assisting the rural home-makers to contribute their small bit in solving many of these problems, as they perform their routine functions.

Home science extension work can result in a raised standard of living for the rural families, and a more satisfying and dignified life for them. The raised aspirations of the rural family, as a result of home science extension work, will in turn help to create the necessary motivation among its members for the efforts to increase farm production. Increased farm production is a means for raising both the level and standard of living. Home science extension and agricultural extension are thus complementary to, and dependent upon, each other.

UNIQUENESS OF THE EXTENSION PROGRAMME IN INDIA

India's extension programme covers the community development programme also. It combines all the activities related to the promotion of the all-sided development of village communities, including political, social, cultural and moral improvement. Some people have called it an unique programme.

OBJECTIVES BEHIND EXTENSION EDUCATION PROGRAMME

Broad objectives

"The programme aims at the rapid increase of food and agricultural production, the promotion of education, improvement in health, introduction of new skills and occupations, so that the programme, as a whole, can raise the rural community to a higher level of economic organisation and arouse enthusiasm for new knowledge and improved ways of living. By this, the three most important levels of the country's economy, i.e., hunger, disease and ignorance, would be tackled through coordinated, planned effort on intensive lines. Its general objective is to secure the fullest development of natural and human resources of the area selected, called as blocks."[1]

The aim of the C.D. blocks is not merely to strive for ample food, clothing, shelter, health and recreation facilities but more important than these material improvements, the realisation that what is required is a change in the mental outlook of the people; instilling in them an ambition for a higher standard of life, and the will and determination to work for such standards.

In the words of C.C. Hearne, the objective behind the extension programme in India is "to raise the standard of living of the village population, and the right use of land, water and livestock".[2]

To sum up in one paragraph, we can say that it is to assist each villager in planning and carrying out an integrated, multi-phased family and village plan, directed towards increasing the agricultural production; improving existing village crafts and

---

[1] Second Five-Year Plan, Government of India.

[2] "Extension", a Journal published by Government of India, Comm. Project Min. Article 1956, by C.C. Hearne.

industries and organising new ones; providing minimum health services; required educational facilities for children as well as for adults, recreational facilities; and, improving housing and family-living conditions for village women and youth.

Specific objectives

(1) To change the outlook of the villagers. Unless the people develop rising expectations for a higher level of living, there can be no motivation for the people to provide the required leadership, to assure that village development will become a continuous people's programme.

(2) Development of responsible and responsive village leadership and of village organisations and institutions.

(3) To develop village people to become self-reliant responsible citizens, capable and willing to participate effectively, and with knowledge and understanding, in the building of the nation.

(4) Continued emphasis is focussed on improving and modernising agricultural practices and methods essential for increased agricultural production.

(5) Improvement of existing, and organising the new, cottage industries and other small-scale industries towards increasing employment and income.

(6) Need of food, clothing, shelter, recreation, health and religion are crystallised within the family and the motivation for their achievement comes from within the family.

(7) To upgrade the social status of the village teacher and to enable him to participate in the programme.

(8) To cut down the high toll taken due to illness, etc.

Financing

The resources for the programme are drawn from the people and the Government. For each block area, development schemes are conditioned by a qualifying scale of contribution from the people in kind or labour. When State assistance is offered for the execution of such projects, expenses are shared by the State and Central Governments equally in respect of recurring items and in the proportion of 3:1 in the case of non-recurring items. For productive works like irrigation, reclamation of land, etc., necessary funds are advanced by the Central Government to the State Governments in the shape of loans. The Central Government also bears half the expenditure on personnel employed by the blocks.

Extension as a programme and process

According to Carl Taylor, "although India has borrowed much from extension programmes in other countries, she has brought out both methods and administration of a programme which are unique in the so-called "Underdeveloped Countries."[1]

The country has chosen the goal of raising the standard of living of the 80 per cent who live in 0.58 million villages through aided self-help improvement undertakings.

[1] C. Taylor: Critical Analysis of India's Community Development Programme—issued by C.D. Administration, Government of India, 1956 p. 27.

India's programme is unique in the sense that it is both a community development and extension programme. It is a community development programme in that its major objective is to develop the village communities using methods which will stimulate, encourage and aid villagers themselves to do much of the work necessary to accomplish this objective. It is an extension programme insofar as it develops channels between all higher centres of information and the villages, and develops trained personnel to carry agricultural and health education and all other types of scientific and technicial knowledge to more than a million villagers."[1]

Extension, as discussed in the previous pages, is educating the villagers in changing their attitudes, knowledge and skills. Under this programme, Extension worker, by working with village people finds a solution for their needs and wants. He does this by 'helping people to help themselves'. The two important principles (1) "Learning by Doing", and (2) "Seeing is Believing" are always kept in view. The villagers are taught "What to want and how to work out the ways to satisfy their wants?"

Extension is the development of the individual, village leaders and their society through their day-to-day living. It is a continuous educational process in which the villagers and the extension workers contributes.

According to Ensminger, "Extension is a programme and a process of helping village people help themselves, incresase their prodction and to raise their general standard of living."[2]

We call it a programme because in it the extension worker is backed by technical staff, available on call, to help in dealing with specific problems, e.g., in the case of spread of animal disease, the extension worker calls in the veterinary expert located at the Block Head Quarters, or the subject-matter specialists in the Agricultural University or College and draws up a programme to prevent the disease from spreading further, and to cure the sick animals. This programme is operated through the villagers.

We call it a process because for the successful working of the programme, the extension worker is required to approach the villagers and win their confidence while on the other hand, the villagers also have to accept him as their guide.

Extension can be called in other words, a specialised system of agriculture and rural development and an out-of-school method of education for the people. In it the people are motivated through a proper approach, to help themselves by applying science in farming, home-making and community living, etc.

Ensminger also calls extension a process of teaching under practical living situations and, at the same time, a definite organisation for undertaking this teaching. As a teaching process, it can be used by anyone working with the people outside the organised class room.[3]

Field covered by extension

The field covered by extension is wider than that of formal education and the subjects studied are many more. It works with adults and young persons in actual life

---

[1] Ibid, (adaped)
[2] Ensminger, D., "A Guide to Community Development" C.D. Administration, Government of India, p. 56
[3] Ibid.

situations, where as formal education in the class room is concerned with the educational growth of children and young persons preparing for life. Extension generally deals with the problems concerning everyday life. It teaches people how to do and how to work out ways and means to satisfy their felt needs.

Agriculture extension brings about:

(1) Changes in things known to farmers.

(2) Changes in ways of doing things in farming.

(3) Changes in crop raising attitudes and behaviour.

(4) Changes in things valued or appreciated by the Client System.

(5) Changes in things comprehended, the understanding with which work is **done.**

Characteristics of extension

Extension is:

(1) Cooperative;

(2) Educational;

(3) Teaching;

(4) Informal;

(5) Flexible;

(6) Broad in scopes;

(7) Family centred; and

(8) Voluntary.

ROLE OF AGRICULTURAL EXTENSION IN DEVELOPING COUNTRIES

Singh, M.P. (1966) recognised that there can be no one pattern of organisation for agricultural extension work. Each country has to develop its extension organisation according to its own social, cultural and economic conditions at a given stage in its development. There are, however, certain broad generalisations which can be made. These are:

(1) Extension work can be most effective only when it is entirely educational in nature and free from regulatory and other Government responsibilities. It is, however, recognised that in the early stages of development, on account of limitations of the trained staff and resources, it may be necessary to combine "education" and "service" functions. This should be viewed only as a stop-gap arrangement.

(2) As development proceeds, more specialisation at the field level may be feasible and desirable. Experience, however, shows that even in most advanced countries where agriculture is diversified, a generalist (Extension officer) who can look at the farm operation as a whole is needed at the field level (except in areas with a single enterprise, e.g., Citrus culture, Cocoa cultivation).

(3) The successful work of the generalists at the field level depends upon their being supported by specialists at the next higher levels of administration. As agriculture progresses, both the necessity and possibility of providing specialists at lower administrative levels will increase.

(4) Efforts should be made to keep Extension and Research closely related to each other. This can be achieved by:

(a) The setting up of an institutional channel and employment of subject-matter specialists in the extension service.

(b) Periodic contacts between research and extension staff through meetings, conferences, field days, etc.

(5) Extension work must be directed towards the family as a whole—men, women and children. Work with youth and farm women is important.

(6) In the interest of providing maximum effective service within the limited resources, there is an urgent need for effective coordination of all the agencies serving rural people.

Extension services have to make available to rural people scientific and functional information in a manner that can be used by them to solve the problems of agriculture. This involves:

(a) Getting the new knowledge from a source—usually Agricultural Research Stations.

(b) Interpreting the knowledge so that people can understand it.

(c) Transmitting the interpreted information, in an effective manner, to the people who will use it.

An Extension Organization, in order to perform its functions efficiently, must keep these considerations in view. A provision must be made in the organisational set-up for:

(a) Flow of useful information from the research stations to the farmers and of farm problems back to the research stations.

(b) Production of teaching materials and teaching aids for use in extension work. This involves setting up of an Agricultural Information Cell within the Extension Division of the Ministry.

(c) A capable and trained extension staff who can transmit the useful information to the farmers and assist them to organise farming as a "business".

(d) In order to facilitate this movement of information back and forth, the number of levels of Extension Admininistration should be kept as small as possible.

Because of the shortage of extension workers and lack of other resources in a number of developing countries, "there is an increasing tendency to concentrate them in limited areas, e.g., on Land Development Projects or areas which have greater potential for rapid agricultural development, rather than spread then thinly over the entire country."

PART II

EDUCATIONAL PSYCHOLOGY
AS APPLIED TO DEVELOPMENT

CHAPTER 7

EDUCATIONAL PSYCHOLOGY: CONCEPT AND HISTORY

Psychology is defined as the science of mental activity of organisms, with the idea that "mental activity" is virtually the same as behaviour or as adjustment to the environment.

CONCEPT OF PSYCHOLOGY

(1) As a science of mental life

Psychology as defined by William James is "the science of mental life, both of its phenomena and of their condition." It studies such phenomenon as feelings, desires and different modes of cognition. The student of psychology tries to know mental facts, classifies them in certain categories, and makes an attempt to determine their causes. Psychology in the past was a speculative science. The psychologist sat in his room and it reflected on his mental status. But modern psychology is approximating its methods and procedure to the Natural Science like Biology and Physics.

(2) Science of soul

Psychology as a separate branch of study is more than 2000 years old. It was the genius of Aristotle that gave birth to this science. Yet, in its modern form, it is one of the latest of all mental disciplines. It has been changing its meaning from time to time. Rudolf Goeckel whose book on the subject was published in 1590, named it as *Psychologia*. This word is built up from 'Psycho' meaning "soul" and 'Logos' meaning "talk about" or "science of". Thus, psychology meant "the science of soul". By soul was meant a being dwelling in the body which could at times even leave the body and go on a sojourn. A more advanced view regarded soul as "a vital principle inhabiting and animating each human body and somehow the ground of each individual's experience". But psychology did not make much progress so long as the thinkers did not give up their theological bias. Soul in the theological sense is an entity inaccessible to scientific investigation.

(3) Science of mind

Psychology in the eighteenth century was conceived of as the science of mind. But according to one school, the mind itself was nothing but an assemblage of ideas. Thus, the "Associationist School" of Hume, Mill and Bain construed a psychology without a soul. Hume said: "all we know directly is the stream of ideas and what we call the mind or soul is a mere empty stage which we unnecessarily assume to exist on the scene upon which the ideas play their part".

(4) A collection of perceptions

He further said that man is "nothing but a bundle or collection of different perceptions which succeed each other with an inconceivable rapidity, and they are in a perpetual flux and movement". The Budhists of India, who were psychologists of an advanced type also regarded mind as a perpetually changing stream of ideas.

(5) Science of consciousness

Psychology was regarded later as "the science of consciousness." According to James, our mental life is a stream. We have to study the "stream of thought" as we defectly know it. But to define psychology as the science of consciousness is, in a way, misleading. In the first place, the definition is not comprehensive enough, for psychology these days studies not only our conscious mental life but the unconcious also. Besides, it studies the relation of conscious life to bodily behaviour. In the second place, "consciousness", as McDougall points out, is a word that has "the form of a substantive which cannot be used as a verb" and allows us to forget that it stands for the fact of being conscious of something, and that it implies someone who is conscious of that thing.

Thus, we see that the definition of psychology as the science of mind or the science of consciousness is too narrow and even misleading. Most of the writers on the subject, however, retain the definition of psychology as the science of mind in spite of the inadequacy of the definition. Thus, McDougall defines psychology as "the science of human mind, positive and empirical". The word "positive" is added to distinguish it from Normative Science like Ethics and Logic and "empirical" to mark the fact that psychology relies on the method of investigation common to all natural science.

(6) Science of human behaviour

The latest definition of psychology is that it is "the science of human behaviour". Thus, McDougall defines psychology in his "Physiological Psychology" as "the positive science of conduct or behaviour". It is the science which aims "to give us better understanding and control of the behaviour of the organism as a whole".

This definition lays stress on objectively observable facts of outward behaviour or bodily action in which mental activity express itself. It is free from many of the logical and other difficulties involved in other definitions.

According to Skinner, R.F. psychology deals with responses to any and every kind of situations that life presents. By response or behaviour it meant all forms of processes, adjustments, activities, and experiences of the organism. Human Psychology is concerned chiefly with such activities as attending, perceiving, imagining, feeling, thinking, remembering and acting. Psychology attempts to collect, organise, describe explain and interpret the facts of experience and behaviour.

Educational Psychology deals with the behaviour of human beings in educational situations. This means that Educational Psychology is concerned with the study of human behaviour or human personality, its growth, development guidance, under the social processes of education. Education is possible in human beings, hence human learning is the central core of educational psychology (both internal and external factors condition the organism).

The Behaviourist School of Psychology understands the term "behaviour" in a sense different from the one held by McDougall. McDougall would not discard the hypothesis of the mind as something different from "the brain" or the body. According to the behaviourists, psychology has nothing to do with consciousness or mind. It is like every other Natural Science, objective and experimental. Every law of psychology is verifiable even as the laws of other sciences are verifiable through observation and experiment. Its subject-matter is the behaviour or activities, of human beings. Behaviourism discards consciousness because the factual data required for a natural science cannot be provided by it. As the facts are not available for objective study, they may provide speculations for a philosopher but they cannot advance the progress of a science.

Psychology thus gradually lost one by one the various entities it postulated. The Psychologist is no longer an introvert, but rather an extrovert. From being the study of an intangible entity called soul, it has become a study of the most tangible facts of bodily behaviour. According to some writers, the change has been responsible for the great advance made in the subject. The various ramifications of psychology are due to it. At least Educational Psychology and Child Psychology are greatly indebted to Behaviourism. But for the objective attitude that Behaviourism brought to bear on psychological studies, the vast amount of educationally valuable data could not have been collected. Obviously, the child's mind cannot be introspectively studied and whether light reflection on one's experience may throw on the facts of child behaviour, certainly it is the objective study of the behaviour as such that is truly the basis of Child Psychology or Educational Psychology.

BRANCHES OF PSYCHOLOGY

Psychology now has several branches. Thus, we have Individual Psychology or General Psychology, Social Psychology, Abnormal Psychology and Animal Psychology. These names are given according to the data which the particular branch of the psychology studies. Names are also given according to the particular method of investigation followed. Thus, we have Analytic Psychology, Genetic Psycholoy, Experimental Psychology, Comparative Psychology and Educational Psychology. It is worthwhile to explain the terms used to name the several branches of the subject more fully.

(1) Individual or General Psychology studies the various mental processes and behaviour of an individual more or less is isolation from the group in which he lives. Social Psychology deals with the behaviour of individuals in relation to society. Thus, for instance, there is an inherited tendency in every animal to imitate others. This innate tendency is studied in general psychology as well as in social psychology, but

whereas the former studies the origin, the development and modification of this tendency from the point of view of the individual, the latter studies it from the point of view of the group. The latter is more concerned with the characteristic manifestations of this tendency and the law of its working in society. It tries to reveal its social significance.

(2) Abnormal Psychology studies the individual as he thinks feels and behaves in an abnormal state of mind; it studies, in other words, his abnormal thoughts, feelings and modes of behaviour. Such phenomena as dissociation of personality, insanity, hysteria, fixations, obsessions, and dreams form the subject-matter of the study of Abnormal Psychology. Psycho-analysis which also studies abnormal phenomena of the mental life of an individual is an offshoot of this science. The former has developed into a science only in the present century and its study is proving to be of much value to educators.

(3) Animal Psychology or comparative psychology studies the behaviour of animals in different situations. This study has proved of immense value in throwing light on the origin and development of certain tendencies which we find in a very modified and complicated form in man. The true nature of our instincts is known in this way.

Sanford has devised a very good diagram to enable one to remember the various divisions of the subject (Fig. 7.1). The diagram is given below:

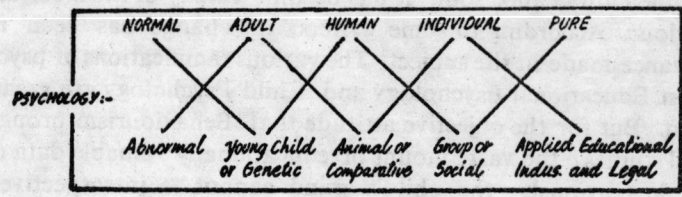

Fig. 7.1

"Each term in the upper line is contrasted with the one immediately below it—Normal with abnorals; human with animals and pure with applied. The lines and the crosslines indicate the various combinations which are to be found." The chief divisions of the subject are—Normal Psychology, which studies the behaviour of normal adults and normal children. Abnormal Psychology which studies the behaviour of abnormal adults and abnormal children, similarly, there are other branches—Adult Psychology, Child Psychology, Human Psychology, Animal Psychology, Individual Psychology and Applied Psychology. Of course, these divisions are not absolutely exclusive of each other.

Educational Psychology is a phase of education. It is a science that supplements the process of education. It is a branch, a segment of education. It describes the behaviour of subject and seeks to explain it in terms of his inner urges, motives, drives and the environmental influences to which he is subjected. It is a study of a child's mental life in its various aspects with reference to its application in the education of the child.

Life is a long continuous process of learning and adjustment. Education is to facilitate, to ease and to further this process. Educational Psychology is to study and to investigate the ways in which this can take place. Thus, Educational Psychology provides the teachers and the educators with a fund of knowledge that may help them in giving to the pupils the best kind of education—the education that causes an all-round development of the pupil's personality.

Educational Psychology studies the problems of education in terms of psychology. In other words, it is a psychological approach to education.

Education and educational psychology

Educational Psychology is not identical with Education. The part cannot be identical with the whole. Educational Psychology, though a phase of education, is quite different from it in certain aspects. Educational Psychology is limited. The following are the main points of difference:

(1) Education is a comprehensive scheme of life. It is very much concerned with aims, ideals, purposes, values and standards of life which are beyond the scope of educational psychology. The aims and ideals of education are determined by Philosophy, not by educational psychology.

(2) Educational Psychology is a positive science. It deals with facts as they are. It studies the laws of the child's nature as they are and as they operate. It has nothing to do with what they "ought to be". Thus it is not a Normative Science. Education is a Normative Science which has got certain norms and standards. Educational Psychology gives the educator only an insight for devising the best means of achieving norms and standards.

(3) Education demands the Educator to know the child as well as the subject. The first demand of knowing the child is fulfilled by the science of Educational Psychology. Educational Psychology helps the teacher in adjusting the process of teaching to the needs and capacities of the child. Thus, Educational Psychology puts into the hands of the teacher the best means of educating. The aims of teaching he has to borrow from another science. Educational Psychology tells the teacher how to teach the child with maximum efficiency and greatest effectiveness. Educational Psychology brings a message to the teacher that environment carries great weight in the education of the child. It reveals to him that every child has a psychological nature and all teaching should be adjusted according to that. Thus, education is benefited by Educational Psychology.

(4) To some, education appears to be only Applied Psychology. This is not true. Education is one word, but many things. Education includes both the means as well as the ends of education. Educational Psychology studies only the means. Ends are outside its purview.

General psychology and educational psychology

Sometimes, Educational Psychology is confused with General Psychology. Though there is much that is common to both, yet their objectives are very different from one another. The field of General Psychology is wider. It deals with every kind of human behaviour and with every kind of problem related to life. All forms of life processes, adjustments, activities and experiences of the organism may become the scope of General Psychology. General Psychology deals with, and explains and interprets the facts of human behaviour and experience in a general way.

Educational Psychology deals with the behaviour and experiences which are related to education only. It selects from the whole field of General Psychology those facts and principles that are of specific significance to learning and teaching.

Thus, Educational Psychology is just a specialised branch of General Psychology and is a science which studies actual events in a scientific way. It studies reasons for the differences in ability to learn quickly or slowly, for failure or success. It studies: (1) how man has always been interested in himself and has always attempted to find answers to questions concerning the "why" and "hows" of experience and conduct; (2) how man has tried to understand his own impulses, feelings, strivings and acts; (3) because of mere curiosity or for more practical reasons, how man has attempted to estimate the ability and personality characteristics of himself and of other people; (4) how most people have opinions, beliefs and explanations of the motives that impel individuals to work or not to work, to accept some ideas of new knowledge or not to do so. The methods of study of psychology are scientific. They are designed to ensure some degree of reliability, accuracy and dependability.

Historical development

The development of educational-psychology may be studied under five major periods of development: (1) Early period of primitive notions (2) Period of ancient philosophy, (3) Period of authority, (4) The Renaissance and the dawn of science, and (5) Period of modern science.

(1) *The early period of primitive notions*

People thought that a ghost dwelt in the body, making the body alive and conscious. At death this ghost withdrew permanently, and during sleep it wandered away to return again when the person woke up. All body activities were activated by this ghost. They believed that similarly all animals, plants and even inanimate objects such as rivers, wind and thunder, were activated by spirits. There still exist many indications of this primitive notion in our modern thinking.

(2) *Period of ancient philosophy*

About 7th century B. C., a number of wealthy Greek citizens, who had the time and interest for study and observation, turned away from political and civil wars to reflect human life. One group of these philosophers called *monists* used elemental substance to explan the whole universe. Another group called *pluralists* looked for many such elements to form the basis for their explanations. The third group *sophists* turned to an interest in man himself. In the 4th century B.C. the Greek philosophers Plato and Aristotle produced their system of thought. Aristotle collected a large mass of obervations of physical and biological facts of nature. He wrote many books covering the range of science and philosophy and in his catalogue of science, he included psychology, which he defined as "Science of Soul." For centuries, psychology was known as the study of the soul of man.

(3) *Period of authority*

For about 1000 years A.D., there was little advance in the ideas about man, his nature and his conduct. Knowledge and education were based on the authority of the

Church and the Ancient Greek philosophers. There was little original thinking or careful observation.

(4) *The renaissance and the dawn of science*

In the 15th century, there was an awakening. Emphasis was laid on the individual man and his rights, so it is called the period of humanism. In the phase of development there was the Protestant movement in the Christian Church. Some persons like Columbus, Copernicus, Galileo, Newton, Harvey and Bacon made discoveries, and opened the doors to new worlds of study and research in both Physical and Biological Sciences.

(5) *Period of modern science*

In the 18th and 19th centuries, because of the development of knowledge in experimental methods, psychology adopted the experimental methods, speculation and arm-chair philosophising were replaced by measuring and charting activities of man in systematic way. In 1879, Prof. W. Wundt in Germany started the first psychological laboratory in which experiments were conducted with the behaviour of man as the subject-matter. Since that time, there has been great progress in this field.

NATURE OF PSYCHOLOGY

As regards its nature, psychology is a science because its methods of getting information are based on the research methodology.

Methods of getting information in psychology

Many times the Extension Workers form their idea about the villagers in a haphazard way and are influenced by current opinions and prejudices. They accept many popular misconceptions that pass as proved facts, when they are nothing more than the product of someone's fertile imagination circulated as truth. The every day thinking of farmers and other villagers is full of opinions, bias, beliefs and ideas which although form their basis has been lost in the dim past, but still they are willing to defend vigorously. It is not a very simple matter to ensure that the observations of human activities are complete and accurate. This accurate observation is difficult and requires as many safeguards as it is possible to arrange. The methods of study of psychology require this scientific approach so that the facts are true and applicable to conditions as results of science are. The methods of study of psychology which support that it is a science can be given as follows:

(1) *Experimental method*

This method is one of controlled observation, which ensures the greatest possible degree of accuracy. One technique in this method is to train the observers because it increases the accuracy. All people can observe many things in the activities of children but if the conclusions are to be of certain practical value, the observer must be so trained so that he will know what to look for, be able to concentrate his observation of the particular feature of the activity selected for study and also be able to record and keep the information in systematic way so that the results are intelligible, useful and accurate.

The training of observers must also be such as to remove all prejudices like: all red-haired individuals are likely to be more hot-tempered. There may be beliefs that persons with longer ears are more intelligent, or similar ideas about persons having small necks, grey pupils in the eyes, one-eye, etc. The scientific observer must be trained to discard all such preconceived notions and observe with an open mind. The accuracy of observations is often increased by the use of mechanical devices of various kinds. The moving picture camera has proved to be of great value in obtaining an accurate record of the behaviour of children in some situations. Instruments that record pulse, respiration and circulation of blood during an emotional experience, have increased the knowledge in psychology on emotions.

In the psychological experiment, the *subject* may be either the observer himself or some other person or persons. When the observer studies his own activity it is called *introspection* and when the subject of the observation is another person, it is an *objective* observation. Introspection is useful for getting information on thinking, feeling and emotion.

(2) *Genetic method*

This is an experimental method. In it the observations are also recorded as they take place. The observation is made by trained observers and precautions are taken to ensure accuracy of results. The main difference is that in it the conditions are not so rigidly controlled and the specific features to be studied are not to be isolated from others. It is the study of development as it occurs. An aspect is anticipated and the development observed carefully, accurately, without interfering with that development by changing the environment conditions, e.g., to observe a child about to start to walk, or to learn to talk, etc.

(3) *Case history method*

In this method, the psychologist collects information about the subject's past history and present circumstances by bringing him to the observation place or clinic. He tries to find what factors contributed to the present conditions and what should be done to readjust the subject (e.g., a juvenile delinquent) to life or society. It is a method for dealing with individual cases. We cannot formulate general principles of behaviour. It can vary as a source of general information if used with necessary caution and supplemented by a control group, e. g., to collect information about 500 delinquents and then collect data about how many of them come from broken homes. If it is found that 20 per cent of delinquent children come from broken homes, it can be interpreted that broken homes are important in causing children to be delinquent.

SCOPE OF PSYCHOLOGY

The work of psychology is to discover the general laws that explain the behaviour of living organisms and the most important living organism is man himself. The individual responds to this stimulation and by such responses adjusts to the world. This continual adjustment constitutes the activity of the individual during this lifetime.

Psychology is seeking to discover what particular conditions produce a given type of activity, so that eventually the psychologists will be able to control and direct human activity by controlling these conditions, e.g., if we know the cause of emotion of fear, we could prevent fear by manipulating the conditions in such a way that the adequate causes of fear would be absent.

The activity of an adult human is very complex and difficult to unravel, but much light can be obtained from a study of the genetic development of activity in the growing child, as well as from the less complex activity of lower animals. Psychology, therefore, at times makes use of child and animal subject in its experiments. The understanding of the normal individual is increased when we study the abnormal individual, for he may show in somewhat exaggerated form some of the characteristics of the normal. So psychology studies the abnormal as well as the normal person.

According to Bernhardt, psychology attempts to discover the source of knowledge, beliefs and customs and to trace the development of thinking and reasoning so as to find the kinds of environmental stimulation that produce certain types of activity; to analyse feelings and emotion, so as to understand how the crude, unorganised activity of the new born infant becomes systematised into useful forms of adult conduct; to trace the modification of activity in learning so as to develop methods for the measurement of the activities and abilities of individuals, and many other similar problems related to human nature and conduct.[1]

This knowledge of psychology is useful to extension workers and change agents because it will help them to find causes of prejudice, the habit of sticking to old practices and ways of doing things, the doubts and lack of confidence and factors affecting motivation. It will help them to know the emotions and feelings of farmers, how villagers or farmers learn new practices and what type of approach should be adopted and teaching aids be used.

EDUCATIONAL PSYCHOLOGY AS APPLIED TO EXTENSION

In education, especially in extension programme, we are concerned with behaviour psychology which includes educational, industrial and religious psychology.

Aims of psychology

These include: (1) environmental adjustments, (2) group behaviour, and (3) improvement of the environment.

Problems in psychology

This aspect has three parts: (1) to understand the characteristic of behaviour, (2) to analyse behaviour, and (3) to interpret or find meaning in this analysis.

Understanding the characteristics of behaviour includes: (a) sensing, (b) perceiving, (c) thinking, (d) feeling, (e) willingness, and (f) doing. The concept of man, according to

[1]Bernhardt: *Practical Psychology*, II Ed., McGraw-Hill Book Co., N.Y., p. 8.

psychology, is that he: (a) is an organism, (b) is able to adjust himself to the environment, (c) desires self-preservation, (d) desires race preservation, (e) has learning capacity, and (f) thinks.

For these purposes, he is provided with: (a) receiving mechanism, which includes all sense organs—eye, ear, nose, tongue and skin, (b) a connecting mechanism—brain and nerves, and (c) a responding mechanism—glands, muscles, etc.

Objective and contributions of psychology

In extension, we are concerned with changing behaviour in general, with improvement based on certain goals and objectives. Success or failure of our extension work very much depends on how we approach people and how much we are able to mould them and affect their actions. The objectives of psychology are to describe, understand, predict and control behaviour of the people with whom we work in extension, or whom we try to educate. The study of psychology helps its readers:

(1) Gives information about the personality of village people with whom we are concerned in our extension programme.

(2) It is man/woman centred as it places emphasis on ability and attitudes of human beings.

(3) Says that a farmer or home-maker is not a clean slate but he or she has with him/her certain traits so that extension workers may create suitable environment. The extension worker simply guides the farmer/farm-wife/youth.

(4) Tells that first six or seven years of the child are the most important in the development of the child for his/her future career. This gives rise to the Multiple Factor Theory: 'Why people behave as they do'?

(5) Tells us that the person who behaves differently is mentally sick and needs our sympathy and treatment. This requires a change in attitudes of extension workers towards such mentally sick persons.

(6) Makes emotional experiences clear which extension workers can make use of in his approach.

(7) Gives knowledge about level of intelligence of clients with whom extension agent work.

(8) Gives knowledge about individual differences so that extension workers are able to adjust their teaching according to the differences.

(9) Gives knowledge about the stages of development so that extension workers can handle the individual farmers, housewives, etc.

(10) Gives knowledge about the aptitudes, inclination and interests of human beings, so that extension workers can suggest projects to their taste.

(11) Gives knowledge about achievements, so that further programmes may be prepared.

(12) Gives knowledge about psychoanalysis of the "problem man" and how he can be handled in learning meetings or projects in the villages.

(13) Gives knowledge about sense experiences, learning and thinking which can make extension work more effective.

(14) Analyses the causes of feeble-mindedness in persons and other drawbacks which help in solving such problems and also in approaching people with a friendly attitude.

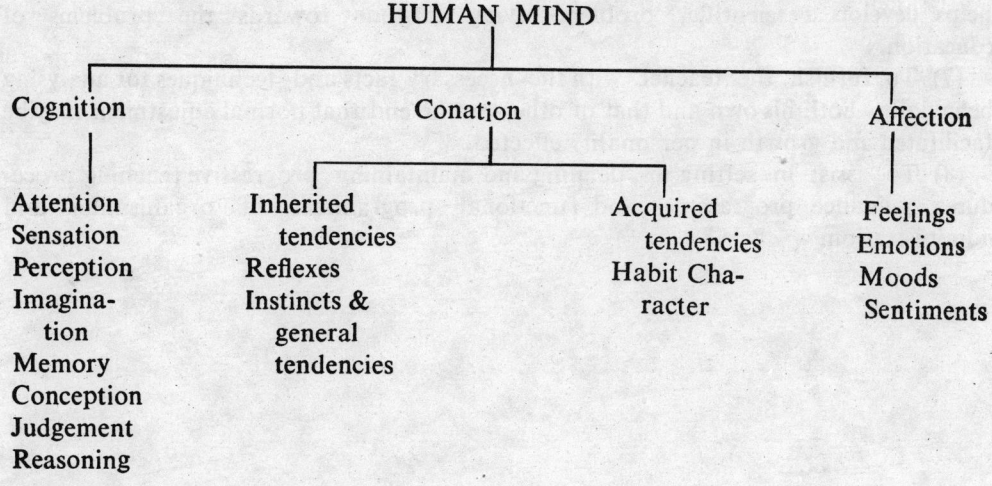

Aims of educational psychology

According to Skinner (1968) the general aim of educational psychology is to provide a body of organised facts and generalisations that will enable the teacher to realise increasingly both cultural and professional objectives. An analysis of the general aim reveals many specific aims. Some of the more important of these specific aims, or results, that may be expected from the study of this subject, are the following:

(1) To develop a conviction and realisation of the extent that growth can be promoted, learning acquired, social behaviour improved and personality adjustments effected. The realisation of this objective will produce an increasing appreciation of what educational psychology contributes to the teacher.

(2) To assist in defining and setting up educational objectives and standards in terms of desirable behaviour (conduct, attitudes and so forth) that ought to be the goal of all teaching efforts.

(3) To aid in developing an impartial but sympathetic attitude towards children so that their behaviour will be regarded objectively.

(4) To assist in achieving a better understanding of the nature and importance of social relationships and the methods of developing in children such modes of social functioning as getting along with others, participation in group efforts and cooperation.

(5) To provide a body of facts and principles that can be used in solving the problems of teaching; how the materials of instruction can best be selected and organised into a graded series of problem-projects, units or contracts; how these materials can be used intelligently as means of attaining the desired outcome; how the learning process can be so guided that the materials and methods will not obstruct learning; and how the entire process can be directed so that what is learned, functions not only here and now, but anywhere and at any time, in school or outside.

(6) To aid in affording the teacher a better perspective for judging both the results of his own teaching and the educational practices of others. Educational psychology

helps develop a scientific, problem-solving attitude towards the problems of education.

(7) To furnish the teacher with the necessary facts and techniques for analysing behaviour—both his own and that of others to the end that normal adjustment may be facilitated and growth in personality effected.

(8) To assist in setting up, defining and maintaining progressive teaching procedures, guidance programmes and functional programmes of organisation and administration.

CHAPTER 8

INTELLIGENCE

Educators can increase their effectiveness by using appropriate language and teaching methods for the individual and groups with whom they work. Understanding the nature of intelligence and how it varies from one person to another and how to recognise these varying degrees of intelligence, will assist the educator in achieving good human relations to introduce the programme of change of the people.

Definitions: Psychologists have evolved many definitions of intelligence:

Norman-Munn: Intelligence may be defined as flexibility or versatility and is a function of the living organism.

Brown: Intelligence is the ability of an individual to adjust himself to the conditions that arise in his environment.

Wechsler: Intelligence is the aggregate or global capacity of the individual to act purposefully, to think rationally and to deal effectively with his environment.

Thorndike: Intelligence has been defined as the ability of an individual to cope with his environment. It may be thought of as a composite or organisation of abilities to learn, to grasp broad and subtle facts, especially abstract facts, with alertness and accuracy to exercise mental control and to display flexibility and ingenuity in seeking the solution of problems.

Intelligence characterises the whole behaviour of an individual (global) and is a sum (aggregate) of his abilities which are quantitatively differentiable, though it is not simply the sum total of these abilities for the following reasons:

(i) Number, quality and manner in which these abilities are combined.

(ii) Factors other than intellectual ability (drive, incentives).

(iii) Excess ability, above that required for intelligence behaviour, in one particular ability may add little to the effectiveness of behaviour as a whole.

Psychologists usually distinguishes between three areas of intelligence:

(1) *Abstract intelligence:* Persons having the ability with ideas, as in language, mathematics, science, words, numbers. Professional people are generally high in abstract ability.

(2) *Mechanical ability:* Persons who understand things as in skilled trades, has much of science, manual skills combination. Individual and building traders are higher in mechanical ability.

(3) *Social ability:* Persons who understand persons, mixes with people, such as salesmen, ministers, diplomats have social ability.

Thus, intelligence is the product of heredity and environment. The opportunities to learn vary widely, yet the inherited capacity as modified by maturation accounts for a greater part of the individual variability.

NATURE OF INTELLIGENCE

Previously, intelligence was regarded to be a faculty of the mind. But in the 18th and 19th century, different theories were evolved to explain the nature of intelligence. Following are the main theories: (1) Monarchic (uni-focal), (2) Oligarchic (multi-focal), (3) Anarchic (non-focal) and (4) Electric (two factor theory).

(1) Monarchic

The theory believed in one great power of mind dominating over others. Spearman defined this to be an "all pervading mental power" or to put it in the words of Ross "conscious adaptation to new situations" or "inborn all-round mental efficiency". According to this view, a person who can perform an intellectual task very well, can also perform another task equally well. Johnson said that if Newton could have turned his mind to poetry, he would have been as great a poet as he was a mathematician.

(2) Oligarchic

It holds that cognitive abilities are manifestations not of a single commanding faculty, but of a few main intellectual powers of groups of abilities. Thus, a boy may be quite clever at languages, or music, but he may have no head for mathematics. Another boy may have a good mathematical ability but no ability for music or languages. In related subjects he does fairly well but fails in unrelated subjects.

(3) Anarchic

Thorndike advanced the theory known as anarchic. According to him, the mind is a host of highly particularised and independent faculties. The theory maintains that from a man's ability to do one kind of work we can infer absolutely nothing as to his ability to do another kind of work. Average of all energies is intelligence.

(4) Electric theory

According to this theory, intelligence is that ability of the mind which is a combination of two factors 'g' and 's'. The 'g' is the general factor and 's' is the specific factor. In any performance of a person say in solving a problem in mathematics, both the general abilities of a man and specific abilities are exercised. In other words, in every act that requires the exercise of intelligence there is 'g' as well as 's' present. Now this 'g' factor is always the same whatever be the test that a man does. The 's' factor will differ in the same man from test to test. He may do music better than mathematics, since he has more special aptitude for the former. Thus the 'g' factor is always the same for the same individual and the 's' factor varies from test to test according to its nature. But there are differences in the general abilities of different individuals as well as in their special abilities. Thus, different individuals differ both in their 'g' as well as 's' factors.

The 'g' factor is gifted and cannot be increased even with all one's best efforts. If this conception of intelligence is accepted the success of a person's achievement in a particular activity depends upon the play of these two factors 'g' and 's'. This may be presented as: A: 'g'+'s' (Achievement: general ability and specific ability).

Characteristics of 'g': (1) It is gifted and constant; (2) It runs through all activities in whatsoever quantity it be; (3) It varies from one individual to another; and (4) Presence of the high 'g' guarantees a good quality and quantity of success.

Characteristics of 's': (1) It varies from individual to individual; (2) It varies from activity to activity; and (3) Presence of the high 's' guarantees a high success in that very activity but without a high 'g' it cannot succeed to that very extent.

Spearman did not identify 'g' with intelligence. To him it is a highly technical and mathematical quantity which plays high role in all mental operation. He tends to view it as mental energy. Thus 'g' seems to be a perceiving capacity of the mind for analysis and synthesis. Spearman announced his two factor theory in 1906. He modified it and added to certain group factors g-v (capacity of writing, thinking, imagination).

Factorial analysis

Thurstone found out eight mental abilities which made intelligence. This analysis is different from that of Spearman. He resolves the performance wholly into primary abilities, the equivalent of group factor, and then takes the general factor as whatever the primary abilities have in common.

He gives the following abilities:
(1) Perceptual ability (P).
(2) Numerical ability (N).
(3) Verbal ('V').
(4) Memory ('M').
(5) Reasoning ability ('R').
(6) Spatial ability ('S').
(7) Fluency in dealing with words ('W').

FACTORS AFFECTING INTELLIGENCE

As Munn has stated intelligence is flexibility and versatility and is the function of the living organism. In this reference, Brown also suggested that intelligence is the ability of an individual to adjust himself to the conditions that arise in his environment. Thus psychologist pointed out that there are numerous factors which directly or indirectly affect the intelligence or ability of the individual and which make up the behaviour pattern of the individual. These factors may be of the following forms:

(1) *Heredity and Environment*

Heredity provides the physical body to be developed with certain inherent capabilities, while environment provides for the maturation and training of the organism. Extensive studies have been conducted on this problem which showed the relationship. In 1940, Newman concluded that variation in the I.Q. were determined about 68 per cent by heredity and 32 per cent by environment. This was an average statistical determination.

An individual's life variations in I.Q. must be due to environment since heredity cannot change. Cases are recorded where this change is as much as 20 per cent. Improved nutrition, health and stimulus situation would account for this change. Environment of children of 2-4 years age appear to be critical, since the child normally learns the language at this time. Better home, school, medical care and less economic discrimination provide a means for achieving a mentally abler population.

(2) Age

A person who is bright or dull in childhood tends to remain bright or dull throughout his life. The evidence shows that a person achieves his maximum I.Q. at about 20 years and remains relatively stable until around 70 years when it rapidly decreases, if health and other factors do not interfere.

Some abilities remain constant, while others decline rapidly due to declining physical efficiency.

For example—A base-ball player at 35 years age is considered to be old. This decline in I.Q. may also be caused by decreasing flexibility in breaking of old habits and establishing new ways of grouping associations or looking at situations. In most mental activities, the older person will be able to excel or at least keep up with younger persons because of experience and wisdom through his I.Q. which may have declined slightly. Therefore, the consideration of age is of minor importance.

(3) Health and physical development

Physical and mental health may be related to one's ability to gain desirable achievements in mental activity. With delicate health, one may not possess enough energy to engage in mental activity to the extent to achieve necessary success. Physical defects such as related or incomplete maturation of brain cells may result in subnormal intelligence. Blindness, or near blindness, and deafness and other sensory and physical handicaps may interfere with observable intelligence behaviour. Conditions such as glandular imbalance, enlarged adrenoids and diseased tonsils also affect intelligence. An emotional block may interfere with one's ability to give evidence of intelligence which one actually possess.

Although unfavourable health conditions may seem to affect mental status, actual mental ability is not reflected in any appreciable degree in remediable health handicaps. In those cases in which the physical or mental health handicaps can be removed or mitigated, a decided improvement in intellectual behaviour can be observed.

(4) Sex

It is popular belief that boys and men are more intelligent than girls and women. Studies revealed that high school boys are supposed to excel in more abstract areas of learning such as Mathematics and Physical Sciences. Men are supposed to be more mechanical than women. These differences between sexes, to the extent to which they give evidence or existing, can be traced to varying environmental conditions, especially in homes where the experiences of boys and girls reflect the acceptance of such sex differences. The administration of tools of intelligence to the same group of boys and girls appears to yield the following general results:

(1) The rate of physical growth is more in girls who seem to surpass boys during the childhood and early adolescent years.

(2) During early childhood, there is no difference in mental ability between the sexes.

(3) During later adolescence boys may show slight superiority over girls, but the difference is negligible especially since there are wide divergences among the members of both sexes.

(4) Analysis of performance on scientific items of intelligence tests appear to show that there is a slight superiority of boys in questions that involve mathematical material and scientific concepts, and that girls excel in material that deal more directly with the humanities (Crow & Crow). It appears then that children become interested and learn what the culture dictates, a boy and girl should know.

(5) Race

There is no convincing evidence to show how far face is a factor in determining intellectual level. However, when differences exist between families, as a result of environment, they will be more marked between racial and national groups. For example, in American culture it is observed that Negroes make lower scores than do the whites, but Buckman found that Negro children in New York City made approximately the same scores as white children of the same socio-economic level. Southern-born children of Negroes, however, scored substantially below the white norms. This suggests that differences in attitudes towards the speed of work, towards the significance of symbols, or towards the test situation itself, was cultural in nature (Ross & Karwoski).

An additional cause for this difference may be the difference in opportunities for training in early years.

All evidence indicates that there is little or no difference in inherited intellectual capacity due to race. There are, of course, differences in opportunities for training and learning. The old idea of inferior and superior races due to heredity is not true. Therefore any differences which exist can be overcome through motivation and training opportunities. It is significant that nations which have recently achieved independence are placing great emphasis on expanded educational opportunities for their people.

(6) Culture

Culture influences the intelligence of the individual to a degree. The test in this respect should be standardised from one culture to another culture. In India, the Education Department is developing and standardising test to measure mental age (MA). Knowledge gained from such studies will be available soon.

(7) Social and economic conditions

As the home plays a significant role in the early developmental years, it can be expected that home conditions can exercise considerable influence on behaviour and attitudes. The activities, interests and financial status of parents, and of other adults in the neighbourhood environment may provide for the child poor, relatively meagre or an extremely rich series of experiences. The amount and kind of mental challenge to which the person is exposed at various periods of his life determines to great degree, the amount and kind of mental activity in which he engages. Apparently, low socio-economic status may result from factors outside the immediate control of parents, such as a period of economic depression. The parents, themselves, may possess a high degree of intelligence but be the victims of circumstances.

In such cases, the child's inherited, intellectual potential usually is able to assist him to get over unfavourable living conditions, and he gives evidence of intellectual behaviour in spite of a meagre social and economic background. As opportunities are presented, he will tend to achieve according to his intellectual capacity. Drive and motivation can operate to overcome social and economic handicaps.

MEASUREMENT OF INTELLIGENCE

The social stimulus value of the individual, i.e., the individual's inner dynamics and traits must be understood and measured by standard tests and observations.

Characteristics of a good measuring instrument

A good measuring instrument should have: validity, reliability, objectivity, and standardisation.

(1) *Validity* is that device which measures what it is supposed to measure.

(2) *Reliability* is determined by a device which shows consistency in giving the same score for the same group or similar groups, for each test.

(3) *Objectivity* means that the two or more people using the same measures will get the same results.

(4) *Standardisation* means that norms or standards have been established so that an individual's score can be compared with scores of others of a defined group.

Classification of psychological tests

There can be five classes, as follows:

(1) According to the aspect of the individual's behaviour.

(2) Verbal or non-verbal.

(3) Group or individual.

(4) Ability to perform certain tasks in a certain time (speed test) or the degree of difficulty of tasks the individual can accomplish. This may be called a power test.

(5) Tests may be analytical or situational:

(*a*) An *analytical* test is one which measures the separate component traits into which complex performance patterns may be analysed.

(*b*) *Situational* tests are those which present a miniature life situation and measure performance, under conditions which require traits to be organised into functional units.

Intelligence tests

There are two important tests: (1) The Standard-Binet Scales for measuring general intelligence; and (2) The Wechsler-Bellevue Scale.

(1) *The Standard-Binet Scale*

It was originally developed by the French Psychologist Alfred Binet and later revised by an American Psychologist, L.M. Terman of Stanford University. If a child can perform most of the tasks of the test that most 10 year olds can perform, he has a "mental age" of 10, regardless of whether his actual or chronological age is 6, 8 or 14 years. These tests may be:[1]

For a child of four years

(1) *A picture vocabulary:* The child must recognise and name everyday objects as seen in pictures.

(2) *Naming objects from memory:* Small toys representing common objects named for him. Later, he must remember the name of each object.

(3) *Picture completion:* An incomplete picture of a man is shown which the child must complete.

(4) *Pictorial identification:* The child must identify pictures of objects presented to him on a card.

(5) *Discrimination of forms:* A child must recognise a number of simple geometrical forms.

(6) *Comprehension:* A series of "why" questions are asked to which sensible answers must be given.

For persons of the age of 13

(1) *Vocabulary:* Subject must correctly define 14 words from a standard vocabulary list.

(2) *Verbal absurdities:* Subject must be able to determine what is "foolish" in a series of statements.

(3) *Responses to pictures:* Subject must be able to tell what a picture is about.

(4) *Repeating 5 digits:* The examiner reads 5 digits in a forward order and the subject must repeat them backwards.

(5) *Abstract words:* The subject must define abstract words like "constant" and "charity".

(6) *Sentence completion:* The subject must provide the missing words in incomplete sentences.

For average adults

(1) *Vocabulary:* Subject must define twenty words from a standard vocabulary list.

(2) *Codes.* Subject must learn two codes and write messages in the code terms.

(3) *Difference between abstract words:* Subject must tell the difference between dfficult and abstract words.

(4) *Arithmetical reasoning:* Subject is required to solve arithmetic problems mentally.

(5) *Proverbs:* Subject is required to interpret proverbs.

(6) *Ingenuity:* Subject is required to solve the problems requiring "mental manipulation."

(7) *Memory sentences:* Subject must reproduce long and involved sentences after a single hearing.

[1]This apply to highly educated and advanced societies like in the U.S.A.

(8) *Reconciliation of opposites:* Subject must tell how words denoting opposites are alike.

Similar tests can be framed for farmers, village leaders, members of youth organisation in villages, village women, etc.

Intelligence Quotient (I.Q.)

After the above tests are given to the subject, his mental age is determined, or, in other words, his Intelligence Quotient is calculated. Abbreviated I.Q.

The I.Q. is the ratio between the subject's Mental Age (abbreviated M.A.) and his Chronological Age (abbreviated C.A.). In order to avoid factions, the ratio is multiplied by 100. The I.Q. formula thus becomes

$$I.Q. = \frac{M.A.}{C.A.} \times 100$$

According to the formula, a child with an M.A. of 10 and a C.A. of 8 would have an I.Q. of 125. The levels of intelligence may be indicated as follows:

Levels	I.Q.
Idiot	0-25
Imbecile	25-50
Moron	50-70
Border line	70-80
Low normal	80-90
Normal	90-110
Superior	110-120
Very superior	120-140
Near genius	140 and over

Some characteristics of I.Q.'s are as follows:

(1) I.Q. tends to remain constant unless there are extreme changes in environment.

(2) An individual's intelligence is influenced by heredity and environment.

(3) Cultural factors influence test results in measuring intelligence, so that the test must be designed to consider the language, physical environment, habits and kinds of experience of the person being tested. The tests in use in the U.S.A. cannot apply to people in India.

(4) Some special factors must be considered in studying intelligence. These are: (a) First-born children are usually slightly inferior in I.Q. to those coming later in the family, (b) A thyroid deficiency in early life interferes with initial development of intelligence, (c) Boys excel girls in problem solving while girls excel over boys in world fluency and memory, (d) Verbal ability and performance on informational tasks may actually improve up to 60 years of age and then remain almost constant. Visual and motor factors also begin to decrease after a certain age.

The I.Q. test is most often used with children over an age range 4 to 14.

The Wechsler-Bellevue Scale

It is designed for adults. Some of the tests in this scale are verbal, dealing with arithmetic, reasoning, general information, comprehension, memory, span for digits and vocabulary. Other tests are of a performance type, i.e., they do not depend to a great extent upon language. A sample performance type test is one in which 16 small cubes coloured differently on their faces are presented to the subject whose task is to arrange the cubes so as to reproduce seven designs presented on the cards.

This test does not yield a mental age but it does produce an I.Q. scoring so adjusted that the average I.Q. for each level is 100. Thus, a person of 50 years age who earns an I.Q. of 125 is superior to 30 years old in general.

Aptitudes testing

The aptitudes are special abilities in such areas as agriculture, architecture, mechanics, clerical activity, handling animals, etc. To measure these aptitudes, some of the tests that have been designed are:

The Minnesota paper form board

This consists of a series of two dimensional diagrams cut into separate parts. From each diagram there are five figures with lines indicating the different shapes out of which they are made. The subject's task is to choose the one figure that is composed of the exact parts of previously reported diagrams.

The satisfaction to be derived from any educational or vocational pursuit depends to some extent upon the individual's interest in the activity that he engages in. Many people have similar abilities but differ markedly in their interest in activities. Interest tests distinguish between real and superficial interests. These can be:

(a) *Strong Vocational Interest Blank*. This is a questionnaire. It consists of 420 items to which the person being tested responds by indicating whether he likes, dislikes or is indifferent to the object or activity named. The test items include names of occupations, hobbies, personal traits, school subjects and amusements.

(b) *Duder Preference Record*. This is score for the types of occupational areas including outdoor, mechanical, computational, scientific, persuasive, artistic, literary, musical, social service, clerical, etc. The examinee is presented with items with instructions. e.g., to punch with a pin the whole to the right of one activity of 3 that he likes the least, and to the left of the activity that which he likes most. The pin-punches make a pattern on an underlying sheet from which the examiner can count the area: the literary, the mechanical, and so on. The scores are finally translated from a table into percentages.

Unlike intelligence tests and tests of special abilities, interest tests are much more concerned with the measurement of motivation than with ability.

Measuring speed or reaction

This is the most direct way to measure the processes of perception, choice and discrimination. In it we determine the time that is taken by a person to perceive and report upon the differences or similarities among various kinds of stimuli. The time that elapses between the occurrence of a stimulus and the beginning of a response to it is called the reaction time. These times are measured by a mechanical or electrical clock-work instrument known as a chronoscope, and a number of pieces of accessory equipment.

Measuring the more general traits of personality

This consists of a wide range of techniques popularly called personality tests. Because of their success with the quantitative measurement of intelligence, special abilities, sensory abilities, interest and reaction times—all of which are, of course, personality components—psychologists have been encouraged to extend their efforts to measuring such personality traits as dominance, sociability, irritability and suspiciousness.

One way to test the above is the use of a questionnaire—the Allport Ascendance—Submission Reaction Study—which aims to discover the tendency of an individual to dominate his fellows, or to be dominated by them, in various face-to-face relationships of everyday life.

For example, when you see someone in a public place or crowd whom you think you have met or known, do you inquire of him whether you have met before.

Sometimes...........................
Rarely................................
Never................................

Other questions may be: Do you walk in your sleep? Yes.........no; Do you feel tired most of the time ? Yes.........no; Do you make friends easily? Yes............no; Do you get rattled easily? Yes.....................no.

This knowledge is helpful in selecting extension workers who have aptitude for village work and social service and who can instruct farmers or home-makers in the scientific ways of farming, livestock raising and home-making, or educate village women in managing their homes and raising their children in better ways. It will make extension workers effective in their approach.

CHAPTER 9

EMOTIONS

We experience in our life various feelings of anger, fear, disgust, repulsion, etc. Seeing a snake in our path we are frightened, more so if we suspect that it might attack us. When an action we do not like is repeated we are angry. These feelings are termed emotions. These emotions largely determine human behaviour and we should learn how to utilise them for the purpose of education of those with whom we work.

WHAT IS EMOTION?

Jersild says that emotions denote a state of being moved, stirred up or aroused in some way. Emotions involve feelings, impulses and physical and physiological reactions. These impulses, feelings, physiological reactions, etc. occur in an almost unlimited variety of mixtures and gradations.

Rass: Emotions are modes of being conscious in which the feeling element is predominant. In other words, these are well-defined states of consciousness, or the feeling tone of a particular quality, the affective colouring of the experience.

Munn: Emotions are acute disturbances of the individual as a whole, psychological in origin, involving behaviour, conscious experiences and verbal functioning. The word emotion has three distinct connotations

(1) Emotion is a kind of reaction pattern in an individual which we observe when he seems to behave in a certain manner and describe as angry, affectionate, afraid, anxious and excited. This type of behaviour is said to be emotional and is objectively observed.

(2) Emotion is a kind of experience within the individual. Those experiences we feel and can talk about without being subjective and are never really known to an outside observer.

(3) Emotion is a kind of somatic condition or set of physiological processes when organic functions are disturbed. This aspect of emotion can scientifically be studied.

McDougall: Emotion is the mode of experience that accompanies the working of an instinctive impulse. An emotion which is accompanied with the working of instincts is known as a primary emotion and all other types of emotions are secondary. Before we discuss about the development of the nature of emotion, it is necessary to understand the instinct, as emotions are mostly associated with instincts.

Instinct

There are certain activities of an individual which are associated with instincts. Love of a mother for her child, suckling of a baby are instinctive acts. Instinctive behaviour is the key to understanding the human behaviour. McDougall says instincts are a native or inborn capacity for purposive action.

Instincts are concrete facts of mental structure, which is the main, we infer from facts of behaviour and experience. Every individual in this world is born with some native endowment. These innate dispositions form the basis of specific modes of behaviour in certain specific situations which are unlearned.

According to McDougall, instincts are innate tendencies which have (1) cognitive aspect, that is, to attend to and to be interested in certain types of objects or situations. (2) Emotive aspect to feel certain emotions towards these objects, (3) To act towards them in a particular way. The conative aspect regards instinctive behaviour and includes all the three modes of mental experience, i.e. cognition, affection and conation or knowing feeling and witting.

Behaviour is a process which is a passing event. Instinct is a lasting, existing mental disposition. It is responsible for behaviour. Instinct is the fact of mental structure while instinctive behaviour is a function. Instincts are responsible to a great extent for the behaviour of the organism and we call it "instinctive behaviour".

Emotion is the complex state of an individual in which certain ideas, feelings and usually motor expressions combine to produce a condition recognisable as such by the individual and frequently by others.

Theories of emotions

(1) Emotions are adjustments which favour the execution of instinctive activity, e.g. in a state of fear, the body prepares for swift locomotion, in anger for successful combat and in the case of creative impulses for creation.

(2) Emotions are emergency equipment. In emergency, we fight, or flee, or do nothing at all, according to the circumstances. In the same kind of emergency an individual may become angry and fight while at another time he will be afraid and take to flight, and again he may not do anything.

(3) During emotional excitement, the muscles responsible for involuntary movements become very active and sometimes the behaviour is uncontrollable. Emotions have a tendency to persist in the forms of moods and anxiety. Anxiety is some kind of persisting fear.

(4) Emotions may be aroused either by stimulus outside perception of objects or by organic change (alcohol or intoxication). For the same reason, temper changes with our changing state of health.

(5) The same emotion may be aroused by a large variety of stimuli, e.g. love for a particular subject that is taught may be aroused by the various stimuli like method of teaching, inspiration from the teacher or extension worker or leader, contents of the course, etc.

James Lange theory

To account for the bodily changes which accompany an emotion, the James Lange theory was developed. This theory indicates that emotional experience is nothing but the experiencing of the organic changes produced by the evoking stimulus. According to this theory *we feel sorry because we cry* not we cry because we are sorry.

This theory does not give complete account of emotional experience. It is wrong to assume that emotion is nothing but those bodily states and their apprehension by the mind. The feeling-tone and experienced impulse are equally essential. Among the arguments put forward against this theory, the important one is that the viscera are not only insensitive but they are also slow to react. Emotional experience may occur in less than a second after it is presented, yet the viscera respond only after a matter of seconds. It seems that emotional experiences precedes visceral change.

Cannon theory

This theory holds that emotion is essentially a preparatory reaction of the organism of biological survival value in times of danger. According to it, all the physiological responses are associated with biological preservation of the organism, and with the defence of the organism against attack.

Nature of emotional behaviour

The emotions hinder voluntary movement and behaviour, and they develop external expressions. These may be overt behaviour-pattern, facial expression and vocal expression.

(1) *Overt behaviour-patterns*

(a) *Destruction:* In anger emotion, the attack from the animal or human being.

(b) *Approach:* In pleasant emotions, the essential response is approach. The biological function of approach to the stimulus object is to permit further stimulation.

(c) *Retreat or flight:* Fear typically involves retreat or flight. Flight from a dangerous situation may be physical or symbolic and is often the best mode of adjustment. In civilised life, we retreat through words—apologies, compromises, discussions or through other ways of the psychological mechanism of withdrawal.

(d) *Stopping of response:* Gloom or severe grief is the condition and the individual refuses to respond to some of the potent stimuli. They even stop eating and may have to be sent to a mental hospital.

(2) *Facial expression*

In normal social conversation, we can, more or less, successfully follow the effects that our words have on the other person by carefully observing the expressions on his face. There are different expressions when one receives a good message which thrills, joy, surprise and annoyance, fear are facial expressions. They are an indication, or a barometer, of the emotions. There are persons who can control facial expressions to a limited extent.

(a) *Empathy:* This is the ability to understand and, to some extent, share the experience of another person's feelings. It depends greatly upon our being able to interpret an individual's expressive behaviour. Everyone of us, in our personal contacts, learns to judge with some accuracy the emotional reactions of the people with whom we work or play in our daily life.

(b) *Vocal expression:* Due to emotions, the human voice gives different expressions. If a person is surprised, doubtful or incredulous, the word WHAT ? takes on a rising inflection. When a person fails, the voice is slow, a dragging monotone reflecting defeat and dejection.

Physiological changes during emotional states

Due to emotions, there are physiological changes. These are Glandular Responses, Neural Responses and Electrical Responses.

(a) *Glandular responses:* In a person experiencing a strong emotion, such as anger, the medulla of the adrenal gland pours an excessive amount of its secretion, adrenalin, into the blood. Travelling through the blood-stream to the various part of the body, this secretion is responsible for many characteristics of strong emotional experience. Under its influence the liver releases stored sugar into the blood and chemical changes occur which cause the blood to clot more quickly. Blood pressure rises, the pulse beats more rapidly and more vigorously and the air passage into the lungs is enlarged to admit more air. The pupils of the eyes dilate so that light may enter. Sweat breaks out all over the body, particularly on the palms of the hands. The temperature of the body may rise or fall several degrees.

Another secretion of the adrenal medulla, adrenalin, brings about constriction of the blood vessels at the surface of the body, thus making more blood available to other parts of the body.

(b) *Neural response:* For every emotional response, there is a neural response. The brain gets disturbed. All parts of the nervous system get involved in the emotions.

(c) *Electrical responses:* Closely associated with the visceral and neural activity occurring during emotion are certain significant changes in the electrical properties of the body. There is a galvanic response in which perspiration appears on the surface of the body. The tissues actually generate an electromotive force (voltage) and the electrical resistance of skin is changed.

Expression of emotions

A child expresses his emotions fairly clear by in his facial expression. As the child grows, he learns to moderate his expression of fear and anger, joy and disgust. Now there is a race between concealment of emotions and the reading of emotions. Social custom dictates that emotions be not paraded in public, and yet social customs demand that we act in accordance with the feelings of other people.

Mood: Mood is usually of long duration, and rather mild. These reflect, to a considerable extent, the organic condition of the individual. Moods are the results of events and experiences, e.g., success in a project produces a mood of cheerfulness and optimism, while failure is likely to induce a gloomy, resentful mood.

Sentiments: These are complex, emotional states directed toward some specific object or person. Love and hate are two important sentiment.

EMOTIONAL CONTROL

Daily happenings and the efficiency of an individual depend on his ability to control and manage his emotions. The feelings and emotions in him can make his life miserable or happy, depending on the control that he has achieved over them. A person who swings frequently from extreme elation to deep depressions needs emotional reeducation. Worry can make any person not only miserable but inefficient as well. Emotions are subject to training and education because these are matters of habit and habits can be changed.

Emotional states also affect the health. When a person has unhealthy fears, he cannot maintain his health. Worry, vague fears and frequent emotional upsets bring illness, so emotional control is necessary. The best time for emotional control is during development, but even in adulthood it is not too late. This makes it necessary for everyone and specially educators or extension workers to know how emotions can be controlled through training and learning how to adjust. Emotional control is necessary for health, happiness and efficiency.

Training in emotional control

The control on emotions does not require the inhibition of emotions, or the removal of emotional experiences, but it does imply the harnessing of the energy of the emotions to a useful purpose. Fears are very often hindrances in our efficiency and most fears can be unlearned. Anger is often a spur to action, but if anger is out of control the action that results is not useful or efficient.

Dealing with children

Children, while under training for emotional control, are to be dealt with in two ways: (a) removing their fears, and (b) dealing with their anger.

(a) *Removing fears in children*

(1) *Frequent application:* The child starts life with very few fears but soon he acquires a variety of them. He loses some of these as he grows older. One method, which proves helpful in removing the fears of children is disuse, i.e., keeping the feared object away from the child for some time. But this may be ineffective in some cases because when the child sees the object of fear after some time, his fear is again intense.

The "familiarity breeds contempt" idea, or frequent contact with the feared object in the hope that the child will become accustomed to it and thus not fear it. But frequent presentation without the child being helped to adjust in some way, succeeds only in making the fear more intense than it was before.

(2) *Ridicule:* This is making a fun of the child's fears. This is a dangerous method because it can cause him to hide his fear. Because he thus bottles up his fears without making a satisfactory adjustment, the fear sometimes becomes more serious than before.

(3) *Verbal appeals:* This is telling the child that there is nothing to be afraid of. This is also wrong because it confirms in him that there is something to be feared.

(4) *Social imitation:* In this method the child is exposed to the fear-situation in the company of someone in whom he has confidence and who does not show any fear, e.g. a child afraid of a dog, when he plays with a child who is not afraid of dogs, learns to overcome his fear of dogs. This method gives occasional success.

(5) *Reconditioning method:* In this method, the feared object is presented along with something else which calls forth a happy feeling and a positive reaction. If skillfully arranged, the happy feeling and the positive reaction become transferred to the feared object and the fear disappears.

(6) *Skill in adjusting:* Fears can be combated by building up the knowledge and skill for adjusting to situation. They should always be brought out into the open and discussed. The individual should be helped to make an adjustment to the situation producing the fear. .

(7) *Increase in knowledge:* Ignorance and inefficiency bring in the learning of fear. Most of the fears of children are irrational and founded in ignorance and lack of understanding and skill. The child should be given the real knowledge.

(b) *How to deal with anger in the child*

When the environment restricts the activity of the child, and when he does not understand the necessity for such restrictions, or when he fails to get his own way, anger may result. The child expresses this anger by temper tantrums, i.e. by kicking, screaming and loss of control. This temper tantrum should not be allowed to be successful, so that the child does not influence other people to cater to his wants by this method. In this situation, there are two methods for dealing with the child.

(1) Remove the child's audience, or the child himself. He will learn that he cannot succeed through these methods and is helped to discard this method of trying to achieve his ends.

(2) When anger explosions are frequent in the child, his environment should be examined. It may be that some children with whom he plays have this behaviour or that his parents, or even teachers, use this method. Also, there may be so many restrictions that he is forced to explode in order to feel at all free to express his own individuality. Or it may be that he does not get sufficient sleep and gets fatigued.

So the child, as he grows and develops, needs help in learning desirable emotional expressions—not merely in suppressing emotions but in adjusting to emotion-producing situations, and in producing the emotional conditions in a manner that is socially acceptable.

Emotional adjustment in adults

The individual can reduce emotional disturbance through careful management of his environment by:

(1) *Avoiding emergency situations:* That are emotion producing.

(2) *Emphasising reasons:* By an emphasis on the rational and intelligent features in any situation, emotional disturbance may be avoided. When the individual succeeds in "keeping his tail up" in any situation, he usually succeeds in preventing an emotional disturbance.

(3) *Being active:* When the individual feels fear or anger developing, he should find something to do. Hobbies and varied interests, sports, or manual work in a kitchen garden are helpful for such persons or situations.

(4) *Keeping oneself in humour and laughter:* Laughter is a good outlet for emotion. A person who manages to remain always in humour and to laugh rarely develops anger or fear.

(5) *Creating confidence:* About three-fourths of all people have an inferiority complex in some form or other. This feeling of inadequacy began to develop in childhood. At that stage the child is made to feel inferior because of his lack of knowledge and experience as well as lack of skills. In some cases, this disappears when the individual learns more and overcomes his ignorance and inefficiency. But in other cases, it continues even though a person has been successful in acquiring knowledge and skills. The traditional examination system prevalent in countries like India is also responsible for such fear, for a failure in examination is often considered a failure in life. As only one student in a class can come first, the others become inferior to him and this fosters an inferiority complex. Because of this fact, some of the Universities in the USA and in India do not grade the candidates with numerical or A, B, C, D, grades, etc. but simply as (S) Satisfactory and (U) Unsatisfactory.

Suggestions for developing self-confidence

(a) The individual should make a fair appraisal of himself. He should make an impersonal and objective inventory of his strengths and weaknesses. He must be careful of the standards of uses in making his appraisal. Comparing oneself with the best and not with the average is not fair, it is very unlikely that anyone can be the best in everything. He should also assess his weak points, i.e., the things that he cannot do better than the average person or of knowledge in which he has little information. Some of these drawbacks can be overcome by a careful, planned programme of learning. There may also be personal limitations which cannot be overcome.

(b) Success in small things motivates the individual to seek further success in the same field or related fields.

Emotional problems of old age

In old age there is deprivation. Family relations change, occupational status is lost and friends also die. There is decreased vigour. Many former pleasures are given up. Financial resources may become limited. Older persons become rigid in their habits and cannot adapt to new conditions. They tend to respond to new emotional situations with whatever behaviour has served them well in the past.

A few rules for emotional control

Guilford (1952) has suggested the following few rules for emotional control:
1. Avoid emotion provoking situations.
2. Change the emotion-provoking situation.
3. Increase skills for coping with the situation.
4. Reinterpret the situation.
5. Keep working toward your goal.
6. Find substitute outlets.
7. Develop a sense of humour.

IMPORTANCE OF THE STUDY IN EXTENSION EDUCATION

(1) The extension worker is like a teacher. He can achieve greater success in

his work by arousing the emotions of the learners i.e., village people. Without emotional appeal, the subject cannot be made interesting, and an uninteresting meeting will remain ineffective.

(2) When emotionally excited, farmers or learners can do extra-ordinary things. The extension worker should utilise this fact in his work.

(3) Strong emotions may help to break up some other crude and undesirable emotions.

(4) Emotions are strong motivating forces of action. The extension worker should arouse the right type of emotions, by preparing subjective conditions of learning for village people.

(5) The emotions of people should be given due consideration in the extension programme if it is to be a success.

CHAPTER 10

MOTIVATION

Motivation is the process of initiating a conscious and purposeful action. Motive means an urge, or combination of urges, to induce conscious or purposeful action. It is ordinarily a compound of feelings, appetites, inclinations and instinctive impulses. It becomes objectified as an interest and, unless impeded by internal or external obstacles, leads to actions in pursuit of that interest.

It is goal-directed and need-satisfying behaviour. It explains why people do the things they do. It influences a person to do a thing in a certain way.

NEEDS WHICH MOTIVATE

(1) Organic needs or appetites

Man is constructed in such a way that he requires certain things in order that he may keep living. He is also so constituted that these needs initiate the activity that will eventually satisfy them. The needs are air to breathe, food to eat, liquid to drink, rest after activity, sleep, a changing environment, the elimination of waste products and sexual expression. These are all basic organic needs, which demand periodic or continual satisfaction. They are motives or directing influences because they initiate and sustain activity and also direct the activity until the need is satisfied. They may be called appetites, and can be defined as follows:

(a) *Appetite of hunger:* This occurs every day. Its basis is found in the organic sensations arising from an emptied stomach. In it, habit or custom play great part. We need 3 or 4 meals a day from habit rather than need. In the beginning, the child eats many times and later on its night feeding is done away with.

(b) *Appetite of thirst:* The stimulus for the activity is the need for moisture, this is indicated most acutely by sensations from the throat region.

(c) *Appetite for sex:* Sex is not all of life, by any means, nor is it all of the marital relationship. The delay and thwarting of the sex appetite by economic and social taboos have forced it to find other outlets in behaviour. The secrecy, shame and suggestion of indecency connected with sex activity provide the soil for perversions of habits and thoughts that originate from an entirely natural and decent but persistent appetite. Better management of this appetite is required. The outlets may be companionship with the oppsosite sex in reading, in the enjoyment of art, or production of art, etc.

(d) *Appetite for rest or sleep:* It is a protective function. Rest after activity is not necessary but satisfying. Sleep is a condition brought about by the reduction of stimuli or by neglecting the respond to stimuli.

(e) *Appetite for change or variety:* Just as there is an appetite for rest or sleep, there is an appetite for activity, for change, for differerent stimuli. In modern industry, specialisation often denies this appetite for change and so breeds discontent and boredom. This results in the search for pleasure and recreation as an escape from drudgery.

(2) Wants

Each individual acquires his own unique set of personal wants. People acquire likes and dislikes for specific foods, sex, play. Once a want has acquired the functions of a need, a person cannot be happy unless he finds some way to satisfy it. However wants are modified through experience and changing pattern in the development of a person from infancy to old age.

(3) Emotions as motives

Under the influence of fear, anger, etc., people may do many things that they would not do normally. Many times, parents use this fear to direct the conduct of their children. The Government and other organisations use fear to produce a desired form of behaviour. Anger motivates individuals to fight, to attack and to say things that would be beneath their dignity if they were not dominated by this emotion. The milder forms of emotion are sentiments and moods.

(4) Feelings and attitudes as motives

An individual's experience activity is evaluated by him as pleasant or unpleasant. Every experience can be located between these two—pleasant or unpleasant. When experience is evaluated as pleasant, the individual has an attitude of approach to that experience. He may prolong or repeat the activity. When he evaluates the experience as unpleasant, his attitude is of withdrawal, i.e., he discontinues that experience and tries to avoid it in furture.

(5) Social motives

There is a universal tendency to strive to excel and succeed, to win out ahead of others, or to overcome obstruction or difficulty. This tendency of self-assertion can be traced through a great many actions of the individual.

There is also a tendency in human beings to submit, to give in, to subordinate themselves to other authorities. This tendency may be called self-submission or self-negation. In most people, there is strong desire to achieve social approval. To gain this social approval, people try to improve their personal appearances through clothes, living in better houses, having a car, the amount of life insurance, social connections, wealth, success in business, being a progressive farmer or Krishi Panau, athletics, a generous and good homemaker or the best fruit preserver, thus people want to feel that they belong to some high standards and then feel that they are liked and accepted in the world. This is what makes a man strive for status and position.

(6) Others

(a) *Habit:* Habit may also be a motive, because once a habit has been establised it becomes almost automatic and requires only a stimulus to set it in action.

(b) *Objective environment:* People act differently in different situation. The objective environment produces a "set" or readiness to respond in a particular way.

PROBLEMS OF ADJUSTMENT

Human beings have wants and cravings and the motives to satisfy these wants call forth persistent activity until some degree of satisfaction is attained. If a need remains unsatisfied it causes unpleasantness. Because of the environment and society there are always some situations where desires, urges and wants cannot be satisfied and these cause frustration. Frustration is an emotional tension produced by failure to attain a desired goal or to terminate an act successfully. It is inner conflict arising as a result of opposing wishes or by external worries to the fulfilment of one's desires.

If the adjustment to conflict, difficulties and obstacles is a happy one, it is better for the individual and the society in general. If it is the reverse, the individual and society will suffer the consequences. People learn to adjust to the unpleasant situations by rationalisation or by habit. Happiness and peace of mind, as well as success in social and vocational situations, depend to a considerable extent on these habits of adjustments

Types of adjustment

(1) *Overt form:* It is more primitive and takes the form of attack and combat, e.g., when the toy of a child does not work, the child may adjust to this difficulty by ruthless attack on the toy that is thwarting his pleasure and destroy it. Overt or immediate adjustment of this kind is rarely throughout, and is often irrational, impulsive, destructive and socially unacceptable. If one nation like India is thwarted by China or Pakistan, the result may be war.

(2) *Covert or inner adjustment:* Here the battle is waged within the individual. As the conflict is within, the adjustment is usually made in some indirect way. A hungry man who sees food in a glass window has to decide whether to satisfy the hunger without caring for social disapproval or to remain hungry and respect the social values that he should not steal anything. When he weigh the two sides there is conflict. These conflicting motives influence his behaviour. In this case, the battle may be won by appetite of hunger, or the fear of punishment may lead the hungry man to find some other means of satisfying hunger than the direct means of taking the food.

Common methods of adjusting to frustration

(1) *Direct attack*

(a) *Surrender:* A person who gets frustrated may give up, submit to defeat and admit failure. Failure produces an attitude of "what is the use"? that kills **chance** for success. It fosters a feeling of inferiority. The individual shrinks from **trying** because he expects to fail and hates to have anyone find out that he is not as good as others. This form of adjustment from childhood is unconstructive and is detrimental to normal development.

(b) *Direct attack:* This may be in terms of either an anger adjustment or of an intelligent rational attack on the difficulty. Anger as an adjustment to difficulty, while common enough, is rarely adequate or efficient, as it always represnts a certain loss of control. Direct attack may also be made with intelligence and insight, and in this case, it is the most healthy as well as useful form of adjustment.

(2) Indirect attack

(a) *Introversion:* This is turning inward, and a purely mental adjustment. This is really a partial surrender; the giving up of the outward struggle while carrying on the thoughts and imagination. Here imaginary success is substituted. Much of the day-dreaming in children as well as adults is of this nature. In his imagination any body can be a great singer, orator or athlete. The danger lies in carrying this to extremes. It may even lead to a case for a mental hospital. Such a person is called:

(i) A conqering hero.

(ii) Suffering hero. For example a small boy has been punished by his parents unjustly, he does not have the courage to go home. He would like to run away. He sets in a corner and thinks that he has run away, has had an accident, and is badly hurt or perhaps killed. He sees his parents weeping when they hear of his death. At some time, every person says that "like you will we be sorry some day". This is a sort of adjustment. The psychologists say that it would have been better if he had run away.

(iii) The third form of introversion is identification. We see a film, drama, etc., and the characters of the actors and actresses: we identify ourselves with them.

(b) *Rationalisation:* This is fooling ourselves, and others, as to the real reasons for our actions or failure. If a student fails in examination, for instance he may say that the questions were unfair, the teacher was poor or the examiner was prejudiced. By such rationalisations, one escapes the anoying necessity of admitting failure and achieve some degree of satisfaction in an unsatisfying situation by being able to fix the blame on circumstances. The rationalisation may be of two types: projection of blame on others or making excuses. If a person losses his job, he says the job was not good; if a person is poor, he says money is the root of all evil; if a person does not have a beautiful wife, he says that beautiful girls are always unfaithful, so he liked a faithful girl.

(3) Escape method

(a) *Defence mechanism:* This is an organic condition of some kind produced by a situation that is too difficult or pleasant. This condition comes after a very serious conflict or struggle between opposite motives. Adjustment that is made non-voluntarily is the production of symptoms that keeps the individual from participating further in the disagreeable situation. An example may be the examination nausea that keeps the ill-prepared student from failure. A real but induced headache that keeps someone from a difficult social situation where he may not be able to face the audience or make a contribution by speech, etc. is another example.

(b) *Escape by means of alcohol or drugs:* Some persons drink intoxicants for temporary adjustment because it keeps them diverted for some time.

(c) *Escape by running*: This may be called nomadism. In this adjustment, the frustrated person moves from one job to another, from one town to another or changes a course in the college or school. He takes all the frustrations with him and this is no remedy for his problems.

(d) *Regression:* This is an attempt to find satisfaction in a form of activity that in earlier development was quite acceptable and satisfying, but which he has outgrown e.g., a child when he was a baby derived satisfaction from sucking his thumb, later, in school, when he finds a difficult situation, he reverts to the thumb-sucking activity.

(4) New outlets

(a) *Sublimation:* The individual, when he feels frustrated, finds new outlets, e.g., a person who does not get married tries to satisfy his sexual desires by going to dancing clubs, games, athletics and other forms of social activity where he can meet the opposite sex which satisfies his sex motive.

(b) *Compensation:* An unprepared student fills his answerbook with irrelevant material to increase the volume. A man forced to be submissive and obedient at work, may be overbearing and dictatorial at home. Addiction to alcohol or drugs as compensation for failure in business is another example. There may be some wise compensation when a person shifts to art, literature, research, poetry, etc.

INFLUENCING OTHER PEOPLE

All societies have built up many elaborate techniques of influencing the action of its members. Education, advertising, fashion dress, speech, habits are ways of influencing others. Rewards and punishments of various kinds are the usual techniques for motivating and coercing people into definite lines of action. Praise, flattery, persuasion, threats, commands, gossip, rumour, propaganda are few of the uses of language, that are designed as ways of influencing the behaviour of others. Most of these techniques work through the basic motives that have been discussed in the previous pages.

Influencing involves: (1) suggestion, (2) conditions, (3) techniques of influencing others, and (4) the effective speaking.

(1) Suggestion

Suggestion has three characteristics: (a) idea enters the mind from without, (b) the idea may tend to produce actions, and (c) the idea is accepted uncritically.

(2) Conditions

There are a number of conditions that are conducive to an effective state of suggestibility. Indirect suggestions are more effective than the direct. Some people accept the suggestions of others very easily: a child is usually submissive to an adult. Similar conditions may differ in experience, reputation of a man, strength, social position, etc.

(3) Techniques of influencing others

(a) *Capturing attention*: A person who can capture the attention of others by that dramatic movements and actions, by arousing their curiosity, will be able to influence them. The pedlars selling their things on the roadside. and in the railway compartments become very expert in this art.

(b) *Sympathetic induction of attitudes:* In order to produce in others a desirble set of attitudes, the essential thing for the person who wants to influence others is to display these attitudes in himself. A frank cheerful manner tends to produce the same return. If we try to create interest in something we want, it is necessary to show an intense interest from outside so that it becomes infectious.

(c) *The "Yes" technique:* In order to influence the individual in any line of activity, it is much harder to get him started right. It is much harder to change a "no" into a "yes" than it is to keep a person saying "yes" once he has begun. A door-to-door salesman of medicine, etc., finds the names of some persons specially ladies, in a colony with the numbers of their houses and then starts: Are you Mrs. Sharma? She says "yes". You have three children? (also collected from somebody who gave other information about their home). Again, she says "yes". And they have same cold sometimes, then she says "yes"; this continues until she leads herself into buying expensive medicine from the man.

(d) *Use of newness:* This requires a judicious mixture of old and the new things to catch the attention of people and influence them. This newness should not be too different or unfamiliar, because the people are little afraid of things that are too strange and different.

(e) *We should recognise the limitation:* One should not try to do too much to draw attention of a person, as there are some limits beyond which he will feel annoyed and make it known to others.

(f) *Our suggestions should appeal to the basic wants and needs of a person we want to influence:* The information we want to give to a person should appeal to his basic wants and needs. If a boy is not eager about health or hygiene, he will not care for the facts given to him by his parents, teacher, etc. But if he is interested i n games and is instructed by somebody in this field, he will make use of such suggestions.

(g) *Making appeals vivid:* In making an appeal, e.g., getting donations for crippled children, just using words may not be as effective as showing the picture of a crippled boy while making the request for a contribution. This use of visual-aid—pictures, etc., move the person and often they will donate.

(h) *Breaking down defences:* To influence others, we must arouse their latent sympathy and break through their first line of defence. We may ask some questions from ourselves.

Does my presentation move? Is there any dramatic suspense? Will it arouse curiosity? Are my attitudes, manners and feelings of the kind I want to see in other persons? Is there anything new or different? Am I trying to do too much at one time? What need or want am I going to tap? Is my appeal vivid? How am I going to get past the defences of the individual? and so on.

(4) Effective speaking

A person who wants to influence others through his speech, can be effective by taking the following points into consideration:

(a) He should be prepared: by keeping his facts on a piece of paper and arranging them in such a manner that the audience follows the speaker's thoughts to see where he is going.

(b) Thinking of the audience: The speaker should have in mind the interests, of his audiences.

(c) The speaker should look at the audience while speaking.

(d) Try to keep your audience active, so that they think along with you.

(e) If possible speak the language of your audience.

(f) Use humour to make the atmosphere better.

(g) Avoid the extraordinary examples.

(h) Stop when you have finished and before the audience feel disinterested.

MOTIVATION IN EXTENSION

Importance in extension

Motivation is necessary for mobilising the village people and the extension workers both, if our extesion programme is to succeed. In pre-Independence India, the development programme could not bring the desired results because there was no motivation in the extension workers. Because the extension workers were not properly motivated to achieve the results, their efforts could not motivate the village people. In the administration, there was the absence of:

(1) Patriotism which could only be infused by the national leaders.

(2) Zeal and enthusiasm for service to the nation.

(3) Recognition and appreciation for their work.

(4) Monetary reward and advancement in cadre.

(5) Stimulus and incentive.

(6) A code for personnel administrators.

(7) Educative behaviour of the superiors.

(8) Proper training and orientation of extension workers.

(9) Recognition of the importance of extension work and extension workers.

In the absence of these factors, the approach of the extension workers was like that of a boss, and not of a missionary and servant of the nation. Now efforts are being made to change this attitude. This section deals with how we can motivate our subordinate staff and the village people with whom we are concerned in our extension work. How to increase this motivation so that the programme is a success?

In this study, we are concerned with how all the conditions associated with the various needs arouse and direct the behaviour of the organism towards the satisfaction of those needs. Internal stimuli associated with needs can either initiate activity independently or with those of the various stimuli coming from the environment.

The motives or stimulus conditions, which direct our response fall into two groups: Biological drives and Psychological and Social drives.

Drives

The term drive refers to any internal stimulus condition of the organism, which impels it to activity.

(1) *Biological drives:* Resulting from tissue needs. These drives motivate the behaviour of the organism in directions that lead to satisfaction of those needs, e.g., hunger drive motivates the organism to seek and eat food which is necessary to maintain the metabolism. Prolonged failure to satisfy hunger may result in disease or even death. The biological drives are: hunger, thirst, air-hunger, fatigue, the need for sleep, heat and cold (below 57° F we need heat), and the sexual drive. Knowledge of these drives will help the extension worker to understand the problems of the people. He will be able to handle them sympathetically if he understand these drives.

(2) *Psychological and social drives:* There are many psychological and social drives that are necessary to keep the individual in equilibrium to perform his normal behaviour. They are closely tied up with his relationship to other people and thus with his happiness in life. These needs constitute the chief values of the people. The extension worker must have the knowledge of the basic psychological and social drives of the people with whom he has to work.

This will help him to formulate the programmes and make effective approaches in changing their attitudes. He should always bear in mind the fact that incentives for change are to be planned in consideration of the existing situation and the cultural groups in question.

People differ in their social and cultural set up. Some are friendly while others are suspicious. Some are progressive while others may be easy-going. The extension worker has always to consider the various motivational forces of the people. Similarly, the supervisor has to take into consideration the limitations with which his subordinate has to work in an area. If he is considerate of these, then, there will not be a conflict or tension. These motivating forces may be: physical needs, growth urge, need for security, need for new experiences, need for affection, recognition and approval, the need for submission and conformity, the need for prestige, mastery and self-realisation, interests, values, habits, power, religion, recreation, joy and pleasure, etc.

Value aspects of motivation

Motivation has two value aspects: (a) intrinsic, and (b) extrinsic.

(a) *Intrinsic values:* These are what a learner does for the sake of engaging in the activity itself. This is to be desired in learning and it is more immediate.

(b) *Extrinsic values:* These are when an incentive or goal is artificially introduced into the situation to cause it to accelerate activity. Psychologists have found that sociological or psychological drives are acquired through past experience. To a considerable extent, they are the product of a learning experience caused by the rewards or punishment. Rewards and prizes are greatly helpful in extension work as motivators. The nature of the reward will have to be worked out in consideration of the total conditions.

Awards and rewards should not be substituted for teaching of knowledge, skills or understandings. They do not replace the practical learning. They can modify the learning process. Rewards can provide the individual with desire for attention, prestige and recognition. Rewards, in themselves, should not be ends but means to an end.

There is every possibility of a reward being used as an end which should however, be avoided. Punishment is also an effective way for motivation but this should not be practiced in extension.

MOTIVATING THE VILLAGE PEOPLE

Awards and their effects in motivating people in extension work

Rewards in extension may be in the form of material, money, symbolic, public recognition, etc. They are effective devices to motivate the rural people as well as the extension workers. Recognition of "Krishi Pandits" distributing amount of money to farmers—regionwise or statewise, or giving cycles to village level workers, etc., for the response to the extension programme, or fruitful results in their work, have given very beneficial results. However, the following considerations must be made while administering the award system in our areas.

(1) Award should be designed to encourage wide participation and activity. They, therefore, should be given adequate "spread".

(2) The potential ability of competitors should be a consideration, i.e., age, training, experience, etc. So that awards, as nearly as possible, are equally attainable by all contestants.

(3) The 'learning experience' as a result of 'award motivation' should be the objective and should be geared towards improvement which is of definite value to the contestant.

(4) The criteria for allotment of awards should be planned, publicised and understood by all concerned.

(5) Awards should be made for "personal" resources rather than physical resources, and should include: achievement, cooperation and leadership.

(6) Awards should be planned to reward the work of the competitor himself, or his group, and not that accomplished with outside help.

(7) Awards should be in keeping with the honour won, the effort expanded, and the stage of development of the participants, with strong emphasis placed on consistent achievement. Group approval and a sense of accomplishment are important by-product.

(8) The activity learned as a means of obtaining the reward should be one which is desirable as a "habit".

(9) An award should be attainable within a reasonable period after it is earned.

(10) Awards should be of durable nature, preferably of the intrinsic type which will encourage further knowledge or skill in the field of interest of the participant. Intrinsic awards, when used, should be well-chosen to perform a similar function, i.e., books, scholarship, etc.

(11) Awards should, where possible, be made on a "Group" or "Club" basis to develop cooperation rather than egoism.

(12) Competent, impartial judges should determine the winners and the basis for awards should further encourage, motivate and prepare for future competitions.

(13) Major awards should not be attainable by an individual too often. But this regulation should not discourage participation on the part of past winners.

(14) Presentation of awards should be timely, effective, and presented by

important persons.

(15) The award system should be continually evaluated to ensure progress.

Basic elements we need to know to motivate the villagers

What we discussed in the previous pages gives an idea how the true objectives of those who are engaged in "helping villagers learn how to help themselves", or who have "educational ends", can only be accomplished to the extent that they are able to bring about change in the knowledge, attitudes, skills and behaviour of our villagers.

In our educative process of extension, we have to take into consideration the following four basic elements:

(1) *The villager himself*

(a) The villager is an individual human personality. He has inherited traits, tendencies and capacities which tend to shape what he thinks, what he does and how he does it. He is an independent unit in his social system. His personality is the product and sum total of inherited traits shaped by forces in the environment in which he has existed. So the villager is an individual personality capable of independent action as well as group action within his community or society.

(b) The villager has a brain just like any human being. He has the capactiy to learn things, to reason, to understand, to judge, to decide. This controls his behaviour. As extension workers, we have to recognise and remember that change in the mind of man/woman always precedes change in the motion of his/her hands.

(c) The villager also has a heart. Just like any human being, he feels emotions of love, fear, resistance, sadness, or happiness. Through these he expresses his attitudes or tendencies to accept or reject things told him by the extension workers.

He has the desire to resist innovation, imposition, force unfriendiness and strangeness. We have to take these into consideration while approaching him.

(2) *The villagers, environment*

Regardless of his economic and social conditions, there are usually external forces in the village environment that the villager has to be taught to deal with and overcome, to survive and make progress. These are: low production of crops and animals, poor housing conditions, low education, the importance of family planning, uneconomic size of holdings and scattered plots, lack of capital, underemployment, etc. He needs help to solve such problems.

(3) *The device created by man to improve himself*

Religion, Indian history, the natural calamities, the apathy of the British administration and even the Mohammedan rule, the approach of the development department in pre-independence India, have all puzzled the villager. Due to it he is still not fully convinced that our programme is really going to improve his conditions. Some of the recommended practices he wants to try-out before he accepts. Here comes our difficulty. We have a big job of bringing this change in his behaviour. The new practices cannot be promised from without. It needs education. If changes are to be found socially, permanently and physically, they must come from the villager's own decisions to act, to result from his own effort. Internal changes in the knowledge, understanding, desires, feelings and capacities of villagers must precede the outward expressions of changed ways of doing things for their own improvement. In other words, it can be said that change in the mind of the villager must proceed change in the action of his hands.

The villager, as any human being, is endowed with internal desires for improvement. He needs only to be shown the path clearly and convincingly and helped to gain the necessary skills.

External stimuli must be created by the villager himself. History shows that in societies without these man-invented institutions and forces for application of external stimuli in the direction of economic and social improvement, progress in these directions has tended to be slow. India is a good example of it. If we compare the progress made by our extension service during the pre-independence period from 1904-51 and after 1952, the changes have tended to be rapid after 1952. Even during the early years of this new approrch there was little progress, as compared to the past 5 or 10 years.

So the primary role of the extension worker is to provide a "Triggering" device, as Leagans calls it, that puts into action the inherent powers of the people in the direction of real progress. This job done well can, in time, create a "chain reaction" that results in better people, living in better homes or better farms. This is the objective behind the extension programme. The extension workers have to keep these points in mind so that they are able to handle the villagers.

MOTIVATING EXTENSION WORKERS

We have already discussed how we can motivate our villagers to accept the new practices and recommendation of our extension workers. It is of equal importance that our extension workers themselves get motivated first; that they have a feeling of belonging to the organisation, love for the profession, are true to their duties and have a missionary zeal. The answer is that they have a high morale and from that are motivated towards the goal. This could possibly be achieved if the following factors are given due consideration:

(1) Selection and training of workers.
(2) Proper stimulus or incentives.
(3) Development of an effective code of ethics for extension workers.
(4) Orientation of new workers towards the goals of the extension programme.
(5) Effective supervision.
(6) Development of a high morale.

A motivation model for extension (Fig. 10.1) can be used as a good source of system analysis and for accelerating the motivation process in the context of an organisation.

RESEARCH IN MOTIVATION

Different patterns of motivation were reported among the farmers in a study con-

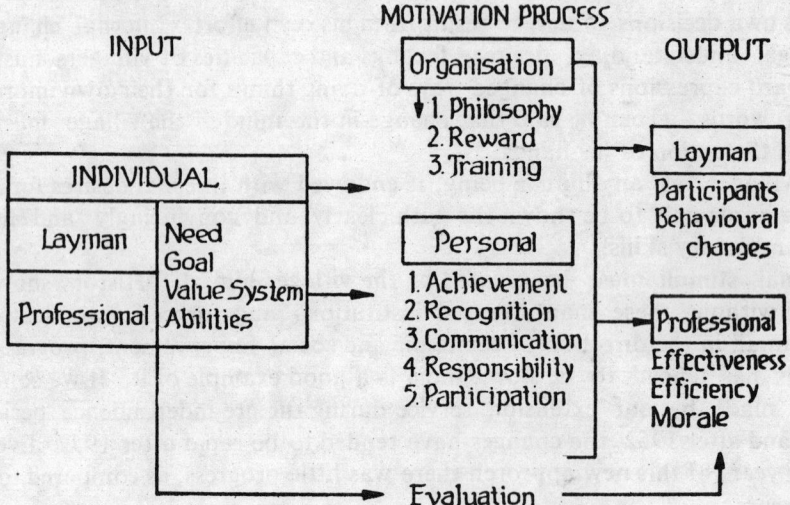

Fig. 10.1. A motivation model for extension.

ducted by the Indian Agricultural Research Institute, New Delhi. These are indicated below:[1]

    (1) To provide better food, clothing and education for one's children (Economic);

    (2) To make the country self-sufficient in food (Nation's Welfare);

    (3) To explore new ideas and adventure (Innovative);

    (4) To make the best use of one's abilities (Self-achievement);

    (5) To be free from debt (Economic);

    (6) To be the best farmer of one's village (Prestige);

    (7) To provide for security in old age (Security);

    (8) To be in confirmity of the community (Affiliation); and

    (9) To wield power (Dominance).

An overall view of the above indicates that the economic motive seems to be much more predominant, followed by national welfare, innovativeness, etc. in that order. Among the economic motives also, providing better food, clothing and education for one's children seem to be dominant motives.

Techniques of motivation

According to S.V. Reddy, (1975). the Techniques of Motivation are:

(1) Need based approach

It is possible for the extension educationist to motivate people to satisfy the five categories of need by knowing the level of motivation and patterns of motivation among them. If there is a desire among farmers for satisfaction of physiological need, they can be motivated towards the direction of achieving higher yields. If there

[1]Rao, D.G., Singh, K.N. and Pal, K. (1971), A study of the Motivation Patterns of Farmers Towards the Adoption of H.Y.V. of Wheat, Behavioural Sciences and Community Development, Vol. V, No. 1, N.I.C.D., Hyderabad.

is desire for security, the farmers can be motivated to adopt new practices by convincing them that the new practices will increase their income and enhance their security. If they have a desire for new experience, the extension teaching can be oriented towards imparting new knowledge and new skills. The desire for response can be satisfied by encouraging people to work in groups. Similarly, the desire for recognition can be met by working with village leaders, by awarding prizes and certificates to winners in crop competitions, etc.

(2) *Training to set a realistic level of aspirations*

Whether a person experiences success or failure as a result of some understanding depends upon the level of aspirations which he has set for himself. Generally, it has been found that the farmers' aspirations are realistic. They seem to be cautious in aspiring for more of the material things like furniture, livestock, agricultural implements, etc. which involve expenditure.[1] Therefore, it is important first to improve their general resources before leading them to aspire for professional items. Any attempt to raise the expectations of the farmers should be done with full understanding of their socio-economic status. For instance, if a farmer has no land of his own, it is better to create an aspiration in him for possession of one or two acres. Again, if one's level of production is 30 tonnes per acre, it is better if he is made to aspire for 40 tonnes per acre, so that he can progress slowly and steadily. Likewise, work orientation is related to aspiration. It is better not only to select progressive farmers to accelerate agricultural programmes, but also to select farmers whose work orientation is positive.[2] The extension educationist, therefore, should not make false promises that miracle varieties evolved will give them thrice or four times more yields than the local varieties. If their aspirations, once aroused, cannot be met with, then frustration crops in which will thwart them in taking up any new agricultural innovations further.

(3) *Participation*

The involvement of farmers in the programmes of agricultural change acts as booster of motivation not only for the immediate participants but also for others.

(4) *Use of audio-visuals*

The role of audio-visuals in motivating farmers needs no emphasis. The proper selection, combination and use of the various audio-visuals for the appropriate purpose will act as lubricants for motivation.

[1]Muthayya, B.C., *Farmers and Their Aspirations*—A study conducted in West Godavari of Andhra Pradesh, N.I.C.D., Hyderabad.
[2]Ibid.

CHAPTER 11

PRINCIPLES OF TEACHING AND LEARNING

Education aims at bringing desirable change in the behaviour of the learners. This change requires about a change in their knowledge, skills, attitudes, values, beliefs and understadings. The teaching in our universities and any type of educational centres should reflect this philosophy. As an example, we may say that in the Agricultural Universities this is to be achieved by: (1) producing effective and dedicated research workers who are able to find solutions to the farmers' problems of the Country/ State or region concerned; (2) producing effective and dedicated extension workers who are able to thrash out farmers problems on which technical knowledge is to be disseminated and then are able to take back the required information to solve the village problems in acceptable form so that farmers can adopt it; and (3) producing effective and devoted teachers who can improve the future education. *Poor education if allowed to continue for a longer period will suck the sap of the nation and ultimately kill it.* India is in a very critical stage, and if we do not improve our education and make our teaching effective and useful we are bound to suffer and further deteriorate.

LEARNING

The learning process

By this process the learner experiences a change in his/her behaviour through his/ her own efforts. Learning occurs within the learner. People learn through the experiences, i.e., through their activity. The teacher should provide such experiences to the learners that they may change their behaviour in the desired direction. *Any change of behaviour which takes place as a result of experience may be called learning.*

The learning experiences

The learning experience is the mental and/or physical reaction to seeing, hearing or doing the things to be learnt and through which one gains meanings and understanding, useful in solving new problems. Learning can take place only when the learner reacts to what he sees, hears and feels. In other words, the learner has to be active in order to learn. *We as teachers* should provide some activity related to the topic of the day as planned in our course outline, in which the learner can react in a desired way. The situation created by the teacher to make the learner active must be very carefully planned to bring specific change in his behaviour.

Laws of learning

Thorndike's four laws of learning are:

(1) *The law of readiness:* The learners will become ready when they feel that their *motives will be satisfied by learning* the new behaviour. Therefore the teacher has first to study the *felt needs of the learners* and help them to focus their attention on the problems which block the satisfaction of those needs. In this way the learner will become ready for learning. The teacher should further see that once the learners are ready to act they are provided with suitable activities, otherwise they will be frustrated and feel annoyed.

(2) *The law of exercise:* This law puts more emphasis on practice by learners. Continued practice is considered necessary for retention of what is learnt. The teacher must help the learner to practice and review the desirable behaviour as many times as is found necessary. When a response is *repeated several times it tends to become habitual*. If these habits are desirable they help in developing the personality traits of the learners. It is a self-activity.

(3) *The law of effect:* People learn more rapidly and permanently when the learning experience is pleasant or enjoyable. As teachers, we have to see that the effect of the learning experience is desirable to the student. The learners must be helped to know the success and errors of their activities. The teacher must help the learners to fix the goals in advance and also help them to keep those goals in focus throughout the learning process.

(4) *The law of belonging:* The law indicates that the teacher should help the learner to perceive the relationships. The relationship between the various elements which may be: (a) cause and effect relationship, (b) known and unknown relationship, (c) old and new relationship, (d) specific to general relationship, etc. Whenever the new behaviour to be taught to the learners it must be related to the situation of the learners or with the background of the learners. Then only will the learners be able to see the meaning of what he learns.

Principles of learning

(1) Learning is facilitated when a new behaviour *contributes in satisfying* felt needs on the part of the learner.

(2) Learning should be *meaningful:* The student must be helped in understanding why he is learning the new behaviour and should also be made aware of the general pattern of knowledge.

(3) Learning is facilitated when *two or more senses are used at a time* by the learners. This demands that the teacher should provide varieties of activities in which the learner may get the opportunity to use his sences.

(4) (a) *Effect of senses on learning.* The researches show that we learn: 1 per cent through taste, $1\frac{1}{2}$ per cent through touch, $3\frac{1}{2}$ per cent through smell, 11 per cent through hearing, and 83 per cent through sight.

(b) *Leaners possess the ability to retain :* Ten per cent of what they read, 20 per cent of what they hear, 30 per cent of what they see, 50 per cent of what they see and hear, 70 per cent of what they say as they talk, and 90 per cent of what they do a thing.

(5) Learning is effective when the *learners participate actively*. This demands that the teacher should help the learners to set goals and to maintain an active attack on the problems which act as a block in achieving goals.

(6) Learning is effective *when there is repetition* by the learners. The repetition should be distributed over more than one period of time. According to this principle the teacher should provide the learners with the preview of the new behaviour on one day, the detailed study on the next, and review on the third day.

(7) Learning is facilitated when the *situations* are real and *lifelike*. These can be provided in farms, farmers' holdings, villages, the offices of the cooperative society, observation trips or bringing in specimens to the classroom or laboratory, using teaching aids, models, resource persons, photographs, slides, flannelgraphs, flashcards, stories, charts and maps, etc. The researches on effectiveness of methods of instruction shows that (Table 11.1).

Table 11.1
Effectiveness of methods of instruction

Method of Instruction	Recall 3 hrs. later	Recall 3 days later
Telling when used alone	70%	13%
Showing when used alone	72%	20%
When a blend of telling and showing is used	85%	65%

(8) Learning is facilitated when the *learners are ready* to learn. Before teaching the new behaviour the teacher should prepare the learners and draw their attention to the topic to be learnt.

(9) Learning is facilitated when the learners *are provided* with knowledge of the progress of learning. They should be encouraged to take notes and prepare the outline of the matter as they read it.

(10) Learning is more effective when the *teacher uses praise and gives* rewards judiciously.

(11) Learning in facilitated when the learners *know their progress of learning*. This requires self-evaluation on the part of the learners.

(12) Individuals *differ in their learning ability*. The teachers should adjust his teaching procedures in such a way that it may be in line with the learners ability.

TEACHING

Teaching process

Teaching is *directing the learning process*, the process by which one through his own activity, becomes changed in behaviour (Hammonds, 1950).

It is a process of creating situations that facilitate the learning process. Creating situations includes *providing activities, materials,* and guidance needed by the learners. The situations created should be such that they may help in bringing desired changes in the behaviour of the learners. The situation created by the teacher may be formal or informal but must be suitable to the learner's ability. So the job of the teachers is *to create learning situations*.

The teaching methods employed by the teacher of extension directly influence the effectiveness of the student. The method, or combination of methods, is sought which is likely to be more effective than other methods in attaining the desired goal.

Principles for consideration in selection of teaching methods

(1) The more senses are involved in the learning process, the greater is the learning.

(2) By maximising responsibility of learner, you maximise learning.

Types of teaching methods

(1) *Trainee-dominated method:* (a) Use of library, (b) Use of laboratory, (c) Questionnaire, (d) Survey, (e) Field trips or observations, and (f) Project method.

(2) *Trainer-dominated method:* (a) Lecture method, (b) Counselling, (c) Case work, and (d) Demonstration—result, method.

(3) *Cooperative method:* (a) Apprenticeship, and (b) Group-discussion—(i) Seminar, (ii) Symposium, (iii) Panel, (iv) Question-answer session where the teacher also participates.

(4) *Functional method:* It emphasises on the developing of skills through instruction rather than lecture. It develops ability to do.

A. Teaching how to acquire knowledge by problem-solving

This is a group process, careful planning and preparation on the part of the teacher and the students are essential for this process. The following steps may be followed:

Step 1. *Introduction of the problem by the teacher.* The teacher describes the situation that gives rise to the problem. He give facts related to it. He helps the students in arriving at some solution.

Step 2. *Stating the problem.* The teacher should let the students help state the problem, i.e., getting the statement phrased from the students' viewpoint so that they think over it.

Step 3. *Finding the facts that have a bearing on the solution of the problem.* Ask the students the correct solution to the statement of the problem. Each student who gives a solution should be asked why he thinks his solution is correct. Then the answers should be placed before the group and with the help of students, each answer must be tested to determine whether it applies to the problems under consideration and whether it is based on the facts or not. The teacher then introduces the pertinent facts that have been considered, after the consideration of all the facts known by the students. This may be done by any or combination of the following ways:

(a) Illustrated lectures supported by charts on big sheet of paper which are easily visible, or on epidiascope, overhead projector, sides or filmstrip.

(b) Using flash cards, exhibits, specimens, etc.

(c) Taking the group on field trips to a village, C.D. Block office, Panchayat ghar, etc.

(d) Having a resource person speak to the group.

Step 4. *Reaching a conclusion.* All facts are weighed as to their importance to the solution of the problem, and a conclusion is reached as to the method of correcting the difficulty that causes the problem. This is done by the students.

Step 5. *Implementing the decision.* Both the students and teacher decide that skills must be acquired by the students in order to implement the decision. The students must be made to realise the importance of becoming skilled in the things decided upon. These may be: (a) The plan of attack, (b) The materiels needed, and (c) The skills the students should have for extending teachings in the villages.

Implementation of the decision should take into consideration the following points:

(i) *The classroom teachings and discussions:* These are important for establishing of understanding and finding solutions.

(ii) *The learning of skills:* These may be done by practice in the visual or audio-visual aids, laboratory workshop, farm or similar places.

(iii) *The application of solutions:* This involves the understandings and the skills in the villages with village people.

B. Teaching manual skills

Facts which teachers should keep in mind before attempting to teach skills to students:

(1) Learning a manual skill requires thinking on the part of the learner. The degree of perfection attained and the rate of progress made depend to a large degree on the amount and the quality of thinking by the learner.

(2) The learner must have a proper "*feel*" for the skill. The feel or sense of each skill can only be acquired by actual practice of the thing to be done. Actual materials, tools and time for each trainee should be provided.

(3) The student must have a pattern in his mind of the recognised goal—the perfect object or the perfect performance he is learning.

(4) Teach skills by "*whole method*" rather than by part.

(5) See that practice is not done incorrectly.

(6) Skills and interest go together.

The teacher must get ready to teach by having:

(a) A time-table—how much skill do we expect the student to have and how soon.

(b) Break down the job—list keypoints.

(c) Have equipment and materials ready before actual training begins, and

(d) Have the workplace properly arranged.

C. Developing desirable attitudes for working with villagers

(1) Supervised field practice; and (2) Mastery of skills.

The mastery of skills and practice of things is necessary because the studies show that learning is affected by various factors like:

(1) *We learn:* One per cent through taste, $1\frac{1}{2}$ per cent through touch, $3\frac{1}{2}$ per cent through smell, 11 per cent through hearing, and 83 per cent through sight.

(2) *Learner ability to retain information studied:* Ten per cent of what they read, 20 per cent of what they hear, 30 per cent of what they see, 50 per cent of what they see and hear, 70 per cent of what they say as they talk, and 90 per cent of what they say as they do a thing.

This has some implication of *methods in teaching* as shown by this information earlier (Table 11.1),

This necessitates some equipment in our classrooms. These can be:

(1) An overhead projector, with transparent material over which we can use letters or figures prepared in advance, or can write in the classroom itself.

(2) An epidiascope—where we use opaque material, pictures, diagrams, written matter, etc.

(3) A chalk board.

(4) A flannelboard.

(5) A hanging wall screen hung.

(6) Other things like: tape-recorder, a frame supporting the pictures, slide projector, movie projector, models, specimens, philip chart, flashcard sets prepared for different lectures.

D. Reviewing the teaching-learning process

It is important because we should know how well the information is retained by the students, how effective our teaching is and whether the students are attentive when we teach, do home work and are serious about their studies, for it we require:

(1) To put up demonstrations because these are useful tools to use in the follow-up process.

(2) Asking direct questions and holding individual conferences with the students outside the classroom.

(3) Noticing the behaviour of the students in the classroom gives clues, *how well* or *how badly* a teacher is teaching. There are indications that the students are on a *mental holiday* i.e., they are physically present in the classroom but mentally are absent by thinking about something else or day-dreaming. Some show restlessness, shift positions, give blank stares, sleep, whisper, read newspapers or do such other things.

(4) Class discussions can reveal very well whatever misconceptions the students have.

(5) Give home work, such as term papers, preparing for seminars, presentations in class, etc.

(6) *Written examination, quizes, tests, etc.:* A test should:

(a) Measure what is supposed to be measured—it must have *validity*.

(b) Measure accurately and consistently, i.e., it should be *reliable*.

(c) Fair to the students to avoid personal judgements while grading—it must be *objective*.

(d) Separate the good students from the poor—it must be *discriminating*.

(e) It must be *comprehensive*.

(f) Easy to use, simple to give and easy to score.

Types of tests

(1) Essay-type: and (2) Objective-type or short-answer test including (a) True-false test, and (b) Multiple-choice test.

Essay-type: (1) It should be used only when the educational objectives of the course can be better evaluated by this method than by the use of the more precise objective short-answer test. (2) The question should be as specific and definite as possible calling for the exact mental process to be evaluated. (3) Students should be given enough information concerning the question. (4) All students should be required to answer all questions. (5) Questions should be arranged in order of difficulty and the length of the examination should be such that all students may be expected to attempt to answer all the questions.

Grading essay-type examination

(1) Answers to each question should be written out, including each point that is expected to be covered.

(2) Each question should be graded in all papers before grading the next question. Grading may be superior, good, average inferior and poor. All the papers can then be sorted and graded accordingly. Better do it anonymously, so that the reader does not know whose paper is being graded.

True-false test

It can be used to review previous lessons or to motivate students to learn new material. It is especially useful when there are only two responses to a question.

Its limitatoins: (1) It encourages guessing, (2) It is sometimes difficult to frame a question that is completely true or false.

Multiple-choice test

(1) One correct answer to be chosen from 4 to 5 suggested responses.

(2) In constructing it the following points should be kept in mind: (a) the number of alternatives should be 4-5, (b) grammatical correctness should be maintained, and (c) the first part of the item should contain a simple problem completely stated rather than simply an incomplete statement.

Teacher evaluation

At the end of each Trimester and Semester/term each teacher should handover a questionnaire to the students to give their replies so that the teaching in the next trimester or term may be improved. The students should not write their names and should be explained the purpose behind it. Better some other teacher is deputed to collect these from the last class of the term. The question can be like:

(1) Organisation of class meetings: Lack of organisation/satisfactory organisation/ exceptionally well.

(2) Teacher's interest in the subject: Mild/strong/intensely interested.

(3) How interesting were the class meeting: Usually dull/mildly interesting/high level of interest maintained.

(4) Physical conditions maintained by the teacher: Was indifferent/had some concern/actively concerned in maintaining light, air, ventilation, water arrangement.

(5) Knowledge of subject-matter: Adequate/broad and thorough/knows every thing there is to know.

(6) Clearness of explanations: Usually not clear/usually clear/explanations complete.

(7) Freshness of presentation: Follows routine/some freshness/fresh and up-to-date.

(8) Class discussion: Usually waste of time/often of some value/usually **highly valuable.**

(9) Teacher/taught relationship: Indifferent/are friendly/mutual goodwill.

(10) Self-confidence: Lack of self conf./Good self-conf./Admirable self-conf.

(11) Tolerance: Unconcerned about students opinion/respects students' thought/encourages students to think for themselves.

(12) Was the teacher easy to talk to and get help from: Sometimes difficult to get help/available for and helpful in conferences/friendly and specially eager to be helpful.

(13) Does the teacher talk in a way that you can understand: Instruction is regularly too advanced for me/is occassionally too advanced/I can always follow readily.

(14) Stimulus to thinking: I rarely think of material except when studying or in class/I occasionally think or talk about subject outside of class/Material provokes a great deal of discussion and thought outside of class.

(15) Fairness in grading: Grades sometimes seem to be unfair/grading seems to fair on the whole/very careful and just in grading.

(16) Use of examination as a learning device: Students are left uncertain of mistakes/usually explains and helps students improve/carefully goes over examination paper and helps students improve.

(17) Major objectives of the course: Major objectives never mentioned or made apparent/objectives vaguely expressed and rarely emphasised/objectives **clearly** explained and made obvious throughout course.

(18) General rating of the teacher: poor/good/one of the best.

(19) Suggestions invited;

The teacher should:

    (a) speak more loudly

    (b) speak more clearly

    (c) speak with less monotony

    (d) use more familiar words

    (e) present material slower

    (f) use more humour in class

    (g) make blackboard writing more legible

    (h) leave material on the board longer

    (i) be more prompt in ending class on time

    (j) get better acquainted with his students

    (k) improve his personal appearance

    (l) try to eliminate annoying mannerisms.

(20) The teachers effectiveness would be increased by:

    (a) a more effective use of visual aids

    (b) handing out mimeographed outlines

    (c) giving tests and examinations more often

    (d) making assignments more clearly and understandable

    (e) having more class discussions and questioning

    (f) choosing a better textbook.

(21) This course should require less work/more work for the Cr.

(22) Your suggestions for the improvement of the teaching of this course:

      (a)   (b)   (c)

      (d)   (e)

(23) What is it about this course you have *liked the least*.

(24) What is it about this course you have *liked the most*.

Guidelines for the teacher

Based on the above questionnaire the teacher should be frank enough to bring out a guideline for himself in this way:

(1) The teacher should know his subject matter, be enthusiastic about his subject and about teaching it.

(2) The teacher should state where the learner is.

(3) The teacher should have a sympathetic attitude towards the students.

(4) His methods of teaching should be appropriate and varied.

(5) The teaching plan should be flexible.

(6) The teacher should stimulate and guide rather than dominate.

(7) The teacher should practice what he teaches and must set right examples.

Principles of teaching

(1) The student should subscribe to and understand the purposes of the course. The teacher at the first meeting, should introduce what is to be covered. If it is very senior class, the teacher must know from the learners the specific goals that are meaningful for them:

(2) The students should want to learn.

(3) The teacher should keep a friendly and informal climate so that the learners can ask things they do not follow.

(4) The physical conditions should be favourable and appropriate.

(5) The teachers should involve the learners so that they participate and accept some responsibility for the learning process.

(6) The teacher should make use of the learners experience.

(7) The teacher should prepare well for the class, should keep his teaching aid handy and should be enthusiastic about teaching it.

(8) The methods of instruction should be varied and apporopriate.

(9) The teacher has always to be a learner and change his teaching notes with the availability of the knowledge on the topic or subject. He should be keen enough to learn more and prepare material for his teaching.

Qualities of a good teacher[1]

A good teacher possesses the following qualities.

(1) *A true student, a sincere scholar in his subject:* He has to search for more information to keep up-to-date in his subject.

(2) *Enthusiastic about teaching his subject:* Likes to teach and is thoroughly prepared

[1]Adapted from "The tributes of a good teacher" by Doan K.E. Gardener, University of nois, JNKVV publication (Mimeo).

for the presentation.

(3) *Has interest in his students:* He likes his students to learn and tries to find time to make clear any part that was not understood. He has patience. He knows that learning proceeds at varying rates among students and at varying rates within the individual student, depending on the topic. An interest in students as persons outside the classroom usually results in good communication inside the classroom.

(4) *Is fair minded:* Has no favourites and treats all students fairly. His examinations are composed of questions and problems which are clearly stated and are representative of the material he has stressed in lectures, practicals and reading assignments.

(5) *Has clarity of expression:* He expresses himself well. Students are not left in doubt as to the meaning of what he has said.

(6) *Is not satisfied with poor performance:* His examinations help him determine whether his class is learning.

(7) *Personable and likeable:* He has a fine sense of humour. Is pleasant and congenial. He does not allow his class to be dull and tiring.

(8) *Alert and perceptive:* A teacher is alert enough to observe whether he is teaching at the level of the understanding his students. He *pitches himself* at their height. He is alert to observe dishonesty in examinations. He is alert to perceive whether he is hitting the mark.

(9) *Has wide experience and broad interests:* He is not narrow in his experience and his interests. He is well read, current and an interesting person. He knows the relationship of his specific discipline to the need of the society and he can explain this relation out of the wealth of his experiences.

(10) *Encourages and motivates his students:* A compliment on a term-paper or examination paper, *when sufficiently earned*, stimulates the student. He shold have in mind that "students and teachers are not adversaries", they have to work towards the same goals of "*enlightenment.*"

An understanding of the learning process and principles and laws of learning, which we have discussed above, is very essential for the teacher. Teaching is the process of creating learning situations by the proper application of principles and laws of learning. The important thing is to know how to apply the principles and laws of learning. While planning for teaching the teacher has to remember to plan in advance to apply the laws of learning in a teaching unit.

Suggestions

(1) Study the lesson plans prepared by good teachers and find out which principles of learning discussed here he has planned to apply.

(2) Observe the teaching of a a good teacher and try to find out which principles he applied and in what way. Discuss your ideas with him.

(3) Revise the lesson plans prepared by you by including creative ways of applying the principles of learning.

(4) Study the differences in impact on students due to the different ways of applying the principles of learning. Improve your lesson plans on the basis of those observations.

ESSENTIALS OF A TEACHING PLAN

Any teaching plan has five major parts. These are:

(1) Objectives—or, if you prefer, goals, aims, purposes, outcomes.

(2) Content—what is to be taught. The subject matter stated in the form of facts, principles, generalisations.

(3) Learning experiences—the activities and procedures employed to help students progress toward the objectives.

(4) Teaching aids and facilities—the tools used to aid students in progressing toward the objectives.

(5) Means of evaluation—methods employed to help to ascertain the student's progress toward objectives and the effectiveness of the teaching.

Considerations in developing educational objectives

What should a student style ? How can I help a student learn? How can I tell when a student has achieved this learning ? These are three questions frequently raised by teachers. Well-stated educational objectives can help determine the answer.

An educational objective is a statement of intent, of hoped-for behaviour (desired learning, proposed change) on the part of the learner which may result from instruction.

Learning is a change in capability which is inferred from a difference in an individual's performance from one time to a later time.

Therefore, it follows that:

(1) We must have some type of data, in terms of the individual performing in some way, in order to infer that learning has taken place;

(2) In order to collect data from which learning is to be judged, statements of hoped for learning (educational objectives) must be specific enough and clear enough so that we know that we are looking for;

(3) The degree of specificity (how detailed to make the objectives) should be at the level of generality of behaviour that one is seeking to help the student to acquire, and identify a performance which can be valued in and of itself as being effective in the student's life. Each objective should express a *purpose* which makes sense within the larger purpose of the person's life goals, and this purpose should be distinguishable from others;

(4) Since performance seems to be the key, a description of hoped for behaviour must contain a good "strong" verb, a verb referring to observable human action. Well-stated educational objectives guide the behaviour of the teacher. They help him to communicate himself and to his students (as well as to other teachers sharing his materials and responsibilities).

(a) Objectives tell teachers what the intent of instruction is so that appropriate experiences can by provided to give opportunities to learners to move toward the desired objective, and by appropriate evaluation materials can be devised to measure growth toward, and achievement of, the objective (the desired learning).

(b) Objectives communicate to students where they should be going. Unless the students know what the objectives are, they are likely to resort to memorisation and mechanical completion of exercises rather than carry out relevant sorts of learning activities. There should be less of the students' trying to guess what the teacher wants and less surprise on the part of students when they are evaluated on one premise (the one the teacher had in mind) when they had studied and learned on another set of assumptions.

Learning experiences

(1) Learning experiences should contribute toward the achievement of the objectives. They should be appropriate to the objectives.

(2) Learning experiences should lead to the development of significant content.

Students should have opportunities to arrive at conclusions on their own. They will need help in understanding the basis for sound conclusions. Such questions as the following may be helpful. Is there evidence in research, or accepted theory for the conclusion? Does one's own direct experience or observation tend to support the conclusion? Is it a conclusion that is generally applicable in situations similar to the one where it was developed?

(3) Learning experiences should be suited to the needs and concerns of students.

(4) Learning experiences should provide for continuity and sequential development.

(5) Learning experiences should provide for variety with respect to the media and senses employed.

Thus, provision may be made for individual differences in ways of learning, and for greater student interest.

(6) Resources should be available for carrying out the learning experiences.

However, one should not easily be daunted by a lack of resources. Frequently, these can be obtained with some effort or one may improvise resource materials that will serve the purpose.

(7) Learning experiences should provide for the development of the ability of the student to think and allow for the development of a problem-solving ability.

(8) Learning experiences should contribute to the interest in and desire for more learning.

The teacher

"Today our great and pressing need is for great teachers. This cannot wait. Research is necessary, but it does not translate into immediate results. Our greatest need at the moment is not for more and better information, it is for more and better dissemination of the information we already have, it is to hold the student, to prevent him for becoming a drop out, a welfare recipient. For every student that fails or drops out, every teacher—and society as a whole—has failed just that much. These are the days of educational decision. We educators succeed or fail in the first great opportunity that society has given us to prove the cause of education; and it must be education for the 21st century. I remind you of the great educator who said, "I educate my students for the future; the future is where I plan to spend the rest of my life."[1]

[1]Allen, Robert, "Can Education Meet the Challenge of Affluence?" *Phi Kappa Phi Journal*, XLVII: 4, 20-27, Fall, 1967.

PROFILES OF "BEST" AND "POOREST" TEACHERS

Best teacher	*Poorest teacher*
Sharp sense of humour	Insufficient knowledge of the subject
Excellent knowledge of subject	Poorly organised classes
Holds student interest	Shows partiality in grading
Always prepared for each class	Refers to only a few students
His exams make you think	Ridiculed by students
Fair in grading	Does not really enjoy teaching
Shows no favouritism	Gives no help to students
Respects students' views	Jumps from one point to another
Loves his work	Often late to class
Never too busy to help with problems	Lacks enthusiasm
Uses examples in teaching	Dresses sloppily
Always plenty to do in class	Unsympathetic
Friendly	Bad-tempered
Neat in dress	Talks to the blackboard
Admits own errors	Self-centred
Encourages students to do better	Inaudible
Recognises cause of students' errors	Late in returning graded exam papers
	Avoids questions
	Fails to convey information
	Unable to keep discipline

CHAPTER 12

THE PSYCHOLOGY OF LEARNING

Learning is a process which brings about change in one's way of responding as a result of practice or other experience. If the Extension Worker knows what factors stimulate learning among villagers, he can be more effective.

THEORIES OF LEARNING

There are two "Schools of Learning".

Associationism

Thorndike proposed (before 1900) a law of effect as one of the principles of learning (fundamental): the connections which an organism forms between a stimulus situation and a response is "strengthened" when the response is followed by some satisfaction or need reduction.

Field theory

This theory is an extension of the principles formulated by the Gestalt School of Psychology (during World War I). The term "field" refers to the gravitational or electro-static forces surrounding an object which help to determine its physical properties: that the organism exists in a constantly changing environment in which the whole is more than the sum of its parts.

FACTORS AFFECTING LEARNING

Some factors are related to characteristics of the subject-matter or of the external situation in which learning takes place. Others are characteristics of the learner himself and what brings to the learning situations.

A. Factors which are within the control of the learning

(1) *Influence of motivation on learning*: (a) Intent to learn, (b) reward and punishment, (c) extrinsic and intrinsic motivation—*extrinsic* includes hunger, thirst or escape from electric shock, in *intrinsic* the learner is interested in the learning task and is

anxious to learn for its own sake, (d) long-term goals, (e) influence stress, and (f) group participation.

(2) *Characteristics of material to be learned:* (a) Amount: it should be within the memory span: 6 to 8 units can be remembered at one time, (b) Familiarity, and (c) Meaningfulness.

(3) *Efficient conditions of practice:* These include: (a) knowledge of results, (b) distributed versus massed practice, i.e., short well placed learning periods and long concentrated learning periods, (c) leading versus reciting, (d) whole versus part learning, (e) influence of prior activity, (f) verbalisation in motor learning, (g) guidance as an aid to learning, (h) special aids to learning: films, visual aids, television, etc.

(4) *Learning under special conditions:* (a) learning during sleep—studies have shown that there is no learning during sleep but, (b) there is some evidence that improved learning may be achieved under hypnosis.

B. Factors to be taken into consideration by the teachers or extension workers in teaching the learners/farmers, housewives

(1) *Learning is growth-like and continuous:* (a) It must begin where the learner is, (b) it is more effective if the new is related to the old, (c) it is effective if the pace is adjusted to the learner's capacity, and (d) is more effective if the idea is brought to the attention of the learner repeatedly.

(2) *Learning is purposeful:* (a) learning is more effective if it makes sense to the learner, (b) if progress is consistently appraised and redirected, (c) if the objectives of teaching are clear to the learner and also to the teacher or extension worker, and (d) if purpose is kept in short focus.

(3) *Learning involves appropriate activities that engage the maximum number of senses—seeing, learning, doing, etc.:* (a) Learning results through self-activity, and (b) learning is more effective if activities are appropriate to the learning situation.

(4) *Learning is more effective if it is challenging:* (a) It is more effective if it is more appropriate and timely; if recognition is given to the learner's achievements, and (b) if the standard demands of the learner are suited to his ability, e.g., if the teacher or the extension worker helps the learner to build a mental picture of himself in the new situation.

(5) *Learning is more effective if it results in fundamental understanding:* (a) Memorising is useless unless there is practical application to it, (b) activity that stimulates the actual situation is most effective, and (c) there must be need for information.

(6) *Learning is effected by the physical and social environment*: So the teacher should see that the physical conditions are appropriate and the learner has no fear.

(7) *Learning is a gradual process:* Usually requiring several exposures before change is noticed; for effective learning, several exposures are to be made to get over each point.

(8) *Learning ability varies widely among individuals.* So the extension worker/teacher should have his level of teaching in line with the learner's/villager's ability.

(9) *Learning capacity starts at about the age of six.* Increases rapidly until the age of 20, then it begins to level off until around 50. The rate of learning declines very slightly after around 35 years of age.

(10) For effective learning, arrange and use equipment that all can see clearly.

(11) *Adults comprehend the spoken word:* With less difficulty than the written word at every rate of presentation. So for effective learning: (a) speak loudly, (b) choose words carefully, (c) arrange room for perception, (d) continue to build on the learner, (e) if it is necessary, reward the progress, and (f) avoid ridicule, punishment etc.

(12) *Learning is effective if it* is taken as an active process on the part of the learner:

It is what he does when he learns:

skills—the learner must practice them,

facts—the learner must relate them,

attitudes—he must change them,

appreciation—he must develop it.

TYPES OF LEARNING

Learning can be grouped as: (1) conditioning, (2) verbal learning, (3) motor learning, (4) perceptual learning, (5) attitude learning, and (6) problem solving.

(1) Conditioning

Through conditioning, the organism learns to make various responses to a wide variety of stimulus situations. It can be: (a) classical conditioning, and (b) instrumental conditioning.

(a) *Classical conditioning*

The type of behaviour observed in classical conditioning is sometimes described as elicited behaviour. It is some recognisable physical stimulus in the organism's environment which is employed to elicit a response that is already in the programme. Thus, experiments in classical conditioning commonly employ such stimuli as electric shocks, loud sounds and puffs of air on the body, which will produce certain physiological responses. Mr. Ivan Pavlov, a Russian physiologist, discovered the conditioned responses in an experiment while performing a series of psychological studies on the salivary response in dogs.

(b) *Instrumental conditioning*

This is called omitted behaviour. In it the response which is rewarded is reinforced, and those which are not rewarded drop out. In it the subject is merely placed in experimental response which is then reinforced by reward.

(2) Verbal learning

The ability to manipulate symbols, as in language, makes it possible for us to learn many things. The experiments in verbal learning include memory drum employment, serial learning and paired associate learning.

(3) Motor learning

Such learning involves primarily the use of muscles of the body. In it the individual requires new muscular co-ordinations as modes of response to some situation, e.g., typing, swimming, cycling, driving a tractor, threshing machine, sewing machine, etc.

(4) Perceptual learning

As a result of past experience, people perceive a situation differently. One way of changing a person's habit of responding is to change the way in which he perceives his environment. A considerable amount of human learning is of this sort: the recognition of sensory stimuli into new perceptual patterns.

(5) Attitude learning

An attitude is an emotionalised system of ideas which predisposes us to act in a certain way under certain conditions. Much of our learning involves changes in our attitudes: our disposition to give favourable or unfavourable responses to objects, persons, situations or abstract ideas.

(6) Problem solving

Whenever an individual finds himself in a novel situation in which he is motivated to achieve a certain goal but in which his progress towards the goal is blocked by some obstacle to which he has no ready-made response or means to overcome, he is confronted with a problem. Solution of the problem involves the development of some mode of response which will eliminate the obstacle.

Problem solving involves utilisation of the products of previous learning experiences and the learning experience itself. Higher mental processes may also be called into play: reasoning, forming concepts, making and testing hypotheses and so on.

MEASURING LEARNING

(1) *Criteria of measurement of learning may be*

(a) Accuracy of response, (b) Speed of response: in this learning is indicated either by a decrease in the amount of time required to perform a task or by an increase in the work done in a given amount of time, (c) Strength of response: in this the experimentor often measures the amount of some physiological activity, such as the number of the drops of saliva or the intensity of the galvanic skin response, which occurs in response to the conditioned stimulus, (d) Probability of response, and (e) Effort in response.

(2) *Plotting learning curves*

The learning curve is a graphic device for showing the amount or quality of a subject's performance after successive units of practice. The curves may be of six different types:

(a) Curves for equal returns, (b) Curves for increasing returns, (c) Curves of diminishing returns, (d) Shaped curves, (e) Plateaus: when for some types of skills there are levelled out places on the curve, and (f) Cyclical curves: when there are ups and downs.

(3) *Measuring retention*

There are four methods by which we can gauge this loss:

(a) Method of Recall, (b) Method of Recognition, (c) Method of Rearrangement, and (d) Method of Re-learning (4 R's).

FORGETTING AND RECALL

Forgetting is failing to remember what has been acquired. A convincing body of experimental evidence points to the conclusion that intervening activities, rather than the passage of time per se is the cause of forgetting.

The more meaningful the material that is learned, the greater is the likelihood that it will be remembered. This is so because there are greater reinforcement effects during the learning of meaningful material.

There is some evidence that painful or unpleasant experiences, although originally well-learned, are difficult to remember. This type of selective forgetting is called *repression*. Apparently, unpleasant experiences are easier to forget by an individual because the effects are distasteful.

Evidence to show that remembering is a selective and organised process, is abundant. Repression is a case in point, so is the demonstration that unfinished tasks linger on in one's memory more than finished tasks. Most everyday memories, if analysed carefully, show accurate retention of only a general plan or arrangement with a filling in of details that are usually wrong.

Retention is measured in four ways: (1) through recall, (2) recognition, (3) rearrangement and (4) re-learning as given above. The essential difference between recognition and recall is that in the former the stimulus is actually before the perceiver, whereas in the latter it is not. Even though one cannot recall or recognise something that has been learned, there is evidence that it is remembered if it takes less time to learn the material a second time that it did for the first.

Forgetting usually is most rapid immediately after the learning period. The degree of reminiscence evidently depends on:
(1) Meaningfulness of material.
(2) Determination to recall.
(3) Degree of mastery, and
(4) Length of time involved.

This phenomenon suggests that forgetting involves dynamic forces that remain active long after the learning situation ends. The activity that follows learning can either help remembering or hinder it. Sleeping results in the least forgetting, and engaging in an activity closely similar to the original learning causes most interference.

TRANSFER OF LEARNING

Another all-pervasive problem in the field of training and extension work concerns the extent to which the acquisition of skills, understandings and attitudes in one situation, have a facilitative influence upon skills, knowledge, understanding, and attitude in a different situation. Many teachers or Extension Workers go about their business unaware that the problem exists, or at least, that some desirable influence or positive transfer may not occur. For years, students were subjected to subject like Latin or Sanskrit in the belief that if these subjects were difficult, the mind was generally disciplined for all mental work. There is now abundant evidence to show that this is not true. If a school boy is drilled in arithmetic computation, will this learned skill help him in arithmetic problem solving? Weli-controlled experimental studies give a negative answer. Does practice in memorising poetry help in memorising prose? Experimental studies again give a negative answer. If children are taught neatness in school work, will these habits of neatness transfer to habits of dress? Under one set of conditions, we can say, "yes". The problem of positive transfer obviously requires for its solution a careful analysis of the conditions that lead to various kinds of transfer effects. An analysis of a case where positive transfer is known to occur will help to clarify the practical aspects of the transfer problem. Training must be organised in terms of *real life* situations, if a significant amount of transfer is to be expected. In other words, the child at home, the student in school or college, and the worker on the job, must be trained in doing what those real situations demand, not in paying lip service or telling theoretically what should be done in those situations.

GROUP PSYCHOLOGY AND ITS EFFECTS ON LEARNING

Many human goals can be achieved more efficiently by cooperative effort than by individual endeavour. One obvious factor contributing to the greater output of the group in such situations is the fact that various members of the group can work at different parts of the task at the same time, whereas an individual working by himself can handle only a relatively small part at a particular moment. Moreover, fewer errors tend to creep into the final product of a group effort, since the errors of one individual are more readily detected and corrected by someone else. In problem-solving too, group performance may yield better results than individual effort.

Feeling membership or belonging and individual status are among the most important factors contributing to the morale of the members of a group. When the channels of communication are restricted on the other hand, the individual members of a group tend to feel isolated or rejected. There is little to create a feeling of belonging, and group morale deteriorates.

Principles of group dynamics

"Group dynamics" is doing much to show how a group can best operate so that each member will make a maximum contribution. Group behaviour is the result of dynamic interaction between individuals in a social situation.

It is important to remember that "group members are made, not born". People must learn how to work together—to see their own efforts in relation to those of the groups as a whole, and to apply certain proven principles for making group activity most effective. There are eight general principles which improve the effectiveness of cooperative activity:

(1) *Atmosphere:* A physical situation that makes members of the group feel equal. Special seats should be abolished. The principle that every member is a teacher and every member is a learner should apply. There should be an informal workshop atmosphere. The size of the group should be kept small: 12 or 15 members.

(2) *Threat reduction:* The members should not feel like strangers. They should be

introduced to each other. In the beginning, there should be some humour. Introductions should be given by the members themselves in detail.

(3) *Distributive leadership:* Groups can function effectively without formal leaders; the various functions of leadership can be shared by different members of the group. Such sharing of leadership causes each person to feel more confidence in both himself and others. The leaders in the democratic group situation are not under the tension of the autocratic leader.

(4) *Goal formulation:* A group that cannot show each member that he has something to contribute and something to gain from membership, is an unproductive one and has no reason to continue.

(5) *Flexibility:* The planning of meetings should be flexible enough to permit last minute changes to meet unanticipated interests of the group.

(6) *Consensus:* Formal voting tends to create fractions in a group and to destroy its cohesiveness. In effective group work, the members continue to discuss the issue until it becomes obvious that everybody is satisfied with the solution.

(7) *Process awareness:* People who are relatively insensitive to the needs of others can learn much by paying close attention to the process of their own feelings.

(8) *Continual evaluation:* The group must continually evaluate its activities and goals, making whatever changes that are suggested by the evaluation. Without evaluation, the members of the group will tend to loose interest and the group may eventually disintegrate.

PROBLEM SOLVING

Where an individual or a group finds itself in a novel situation in which it is motivated to achieve a certain goal, but in which individual or group progress toward the goal is blocked by some obstacle which he or the group has no ready-made response to overcome, he or the group is confronted with a problem situation. Solution of the problem involves the development of some mode of response which will eliminate the obstacle.

Problem solving involves utilisation of the products of previous learning experiences. Higher mental processes may also be called into play: reasoning, forming concepts, making and testing hypotheses, and so on.

Many problems can be solved more efficiently by cooperative group effort than by individual endeavour. This is because various members of the group can work at different parts of task at the same time, whereas an individual working by himself can handle only a relatively small part at a particular moment. Secondly, fewer errors tend to creep into the final product of a group effort, since the errors of one individual are more readily detected and corrected by someone else. In the group situation, the needed variety in elements is more likely to be presented when an individual is working alone. This probably helps account for the fact that where there is ample inter-communication and pooling of ideas, group sanctions are usually better than individual ones.

ADULT LEARNING IN EXTENSION

The fact that adults *can* learn is very important in India where adult learning especially learning new practices, is so essential to increasing production of foodstuffs and improving standards of living. Too often adults learn less than they might, partly because they underestimate their ability to learn, partly because of the narrowness of their interests and most probably, because of the attitudes and values which they hold. The traditional ways of village people are a real block to getting them to learn new ways.

The power of adults to learn

The central problem in getting adults to learn as has been shown, is that of motivation. Social scientists feel that motivation largely determines the rate of learning. Desire to learn must be aroused by teachers adapting their methods to the situation; to learn, the adult must find meaning and significance in the subject matter to be learned.

There is considerable evidence from scientific studies to prove that most of us underestimate the power of adults to learn. Nor need illiteracy stand in the way, for almost all people without the basic tools of learning can achieve them if well taught and properly motivated. Nor is age the hindering factor that many have supposed, for tests have shown that throughout life learning ability does not change significantly; and there are no sex differences in learning power.

Another important fact about learning is that it brings about change; in knowledge, in group belonging-ness, ideology and in skills. Learning involves what the psychologists call retention, or the ability to use the thing taught in future situations, for learning which is not related to memory, is not truly learned.

In general learning is more rapid and efficient when the learner is a participant rather than a simple spectator. There is high value in knowledge of the results of learning. Group learning is more effective than individual learning. The greater the number of sensory channels used in the learning process, the greater the actual amount of learning must be used to be retained. These are basic principles of learning that apply to adults as well as to children.

This brings us to the subject of motivation to learn. By motivation, according to social psychologists, is meant "goal-directed behaviour". This definition places emphasis upon well-defined goals for particular programme; of clear statements about the difficulties and possibilities of achieving these goals, and, if total achievements is remote from planning, the programme in clear stages which can be successively attained; and of allowing each individual to have some knowledge of his achievement at appropriate points.

A simple approach to understanding motivation to learn is that in adult education the main incentives can be classed under such categories as "people want to gain", "want to be", "want to do", and "want to save". These relate to the four wishes which the famous sociologist Thomas outlined and which have become classical in sociological literature: desire for security, response, recognition and new experience.

One fact which many extension people soon learn is that motivation is related to the level of aspiration, and it does not begin until one has formed something of a self-image which carries with it the desire to attain or preserve a certain status. This is related to the development of one's image, sense of pride and goals are often set in terms of one's self-image. Self-evaluation is not done in isolation. It is a social phenomenon, one in which the individual compares himself not only with what he finds he can do but also with what he sees others can do. And all groups, no matter what their reference group for the task in question set their aspiration levels relatively low when they themselves have no experience with the task.

Learning and goal formation

We come then, to the matter of goal formation. For personal adjustment as well as for learning, it is important that goals be well-defined and clearly related to action. The individual must not only have a current and well-defined problem arising out of specific situation, but he must be aware of some course he can follow in getting a solution to his problem.

Goal directed behaviour as a motivating force may be similar to what sociologists call expected satisfactions. The formation of these expectations do not come over-night, rather they are formed over a period of time as an individual sees, becomes interested in, and experiences the results of a new method.

Motives differ with different persons and may relate to such factors as intellectual curiosity, interest in the subject, desire for mental stimulation, the desire to be neigh-bourly, the desire to work for a better kind of life for one's self and one's community, to aid in strengthening group solidarity, and for the sheer enjoyment derived from learning new skills and knowledge.

As one grows older in this he becomes better developed. The things which motivate him are increasingly socially defined and channelled, and new motivations are learned from the social systems of which he becomes a part. As this social system changes, or as the individual changes from one social system to another, the basic motivational forces change, and these must be understood if the adult educationist is to make progress in his field.

The role of attitudes

We have discussed what learning is and some of the forces that lie behind motiva tion. Of importance in the field of motivation is the matter of attitudes, for they influence the process of learning fundamentally. The adult educator must be put on his guard by remembering that bias can retard learning. If one were to use a simple definition of "attitude" it probably would be that "attitudes are learned responses" and they are always formed in relation to objects, ideas or persons. Attitudes may reflect one's central values, show one's consistency in ways of reacting, or ways or gratifying needs. Or they may form a part of an attempt to construct for oneself a meaningful world within which one can order his life, or can express his identification with or promote his acceptance by favoured social groups.

Motivating forces affecting attitudes include such basic appeals as fear-arousing appeals, or threats, the force of the group from which the individual attains his basic values, or through which he substains them. These are used differently by different leaders. Appeals to a person in a democratically oriented society to become a leader may take either one or both of the following forms:

(1) A seeking of personal gain or glory.
(2) A genuine joy and satisfaction in serving.

Important to the latter value system are such beliefs as:

    (i)   that every individual is worthy,

    (ii) that each is unique and different,

    (iii) that the way a person lives he becomes,

    (iv) that the potential and capacity for learning exists in every individual.

    (v) that love, as expressed in concern for one's fellow-man, is a reality, and

    (vi) that dedication, values and ideals are the stabilisers for personality.

Thus, we have seen that adults can learn, that learning brings about change, that the basic motivation to learn is goal formation, that such goals must be related to expected satisfactions, and that attitudes affect the process of learning fundamentally. These facts are important to the change agent if he is to bring about change in the village in India.

PSYCHOLOGICAL FACTORS IN ADULT LEARNING

The communication media with which an extension agent can work are limited, as we all know, by the fact that eight in ten of the cultivators in India are illiterate. This does not mean they are not intelligent. It means that communicational media are largely limited to the spoken word, and pictures and demonstrations to go with the spoken word. This means extension agents and their fellow-workers must make *personal contacts*, both individual and group, and establish *rapport* and *empathy* with these cultivators. You can reach and influence to change them in no other way if you are to use educational and democratic methods.

A. Rapport and empathy

Important to the extension workers is rapport and empathy. But you must understand what rapport and what empathy mean, and know how to use these concepts before you can put to use other understandings of the psychology of the farmer or cultivator in India. You establish rapport with the cultivator only when he accepts you, has confidence in what you recommend and comes to you for advice in improving his practices. This rapport can only be established, on your part, by demonstrating your genuine concern for the welfare of the cultivator and his family, your understanding of the problems he faces, and the successful demonstration of your practical knowledge of how to meet these problems, especially in the area of increasing production. You and those you work with to re-educate the farmer must be able to demonstrate convincingly that the new practices you recommend are better than the ones now used by the farmer. He will know they are better only when he has tried them out and found out for himself that they are better than the ones he is using.

To establish rapport without empathy, however, can mean failure to effectively reach the cultivator, even if he has accepted some of your suggestions for change. For if he suspects that you do not really understand his problems, or sympathise with him, that is, look at the problems from his point of view, he may very likely lose confidence in you. The faculty of putting yourself emotionally in the situation of the farmer will help you to best use your knowledge in finding a solution to his problem. For, whereas he sees the problem as insoluble, you can see why he does and have the advantage of being able to see it in terms of solutions you know will work, as well. You are thus in a better position to guide him in trying out the new practice for himself, leading him to discover for himself with your guidance, the way to solve the problem. By these tactics you have established both rapport and empathy: rapport means that the cultivator has confidence in you, and empathy that ‹you can rejoice with him in the solution of the problem, in getting better yields as a result of the use of the new practice, or in getting the home improved by convincing the housewife to accept your ideas.

B. The four basic wishes

With this introduction, we come to the question of what are the basic wishes or desires of man, and this includes the cultivators of land in India. Sociologists have listed four basic wishes, namely: (1) the wish for security, (2) the wish for response, (3) the wish for recognition, and (4) the wish for new experience. As you analyse these four wishes, you will see that they find expression in one way or another in all people including the villagers with whom you work. Let us, therefore, make our analysis in terms of the villagers in India.

(1) *The wish for security*

It is universal and includes security in childhood, in one's occupation, in family life, in group relations in the nation and the world in which one lives. The lack of security, or the fear of losing one's sense of security, brings on a wide variety of fears, suspicions and resulting actions which can lead an individual to act rashly or violently. The promise of greater security leads one to greater efforts to attain it.

The average cultivator in India lives very close to the margin of insecurity. A single crop failure can cause an entire village or even a tract to be thrown into panic and despair. It is for this reason that most cultivators hold fast to the old "tried and true" methods, and are afraid to try anything new that will upset this delicate balance between his present security and possible insecurity. The wise extension worker will not, therefore, insist upon a wholesale change to new methods; rather he will encourage the cultivator to try out the new practices in a small way, e.g., in only one part of a field.

Because the majority of cultivators are so close to the insecurity margin, the extension educator, or the change agent, as he is frequently called, is inclined to work with the cultivators, in the village who can afford to take chances with new methods. As we study the process of diffusion and the group structure in the village, however, we may find that this policy will delay or defeat widespread acceptance of new practices. The well-to-do farmer in the village can do things others cannot do. This is part of the psychology of the villagers in India and a part of the pattern of expectations in the village. The rich farmer of the village expects to be different and others expect him to be different, so they will not necessarily expect to do the things he does. This is why the change agent must try to break through to the ordinary cultivator and get him to try out new practices, at first in a small way.

We know economic security is important to the average village cultivator. It is related, of course, to security in other ways: security for his family, security in his caste, and security in his old age, security in the eyes of his fellows. These socioeconomic relationships must be recognised by the change agent. He must know, for example, who it is in the local situation who looks with fear on the new practices, and why his wife may find in it a necessary change in her duties or responsibilities and so oppose the change. Or the money lender, to whom the farmer is indebted, may look with disdain on the new method, especially if it will deprive him of his advantage. The farmer, moreover, may be prevailed upon by his caste, or his guide in family affairs, to hold on to the old methods. The reasons they give can be far from rational: based on tradition, superstition, or actual religious belief.

(2) *Desire for response*

Fortunately, every individual has other basic desires, one of which is the desire for response. If a cultivator comes to the point that he is willing to try out of a new method, the response to his efforts is all important. He may be promised certain things by his government in response to his asserted willingness to cooperate, such as the means to prepare his field for fertiliser use. If he fails to get a response, such as getting the fertiliser on time or getting better yields from the fertiliser, he will turn away from the new method, and it will be difficult to get him to try again. So also with his peers those to whom he looks for respect—his neighbours, and his family: if he gets a favourable response to his new methods, they are likely to applaud and approve and may follow his example. If he fails to get response, he loses face in their eyes and this is a painful thing for any villager in India to have to face.

(3) *The wish for response*

It is closely related to the wish for recognition. Success in the use of a new practice which will bring recognition, or should, on the part of the change agent. Even in working toward getting a new practice in operation, if the cultivator discovers a new way for himself, to be given recognition for his achievement is all important. Such recognition brings new status to him in the eyes of his peers.

What, then, can we say of the wish for new experience? Is it true that the average villager is so enmeshed in the life and traditions of the village that he actually shuns new experience? This depends, of course, on the age and degree of security of the individual. If the new experience enhances rather than endangers security, pleasures and promises, even the old may welcome it.

(4) *The desire for new experience*

This is held by every person. The wise and tactful change agent can use it as a means to instill the experimental attitude into the mind of the farmer, especially the young farmer. This attitude is related to the tendency for some to wonder what would happen if they were to try out a new idea. Closely related is that somewhat rare quality of some of our people to ask why things happen as they do. It is not unusual for one to see clumps of tall wheat in fields of ordinary wheat, for example. The rare individual would ask himself why this happens, and the change agent in going to a farmer's field must always question why some plants or patches of crop are so much better than others. This questioning attitude is related to the wish for new experience, and it has led to the discovery of many very useful innovations, such as new crop varieties, that mankind now enjoys.

C. Emotionality and rationality

We have touched upon the role of emotions and rationality in our discussion of the four basic wishes and also in previous chapters. But let us move further into those elements in the psychology of rural people, for they affect the extent to which and the rapidity with which, changes in practices can be made.

Everyone knows the difference between emotionality and rationality. Emotions, as we know, are related to feeling and have little rationality in them. Rationality relates to the working of the mind, to looking realistically and practically at a problem. One can become emotional about results obtained from rational effort. It is probably more likely that feelings about something will stand in the way of a national approach to it. Emotion, however, can be used as a means of motivation to learn.

Here we come face to face with the needs of the individual and of the group of which he is part. Much of the motivation to learn comes from *personal and social needs*. Personal needs and satisfactions have a definite emotional or "feelings" base. A person must "feel" right in the society of which he is a part. His attitude toward himself is acquired through attitudes of others toward him: feelings of modesty, vanity, confidence, timidity, fear, courage and belongingness. Many of these personality traits come out of the culture into which the individual is born. This is the reason he must learn all he can about rural culture.

Personal and social needs, then, are closely related. Each individual growing into a culture learns to play a role, or different roles in different situations. There are times in the life of the individual when he must learn a new role such as being a parent, becoming a member of a cooperative, or finding his place as a respected and successful farmer. It is at these times that someone must help him learn his new role. If he learns it on the basis of tradition and custom, the chances are there of much feeling, emotion, belief and possibly mysticism being in it. But if he must learn it strictly in terms of being able to hold a job in an industrial or technical society, his learning must be based largely on reason or rational action.

The situation in India today is such that it is difficult to discern where feeling and emotion leave off and reason and rationality begin. It is evident that when a farmer is ready to discard such ideas as that an iron plough, or fertilisers, poison the soil or that planting must be done according to the proper sign in the zodiac, and uses the results of scientific experimentation in his farm plans and operations, he comes into the sphere of the rational.

Social psychologists are still baffled by how these forces—feelings and thinking—affect learning. Two things seem somewhat clear: (1) that individuals must be aware of education as a positive value for solving problems, and (2) they must have had an experience which had demonstrated that education can bring happiness and success.

However, we can *rationalise* about the need for education but until the villager can attach an emotional element to it, he is likely to look upon it merely as something good for someone else. He can become emotional about it, however, in wanting his children to have a better life than he has had, and finding in education the way to accomplish this goal. If education for himself, such as learning that a new practice will bring better yields and hence more income, is accepted by the cultivator, he will have taken the first step in the direction of a rational rather than emotional or tradition-directed farming.

D. Suggestibility and suspiciousness

The first reaction to the approach of a new person or a new idea is to be *suspicious* of him or it. There is always a fear of the unknown. It is important, then, that this unspoken fear or suspicion be removed before one can suggest to a farmer that he change his practices. It is difficult to know why a farmer is suspicious. Not too infrequently it is that he has been taken advantage of by others holding similar positions to those held by you. If these other persons have made promises and not filled them, or encouraged practices that have failed, the farmer is naturally suspicious of anyone else coming to encourage him to do things like those which have failed. This brings us back to the problem of *rapport*. The change agent in establishing rapport, must overcome these feelings of suspicion. Only then the farmer will be open to new ideas.

In an educational system, one can *suggest* that an old practice be replaced by a new one. If this carries with it an appeal, and if the new idea is related in some way to prese*nt* practice or experience, it may reach through the natural resistance on the part of the farmer toward change. Suggestions that old ways are wrong may intensify resistance, but suggestions that the old ways are good and can be improved may lead the farmer to consider the new. If, in the discussion, the farmer is led to make the suggestion himself, a big step has been taken in getting him to accept a new practice.

E. Imitativeness and assertiveness

Most of us are imitators. We tend to follow in the path of those who lay the trail. As childern learn to speak and act through imitation, so all through life we come to do things by imitating others. We imitate others in dress, food habits, work habits, in short, in all those ways in which we find favour in the eyes of those whose respect and affection we covet. We do not want to be different, although each of us is different from others. We prefer to conform and follow the usual ways of the group.

Change in practice can come through imitation. If one farmer takes on a new method and he has influence in his village—has the respect and confidence of his neighbours—others may imitate him. This is the basis for the finding that neighbours are the most important factors in influencing farmers actually to take on a new practice.

Assertivenss may be a trait arising out of a desire to be different. Whereas in a group most members tend to conform to group norms, there are always one or more individuals who tend to deviate from these norms, they assert themselves This may be used as a positive force, or it may create a negative situation. The deviant, as he is called by sociologists, may be the one who first breaks entirely from the group. If his desire for self-assertiveness can be sanctioned by the natural leaders of the group, a way is left open for the others to imitate him in case his efforts prove successiui. It is in the interest of the change agent that his action be sanctioned and that his efforts be successful. Otherwise, his deviant action may result not only in ostracising him from the group, but in destroying the influence of the change agent with the group.

F. Group loyalty and individualism

Group loyalty and conformity are related. Naturally, when a person becomes a member of a group, he is *expected* to be loyal to the aims and objectives of the group and to work actively for their accomplishment. In becoming a member of the group, the individual plays an assigned role in the group and his status may either be ascribed or acquired. If the status is ascribed, it is dictated by the group a child born in a village is ascribed to the *caste* of which his parents are part. If the status is acquired it is usually because of a role of *value* that the individual has played, or can play, for the group.

Group loyalties are brought about through expectations. The individual becomes a member of a group because he promises to do what the group wants him to do. He remains a member of the group so long as he gets what he expects from the group, unless, of course, he is bound to the group by tradition or force.

Group loyalties do not prevent an individual from expressing his individual desires or wants. In a democratic society, he is expected to contribute his individual thoughts and suggestions so long as they promise to contribute to the work or programme of the group. In purely democratic societies all decisions are made in this way: individuals make their suggestions, all suggestions are considered, and the group *comes to a consensus* as to what is the best action.

Individualism can be equated, of course, with resistance to conformity to group norms, then the individual becomes a deviant. By being isolated from the group, he may no longer have an influence with the group. Yet in his individualism, he may be freed to do what he feels is best and thus to try out a new practice. He then becomes an innovator. He may or may not be imitiated. If he is, then the process of group acceptance has begun—he again becomes a member of the group, but by this fact makes a change in the group.

The change agent must be aware of these group processes, and be able to determine at what point the desire for individual action can lead to group approval and sanction. This appraisal must include an assessment of the nature of the group, the degree to which it is democratic, and hence the degree to which attention and consideration are given to new ideas and practices which he wants to see adopted.

G. Adherence to tradition and changeability

We all know that a primitive society is usually steeped in tradition, and that change comes most rapidly in the society which has accepted science and looks eagerly for new developments in science. Each change agent must assess the society in which he works in terms of the influence of tradition as against science.

The fact that the average village cultivator in India lives in what is called the ox-cart age does not necessarily mean that he is completely tradition-bound. Our experience and researches lead us to believe that farmers welcome anything which will improve their material welfare consistent with the mores of the society of which they are a part. This means the change agent must know what the mores are which tend to limit the practices that a farmer can be led to consider. Mores are sanctions and carry the possibility of group punishment for the individuals violating them. In India, one soon becomes aware of the fact that it is easier to get practices adopted which relate to crops than to livestock. So at the outset, primary efforts to get changes made must relate to crops. But change can also be made in livestock practices which do not violate local mores, or in a society in which restrictive mores are working.

H. Creativity and pragmatism

Every individual has latent creative capacities. That society which gives widest play and encouragement to this creative impulse can be much more advanced and enriched than one in which this human resource is neglected or suppressed. A real task of the change agent in a democratically oriented society is to encourage the discovery, training and use of this talent. The development of youth clubs with wide opportunity for individual expression is certainly one way to bring this about.

The pragmatic individual is one who may be tied to form or order to the practical, or be may he officious, opinionated or a busy body. This pragmatic characteristic may be often seen in the Indian village in the person holding an official position. He may come to feel that that which is according to the law is the only thing that is practical. And since he may hold a position of authority, whereby his sanction must be given to actions affecting the community, what he says is of importance to the change agent and to getting new practices adopted. For some, it may even mean a change in rule or law before the practice can even be discussed.

I. Artistry and devotion to forms

There are lovers of beauty for whom there is more in good practice than merely material gain. There are in some countries, for example, breeders of livestock who take pride in beauty and quality of the stock they produce. This artistic tendency in farmers is to be valued especially if with it can come a realisation that with beauty there can be utility as well. Man does not live by bread alone.

So far as devotion to form is concerned, we can be confronted, especially in a tradition-bound society, with actions that prevent acceptance of a new practice. Where the feeling is prevalent that a thing should be done in a certain way, it is difficult to convince the person that another way may bring equally good or better results. Devotion to form comes most rapidly in a society in which the individual has been taught over the ages that these forms are sacred and are not to be tampered with. If some means can be developed in these forms to give sanction to new ways, then the form may remain the same and the new practice take the place of the old.

J. Religiousness and scepticism

The sceptic is one who is given to doubting. The doubting may relate to new methods, or to beliefs, or even to knowledge of truth itself. The sceptic is the man who suspends judgement, who is critical, and he may carry this characteristic to extremes, standing in the way of any new idea or practice. One must know what influence a sceptic may have in a community to be able to deal with him. If he is a natural leader, the task is very difficult, for he must be won over to an acceptance of the new way. It may be that the only way to do this is to bring influence on his peers so that he must either abandon his position of scepticism or suffer a lowering of status among his friends.

Religiousness is quite another matter and may be the very opposite of scepticism. Religion ranks with education and government as a basic force. It is a universal force relating to beliefs about life and death and man's place in the Universe. In rural areas, it is likely to be related to all life, manifesting itself as a supernatural power in nature. It is of importance, therefore, that the change agent know what are the religious beliefs that are related to the new practices that he is seeking to get adopted. It may be that there are elements in the religious beliefs which, if properly interpreted, would support the adoption of the new ways.

K. Relating negative traits

A trait, from the social points of view, is a persistent behaviour pattern or attitude held by a person. It may be positive or negative in its effects. Some positive traits are cheerfulness, reliability, sincerity, truthfulness, cooperativeness, kindness, compassion, tolerance, etc. Negative traits include such things as secretiveness, cowardice, imprudence, credulousness, dishonesty and others.

Some of these traits may be called vices, springing out of the above-described psychological characteristics. Lack of foresight is one. This comes as result of dependence on the judgement of others, doing things on the spur of the movement, jumping at others, discussing and thinking through the problems and looking at the consequences. In this case, the training the change agent has had in the art of planning is all important. He must encourage every farmer to plan ahead in terms of a balanced farm plan, trying by the adoption of new methods to avoid possible set-backs in such plans. Elements in good farm planning are sound land use and soil conservation, crop rotation and field arrangement, high crop yields, efficient and suitable kinds and amounts of livestock, carefully planned use of labour, effective use of power and machinery, conservation of buildings and other constructions, study of price trends and changes, having enough land and resources to produce the required income, constant study of purchase and sale of transactions, timeliness and regularity, kindliness, cleanliness and thoroughness, the will to do a good job, and love of farm life and work.

A second negative trait often found in individuals is imprudence, which is about the same as bad judgement. This, of course, comes out of impulsive thought and action and lack of reasoned planning. All change agents may have to deal with such imprudent people from time to time. It is best to deal with them through the medium of local natural leaders with whom rapport has been established.

A third trait is that of credulousness, that is, a tendency to believe all one hears. Such a person is likely to be taken in by a "smooth talker" who has little regard for the truth. He may be a deviant in that he prefers these "bad" characters for they conjure up for him visions which please him, but which are completely beyond his potential capacities. Unfortunately, such an individual may blame his failure to realise his vision on his more mature associates who, seeing the folly of his resolves, restrain him. He then becomes frustrated and may rebel completely. The change agent should be on guard against such an individual and, through the more sober-minded leaders of the villages, endeavour to show up the falsity of the fancies possessed by this credulous individual.

Conservatism may be called a vice if it really stands in the way of progress. In some cases, the conservative individual can be worked with gradually, for when he has had a new way conclusively demonstrated, he becomes as conservative, that is, careful in its use, as he was in holding on to the old ways. Hence. the conservative may help the change agent in the development of as clearly fool-proof demonstrations as possible.

Immobility may refer to the fact that a person or group holds to one place of living; or it may refer to holding to one way of doing things. Two are related and contribute to what is called provincialism. It is through tours and conferences, where-in the farmers of one village come out of their environment and see how things are done in other areas, that this trait of provincialism can be partly overcome.

The liability to exploitation may not be a negative trait but a danger to which all of us may from time to time be exposed. If the individual is credulous of course, he is more liable to be exploited than if he is careful in making choices. He should be encouraged to be careful in his choices, or even conservative, in this regard. Yet, even in spite of the alleged conservativeness of farmers, it has been true that some are easily exploited, especially by the unscrupulous. This makes them suspicious of new people and new things, of new systems such as the Extension Service, which may have grown out of the same government system which previously have exploited them. Hence, it is important for the change agent to establish rapport and empathy.

One of the most widespread conditions found in villages is unresolved conflicts. These are social situations in which individuals or groups seek to thwart each other's purposes and to prevent satisfaction of each other's interests, even to the extent of injury or destruction. If most or all of the people in the village are involved, as is sometimes the case, such a conflict often stands in the way of constructive planning and action. Therefore, the resolving of conflicts in the village is important to the change agent and his desire to get new practices adopted. Probably, the best approach is to get both parties working, independently or through natural leaders, toward a common and highly desired goal. One toward which both factions will strive. Effort should be made to get at the cause of the conflict and, if possible, to remove it. Often government officials are at the source and by proper action can remove the cause, or induce cooperation on a common objective.

A complex is a different thing. Psychologically, it is a system of impulses or of ideas with emotional elements attached to them—a set of memories, beliefs, ideas, words, attitudes, wishes, etc., related to each other through memory, emotion, interest or goal. People with complexes often need the help of psychiatrists. But there may be social complexes in which the use of a practice is tied in with a number of ideas, beliefs, attitudes or emotions. Where this is the case, a real problem faces the change agent. He must try to isolate these other influences and, with the help of those in the village with whom he has established rapport, gradually overcome them.

The virtues springing out of the positive traits described above include an apprecia-tion of sincerity. This is a trait which every change agent should possess. He can-not be evasive nor must he mislead or make promises he cannot fulfil. His attitude, regarding practice adoption, must always be that he will promise good results only if the cultivator follows completely the method recommended for the practice. Hence, he must be sure of what he is to teach, and teach it thoroughly.

The average farmer is likely to adopt a new practice that he is convinced is better than the old. This is the reason method and result demonstrations, carefully planned and carried out, are so important. They are much more effective if the cultivator does most of the work under the guidance of the change agent.

It is best if all teaching can be done in a group setting. Thus, individuals learn to work in a group and the change agent can teach proper methods of group action. Of course, the individual who is amenable to group work is much easier to work with in group situations but this comes largely through experience in group activity. We must point out in this connection, the importance of group work in Extension. India simply does not have the resources to permit individual attention even on the part of the VLW, except for demonstrators and those who will act as voluntary leaders in groups in their own villages. It is only through the group that effective contact can be made with the mass of villagers in India.

This brief discussion of basic urges and traits as related to village life in India had to be brief; it should suggest further study. A few items remain which are of enough importance to be included. They are the urge to aid, the urge for fair treatment, the urge for freedom and the urge to be creative. None of these need much discussion but they need the concentrated attention of the change agent.

Those of us who have worked directly with farmers believe that, as a whole, they have the urge to aid their fellowmen. The very widespread evidence of mutual aid in farming areas all over the world bears this out. This urge needs to be nurtured. So too with the urge for fair treatment. This is at the basis for many of the agrarian reforms which have taken place all over the world. If the farmer can feel that the change agent backs him up whole-heartedly in his fight for fair treatment, he will work closely in many other ways with his change agent.

Farmers have always been individualistic. A better way to look at it is that they want freedom to act, produce and live as human beings. This desire is related to the desire to be creative. The farmer lives in an environment in which creation is almost a daily phenomenon. He has a hand in this creation as he plants the seed in the soil and nurtures the plant to maturity. The challenge to the dedicated change agent is to help make the farmer become free in many ways by releasing him from the bondage of ignorance, poor health, debt, outmoded practices, low living levels, restrictions to personal expression and from repressive tradition. He equally challenges the creative potentialities of the farmer by opening for him the vast opportunities that scientific agriculture holds for him, increasing production, advancing his income and attaining better living conditions for himself, his family, his village and his nation.

CHAPTER 13

OTHER PSYCHOLOGICAL CONCEPTS

The extension worker needs some knowledge of other psychological concepts also. For him, we give here a brief outline of: Development of an individual; Senses provided to the human beings; Attention and perception; Thinking; Communication and group processes; and Problems in group living.

DEVELOPMENT OF AN INDIVIDUAL

A. What determines human development?

(1) Man is said to be the product of his nature and his nurture.

(2) Heredity determines the capacity a person has for learning.

(3) A person's environment has a great effect on his progress towards achieving learning capacity.

(4) The development process can be shown by the equation: heredity × environment × time = development level.

(5) The factors in the maturation process are, said to be:

(a) Maturation follows an orderly sequence.

(b) Due to hereditary factors maturation is not uniform for all children.

(c) The maturation process is said to have usually three levels:

   (i) A level of global, undifferential mass activity.

   (ii) A level of differential parts, each acting more or less autonomously.

   (iii) A level of integrated action based upon interdependence of the parts.

(d) The principle of motor primary, or the individual's maturation level at any given time limits the effectiveness and his environment in stimulating development.

(e) Girls and boys have different rates of growth and maturation.

(f) The endocrines (ductless glands) have major effect on development:

   (i) They release their substance (hormones) directly into the blood streams.

   (ii) They are regulatory in nature and control the rate of growth of certain bodily processes in maturation.

   (iii) They affect metabolism, flow of and the tendency for the body to maintain its chemical equilibrium (homeostasis).

   (iv) The master control for these glands probably lies in the hypothalmus.

(v) Certain endocrine glands seem to have the greatest effect on the maturation process. These can be given as follows:

(1) The pit controls the growth of the skeleton, muscles and various internal organs (malfunction of these glands causes dwarfism or giantism).

(2) The thyroids affect body metabolism and help control the rate of growth. They have an influence on the structure and function of the nervous system, especially in the development of intelligence.

(3) The inner adrenal (adrenal medulla) helps individuals to adjust to emergency and strong emotional situations and the outer adrenal (adrenal cortex) which acts with the sex glands in affecting maturation of sexual characteristics of masculinity and femininity.

(4) The glands work with the adrenal cortex in affecting masculinity and femininity.

B. Environment and maturation affect learning

(1) Environment opportunity is very important in determining the level of development of a person.

(2) Maturation will greatly affect the rate of learning.

C. How psycho-social development stages are related to development tasks?

Some developmental tasks, according to the various stages from infancy and early childhood to later maturity, can be given, in case of human beings, as follows:

(1) *Infancy and early childhood.* Learning to:

walk,

take solid foods,

talk,

control the elimination of body wastes,

sex differences and sexual modesty,

achieving psychological stability, and

forming simple concepts of social and physical reality.

Learning to relate oneself emotionally to parents, siblings and other people. The child learns to distinguish right and wrong and also develops a conscience, i.e., there is a development of sense of a trust, a sense of autonomy and a sense of initiative.

(2) *Middle childhood:* Sense of duty and accomplishment: The child learns physical skills necessary for ordinary games. Learns to build wholesome attitudes towards himself as an organism. Learns to get along with his age mates. Learns appropriate masculine and feminine social roles. Develops fundamental skills in reading, writing, calculating, etc. Develops concepts necessary for everyday living. Learns to develop a conscience, morality and sense of values. Tries to achieve personal independence and also develops attitudes towards social groups and institutions.

(3) *Adolescence:* Sense of identity and sense of intimacy.

At this age, the child learns to achieve new and more mature relations with age mates of both sexes, achieves a masculine or feminine social role, tries to build his physique and learns to use the body effectively, achieves emotional independence from parents and other adults, tries to achieve assurance of economic independence and even may select his future occupation and prepare for the same, in Western culture, may prepare for marriage and family life. In countries like India, he or she shows his or her preparation for marriage to the parents. Develops intellectual skills and concepts necessary to civic competence. Tries to achieve socially responsible behaviour. Acquires a set of values and an ethical system as a guide to behaviour.

(4) *Early adulthood:* Parental sense.

In Western society, the individual selects a mate, while in cultures like that in India the parents, or even oneself, select mate for marriage. After marriage he learns to start a family life like rearing children, managing a home, gets started in an occupation, starts talking about civic responsibility, and tries to find a social group to his liking.

(5) *Middle age:* If not the eldest in the family or not a member of a joint family, learns to achieve adult, civic and social responsibility. Establishes and maintains an economic standard of living, assists teenage children to become responsible and happy adults, learns to develop adult leisure-time activities. Relates oneself to spouse as a person, and accepts and adjusts to the physiological change of middle age. Adjusts to aging parents.

(6) *Later maturity:* Learns to adjust to decreasing physical strength and health, prepares for retirement, reduced income, when the spouse dies tries to adjust to the situation, establishes an explicit affiliation with one's age-group, becomes more religious, tries to meet social obligations, establishes satisfactory physical arrangements.

THE SENSES PROVIDED TO THE HUMAN BEINGS

A sensation arises when a physical force or substance acts on one of the specialised end organs of a sensory nerve.

In a sensory response, the following four conditions are essential:

(1) *A stimulus*

(a) Supplied internally or externally. This stimulus is some form of radiant chemical, or other energy that invites a receptor or more often a large group of them.

(b) The stimulus stirs certain receptor cells into activity.

(c) Nerve impulses travel from the receptor cell through the nervous system, the main connecting mechanism.

(d) These impulses may finally arouse activity in the effectors (Muscles at glands) and/or produce conscious, sensations.

Each of these four conditions is necessary for a sensory response. If any steps were missing, we could not adjust to the world around us.

A sense organ is the specialised apparatus at the end of the nerve that receives the stimulus. Every sense organ responds only to certain substances or forces.

(2) *Vision*

It is one of the most important senses.

The eye is a complex organ, so structured that it can make rapid changes without blurring. Eye movement and adjustment make it possible for an object to be kept in focus and seen clearly.

(a) Eye and camera have certain structural parts that are similar, although they are somewhat different in shape.

(b) Light rays from an object enter the eye through the pupil.

(c) Light rays are focussed by the lens on to the retina which contains visual receptor cells.

(d) Nerve impulses travel from the receptor cells in the optic nerve to the occipetal area of the brain.

(e) The visual receptors are of two kinds:

(i) The ones of receptors which produce sensation of both hue and brightness. The cones are cylindrical in shape.

(ii) The rods: which produce sensation of brightness alone. They have a tapered shape.

The colours as determined by one's vision have three qualities:

(a) Hues, which is determined by the frequency of light waves.

(b) Saturation which is determined by the complexity of the light waves.

The primary colours—red, green and blue. By mixing these we can have many colours.

(3) *Hearing*

Like colour, sound has three dimensions:

(a) Pitch—determined by the frequency of the sound waves.

(b) Loudness—determined by their intensity.

(c) Timbre—determined by their complexity.

ATTENTION AND PERCEPTION

A. Perception

Through our perceptual processes, we organise and give meaning to the information we receive through our senses. It enables us to identify objects and situations in our environment. A perception can be regarded as a meaningful sensation. It is the process of filling in, enabling us to interpret a series of fragments as a whole when sensory data are incomplete. Perception organisation is dependent upon the characteristics of the stimuli object such as nearness, likeness, inclusiveness and part or whole relationship. Perception is of very basic importance to the individuals in educational programme. A perceptual accuracy depends upon an individual's past experience in each area in which the stimulated mental activity functions. No two persons have the same perceptual capacity.

B. Attention

It may serve as a preparation for perception. Attention can be defined as the process of focussing upon certain phases or elements of experience and the neglecting of others. The relative clearness of perception depends upon the intensity of the attention process.

What an individual perceives is limited by physiological and psychological sensitivity.

Attention is (1) an adjustment of the body and its sense organs;

(2) clearness and vividness in consciousness; and

(3) a set towards action.

Direction of attention

The conditions of attending are:

(1) Involuntary attention,

(2) Voluntary attention, and

(3) Habitual attention through practice only.

Some specific factors influencing the direction of our attention in a given situation may be:

(1) Change: in any direction—from one place to another, from one intensity to another, from absent to present, etc.

(2) Size.

(3) Prepotency: Some stimuli are more potent in attracting the attention of the others.

(4) Repetition: A weak stimulus frequently repeated may be as effective as a strong one presented once.

(5) Organic conditions.

(6) Interests.

(7) Social suggestion.

Shifting attention

Individual's attention adjustment is not stable and fixed but shifts constantly from one aspect of a situation to another.

Distraction

It reduces efficiency because our attention shifts involuntarily.

C. Factors determining what we perceive

Characteristics of the stimulus objective: (a) Nearness, (b) Likeness, (c) Inclusiveness, and (d) Part of relationships.

Characteristics of the perceiver: Organic conditions.

When sound waves strike the ear, they cause the eardrum to vibrate. It in turn transmits the motion to the hammer, anvil and stir up bones, whose movements cause a vibration of the oval window a membrane between the middle and inner ear.

D. Cutaneous senses

This group includes pressure, pain, warmth and cold. All these senses shows a point distribution rather than a continuous one.

E. The sense of taste

It includes a sweet, sour, bitter and salt taste reaction. This sensitivity is aroused by a substance in solution as they contact the taste gland. These receptors are small bulks, that lie on the surface of the tongue and in certain areas on the sides of the cheeks. These taste buds are hair-like cells which project into the papillae.

F. Sense of smell

It is also called olfactory sense.

THINKING

Definition

The process of using symbols to manipulate implicitly ideas or objects not physically present, to the senses is called thinking. These symbols include words, numbers, gestures, pictures and visual images.

Mechanics of thinking

It involves languages, concepts, manipulation of images, muscular contractions.

(1) *Imagery in thinking:* These are:

(a) *Idiotic imagery:* Strong images usually visual. Some people can repeat the whole page of a book which they remember.

(b) *Synthesia:* Translation of sensory experience from one sensory mode to another.

(2) *Language in thinking:* It includes: Concepts in thinking, forming concepts and language structure and thought.

(3) *The context of thinking:* It includes that which we learned from past experience, our motives and attitudes and our particular "set" at the moment. Context acts as a selective and regulatory mechanism which influences the direction of our thought.

Kinds of thinking

(1) *Autestic thinking:* It deals with fantasy, dreams and wishful thinking. This kind of thinking is an end in itself.

(2) *Realistic thinking:*

(a) It helps us to adjust to real world and is mainly used in problem-solving.

(b) It follows a definite sequence:

(i) To become concerned about or interested in a problem.

(ii) Assembling the material with which to work.

(iii) To derive a number of possible solutions.

(iv) To evaluate the suggested solution.

Avoiding cloudy thinking

(1) *Cloudy thinking can be avoided by care:* Past experience may be either helpful or hindrance but when understood, they will become more helpful, e.g.,

(i) When we encounter similar or relevant situations, they are helpful.

(ii) They may be a hindrance for one through mechanisation, that is, a rigid continuation of behaviour in the face of different situations, etc.

(2) *Factors that help or hinder Effective Thinking*:

(a) Past experience.

(b) Mechanisation (Rigidity).

(c) Functional fixedness.

(d) Reducing rigidity and functional fixedness.

Common pitfalls in thinking

(1) All or nothing thinking.

(2) Desire to believe.

(3) Being misled by big words—difficult language may give the wrong meaning to some person.

(4) Words versus meanings—the same word may have different meaning for different people.

    (a) Materials meaningfully organised are not forgotten as readily as nonsense material. Mastery of subject-matter becomes more stable the longer it is retained, making less review essential.

    (b) Tasks interrupted before completion are more likely to be remembered than completed tasks but when stressful conditions are involved, the reverse may be true.

    (c) A person tends to learn something faster and remembers it better when it agrees with his own attitudes.

COMMUNICATION AND GROUP PROCESSES

Information theory

The principles that make for understanding, control and predictability in communication is the communication theory.

Communication is the essence of the teaching-learning process.

It implies to transmit to share or to make common. By better communication, we can influence people in a better way.

(1) It includes the following parts:

    (a) source,

    (b) transmitter,

    (c) channel,

    (d) receiver, and

    (e) destination.

(2) Source is the starting point; transmitter encodes and sends the message; receiver decodes the message and destination is the end where the message is usable.

Importance of feedback in communication

(1) Feedback is the interchange of information on the part of human beings.

(2) It enables the sender to know the reaction to the information at its destination, and

(3) It enables integration of an individual with a group.

Group dynamics

(1) *Group behaviour:* Group behaviour is the result of dynamic interaction between individuals in a social situation, and group dynamics can do much to make cooperative activities more democratic and more effective.

(2) *Effectiveness can be improved by the following:*

    (a) An informal workshop atmosphere.

    (b) Feeling of security through threat reduction.

(c) Distributive leadership.
(d) A sense of purpose through goal formation.
(e) Flexibility in plans.
(f) True consensus.
(g) Process awareness.
(h) Continual evaluation.

Effective leadership

(1) *Responsibilities of leadership*
    (a) Structuring the situation to interpret it, and objectively focussing the goals.
    (b) Controlling group or individual behaviour to the best interest of the group.
    (c) Speaking for the group by having an awareness of group feelings, and to be able to express these.
(2) *Kinds of leadership*
    (a) Authoritarian.
    (b) Democratic.
(3) *Methods used by leaders in performing their functions*
(1) Force: Vested in law. Now its use is decreasing. At present it is not used in USA.
(2) Paternalism: Hopes to gain their loyalty and obedience.
(3) Attempting to explain the impacts under a single hypothesis rather than searching for alternative hypotheses.
(4) Incomplete or faulty information about the topics.
(5) Overlooking some data.
(6) Mistaking correlation for causation.

Ways of Avoiding the Pitfalls

(1) A person can check his thinking and opinions by getting another person's judgement.
(2) Using formal logic.
(3) Avoiding the atmosphere effect.
(4) Using semantics. Semantics emphasise a point frequently lost sight of which is that concepts are abstractions from real things, and that the word which stands for the concept is removed by still another step from original perception.

Education for democracy

(1) *The aims of education*

A teacher's purposes influence what he teaches and how he teaches it: a pupil's purposes influence what he learns and how easily he learns it. Ideally, the purposes of teacher and learner should coincide, but this seldom happens without careful planning.

(a) *Learning as behaviour change:* Teaching, today, is usually defined not merely as the process of transmitting knowledge but also as fostering, guiding and identifying desirable behaviour changes.

(b) *Learning through experience:* American education has come to be guided by the principle of *learning by doing*. One of the basic tenets of all experimental psychology is that without experience there can be no learning.

(2) *Allowing for individual differences:* It has been found that there are slow learners and fast learners. This the teacher should take into consideration. The social and emotional needs of the students should also be considered.

(3) *Curriculum design:* This has three plans:

(a) Unstructured or child-centred;

(b) Integrated or core; and

(c) Subject or traditional.

Each has its supporters but in all three there is a general trend toward integrating subject areas with each other and with the child's out-of-school experiences.

Most important is the selection of materials and learning experiences appropriate to the learner's level of maturity

Today, there is increasing integration of opposing theories in education—including those of progressive and traditionalists.

(4) *Group dynamics:* Group dynamics as applied to education is called *participative action.* It represents group-centred, as opposed to teacher-centred, methods in the class-room. It has been indicated by some studies that students prefer the older method—authoritarian approach but the permissive approach has the advantage. "Authoritarian leadership" in the classroom eliminates the "incidental learning" of many kinds of personal and social skirmishes.

Propaganda

In America, two-third of the editorial material in newspapers is slanted by press agents and public relations men. The various principles of persuasion recognised by people are:

(1) One-sided argument   (Effective with those in initial agreement).

(2) Two-sided argument   (Effective with those initially opposed).

(3) The appeal to fear   (Relatively ineffective).

(4) The sleeper effect   (In which a communication is first rejected as propaganda and later accepted as fact)

PROBLEMS IN GROUP LIVING

Problems and causes of success or failure of marriages

(1) *Length of courtship:* During courtship, the couple has the opportunity to become well-acquainted; to discover areas of agreement and disagreement.

(2) *Age of marriage:* If very early, people are supposed to be too irresponsible and older, to be too set in their ways. Before the age of 21 it is risky because they are poorly adjusted. It has been found out that in USA that women who had married at 30 or older and men who had married at 35 or older had the shortest mean duration of marriage.

(3) *Age discrepancies:* It has been found that this factor is not related in any important degree to happiness in marriage.

(4) *Education:* Deviation from the required standard for the partner or difference in the degree of education appears to jeopardise the chances of happiness.

(5) *Religion:* It is not a cause of failure of marriage.

(6) *Marital adjustment of parents:* Happily married parents pass on a kind of

upbringing to their children to lead a happy married life or to adjust with the partner.

(7) *Pre-marital sex-relation:* In USA, it has been found out that there is a low correlation between non-virginity and happiness of marriage.

Because of their social system and other factors the divorce rate has increased tremendously. The data shows that of all the teen-age marriages in the USA 40 per cent involve pre-marital pregnancy and 50 per cent end in divorce within a 5 year period (See Fig. 13.1).

OF ALL TEEN-AGE MARRIAGES IN THE USA.

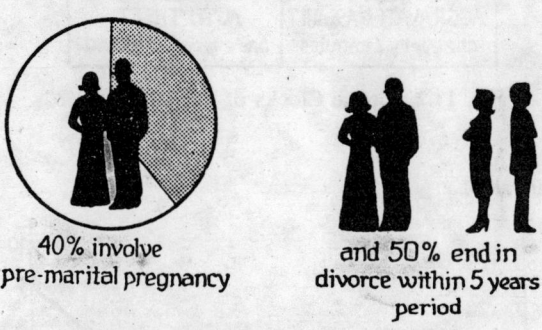

40% involve
pre-marital pregnancy

and 50% end in
divorce within 5 years
period

Fig. 13.1. Teen-age marriages in the USA

(8) *Economic factors:* If both partners have a similar status, there are more chances of success. At lower occupational levels, there are divorces.

(9) *Desire for children:* Desire for children is correlated with happiness in marriage.

(10) *Interests:* Happiness is positively related to sharing of familistic interests.

(11) *Personality pattern:* Emotional stability of one marriage partner has been shown to be significantly correlated with the happiness of the other partner.

(12) *Cooperative attitude:* When the wife is dominant, trouble is almost inevitable in the sphere of social and sexual adjustment.

Problems of illegal behaviour

Delinquency is defined as legally prohibited behaviour committed by minors.

A. Causes of illegal behaviour

The causes of illegal behaviour are the following:

(1) Poverty.
(2) The influence of transitional areas.
(3) Family breakdown—differential treatment.
(4) Emotional maladjustment.
(5) Intelligence—It has little influence in making a criminal.
(6) Effect of movies, television and comics.

B. Crime prevention

Major avenues to crime prevention are:

(a) Involving social organisations.

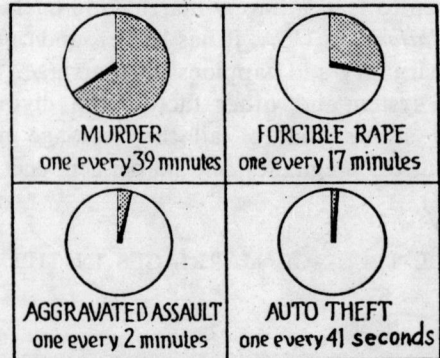

Fig. 13.2. Crime Clocks of the USA—1968.

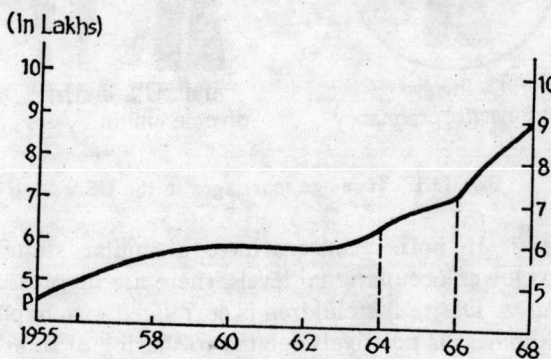

Fig. 13.3. Trend of total crimes in India.

(b) Slum-clearance projects.
(c) Professional social workers.
(d) Self-help neighbourhood drives.
(e) Judicial action.

Racial antagonism

(1) Human differences are being continuously produced through the inherent variability of genetic materials and through gene mutation. Therefore, any scheme for classifying races can have validity for only a brief time.

(2) Physical characteristics are unreliable indices of racial differences and psychological characteristics seem to result from environment rather than hereditary influences.

(3) It has been suggested that ethnic group, a primarily social division, be substituted for race, a biological division.

(4) Man is not born with prejudice. He is conditioned to prejudice by isolated experiences, or very frequently, by exposure to the prejudiced attitudes of his parents, teachers and companies.

(5) Some people seem to be antagonistic toward all groups other than their own. This generalised prejudice is often the result of a striving for personal security.

(6) Aggressive feelings growing out of frustration, guilt, fear and anxiety, or the need for self-glorification are often turned against a minority group. Such scapegoating is the primary mechanism underlying prejudice, but scapegoating does not always seem to operate and, alone, it does not explain the development of a particular prejudice, which may result from a variety of social, economic and cultural factors.

Cure of Prejudice

There is no single cure for prejudice but these can be given as effective measures.
(1) Education, (2) Inter-group contacts, (3) Legal action, (4) Bargain. It involves the principle that the leader and members can work out a "trade" to satisfy the desires of each, and (5) Mutual means.

Characteristics of leaders

The leaders have generally the following three characteristics:
(a) They have an awareness of the group attitudes.
(b) They have the ability of abstract thinking.
(c) They have emotional ability.

Use of competition and cooperation in educational work

(1) Competition has long been used as an incentive.
(2) There should not be too much emphasis on competition because it may encourage children, or even adults, to employ dishonest means. This should be avoided.
(3) Competition tends to act as a wider barrier between individuals and groups.

Planning for effective competition

(1) Rewarding improvement rather than rank.
(2) Setting up sub-groups of individuals of equal ability.

How to improve group activity

(a) By improving the group setting and improving the atmosphere.
(b) Reduction of threat.

RURAL PSYCHOLOGY AND PERSONALITY

Here we study the picture a given villager has in his mind regarding his role as a member of society. More specially, what images he has of his mother, of his father or of members of another and competing racial group. How does he conceive of his place, as citizen, workingman or businessman. What are his concepts of right, justice, liberty and other values which he has acquired from his particular class or country.

In dealing with such matters, we have to examine the nature of the person's social and cultural training, so as to find out, how he derived his particular prejudices, stereo types, convictions, values and frames of reference as they affect his conduct.

Factors determining the rural mind

In the psychology of the rural person, the dividing line between the conscious and the non-conscious is most thin and vague. His thought is conditioned by instinct, intuition and habit. The opinion of the family, caste or village tradition, even superstition, pre-determine his will and wishes. His own thinking has little independence and is part of an intangible whole, to a degree, inconsistent with his social and cultural evolution. The causes of this type of mental attitude of the Indian villager is related to his history. For the last about 2000 years, the life of the villagers in India has been on the defensive watching thundering invasions and conquests of the foreigners, since Alexander the Great. So accordingly, the Indian villagers have been conditioned to accept external changes in the same way as natural calamities.

The frequent violent effect of the natural calamities on his only occupation of crop raising has reinforced his defensive attitude, due to the extent that the cultivator has clung to his beliefs and habits. He did not think or incline towards making a change in the technique of production, which has resulted in his being conservative against all arguments, factual or verbal. His ignorance is both, the cause and result of this type of attitude. Penalties, at the hands of family and caste, threaten and restrain adventure into anything new and unknown. To the fear-complex is added the hard-complex, and the village consequently remains fortified against the march of time and progress being made in other parts of the world.

Natural opposition to change

Some cultures, in some of the tracts of India, are so tightly integrated that any change threatens the whole. The villager cannot regard it as a new technique to that they are already following. They are not accustomed to analysing things. Even if the superiority of the new technique is demonstrated, they feel suspicious about it. This may be because in the past, the Agricultural Departments were holding the demonstrations on Government farms where the technique was above the normal. This practice created a general feeling amongst the villagers that it is easy for the extension worker with the above-normal conditions, i.e., the fertilisers, means of irrigation, type of soil, extra labour, etc., to get better yields. But for normal people, who cannot afford the use of improved fertilisers, or the waste of labour in works like marking lines, levelling of fields, etc., it is not so easy.

Agriculture and religion

Agriculture and religion, in some of the tracts of India are so closely related, that what may be regarded as technical change of little consequence is not easily understood by the villagers. There are examples where some of the operations are not done or some of the implements are not used or the trees are not cut or the useless stray cattle are not killed because there is a religious sentiment or superstition attached to it. The people of the *Baiga* tribe refuse the use of an iron plough because this would be unkind to the earth which they worship. Similarly, there is religious prejudice against the use of fertilisers and even flooding of some land or the cleaning of land by uprooting the *Peepal* trees or killing of monkeys or birds who destroy crops.

Standing habits

Some rural people are habituated to use a particular thing or to follow a particular practice and they cannot change it, or do without it. In some rice-eating areas, people would not be convinced to use unpolished rice or to reduce the quantity of rice by substituting it with some other better, nutritive food to balance their diet. They do it, because they are used to eating rice only. Similarly, the use of dung cakes as fuel cannot be replaced by fuel wood even if it is available cheaper because they feel that dung cakes fire is more suitable for the cooking of certain things.

Conflicts

As the houses of the villagers are huddled together there are numerous contacts and so if there is some conflict between two families, or groups of families, this conflict may pass on from generation to generation. Such factions make it difficult to take up any work where the cooperation of these groups is required.

The second antagonism is between the rich and the poor, the landowners and the landless labourers, the money-lenders and the debtors. Either the rich will be against the technical change or the improvement in their traditional methods, because they fear that the poor may get extra advantages which would endanger the established position of the rich or the zamindars or money-lenders or the poor are reticent to following new practices because they feel that the proposed measures are only for the rich, or for those who can afford them.

Similarly, the landless labour class feels that the whole programme of extension is going to improve the position of the owners of land and that unless their wages are increased, they cannot get any advantage out of the National Extension Programme.

Under the joint-family system, the aged persons who are heads of the families, or those who have some say in matters, do not like to accept the suggestions of the new blood who may have technical knowledge, experience or training. They like to see their sons or younger brothers passing B.Sc. (Ag.) and managing the farms of the governments, or others, but they consider such graduates to be incompetent to guide them in their occupation, or household affairs because this would lower their position.

Basic principles in rural psychology

Extensive research material and accumulated world experience relating to man's behaviour and the educative process has provided us, the extension workers, with a number of highly valid and useful guides. These basic principles, in rural psychology, have universal application and will be of much advantage in our extension progamme.[1]

(1) Man everywhere is in a constant state of attempting to create and maintain a satisfying adjustment between internal forces created by the human desires, traits and capacities he inherited, and external conditions and forces imposed by his environment natural and man-created.

(2) Man is constantly out of adjustment in certain ways with the forces in his environment. Usually, he is not in a utopian situation. He rarely if ever is in complete

[1]Leagans, J.P., Cornell University, Ithaca, N.Y., *A Talk to Trainees* at National Institute, Mussoorie, India.

harmony with his environment. He probably always has problems. There is usually some conflict situation existing between internal forces represented by feelings, desires and external forces, with which he must deal.

(3) To the extent that man's inner forces are out of adjustment with outer forces in his environment, he has needs. Indeed, this is the source from which people's needs emerge. Man's needs are represented by the gap existing between what is and should not be, and should and can be, in his situation.

(4) Man's attempts to narrow, or close, the gap between his inner drives and the conditions imposed on him by his environment represent, in true form, his real struggle for survival and improvement economically, socially, aesthetically and normally.

(5) To help man narrow, or close, this gap is the true objective of the educator or extension worker using education as his tool. It is change in what people know, what they believe, what they can do and in what they actually do that holds the key to progress.

(6) Permanent change in man's behaviour comes from within. It cannot be successfully imposed from without. This requires education. If changes are to be sound socially and permanent physically, they must come from people's own decisions to act, resulting from their own efforts. Internal changes in knowledge, understanding, desires, feelings and capacities of people must precede outward expressions of changed ways of doing things for their own improvement. In short, changes in the mind of man must precede changes in the actions of his hands.

(7) Man is endowed with internal desire for improvement. He needs only to be shown the paths clearly and convincingly and helped to gain the necessary skills to travel them.

(8) In the process of adjustments between internal desires and external forces, man tends to be concerned with the biological, economic, social and aesthetic needs in that order, with moral values pervading and influencing both the form and content of the entire process.

(9) External stimuli must be created by man himself, designed for and used to promote his progress. Historically, in societies without these man invented institutions and forces for the application of external stimuli in the direction of economic and social improvement, progress in these directions has tended to be slow, or almost non-extent, for example, in India, before independence. In contrast, societies with effective man-created agents of change have tended to progress comparatively rapidly, for example, India since Independence, and particularly since the introduction of community development and extension service in 1952.

PERSONALITY

Meaning of personality

From the sociologist's point of view, personality is defined as, "that dynamic organisation of ideas, attitudes and habits which is built upon the foundation of the biologically inherited psycho-physical mechanism which embodies all the adjustments of the individual's desires and purposes to the requirements and potentialities of his social and sub-social environments."[1]

Among the psychologists, Watson defines personality as a sum of the activities that can be discovered by actual observation of behaviour over a long enough time to give reliable information. He further says that, "personality is the end product of our habit systems."[2] Woodworth defines personality as the quality of an individual's total behaviour, i.e., how he acts when his activity is considered as a whole. Personality comprises an individual's experience, his knowledge, skill, temperament, attitude, habits, character and physical traits. Wickens and Major say that personality refers to the motive and the organisation of motives, which characterise an individual and the manner in which he behaves in satisfying or attempting to satsify them.

Analysis of personality

Personality includes; (a) the focus of consciousness. (b) the preconscious area of sensory-motor experience and of unrepressed memories, ideas, wishes, attitudes and purposes, (c) the unconscious, including repressed, memories, ideas, wishes and attitudes, and (d) patterns of behaviour which can be overtly observed and operated upon by others.

Personality traits

The dimensions of personality can be divided into; (1) physical traits, and (2) behavioural traits.

(1) *Physical traits*

Biological inheritance is responsible for the individual's physical aspect. Genes which are inherited are responsible for the physical traits, e.g., colour of hair and eyes, complexion, etc. But some physical traits are also effected by environment, e.g., development of muscles depends on the food given to the child. This indicates that the relationship between environment and heredity is one of interaction.

The human organism is the product of many forces in interaction with each other. As it is difficult to differentiate between the hereditary and environmental factors it is convenient to use the term constitution, which represents both the forces. Constitution comprises; (a) drives, (b) temperament, and (c) capacities.

(a) *Drives:* A drive is a form of motivation in which the organism is impelled by factors, essentially beyond its control, to act without foresight of ends. These consist of inner energies, tendencies, and urges that interact with outside forces and become dynamic patterns of response as a result of this interaction. The different types of drives may be: visual drives, hunger, thirst, sex activity, defence, etc. The action of satisfying these drives calls for adjustment to one's social environment and thus the individual develops personality.

(b) *Temperament:* This is the characteristic mood of an individual which may bring elation, depression or confidence in him. The endocrine glands play a vital part in

[1]Henry Pratt Fairchild, et al., *Dictionary of Sociology and Related Sciences*, Patterson, N. Jur., Littlefield Adams & Co., 1961. p. 218.
[2]J.B. Watson: *Behaviourism*, W.W. Norton & Co., Inc. 1924, p. 220.

determining the type of temperamental reactions which the individual exhibits. These glands secrete directly into the blood stream certain chemical substances known as hormones, which in turn exert a profound effect on behaviour.

(c) *Capacities:* Personal capacity is a sort of inherited potentiality or adaptability which enables the organism to acquire the ability to do a certain task or to solve a particular type of problem. Thus, from an individual who inherits an aptitude for learning how to solve mathematical problems quickly and easily, one might infer that he was endowed to more than the average degree with a mathematical capacity.

Ability and capacity are not the same. Ability is equal to inherited capacity plus training. We can assume that unless a person has certain inherited capacities and has them in certain proportions, he cannot develop the abilities. So our abilities are the product of both experience and inherited capacities.

(2) *Behaviour traits*

The important elements which influence the individual's behaviour are his ideas, habits, attitudes and wishes. The individual learns these through the process of inter-personal interaction and thus, these elements become an integral part of his personality. These may be considered as follows;

(a) *Ideas:* Under these, we include all mental pictures, concepts, impression, notions, factual knowledge, and the like, which we carry in our heads.

(b) *Habits:* These include all the acquired ways of feeling and doing, which tend to repeat themselves under appropriate conditions.

(c) *Attitudes:* An attitude is acquired, or learned and established tendency to react toward or against something or somebody. It is evinced either by an approaching or a withdrawing type of behaviour, and the object of the reaction becomes thereby either a positive or a negative value respectively, from the subject's view point. An attitude may be largely latent, subjective, unexpressed, or it may represent any degree between two extremes. An attitude may be characteristic of a person, towards other persons, social groups, society, or the universe. An attitude may be social in the sense that it is characteristic of homogenous groups of persons.

All attitudes are habits, but not all habits are attitudes. The attitude has a dynamic quality, which is lacking in some habit patterns. It involves an evaluation of the object or situation towards which it is called out.

(d) *Wishes:* A wish is one, or a set of attitudes, focussed on a goal. An attitude is a pre-disposition to want (or to avoid) something, while a wish is actual wanting. There is no action without a wish and no wish without action. Wishes help to explain human behaviour.

There may be four universal wishes;

(1) New experience includes wishes for new activities, new sights, excitement, variety, change, etc.

(2) Security may be based on fear and covers wishes to be safe. Wishes due to fear may be for security for old age, for security of children after one's death, for security from unemployment etc.

(3) Response covers the desire for affection, friendship and love, for inter-personal acceptance, warmth and appreciation.

(4) Recognition refers to wishes for a favourable position in one's social group;

getting an award, or being a Krishi Pandit, first in crop competition, progressive farmer, best poultry breeder, good home-maker and so on.

The process of self-development

The individual is influenced by heredity, his geographical and physical environment, the culture of the group in which he is born and the unique experiences acquired by him through inter-personal interaction. These can be described as follows:

(1) Heredity

The role of heredity is not to develop human nature alone and unaided, but to furnish materials out of which experience will mould the personality. Although this raw materials includes the whole human body and all of its mechanisms, certain biological traits are more significant than others in the bearing they have upon personality. The more important mechanisms are the nervous system, the ductless glands, the organic drives, the emotions and the capacities for mental behaviour. These materials may lead to differences in personality. Pronounced variations in intelligence as in case of the idiot (having I. Q. below 25) and the imbecile are such as to leave an indelible stamp on personality.

Hereditary influences upon personality are both direct and indirect. Indirect influences are those exerted through group evaluations of genetic traits, e.g., physique. Direct influence come from the degree of emotional drive and mental alertness; an individual may be energetic because of his heredity, but whether he is active on his own behalf or on behalf of others, is a matter of his training.

(2) Physical or geographical environment

Food and climate may be the most significant aspects of the physical environment as they influence the individual's biological development and, as such personality. Some traits, such as the development of muscles, can be attributed primarily to environment. Even at birth, the human organism is already the internal product of a very complex heredity potential and a specific physical environment in the uterus. The environment is not the same in all mothers. It varies from child to child. This is most easily understood in terms of the nutrition available to the foetus.

(3) Culture

What the child gets from his culture are things such as clothes, tools and skills, speech and occupation. These have both a direct and indirect effect on his personality. In addition, culture undertakes specifically to shape his attitudes and habits through such avenues of influence as folkways, customs and group ideals. These aspects may be called material. Thus, culture provides a framework in which the individual develops his own personality. A child acquires his culture by conditioning. Individuals come under different aspects of the social heritage and develop distinctive personalities. Many factors determine the phases of culture an individual will experience, but in general it may be said that the governing one is the individual's group affiliation.

(4) Unique experiences

Ideas, habits, values, motives are the integral parts of one's personality and are acquired through the process of inter-personal interaction. This interaction is unique to the individual. Two twins, though they have the same kind of physical and cultural environment, still develop different types of personality. The unique experiences which they gain account for this difference, as it is unique to each one of them.

The interaction between persons communicates more than culture. Individuals develop ideas, attitudes and values according to their experiences as they are unique or peculiar to them, and in the process of interaction, they try to pass them on to others. In the process of personality development, the early years are most important in laying down the basic personality pattern as the child learns the ways of the world.

What is "Self"

What a person or an individual consciously or unconsciously conceives of himself is "self". It is the sum total of his perceptions of himself and especially his attitudes towards "self". That infant has no self. So distinguishing oneself as a person is not that one requires a certain amount of experiences, but it requires experiences with other persons. So self is a social product. In the words of Cooley, "self-ideas or self-attitudes develop by a process of imagining what others think of us by a kind of looking-glass process." We try to imagine how we appear to another person, or what his judgement is of that appearance, and this generates a sort of self-feeling, pride and shame.

Theories of personality

Personality is a very complex pattern. It cannot be completely and accurately described in one work. The two theories most prevalent are: (a) the type theory, and (b) trait theory.

(1) The Type Theory

This theory is based on (see Table 13.2) the assumption that all persons can be classified into a limited number of personalities. Each type has certain related response tendencies as an individual. It implies that all the acts of an individual are related to each other. It also implies that all the individuals of a type, are alike in behaviour.

By knowing the type of an individual, his actions in one situation can be predicted in other situations. Behaviour, according to this theory, is of the following three types: (a) introvert, (b) extrovert, and (c) ambivert.

(a) *Introvert:* An introvert limits his acquaintance to a few. This person is very conservative and suspicious of the motives of others. He is not social, likes solitude, prefers to remain in the background on certain occasions. He avoids embarrassment and public speaking. He is very reserved, self-centred, introspective, absent-minded, remains worried and is always day-dreaming. He is generally slow and hesitant to take the initiative. Philosophers, poets and scientists are generally introverts.

(b) *Extrovert:* An extrovert is social and sociable. He likes to make friends and very soon creates a circle of friends around him. He prefers working in company with other people, does not like solitude, is talkative and fond of talking. He is proud and self-assertive and generally takes things lightly. He never feels embarrassed. He has a keen sense of observation and is attentive. Reformers and social workers are generally extroverts.

(c) *Ambivert:* Ambiverts are partly introverts and partly extroverts. They have a liking for people as well as liking for thought. It is very difficult to draw a line between introverts and extroverts. The same individual have certain qualities of the one and also of other.

This theory of types is regarded as unsound, because: (a) it is difficult to find one hundred per cent introverts. So it is difficult to see just what is the behaviour of, ambiverts, (b) no two individuals will be exactly alike in behaviour under all circumstances.

(2) Trait theory

According to this theory, there are a limited number of basic characteristics of behaviour, and it is possible to describe an individual's personality by stating how he stands on each of these characteristics. The traits are independent of one another in the sense that there may be little or no relationship between an individual status and a trait, such as shyness, emotional stability and intelligence: (a) socially ascendent excitable, intelligents, (b) socially submissive excitable intelligents, and (c) socially ascendent, calm but dull.

Trait profiles include: (1) intelligence, (2) emotional stability, (3) aggressiveness, (4) social receptivity, and (5) persistence.

Researches have shown that traits are independent of one another, though certain traits always tend to cluster together.

Table 13. 1
Traits used in Personality Descriptions

Trait cluster	as opposed to
(1) Easy-going, adaptable, warm-hearted, expressive	Inflexible, indifferent reserved, suspicious.
(2) Intelligent, thoughtful, persevering (continues to attempt).	Unintelligent, uneffective, quits easily.
(3) Emotionally stable, realistic, calm and thorough.	Emotionally unstable, unrealistic, excitable, careless.
(4) Self-assertive, aggressive, adventurous.	Submissive, makes complaints and is timid.
(5) Cheerful, social, energetic and witty.	Pessimistic, retiring, languid and dull.
(6) Perserving, responsible and ordered.	Fickle, frivolous and relaxed.

It should not be assumed that these traits are fixed and a final way of describing personality, but they serve the purpose in the absence of something better.

TEACHING FARMERS

The inherent capacity for motivation exists among the farmers, but it is the role of the Extension Educationist to arrange the effective 'teaching-learning situations' conducive to the acceptance and adoption of any innovation.

Table 13.2
Comparison of Type and Trait Theory

Type Theory	*Trait theory*
(1) Assumes that there are significant relationships between all the responses of an individual.	Significant relationships are found only among those responses related to the trait in question, but not between them.
(2) Implies that we need to know only the type, to predict an individual's behaviour.	This implies that we must know the status of an individual on all aspects and the responses related to some individuals.
(3) Ii is over-simplified. People do not prove to be true to the type in all situations.	The traits predicts behaviour more accurately.

A learning situation is a condition or environment in which all the elements necessary for promoting learning are present, namely Instructor, Learner, Subject-Matter, Teaching Material and Equipment, and Physical Facilities (see Fig. 13.4.).

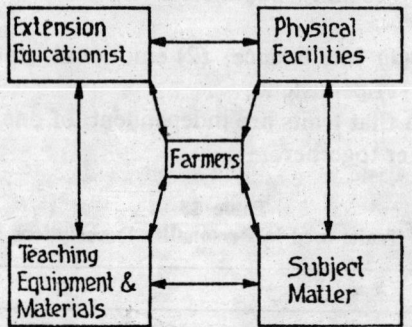

Fig. 13.4. The relationship between the elements that promote farmers' learning.

The nature of each of the above elements, their relationships to each other, their roles in the educational process should be properly conceived in order to make the learning situations effective.

Extension educationists engaged in massive farmers' training programmes, in addition to the above, need to understand the conditions, home life, problems, hopes and needs of the farmers. The type of understanding required from the extension educationists must go deeper than a superficial acquaintance with a farmer's personal characteristics and concerns. It requires sympathetic attitudes and the unyielding patience which most often results from direct, simple, personal contacts with farmers themselves. Besides the above, the extension educationist, as a teacher, can also better determine when to teach, how to teach as well as what to teach, when he knows about the characteristics of farmers as adult learners.

Desirable conditions for teaching farmers
(1) They must want to learn:

We should not waste time in forcing them into training.

(2) Farmers learn only when they feel a need to learn:

They learn best when they expect immediate benefits, and when knowledge or skills are directly useful in meeting a responsibility.

(3) Farmers learn by doing:

The importance of active participation in the learning process is greater among them. They learn only about 25% of a lecture; 50% of what they learn is forgotten within one year and 80% in two years.

(4) Farmer's learning centres on problems, and the problems must be realistic:

Let them begin with special problems deduced out of their experiences.

(5) Farmers learn best in an informal environment:

They will respond to extension programmes in an inverse relationship to the degree they are reminded of their past experiences.

(6) Experience affects farmer's learning:

New knowledge must be related to and integrated with accumulated results of life-time learning experiences.

(7) Farmers favour a variety of teaching methods:

Learning proceeds more quickly among farmers when information reaches them through more than one sensory channel.

(8) Farmers want guidance and not paper grades:

They learn best under continuous guidance. They revel very much against grades.

(9) They want desperately to know how they are *doing:*

They should be encouraged to measure their own progress. Guided self-evaluation is the best step for evaluating their progress.

Some characteristics which distinguish under-educated adult farmers from better-educated adult farmers as learners.

(1) They are difficult to identify.

(2) They are difficult to involve.

(3) They are more than likely to be culturally disadvantaged.

(4) They are more than likely to be living under conditions of severe economic disadvantage.

(5) Their social values, attitudes and goals differ widely.

(6) They live for today, not for tomorrow.

(7) They are easily discouraged if evidence of progress is not regularly recognised.

(8) They are sceptical of the system and of those who appear to represent the system.

(9) They are doubtful of their ability to learn.

(10) They are uncertain of the relationship of their education pursuits to their vocational, social and community adjustments.

The extension educationists working with adult farmers in villages will come across certain psychological barriers in addition to the others.

PSYCHOLOGICAL BARRIERS

When farmers are confronted with new opportunities, acceptance or rejection of an innovation depends not only on their motivational patterns, on a favourable social relations and in economic possibility, but also upon psychological factors.

Perception

It is how one feels about a thing and interprets in one's neural mechanism. The farmers and the extension educationists should perceive in the same way to bring out an effective change about an innovation. Differential perceptions have affected agricultural programmes in many villages. When an extension worker in an Indian village introduced the improved variety of pea for seed multiplication, the farmers misconceived it and used it for fodder purposes. Consequently, the very purpose of the extension worker in introducing the variety has suffered a serious setback.

Most of us associate differential perception with a gift.[1] In some areas, where horticultural plants were distributed free of cost, people came forward. After an year the Village Development Officer (VDO) found that out of 200 plants distributed, only 20 were surviving. When another VDO distributed the plants at a nominal cost, though initially a few came forward, the total number of plants that survived in one year was more. Hence it is better that the extension educationists introduce innovations at nominal costs. Similarly, the perception of purpose and differential role perception also serves as barrier for the acceptance of new farm technology.

Communication

Communication is a sine-quo-non for development. While communicating we use certain symbols. Unless they are properly understood by the receiver (farmers), the communication becomes ineffective. Hence the communicator's fidelity (the accuracy with which the message from the source reaches the receiver) and the communicator's credibility (trustworthiness and expertises of the communicator) have a bearing on the adoption of farm technology.

Demonstration dangers

When an extension educationist demonstrates something, he should do it in the right way. If one fails, it may have adverse effect on further recommendations. Any new farm technique should have been proved suitable to the local conditions, prior to its recommendation by the extension educationists. This necessitates the adoptive trials which form a prerequisite for a confident recommendation for large scale adoption.

Learning problems

The adoption of new ideas and techniques means that farmers must learn. The psychology of farmer's learning has been amplified in the previous pages. Tasks, which seem to be simple to one who has mastered them, may appear difficult, or perhaps not worth attempting, to those who have no opportunity to handle them. Therefore, the psychology of learning of both small and rich farmers, should be thoroughly understood by the extension educationists and, accordingly, differential communication strategies should be adopted for teaching them.

[1]Foster, G.M.; *Traditional Cultures and the Impact of Technological Change*, Harper &Row Publishers, New York, 1962.

Part III

RURAL SOCIOLOGY AND PLANNED SOCIAL CHANGE

PART II

RURAL SOCIOLOGY & RURAL PLANNING AND GOVERNANCE

CHAPTER 14

RURAL SOCIOLOGY—SUBJECT-MATTER AND IMPORTANCE

DEFINITION AND MEANING OF RURAL SOCIOLOGY

In this scientific age, knowledge is being developed about everything related to human beings. Social Science studies the various activities related to human society. It is more precisely the systematic study of human relationships, the study of psychic interactions between individuals; who come into association in groups, with the necessary and accompanying study of the inter-relationships of groups and of social systems.[1] When its field is limited to a particular area it can be named Sociology of Family, Urban Sociology (dealing with urban people), Rural Sociology (dealing with rural people), and so on.

Sociology

Sociology is the science of society.

It may be defined as the study of the ways in which social experiences function in developing, functioning, maturing and repressing human beings through inter-personal stimulation. Since these ways of making and re-making the members are social processes, sociology may be said to be a study of social processes.

Sociology is really a body of facts and principles which are based on scientifically organised knowledge. To study the social relationship is its subject-matter.

Rural sociology

It is the study of the sociology of life in the rural environment which systematically studies rural communities to discover their conditions and tendencies and to formulate principles of progress.

It is made up of two terms: Rural+Sociology, so it is limited to the study of various aspects of rural society. Its function is "to assemble . . . the essential facts and the baisc principles that have been derived from the application of the scientific method in the study of rural-social relationship."[2]

---

[1]F. Gibbert, *Fundamentals of Sociology*, Orient Longmans, Bombay, 51, p. 3.

[2]T. Lynn Smith, *The Sociology of Rural Life*, 53, p. 3.

According to F. Stuart, the Sociology of rural life is a study of rural population, rural social organisations and the social processes operative in rural society.[1] Probably, it is more logical, however, to refer to it as systematised knowledge of rural social relationships.

So it is clear that rural sociology is related to the organised and scientific study of the life of rural people and their inter-personal relationship. According to Chapin, the sociology of rural life is a study of rural population and the social processes operative in rural society.[2] In this way, under rural sociology, we study all the phenomenon of rural life. Supporting this view, Smith says, "Some investigators study social phenomenona that are present only in, or largely confined to the rural environment, to persons engaged in the agricultural occupation. Such sociological facts and principles as are derived from the study of rural social relationships may be referred to as Rural Sociology."[3]

According to Desai, "Rural sociology is the science of rural society. The laws of the structure and development of rural society in general can aid us in discovering the special laws governing a particular society."[4]

NATURE OF RURAL SOCIOLOGY

Whatever may be the subject-matter, the question arises whether its way of achievement is scientific or not. On this basis, we can judge the nature of Rural Sociology. In the collection of facts for any knowledge, when we apply a scientific method, it is called a science. So science goes with the method, not with the subject-matter.

Before discussing the nature of Rural Sociology, it is necessary that we understand the meaning of scientific method. Discussing this topic, Lundburg says, "Scientific method consists of systematic observation, classification and interpretation of data."[5] On the various aspects of scientific method, Bernard writes, "Science may be defined in terms of the six major processes that take place within it. These are testing, verification, definition, classification, organisation and orientation, which includes prediction and application."[6]

Further Lundburg says that "Social scientists are committed to the belief that the problems which confront them are to be solved, if at all, by judicious and systematic observation, verification, classification and interpretation of social phenomena. This approach in its most vigorous and successful form, is broadly designated as the scientific method".[7]

Various steps in the scientific approach can be:

(1) Formation of provisional or working hypotheses,
(2) Selection of apparatus of questionnaire or schedule,
(3) Observations and collection of data,

[1]F. Stuart Chapin, *Rural Structure in Rural Society*, p. 7.
[2]Ibid.
[3]T. Lynn Smith, *The Sociology of Rural Life*, 53, pp. 9-10.
[4]A.R. Desai, *Rural Sociology in India*, 159, p. 106.
[5]George A. Lundburg, *Social Research*, 1942, p. 5.
[6]L.L. Bernard, *The Field and Methods of Sociology*, 1934, p. 234.
[7]George A. Lundburg, *Social Research*, 1942, p. 1.

(4) Recording,

(5) Classification and organisation of data; and

(6) Generalisation and formulation of laws.

For this scientific method, the research worker in the social sciences is required to have a scientific bias. As ordinary man cannot have it. This scientific process is called the scientific method. Its important elements are: urge, speciality, enthusiasm, hard labour, critical thinking, unbiased opinion. Really speaking, the scientific approach is very difficult.

If we examine the scientific nature of Rural Sociology, we would find that the earlier efforts made in the rural areas were mainly related to economic standards. Several studies made in the field of agriculture had a relationship with the welfare of a rural society. Rural sociology studies the rural society with many purposes. So we find that rural sociology besides studying the various social systems also finds a solution to its problems. In 1937, at the Sociological Conference held in the U.S.A., it was decided that the scientific way of study for rural sociology may be defined and all the rural problems may be studied with reference to such a definition. So the nature of rural sociology is completely scientific and it is a social science.

Rural sociology as a science

As a science it is to be judged by the criteria: (a) the reliability of the body of knowledge, (2) its organisation, and (3) its method. Rural sociology as described here, fulfills these three conditions.

(1) *Reliable knowledge:* In order to have a science, an organised body of knowledge must be developed which has been tested for validity and reliability by the best known scientific methods. As to its body of reliable knowledge, rural sociology, though a young science, has made a very good beginning in studies like: population, the family, group behaviour, the evolution of institutions, the processes of rural social change, etc. Despite the difficulties involved in the scientific and systematic way of studying sociology the general knowledge and data are reliable. Keeping in view the difficulties of rural sociology is facing, its knowledge and data are reliable.

(2) *Organisation of knowledge:* The organisation of a science rests upon the relationships which the parts of knowledge bear to each other. In sociology, there are many inter-relationships, that require many tools for discoveries.

(3) *Rural sociology as a method:* Just as in a laboratory experiment in physics accurate observations are made, so in rural sociology, we try to do essentially the same thing, not in a laboratory, but with statistics. For instance, if we want to know whether families with low incomes have more infant deaths, we do not get 500 rich mothers and 500 poor mothers and put them in a room and watch the babies die. Instead, we collect statistics or data. But first we must hold constant the type of food, the customs associated with ethnic groups and finally the race. By studying and varying the factor of income and infant deaths, and by keeping other factors constant, it is shown that by increasing the income alone can we save the lives of babies.

So in rural sociology, the scientific method of study is strictly followed. All the steps of scientific approach are necessary in analysing and planning a community development programme scientifically. In the study of rural society, we need social statistics, social surveys, case studies, community studies, etc. In the absence of a scientific approach, the village problems cannot be studied. In such studies we formulate generalised principles and laws on the basis of which to forecast future trends. In rural sociology, an attempt is also made to find the relationship of cause and effect, which is the first necessity of science. As this science has all the qualities expected in a social science, we can conclude that rural sociology is a science.

Limitations

Of course, there are some factors which limit the scientific nature of the subject. These are: (1) It is impossible to draw a line between the rural and urban fields, (2) The science is still not fully developed, (3) It cannot have a laboratory just like the physical sciences, and (4) We cannot measure the subject with a yard stick. But these are minor limitations. A scientific approach in rural sociology is difficult, not impossible.

SCOPE OF RURAL SOCIOLOGY

Rural sociology is a study of rural social happenings. Regarding the scope of the subject, all the writers have different views. Some of them have limited it to rural development only. On its scope, Desai writes: "Should rural sociology only provide scientific knowledge about rural society and laws governing its development, or should it also serve as a guide and suggest practical programmes of reform or reconstruction of that society in the economic, social or cultural fields?"[1]

Generally, all writers agreed that rural sociology is the analysis of the life of rural people. Smith supporting this view writes: "All of them unanimously declare that the prime objective of rural sociology should be to make a scientific, systematic and comprehensive study of the rural social organisations, of its structure, functions and the objective tendencies of its development."[2]

Rural sociology studies the relationships and interaction in the village society, so its scope is very wide. From this, it is also expected that it will study the non-material culture of village people and the effect of the material culture of the urban population on rural people.

The studies in rural sociology include:

(1) The social psychology of life,

(2) The rural social organisation, and

(3) The social values, which are of advantage for any development programme of a society.

Rural sociology has become an important aspect of the science of sociology and has made a unique contribution on its own. Most of the people of the world are rural and most of them live in the so-called, under-developed areas. These people are reproducing at a faster rate than those in the more advanced areas and if these trends continue, will finally dominate the world.

[1]A.R. Desai, *Rural Sociology in India*, 1959, p. 9.
[2]Ibid., p. 10.

ELEMENTS OF RURAL SOCIOLOGY

Following are the elements of rural sociology:

(1) *Rural structure:* Village life gives birth to a type of settlement. So it is necessary to study the pattern of settlement in various parts of the world.

(2) *Rural social organisation:* This includes the study of family life, marriage systems, social stratification, etc.

(3) *Characteristics of village life:* As compared to urban life.

(4) *Study of rural problems:* In the beginning, rural sociology developed with the study of village problems. Taking the village as an economic unit, we study the village problems in detail and find the solution of these problems based on our researches.

(5) *Rural moral teaching:* From the very beginning, it was expected that, based on its principles and rules, rural sociology would act in the field of moral education.

(6) *Rural social life:* It studies the social, economic, educational, religious, cultural, philosophical, material and non-material aspects of the rural people.

(7) *Rural reconstruction:* After studying the various aspects, characteristics and problems of village life, rural sociology studies the various factors which can help in the rural reconstruction programme. According to the views of the Utilitarians, rural sociology is a science of the study of rural reconstruction.

This shows that the scope of rural sociology is as wide as the presentation of the whole of village life. In countries where agriculture is the main occupation, this becomes more important.

SCOPE OF RURAL SOCIOLOGY IN INDIA

India has been described as a country of villages. In India, about 75 per cent of the population lives in about six million villages. This means that India's sociology is the sociology of mainly the rural life, or rural sociology. Because of this fact, India's struggle to achieve political freedom was the struggle for Rural Development Programmes. After achieving political independence, the Indian Government launched the Rural Development Programmes. These are; (1) The Five-Year Plans, (2) Community Development Projects, (3) Reviving the Village Panchayats and Democratic Decentralisation through Village Panchayats, (4) Development of Cooperatives, (5) Rural Educational Programmes, and (6) Bhudan Yajna, etc. These will be discussed in the succeeding part of the chapter.

ORIGIN AND DEVELOPMENT OF RURAL SOCIOLOGY

Rural sociology in an organised and scientific way has developed only during the 20th century. This is a branch of sociology. Besides the scope of the subject, all other things are common to both. This is the fact that rural sociology could develop even in such a short time.

The study of rural sociology started in the latter part of the 19th century in the U.S.A. It grew out of a humanitarian philosophy and a concern for the disadvantages and problems in rural life. It was characterised by pity, sympathy and a burning desire to improve rural conditions. Its primary thrust has been to place emphasis on improving the welfare of people, solving the population problem, mobilisation of labour, economic problems, food problem, idleness, etc. The study of such problems and finding out their solutions led to the rapid development of Rural Sociology in the USA. Under the impetus given by grants of money to rural sociologists in Land Grant Colleges, studies were conducted analysing the practical problems faced by the rural people in the USA.

Rural sociologists from the USA have also made significant contributions to the solution of problems in other countries. Some of the significant works are: (1) Analysis of the need for implementation, University of Illinois, (2) Creation of the Community Development Movement in India, by Dr. Douglas Ensminger of the University of California, (3) Setting up Adult Education Programmes in rural areas in Greece by Howard Beers, (4) Work done by T. Lynn Smith in Brazil, (5) Participation by Robert A. Polson, of Cornell University in Development of Rural Reconstruction Movement in the Philippines, and (6) Works of Carl Taylor in Argentina and other countries,

The main contributions by Indian rural sociologists are: (1) Rural Sociology in India by A.R. Desai, (2) India's Changing Villages and Surveys in Hyderabad and Saharanpur (U.P.) by Dr. S.C. Dube, (3) Rural Sociology by R.B. Singh Tomar, (4) Works by R.D. Singh, (5) Extension and Rural Welfare (a book) by Dr. O.P. Dahama, 1958, 62 and later editions; Rural Sociology in collaboration with Dr. Lindstrom, (6) Hindu Society at the Cross Roads by K.M. Panikkar, (7) Blossoms in the Dust by Kusum Nair, and (8) Gaon Sathi by Dr. Chitambar and Dr. Barnabas of Allahabad Agricultural Institute.

Areas of contribution by rural sociologists

The areas in which rural sociologists have made contributions are: (1) Understanding the changing rural society, (2) Making analyses and defining concepts towards the development of a Theory of Rural Society, (3) Developing new methods of research, (4) Formulating public policies for rural life, and (5) Traditional subjects like the nature of rural society and the social aspects of rural living, the diffusion of farm practices, demography, rural groups and social participation, levels of living, studies of public agency programmes, farm tenure and the labour force, the rural community, the rural school, rural health and rural social security.

During the Second World War, the need for trained rural sociologists was greatly felt. The U.S. Government felt the necessity of directing rural activities in various countries and appointed Pearl Harber, an expert in rural sociology as its director. This programme gave impetus to the development of rural sociology.

Beside the efforts of the rural sociologists in the USA, the League of Nations, U.N.E.S.C.O., U.N.I.C.E.F., U.S.A.I.D., programmes and philanthropic organisations like the Ford Foundations, Rockefeller Foundation, Colombo Plan, etc., have helped in the advancement of rural sociology by their grants to institutions for studies, extension wings, training of rural social scientists, establishment of agricultural universities, etc.

Rural sociology in India

In ancient times, India was regarded as a developed country as regards knowledge, science and agriculture. Many of the important researches made during the present age were known to people in those days. But all this deteriorated because of the destructive efforts of the foreign rulers. India lost many good things known to our forefathers. The social life in olden days was very well-organised. Now, after the achievement of political independence, efforts are being made to revive some of the important institutions and organisations so that life in the village becomes happier and prosperous. To achieve this, rural sociology has to play an important role. Various experts and organisations are engaged in it.

The sociologists of India have very recently thought of giving more importance to rural sociology. In the syllabi of B.A. and M.A., most of the universities have added papers on rural sociology. In nearly all the universities imparting training for the M.Sc. (Agriculture) in extension there is a compulsory paper on rural sociology. All the Agricultural Universities offer courses in rural sociology. The theses for the M.Sc. (Agriculture) Degree in Extension are adding research data to the field. The Programme Evaluation Organisation; The Orientation and Study Centres, The Planning and Action Institute, Lucknow, The National Institute for Community Development, Hyderabad, I.A.R.I., New Delhi and the Agricultural Colleges and Universities are important centres of Rural Social Studies.

Because of the great number of villages and the variety in language, culture and social institutions, depending on the geographical and other factors, there is no social uniformity. This necessitates a series of studies of village communities from different parts of the country, which may cover many divergent patterns of organisation.

Besides the experts in the institutions and organisations, the Government social workers and reformers are making efforts to raise the standard of living of the rural masses through Community Development Projects, Cooperative Societies, Bhoodan Movement, Reorganisation of Panchayats, Five-Year Plans, educational programmes, etc. and also through family planning, farm planning and educational programmes of the extension services for training the farmers in adopting better ways of raising crops, livestock, etc.

So, for the all-sided development of rural society, the statisticians, economists, social scientists, social reformers, and political organisations like Bharat Sewak Samaj, etc., centralise their work on the study of human life which lie in the midst of material and cultural poverty. Really speaking, the work in rural sociology in India started after the Community Development Projects created the need for this knowledge to be given to the extension workers and community development workers.

IMPORTANCE OF THE STUDY OF RURAL SOCIOLOGY

Rural sociology presents a scientific picture of rural life.

Villages are important for many reasons because they are the springs to feed urban areas. So rural sociology is an important subject. This importance can be put under the following heads.

Science of human relationship

Besides knowing the natural, unnatural and non-living things around him, man has an urge to know human relationships from close. This urge can be satisfied through rural sociology.

(a) *Majority of rural population*

In every part of the world, the rural population is more than the urban population. On this basis also, it can be said that rural sociology is more important than any other branch of sociology.

(b) *It gives complete knowledge of rural life*

Rural sociology gives us complete knowledge of village life. The first unit of development in a country is the village and the village is the centre of culture of any country.

(c) *Rural reformation*

Rural sociology started with the aim of bringing reformation and welfare in society. Rural reformation is its first aim. For this purpose, it helps in the following works:

(i) *Organisation:* Village units which seem disorganised can be reorganised through the study of Rural Sociology. Side by side, uniformity can also be brought through it. It improves the coordination between various units and helps in bringing an improvement in economic, social and health conditions.

(ii) *Economic betterment:* Through detailed studies of village problems and observations, rural sociology lays stress on the importance of increasing the quantity and quality of production. This results in raising the standard of living. This is an important function of rural sociology.

(iii) *To provide technology and systematic knowledge and reforms in farm production:* The main occupation of the 80 per cent population of villages is agriculture. For the purpose of improving this main occupation of the rural people, the earlier researches in rural sociology were conducted in agricultural colleges.

(iv) *Solution of pathological social problems:* Every branch of sociology attempts to study social relationships and the solution of human problems. The study of rural sociology shows that it examines the social pathological problems and based on scientfic methodology it suggests ways for improving the village conditions.

(v) *Education:* The improvement, progress and development of any community depends on its education. Because of this fact, rural sociology lays stress on education for the solution of rural problems.

(vi) *Planning for development:* Rural sociology encourages development of various plans for any rural development programmes. For making progress in the rural society, work is carried out according to these plans.

(d) *Rural sociology develops a relationship between the village and industries*

(e) *Rural sociology is most important in agricultural countries*

About 90 per cent of the progress of the world is based on agriculture. It is only in agricultural countries that people realise the importance of rural sociology. For some years before, when the U.S.A. was mainly an agricultural country, rural sociology started playing its role there. Similarly, for India's all-sided development, the development of rural sociology is very important.

The importance of the study of rural society in India can be discussed under the following heads:

(1) The village is a basic source of Indian culture. India is a country of villages and

the birth and development of its culture took place from the villages. India's progress is based on the progress of the villages. Thus, it is necessary to develop the villages.

(2) Indian sociology is rural sociology.

(3) Complete knowledge of society for social development is needed. This helps Change Agents or Community Development Workers in knowing the felt needs of the society, and then they can help the villagers in satsfying them.

(4) Rural sociology can help in organising the disorganised Indian rural structure.

Importance in development programme

(a) *Planning*

For those who are to engage themselves in the country's planning, it is necessary that they should have knowledge of Indian rural sociology. In independent India, for its all-sided development, various programmes, like the Five Year-Plan and many other schemes regarding the village improvement are being prepared, and in these rural sociology has a part to play.

(b) *Community development (C.D.)*

The various programmes of C.D. are directly related to villagers. These programmes are discussed in other chapters.

CHAPTER 15

IMPORTANT SOCIOLOGICAL CONCEPTS

PLACE OF CULTURE IN RURAL SOCIETY

Definition of culture

To Sorokin and MacIver, cuture stands for the moral, spiritual and intellectual attainments of man. David Bidney defines culture as the self-cultivation of the natural geographical environment. He says that culture is the product of agrofacts (products of cultivation), artifacts (products of industry), sociofacts (social organisation), and manifacts (language, religion, art, etc.). To Malinowski culture stands for a total way of life, which secures for an individual the satisfaction of his biopsychic drives and the fulfilment of other wants and cravings and, ultimately, invests him with freedom. Radcliff-Brown regards culture as cultivation, the process of handing down and acquiring traditions, as a result of which society is perpetuated. Tylor says that culture stands for the beliefs, ideas, customs, laws, morals, arts, and other capabilities and skills acquired by man as a member of society. He says that culture is a social heritage. It is the gift of society to an individual.

There seems to be little unanimity among the authors. Truly speaking, there cannot be one definition for all societies, countries or even groups. This is because the culture of a given group of people is an historically-created design of living. This suggests that the experience of their ancestors provides the group members with a pattern of ways for satisfying their needs, getting along with each other and coping with their environment. There are a variety of designs in different parts of the world. Some satisfy the basic needs of its members more adequately than others. But if a design does not work well then it affects not only the passive receivers and carriers of culture, but also its creators and modifiers as well.

The *Sanskrit term* for culture is 'Sanskriti' derived from Sanskar, meaning ritual performance. Man is born as a social being, he attains sociability by going through the Sanskars.

In agriculture, man deals with soil, plants, animals, tools, means of control of disease and insects. The "culture" is adapting, so there is social change as affected by various exogenous forces.

Ethos and Eidos

According to Kroeber 'Eidos', the formal appearance of a culture derived from its constituents. 'Ethos' is the disposition of a culture which determines its quality, its main themes and interests.

Ethnocentricism

Generally, the members of each group think of their culture as the best. This attitude is called ethnocentric. The ways of other groups are assumed to be inferior. This is because the newcomer in the world cannot help but learn the ways of his group. Once he has acquired the ways of his group, they become part of him and so seem to be natural, and thus look superior to other ways.

Nature and analysis of culture

Explicit: Such regularities as may be perceived with the aid of the eye and the ear are the explicit items of culture.

Implicit: Those which would be perceived by us only after we are specially trained to look for all that is not obvious. The motivations and impulses underlying human action of which the actors themselves may not be conscious, are included in the implicit.

Content of culture

The content of culture consists basically of non-material phenomena—ideas, knowledge, techniques, symbols, patterns, view-points, etc., and not the visible and tangible material things or objects. Sociologists generally hold the opinion that only the knowledge of techniques, for making and using these articles, and their meaning to their makes and users are parts of culture. These objects are known as "cultural objects". For any cultural object, actual culture consists of: (1) an associated technique of fabrication and manipulation, e.g., part of building a bridge, printing a book, etc., and (2) a set of questions or usages governing the objects of utility and social significance. Cultural objects also include natural objects which have been given a certain meaning or use, e.g., sacred stones, rivers, plants, animals, etc.

Functions of culture

The profession of a common culture gives the members of society or group the feeling of unity with the group. It also enables them to live and work together without too much confusion and mutual interference. The important functions are:

(1) Culture provides a series of patterns whereby the biological demands of the group members can be met, e.g., for sustenance, shelter and reproduction.

(2) Culture provides a set of rules to insure the cooperation of the individuals of a group in adjusting to the environmental situation. The group is thus able to act in certain situations as a unit.

(3) Culture provides channels of interaction for the individuals within the group.

(4) Culture provides methods of adjustment of the group to its external and internal needs. It provides a pattern for the development of the individual.

(5) For the individual in a society, culture provides: (a) ready-made adjustments to

a number of situations, and (b) a series of familiar stimuli to the individual, to which he has only to respond in a familiar way.

All these functions are controlled through norms or rules made in society. These norms may be governed by sanctions or punishments. So the study of norms, mores, folkways, laws, etc., is necessary for knowing the culture of a society.

Culture norms

Norms are blueprints for behaviour, setting limits within which individuals may seek alternate ways to achieve their goals. All societies have such norms or rules which specify appropriate and inappropriate behaviour. Individuals are rewarded or punished as they conform to, or deviate from, the rules. Norms are based on cultural *values* which are justified by moral standards, reasoning or aesthetic judgement. Norms obviously vary in strength and are classified as: (a) mores, and (b) folkways, according to the intensity of feeling associated with them and the degree of conformity expected. These are illustrated in Fig. 15.1.

(Mores)	Norms		(Laws)
Strong sanctions	Cannibalism Strong feelings & control	Killing	Severe penalties
	Drunkenness	Domestic relations	
Weak sanctions (Folkways)	Style of dress Weak feelings & controls	Routine licensing	Minor penalties

Fig. 15.1. Types of Norms[1]

As shown in the figure above, mores stand at the upper range of the scale and folkways at the lower range of non-institutionalised norms, i.e., norms that have not been transferred into laws.

Mores

Mores are the folkways which deal with moral aspects. These are ways of doing and thinking, and if they are violated the group may be divided or disturbed. They are the group-shared understandings about what to do in any situation. They define the expected types of behaviour for various situations. They guide our decisions, usually without conscious thought. Consequently, our behaviour corresponds with what others expect.

Folkways

Folkways are group habits. Sumner says that our social heritage is composed of group habits of thought, and these can be called folkways. These are the customs or

1 Broom and Selznic, *Sociology*, page 53 (2nd Edition).

usages that have developed out of experience and are handed down by tradition, without purpose. They are seldom the results of any conscious advanced planning. Folkways are norms or standards of conduct. They are not conceived to be highly important to group welfare. Violation threatens no one. Punishment does not follow. They are simply the usual expected types of behaviour. To be regarded as a good fellow and to be like other folks, we hesitate to depart from group-rituals, and thus folkways are to some extent compulsive.

Mores, of course, are much more compulsive than folkways. They are not norms but rather guides for behaviour.

Laws

These are consciously and deliberately formulated behaviour patterns. Men are aware of having created them or certainly of having codified them. They are rational and practical in character, which is lacking in mores. In mores, there are elements of sentiment and faith, whereas in laws, fixed punishments are prescribed for disobedience. The enforcement of laws is placed in the hands of designated functionaries, such as judges. Laws generally grow out of mores, As societies become larger and more complex, codification of some of the mores tends to take place.

Institutions

An institution is a set of folkways and mores that centres in the achievement of some human end or purpose. It is essentially a pattern of usages which define the roles of the participating group members in such a way that their aims can be achieved through the resulting cooperative behaviour. The relationship between institutions and folkways and mores is a genetic one. Certain folkways and mores develop into institutions. Our current institutions in the fields of government, trade, education, religion, all with their fixed rule patterns and their elaborate regulations and ritual customs, are at root only aggregations of folkways and mores built together around central unifying concepts.

Conformity to and deviation from norms

Most norms are regarded as binding rules by most people but they may change in importance over a period of time. Norms, however, may or may not be followed or even deviated from. There are a number of reasons why norms are not followed or deviated.

(1) Some norms are perceived as less important than others. A driver, who hits another motor-car to avoid hitting a child, has violated one norms so as to conform to another.

(2) Norms may conflict with each other so that the individual must disobey one if he is to conform to the other. A student who sees a friend cheating in an examination must choose between conflicting norms. One norm instructs him to see that honesty is upheld, and another tells him to be loyal to his friend.

(3) An individual may evade a norm because he knows it is not well enforced. Using company stationery for personal letter writing and taking home company supplies are rarely punished, but they are wrong according to the norms.

(4) Some norms are not learned by all people even in the same society, e.g., there are class differences in etiquette and life style.

Culture patterns

According to Bogardns,[1] a culture pattern is an objective expression of a way of doing or believing that is common to a number of people. It ranges from the very simple to the very complex. It becomes the behaviour trait of children, youth and adults. Culture patterns become "established as patterns of habitual response" of persons. They have two special characteristics: (1) they are shared, and (2) they are transmitted from one member of a group to another, from one generation to another.

A *culture complex* is a combination of unnaturally attached culture patterns such as the swagger stick carried by a democratically-minded person in the U.S.A.

A *culture area* is the region wherein a specific culture pattern or culture complex may be found. It is the regional base for a way of acting or believing, as for example, Punjabi culture, or Maharashtrian culture.

A *culture centre* is the emanating point of a culture pattern. Paris has been the culture centre of new styles in women's dress for the Western world.

Universal culture patterns

All cultural patterns fit into universal culture patterns, i.e., a basic pattern, common to all people everywhere. The following may be common to all people everywhere: (1) all people have a family system, (2) all have a communication system or a language, (3) all have physical living systems relating to food, clothing, shelter, and occupational systems, (4) every tribe and nation has some kind of government and social control patterns, (5) property systems are found in all lands, (6) people in all groups have art patterns in one or more fields, (7) people in all groups worship a higher power, and (8) informal educational patterns function among all mankind.[2]

Culture heritage

A culture heritage is the sum total of the cultural patterns that a person receives from the various social groups of which he is a member. Everyone of us is indebted to preceding generations in so many cultural ways that we can scarcely realise how deep is our indebtedness.

Social groups vary greatly in the extent and quality of their cultural heritage. One group may have an extensive heritage of primitive culture patterns. Another group may have a replete heritage of complex and carefully thought-out culture patterns, and striving to improve the scope and quality of these patterns. Still another group may have an unusually wide variety of culture patterns, but has become so self-satisfied with its glorious culture that it offers no encouragement to any of its members to develop new patterns. In fact, a group may penalise anyone who criticises the group's traditions or custom. An autocratic class, satisfied with its own influence and affluence,

[1]E. S. Bogardus, *Sociology*, New York: Macmillan Co., 1937, p. 36.
[2]Clark Wissler, *Man and Culture*, N. Y., Thomas Y. Cromwell, Col., 1923, Ch. V.

may crush out any attempt to incubate new ideas. The extension workers must **be on** the alert for these in their approach to a village.

Culture history

(1) The earliest period in culture is called the Old Stone Age or the Palaeolithic Age. At that time metal implements were unknown and stones, bones, horns, shells and wood served in the manufacture of tools and weapons. Animals were not domesticated and fire was unknown. Food was chiefly of uncooked vegetables, fish and animals were eaten raw.

(2) The next stage was the New Stone Age or the Neolithic age. The implements of the people of this age were superior and of a higher order as compared to the Palaeolithic Age. Pottery and agriculture developed in this age. Cooked foods were used. Domestication of animals began. Monuments indicating the nature of religious rites were developed.

(3) Then came the Bronze Age of human culture, when metals were developed. Copper was used in place of cattle for money. The iron age merged into the steel and oil ages.

(4) The present age may be called the Electric Age or Technological Age, where techniques and machines handle the work done by a labour on a large scale. The world is now moving into the Atomic Age.

The chief emphasis of human society has been shifting. In addition to the invention of material objects of culture, increasing attention has been given to psychical and social phenomena. Social attitudes and values are now central data. The development of constructively-minded and wholesome personalities in and through group life has become a theme of far-reaching significance.

Outstanding in the history of human groups is cultural growth and advancement. For example, compare the loose family life of the best people among tribal people with the developed forms of love and affection that now characterises family life at its best. The change from magic and witchcraft to medicines, the shift to the banking system and the invention of printing reveal the tremendous role of a changing culture in our group life.

Culture diffusion

The spreading of a culture pattern from one group of people to another and from one culture area to another, is called culture diffusion. Culture patterns spread in two ways: (1) incidentally, and (2) by direction. Whenever a person migrates from one culture area to another, he carries culture patterns with him. If these appeal by their utility or uniqueness, or irrespective of their utility or uniqueness, and irrespect of utility to many people culture diffusion is likely to occur. This is culture diffusion by incident.

Culture diffusion by direction is in case of: (a) sending missionaries to other countries, or (b) colonisation. This happened, e.g., in the diffusion of European culture in East Asia, and diffusion of Punjabi culture in parts of India or in Israel.

Cultural lag

Cultural lag means that some parts of a people's culture do not change as do other traits. It means that one or more phases of culture have moved ahead, and that all other phases are lagging behind. Lag is a term which suggests more progress at some points than at others.

Marginal man

Difference in culture produces a marginal man. A person who is living in two cultures is likely to be occupying not the centre of either, but the margins of both. He is the man who belongs to two or more cultures but is not fully accepted in any. An immigrant, who has moved into a decidedly different culture area from the one in which he grew to manhood, is likely to be a marginal man.

Ways in which culture is involved in group life[1]

(1) *Descriptive:* Culture includes customs, beliefs, morals, art, and knowledge.

(2) *Historical:* Culture is the sum total of social heritage.

(3) *Normative:* Culture is composed of the traditions, attitudes, ideas, that control human behaviour.

(4) *Psychological:* Culture is the means by which people try to obtain their goals.

(5) *Structural:* Culture is an organisation of conventional understandings and learned behaviour.

(6) *Genetic:* Culture arises from and includes all the products of social interaction.

SOCIAL ACTION

Social psychologists have formulated what is called as "construct of social action". It is an elaboration of five basic stages in the process of thinking. These are: (1) a recognition of need and the facing up to a problem, (2) the tendency of the mind that is working to jump to a solution of the problem, (3) the need on the part of the change agent (Extension Worker) to get the group to list and consider alternate solutions to the problem presented by the members, (4) the testing of each proposed solution in the light of known or discovered facts, or by experimentation, and (5) the decision to act upon an agreed solution.

Elements of social action

The pattern of social action may follow, as well as involve, these fundamental steps:

(1) The recognition that all social action takes place in a social system. The social system may be a village. It may involve inter-village organisations and block, district, state or even national systems as well. The village may be looked upon as a "target system" and the "overhead" elements or the organisational set up as "the Change Agent System".

(2) For every social action, there is some past or present experience on which the action must be based. In Indian villages, the hold of traditional usage is very strong. If a new practice is suggested and it involves a major change, farmers may take a long time to adopt it. Those involving a minor change may be accepted and adopted

---

[1]A.L Kroeber and Clyde Kluckholn, *Culture*, Peabody Museum of American Archaeology and Ethnology, Cambridge, Massachusetts, 1952.

in a shorter period. Introduction of the new, in any case, must be tied to what is now being done or what has been done.

(3) Social action usually is initiated by two or more people who agree that some kind of problem exists. If two or more persons recognise the problem and agree that something must be done, the actual process of social action can begin. If the problem is one facing all of the people of the village, it is possible that all of them can be finally involved. Action taken by the initiators must take this into account. These initiators may come from within the social system, or include both within and those without it; or only outsiders, but eventually insiders must be involved.

(4) People other than initiators must come to realise that something must be done about the problem. This is *involvement*. The originators of the action must get help of others so that even in the beginning, there are several sets of initiators, outsiders, outside-insiders and insiders. Through discussion with these small groups, ideas may be added, alternatives may be listed, and the nucleus or the plan of action be decided upon.

(5) Before action can take place, it must be approved or *legitimised* by those holding such power in the village, or the group, or the social system, whatever we may call it. In *legitimation*, before the action is carried very far, the approval of certain people in positions of authority or power must be secured. These may be administrators, officials, leaders, heads of castes or factions who hold power according to a value system. To "by pass" such leaders may cause opposition and it may result in the failure of our programme.

(6) The idea of the need for social action must be diffused among the masses in the social system. This is *diffusion*. Once approved the action proposed can be taken to the people. The right person, or persons, need to be chosen for task. These may be leaders, as defined above, or those to whom they delegate their authority. Mass media and other forms of communication, designed to reach and influence the villagers, can be made use of in this phase of programme.

(7) This step has as its objective to make the problem, the *People's Problem by definition and acceptance*. After we have made the people aware of the problem and the means proposed to solve the problem, we should make efforts to get popular approval of the proposal. At this stage, small group discussions leading to group decision need to be arranged. They must include a decision on the part of the people to do something about it. Once they know what the goal is, they will accept it.

(8) This recognition of the problem must be followed by *commitment* following the decision of the people to do something about it. This probably must come through caste, factional, economic, or other group leaders. But it is important also to get approval from the rank and file of villagers.

(9) Goals must be defined. At this stage, the people learn exactly what must be done, how it must be done correctly, and what can be expected if the job is done right. Here means and goals are considered.

(10) In discussing alternative means, there may not be agreement as to the one best method. As various methods are discussed and some tried out, some are discarded, and others which stand up to the test are accepted. At this stage, the previous experience of the worker or Change Agent is important. After a method is used, it needs to be evaluated as to whether our recommended practice of farming can be

accepted by an average farmer, or whether the practice will be successful in this village.

(11) Decision on a plan of action requires the village leaders to work out the details of what is to be done, how it is to be done, who is to carry out various parts of the plan, what must be or can be done in meetings to finalise plans, and to provide materials, finances and publicity needed for the work.

(12) The mobilisation and organisation of resources and people. In this stage, the people are brought together and organised into groups so as to carry out the plan of work. The materials and equipment needed are arranged for in such a way that they are at hand when they are needed.

(13) In launching the programme, the work is actually started. This may be by inviting a popular leader, or having a ceremony, or a method demonstration.

(14) To carry out action, the plan is put into operation, step by step. The village forces need to be so organised that one phase, when completed, may be followed by another in the logical sequence.

(15) In evaluating the results, to find out whether proper steps have been taken and to find flaws in the method, each stage is examined. At the end of the programme, there should be a final evaluation. This will show how good the methods were, how effectively the measures were used, where the programme failed, what were the causes of failure, how to plan differently next time, what was learned of value in these first efforts, and what next steps need to be taken. This information can be of use to other workers also. These stages can be grouped as:

A. Initiation stage including point 1 to 4.
B. Legitimation stage, point 5.
C. Planning for action stage, points 6 to 11.
D. Action stage, points 12 to 13. (See Fig. 15.2)

SOCIAL VALUES

A person becomes socially accepted by behaving according to a set pattern, fixed and approved by the society. He is all the time influenced by the natural and the social enviroments. He is isolated and left to himself after his birth. On the other hand, the most important and the basic institution of the family is there to guide him and shape him in the way it likes, and on the set patterns which the parents themselves have learnt from their parents. Besides family, there are various other groups which approve ideas and patterns of behaviour which are very old. These ideas are known as "Social Values". Social values are ideas which help an individual to discriminate whether a particular object or behaviour is good or bad, desirable or undersirable. There are at same time rules which govern the action of an individual directed towards achieving values and they are known as "Norms". People are expected to behave in accordance with the values held by the groups to which they belong, and their expected behaviour is "normative behaviour".

Formation of social values

(1) *Norms:* Norms decide the formation of particular social values in a group. or a particular situation or time. The social values change along with the change in

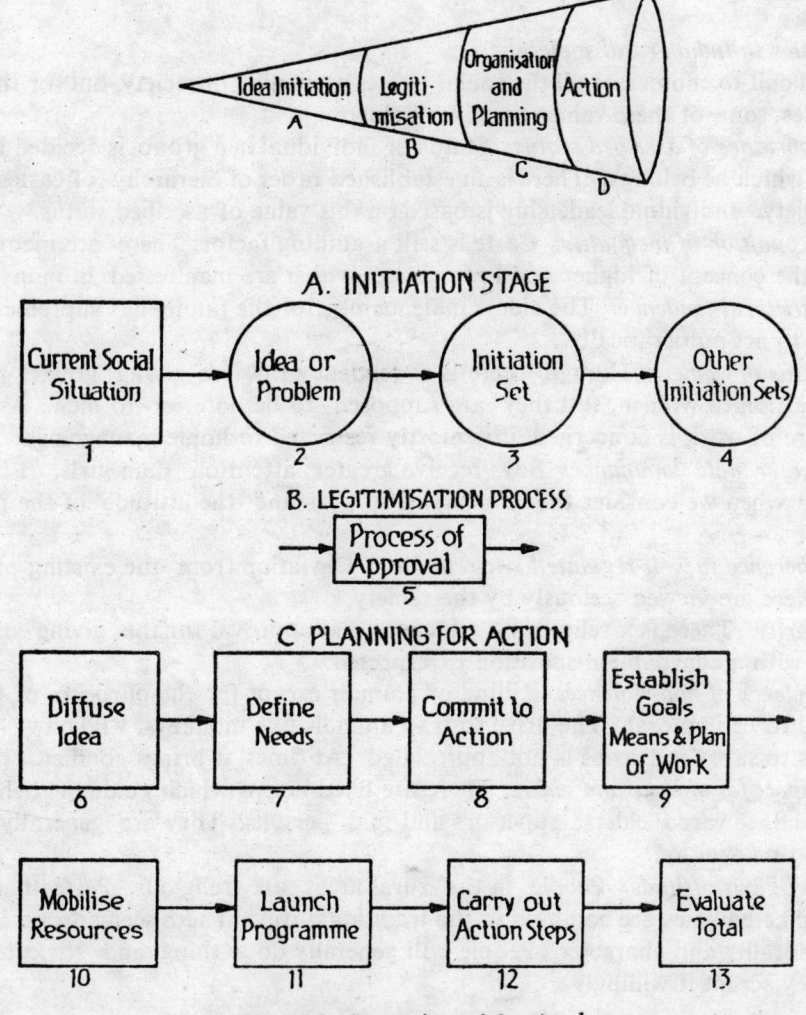

FROM IDEA TO ACTION

Idea Initiation | Legiti-misation | Organisation and Planning | Action
A | B | C | D

A. INITIATION STAGE

Current Social Situation → Idea or Problem → Initiation Set → Other Initiation Sets
1 | 2 | 3 | 4

B. LEGITIMISATION PROCESS

Process of Approval
5

C PLANNING FOR ACTION

Diffuse Idea → Define Needs → Commit to Action → Establish Goals Means & Plan of Work
6 | 7 | 8 | 9

Mobilise Resources → Launch Programme → Carry out Action Steps → Evaluate Total
10 | 11 | 12 | 13

Fig. 15.2. Stages in social action.[1]

'norms'. By constant use and application a value gets internalised' in an individual and forms a part of his nature.

(2) *Formal and informal education:* Social values are learned through both formal and informal means of education.

(3) *Social change:* Change in Economic, Political, Religious, Cultural and other social concepts to modify social values.

(4) *Scientific and technological change:* With change in technology, there comes a

[1] Adapted from Joe Bohlen and George Beal—Iowa State College and Federal Office, Task Force on Programme Projection.

change in values and scientific knowledge results in the modification and formation of new values.

Social values in Indian rural society

It is difficult to enumerate all the social values prevailing in society, but for the sake of examples, some of these values are given below:

(1) *Importance of ascribed status:* Status of individual in a group is decided by the groups to which he belongs. There is an established order of hierarchy of castes in the Indian society. Individual leadership is based on this value of ascribed status.

(2) *Recognition of inequality:* Caste is still a guiding factor. There are inequalities based on the concept of higher and lower castes which are manifested in many ways.

(3) *Patrilineal tendency:* The eldest male member of the family has supreme power and tends to act autocratically.

(4) *Status of women:* Though there is a tendency towards giving greater respect and recognition to women, still they are supposed to be inferior to men. As far as their sphere of work is concerned, it is mostly restricted to home management.

(5) *Greater male dominance:* Boys receive greater attention than girls. It is more spectacular when we consider the education of girls and the attitude of the parents towards it.

(6) *Adherence to well-regulated sex-relations:* Deviation from the existing patterns in this sphere are viewed seriously by the society.

(7) *Charity:* There is a religious significance and approval for the giving of alms. A person with a charitable disposition is respected.

(8) *Tendency of non-violence:* Killing of animals except for the purposes of food is considered to be immoral. The drive to trap animals like monkeys, wild cow (Nilgae) and others to save food crops is not appreciated. At times, it brings conflict.

(9) *Respect for old age and elders:* There are fixed norms which guide the behaviour of individuals towards elders, superiors and old persons. They are generally given respect and recognition.

(10) *Religious attitude:* People in the rural areas are religious. Performance of rituals and ceremonies are common in the traditional way. There seems to be a great sense of morality and character. People will generally do a thing, and stick to ideas if once they accept it willingly.

Desired new values

In view of the fact many changes are taking place in Indian Society, there is need to consider as to whether the existing values need modification. The following are some of the social values which may be relevant in the changing circumstances.

(1) *Acquired status:* In place of the ascribed status or along with it, we have to consider how we can provide opportunities to all, irrespective of differences in caste and creed, for progress. Steps have been taken by the Government to eliminate preferential treatment.

(2) *Equality for all:* In the present set up of the world where democracy is the main value of the day, the differences on the basis of caste, creed and sex have to give place to the provision of equal opportunities to all, in all spheres of life.

(3) *Modification in marriage norms:* While retaining all the good points in exist-ing social values in this regard, efforts are to be made to provide for certain relaxa-tion. We can think of providing some basic sex education to the youth. Inter-caste marriages can also take place to gradually reduce the caste feeling. All this requires modification in the existing values.

(4) *Charitable disposition:* Charity and donations which, at the moment, are mostly going to the beggars and mendicants, irrespective of their eligibility for it, can possibly be channelised towards the needy and the welfare institutions.

(5) *Attitude to non-violence:* It should not prohibit the removal and destruction of animal spoiling the food crops in the midst of a shortage. It can be developed into peaceful and corporate living and creation of fellow-feeling. It has to be rationa-lised.

(6) *Respect for the old and elders and consideration for the younger generation* The old and the elders are to be respected, and they on their part have to give weighᵗ and recognition to the opinions of the younger generation. A mutual give and tak e process will be more useful. The youth, learning new ways, should be allowed to work on improved methods. This is possible only when the elders change the attitude that the young generation has simply to carry out the dictates of the elders.

(7) *Religion and technology:* Along with faith in religion, the people have to develop faith in science and technology.

SOCIAL VALUES IN RELATION TO FARMING

S. N. Singh et. al. (1965) studied the social values in relation to farming. The final hierarchy which emerged as a result of their study apportions importance to these values in the following order, the first one denoting the most preferred value:

(1) Hard work,
(2) Familism,
(3) Traditionalism,
(4) Freedom,
(5) Scienticism,
(6) Economics,
(7) Security, and
(8) Leisure.

The low ranking of economics has been interpreted in terms of the losing battle the farmer wages against environmental forces, and also in terms of his being a passive observer of other people getting rich on his labour. This attitude is seen as a defence mechanism to overcome his frustration.

The authors suggested that any devices towards adoption of improved practices stand a chance of being successful only insofar as these programmes are able to incorporate the traditional values like hard work, familism, traditionalism and free-dom, which the farmer wants to cling on to. Programmes which emphasise this aspect, and seek to introduce values of economics and security as adjuncts, stand a better chance of being accepted with clarity. The importance given to scienticism is seen as a growing awareness among the farmers of the advantages which might accrue by the adoption of improved practices.

Y.P. Singh, and V.K. Babu, (1968) from their study on the "adoption of improved farm practices as a function of positive values" drew the following main conclusions:

(i) Profitability and productivity preference were the highest ranked values for the adoption of improved farm practices.

(ii) Scienticism was amongst the lowest ranked values as related to the adoption of improved seed, improved implements and improved irrigation practices.

(iii) In the adoption of fertilisers, the farmers were influenced by the value of profitability at the top, while 'simplicity of adoption' found the lowest rank in the order of values playing a role in the process of influencing the adoption.

The study suggested that, in general, the Indian cultivators are profit-minded. What cultivators need is assurance of high profit and greater productivity.

SOCIAL CONTROL

Change is involved in the process of community development. But there are certain factors which may come in the way of progress. Social control, besides helping in the maintenance of desired social values, involves agencies which make modifications in the existing social values very difficult and slow. Social control has been defined as the pattern of influence which society exerts on the individual to maintain order and establish rules in society. The group itself is frequently able to exert more effective control over the conduct of its members than can any outside individual with special authority. Social control is much more effective in primitive groups, because social selections are of primary nature.

AGENTS OF SOCIAL CONTROL

The following have been identified as agents of social control:

(a) Gossip,
(b) Rumour,
(c) Ridicule,
(d) Public opinion,
(e) Custom,
(f) Traditions—folkways and mores, and
(g) Law.

These agents of social control work through the following groups,

(1) Family,
(2) Neighbourhood,
(3) Play,
(4) Age,
(5) Sex,
(6) Caste,
(7) Class, and
(8) Associations, organisations and Institutions.

Some of the agents of social control which require certain classifications and illustrations are as follows:

Folkways

Folkways are informal rules of behaviour based on habit and tradition, mostly found in usages. A child will eat with hand or spoon, will put on a dhoti or a trouser, etc., as decided by the present modes in the groups, or the society, of which he is a member. Customs and traditions are nothing but folkways which have persisted over a relatively long period of time and have attained a degree of formal recognition so as to be passed from one generation to another. Benedict has very clearly given the role of custom in the life of an individual. From the movement of his birth, the customs into which he is born, shape his experience and behaviour. By the time he can talk, he is a little creation of his culture and by the time he is grown up and able to take part in its activities, its habits are his habits, its beliefs his beliefs, its impositions his impositions. A clear knowledge and understanding of these values therefore becomes imperative for a development worker. He has to know the background of these values and the processes which give them strength.

Mores

Some of the values take the form of mores, like folkways, they are popular usages and traditions. "They are behaviour patterns of a group to which conformity is required, on pain of group coercion." Whether a person in utter poverty will accept charity or not is decided by the mores, whether a hungry person will enter a shop and steal bread and satisfy his needs or he will die of hunger is decided by the mores of the group. Mores are more powerful than the folkways in conditioning man's behaviour. They are more or less obligatory.

Law

Social values are given the shape of law for strict adherence and compliance. But some of the laws do not receive the desired acceptance by the people and their legal enforcement creates so many other social problems. Such laws may not represent public opinion in the true sense, though they may be for the public good.

People need to be properly educated to obey the law.

Thus, we see that social values and social controls are effective means of guiding and controlling the behaviour of the people. Desired social values will help in the proper growth of social structure and social function. The outward values may isolate a group from the rest of the society by the rigidity of their use. Giving importance to 'groupism' and 'casteism' through these values will surely hamper the cause of the society, the nation and the world. The development worker has always to keep these things in mind while working with the people. People do not function in isolation but rather in a complex framework. They are influenced by so many factors of which. 'Social Values' and 'Social Controls' are the two patent factors.

RURAL AND URBAN LIFE

Environment effects human life to a greater extent. Human beings live into two types of environments—namely rural and urban. There is a difference in the social life of both these environments. Here we shall attempt contrast between rural and urban life. Before we differentiate between rural and urban life, we must study the characteristics of both.

Characteristics of rural society

We can study a rural society on the following basis:

Close contact with nature

Rural society has close contact with nature. It means that the rural people are primarily influenced by the natural environment. Sorokin and Zimmerman[1] have written, ' Further he (the farmer) is in as much greater proximity to and in a more direct relation with nature, soil, flora, fauna, and so on than an urbanite... ..Only the walls of his farm-house or hut separate him from nature, when he is in doors. While he is outdoors, he is at all times amidst nature, whatever it may be."

The villagers have to depend so much on nature, that it becomes the significant part of their life. For them nature is the all in all. In their day to day life, they have to face storms, fogs, heat, etc. Bertrand[2] has remarked, "In so doing, he develops customs, practices and personality traits compatible with his struggle with nature". The villagers have association with land because land is their real mother. Only the land gives them food to eat and cotton for clothes. Land is their property and they depend on it throughout the life. The close contact of the ruralite with the soil tend to make his view of land as the most precious of possession.[3]

Agriculture as the main occupation

Agriculture is the fundamental occupation in the rural society. According to Smith[4] agriculture and its enterprises are the basis of the rural economy, 'farmer'. Agriculture is such an occupation, in which a farmer is concerned with national goods such as plants, trees, animals, etc. An agriculturist has multifarious needs and he has to learn so many things. In other words, he has to become a jack of all trades (carpenter, blacksmith). Agriculture is an occupation in which the assistance of so many persons are needed. Ordinarily the members of the entire family have to share in agricultural functions. Nelson[5] has remarked that "Farming is family enterprise". Much of the significance of family is due to its participation in agricultural performance. Most of the thinkers are of the opinion that rural society is familistic. Not only this, the neighbour of the agriculturist are also agriculturists, that is why they have close contact and also cooperate in their day to day activities. The majority of the population in the village is engaged in agriculture.

Smaller in size

The village communities are smaller in size in comparison with urban communities. As Smith[6] has remarked "Small community and rural community have become syno-

[1]P.A. Sorokin and Carle Zimmerman, *Principle of Rural-Urban Sociology*, p. 17.
[2]Bertrand, et. al., *Rural Sociology*, p. 25.
[3]Ibid. p 27.
[4]L. Smith, *The Sociology of Rural Life*, p. 18.
[5]Lowry Nelson, *Rural Sociology*, p. 18.
[6]T. Lynn Smith, *The Sociology of Rural Life*, p. 20.

nymous". We know that agriculture is the fundamental occupation in the rural communities. For agriculture, some land is required. The minimum size of land should be at least one acre per cultivator. In case, there are about hundred cultivators, they need at least one hundreds acres of land. Whereas in urban areas thousands of people live on hundred of acres of land. In urban areas, there is scarcity of land, but not in rural areas. Robert Redfield has called the rural community the *Little Community*, because of its smaller size.

Less population

In a rural community, the density of population is low. Low density is due to its fundamental occupation. Sumner and Keller[1] have remarked, "Out of the blocks of customs thus evolved, controlled issue of all human institutions. Hence, the type of society institutions derives ultimately from the ratio of men to land. Because of low density of population, the inhabitants of the community have intimate relations. Coley has termed such relations face to face or primary relations. There is no problem of overcrowding or hue and cry. The atmosphere is quite peaceful and calm.

Homogeneity of population

Village communities are homogeneous in nature. Normally, most of its inhabitants are agriculturists or are indirectly connected with agriculture, although the rural population consists of people belonging to different castes, religions, and classes.

Social stratification

In rural society, social stratification is traditional one. It is not divided into many stratas. Theosophical classes are found less in number in comparison with that of urban society.

Social interaction

The frequency of social interaction is low in the rural communities, that is why the processes of interaction are few, but they have greater stability and continuity. Normally, the processes of cooperation and conflict are seen in the village life.

According to Sorokin,[2] "The rural social telephone system is composed of permanent private lines, which go directly from farmer to farmer, often without the mediation of a central station, and are used by each individual, so to speak, permanently. Lines are few, but permanent and direct."

Social mobility

The rural society is not so mobile as urban society is. The rural people hardly shift from one social status to another. It is because of the fact that social status and occupations are limited. Further the process of social change is also very low. The villagers hardly prefer to go from one place to another. According to Sorokin and Zimmerman[3], "The rural community is similar to calm water in a pool".

[1]Sumner and Keller, *The Science of Society*, Vol. I, page 4.
[2]Sorokin and Zimmerman, *Principle of Rural Urban Sociology*, p. 52.
[3]Ibid, p. 44.

Social solidarity

The rural communities are stronger than urban ones. In other words, the degree of social solidarity is greater in the villages. Common experience, common aims, common purposes, common customs and traditions are the basis of the unity in the villages. Giddings formulated the concept of consciousness of kind on the basis of such a unity. The basis of village unity is informal relations or direct relations. According to Smith[1] "In essence it is based upon very informal and non-contractual relationships".

In the preceeding pages, we have talked about the characteristics of rural life. Before we make contrasts between rural and urban life, it would be better to study the characteristics of urban life too.

Characteristics of urban life

(1) *No fundamental occupation:* There is no fundamental occupation in urban societies. There are numerable occupations. Such multiplicity of occupations are responsible for differences from rural life.

(2) *Over population:* The cities are densely populated. Such density is primarily responsible for the different social problems, such as slums, housing, crime, juvenile delinquency, etc.

(3) *Heterogeneity of population:* Different types of population are seen in the cities belonging to different places, religions, castes, classes, races, communities, etc. Economic differences are also found in the cities along with cultural differences. Such differences give rise to many problems in social life.

(4) *Secondary relations:* In cities, the social relations are secondary and formal. They can be called indirect. There is a lesser degree of intimacy.

(5 *Division of labour:* Because of the multiplicity of occupations, division of labour specialisations can be seen in the cities.

(6) *Interdependence:* The entire urban life is interdependent because of the division of labour and specialisation.

(7) *Social mobility.* The degree of social mobility is greater in cities. The people frequently shift from one occupation to another or from one place to another place, also leading towards a change in their social status.

Contrast between rural and urban life

It is not an easy job to put contrast between rural and urban life. Sometimes, to decide which should be called a village or which should be called a city. Secondly, there is no universal definition of a village or a city. Thirdly, the difference between rural and urban life is a matter of degree. Fourthly, the changing character of a village and a city is also creating a problem in distinguishing between rural and urban life. Bergal[2] has remarked, "Everybody seems to know what a city is but no one has given a satisfactory definition. MacIver and Page[3] have also pointed out that between the two, there

---

[1] T. Lynn Smith, *The Sociology of Rural Life*, p. 36.
[2] Bergel, *Urban Sociology*, p. 5.
[3] MacIver and Page, *Society*, p. 311.

is no sharp demarcation to tell where city ends and country begins". In this context, Gist & Halbert[1] have remarked. "Thus the frontier dichotomy between rural and urban is more of a theoretical concept than a division based upon the facts of community life."

CHAPTER 16

VILLAGE PATTERNS AND MODES OF LIVING

ORIGIN OF VILLAGES

The origin of villages takes place in two ways:

A. With the development of knowledge, members of a group or tribe leading a nomadic or unsettled life come to a settled one. This has happened in nearly all the old settled countries like India, China, etc.

B. Development of villages by transfer or shifts in population, which has been the case in the USA, Israel. The villages are also rehabilitated by settling the refugees as has been done by settling of refugees from Pakistan in India.

EMERGENCE OF VILLAGES

First method

The emergence of villages at a certain stage in the evolution of the life of man and its further growth and development in subsequent periods of human history depend upon various types of structural changes, the industrial revolution, etc.

This emergence of a village signifies that man has passed from the nomadic form of collective life to the settled one. This was basically due to the improvement of tools and implements of production in agriculture, which made agriculture their occupation and the settled life on a fixed territorial zone became possible.

The village development study covers how humanity in different parts of the world passed from the nomadic, hunting and food gathering stage, to that based on hoe-agriculture, and after that to a settled plough-agriculture where the use of draft animals was also adopted.

With the emergence of the plough, man made agriculture as a stable profession, and a basic source of assured food supply. He left nomadic life. The settlement was made on a definite territory and its organisation was based on agricultural economy. With differences in geographical environment, villages developed on different pattern underwent changes in the technical, economic and various social aspects.

Second method

When the population of a place shifts from settled villages to rehabilitate a new area, they try to settle, villages according to the new conditions and also find a new pattern which is convenient to them, as regards, to their municipal and community services. They try to avoid the drawbacks of their previous settlements. The USA, Israel, and some other countries have made such trials and Israel provides a sort of laboratory where different villages and patterns of living are available.

TYPES OF VILLAGES

There can be four criteria for classifying villages:

First criterion

(a) *Migratory villages:* In such villages, people live for months, arrange food supplies from natural sources in the form of wild fruits, animals, etc. When the food supply of a place is exhausted, they shift to another place, where they can find better supplies.

(b) *Semi-permanent villages:* The inhabitants stay at a place for a few years and afterwards, when they feel that the place has exhausted its capacity to provide food supplies and the soil has been also depeted to produce better crops due to their wrong way of cultivation, they move to another place, and settle in new villages of the same type. They keep animals like goats and cows, graze them and eat them. They generally burn the small trees, bushes, etc., and spread seed over this ash and it gives them some crops after rainfall. The soil is not cultivated or ploughed, and so most of the food material from the soil is washed during the rains. The Jhum cultivation in some parts of the tribal areas of India is a typical example.

(c) *Permanent villages:* In such villages, the settled human aggregates live for generations. They develop their farm practices, village organisations and social relations with the neighbouring villages. After some time, they organise a local or regional government. The villages of India, USA, England, Germany, etc., where the residents form a compact village group, fall in this category. This settlement may be of any type, which we shall discuss under separate heads, but the residents should stay permanently. The population of each village varies from a few households or families to even 10,000 persons as in the Indian villages, which are given a status of Town Area when they exceed this number of inhabitants. Loomis and Beegle have given the name 'hamlet' to villages which have less than 250 persons, from 250 to 999 villages, from 1000 to 2499 towns, and places over 2500 cities. In the USA, the position is different because of lesser population.

Second criterion

According to another classification, the types of villages can be given on a settlement basis such as:

(a) *Grouped or nucleated villages:* In the grouped or nucleated villages, the residents dwell in a cluster. Their farms are spread around the village dwellings. Their farm land may be in a block or the fields may be scattered in many plots. As they dwell in a single habitat, they develop a compact life. They have the advantage of municipal and other services. Their life is more social but when the fields are far away, they have to spend sufficient time on going to and coming back from their farms.

(b) *Dispersed villages:* In the case of dispersed or non-nucleated villages, the farmers live separately in their respective farms. Their habitats being thus dispersed, their social life assumes a different form.

Third criterion

The third criterion can be based on social stratification and ownership of land. According to this, village aggregates can be grouped into:

(1) Peasant joint owners,

(2) Peasant joint tenants,

(3) Farmers who are generally owners, including some tenants and labourers,

(4) Individual farmer tenants,

(5) Employees of big landowners, and

(6) Labourers and employees in the State Government, or corporation, or mines, or industries, etc.

Fourth criterion

This criterion is based on an organisation systems of villages.

(a) *Cooperative villages:* Individual farmers may cultivate their land separately or in joint groups, and may receive their common services from a cooperative store, cooperative implement shed and common municipality services. The *Moshav Obidim* type villages of Israel, cooperative villages of India, saxon villages of Germany, etc., fall in this group.

(b) *Semi-collective villages:* In such villages, the land belongs to the collective body of the villagers. People work on their farm as a collective body, i e., all production sources are owned and worked as a collective unit. As regards the consumption each gets a monthly or annual quota fixed according to the income of the whole village and purchases his supplies quota as he likes. He can save, or overspend, but the collective village has not to be worried about it. The Moshavim Shitufim type villages of Israel and the present working of the villages, received by Vinoba Bhave as, 'Gramdan' in India are settled along these lines. In these villages, income has nothing to do with the number of hours put in by a member or family, but the families receive their quota based on the number of members. The Kolkhoz villages of the USSR differ in that there people get their income according to the number of labour units provided by the members.

(c) *Collective villages:* These are communal, collective settlements, where all property is collectively owned and worked in an organised way on a collective basis. The land, and all property, belongs to the village, the members give their labour to the common pool and get all supplies of food, housing, clothing, education, cultural and social services and whatever is required and is within the means of the village. There is one dining hall for the whole village, which also have a communal kindergartens and children's houses, with common stores. Individual houses are provided to couples or bachelor quarters are given to the unmarried. The old people are also maintained from the common pool. It gives full security for life to a person and his children and dependents. Wives and husbands are separate members. There is no entrance nor membership fee when one joins and nothing is to be distributed when a member leaves a village. The collective villages of Israel are a good example. These are called Kibbutzim in Hebrew (singular Kibbuta).

PATTERN OF SETTLEMENT

According to pattern of settlement, the following classification is given:

(1) Village settlement.
(2) Scattered settlement.
(3) Cross-road settlement.
(4) Line settlement.
(5) Circular settlement.
(6) Regional settlement.

(1) Village settlement

(a) *Unplanned nucleated villages*

Such villages exist in all the older countries, where people developed their houses around a centre, or nucleus, generally the village office, chapel or community centre. The roads and streets are laid zigzag. As they are developed in the absence of a plan organised by local governments, they took any shape. Generally, people with high position in the village society have their houses in the centre and the people who serve these rich or high strata, reside on one side of the village. In villages in India, the *Chamars*, *Bhangis* and shepherds (lower strata) generally live on the outskirts of the village (See Fig. 16.1).

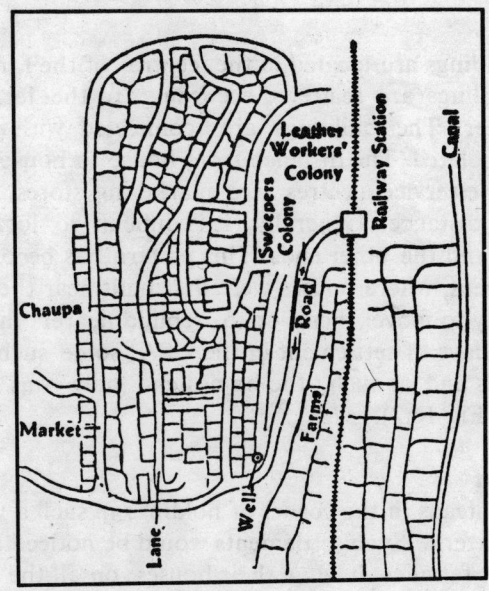

Fig. 16.1. Unplanned village Khekra, Meerut (U.P.) Patti—Tampur.

(b) *Planned village settlements*

In countries where people came from some other region or country and formed new villages during the past 100 or 200 years, they have planned villages. This type of villages are organised in the USA by placing the farmsteads in a compact unit and the number of farm families that can be brought together in a given village is theoretically limited. The size of a village is generally a compromise between the disadvantages of travelling considerable distances from village residences to the farm operating units on the one hand and the social and institutional advantages which accrue from having a relatively large cluster of families per village.

The farmers of the USA who are living in such settlements generally give the following advantages of these villages: (1) that the size, shape and organisation of the farm need in no way be conditioned by the location of the house and other farm buildings upon it, since it is purely a farm-operating unit and not a given farm family to own a number of pieces of land, each adapted to a particular type of use but located separately and at considerable distance one from the other, and (2) that there are great social and community advantages in the village type of settlement ranging from maintenance and support of such standard institutions as schools, churches, etc., for more sociability.

But there are some disadvantages too, which are: (1) the travel between the residence and fields and pastures increases costs and jeopardises immediately the constant supervision, especially of livestock, (2) the location of the livestock in the villages, especially during the winter months, creates problems of sanitation and makes necessary the hauling of animal manure to a considerable distance from the village to farms, and (3) fragmentation of holdings. It has been seen among the Russians and Hebrews, and among the early New Englanders and also among some Normans in the USA.

(2) Scattered settlement

In this the farm buildings are located in the centre of the farm area of a farmer and in this way the buildings are scattered according to the farm areas owned or cultivated by each farmer. The buildings are connected with the county service road. The families are isolated. The distance from house to house varies according to the size of holdings. The service centres like marketing stores, cafe, schools, hospitals, etc., may be at a distance. Generally, it is difficult to locate in some areas, where one village starts and the other ends. This pattern has become almost universal in the USA. In many areas, where houses were first built near the centre of the unit, there has been a tendency to move them or to rebuild nearer the road and edge of the farms. In the early days of settlement in the USA, some such houses were at a distance of up to $1\frac{1}{2}$ miles and as such, the homestead area was separated from the nearest neighbour (See Fig 16.2).

(3) Cross-road settlement

Establishment of farmsteads in the corner of holdings in such a way that several lie juxtaposed makes this pattern. Such settlements would be noticed in sporadic patches at many places, e.g. four families having their houses on all the corners of a cross-road. There are numerous examples where farmsteads in America, previously located on individual farms as scattered houses, turned themselves into cross-road settlements. In the USA, two patterns of small clustered settlements namely *hexagon form* and "*E*" *Pattern* were sought to be planned years back, but they could not be given the practical shape. In 1896, Mr. William Penn is said to have considered using a hexagon pattern for Nebraska in the USA. It is believed that this form would have

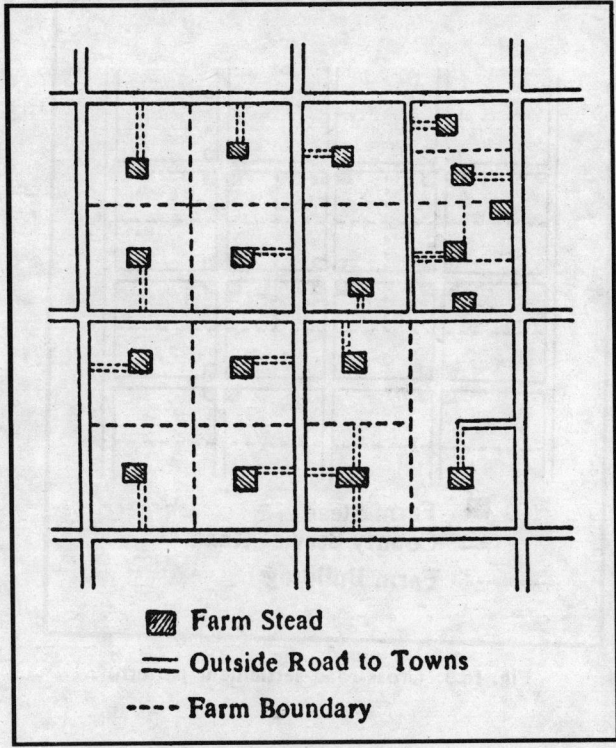

Farm Stead

Outside Road to Towns

Farm Boundary

Fig. 16.2. Scattered village.

been a drawback because practically every field and every crop row within a field, would have turned at an acute angles (See Fig. 16.3).

The "F" pattern of settlement groups have eight farm houses. The houses are located on the county service road (See Fig. 16.4).

(4) Line settlement

In this type of settlement, houses can be located on the individual farms according to the choice of each farm family. They can be evenly spaced with equal distance between them, grouped by two or four at the corners of the farms, be located exactly opposite each other or systematically staggered on the two sides of the road if it is preferred to have the farmstead near the centre of the farm. These can also be called "string towns". Such villages in the USA came into existence chiefly under French influence. They also developed in the Southern New England area of the USA (Connecticut Valley), the Quebec Province of Canada and France. In such settlements, the relationships of the farm family to the land are constant and unbroken, economic activities are highly integrated and coordinated, but social activities operate more haphazardly. Children may be sent in one direction to school; the family may go in another on Sunday to gather at some church. For meetings, they have to build a central place on the road-side. Similarly, village trading centres are developed for disposal of produce or purchase of their goods (See Fig. 16.5).

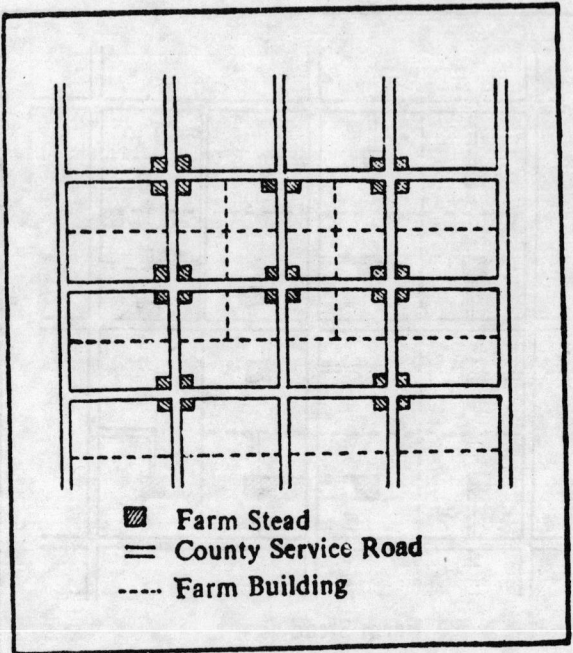

Fig. 16.3. Cross-road settlement pattern.

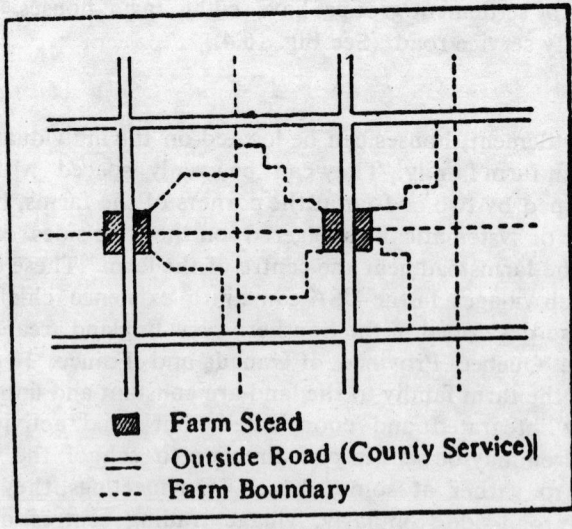

Fig. 16.4. Cross-road settlement pattern 'F'.

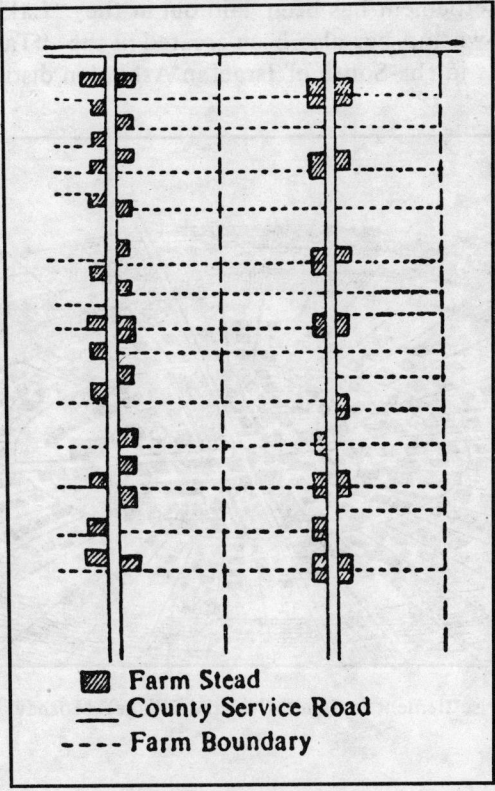

Farm Stead
County Service Road
Farm Boundary

Fig. 16.5. Line settlement pattern.

(5) Circular settlement

The Nahalal village of Israel, in the Gallilee area (North), is a good example of it. It was founded in 1917. All the common buildings like village dispensary, veterinary hospital, cooperative stores, schools are located in the centre. Around there is a circular road and then the farmsteads-residential building in the front, then dairy shed, poultry building, implement store and other such buildings. Behind each farmer's building is his farm area spreading out to the out-boundary of the village. It.has the disadvantages that the farm plots have to be broader on one side towards the outskirt and narrower towards the centre of the village or face of the buildings. If plots are to be made rectangular, some land on the sides has to be left unused. Due to this defect, they had to leave the idea of planning such villages. The aerial photo of the village is just like a bullock-cart wheel and looks very nice, as shown in Fig. 16.6.

(6) Regional settlement

About 4 to 8 (marked A in Fig. 16.7) villages are located around a centre (marked B) having marketing, school, hospital and other such facilities. Again, five more such centres are grouped in a large unit (marked C) having wider facilities like a college, big hospital, veterinary hospital, industrial area, etc., and formed into a township. All the villages have a good approach from different angles to their central or regional area. Such a regional settlement has been laid out in the "Lakhish area" in Israel since 1954. A similar township has also been created in the "Tanakh area" of Israel in the North. Lakhish is in the South of Israel in Ashkalon district.

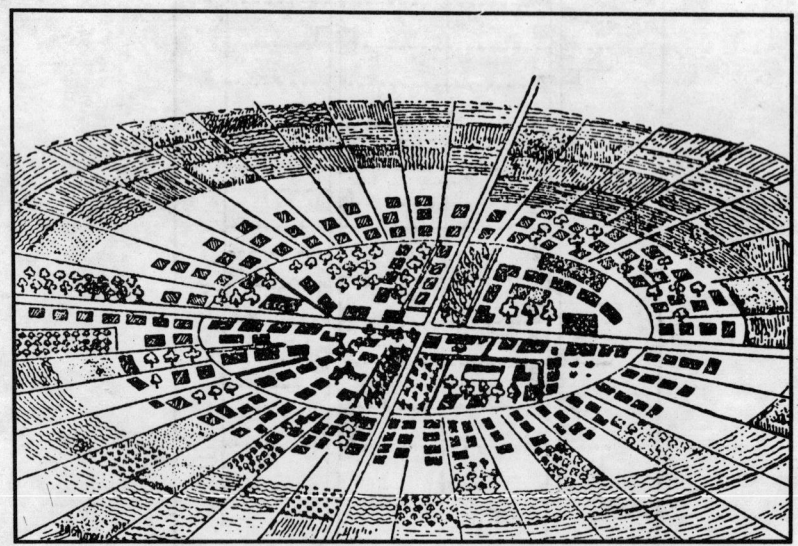

Fig. 16.6. Circular settlement in Israel (Nahalal village) Moshav Ovdim type.

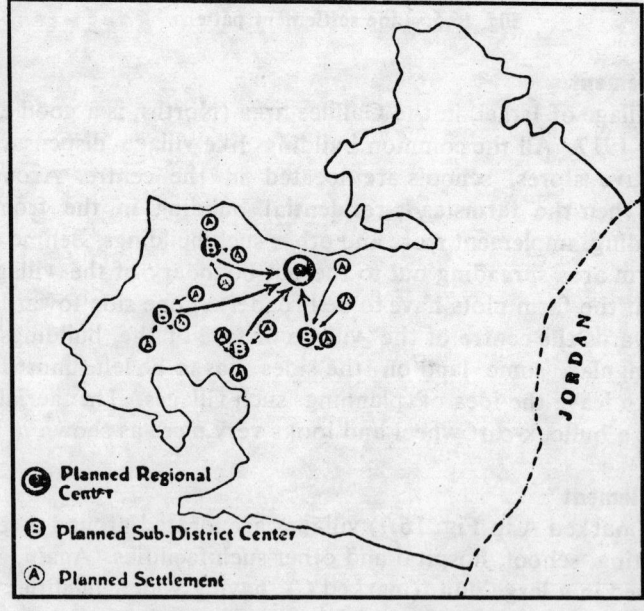

Fig. 16.7. Regional settlement, Lakhish (Israel).

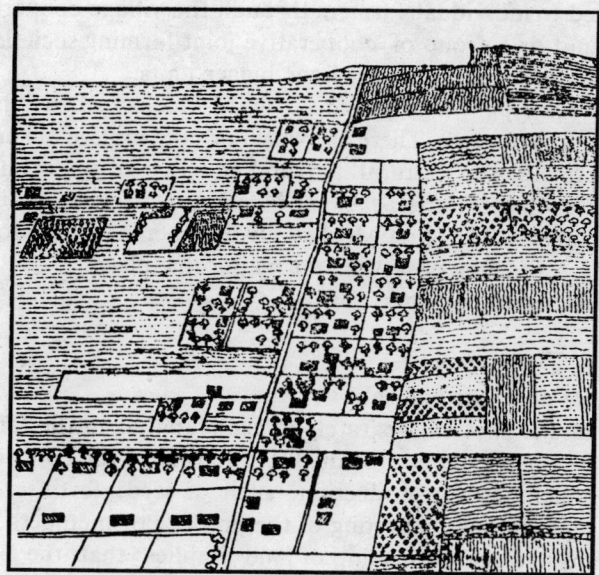

Fig. 16.8. Cooperative village of Israel (Moshav) private homes,
individual and collective plots.

VILLAGE TYPES ON LANDOWNERSHIP BASIS

(a) Landlord villages

In such villages, the land is owned by an individual family or a number of families or owners. This co-sharing or landowning body has proprietary rights over the land and gives it to the tenants, who may again sub-let it to other tenants. The landowner charges a rent from the tenant and pays out of it a certain percentage to the government or king or any superior authority as revenue. He keeps a good percentage for himself and his family. Such type of villages existed in India before the abolition of the Intermediary Landlordism System in India i.e., before 1952, when the Zamindari (Landlord) system was abolished. There are still some countries where there are such villages.

(b) Peasant proprietor's villages

In such villages, the farmers themselves are the owners of the land they cultivate. They pay to the government certain revenue direct without any intermediary. Such villages are known "Ryotwari" villages in India, where the land is owned by "Ryot" or cultivators, who they are responsible for payment of the Government revenue to the treasury. After abolition of landlordism in India, all villages fall in this category. In countries, where there is no intermediary between the Government and the man cultivating the land, the peasant proprietary system is prevalent.

(c) Cooperative villages

In such villages, land may be owned by the individual farmers, or by the whole village, or a common body, as in Israel where land is owned by the Jewish National

Fund. It is alloted to individual farmers through the village cooperative, and cultivated as one farm unit or a group of cooperative joint farming societies, system that is being pushed in India to make the holdings bigger units.

(i) *Moshav Ovidim type village of Israel* (plural Moshavim Ovidim): This is a good example of cooperative village. There are workers' cooperative of small holders' settlements based on principles of natural aid and equality of opportunity. The farmers who founded these villages in Israel were idealists who believed in self-labour, and equality of all members. The first Moshav Ovdim, Nahalal, a circular village, was founded in 1917. A Moshav observes four main principles:

(a) National ownership of land,

(b) Self-labour,

(c) Mutual aid, and

(d) Cooperative purchase and sale.

In these, the land is allotted separately to each family and the farm operations are also carried out by the members individually. The role of the cooperative largely consists in providing facilities for production, such as seed, fertiliser, plant protection, etc., and also in undertaking marketing of the produce of members of Moshav.

The principle of national ownership of land implies that the land in this type of settlement is not the property of the individual members. Their right is essentially the right to cultivate and pass it on to their descendants. They cannot sub-divide or alienate the land. The area per family differs from one village to another, but within the village, a member is allotted as much land (partly irrigated and partly otherwise) as he can cultivate himself with the help of the members of his own family. All members in the village get an equal area of land. No member can employ hired labour without the permission of the cooperative, because they enforce the principle of self-labour. The intention behind it is that there should be no exploitation of hired labour.

A large number of activities in these types of villages are carried out on a cooperative basis, and, to a certain extent, these activities correspond with the activities generally associated, with a village multipurpose cooperative society in and country like India. Besides these, it carries out municipal functions, such as sanitation, education, health, etc. Entertainment is also handled by it. In some settlements of this kind, there may be separate organisations for a group of functions. It tries to function on a no-profit, no-loss basis in respect of each branch of activities. The annual surplus is distributed amongst the members in proportion to purchases from or sales to the cooperative. In case of loss, the amount is recovered from the members on a per capita basis. In this way, the members who do not use the local store for buying, but divert their shopping to a nearby town, may be called upon to make up the loss caused by the diminution of the turnover. As they do not make any profit, no income-tax is to be paid. If they need some reserve, members meet and decide the share capital and amount of share for each member. This is deducted from annual sales.

(ii) *Middle class farmer's cooperative villages of Israel:* They are just like Moshavim Ovidim but in these members do not have any ideological objection to engaging hired labour to assist them in agricultural operations.

(d) Collective villages

Such villages have been organised in the USSR, Israel and China. In the USSR, they are called "Kolkhoz" and in Israel "Kibbutz". About 25 per cent of the total agricultural population of Israel lives in such villages. Their number is 230 at present. About 45 of these are 15 years old, or more, and their population varies between 500 and 1500. About 100 are 15 and 44 years old. The rest have been found after 1948 when Israel became free from British rule.

Working in a Kibbutz: The plural is "Kibbutzim". It is a Hebrew term representing a mode of collective life—a commune or kuvtzc. It is free association of people, where all property is jointly owned and there are no individual shares, entrance fees, or distribution of property when a member leaves the settlement. Every member has to act as a part of the community, and acts on its behalf. He never fulfills any economic function in a private capacity. The wife and husband are members separately. The members give their labour to the common stock and receive from the settlement the satisfaction of their needs in accordance with the principles and financial means of the settlement.

For running the various activities of the village, the following committees or bodies are formed: (1) General body, (2) Farm committee, (3) Work committee, (4) Purchase committee, (5) Special farming committee, (6) Educational committee, (7) Cultural committee (8) Member's committee, (9) Health committee, (10) Security committee, (11) Relative's committee, and (12) Special Committees for Games, Political Affairs, etc. The various committees work in close coordination with each other.

Agriculture in a Kibbutz: Due to high organisation and specialised training of the farmers, the per labour unit return is very high. The competition of the national organisation of Kibbutzim with national organisations of other types of settlements, the pioneering spirit of the settlers, the competition amongst the Kibbutzim themselves, the hope of higher security and higher standards of living and the love for the country of the new immigrants, etc., has helped them to attain a very high standard of production. At present, about 36 per cent of all agricultural production in Israel comes from Kibbutzim. The average milk production in many old established Kibbutzim is over 8,000 kg., annual egg production per lying hen is over 230 (See Fig. 16.9).

The Einsurim village in the South gives a clear picture how the Kibbutzim have given a higher standard of living to Israelies as compared to a typical Arab village on the opposite side of the settlement. This village had a bull "Marshall 575", whose 80 daughters gave an average of over 8,000 kg of milk till 1956.

Needs of the people: The Kibbutz provides housing facilities together with furniture and other equipment. It runs a common kitchen and a dining hall, where food is provided free to all members and their families. It provides free clothing and gives choice in design. It provides free medical aid and looks after all the requirements of the members.

Work: The Works Committee elected each year, just like the other committees, evolves a workable system. Most of the members are given permanent assignments to suit their aptitude and training. In some cases, where jobs are not so skilled, they are rotated.

Every evening, when members are in the dining hall for their supper and recreational programmes, the branch committees have their meetings and work out their requirements of labour for the coming day. The Work Committee finds out the changes to be made for the following day's work and assignments, prepares the list of

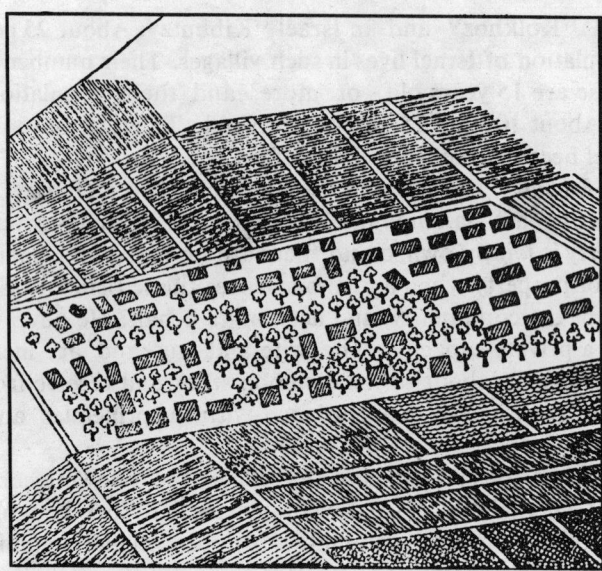

Fig. 16.9. Collective villages of Israel (Kibbutz) houses in the mid and farms, dairy, poultry, etc. outside.

changes and puts it on the notice board before the members leave for their homes to sleep.

Other specialities

(1) *The Kibbutz believes in equality:* In case it is short of any supply, all share equally in the hardship. Sometimes, in cases like distribution of houses, seniority of a member in the village, i.e., the date a member joined the Kibbutz, is given a priority.

(2) *No money transaction.*

(3) *It is a classless society:* The senior author, while he was in Kibbutz Givet-Hayim, in the north of Israel in March, 1956, saw a member of Parliament, a representative from this tract and a member of the Kibbutz, serving food to other members and collecting dishes for washing. Similarly, the Minister of Agriculture, who was a member of "Digania Aleph", the first Kibbutz settled in 1909, stayed in the village and worked as member when he had not to attend the Parliament and other offical meetings. The ex-Prime Minister of Israel, Mr. David Ben Gurion founded a new village in the desert area of Bersheba, and used to shear his sheep just like any farmer.

(4) *Motivation within a Kibbutz:* For an outsider who has not stayed in a Kibbutz, it is hard to believe that the Kibbutz does not believe in assessing the work of its individual member on the basis of any norms, and that no wages are paid, since each member receives from the Kibbutz, by way of services and goods, whatever he needs, and the Kibbutz can afford. It is certainly not for economic or individual gain. The senior author put this question to Mrs. Lili of Kibbutz Givet-Hayim and also verified it from the Indian Jews, who have settled in that Kibbutz, and then watched it for two weeks by living with them and working with them in each branch. The settlers very

proudly said that the Hebrew language a special term 'Hakkara' signified the sense of moral responsibility felt by every member of a Kibbutz towards realisation of its goals. The term explains the intangible factors providing the motive power for action within a Kibbutz. A high sense of duty, devotion to a cause, the spiritual satisfaction, the prosperity of the village hoped for by the members, and the security for them and their coming generations motivates them.

What facilitated the establishment of kibbutzim in Israel

Before 1948, the Kibbutz movement was helped by the consideration that it provided an effective weapon in the struggle for survival by the Jewish settlers in Palestine. New membership also continued to flow into the Kibbutz through recruitment from the Jewish Youth Movements, which were flourishing in various European countries. Another extraneous factor which facilitated the establishment of Kibbutzim was the national ownership of the land.

Can Kibbutz be an ideal village for other countries who want to change the old pattern of settlements ? A case for the Gramdan Movement[1] villages in India.

The Kibbutz movement was the result of the peculiar faith which animated its founders and its subsequent adherents. Such faith is, however, generally absent in the new Jewish immigrants who have come into Israel from various Asian and African countries. That is very well indicated from the fact that during the last about 22 years or so, no new Kibbutzim have been established. It has been observed that within the Kibbutzim itself, in recent years, there has been a perceptible tendency towards relaxation in some of the practices, which had characterised a Kibbutz in the early period. For instance, collective dining used to be insisted upon in all Kibbutzim. Now, some of the members are allowed to carry food, on certain days, from the common kitchen to their quarters. Similarly, each member of the Kibbutz is assigned some money for purchasing some items of his or her personal choice. Sufficient choice is given in selecting the clothes in the stores. These developments indicate that the Kibbutz is gradually transforming towards the semi-collective settlements called Moshavim Shitufim where production is collective, while consumption is on individual basis.

In the beginning women used to work for most of their time in pursuits which are done in other countries by males. Now, the tendency is that more and more women work-hours are being given to house-keeping, etc. Many women have also not reconciled themselves to the system of children's education and upbringing as it seems to have frustrated their deep seated natural maternal instincts. There are many instances where families have left a Kibbutz for the reason that the wife could not accept the way of living in a Kibbutz.

The very example of Digania "A", the collective village where children are kept with their parents throughout night, proves that they feel that it is not good to keep young children away from their parents in the night. They have found out that in the case of young children, the beds were soiled a greater number of times when they were away from their parents in the Children houses, than when the children spent the nights with their parents.

---

1 "Gramdan Movement": These villages have been received by Vinoba Bhave as donations, which we have dealt in Chapter 40 of this book.

Thus it shows that it was for a certain cause that the Israelies were forced to live for others who were not in the same condition or do not have similar problems. The movement had a strong fascination for persons, who had and still have a high moral faith. Living in a Kibbutz is considered to be living on "the crest of the wave of the Jewish Renaissance in Israel".

(e) Semi-collective village

It is a hybrid form, synthesising certain features of the cooperative village with those of the collective 'Moshav Shitufi'. It is an agricultural settlement in which members conduct all farm and other operations, jointly, with the pooling of land, equipment, etc., while the individuals have separate homes and lead their own private lives separately. Thus, on one hand, by collective production, it is like a Kibbutz, while the consumption side or living is like Moshav Ovidim. Each family is paid a certain amount according to the number of members in the family and also according to the financial position of the village. Out of this amount, they make their purchases from a cooperative store, as they like. As in the case of Kibbutz, the main activity of Moshav Shitufi centres around joint management of the agricultural economy. Most of the techniques and practices followed are similar. There is a labour committee which assigns work to various members. The women are full-fledged members of the cooperative and may work in their own homes or in their vegetable gardens. On the basis of the age of the children in a family, calculations are made to determine the hours to be devoted to household work by a woman. Her public duties, if any, are only supplementary to the housekeeping hours. If any woman falls ill and is unable to attend to her household duties, some other woman is appointed by the labour committee to look after her household duties.

The first settlement of this type was founded about 30 years back. Since then only 30 settlements of this type could be established. Mostly, the ex-servicemen have favoured it. They had developed a comradeship during their active services, but did not like the common kitchen and dress, etc., of which they were fed up.

Moshav Shitufi Pattern for India: In India, during the past few decades, the joint families have changed their shape. Formerly, they did not divide their sources of production, i.e., land and other allied occupations. Now, due to the adjustment difficulties of the new blood, i.e. the daughters-in-law, who come from other family, cannot adjust to their mothers-in-law what they were expected to be thirty years back. They eat and cook separately and make arrangements whereby separate rooms, or even a house, is given to them to live as a separate family. However, they still have to take part in the common family occupation as members of a team. This was found to be a good adjustment to the changing conditions. It enabled the family to maintain an economic and cultivable size of holding and to pull on, with the joint family as a member of the production unit. At the same time, the separate and independent entity of individual living is there, because the wife, the husband and their children cook and sleep separately, and can claim that what they have in their room or house as their's.

This adjustment clearly shows that there is a scope for Moshavim Shitufim type of villages in the villages donated to Shri Vinoba Bhave, under the Gramdan movement, totalling about 5807 in number.[1] But adjustments are essential for adapting it under Indian conditions. It is a fact that when Indian Jews can adjust in Kibbutz in Israel, their brothers and relatives left in India can also very well adjust to semi-collective life. Since our holdings are very small and we want cooperative farming, it is easier to mix it with the present life of our disintegrated joint families and turn a few villages, first as pilot experiments, towards Moshav Shitufi type villages.

CHAPTER 17

VILLAGE LIFE AND
RURAL SOCIAL INSTITUTIONS IN INDIA

VILLAGE LIFE IN INDIA

The study of the Indian rural society, which varies from region to region or even district to district due to the extreme geographical, economic, historical, ethnic and other peculiarities, is very essential for carrying out a programme of rural extension. India, being a classic land of agriculture, has a complex organisation and religious life, varied cultural patterns and also diversification of customs, traditions, mores, governed by caste and community rules.

Concept of community life

Wherever the members of any group, small or large, live together in such a way that they share the basic conditions of communal life, we call that group a community. A person's social relationship is found within this community, and the work of the community is to provide conditions that one's life may be lived wholly within it.

Human beings and families come together for specific purposes because of their common interest and thus form themselves into communities. There are religious communities, economic communities, social communities and so on.

With the development of agriculture at a certain level, mankind took the leap from a totalistic collectivist, clan society to a territorial civil society with its distinct mutli-class social structure and the resultant institutions of the state.

Civilisation thus began with the development of agriculture. The village, the first settled form of collective human habitation and the product of growth of agricultural economy, thus historically gave birth to rural society and from the surplus of its food resources nourished the town, which subsequently came into existence.

Structure of rural society

Rural society comprises of all persons residing in an administrative unit of a village. It is characterised by isolation, and hence the economic features develop around its regional self-sufficiency. The unit of production is the family, which tries to produce much of its required goods. What it does not produce is produced by artisans, residing mostly in the same, or neighbouring villages. There is a lesser degree of competition for goods, power and status. Agriculture and industries are closely connected and are mainly characterised by local environment. Culture tends to be regional and develops out of local environment.

The structure of the society can be studied under heads like family life, racial element, caste system, etc.

FAMILY LIFE

The groupings that come into the existence in the villages may have for their immediate cause and as binding force, several principles of integration. The simplest and most obvious of these is the principle of kinship, i.e., relationship between different members of a family based on marriage and on descent. This relationship can be of three types: (1) that between husband and wife, (2) that between parents and children, and (3) that between siblings.

Family as a functional unit

The family grows out of biological needs, particularly those of the expectant mother and infant child who cannot support and live by themselves. Another contributory cause is the need for exploitation of environment which cannot take place without co-activity. By cooperating with other members of the family and dividing work with them, the man is able to satisfy his own basic need for food and of those other members who are cooperating with him. The family acts as an educative unit and a socio-cultural agency. Its twin fuctions are procreation and recreation.

Family as an association

The basic grouping of the mates and their children has been called: (1) nuclear, the primary family, and (2) extended family, where some closely related kins is added to the primary family. The Hindu joint-family is an extended family.

The nuclear family may be consanguinous family, where the man goes to live in the house of his wife's family or the conjugal family where the wife comes to live with the family of her husband.

Other forms of family

Family of origin or orientation

The family in which one is born.

Family of procreation

The family which one sets up after one's marriage.

Polygymous family

Where a man marries more than one wife.

Polyandrous families

In which husbands are more than one e.g., the people of Khasa Tribe of Jaunsar-Baber, U. P. (Dehradun distt.) where several brothers marry one wife without any exclusive right of co-habitation for any one spouse.

Joint family

Collection of more than one primary family, on the basis of close blood ties and common residence, is called the joint family system. This is again grouped as:

(1) *Matri-local joint families:* Where the husband goes to live with the family of his wife, and the family line goes with the mother.

(2) *Patri-local joint families:* When the married couple and their off spring put up with the husband's family or in a new household, which he sets up on his own.

(3) *Patri-lineal:* When property inheritance and reckoning of descent takes place along the male line.

(4) *Matri-lineal:* When it is along female line.

(5) *Patronymic:* If offspring inherit the father's name.

(6) *Matronymic:* If the name goes with the mother's name.

The characteristics of patriarchical rural joint family

(1) The rural family is far more homogeneous, stable, integrated and organically functioning than the urban family. The ties, binding the members of the rural families for instance, the husband and the wife, parents and children are stronger and last longer than those in the case of the urban family.

(2) Rural family is based on a peasant husband.

(3) There is greater discipline and interdependence in the rural families.

(4) Dominance of family ego. The interdependence of the members of the rural families, wields its members into a homogeneous compact, egoistic unit, strengthens emotions of solidarity and cooperation among them and fills them with family pride. They develop more collectivist family consciousness and less individualistic emotion. A person in rural area tries to protect the good name of the family at any cost.

(5) Authority of the father or head of the family. The head of the family, generally the father if he is alive, otherwise the mother or elder brother distributes the work of the peasant's household among the family members on lines of the sex and age differences; arranges marriages of sons, daughters, nephews and nieces; administers the joint family property according to his wisdom; and trains the youngsters for future agricultural work and social life. Really speaking, he works as priest, teacher and manager of the family.

Property is held in common and the actual shares to which each member is entitled, if there is a separation, diminishes or increases with each birth or death in the family.

The ancestral property, and the income from it, along with the earnings of the individual members of the family, constitute a common family fund out of which the whole family's expenses are met. This arrangement of give and take demands a great deal of mutual tolerance, love, understanding and accommodation on the part of the members.

This system in which all are bound to contribute according to their earnings and where all are entitled to be maintained from the family funds according to their needs, is practically a recognised socialistic way of living.

The joint family system

In the old times, India was a land of vast and rich alluvial plains with less population to be fed. Labour was scant, but resources were plenty. The occupation of cultivating the lands needed larger families. The large family also gave protection from the wild beasts and other enemies.

Advantages

In it, every member gets his first lesson in forbearance, tolerance, and accommodation. It takes all sorts of persons, knit by ties of consanguinity, and provides insurance against unemployment, old age, loss of parents, etc.

It affords the best training in humanity, love and affection, and carries a person beyond a narrow circle to embrace relatives of the second and third generations based on an intimate knowledge of their qualities and feelings and thus helping to develop the understanding and cultivate the emotions. Because of this advantage, Israel has demonstrated that even a whole village can live as a family. The life in a Kibbutz, given in the previous chapter, provides a good illustration to the world that the whole village can live as one family and thus have a more prosperous life. The joint family can also be an ideal way of living. Because of the joint family system in Indian villages, they could face the hardships of over-population, foreign exploitation, etc. It saved rural India from disorganisation, to some extent, as compared to urban areas,

Drawbacks in the joint family system

In the times when there was not much pressure of population on land, and there was prosperity, this system could run without any quarrel in the family. With the increase of the pressure of population, and decrease in the earnings of the families, increase of knowledge, influence of Western culture, mobility of the population towards cities, etc., the joint family system has proved to have some inherent drawbacks and, to some extent, it looks like an out-of-date system. The inherent drawbacks may be given as follows:

(1) The individual in the joint family is not an independent unit, he is at best a coordinating part. Even the gifted and exceptionally intelligent individuals are pulled down by the less intelligent members of the family, because they are elders and the younger members should not show any superiority over them in handling the family or occupational affairs.

(2) The individual attention to children in their upbringing is absent, with the result that the physical condition of the children and their mental outlook, in general, are far from satisfactory. A younger person who wants to keep his children in a better way, as regards education, clothing, etc., cannot do so because his children cannot get this extra expenditure and special care and so he has to sacrifice this desire.

(3) It breeds a kind of authoritarianism. Elders sometimes behave like dictators. It stands as a barrier between the individual and the state as a group within the group.

(4) It creates conservative and reactionary attitudes towards women, their position in the family and prospect of their progress. Most of the girls who come in to such families by marriage are not always happy.

(5) The joint family is so constituted that the sympathy and understanding, affec-

tion and love of the husbands are denied to their wives.

Clan: When primary families link up with each other on the basis of kinship and not residence, it is called a clan or sib. There can be mother-sibs or father-sibs.

Phratry: When a group of clans gets merged together for one reason or another to constitute a still wider grouping, it is called a phratry.

Gotra: It is found among Hindus all over India. It consists of a large number of cognates supposed to be descended from the same ancestor, who lived in the ancient past. The marriage of kins and kiths was not allowed amongst the people of the same *Gotra*. But today, when such *Gotra* consists of a large number of culturally heterogeneous people, it is not given much consideration.

Muslim family system

They present a more or less uniform family pattern which is the outcome of interaction between Islamic law and Hindu influence. *Shia Muslims* have developed a caste structure in India. The Muslim family is like the Hindu family is patronymic and patrilocal. The eldest male runs the family and woman, who generally observe *Purdah* do the domestic work. Property is held jointly, as among the Hindus, and is inherited according to a very elaborate code. The Muslim family is extended like that of the Hindu, but may not consist of all the relatively distant kin who find their place in the Hindu Joint Family.

RACIAL ELEMENT

I. According to Herbert the races of India can be grouped into; (1) Dravidians, (2) Indo-Aryans, and (3) Mongloids.

II. A second classification was done by A.C. Hudden, who disagreed with Herbert's views. According to him, the racial element in India is:

(1) Pro-Dravidian races, (2) Brunette Delichocethals (it included people of Dravidian race having black colour and very big head), (3) Indo-Aryan, (4) Indo-Alpine (who had smaller head and are called Drachycepshal), and (5) Mongols.

III. The third classification was done by J. H. Hutten. According to him, the Indian races are:(1) Negreto: Who resided in India in very ancient times and there are very few of these who still can be said to be Negretos. (2) Proto-Austroloids: They came into India after the Negretos and their original place was Palestine. (3) The first group of Mediterraneans. (4) The last group of the Mediterraneans. (5) The Armenied branch of Alpines. (6) The Pishas or Dard group of Indo-Europeans.

IV. The fourth classification is according to Dr. Guha who has classified Indian races as: (1) Negreto, (2) Proto-Austroloids, (3) Mediterraneans or Dravid, (4) Alpine Dennaric and Armeneid, (5) Nordic or Aryans, and (6) The Mongols.

The racial elements based on differentiation in colour, manner of eating, marriages, place in social hierarchy, etc., gave strength to the development of a system and its presentation throughout this long period.

CASTE SYSTEM

It may be defined as a collection of families or group of families bearing a common name, which usually denotes and is associated with a specific occupation, common descent from a mythical ancestor, human or divine, professing to follow the same calling and regarded by those who are competent to give an opinion, as forming a single homogeneous community.

It is one of the oldest social institutions. Birth determines the whole course of man's social and domestic relations and he must throughout life, eat, drink, dress, marry, and give in marriage according to usages into which he was born.

Status groups

A number of people constitute a group not because of physical togetherness but because they have some common interests and common ways of doing things, as a result of which the society is dvided into higher and lower groups. If a status group is open to entry, i.e., if anybody can become its member by fulfilling prerequisite conditions, like paying admission fee or earning a particular income, then the status group may be called a class.

If a status group is not open to anybody, but only those are allowed to become its members, who have certain ascribed attributes which cannot be acquired by others, then it is called a caste. A caste is a closed class. A person is generally born into it.

The Indian caste system is unique in the world. It is a social institution, deriving sanctions from and intimately interwoven with Hindu religion. Caste sanctions and structures still govern all social, religious and economic activities of the average Indian in the vaillages, and to a decreasing extent in the towns and cities.

The caste stratification is based on the *Chaturvarn* doctrine, *Varn* means colour and it has a racial significance. It is believed that the *Creator*, created three groups from various parts of his body. From the head came the Brahmin, from body the Kshatriya, and from his feet and hands came the Vaishya and each gave rise to a caste. Afterwads, below the Vaishya, without any rank, were put the Shudras, consisting of menials and servants, who provided services to others.

According to James Mill, the caste system developed as the result of the need for division of labour. Thus four functional groups came into being: (1) Teaching and preaching, (Brahmins), (2) Administration and protection (Kshatriyas), (3) Agriculture and Commerce (Vaishyas), and (4) Services and manual labour (Shudras).

Social distance

As a result of belonging to a low caste, a person has to suffer many difficulties and about 70 to 80 millicn people in India belong to the depressed castes. In the South, there was even a caste of "unseeables", the seeing of whom could pollute the Brahmins, and due to it they were not allowed to go out of their localities, could not take water from common well, and so on.

The women develop a conservative attitude, they are reduced to non-entities in the family and the development of their personalities is thwarted. Thus the prospects of their progress towards becoming responsible individuals in the family is blocked.

The basis of such social distance was the fear among the higher castes of pollution from contact with the lower castes.

At present, there are approximately 3,000 castes and tribes in India and there are probably as many theories on caste origins as there are those, who have written on the subject

Functional basis

The social hierarchy in every part of India follows a particular system. Higher caste status is associated with land-ownership or superior rights on the soil, a higher living standard and a ban on manual labour. The gradations of peasants and agricultural castes fill up the middle ranks, the field labourers occupying the lowest status. The artisan castes are regarded as inferior to the farming castes. In accordance with their importance to the village economy, the more important of them assume clean status. In the northern part of India, covering the U. P. tract, the caste alignment follows the following order: Brahmin, Kshatriya, Khatri, Kayasth, Vaishya, Ahir, Kurmi, Kahar and other low artisans, such as Chamar, Pasi and the tribal groups.

HOW THE CASTE SYSTEM PRESERVED AND DEVELOPED HINDU SOCIETY

(1) According to Jod, the caste system tried to link the inhabitants of this vast country to each other. Each caste has its distinct place in society, and so every activity of life, from education to the cleaning of streets, houses or even latrines, etc., goes on as pre-arranged. Every caste thinks that they have to do the work for the society that has been assigned to them by birth and so there is not much dissatisfaction.

(2) Some of the arts have been passed on from generation to generation and particular castes have been sound to specialise in their occupation.

It was only due to the caste system, that Islam could not make Hindus into Muslims. Otherwise, wherever it (Islam) went, namely in Egypt, Iraq, Iran, Syria and Palestine, it abolished their original culture and introduced the Islamic culture.

(4) To maintain the purity of blood and to show the superiority of one caste over the other, the caste system controlled the society from various vices and the practices, which were not recognised by the society.

(5) The caste system provided for its members a club, a trade union and a philanthropic body.

According to Abbe Dubois, a Frehch clergyman, the caste system prevented India from going towards barbarianism, while Europe could not save itself from this drawback.

Utility of the caste system

It provides security to a person. He is assured of employment, shelter, protection and marriage. In the event of disability, he is not faced with disaster.

A caste provides free training and education of members in the skills in which it is traditionally proficient.

Its drawbacks

The system has become a hinderance in the development of some subsidiary industries, like poultry and independent industries, like tanning or shoe-making because such occupations have been relegated in the past to people of the lower castes. A Brahmin cannot keep poultry or swine, because it is considered the occupation of scavengers, similarly, a Chamar in a village, cannot run a dairy, because the Hindus or Jains will not purchase his milk or ghee. The second problem is of marriage. The Hindu custom allows for hypergamous marriage, or Anuloma marriage, under which a man can marry from his own caste or those below, but a woman can marry only in her own caste or above, the father of a Brahmin girl has either to give a big dowry for the marriage of his daughter, or to choose between polygamy and spinsterhood. Hence, the female children in the higher castes are supposed to be a curse.

RURAL SOCIAL INSTITUTIONS IN INDIA

A social institution is the structure and machinery through which human society organises, directs and executes the multifarious activities required to satisfy human needs. By this term, we mean the established forms, or conditions of procedure, characteristic of group activity.

When human beings create an association, they must create rules and procedures for the despatch of common business and for the regulation of the members to one another. Such forms are distinctive institutions. Every association has, in respect to its particular interest, its characteristic institutions. The temple, for example, has its sacraments, its modes of worship, its rituals, etc. The family has marriage, home, the family meal and so on. The State has its own particular institutions such as representative government and legislative procedures.

So, if we are considering something as an organised group, it is an association of a form of procedure and is called an institution. Association denotes membership and institution denotes a mode or means of service. Under it, we study social customs, folkways and the mores of the villagers.

Customs

The accepted ways of eating, meeting folks, wooing, training the young, supporting the aged, etc., are called the customs of society. When we speak of custom, we think of accepted ways in which people do things together through personal contacts.

The custom of marriage which requires the *Kanyadan*, i.e., the gift of his daughter by the father to the bridegroom, the *Home*, *Pani-grahan*, i.e., holding of the bride's hand by the bridegroom and the *Saptapadi*, i.e., the bridegroom taking seven steps, each step being denoted by a coin on the floor, the bridegroom leading the bride and then *Vivah*, i.e., the carrying away of the bride is a custom among the Hindus and is followed with slight variations throughout the country.

Similarly, there may be other customs, like that of giving feasts at the time of marriage of the son or the daughter or when a person arrives to meet some other person, there are customs as to how he should be received and offered something to eat, smoke or to chew, i.e., nuts, betels (*Pan-Supari*), etc.

Folkways

These are recognised or accepted ways of behaving in a society. They include conventions, forms of etiquette the modes of behaviour men have evolved and continue to evolve with which to go about the business of social living. They vary, of course, from society to society and from time to time, e.g., in northern India while smoking the *Hukka* in a group, the first puff is always given to the eldest man, similarly, while sitting on a *Charpai*, the eldest person is given the seat towards *Sarahana*, a younger lady touches the feet of her mother-in-law and other elder ladies or performs *Purdah* in the presence of her father-in-law, the elder males or even her husband in presence of elders.

Mores

The mores represent the living character of a group or community, operating in conscious or unconscious control over its members. They both compel behaviour and forbid it. In their forbidding function, we call them taboos. The wearing of clothes of certain style, for example, represents confirmity with the folkways while the wearing of clothes themselves, is enforced by the mores.

Variety of mores

One group uncovers the head to show respect, another the feet. One group prohibits the marriages of its members with outsiders, another recommends it. One group condemns the remarriage of widows, another commences. One group has a strict sex-code for the married, but not for the unmarried, another group follows the opposite system.

Religion

It is the human response to the apprehension of something of power which is supernatural and suprasensory. It is the expression of the manner and type of adjustment affected by people with their conception of the supernatural. In it, the persons perform necessary actions which bind them with the supernatural powers.

The beliefs and rituals are the two main component parts of religion everywhere.

Ritual

It consists in the observance, according to a prescribed manner, of certain actions designed to establish liaison between the performing individual and the supernatural power or powers. The offering of flowers, pouring of water, saying of some *Mantras* or offering the prayer, all are rituals in the worshipping of the gods or goddesses in the temples and they are to be followed according to a prescribed manner.

Beliefs

These are a charter for the rituals, as also a rationalisation for the same. These beliefs ensure that the rituals will be observed. The people perform some rituals or worship a particular god or goddess because they believe that if they do not do that some calamity may befall them.

The concept of the exact nature of the supernatural as believed by the villagers in India differs from place to place and people to people. For some, the supernatural may be constituted of ghosts and spirits; for others it may be an impersonal power, which pervades everything in this world; for still others, it may be manifested through a pantheon of anthropomorphic gods and goddesses or a single high God and so on.

Taboos

It means to forbid or the forbidden. The word is used to designate all the restrictions communicated through the verbal "Dont", and is generally associated with ritualistic behaviour to which a member of a rural society has to submit.

It is also said to be an unwritten law of society. Its purpose is threefold: productive, protective and prohibitive:

(1) Taboos associated with the process of cultivation are designated to be productive:

(2) Those like keeping women, children, or even men away from certain places, actions and objects are protective.

(3) Those which seclude a person, or limit contacts with him or her, as is done in the case of a menstruating woman when she is not allowed to enter a cow-shed or handle milk, etc., are prohibitive.

Major religions in India

According to the 1971 census, the population of India can be divided under various religions (See Table. 17.1)

Table 17.1
The religions of India in the 1971 census

Religions	No. in million	% of total
Hindus	439.8	83.5
Muslims	56.2	10.9
Christians	12.8	2.4
Sikhs	9.3	1.8
Buddhists	3 8	0.7
Jains	2.4	0.5
Others	1.9	0.37
Total	550	100.00

Hindu Religion

It is very difficult to get a clear picture of the Hindu religious beliefs, thoughts, feelings and practices of the rural people of India. The folklore and myths, religious teachings of saints or poets, contact (darshan) with persons having knowledge of scriptures and popular religious books have all influenced the religious ideology of the people. S. C. Dubey describes Hindu religion as:

"A mixture of animism and polytheism with the occasional appearance of monotheism also, with addition of faith in spirits, ghosts, demons, witches and magic. The complex of all these diverse factors constitutes the picture of the supernatural world as it is understood by the people in the countryside. The doctrine of the classical Hinduism, as known throughout India, with several cults and worship of a purely local nature, adds further to the complexity of the beliefs and rituals of the community. A wide variety of cults is observed by the family, some by the village as a whole, and still others by individual caste groups."[1]

According to D. K. Sharma, Hindus have no fixed time for daily worship except for the Brahmins who do this regularly in the morning before they start their works.[2] Some families have some images of gods or goddesses in a corner of their room or may have a separate worshipping (*Puja*) room for it.

Hindus have great degree of fatalism and demonstrate a spirit of resignation towards predestined facts ordained for them by the supernatural forces of the world beyond. Village people can often be heard to remark, "If it is written in our fate, we must submit to it. Human effort cannot alter the will of God." What is predestined must take its course. But this fatalism only appears when the people have tried their best to solve the problem and still find themselves not any closer to the solution.

Rural ethics in India lay more emphasis on acting rightly as laid down by the traditional norms, because they believe that it is the only way to a better life after death. It is believed that after death, a person either goes to heaven (*Swarga*) or to hell (*Narka*) or may take re-birth. It all depends on a person's actions in the past life (*Purva Jamma Sanskar*).

The other concept is of *Dharma*, not the religion in its literal meaning as Western translators believe, but it constitutes acceptance of certain traditions in the person's caste, observance of fasts (*Vrata*) giving feasts, and undertaking pilgrimage (*Tirtha Yatra*) to places of worship, or bathing in holy rivers, etc. It is belived that through *Dharma* one can make or mould the future. The concepts of sin (*Pap*) and merit (*Punya*) and of ritual pollution are fundamental to the wider concept of *Dharma*.

Certain taboos (restricted acts) must not be broken by any member of the community, irrespective of his caste, because they are sinful (*Pap*). Murder, extreme cruelty, killing of a sacred cow, sex relations with a woman other than one's wife, are placed under this category.

Other religions

Similarly, all religions like Islam, Christianity, Sikhism, Jainism, etc., have their beliefs, rituals and taboos and their marriages, festivals, ceremonies and other activities are controlled by religious bodies.

Festivals

People of different religions have different festivals. Some festivals are common to Hindus, Sikhs and Jains. These important festivals of the Hindus may be given as follows:

Hindu festivals

(1) *Dashehra:* The name comes from Dash+Hara. Defeat (from Hindi word Hara) of Ravana (Dash means ten-headed) the evil by Lord Rama. It falls on the 10th day of the Hindu Lunar calendar in the month of Kuar (end of October). In North India, girls put images of the goddess made from cowdung called *Sanjhi Mai* on the walls

---

[1]Dubey, S.C., *A Deccan Village, India's Villages*, West Bengal Govt. Press, India, p 88.
[2]Sharma, D.K., "An Essay: The Social Structure of Jamania Village" submitted for M.Sc., Cornell University, 1957.

and worship it with earthen lamps for ten days before the actual day of Dashehra. Ramlila—a stage drama of Ramayana is held, where the whole story is depicted to show the various char cters—how Kaikai got Rama sent to exile for 14 years, how Sita was kidnapped by Ravana, how Laxman obeyed his elder brother, the role of Sita (wife of Rama when she was exiled), how Ravana was defeated and killed by Rama, etc., On the last day, there is a procession in the streets and in the evening the images of Ravana and his supporters are burnt.

(2) *Diwali (Dipawali):* This comes from Deep (Hindi term) means light and is celebrated on the 15th day of the Hindu month Kartik, when it is Amavasya. It falls 20 days after Dashehra. On this day, Rama after defeating Ravana and completing his 14 years in exile, came back to his home. When he came, the city of Ayodhya (his hime-town) celebrated his arrival with lights (illuminations), rejoicing, and distributing sweets. Before this day, people clean their houses or if possible, whitewash them, prepare sweets which they distribute among their friends. Two days before Diwali there is a festival of Dhanteras, when each family is supposed to purchase a new utensil, the day before, there is Chhoti Diwali, when some earthen lamps are illuminated; the day after Diwali is Govardhan—the festival of cows, when cows and bullocks are worshipped. The Vaishyas worhip Goddess Laxmi and money-lenders send sweets to their debtors. Rajputs worship their swords, farmers their ploughs and implements, Kayasths their pen. Children burst crackers (Patakhe, Phooljhadi) in the nights. On the third day of Diwali, the Bhaiya Doj—Brother's Day, the sister comes to her brother's house and puts Tikka on his forehead if she is married, and feeds him with sweets, she gets some money on this day. After Govardhan people start chewing sugar cane for there is a taboo that sugar cane should not be chewed before it.

(3) *Nagpanchami:* On 5th day of Srawan month (July-Aug.) the Cobra sanke is worshipped and milk is offered to it by some people in some parts of India. On that day, there is no cooking, in the sense that the Tawa (cooking pan on which Roti is prepared) is not used and people eat only such things where bread is not needed.

(4) *Ganesh Chaturdashi:* In northern India it is celebrated as Teachers' Day on 4th day of Hindu calendar month (Aug.-Sept.) Bhadon. This is in honour of Ganesh, the son of Lord Shiva and Parwati. He is supposed to have the face of an elephant. Images of Ganesh, made of clay or paper mache are worshipped for 8 days in houses, and public places. It is worshipped by singing Arti—'Jai Ganesh, Jai Genesh, Jai Ganesh Deva'; in western U.P. where it is observed as Teachers' Day the children of primary schools along with their teacher, go to the houses of each student and sing songs called Chopai. The teacher is given some presents—sweets and money, depending on the financial position of the parents, ranging from Re. 1 to 10. On the Chaturdashi day, the Ganesh images are taken in processions and immersed in tanks.

(5) *Kali Puja or Durga Puja:* It is named after the Goddess Durga. Her image is displayed in public and then taken out in procession on Dashehra and immersed in water. In Jabalpur, about 100 Kalis are brought in procession from various parts of the city and then form a big procession. People saying 'Jai Kali' bring their goddesses in trucks, on their shoulders, and rickshaws to be taken to some tank or river.

(6) *Holi:* It is celebrated before the harvesting of the winter crop (Rabi) in the month of Phagun (March-April) on Puranmashi (when it is full moon). About 37 days before it, another festival, Basant Panchmi is celebrated and on that day a place is

selected for collecting dungcakes and other fuel. A big pile is collected during this period of $1\frac{1}{4}$ months by the children and even adults.

Throughout the month, people are always in a festive mood, singing and joking with each other. In the nights, they play on Drums, Jhanj, Gharnaval, Kalangi, etc., and sing Holi songs. On this day, at about 10 P.M., the fuel pile is burnt. Next day *Dulehdi*, throwing colour on each other, is celebrated.

(7) *Krishna Janmastami:* On the 8th day of Bhadva month (August-September), when Lord Krishna is supposed to be born, people keep fast throughout the day and in the night at 12 o'clock (when Lord was born) people offer prayers and break their fast.

Other festivals are like Ram Navmi, Teej, Pitramoksh Amavash, Kartiki Purnima, Til Sakranti, Karva Chowth, Holi, Rakhi, Nav Ratri.

Festival of other religions

Jains celebrate Mahavir Swamiji's birthday, and have Rath Yatra, Rishi Panchmi. Sikhs celebrate Guru Nanak's birthday in addition to all Hindu festivals, Muslims have Id and Moharram, etc. Christians celebrate their all festivals like Christmas, Easter, etc.

Marriage

Sex-gratification, irregular or institutionalised, is a basic reason for the formation of the family and the institution of marriage. Besides sex-gratification, getting possession of the paternal property is also a cause. Another reason is the need for a dependable social mechanism for the care and rearing of children and for the transmission of culture. It ensures a biological satisfaction, (that of sex) and a psychological satisfaction (that of having children), on the individual plan, while on the wider collective plan it ensures a two-fold survival—that of the group and its culture.

Marriage involves the social sanction, generally in the form of a civil or/and religious ceremony, authorising two persons of opposite sex to engage in sexual and the other consequent and correlated socio-economic relations with one another.

Forms of marriage

Exogamy: Marrying outside one's clan, because the followers of this system believe that there should not be inbreeding or sexual intimacy between primary kins.

Endogamy: Marrying within one's tribe. It may also be: (a) *Levirate:* The practice of being mate, actual or potential, to one's husband's brother. (b) *Sororate:* When several sisters are simultaneously or potentially the spouses of the same man.

Polygamy: Marrying with more than one person. It may be of two types (a) *Polygamy:* Marriage of one man to several women, (b) *Polyandry:* Marriage of one woman to several men. It is found amongst tribes, namely Toda, Khasa, Kota, Ladakhibota or Tion.

There is another term called Adelphic polyandry or Fraternal polyandry, when several brothers share the same wife as among the Khasa and Todas.

Hydergamy: Under this system in India, a man can marry from his own caste or from those below. Under the caste system, if a high caste woman marries a low caste man, she looses caste status, which is indicative of a degree of ritual purity. Up to marriage, a daughter shares her father's caste status and after marriage, her husband's. But a man himself does loose caste status or ritual purity by marrying a low caste woman. Manu and other law-givers prescribed *Anuloma and Pratiloma* systems. Under these systems, marriages for woman and man can be as follows:

Marriages permissible for women:[1]

Shudra girl to	Shudra, Vaishya, Kshatriya, Brahmin.
Vaishya girl to	Vaishya, Kshatriya, Brahmin.
Kshatriya girl to	Kshatriya, Brahmin.

Marriages permissible for men:

Brahmin man to	Brahmin, Kshatriya, Vaishva, Shudra.
Kshatriya man to	Kshatriya, Vaishya, Shudra.
Vaishya man to	Vaishya, Shudra.
Shudra man to	Shudra.

Ways of acquiring mates

Among the tribal people of India, the ways are: (1) Probationary marriage, (2) Marriage by capture, (3) Marriage by trial, (4) Marriage by purchase, (5) Marriage by service, (6) Exchange, (7) Mutual consent, and (8) Intrusion.

But out of these, the mutual consent, exchange or even purchase methods are adopted by the non-tribal people.

Pre-marital relations

All over tribal India, pre-marital relations are generally free and much value is not set on virginity. But among the non-tribal peoples, pre-marital relations are not allowed and virginity is given much value. No extramarital sex relations are allowed in the rural areas.

Some castes practise widow re-marriage, but high caste people do not allow it, although the Act regarding it was passed long ago.

Marriage is a necessity in rural areas, as without marriage there can be no off-spring and it is believed that without a son, there is no release from the chain of birth, death, re-birth. It is designated as one of those body sanctifying rituals which every Hindu has to perform.

The forms of marriage ceremony

(1) *Brahma marriage:* When the father gifts his daughter to a learned man of good character.

(2) *Dev marriage:* If married to a priest.

(3) *Ashi marriage:* When a prospective son-in-law gives a bull or a cow to the girl's father.

(4) *Asura marriage:* When girl is purchased.

(5) *Gandharva marriage:* Marriage by mutual love.

(6) *Prajapati marriage:* When the father gifts his daughter to a man after duly

---

[1]Brahmin is a priest by caste, Kshatriyas are martial castes, Vaishyas were regarded as agriculturists and suppliers while Shudras were for serving the other three classes.

horouring him.

(7) *Rakshas marriage:* (Abduction or carrying away a girl): In some tribes it is regarded as lawful, but the seduction of a girl while asleep, intoxicated or of unsound mind, is unlawful. It is called also a *Pishach* Marriage.

Marriage as ritual in rural India

About three decades back child marriages were common, but the increase in literacy and the Sharda Act has decreased it to a great extent. Generally, boys are married after the age of 18 and girls after 15 years. Dowry amongst certain Hindu castes, namely: Kayasthas, Rajputs, Vaishyas and Tyagis is very common and so is a great worry for the father of a daughter. But it is decreasing. As we mentioned amongst Caste Panchayats elsewhere, the Jat Community in western U.P. has organised region or village Caste Panchayats and has restricted the dowry, number of Baraties (persons going in a marriage party to the girl's house). Other castes like Agarwals and Brahmins of western U.P. have also imposed certain restrictions.

In the majority of cases, marriage among Hindus is fixed by the parents of the bridegroom. Generally, the bridal couple get no chance to know each other before marriage, because dating is not known to boys and girls unlike in the Western countries. The wedding takes place generally in the bride's house on an auspicious day fixed by both parties on the advice of Brahmin priest. The marriage party of the bridegroom, consisting of relatives and friends, travel to the bride's place by *Rath*,[1] tongas, cars, elephants, bullockcarts, train or bus, as is convenient, but with full pomp and show. In western U.P., in some communities, they stay for three days and are given very special food and all sorts of comforts and recreation. On the first day, there is the performance of marriage rites (*Vivah Sanskar*). The Brahmin priests chants religious verses (*Sanskrita Shlokas*) in the presence of the *Barat* (Marriage party) and other invited guests of both parties. A *Nai* (Barber) is also needed in the marriage party. He is a sort of agent between the two. At this time, there are some rituals to be performed like *Godan* (presenting a cow by the father); *Vida* (departure of the marriage party with the girl), *Kanya Dan*. When the girl leaves her parents and friends and relatives, she shows that she has felt it much. At some places they cry and thus all relatives, girl's friends and ladies bring out tears in their eyes, the scene of happiness and rejoicing is changed to sorrow and grief. The ladies and girls sing songs saying 'Oh girl! you are now leaving us to have a new house with your husband, mother-in-law or father-in-law'. When she goes to her father-in-law's house, there are some rituals to be performed by both—girl and the boy like: *Kangna Khulai, Chak Pujai, Kua Pujai* (worshiping a well). The girl stays in her mother-in-law's house for about a week or so. Then the brother or any near relative comes to take her back to her parent's house. After a year or so, the husband again goes with a few friends for '*Gona*', to take her back to his house and then she becomes a permanent member visiting her parents on occasions. It decreases with advancement in age and increase in number of children or the financial position of her parents and brothers.

---

[1]*Rath* is a special carriage for wedding.

Marriages among the Muslims

Marriage among the Muslims is not a religious sacrament but a secular bond. Prohibited degrees of alliances are few and limited. Marriage between even half-siblings and first parallel cousins can take place. It is polygamous and a Muslim can have up to four living wives. Two sisters or an aunt and niece, cannot be taken as co-wives. A Muslim can marry his deceased wife's sister and also parent-in-law of his children. A Muslim can marry a non-Muslim but idolatrous woman like a Jew or a Christian, a Muslim woman does not enjoy a similar right.

Marriage is solemnised by signing a legal document and can be dissolved. The divorce is almost only the husband's right and he can do it in presence of two persons by saying Talaq three times. A wife can obtain Khula or relief from her marriage by taking the consent of her husband. If separated by mutual consent, it is Mubaraq.

There are three types of marriages amongst Muslims:

(1) *Sahi:* That is a contract, where both the parties take responsibilities.

(2) *Batil:* A marriage which is based on unaccepted principles of the society.

(3) *Phasid:* Irregular marriage.

The marriageable age amongst Muslims for male is 15 years and for girls, after the first menstruation, *i.e.*, about 13 or 14 years.

Rights given to a woman after marriage

(1) After the marriage, the husband gives a settled dowery, which may be the right of *Mahar* and if it is given just after the marriage, it is called *Muaazal* but if after a long period of the marriage, it is *Muvazzal.*

(2) Food and residence for the wife.

(3) Equal love, if the husband has other wives.

(4) Maintenance of children.

Duties of wives

(1) To obey the husband and to live a pious life.

(2) To keep the husband happy.

(3) To suckle the children, if he cannot afford a midwife.

(4) To remain unmarried during the *Iddat* period.[1]

Conception ceremony

In some regions of Madhya Pradesh, when it is known that a lady has become pregnant for the first time by her husband it is celebrated.

Attainment of non-menstrual age

In some castes or religions, when a lady attains an age that her menstruation stops for ever and that she is no more fit for producing children, this is celebrated among Maharashtrians.

---

[1]*Iddat* is a prescribed period after the death of her husband, united the temptation of which the wife is not allowed to re-marry.

Death

Among Hindus, Sikhs or Jains, the corpse is washed, clothed and tied to bamboo bier (*Arthi*). It is covered with a new white cloth.[1] In case of adults, the bier is carried by four persons on their shoulders. They go on foot to the cremation ground uttering "*Ram Nam Satya Hai, Satya Bolo Gatya Hai*". A son or younger brother carries an earthen-pot with fire in front of the bier. The bier is placed on the funeral pyre and a near relative sets fire to it. When the pyre is burnt, people come to their homes, take a bath and change clothes. On the third day, the remaining bone pieces (*Phul*) are collected and immersed in some holy river. After the 13th day in the case of a man and 10th day in the case of a woman, purificatory rites are performed with the help of a Brahmin priest. The near relatives get their heads shaved[2] and the Brahmins and some relatives are fed. It is called *Terahwi*. After one year, *Barsaudi* is celebrated. In the case of child it is buried or even immersed in a holy river as a whole body. *Shradh*[3] ceremony is celebrated every year for fifteen days in rememberance of all adults dead in a family. Any day in Hindu calendar 1-15th which was the day of death within these 15 days, is celebrated as the death day of a particular person. On this day, special food is prepared and Brahmins and unmarried girls[4] are fed. Among some Hindus, those who believe in Math (Karnataka State), the dead body is kept for the whole day in the sitting pose and buried as such.

Rural art

The constituent elements of an art product include lines or surfaces or colours, or all these together or sound of words, suggestive of harmony or melody or both for rhythmic movements, often accompanied by harmonic sounds of musical instruments, and the melody of the words sung.

The artist's joy lies not in creating new ideas and styles but in reproducing those that already exist. Consequently, art in primitive society is more thoroughly social in its character than art in modern society.

Characteristics of agricultural aesthetic culture[5]

(1) It is based on the eternally human phenomena of birth, marriage and death and the emotions of love, joy, despair, jealousy, etc. So the songs, dances, festivals, pictures, stories and fairy tales in which phenomena and emotional arts depicted are placed in agricultural and rural settings.

(2) The agricultural arts, in addition to this general trait, have some specific characteristics of technique, rhythm, style and execution.

(3) They display, as does the nomadic art, culture, methods of selection and survival, differing from the commercialised arts.

(4) At any time, they usually contain fewer modern and more ancient forms than the urban arts.

(5) There are usually some elements of rural art that do not spread to the cities and vice versa

[1] A woman whose husband is alive at the time is wrapped in a coloured cloth.
[2] *Kriya* ceremony.
[3] It is a festival in *Kuwar* month for 15 days.
[4] *Kanya*, they are called.
[5] Adapted from Desai, A. R., *Introduction to Rural Sociology*.

Songs

Songs accompany collective agricultural occupations like hunting, fishing, grain-grinding, threshing, ploughing and seeding, etc. Some of the religious and music songs of the villagers are concerned with love and death.

Tales, legends, dances, festivals, etc.

The dances, plays, festivals, etc., are connected with religious rites, or with work. They are performed to venerate certain deities, to protect the interests of the people, and to secure the fulfilment of their desire. The dances show the harvesting, sowing, ploughing, hunting, war against enemies, worship, rejoicing, taking water from well, etc.

Ornamental arts

These are based on the rural environment and occupations. Trees, flowers, cattle and other domestic animals, birds and peasant houses, etc., are its component parts.

Nature, plant and animal lore

The existence of the people in close contact with nature, and their dependence on it, is reflected in their stories, songs, tales, proverbs, metaphors, theatrical performances, pictures, designs, etc.

Peculiarities of style

Rural art varies greatly in different periods and in different forms. Hence it is impossible to make any generalisation that would be generally applicable to all its numerous varieties.

(1) *Repetition of words:* The songs, narratives, tales, and recitations about in repetition of words and expressions. Sometimes, they are merely exclamations and ejaculations necessary to the rhythm.

(2) *Rhythm:* The rhythm of the various agricultural work songs varies apparently to correspond to the rhythm of the bodily movements in a particular type of agricultural work.

(3) *Melodies:* The turns of agricultural songs are also the product of the agricultural milieu. In some of them, one feels the loneliness, in others the spaciousness of the fields and open spaces.

(4) *Colour combinations:* In their decorations, costumes and ornamentations, the agricultural arts are marked by great richness which may be symbolised by a meadow covered with red, blue, white and green flowers.

(5) *Curved lines:* Among agricultural people the lines composing the design of an ornament and governing the style of costumes are dominated by harmonious curved lines and among urban people by straight lines. The trees, plants, animals, surface, configurations and clouds that constitute the rural environment are beautiful combinations of curved lines.

Rural art in India

Under it we include: (1) Art products—utensils, ornaments, toys, Rangoli (making pictures or images on the ground with coloured water Sanjhi, Jhanki, Mehndi lagana, etc., (2) folk dances, (3) stage acts, (4) processions, Bharat Ram Milap, Kali, Durga, Ganesh immersion.

Art products: It includes printing on cloth, weaving of various designs in cloth. The printed turbans, chunnies and the present printing of quilt sheets, table cloths, saris, etc., are famous. Bhopal purses, Jodhpuri shoes (Indian) with Salma Sitare, Banarasi and Chanderi (M. P.) saris have very good attraction for foreigners as well as Indians.

Utensils and toys: Engraving or printing of colours on utensils or toys at Khurja, Chunar (U.P.), Jaipur (Rajasthan) have been perfected to a very high degree. Flower designs on ornaments, the images of gods and goddesses on golden and silver ornaments, is done throughout India. Bangalore (Mysore) is famous for ivory work. Wooden, papier-mache and clay toys are prepared at Krishna Nagar, Gwalior (M.P.), Sheopur (M.P.) Kodapalli; cloth dolls at Poona and Taj Mahal models at Agra.

Alapna and Rangoli: In Bengal, Madras, Gujarat, Rajasthan, M.P. and Maharashtra coloured pictures are made on certain festive occasions. These occasions may be Lakshmi Puja festival in Bengal, Saraswati Puja in Gujart and on marriage days in M.P. Rangoli has a great importance in the daily life of Maharashtra so that it is considered to be qualification for the marriage of a girl, along with her other qualities.

Sanjhi: In the month of Kuwar (October) before Dashehra, an image of the goddess in clay is made by girls on the wall and ornaments made of paper or clay are placed on the body. The girls assemble in the evening and worship by holding an earthenware lamp and saying:

"Sanjhi Mai Arta,

Arta Ri Arta. . . . . .and so on."

Jhanki: On many occasions and specially on Ganeshotsava and Janmashtami, very beautiful and attractive Jhankis displaying the image of Ganesh, Lord Krishna, or Durga Kali in the middle and putting different shades of light and other attractive things like toys, flowers, etc., around it, are arranged. In the night, people visit each other's houses and appreciate the art of the ladies or children who prepared the Jhankis.

Folk dance: On the occasions of Holi, Diwali, Basant Panchami and even at marriages, folk dances are organised.

Folk dances have a regional touch in India. In southern India there is Bhartnatyam and Kathakali and in Manipur and its surrounding areas Manipuri dance. During the Moghal period, Kathak was the famous dance of Northern India. These dances have also reached foreign countries where artists like Udai Shanker, Indrani Rehman and others have given performances at Universities and other places. Once the Indian Association of Cornell University arranged a dance performance by Indrani Rehman and her troop and the author observed that the American and other foreign students and staff at Cornell appreciated the art very much. Besides these, there are many other folk dances in different parts of the country. These can be given as follows:

ASSAM: Kamurappa, Keli Gopal, Mahar Ras, Vid, (These are held at the time of harevesting of crops) Khasi Nagar Khasi, Naga Khambali, Vori (also harvest dances). In Manipur area Lai, Irimba, Pung, Chholog, Rakhal (are Spring season dances), Jhaval, Jhogvi, Raslila are other dances.

BENGAL: Bratachari, Kirtan, Yatra, Boul, Shantiniketan tradition.

BIHAR: Chao (in Spring), Ba (on festivals), Matha.

UTTAR PRADESH: Diwali dance of Ahirs, Holi, in Brij (birthplace of Lord Krishna), song of Ram Singh and Bulli (Khekra Baraut area) Notanki, Kaharwa, Jhora, Thali, Jhenta, Ras (Brij).

PUNJAB: Bhangra (folk dance of farmers), Gidh.

HIMACHAL PRADESH: Chanwa (dance of farmers).

RAJASTHAN: Jhumar Panihari.

GUJARAT: Garba.

MADHYA PRADESH: Karma, Navrati, Chetdanda, Beejphutni (sung at the time of sowing seed in the field). Goncha (Prayer to Lord Indra for rainfall), Lakshmi, Jagar, Daglar (Bhils—tribal people). Langi, Ghero, Kamarchano, Gopal Kala.

MAHARASHTRA: Lajim, Dahikala, Govinda, Nakta Kol ya Cha Nach (dance of fishermen). Phugari, Korku, Gond Dance (Tribal).

KERALA: Kolattam, Kummi, Thiru Vatirakali and Kaikoltikali.

MADRAS: Kuru, Banji, Kolattam.

ANDHRA: Kuchipudi, Burikatha, Yakshaganam, Lambadi.

MYSORE: Karago, Itari, Atikalanji, Dol Kunita Kolata.

Folk songs: The folk songs of India are related to the life of the people and, side by side, they depict the industry of the people who sing them. There are different songs for different occasions or operations in agriculture—sowing, ploughing, harvesting, etc. Similarly, there are songs which are sung by ladies while spinning, grinding the flour, and songs of fishermen.

There are special songs for ceremonies and occasions like birth, 'Yagyopavit' (thread-taking ceremony), marriage, travel. Some songs are sung to incite enthusiasm or bravery—'Alba'. Some give the character a person should have—Ramayan and Mahabharat.

In different regions, different songs find their place as follows: 'Ramayan' and 'Mahabharat' are read in song by persons when they are idle. Farmers, when they do not have much work on the farm during the rainy season, assemble in the night or even in the daytime. 'Britachari' songs in Bengal, are sung on the occasion of 'Paush Sankranti' festival, 'Bhalari' and 'Sugi' songs are sung at the time of harvest in Maharashtra. Eru-Barwa and Uru Badhai Patt are also crop harvest songs of Andhra Pradesh. While working in the fields, the people of Kurga and Kerala sing 'Katari' song and the ladies of Punjab while spinning thread sing 'Trinjan'. In northern part of U.P., during rainy season, 'Alba' is sung. In northern Madhya Pradesh, 'Languria' is also sung by ladies as well as men.

Folk stage art: It includes 'Ras Lila' of Brij area of U.P. (common in Meerut, U.P.) 'Swang', Notanki, Ram Lila. are also very common in U.P. 'Mach' in Malwa (M.P.), Kathputli (Puppets) of Rajasthan come under the same category.

Processions: Processions with musicians, drum-beaters, Jhankis, etc., are taken out in the streets of town, cities or even villages on certain occasions: In Bengal, U.P., M.P. on "Devi Puja', in Madras on Dashehra, in U.P. on 'Bharat Milap', 'Parikrima' (walking around a holy place in Chitrakut) Banda district of U.P. and Brij or Mathura district, U.P., taking out 'Tajia', during Moharram amongst Muslims, Chalia Sai' amongst Sindhis (Hindus who came from Sindh Province, in Pakistan now), Rani Jhansi in Gwalior. Similar processions are arranged on Independence Day and Republic

(Gantantra) Day all over India.

Other arts: Some arts like 'Chakri Ghumana' (Lattu) of Gwalior which is celebrated every year at Chakri Ka Mela (Fair) at Tansen (The great singer of Akbar's time), Tirandazi (arrow shooting) Yogasan, feats of Nats, playing on certain instrument like Ghara (pitcher), Sarangi, pipe, etc., have a charm for the village people.

Government support to these arts: The National Culture Trust was set up to promote art and culture and foster conciousness of art among the people. These objective are secured through the agency of Lalit Kala Academy (Academy of Arts), Sangeet Natak Academy (Acadmey of Drama and Music) and Sahitya Academy (Academy of Letters). The facilities for mass communication at the disposal of the State have also been utilised to make the people ·conscious of their cultural heritage. A number of institutions have collaborated in the task of popularising traditional arts and crafts.

Art in tribal India: Different tribes have different arts and they are on the decline everywhere in India because of confused judgements. Open condemnation of tribal culture or an implicit disapproval conveyed through movements to uplift have induced in the minds of the Indian tribal folk a distrust, and in some cases, even a distaste, for their cultural traditions.

There is a richness in the folk music and the folk dances of India that can enrich and inspire the efforts of the most advanced and modern artists of India. It is good to note that dance and music performances by the invited representatives of various Indian tribes now form a regular item of the official programme for the annual Republic Day celebrations in Delhi on 26th January.

We may think of development work and the changing of attitudes of these tribal people but the tribal art is so rich, that it has to be preserved and nurtured for the good of the country.

CHAPTER 18

SOCIAL WELFARE AND WELFARE ORGANISATIONS

CONCEPT OF SOCIAL WELFARE

The term social welfare is very comprehensive in its meaning. It includes a large number of activities connected with the uplift and welfare of the weak and exploited sections of society.

The numerous individuals and groups, who desire and strive for the improvement of the material and cultural life of the rural people, can be put into three categories:

(1) The philanthropic group,

(2) The reformist group, and

(3) The revolutionary group.

(1) The philanthropic group holds the conviction that it is possible to ameliorate the conditions of the rural people through direct humanitarian effort, without changing the village institutions and structure. It involves welfare programmes through charity, by opening of hospitals, schools, etc.

(2) The reformists work for a healthy functioning of the social system and its institutions for reforming them. They assert that once this institutional reform is accomplished, it will result in the all-sided betterment of the life of the villagers. This group does not regard it necessary to replace the existing social system and its institutions by new ones and strives only to reform them.

(3) The standpoint and programmatic approach of the revolutionary group to the solution of the rural problems is based on a revolutionary conception. They think that poverty, ignorance and cultural backwardness of the rural population are fundamentally due to the existing social system and the institutions which sustain that system. They believe that both the programme of individual aid and relief and that of institutional reform will be unable to liberate the rural people from want, disease, illiteracy and lack of culture. According to this group, the evils of the rural society are inherent in the rural social system and its institutions, and so it evolves and attempts to carry out a programme for the revolutionary transformation of the rural social structure.

According to another school of thought, welfare workers and groups can be divided into two categories:

(1) Those who do not want any State interference in the economic progress of the society.

(2) Those who base the pattern of society of a socialistic way of thinking and say that the poor or labour class should not be provided the welfare services and amenities on a charity basis but that the Government should compel the industrialists to provide such amenities as education for children, medical aid, recreation, etc., and that labour also should think of these amenities as their right.

Theories of the philanthropic group

There are four theories on which the thinkers of this group base their ideas:

(a) *Theory of natural rights:* Its supporters, like John Locke (1632-1709), are of the opinion that a person should be allowed to make economic progress without State control. An efficient and hardworking individual becomes rich while the inferior one remains poor. We cannot force all to become equal.

(b) *Utilitarian theory:* Its supporters, like Bentham (1798-1832), believe that if a person is made free to find a suitable way, he makes himself fixed to suitable position and so the State need not interfere in it.

(c) *Economic theory of laissez-faire:* Such economists believe that the natural economic man is tied to the natural economic order and he cannot break this organisation. The economic organisation of the world is controlled by the economic laws, e.g., "Law of Demand and Supply", and no person or State can break such laws. Because of this thinking, the followers of this group do not proffer for any State interference and believe that business should be allowed to carry on without any control.

(d) *Organic theory:* The followers of this group believe that as the body develops according to nature's laws, society also develops in its natural way. Just as we cannot develop the body as we wish, so also the society.

Theories of the reformist group

This group includes socialist thinkers like Noyal Boyf, Charles Fourier, Robert Owen, Karl Marx, etc., who believed that the natural resources of a country should be the property of all, and that all the members of a society should be given equal chances of progress.

Noyal Boyf, a French reconstructionist, pointed out that it was very strange in our society that a weaver, who makes cloth for others, remains unclothed himself. He called the proprietors of such industries, enemies of the public. Charles Fourier, another French thinker, put forward the doctrine of collective production in which all the member should get their share in the produce. Another French thinker, Louis Brown, went to the extent of saying that just as the power passed from the hands of the capitalists to the middle class, similarly, it should pass to the labour class.

Robert Owen, an English reformist, decided not to take more than 5 per cent as his profit in his mills and he divided the surplus income amongst the workers.

Karl Marx, the German economist said, that every labourer should get the reasonable wages of his labour and that every member of society should get equal opportunities for education and for increasing the knowledge. The workers should get their wages according to their ability and work. It would reduce the class-conflict because, there would be only one group in society and that would be the group of workers. The real reconstruction could only come when power is in the hands of labour class.

Philosophy of Sarvodaya

The Sarvodaya ideology is the outcome of Gandhiji's way of thinking and his constructive programme. After the achievement of political independence in India, the next step, he pointed out, was to base the country's line of work on principles of "Sarvodaya". By Sarvodaya, he meant doing good to many, in place of doing good to a few members of society. He pointed out that this new revolution, social and economic, was to be brought about peacefully and non-violently.

After the death of Gandhiji, the constructive workers, who were his followers or co-workers, assembled on January 30, 1950, at Sewagram and formulated an economic plan to give Sarvodaya a practical shape.

Difference between Sarvodaya and economic way of thinking

Sarvodaya says that, as in the profession of teachers and doctors, social service is the main aim and money earning is the secondary one. In the same way, in business or industry, social welfare or social service should be the main aim of the owners or the capitalists. In this way, according to the Sarvodaya principles, business would not remain a way of only earning money but will be a ground for social welfare. When this becomes the line of thinking of the businessmen or the owners of industries, there will not arise the problems of conflict between the workers and the owners or capitalists, and strikes and lock-outs.

The second difference is that the Law of Demand and Supply or Competition will not be the guiding principle in determining the prices of the commodities, but the price will be determined by how far the commodities are able to fulfil the needs of society. In this way, the businessmen or the shopkeepers will not let the prices increase in case the demand for the commodities increases. On the other hand, the purchaser will also think of giving a reasonable price and will not make the seller to suffer because the demand has fallen.

Bhoodan

Bhoodan is the fruit of the 'Sarvodaya' way of thinking. Through it, Acharya Vinoba Bhave demonstrated vital and radical changes in the minds of the villagers in India could be affected by awaking and canalising the strength of the people from within.

According to Shri Jaya Prakash Narayan, "Bhoodan, in short, is the Gandhian way to bring about an economic and social revolution. Bhoodan is the theory and practice of a new way of life, a new social philosophy. It is the intimation of a new civilisation." The fundamental ideas underlying the movement, according to Shri Jaya Prakash Narayan are:

(1) "All that man possess belongs in reality not to individuals, but to the society in which they live......But we tend to forget this eternal debt we owe to society and wrongfully appropriate what is society's own."

(2) "Bhoodan is not a charitable movement. . . Man is not the master of what he

possess, but only a trustee of what in reality belongs to society. . . . A trustee should take from the trust not more than what is necessary to fulfil his needs, and give all the rest back to society. . . . Giving back to society is not charity but elementary honesty, the performance of a simple duty, an act of restitution".

The origin of the movement dates back to 18th April, 1951, in the village Ponchampalli of Nalgonda district in Telangana. Acharya Vinoba Bhave, during his stay in the village, received a very pressing request from the landless agricultural workers (*Harijans*) of the village to procure for them some land. Vinoba made a public request, and a land-owner named Ram Chandra Reddi offered 100 acres out of his 200 acres of inherited land. Then Vinoba asked the landless labourers, how much they needed? They said that they could do with 80 acres for their 40 families. This happening, that on one side the donor was ready to give 100 acres and on the other side, the landless and the needy were ready to do with only 80 acres, gave him a true picture of the *Sarvodaya* philosophy. It showed him a way for the solution of the many problems of this materialistic world. He was very pleased to find a way and immediately made it the mission of his life to accept gifts of land from such people as could make them for redistribution amongst the landless. With the help of co-workers and disciples as he has collected over 42 lakh acres of land up to April, 1964. The target is to collect 5 crore acres. Eleven lakh acres of land received in this manner have been distributed among villagers.[1]

The other workers, like Jaya Prakash Narayan joined him and then other ways—collecting money, taking labour from people and workers who could devote themselves for the country—were adopted under the names of *Sampatti Dan*, *Shram Dan*, *Budhi Dan*, *Jeewan Dan*, etc.

Defining *Sampatti Dan* (gift of property) Shri Jaya Prakash Narayan, addressing the Bombay Bhoodan Samiti in June, 1954, remarked that it was the first step towards conversion of capitalism into "the non-violent and just society of the future in which everyone lives for all and for everyone. . . . A climate will have to be created to take the next step towards the transformation of the existing economic order—that of full trusteeship."

Regarding *Shram Dan* and *Prem Dan*, Shri Jaya Prakash Narayan observes, "Whatever we have, we must share with others because they have a right to it. If we have nothing to give, let us give our service—*Shram Dan*, our love and goodwill —*Prem Dan*."

Gramdan

The Bhoodan Movement has now widened out into Gramdan, i.e., donation of entire villages. The ideal behind it is that all land should belong to the village community as a whole.

This gives a better way for cooperative village development. At a conference convened by the Akhil Bharat Sarva Sewa Sangh in September, 1957 at Yelwal (Mysore State), the desirability of the closest cooperation between the Community Development Programme and the Gramdan Movement was emphasised. The matter was discussed by the working group in the Ministry of the Community Development, and after further consideration at the Development Commissioners' Conference held

[1]India, 1965, p. 241.

at Mount Abu in May, 1958, certain decisions were arrived at for closer cooperation between Bhoodan and Gramdan. Gramdan villages are now given preference in the matter of opening Community Development Blocks and starting such other development activities.

State patronage of Bhoodan: Legislation has been adopted for facilitating donations and distribution of Bhoodan land in Andhra Pradesh, Bihar, Gujarat, M.P., Tamil Nadu, Karnataka, Orissa, Punjab, Rajasthan, U.P., Delhi and Himachal Pradesh. Adminitrative instructions have been issued in Maharashtra and Kerala. Special legislation for management of Gramdan villages has been passed in Rajasthan.

Various States are giving financial assistance by way of resettling landless workers on Bhoodan lands, supply of free literature, help to small-scale industries, advancing loans for subsidy to farmers who organise into cooperative societies.

Sarvodaya and the Indian Government: The Government of India has fully accepted the principles of *Sarvodaya* and has decided to base the future of the country on a 'Socialistic Pattern of Society.' It has been adopted that the aim of industrialisation should not be private profit, but social prosperity. The planning is being done in a manner in which wealth will not remain limited to a few capitalists but will be equally distributed in the hands of the society. It provides that the common man is to be given a better standard of living by wealth flowing from a higher level to a lower level. To achieve this end, it has been pointed out by our planners, we cannot copy the economic pattern of other countries but must frame a society of our own type because our problems are different from those in other countries.

WELFARE STATE

Every man or woman has some fundamental human rights and the State, which protects such rights, is called a Welfare State.

What are fundamental human rights?

In 1954, the UNO was organised and its functions were divided into six bodies, of which economic and social, was one. The field of the Economic and Social Council, was decided: (1) To raise the standard of living of masses, to reduce unemployment and to help economic and social development in underdeveloped countries. (2) To solve the international economic, social and health problems, and to increase internal harmony through cultural and educational programmes, to safeguard the fundamental human rights of persons and to remove the differences of caste, race, language, sex, religion, etc., so that nobody is deprived of his rights. The Economic and Social Council prepared an International Bill of Human Rights. According to it, the accepted Fundamental Rights of every person in a Welfare State are:

(1) Everybody has a right to live independently.
(2) No one can be arrested without showing a cause and after arrest he has a right to an impartial enquiry.
(3) Right of protection and right of equality.
(4) Right of moving where one likes, and everyone is free to become a member of any nation.
(5) Everybody can own property.

(6) There is freedom of thought and of religion.

(7) Everybody has the right to vote and the right of independent thinking.

(8) Right of mixing and free assembling.

(9) Everybody is free to take part in Government activities and has that right of social security and the right to employment.

(10) Right of selecting work according to one's choice, equal wages for equal work and the right to take leave and rest.

(11) Right to get education and attend cultural activities.

How far India is a welfare State ?

The Welfare State is a goal towards which every State, which is conscious of its obligations to its citizens, is moving in the world today. India is trying to realise this noble objective and to take her place among the socially and economically advanced countries of the world. Indian Parliament on 26 December, 1949, accepted the fundamental rights of the above-mentioned International Bill, as part of its Constitution, under Part 3 where it has been stated that, in this country, everybody has equal rights regardless of race, religion, caste, sex and place of birth.

All the citizens of India have equal rights to the natural resources. The national wealth is being utilised for the welfare of all and efforts are being made through the Five-Year Plans to ensure that the industrialist or capitalist may not exploit the labour class. We mentioned under *Sarvodaya* that the Indian Government has decided to base the country's future on a socialistic pattern of the society. *Sarvodaya*, the accepted principle for our country's development, is itself a way of making it a Welfare State.

It is the firm belief of our planners that "real progress is not achieved through military success or some kind of violent revolution, but by constructive activity and hard work."[1]

As we may see in Part IV of this book on Planning in India, since 1951, when the First Five-Year Plan of India was inaugurated, the country has endeavoured to harness natural resources and the energies of the people to the tasks of national development. The planners have been stressing from the very beginning that the objective of planned development is not only to increase production and attain higher levels of living but also to secure a social and economic order based on the values of freedom and democracy in which "Justice, social, economic and political, shall improve all the institutions of the national life". It is the primary aim of the country's Plans to provide the basic necessities to all persons within the community, and at the same time, to emphasise the place of human values in economic and social development.

The Parliament of India in December, 1954, declared that the broad objectives of the economic policy of the country should be to achieve the "socialistic pattern of society". Accordingly, the basic criteria in determining social policies and the lines of economic advancement should not be private profit or the interests of a few, but the good of the community as a whole. The existing social and economic institution and the welfare organisations have, therefore, to be judged in relation to their role in national development. It is to be taken into consideration in the development programme that if these institutions do not fulfil the social purposes in view, they have to be transformed or replaced by new ones. In

"Kurukshetra", January 26, 1956.

reconstructing social and economic institutions, a large responsibility rests with the State on behalf of the entire community. The State has to plan its own investment, and to influence and regulate economic activity within the private sector so as to ensure the coordinated development of all available resources. Through its policies, the State has to safeguard the interests of the weaker sections of the community and enable them, as speedily as possible, to come up to the level of the rest.

"A socialistic pattern of society" has to be based on increased production, realised through the use of modern science and technology, and on equitable distribution of income and wealth and the problems of production cannot be viewed in isolation from wider social considerations, for the manner in which productive activity is organised itself determines, to an extent, the relative distribution of incomes and benefits reaching different sections of the community."[1]

WELFARE ORGANISATIONS

The welfare organisations working in the country, can be studied under three heads:

(1) Early welfare organisations.
(2) Recent welfare orgrnisations, and
(3) International welfare organisations working in India.

(1) Early welfare organisations

These organisations can be divided into three schools of thought.

First school of thought

It was formed by the educated Indian people who had come under the Western influence and who began to see each and every Indian custom as out-of-date. *Brahmo Samaj* and *Prarthna Samaj* were their organisations.

Second school of thought

It consisted of persons, who pleaded that the old customs and traditions needed no change. *Ramakrisna Mission* and *Theosophical Society of India* were their organisations.

Third school of thought

It adopted the mid-way and preached that neither the old customs and traditions were totally correct nor were they totally wrong. *Arya Samaj* was their organisation to carry on welfare work.

Institutions of first school thought: The institutions of first school of thought are the following:

(i) *Brahmo Samaj:* It was founded by Raja Ram Mohan Roy in 1828. After his death, Shri Devendranath Tagore, father of Rabindranath Tagore, took up the work of the *Samaj.* In 1857, Shri Keshav Chandra Sen joined the organisation. He differed with

---

[1]Draft Outline of Third Five-Year Plan published by Planning Commission, Government of India, June, 1960.

some of the *Samaj*, and so he organised the *Prarthna Samaj* in Bombay. The main works of *Brahmo Samaj* were for inter-caste marriage, and widow re-marriages, and preaching against child marriage, etc.

(ii) *Prarthna Samaj:* This organisation took up the work of running institutions, like *Anathalayas*, *Widhwa Ashrams*, girls schools and the uplift of lower castes under its *Dalitoddhar* movement. Justice Ranadey, a worker of the organisation, founded the Deccan Education Society in 1889, which started Ferguson College, Poona. This institution was based on welfare principles. Its teachers used to take only nominal pay. The *Samaj* had the patronage of persons like Gokhale and B.G. Tilak.

Gokhale founded The Servants of India Society in 1905. The purpose of the Society is to train national missionaries for service to India, and to promote the interests of the Indian people without distinction of caste or creed. The members of the Society are pledged for life to give the best that is in them for the cause of the country in all secular fields. Its members work in the field of welfare of under-privilleged groups, political reform, labour and peasant organisations rural welfare and cooperation, education and literacy, emergency relief of distress and general social service. It started the Gokhale Institute of Politics and Economics.

Organisations like the All-India Trade Union Congress, the *Sewa Samiti* at Allahabad, Scout Association for India, *Sewa Mandal* for *Harijan Uddhar*, etc., were organised by the members of the *Samaj*.

Institutions of second school of thought: The institutions of the second school of thought are the following:

(i) *Ramakrishna Mission:* Ramakrishna Paramhamsa was a great reformer. His disciple, Swami Vivekanand, founded under this mission the Ramakrishna Math and Sangh in 1897. It aims at carrying on missionary and philanthropic works looking upon all, irrespective of caste, creed or colour, as manifestations of the Divine. The workers of the Mission, who are *Sanyasis*, take up activities like maintaining hospitals, outdoor dispensaries, schools and colleges, women and village uplift, work in labour colonies, and cultural work, etc. Its sources of income are grants, public contributions, fees and charges, sale proceeds of publications, etc. It has branches all over India and also in many other countries.

(ii) *Theosophical Society:* It was started in America through the efforts of Madam Blavatsky and Col. Alkot in 1875. They heard about the work of *Arya Samaj* and, with the consent of Swami Dayanand, opened a branch of their organisation in India, under the auspices of the *Arya Samaj*. Later on, the views of the two organisations differed, because the Theosophical Society workers believed in ghosts, spirits, worshipping of images, etc., while Rishi Dayanand was removing these orthodox ideas and baseless beliefs.

Institutions of the third school of thought: The institutions of third school of thought are the following:

Arya Samaj: It was founded by Rishi Dayanand in the year 1875. He took up lead in conducting a campaign against the role of priests, worshipping in temples, *Shraddha* ceremonies, exploitation of the weak, *Purdah* system, etc., and created an all-round awakening by saying that the real Hindu religion was the *Vedic* religion and in in the *Vedas* there was no mention about *Shraddha*, *Devis*, caste system, superiority of one person over the other due to birth in a higher caste or difference in sex, etc. He also campaigned against the use of English and started *Gurukuls* to adopt Sanskrit as a medium of instruction. He advocated that Hindi should be the national language. He took up works like the uplift of scheduled castes, opened *Anathalayas*, *Widhwa Ashrams* and started a *Shuddhi programme*, under which people who had sometime changed their religion were again converted to Hinduism.

In the Punjab, U.P. and other States, there are hundreds of educational institutions called D.A.V. Schools or Colleges, serving thousands of people.

Welfare Organisations of Non-Hindus: Bahawi Sampradaya and *Ahmedi Qadyami*, organisations among Muslims, *Rahanumal Mazdyasna* amongst Parsis and *Shrromani Gurdwara Prabandhak Committee* amongst Sikhs, did welfare work in their communities.

(2) Recent welfare organisations

Central Social Welfare Board

It was set up in August, 1953, on the recommendation of the Planning Commission. Its function was to aid and strengthen the activities in the field of social work. Among other schemes, directly controlled by the Board, are the Welfare Extension Projects, Urban Family Projects, Training programmes, etc. With a view to decentralising the functions of the Central Board, the State Welfare Boards, consisting mainly of women social workers have been constituted in nearly all the States of India.

Welfare extension projects: This scheme was launched on 2nd October, 1954. Under it, an all-round development of rural areas is being attempted. Each project covers 20 to 24 villages and a population of about 20,000. Each project is divided into five villages each, so that it can be easily covered by a welfare worker. Voluntary workers, representing local welfare organisations, who are members of the Project Implementing Committee, plan the project work. This committee ordinarily consists of nine members, the majority of whom are women social workers and at least one, is a district official concerned with planning. The VLW and *Gram Sevika*[1] is a whole time employee and carries on the day to day work in the project centres.

The details of the programme are determined in relation to the felt needs of the population. About Rs. 25,000 are to be spent on a welfare extension project in a year, and half of this amount is paid by the Central Social Welfare Board.

Youth Welfare: The main objective is to offer an individual youth opportunities of various kinds, complementary to those of a home, such as a formal education and work so as to be able to hold discourse and develop their personal resources of body, mind and spirit and thus better equip themselves to lead the life of mature, creative and responsible members of the society.

A seminar, held by the United Nations in Simla in 1951, stressed the importance of setting up a Youth Welfare Organisation. The Government also viewed this problem and set up a Youth Welfare Section to draw up a programme of work for the youth population. A sufficient amount has been provided in the Fourth Five-Year Plan for taking up this work.

A scheme, regarding Youth Camps and Social Service has been designed, whereby

---

[1] A Lady Village Level Worker (LVLW).

through the camps, youths are engaged in providing manual labour for projects of national utility like the construction of roads, repair of tanks, planting of trees, etc. They also carry out a literacy and sanitation drive in rural areas, and conduct surveys of village conditions and life. Universities, State Governments and voluntary organisations like Bharat Sevak Samaj are taking active part in conducting Youth Camps. The N.C.C. units have also extended a helping hand by inviting non-cadet students to join the N.C.C. service camps.

In some States, youth organisations on the lines of the 4-H Clubs of the USA are being organised under C.D. programme and extension wings of agricultural colleges.

Welfare of women: The Central Social Welfare Board, under their scheme of Welfare Extension Projects, takes up maternity aid, spread of literacy, social education, instructions in crafts and also the community life of women; the economic conditions of their families and their general outlook on life is also being touched.

All-India womens conference: It was registered in 1929. Its objects are, to work for the welfare of women and children in all ways, promotion of the ideals of citizenship and social reform. It holds annual sessions, and the activities include family planning, running cooperatives and vocational training centres, protection of the handicapped, suppressing immoral traffic in women and children, the running of maternity houses, nursery schools, distribution of milk from milk powder, family planning work, etc.

Shri Nehru, the then Prime Minister of India, in his message to the Community Development Conference, held on 20th May, 1958, at Mount Abu, emphasising the work of women welfare, remarked that "In order to awaken the people, it is the woman, who has to be awakened. Once she is on the move, the household moves, the village moves and the country moves and through the woman the children are brought up and given the opportunities of a healtheir life and better training. Thus, through the children of today, we build the India of tomorrow."[1]

Bharat Sewak Samaj

With the aim in view that a national front for constructive work, should be created as a powerful instrument of economic and social progress in the country, this organisation has been set up. Under it, every effort is being made to secure the fullest cooperation of all the bodies engaged in social work. Its aim is to find and develop avenues of voluntary services for the citizens of India, to promote national self-sufficiency and to build up the economic strength of the country, to promote the social well-being of the community and to mitigate the privations and hardships of the less-favoured sections, to draw out the available unused time, energy and other resources of people and direct them into various fields of social and economic activity.

Functions of the Samaj: The functions of the *Samaj* are to render assistance in restoring and improving the health of the community, building up standards of honesty in public conduct, public administration and business relations, creating a social atmosphere and organising public opinion and social action to combat antisocial behaviour, etc.

The *Samaj* makes arrangements to train and equip those who offer themselves for

---

[1] *The Indian Express,* 21st May, 1958.

work in the organisation in order to enable them to render official and useful services.

Principles of the Samaj: The organisation and the activities of the *Samaj* conform to the following principles:

(1) A common platform for the services of the nation, irrespective of caste, creed or political beliefs or affiliation.

(2) Any use of the organisation or its activities for capital or communal purposes is strictly forbidden.

(3) The principle of decentralisation is applied to the utmost extent.

(4) Every effort is made to secure the fullest cooperation and collaboration between the *Samaj* and the official or non-official agencies working in the same field.

Membership of the Samaj: There are founder members, ordinary members, honorary members, life members, associate members and organisation members.

Organisation of the Samaj: The activities of the *Samaj* are organised on a regional as well as functional basis. The regions, and subordinate units, are the same as the administrative areas of the Government, namely Tehsil, District or Province. The activities of the *Samaj* are organised in accordance with a list, provided by the Central Organisation, which can be modified according to the local conditions. There is one head of each division who is responsible for the day to day administration of the affairs of the division. The Central Board appoints an Advisory Committee for each division, to guide and assist the working in the division subject to the directions of the Central Board. There is a similar set-up in each State.

Funds of the Samaj: Funds are obtained from donations; grants from private charities, private or public trusts and public bodies; grants from the State and payment for services rendered.

The main work of the *Samaj* is the holding of Youth Camps, for college, school and village youths. They pay the transport charges, provide free food and other amenities, costing about Rs. 2.50 per head per day for food and Rs. 2 per head towards contingent charges, etc. Any responsible teacher or social worker can get this aid if he manages to enlist half of the students and half of the village youths, totalling up to 30. The duration of such camps should be at least 10 days. During the summer and winter vacations, such camps are organised throughout the country.

The other important work done by the *Samaj* is to help the affected population at the time of floods, epidemics and other such devastations and calamities.

(3) International welfare organisations working in India

Important international welfare organisations have done great work in the development of our resources and the education of our technicians, etc. Such organisations are:

World Health Organisation (WHO)

It was established in 1948. India has been its members since then. It has provided assistance to projects connected with malaria control, child health, nursing, T.B. control through B.C.G. campaigns, etc. Its important works have been malaria control in Tarai, U.P., T.B. control through B.C.G. campaign and starting of T.B. Clinics at Delhi, Patna and Trivandram, etc. It has helped the College of Nursing, Delhi; Physiotheraphy School, Bombay and Nursing Training Schools in Madras, Bombay and Calcutta. During 1959, it provided a sum of 0.9 million dollars for implementation of programmes in India under its regular technical assistance funds, and also sanctioned 0.3 million dollars for Malaria eradication. It holds its annual meeting in different parts of the world to which Indian delegates are also invited. The World Health Assembly was held in 1959 at Geneva and India's Health Minister attended it with his delegation. It awards fellowships in the medical and health sciences for the training of experts abroad.

United Nations Educational, Scientific and Cultural Organisation (UNESCO)

It is directly responsible for all United Nations' social activities. It is very much interested in assisting various projects through technical advice, information, holding conferences and seminars, etc. A social officer attached to the body, for South Asia, is located at Delhi. With the help of Government of India it is running a Public Library Project in Delhi. Its Social Education Department arranges lectures, film shows and holds discussion groups and reading circles. It is running an institution for training youth leaders in India. India is also a founder-member of UNESCO and has a permanent National Commission on it. A Seminar on the implementation of major UNESCO projects was held in Bombay. A refresher course for sociologists from the South Asian countries sponsored by UNESCO, was held at Agra University in December 1959.

Agreements on operational plans were signed in New Delhi on January 15, 1960 for the establishment of the Central Mechanical Engineering Research Institute at Durgapur, and two power engineering research organisations through UNESCO.

United Nations International Children's Emergency Fund (UNICEF)

This is an international organisation having 75 countries as its members. It receives voluntary contributions from governments and individuals of various member countries in money, goods and services which utilises for the welfare of children. It provides basic medical equipment for rural health centres, teaching aids, etc. During 1959, it allocated 5.1 million dollars to India and the total aid received up to 1959 has been 28 million dollars.

Food and Agriculture Organisation (FAO)

Its head office is at Rome and India has one branch office. It conducts surveys, holds conferences, provides training facilities abroad, supplies information of international value. It keeps technicians on its staff and posts them in underdeveloped countries. The FAO Regional Seminar on Food Technology for Asia and the Far-East met in Mysore in 1959. It has formed a World Food Bank to overcome the food surplus and shortage problems. The international meeting on Dairy Problems in Asia and the Far-East and the third meeting of the Plant Protection Committee for South-East Asia and Pacific Regions were held at New Delhi in December 1959.

Colombo Plan

It was born at a meeting of ministerial representatives of the Commonwealth nations in Colombo (Ceylon) in January 1950.

The Plan took all countries constituting what is called South-East Asia. It was inaugurated on July 1, 1951. The plan is to improve the standard of living of the member countries with assistance from developed countries. Assistance is rendered financially and technically and technical assistance is exchanged. Britain, Canada, Australia and New Zealand are financing India under the plan.

Aids from the USA

(a) *U.S.A.I.D. Programme*

This was an abbreviation of United States Administration for International Development. Formely, it was called the Technical Cooperation Mission (T.C.M.). Besides other programmes, it gave aid to Agricultural Colleges and Agricultural Universities in India. In it India was divided into four regions: Northern region, Eastern, Western and Southern. Each Province is attached to one University of the USA. The US Government provides its aid through that University. The aid is in the form of equipment, books, training of staff and provisions of experts from the USA to develop Indian institutions in agriculture and especially Agricultural Universities.

U.P. and M.P. were with the University of Illionis. The training of teachers in the USA under this programme started in 1956. Every year some staff members were sent from each college covered by the programme. A team of experts under a group leader works at various places. Orissa University (Bhubhaneshwar) is being aided by the University of Missouri; Andhra Pradesh University by Kansas State University; Mysore University by the University of Tennessee; Punjab and Rajasthan Agricultural Universities by Ohio State University.

(b) *US Philanthropic Organisations Helping India*

(i) *Ford Foundation:* The Ford Foundation work in India started in 1951. The Ford Foundation gives money to the Planning Commission or appropriate ministries. Besides important programmes in other fields, rural development has been given great emphasis. It has financed 15 Pilot Extension Projects, 43 VLW Training Centres, 25 Women VLW Training Centres, 3 Public Health Training Centres, 5 Social Education Training Centres, 25 Women VLW Training Centres, 20 Village Artisan Training Centres, 3 Centres for Training of Project Executive Officers. It is financing in-service training programmes for rural development; youth organisation and village leaders; organisation of extension wings at Agricultural Colleges; farm youth exchange; evaluation programmes and strengthening the agricultural information and extension services. It posts experts on extension education and rural sociology to work in India. It has financed the establishment of the farm advisory unit at New Delhi. Hundreds of trainees are getting education in the USA on Ford Foundation scholarships.

(ii) *Rockefeller Foundation:* The Rockefellers are a billionnaire family of New York. Their generous help has been flowing into India since 1920, when they firstly financed the studies and control of hook worm. Their early help has been to health programmes. The Rockefeller Foundation is cooperating with the Indian Council of Medical Research. Besides other programmes in extension, it provides about 15 scholarships per year for study in the USA. It gives 250 dollars per month to the trainee and 100 dollars to his wife if she goes with him to the USA. Besides this, it gives return passage for both and also other expenses.

AMENITIES AND SERVICES FOR RURAL DEVELOPMENT

Education

In the present age, education, for any society, is of vital importance. In the community development programme, education also plays a very important role, especially in bringing about social change and the adoption of improved farming practices. Since its Independence, India is making a continuous effort through its Five-Year Plans to increase the percentage of literacy in the rural areas. Literacy, which was only 8 per cent in 1947-48, is now about 29 per cent and the number of institutions imparting education has increased from about 2.86 lakhs to over 8 lakhs during the same period.

There are now facilities for all types of education: (1) general, (2) technical, (3) social, (4) rural, (5) audio-visual, (6) for the handicapped, and (7) medical.

(1) General education

The struggle for India's political freedom was also a struggle to remove poverty and ignorance. In the Constitution it was laid down that the education of a child, up to the age of 14, shall be made free and compulsory up to the year 1960-61. In India, education is primarily the responsibility of the State Governments and the Union Government mainly deals with the coordination of educational facilities, determination of standards of education, research, scientific and technical education. The State Governments took up the question of free and compulsory education up to the age of 14 years and they have done it to a great extent. General education can be divided into: (a) Pre-Primary Education, (b) Primary Education, (c) Secondary Education, (d) Basic Education, and (e) Higher Education.

(a) Pre-primary education

The number of such schools in the country increased from 303 in 1950-51 to 4,70,115 in 1976 and the strength of students during the same period increased from 21640 to 77 lakhs.

(b) Primary education

There is an All-India Council for Elementary Education which advises the Central and State Governments on all matters relating to elementary education and the preparation of programmes for the early implementation of compulsory and free education. Legislation for compulsory primary education has been enacted in nearly all the States. The number of schools has gone from 2 lakhs to over 4 lakhs and the number of students have increased from 1.8 crores in 1950-51 to over 8 crores in 1978-79.

(c) Secondary education

The number of such schools has increased from less than 12 thousand (1946-47) to over 1,52,588 in 1978-79. These institutions now handle about 10 crore students. In 1952, the Government of India appointed a Secondary Education Commission under the Chairmanship of Dr. A. L. Mudaliar and the programme is going on according to the recommendations of this Commission. This education is said to be self-contained and complete and aims to provide instruction up to the age of 17 years to be followed by a 3-year integrated course in Arts or Science, or 4 years in Agriculture or Veterinary Science for the Bachelor's Degree. A Central Board of Secondary Education has been set up to conduct a common All-India Higher Secondary Examination. It will cater to the needs of children of Union Government employees and will make its services available to any secondary school in or outside India wishing to prepare its candidates for its examinations.

To assist in making reforms in the examination system evaluation units have been set up in Assam, M.P., Maharashtra, Mysore, U.P. and West Bengal. The State Bureau of Educational and Vocational Guidance are being strengthened in Gujarat, Mysore, Orissa, Punjab, Rajasthan and U.P.

(d) Basic education

This pattern is mainly based on the principles and philosophy of Mahatma Gandhi. In it, education is imparted through socially useful and productive activities like spinning and weaving, gardening, domestic carfts, pottery, elementary engineering, etc. There are junior basic schools, senior basic schools and post-basic schools. A National Institute of Basic Education was set up in 1956. It conducted reseach and offered training and guidance to teachers and administrators of basic education. It also developed suitable material and literature on basic education. It is now a constituent unit of the National Council of Educational Research and Training. A National Board of Basic Education was established in 1962 to advise the Union Government.

(e) Vocational and technical education

These include schools for agriculture, arts and crafts, commerce, engineering, forestry, industry, medicine, physical education, teachers' training, veterinary science, polytechnics, etc.

(f) Special school education

It includes school for the handicapped and for social workers, school of music, dancing and other fine arts, schools of oriental studies, adult education, etc.

(g) Higher education

Post-secondary education in India is imparted through arts, science, professional and special education colleges, research institutes and universities. There are about 115 Universities. Twenty-eight boards of education, 3582 research institutes, and arts and science colleges, 1834 professional colleges, in all totalling about 52,700 institutions.

(1) *University Education Commission:* In 1948, the Central Government appointed a University Commission under the chairmanship of Dr. S. Radhakrishnan. It reviewed the university education system and recommended that the universities must provide leadership not only in politics and administration but also in the various professions, industry and commerce. They must also meet the increasing demand for every type of higher education—literary, scientific, technical and professional. The Commission laid particular emphasis on agricultural colleges and suggested

that wherever possible, these should be located in rural areas. To coordinate the university education in the country, the Commission suggested the establishment of a University Grants Commission.

(2) *University Grants Commission:* It was constituted by the Central Government in 1953 and given an autonomous statutory status in 1956. The Commission has the authority to make appropriate grants to different universities and to implement development schemes.

(2) Technical education

The number of degree colleges in engineering and technology has increased from 53 in 1951 to 108 in 1978 and the diploma institutions in engineering and technology increased from 89 to 291. There are about 65,000 students in these institutions. Institutes of Management at Calcutta and Ahmedabad, a College of Architecture at Chandigarh, and an institute for training in industrial engineering was set up in Bombay.

Higher education in agriculture and veterinary science

There are about 96 Colleges of Agriculture and 21 of Veterinary Science. These were formerly constituent or affiliated colleges of General Universities. Now, some of these are under the Agricultural Universities. Such Universities have now started functioning on the Land Grant College pattern of the USA. These include: G.B.P. Agriculture University, Pant Nagar; CSAU, Kanpur; NDUA, Faizalabad (U.P.). Punjab Agriculture University Ludhiana, HAU, Hissar; Udaipur University; J.N. Agriculture University Jabalpur; University of Agricultural Sciences Bangalore, A.P., Agriculture University, Hyderabad; Orissa Agriculture University Bhubhaneshwar (Orissa). Four Agricultural University in Maharastra; BEKVV, Kalyani (W.B.), MPKVV, Palampur (M.P.), T.N.A.U., Coimbatore, AAU, Jorhat, Gujarat Agricultural University, Anand; R.A.U., Patna; Kerala Agricultural University, Mannuti and I. A. R. I., New Delhi is also functioning as an university of this type.

(3) Social education

It embodies a five-point programme to promote literacy, knowledge of rules of health and hygiene, improvement of adults' economic status, sense of citizenship with an adequate consciousness of rights and duties, and healthy recreation suited to the needs of the community and the individual. Social education provides an educational base for Community Development Programmes in the country. The Block Programme under it has cultural and recreational activities, utilisation of audio-visual aids and organisation of youths' and womens' groups.

For the training of social workers of a higher grade, a National Centre for Fundamental Education has been established in New Delhi. A similar Social Education Institute has been established at Indore. Janata Colleges and Vidyapiths are providing similar facilities for training the social workers.

(4) Rural education

A National Council for Higher Education in Rural Areas was established in 1956, to advise the Government on all matters relating to the development of rural higher education. The Council has selected 14 institutions for developing into Rural Institutes and these have started functioning. They are Sriniketan (West Bengal), Gandhigram (Madras), Jamianagar (Delhi). Udaipur (Rajasthan), Birouli (Bihar), Bichpuri (U.P.), Sanosara (Gujarat), Coimbatore (Madras). Gargoti (Maharashtra), Amraoti (Maharashtra), Hanumanamathai (Mysore), Travancore (Kerala) and Indore (M. P.). Their diplomas have been recognised as equivalent to the first degree of a University, for employment purposes. It is also recognised by the Inter-University Board and certain universities. Their two year certificate course in Agricultural Science, and the Sanitary Inspectors' course have been recognised by most of the State Governments. A three years' course for general education and teachers' training has been started at Gargoti.

(5) Audio-visual education

A National Institute of Audio-visual Education has been established since 1959. It conducts a Diploma course for 9 month's training at Delhi and acts as a production, research and clearing centre for audio-visual education.

(6) Education of the handicapped

The National Centre for the blind at Dehradun provides an integrated service for the blind. A national library has been started at this centre to produce literature for the blind. A training centre for the adult deaf has been established at Hyderabad. A training centre for teachers in blind schools has been set up at Bombay in 1963.

(7) Medical education and training

There are about 106 medical colleges, 18 dental colleges and 11 other institutions for training in the allopathic system of medicine. The capacity of these institutions has increased from 3,600 in 1955 to over 12,500 now. There is a Central Health Education Bureau which since 1956 coordinates and promotes health education in the country. There is an All-India Institute of Medical Sciences at New Delhi. The hospitals and nursing colleges provide facilities for training the nurses. There are 264 nursing schools for training nurses, midwives, health visitors and auxiliay mid-wives. The National Institute of Communicable Diseases, Delhi, is conducting training courses for health personnel.

Health and medical facilities

In India, there has been very steady improvement in the general health of the population. The average expectation of life has increased from 30 years in 1945 to 52 years in 1978. The death rate per thousand has decreased from 20 in 1945 to 15 in 1976. The infant mortality rate per thousand of population declined from 102.4 in 1958 to 80 in 1964. During the Fifth Five Year Plan, an amount of Rs. 681.66 crores was earmarked for health and medical services. At the end of 1976, there were about 162,000 doctors, 70,000 mid wives, 1,03,000 nurses, and 2,052, health visitors. We require double the present number of doctors.

(1) Nutrition

The average diet of an Indian is about 1,200 calories against the requirement of

2,800 calories per day. Several steps have been taken to meet the deficiency of nutrients especially for infants and feeding mothers, school children and industrial workers. It is being done through school feeding programmes, distribution of skimmed milk, protein supplements, manufacture and popularisation of cheap and nutritious food, distribution of dried milk for school children. An Applied Nutrition Programme has been launched throughout India in cooperation with U.N.I.C.E.F., F.A.O. and W.H.O.

(2) Primary health centres at block level

There are over 5328 primary health centres working in the country. There is a team of health workers in each blocks who visits the villages to provide this service.

(3) Family planning/Family welfare

The Family Planning Programme was started to reduce the birth-rate, to stabilise the population, and to help women to maintain their health by proper gaps in between two births. The Fifth Five Year Plan provided Rs. 497.36 crores for: (a) education and motivation for family planning, (b) provision of services, (c) training, (d) supplies, (e) communication and motivation and (f) medical and biological research. There is a Central Family Planning Board, the Demographic Advisory Committee, the Committee on Scientific Aspects of Family Planning and the Family Planning Communication Research Committee. Family Planning Boards are functioning in all the States. There are district committees for family planning. Full time family planning officers have been employed in most of the States. There are about 5328 regular clinics in the rural areas. Free distribution of contraceptives, sterilisation operations in women and vasectomy on males are done. The use of the loop is also being popularised. Other incentives include increments, pay hike and priorities in promotions, etc. Now this is a family welfare programme since 1977.

(4) Water supply and sanitation

Under the National Water Supply and Sanitation Programme, launched in 1954, about 500 Rural Water and Sanitation Schemes have been completed. A Drinking Water Board was set up in April 1963 to provide liaison between the Central and State Governments. Training in Public Health Engineering is also being provided at the All-India Institute of Hygiene and Public Health, Calcutta, the Engineering College, Guindy, and the Engineering College, Rourkee. A Central Public Health Engineering Organisation has been set up to help State Governments in the preparation and execution of their schemes and to provide technical advice and guidance.

Recreation and utilisation of leisure

If the village youth, and even adults, are not provided with a healthy programme of recreation and utilisation of their leisure period, they can indulge in vices like drinking, gambling, etc., and there will be more quarrels, litigations, wastage of money leading to indebtedness. So there is need for a programme for the utilisation of the leisure period and provision for recreational facilities.

Points for consideration in drawing up programmes for villagers

(1) Because rural people work in the open fields and exert themselves a good deal, games requiring heavy exertion may not be suitable for many. (2) Rural people are mostly illiterates. (3) Programmes have to be of the seasonal type. (4) Villagers are poor and may not be able to afford costly games. (5) Recreational programmes should be of the educative type combined with things which already exist there.

Facilities available for games, sports and recreation

There is a National Plan for Physical Education and Recreation for the promotion of physical education and recreation. The plan aims at popularising a model syllabus for physical education for boys and girls, promoting research in special aspects of physical education including *Yoga*, granting assistance to *Vyayamshalas* and *Akhadas*, holding Physical efficiency weeks and festivals and producing documentary and feature films on physical education. The College of Physical Education at Gwalior started in 1957 offers training facilities for a 3-years degree course in physical education for a Bachelor's Degree and 2 years for a Master's Degree. There is a N.C.C. College for Women at Gwalior. A Central Advisory Board of physical education and recreation has been set up since 1950. It advises the Government on coordination of programmes and activities. There is an All-India Council of Sports and a National Institute of Sports has been set up at Patiala to provide training to coaches from educational institutes in the rural areas. It has a scheme of regional training centres.

The village schools can avail of these facilities. Besides, the Block Programme through social education organisers, provides facilities for the supply of sports equipment to youth clubs. Such youth clubs should be organised for games, sports and recreational programmes.

Recreational Programmes can be: (1) Radio programmes—All India Radio broadcast programmes for rural people. The villagers should be told about such programmes especially dramas or talks on crops, livestock raising, etc., (2) Film shows, (3) Dramas, (4) Folk dances, (5) Songs by professional singers composed on village problems, methods of improved farming and better ways of living, etc., (6) Readings of the Ramayana, Mahabharata or Gita followed by talks or group discussions, on their importance, (7) In some areas during the month of Holi, *i.e.*, from Basant Panchmi to Holi there are special programmes of songs and dancing with the aid of instruments like Drum, Jhanj, Gharnawal, Dhup, Kalangi, etc. This can be revived and special songs can be composed by the village composers on technical material given by the Subject-Matter Specialists or teachers or Extension Wings of Agricultural Colleges. In the months of August and September, the village people have sufficient leisure time and assemble to hear Alha.

This Alha can also have songs composed on the problems of rural people such as cattle breeding, poutlry, etc., and their solutions. Puppet shows dealing with rural problems can also be organised at the time of marriages and it can be followed by speeches or visits to demonstration plots. The Baratis have the leisure for such visits and, moreover, will learn new techniques.

On national days like 15th August, 26th January, Gandhiji's birthday (2nd October), Nehru's birthday (14th November) special programmes of games, sports and recreation can be organised.

CHAPTER 19

SOCIAL ORGANISATION, DISORGANISATION AND CHANGES IN RURAL ORGANISATIONS

SOCIAL ORGANISATION

Definition

It is a state of being, a condition in a society, in which the various institutions function in accordance with their implied purposes. It is characterised by the harmonious operation of the different elements in the society.

Relationship of social organisation with social structure

Social organisation is dependent upon social structure and the degree of agreement that characterises its members. Efficient functioning of the society depends upon: (1) the way in which the members of the group or society assume their roles, and (2) upon the mechanisms by which they fulfil their social needs and purposes. The mechanisms are the social patterns, the institutions, administrative agencies, and other instruments of social control, which the group or society has developed to achieve its goals.

"The degree of social organisation is determined both by the harmony existing between those social mechanisms and the relative willingness of the individual members of society to accept their particular statuses and roles. Where members refuse to accept traditional statuses and roles, the social organisation breaks down."[1]

Social structure: The term applies to the particular arrangement of the interrelated institutions, agencies and social patterns as well as the social statuses and roles which each person assumes in the society or group. Thus, the religious institutions—the church, the temple or Gurdwara or Synagogue; the economic institutions, welfare agencies, educational institutions, the family and all other social controls are interrelated. In the old days, social structure was dominated by religious institutions—church, temple, etc., and all other institutions were closely related with these. Now the government has assumed an increased dominance in the social structure and the status and roles of the individuals have already changed and are still changing day by day. In any society, certain persons direct the functioning of the institutions and others merely take a subordinate position in the process of this function.

[1]Elliot & Merrill, *Social Organisation*, Harper and Bros., New York, p. 6.

The status and the role

The status is the position of an individual in the group or society which he occupies by virtue of his belonging to a sex, age, birth, being married, physical abilities possessed, achievements and designated duties.

The role is the part an individual plays as a result of his status in the society or group. Thus, any individual has a status as: child of his parents, he is young or old, married to a girl or a boy, is younger or older to somebody, is leader or follower, literate or illiterate. An Extension Officer has different roles as: Subordinate to his supervising officer, as husband of his wife, father of his children, son of his parents, guide to farmers, supervising officer to village level workers, member of the social group in the town and so on. So the member of a group must act as they are supposed to act in terms of their status and roles otherwise there will be a threat to organised society.

Types of status

(a) *Aseribed status:* It comes by birth. In primitive and static societies social mobility is restricted. The majority of persons neither rise nor fall from the status ascribed to them by accident of birth.

(b) *Achieved status:* In a dynamic and progressive society, birth in a poor or low status family does not debar a man to reach out high status. If he gets the required status through education, desired abilities, he can achieve it. In the USA, society is dominated by those who have their achieved status. In primitive societies, the sons and daughters of kings, emperors, landlords, etc., dominated, because the ascribed status was recognised. In India, after Independence, a person of the family status of the late Shri Lal Bahadur Shastri, could become Prime Minister. Society has become dynamic and progressive and the country abolished the system of recognising the Rajas, Maharajas and landlords after 1947. In a dynamic society, anyone can aspire to reach the top of the social structure. So status and role differ in different societies at any one time, and within the same society at different times. The success with which a person can play his various roles depends upon his inherited abilities and social situations. Because of differences in individual inheritance and social situation, one person may be more successful than another. In a dynamic society, the social difficulties involved in carrying out the expected patterns of behaviour are proportionately greater while in static society, status and role are more secure, and individual adjustment is proportionately easier. Therefore, in a dynamic society, there is complexity of status and role because of the changes in the patterns and the difficulties of personal adjustment. In recent years, for example, in developing countries like India, there has been an increase in the educational level of the people, rise in the standard of living of labourers, tenants, social and economic position of women. With the change of economic and political status of women, where a lady can be the Prime Minister of India, the role of the husband as head of the family has changed and will change. Similarly, the father of today may not hold the same position in deciding the career of his son. In an advanced country the daughter may not accept a boy selected by her father to be her husband. The father of today, in many communities in India, may not like the family priest (Pandit) and the barber (Nai) to settle the marriage of his daughter as it used to be in 1920's in many parts of India.

Social processes in a dynamic society

The concept of social process refers to all the changes that can be regarded as changes in the life of the group. These can be classified as communication, conflict, competition, accommodation and assimilation. The processes in interaction give rise to social inter-action.

Communication

It is basic to all social interaction and fundamental to all social organisation. Many times, the symbols, words, phrases and ideas, may be understood differently and those may arouse different emotions, e.g., "I will see you some day" if said in anger, with red eyes and straight neck may have a different meaning than saying it politely to somebody. The previous when in anger is an indication of revenge while the other is submission, cooperation. *Dekh Lunga* (देख लूंगा ।) *Zara Soch Samajh Ke Rehna.* (जरा सोच समझ कर रहना ।) *Kyon, Kya Irade Hain.* . . . . (क्यों क्या इरादे हैं ।)

Conflict

If the circumstances are such, communication may result in conflict or competition. If the opposition between persons or groups is conscious, the process is called conflict. In general, conflicts are destructive to the organisation of larger groups. Such social conflicts as feuds, class struggles and wars are fundamentally disruptive and tend to bring about the disorganisation of any society in which they are allowed free play.

Competition

When impersonal social forces are in opposition, the struggle is called competition.

Accommodation

When persons in conflict come to terms we call it accommodation. In this situation, there is mutual adjustment and the persons carry on their various activities with a minimum of friction. If the interests of two groups are at stake, certain definite agreements may be made in which both sides make concessions. When conflicting groups vary in power, subordination of the weaker often results, whatever be the type of accommodation. However, the permanent stability of the social structure is affected. It is often a conscious process and may take place suddenly and deliberately.

Assimilation

There is an unconscious adjustment to a changing social scene. By this process, the people of different cultures are absorbed into a new cultural synthesis. This is gradua, and depends upon some degree of intimate communication between the members of the larger group.

Social change in a dynamic society

Social change occurs whenever there is an introduction of new cultural traits into a given society. This introduction may take place by independent innovation or by borrowing from other cultures. If the process of cultural accommodation is slow, the society is comparatively stable. As the culture base increases the size of complexity by the addition of new traits, the relative stability of the society is seriously threatened. Living in a complex society requires more and more adaptability on the part of individuals and institutions. The material and non-material elements of culture tend to become further and further out of adjustment. Modern economic organisations cannot function effectively with an outworn legal structure. The mores become more and more unsuited to new situations. The function of society totters as inconsistencies between old social theories and new social practices increase in number and intensity.

Areas of social change

(a) *Social techniques:* Inventions and researches give new machinery or things, so old machines and ways are replaced by new techniques. This change is the first in sequence.

(b) *Economic relationships and institutions:* These grow out of technical processes, so they are second in the sequence of social change. New social classes arise about the different productive functions in the industrial society.

(c) *Social institutions:* The family, the school, the religious institutions and the government are in turn affected by the changes in the larger economic and social world.

(d) *Non-material changes:* The folkways, mores, myths and ideologies tend to persist even when there has been change in the above three areas.

Social control in dynamic society

One of the chief difficulties in bringing about any permanent adjustment between the various elements in modern society lies in the relative rigidity of the social control that society has framed. In the midst of changing techniques, economic processes and institutional functions, men cling to certain folkways, mores, attitudes, values and ideologies. These controls which the group or society imposes upon its members impart a certain consistency and stability to human activities. At the same time, they tend to render the task of adjustment to the changing world increasingly difficult.

(a) *Folkways:* The habitual forms of behaviour are handed down from one generation to the next and come to possess definite social value. They become the folkways of the culture or the only acceptable ways of acting. They become the arbiters of conduct and serve as comparatively stable elements in a changing society.

(b) *The mores:* The mores are folkways with a philosophy of social welfare attached. So they carry the implication of greater importance to the well-being of the group. Among individual persons, many violate certain folkways and still retain their status as respectable members of society. But, if their behaviour runs consistently counter to the mores, they are condemned and ostracised by their fellows. These are the standards to which the individual must conform if he wants to remain a respectable member of the society. In all societies, they are compulsive and absolute social norms which must be obeyed without question.

(c) *Law:* These are crystallised mores armed with the authority of the Government which may compel subservience and inflict punishment if it is thought fit. Murder is not only a social taboo, an infraction against the more but also an infringement upon the laws of the country. Society punishes a murderer through a court of law.   laws also embody the mores.

(d) *Institutions:* These are the most entrenched of all the elements in society. They represent values which have become incorporated into a social framework and hence constitute important units in the structure of a dynamic society. They constitute elaborate control devices whose essential rigidity renders difficult the task of maintaining any social equilibrium. The major social institutions are the family, the religious organisations, the school, the government and economic institutions.

They are not only rigid in structure, they tend to produce a group of advocates for status quo on the grounds of its essential validity. The cultural compulsions grow out of vested interest in a culture and represent the group interests in its psychological form.

Normality of social organisation

An organised society is presumed to be normal and a disorganised society abnormal. Normal is conceived to be ethical and the abnormal is immoral and undesirable. The existence of such a value system is important in the organisation of a society.

Social disorganisation in modern society is in no sense an abnormal phenomenon. It is the rather natural result of the gradual breakdown in social consensus that has been taking place for centuries under the impact of an increasing rate of social change. It is a human propensity to consider those phenomena which we prefer as the normal manifestations of a desirable social order and those which we dislike as the temporary maladjustments of that order. Such interpretations make an understandings of individual, family and community disorganisation difficult and render effective social reorganisation more unlikely. In a situation in which the social structure is seriously maladjusted by the rapidity and disparity in the rate of social change, the individual result is some degree of social disorganisation. By the very nature of social process, social disorganisation is as normal as social organisation and social change is as normal as social stability.

Certain human attitudes and activities are the natural result of combinations of circumstances over which the present generation has no control. Such activities—prostitution, crime and political corruption—are the natural products of existing social patterns and biological drives. Crime against property grows out of violation of the mores which sanction private ownership. Prostitution is the inevitable concomitant of such social relationships as monogamous marriage, restriction on marriages of widow girls and pre-marital sex taboos between a man and woman of the same social class. Some societies have solved these problems by allowing widow marriages, accepting pre-marital relations as courtship and preparation for marriage, and making divorce easy and cheap. Political corruption is the result of the operation of a democratic process in a *laissez-faire* economy in which financial success is placed above political honesty. Many of the Ministers and even Chief Ministers proved themselves very good political leaders in the struggle for Independence from British rule but they proved corrupt because when they got such offices, they placed their financial success above their political honesty. They gave the chance of earning money to their sons or relatives by using their own influence or offices.

As society advances in technology, people begin to accept some signs of disorganisation such as mental derangement, prostitution, etc., to be the result of the outdated folkways and mores. Crime may be viewed as a natural result of certain social forces, and not as evidence of deliberate moral depravity. The mores can make anything right. So the definition of the situation is an important consideration. Social definitions are social products which grow directly out of the life of the group or society. The normal stability of the past century was the result of a social order that was relatively static and traditional. The breakdown of this stability was the equally natural result of social changes which dissolved the traditional social ties and rendered more difficult the establishment of new ones. The definitions which are vital in one period loose their vitality for another age. The conditions which originally give rise to the norms undergo such alterations as to be unrecognisable but the norms themselves linger on.

Consensus of social organisation

Without a general social agreement on basic issues, a society cannot continue to exist. All societies have ethos, i.e., shared values, objectives, preferences and the well-founded anticipation of the members that all the others will recognise the rules of that society and will abide by them. A society can exist only when a great number of men consider a great number of things from the same point of view; when they hold the same opinion upon any subject and when the same occurrences suggest the same thoughts and impressions to their minds. A minimum of agreement has to exist before collective action is possible. In the common understandings and expectations which make their consensus, a social organisation is said to exist.

Consensus

It is a process of 'we feeling' by the majority of the members of society on the important matters of their common life. Society is a complex of organised habits, sentiments and social attitudes, which can be said to be a consensus. It takes the form of general agreement upon such matters as nature, role, and importance of religion in society; the duties of the family towards its members and the obligations of its members towards the group itself; the nature of property relationships and the relative importance of these relationships as compared to other values in the society. Consensus applies to the government of a society, the groups which this government serves and its welfare programme for the citizens. It involves basic agreement with reference to the relationship of the individual to the group. When this common point does not exist society is basically in a condition of disorganisation.

So the consensus of the group must continually strengthen and reaffirm the values of the society if it is to remain in a state of sound organisation.

The great majority of the social acts must have social definitions before they are adjudged 'good' or 'bad' by its members. Juvenile delinquency, for example, must be constantly defined as such, by the group before it can be regarded as truly delinquent conduct. When all the members of a given society are in vital agreement on the definition of certain fundamental situations, we call it organised society, but when there is general disagreement concerning the social implications of particular activities or creeds, the disorganisation starts.

SOCIAL DISORGANISATION IN INDIA

Before we examine the process of social disorganisation in our country it would be better to understand the meaning of the term 'social disorganisation' itself. According to Elliot and Merrill, social disorganisation is a process by which the relationship between the members of a group are broken or dissolved.[1] The group may be a family,

---

1 Elliot and Merrill *Social Disorganisation.*

association, community or a nation. The process of disorganisation is found in every society in the world. There is no such society which may be called as an organised society. This is because of the fact that the process of organisation and disorganisation go side by side as we already know the society is dynamic. In other words, society always changes. The changes disrupt the equilibrium of the society or its social structure. The society resists such changes and consequently the clash takes place between the different elements (organising elements and disorganising elements).

Type of social disorganisation

There are different types of social disorganisation:
(1) Individual disorganisation.
(2) Family disorganisation.
(3) Community or National disorganisation.
(4) International disorganisation.

Actually speaking, the process of disorganisation commences from the individuals in a society, particularly those who are disorganised. These are different types of disorganised individuals such as criminals, juvenile delinquents, sex-offenders, truants, drinkers, prostitutes, gamblers, etc. There are multifarious factors involved in their being disorganised. These may be psychological, economic, social, religious or cultural.

(1) Individual disorganisation

In India, the rate of individual disorganisation is increasing gradually, particularly in the urban section of the population. The process of industrialisation and urbanisation has created so many big cities and towns. It is reported that the industrialised cities like Agra, Ahmedabad, Bombay, Calcutta, Delhi, Kanpur, Hyderabad, Madras, Nagpur, etc., are producing a very high rate of disorganised elements. As the population is increasing rapidly, the cities are becoming overcrowded leading towards density of population. This factor is creating problems of housing, due to which the slums have developed. Our late Prime Minister Pandit Jawaharlal Nehru, once remarked that the slums are challenging the nation and are responsible for creating multifarious problems. Different researches have proved that the criminal areas are to be found in the heart of the city or such areas where concentration of population is seen. All of us know that most of the industrial labour belongs to the villages. They come down to the cities to earn their livelihood. In the cities they find a new type of environment which is quite different from that in their villages. They try to adjust with the new situation but they decline in this respect. So they are maladjusted in the new situation and consequently they are disorganised. At the time of coming to the city, they have the idea to earn money to send to their family in the village but when they get insufficient wages in relation to their requirements, the entire dream is destroyed. Further, they are greatly affected by artificial and attractive surroundings. Besides this, they also become victims to different habits into which they are dragged by the bad elements. Such habits are drinking, gambling, prostitution, etc. If once they are involved in these habits they find it hard to get rid of them and are dragged towards starvation and poverty, compelled to borrow money, they become indebted. Once they are involved in indebtedness, they cannot get rid of it because of very high rates of interest. Starvation and poverty along with the bad habits picked up compels them to commit suicide or engage in crimes such as thefts, pick-pocketing, robberies etc. This is the real picture of most of our Indian labourers engaged in industry in different cities.

The slums and overcrowding are equally responsible for the increase in the rate of juvenile delinquency. Different factors contribute towards juvenile delinquency. Technically speaking, juvenile or child offenders are disorganised youths whose anti-social behaviour is in opposition to the existing laws. The factor of age determines the difference between adult and juvenile offender and this varies from one country to another. In India, the juvenile delinquent is an offender whose age is between 7 to 18 years. There are different causes which are responsible for juvenile delinquency. These are broken homes, low economic status, bad neighbourhoods, overcontrol, bad companions, bad schooling, immoral family, ill-health, neglect by the parents, cultural conflicts. unregulated leisure, lack of recreational resources, etc.

In our country most of these causes are responsible for the increase in the rate of juvenile delinquency, particularly in the urban society. In the modern era, the familial control has greatly declined and the children are gradually ignoring the importance of the family. Most families complain about the indiscipline amongst their children. The element of respect for elders has declined to a greater extent in the modern genera-tion. The lack of familial control during chidhood is one of the contributing factors to students' unrest in the country, nonetheless the schools are equally responsible for this.

It is generally reported that the reformatory agencies are also not properly dealing with the problem of juvenile delinquency although in some places such reformatory schools are functioning effectively, particularly in Bombay and Delhi. There is also a reformatory school at Bareilly, U.P. which is primarily handled by the Department of Jails. However, it is surprising that most of the juvenile delinquets belong to the poor classes or castes whereas cases among the higher classes or castes are rare. This does not mean that children belonging to rich section of the population do not express criminal behaviour. The fact is that rich and influential parents are in a position to save their children from the clutches of the law. On the other side, the poor parents are not in a position to save their children. Much is to be done in respect of diagnosing and treatment of juvenile delinquents.

Suicide is another form of individual disorganisation. Suicide means to take one's own life. It is said that the rate of suicide is very high in America. But not only this, the rate of suicide can be directly correlated with mechanisation and urbanisation. In our country, no relevant data is available on the suicide rate because most of the cases are concealed. There may be other cases of suicide also, such as family tension, starvation, mental defects, physical defects, continuous illness and so on and so forth.

Prostitution is one of the problems of the day. Throughout the country, there are brothels which are usually in the heart of the cities. A prostitute is a woman who under-takes commercialised sex relations. Prostitution has been declared illegal by the Indian Government through legislation. The Suppression of Immoral Traffic in Women and Girls Act was passed in 1955. It has brought forth fruitful results even though it is vehemently violated by prostitutes and the people involved with them.

Begging is prevalent in our country. Most of the persons engaged in begging are not physically or mentally retarded. They have adopted begging as their occupation and adopt different techniques to get alms. Begging is also associated with the religious element. Hindus have a firm belief in 'Dan'. Beggars can be seen in large numbers at the pilgrim centres such as Hardwar, Mathura, Banaras, Allahabad, etc. Although begging has been prohibited through legislation, this has not effected it at all as the Hindu sentiment is not against it. Hence it is flourishing and developing in the same form as in the past. Some of the social surveys have proved that the beggars indulge in vices, such as drinking, gambling, adultery, etc. Whatever money they get, they spend in the wrong direction. It is also noticed that some of the beggars indulge in theft and pick-pocketing and have adopted refined ways of cheating and robbing. Therefore it is suggested that begging should be banned outright otherwise it may create more and more problems for society. Begging in India has been very much criticised in the Western countries and society at large is to be blamed for it.

Our industrial labour is the victim of liquor and gambling. In the big cities like Bombay, Calcutta, Kanpur and Ahmedabad, the labourers spend much of their income on liquor. In other words, they are addicted to drinking wine due to which they are dragged into other habits such as gambling, illicit sex relations, etc., and sometimes they commit crimes in a drunken stage. These two elements are equally responsible for social disorganisation.

(2) Family disorganisation

Family disorganisation is another form of disorganisation and rather a significant one. Actually speaking, disorganisation of the family takes place because of individual disorganisation although social factors are equally responsible. Normally, family disorganisation is measured in term of divorce, separation and desertion.

Divorce refer to dissolution of marriage. In India, the divorce rate is very low but in the Western countries particularly in the USA it is very high. Here marrige is considered to be a religious sacrament. It is a bond which can never be broken even in death. Further, divorce is vehemently criticised by the Hindu society. Due to the criticism, no one dares to divorce. Before the enactment of the Hindu Marriage and Divorce Act, 1955, divorce was not legal, but now it can be legally obtained by either of the parties. But the legislation is so complicated that divorce still cannot be easily obtained. Now gradually divorce is becoming popular amongst the educated section of the population. It is just possible that divorce may become one of the major problems in the country. Divorce normally takes place when the tensions between husband and wife become chronic and there is no other solution for them or there may be cultural maladjustments or any other reason.

Separation and desertion are also the consequences of family disorganisation. In case of separation, both husband and wife start living separately because of personal conflicts if, after sometime, the situation does not improve, it finally results in divorce. Desertion means to run away. In other words, when one party runs away and there is no likelihood of return, it is a case of desertion. Of course such cases does occur in our society but the number is small.

Today, family disorganisation in India is primarily in the form of disintegration or disruption of joint families or extended families. Actually speaking, it is the disorganisation of Indian rural families at large. They are disorganising rapidly although the Indian sentiment is still in favour of joint family systems. These families are disintegrating because of the impact of urbanisation, decline of cottage industries, mobilisation, materialism, individualism, and increase in population, etc.

Family tensions are the main root of family disorganisation. But these tensions are of two types: (a) primary tensions, (b) secondary tensions. Primary tensions are those which break up the family whereas the secondary tensions do not. There are so many families which are internally disorganised but externally they appear to be organised. It is not essential that the disorganising elements break up the family. Further, we can say that there is no such family which is completely organised or where no tensions are to be found.

Nowadays, the nuclear, or modern families, are taking the place of the extended families. This provides a change in the family structure. Now the family consists of husband, wife and minor children, whereas formerly it was based on the kinship pattern and was larger in size. However, it cannot be denied that the importance of the family has declared and is still declining. Along with it, the functions of family are also decreasing day by day. Formerly, the family was dominated by the father, but now it is dominated by the children. The clash between the parents and the children are developing because of differences in ideologies leading towards disintegration of families.

3. Community disorganisation

Community disorganisation refers to the disruption or disintegration of the community at large. Such a state of disorganisation is a most serious one. There are different factors which disrupt a community, namely: political, social, cultural and religious. Political corruption as well as the clash between the different political parties, bring about very serious situations. During the period of elections, the different political parties adopt different undesirable means to earn the votes to win the elections. Sometimes. the supporter of one political party does not hesitate even to murder the ring leader of the opposite party or its supporters. Such a situation is detrimental to the masses who are victims in the tussle.

Communal riots also disrupt a community. During the partition of the country into India and Pakistan, millions of Hindus and Muslims were slaughtered. They were innocent but they were victims of the political strategy of the British. Both the countries were disrupted for a long period and so many problems were created.

Unemployment and poverty are the economic factors which also disrupt a society. When the rate of unemployment increases, it leads to poverty and when there is dire poverty, it leads to crime, starvation, suicide, indebtedness, etc. In India, the problem of unemployment is rapidly increasing amongst both the sections of the population, educated and illiterate. Further, there is seasonal unemployment which is the main cause of poverty. An Indian farmer is born in debt, brought up in debt and dies in debt, and our industrial labourer is as poor as the farmer. About 3/4 of the population belongs to the middle and poor classes. The rich are becoming more and more rich and the poor are becoming more and more poor. Although India is a democratic country, there is no equal distribution of wealth, there are no just wages. If the growing rate of unemployment is not checked, it will bring about more and more poverty in the country. The extent of poverty has also increased because of a rapid increase in the general price level. The prices of commodities have gone up 6 to 8 times during the last three years. The rise in prices has greatly affected the masses and is equally responsible for the disintegration of economic unrest in the country.

Blackmarketeering is very popular and prevalent in India. No one is bothered to check it. Along with it people are trying to hold black money by grappling sales tax and income tax in abundance. The producers are exploiting the consumers. Such a situation is equally responsible for community disorganisation.

The clash between two nations also brings about national or international disorganisation. War is a destructive element in a nation's culture and civilisation. Pakistani aggression against India disrupted the civil life of both the countries.

Revolution also disrupts a nation or nations whether its form is political, industrial or social. Revolution brings forth new forces and destroys old ones. Revolution is a sudden change which takes place unexpectedly. However, it is harmful as well as beneficial, for it brings about disequilibrium in a society when it takes place.

In the preceding pages, we have discussed the different elements of social disorganisation with particular reference to India. India may be disorganised internally, but externally it is as strong as the big nations are although its protectors are very concerned to strengthen the foundations of the country. Our leaders are familiar with the problems and their consequences and are trying to root them out.

CHANGES IN RURAL SOCIAL ORGANISATIONS IN INDIA

Social organisations in India have remained quite stable and integrated for quite a long period. Under British administration Indian society experienced some basic changes, but changes in village life were greatly accelerated after the political independence. The systems of social organisation which have been affected by disruptive forces as well as planned and creative forces like development plans, joint family organisation, caste organisation, economic organisation, political organisation etc., are passing through a transitional phase. The evils and bad effects of urbanisation and industrialisation can be seen among the migrants of rural society who have left their villages to seek a better livelihood.

Today every social phenomenon is changing. Of course some aspects of social organisation in the village still maintain their originality and traditionality. The main ingredients of social organisation in village life include family, caste, marriage system, panchayat, religion, school, farmers, woman and youth organisations. The family although disrupted and disintegrated by industrial progress and technological factors still maintain glimpses of the old village life. The caste system, the main determinant of the Indian social structure, plays a great role in organising people according to castes. Religion in village life is still crude, unscientific and based on old beliefs, but a very dominant force in human life. Panchayats are still dominated by influential caste leaders and rich persons. Mahila mandals and youth clubs have started functioning. And at some places farmers organisations like Bharat Krishak Samaj and Tonnage clubs are taking roots.

To study social organisations and the factors responsible for such changes and disintegration is the urgent need of sociologists and anthropologists. To meet this demand to some extent, the Department of Extension Education and Sociology of Agriculture University at Jabalpur through its various campuses in M.P. state has conducted some studies during the past decade. The results may be represented under the heads of: (1) Family life, (2) Caste system, (3) Religion, (4) Marriage, (5) Panchayats, (6) Educational aspects, (7) Youth organisations, (8) Occupational mobility and (9) Women organisations.

(1) Family life

The joint family has been the common form of family organisation in India. Typically it consists of a set of men related to fathers and sons or brothers together with their wives and children. The several nuclear families thus grouped together form a single unit of consumers and function as a single producing unit.

Family structure: Because of the pressure of the Hindu Marriage and Divorce Act, the increasing education of young men and women and increasing opportunities for employment outside the village and the farming occupations, there is a tendency towards a smaller size family. A study made by R.B. Goel in Jabalpur and Sihora blocks of M.P. in 1966-67 revealed that 40% families changed their status from joint to individual types during the previous 15 Years (1951-66). Factors responsible for this change, as pointed out by Goel, were schools, transport and quarrels among housewives.

Another study by A.K. Parwar (1965) in Rewa block of M.P. in 1966-67 revealed that 72% people were living in joint families before 1958, but this came down to 62% in 1966, *i.e.*, 10% reduction in 8 years. Of those who left their families and went out, 93% were the people who got better service and income chances elsewhere. P.S. Tiwari in Sihora block of Jabalpur district revealed that only 39% of the people lived in joint families and 61% had individual families. A decade back 72% had the joint family system. In 69% cases the reason for this disintegration were quarrels among males and females. About 50% of the joint families belonged to the upper castes and 42.7% to the middle castes. U.S. Malviya in Gangai village of Narsingpur district found out that only 46.49 families were joint in form, being controlled by the eldest members of the family.

(2) Caste system

The traditional caste system is the basis of Hindu social organisation. It is the caste system which determines the function and social status of the individual. Malviya, in his study, concluded that in the social hierarchy Brahmins still enjoy the top position and many opportunities. They are followed by Rajputs and Raj Gours. The middle rank goes to Kayasthas, Ahirs, Vaishyas. The lower rank included Malies (gardeners), Dhobies (washerman), and the most depressed were Nais (barbers), Swarnkars (goldsmiths). The untouchables were Bhangies (sweepers), Chamars (cobblers). Social hierarchy in the village was almost synonymous with occupation, *e.g.*, carpenter (Badhai) weaver (Jullahas) etc.

Many changes have taken place in the caste system of India. The most important change has been the weakening of the system. The impact of industiral progress, development of channels of communication, political movements, the awareness among the lower castes and their fight for a raise in their status, etc., have worked significant changes in the caste system.

P.S. Tiwari in his study revealed that younger groups were in favour of intercaste marriages. Older people said that they could go upto talking relations. In the economic and political fields, 74.9% of the respondents favoured participation of people of all castes but they did not favour lower caste people drawing water from their wells, or entering their religious places. In 99.5% cases the religious funtions were still performed by the highest caste Brahmins. But significant changes were observed in the recruitment of teachers. About three-fourths of the teachers were from castes other than Brahmins. Pig rearing was still the occupation of lower caste people. About one-third respondents accepted that there has been a change in their attitudes towards the caste system.

Another study by A.K. Parwar on caste relationships revealed that in maintaining the relationship with the lower caste, 100% favoured talking relations, 89% favoured visiting relations; no one agreed to maintain marital ties with lower caste people. As far as equal participation is concerned, the majority of the respondents (85%) favoured equal participation of all castes in social and economic functions, 51% favoured it in social functions and 56% in religious functions.

A study by Goel pointed out that 65% of the respondents felt that during the last 15 years (1952-67) their feeling of superiority or inferiority complex has changed. Goel further found that 80.7 respondents were in favour of only talking relations with the lower castes, only 9.3% respondents were in favour of social mixing or would accept water from lower caste people and 10% favoured eating relations. None of the respondents accepted marriage with the lower castes. As far as participation of the lower castes in social and religious places 90% respondents favoured the participation of lower caste people in political and economic fields, 77.2% people still wanted to maintain their traditional attitudes towards untouchables. Only 10.7% believed that poultry farming should be limited to lower caste people. About 90% respondents refused to accept piggery as an occupation for higher caste people.

The study by A.P. Tiwari in Rewa block revealed that the majority of the higher caste people (80%) played a significant role in positive attitude formation towards technological change.

(3) Religion

Undoubtedly India is a religious conutry. Every walk of rural life is heavily loaded with religious thought. It has a simple and staunch influence. Even if an Indian farmer is not afraid of anything in the world, he is afraid of God and religion. In recent years religious thought has been influenced by many changes that have taken place.

An effort by P.S. Tiwari to study religious activities, revealed that 97% of the rural people believed in sacred rituals, 96.5% had faith in fasts, and 97.5% favoured celebration of festivals to please the gods, 87.5% favoured pilgrimages and visits to holy places, and 70% to give alms to beggars.

Tiwari further revealed that 64% people still held the old religious concepts, 70.37% people had faith in rebirth and 66.67% people believed in the other worlds of Naglok Pitralok and Parlok. 90.5% believed that smallpox could be cured by pleasing Mata in the traditional way. 42% believed in the cure of cobra bites by the chanting of mantras.

A.K. Parwar revealed in his study that 92% believed in fasting from a religious point of view. A visit to the temple to worship the Gods and deities was observed by 89% people. Many people still believed in treatment by witchdoctors for smallpox and cobra bite. Many staunch religious beliefs or mores are now disappearing slowly.

Castration of bulls, use of insecticides, and acceptance of eggs are no longer opposed blindly and vehemently as was the case 20 years ago.

(4) Marriage

Marriage is still considered to be a sacrament by villagers and Indian rural society still follows the old and traditional forms of marriage institutions. Modern education and urbanisation have brought some changes to marriage system.

Parwar (1965) has revealed that in the selection of a bride, education as a criterion plays a significant role. About 67% people prefer to marry educated girls but they had no such criterion of education in the past. Only 29% people said that they do not want educated girls. Late marriage was preferred by 92%. Only 31% used invitation cards in marriage ceremonies.

Tiwari (1966) revealed in his study that only 6.5% saw their wives before their marriage whereas 93.5% did not have this opportunity. Late marriages were followed by the upper castes only, (65.5%) Brahmins still believed that tallying horoscopes was the best method to ensure a happy marital life.

The divorce rate is still very low. Tiwari in his study found that 89.5% people were not touched by divorce. Only 7% had been divorced.

As far as marriage expenditure is concerned both Tiwari and Parwar reported that people agreed that there was increase in marriage expenses.

(5) Panchayats

Village Panchayats have been reflecting the collective will of the community even in the old days. Gram Panchayats were the media through which every individual had the opportunity to express himself in the progress of the community.

Tiwari, P.S. (1966) in his study reported that 53.5% favoured open elections 16.5% did not favour it, and 30% favoured election and nomination. Women participation was favoured by 34% whereas 66% rejected women participation. Education was favoured by 83% people as a consideration for selection of candidates to panchayats.

Tiwari, S.K. (1967) in his study conducted in Jabalpur block revealed that 46% people expressed satisfaction to the working of panchayats. Of the total members of panchayats 40% belonged to higher caste and 20% to lower castes. More than 50% members had more than 50 years of age. Majority of panchayat members were educated upto primary standard of education.

(6) Education

The significance of education in modern society cannot be overestimated. Tiwari in his study tried to understand the attitude of rural people towards education. He reported that 90.8% people sent their children to schools, 80% people favoured college education for boys and only 5% favoured college education for girls. For girls, 62.5% respondents favoured primary education. This reveals that in village higher education for girls is not liked. Only 2% favoured co-education in colleges. Caste again plays a significant role. Upper caste people preferred high school education for their girls because in such families girls have better chances of getting services and a qualified husband.

(7) Occupational mobility

Impact of technology, education and industrial progress have brought significant changes in the economic life of rural people. People who followed their parental occupation very strictly are now giving them up for the sake of better income.

Parwar while studying occupational mobility revealed that agriculture as a subsidiary occupation has increased to a great extent as compared to the past. Priests, blacksmiths, poultry keepers, barbers still maintain their traditional occupations. About 24% people have not changed their traditional occupation. Among those who have changed their main occupation, the majority (44%) have not changed their subsidiary occupations. Traditionally upper caste people had agriculture as their main occupation, middle caste people had it as a subsidiary occupation, and the people of lower caste generally worked as labourers. Persons who have changed their occupations reported that the majority of them (88%) left their occupations because they could not fulfil the needs of their families. Only 11% said that they changed due to an interest in other occupations.

Tiwari reported that 97.5% people were still following their traditional main occupation but 27.5% of them changed their sub-occupations. Only 39% felt that they may change their family occupations in the future.

Goel in his study reported that 20.7% people changed their family occupations during the last 15 years. Of the total, 91.2% respondents said that they were not interested in changing their occupation in the future. About 75% reported that they were satisfied with their traditional occupation.

(8) Youth organisation

Youths are the hopes of the nation and they are the future citizens of our country. All the aspirations of a country rest on the latent potentialities of our youths. They are the creative force of a society. Therefore, they need to be organised on better lines so as to utilise their potentialities. R.K. Shukla conducted his research on the participation of youth organisations in the community development programme of Jabalpur district. He found out that more than 70% members of youth organisations belonged to middle castes families. The majority of the members were educated and more than 50% members were the sons of parents who had a better social status. They also participated more in games. More than 60% members were interested in community development activities. The members of the youth organisations were better disciplined.

(9) Women organisation

The necessity of women's organisations was felt by the community development programme in 1954. To uplift the conditions of women, Mahila Mandals were organised in each block. Kumari Chaturvedi of Agriculture College, Jabalpur, in her study of women organisations in Jabalpur block (1967-68) found out that 68% members of such organisations belonged to the middle age group i.e. they were below 35 years, 75% members belonged to high and middle caste families only, 37% of such members had education above primary standard. The major participation of women was reported in child education (84%) recreation (81%), preparing new recipes and sewing. Of the total 64% members belonged to the upper caste, 67% always participated. Most of the members of the middle aged group were interested in preparation of recipes and sewing.

IMPACT OF DEVELOPMENT PROGRAMMES ON SOCIAL ORGANISATION

(1) Impact of education

The change of attitudes, habits, ways of thinking and relationships among people is a basic concept of education. Education acts as an instrument by which desirable change can be brought about in the people. Goel reported in his study that in a village where educational facilities were available, it brought significant change (20.6%) in the values of the caste system. Education, to a considerable extent was responsible for weakening the system of untouchability. Caste rigidities weakened with the development of knowledge. Because of education, rural people have started preferring the individual family system over the joint-family. Educated men have started believing in the utility of a planned family. Change in educational aspects was found closely connected with educational facilities. Education has brought significant changes in the status of women. Of the total 58.6% people, because of education, welcomed the participation of women in social activities, 65.5% respondents reported that they were encouraged to change their occupation because of education. The majority (67%) of the respondents reported that they were inclined to educate the girls. People having education were found more interested in organisational activities as revealed by Chaturvedi and Shukla.

(2) Impact of transport facilities

A.C. Guha (1962) in his study of the changing rural scene observed that demands for better amenities for the rural people primary education and roads occupy the top place in almost all villages.

Communications, transport facilities and social change in rural social world are virtually correlated. Goel, pointing out the role of transport reported that 47.6% people, because of educational and transport facilities, agreed that there was change in their attitude towards caste complexes. People were prepared to mix with lower castes because of transportation (20%) and accepted that they mixed with lower castes because of transport. Because of transport facilities 20.5% people left their families to get income from other places. Of the total 15.6% people changed their attitudes towards untouchables where transport facilities were available, about 60% people were in favour of co-education upto the college stage. Transport along with education, helped in the expansion of female education.

(3) Impact of community development

Community development is a programme of change which involves changes in relationships between people. As pointed out by M.S. Rao in his article dealing with analysis of development programme, rural people have become aware of the advantages of the new economic, educational and other welfare opportunities provided by the C.D. programme. Prof. Wilson, Prof. Carl Taylor, Osmen Lewis, Prof. Opler and Prof. S.C. Dubey have attempted to assess the nature of the impact of C.D. programme on the life of the rural people. Parmaroy found out that change in the caste system was seen in cases of people maintaining talking and visiting relations with lower caste people. More than 80% of the respondents favoured participation of lower caste people in social and economic development, and more than 50% favoured their participation in social fun-

ctions and religious activities. According to Tiwari the community development programme could not create any impression on the religious life of the rural people. They
are still maintaining a crude form of primitive religion. Agriculture as a subsidiary
occupation has increased to a great extent as compared to the past.

Suggestions

There is a need for higher education in rural life so that literacy may increase.
The evils of the caste system need to be rooted out. Religious beliefs which are based
on unscientific thinking have to be removed.

To improve female education, separate institutions for girls need to be started in
rural areas. It will be an incentive for those who are reluctant to send their daughters
for co-education.

A good transport system and communication network aids in agricultural and economic development. It helps in spreading education and creates a sense of general awakening in the society. There is considerable scope for road development in villages.

CHAPTER 20

PLANNED SOCIAL CHANGE

I. PROCESSES OF PLANNED CHANGE

The modern world is a world of rapid change. People too must change and acquire the facility of change. To maintain our health and creative relationship with the world around us, we must be actively engaged in the change efforts directed towards ourselves and towards our material, social and spiritual environment.

This help is now being given by providing professional helpers or change agents like extension workers, subject-matter specialists, home science extension agents, veterinary extension workers, etc., and their skills and techniques are constantly being improved. The factors which are components of the processes of change may be given as under.

A. Stimuli forcing human beings to change

Personal and social aspirations for change emerge from the forces pressing towards innovation or adoption of new technology. The four stimuli for change are:

(1) Man is continually making efforts to modify the natural resources to solve problems. These are weather control (coolers and air-conditioners, afforestation, etc.), production of electricity, atomic power; chemical control of pests and diseases, etc. This makes the set up of society complicated and new problems like labour management, new patterns of working and new patterns of leadership and cooperation begin to emerge.

(2) This (given under point 1 above) creates the need to utilise and adjust to the changes that we are continuously creating in our environments. Planners look ahead to adjustments and changes in our way of life. Legislators enact new laws to take account of changed conditions of living and the new resources which have become available; educators organise the specialised units of knowledge, which must be transmitted to our young people if they are engaged in these new processes of utilisation and adjustment; administrators coordinate our adjustmental efforts; and all of us grapple with the problems of changing our personal goals, desires, expectations and patterns of behaviour.

This creates situations in which we are always required to revise our definitions about what is good health, good performance, efficiency, effective use of our resources and so we constantly use innovations, i.e., use of DDT was once advocated, but because of the change of mind due to problem of pollution and its adverse effects on our health its use has now been banned at certain places The problem of Hippies opened the eyes of the advocates of Western culture to the problems of material wealth. People have now started thinking in terms of the values in vogue in Oriental countries like India.

(3) The competitive process of comparing ourselves with others is another impetus towards innovations. It provides us with the motivation for progress through discovering improved or changed ways of doing thing

(4) The pain and disorganisation that arises from finding that our familiar ways of behaviour no longer work in a new environment is a stimulus to change.

B. Problem-solving efforts of different strata of society compel change

Four types of dynamic systems: (1) The individual personality, (2) the face-to-face group, (3) the organisations, and (4) the community are related with change in a society.

(1) *Individual personality:* Different personality systems have various accustomed ways of solving problems. Some personality systems exhibit patterns of trust, while others exhibit patterns of distrust. Some systems try to create a relationship of submissive dependence, others strive for dominance, still others seek an extreme of dependence or minimal contact. As internal or external conditions changes, the personality system is confronted with the challenge and often with the stark necessity of modifying its customary and stabilised patterns in order to cope more effectively with the new conditions. The desirability of improving one's performance may provide a challenge which incites one to seek help, or the pain of personal maladjustment may create a readiness for change. If a person is in a state of considerable frustration because he has recently been dressed down by his boss, he is subject to a conflict between some of his subordinates for instance, his sense of social values may conflict with his need to express hostility. He may be out of mood and be harsh to his wife or his clerk, or other subordinates, or may go out for a vigorous walk and may organise a counterattack against the source of his frustration, or his boss. So it depends on the individual personality how he adjusts or behaves in a particular situation.

(2) *Face-to-face group:* Such groups include committees, staff associations, families, work groups, clubs, etc. We can visualise the internal dynamics of these systems much more easily than the internal dynamics of individual personality systems. We can watch the interaction between sub-parts of groups. We all know of the conflicts between the chairman and members of the committees or bodies, etc. These are face-to-face group difficulties. These call for change so that the conflicts and difficulties may be solved.

(3) *The organisations:* This is a larger social system which comprises the community. These are the parts of the community which have a more or less clearly defined and specialised function requiring the loyalty and a labour of a group of people who are organised in a relatively systematic relationship and whose efforts are coordinated by some kind of formal leadership structure. These are business organisations, welfare

agencies, educational institutions, government bureaus, religious associations, political parties, farmers' organisations, women's associations, youth clubs, etc. The internal process of such systems usually involve interactions among officially defined sub-parts, such as various departments of a business organisation. In organisations, the relationships among sub-parts are likely to be formalised and hence face-to-face interactions are more feasible than in small parts.

(4) *The community:* This is made up of a variety of interacting sub-parts, individual citizens, informal interest groups, organised occupational or political sub-groups, economic and social strata, geographical units, political sub-divisions, etc. The stresses and strains set up by these interacting sub-parts and the necessity of maintaining community services to all constituent units have resulted in a variety of stabilised structural arrangements and problem solving procedures.

C. Notion of planned change

The changes in a system may be in two ways: (1) by mobilising its resources to improve and correct its own operation or structure, (2) or the normal process of maturation and development which may result in the spontaneous evolution of change from within the system. All dynamic systems reveal a continuous process of change, adoption, adjustment and reorganisation.

Change agents: The specialists who introduce change are called change agents. These may be psychiatrists, psychologists, social workers, extension workers, C.D. workers, human relations experts, etc.

Client system: The individuals, groups, organisations, communities with which the change agent works for introducing a change is called the client system.

II. THEORIES OF SOCIAL AND CULTURAL CHANGE

A. Theories of social and cultural change

According to the various schools of thought the theories can be put under four heads.

(1) *Social and cultural changes are non-existent or of little importance:* These believers say that they feel like that because since the human world was established it has always been much the same. There has not been much change in the social system and the culture of the people.

(2) *Social and cultural changes are degenerative:* Such thinkers say that social and cultural changes occur for the worse; That, man step by step, moves towards degeneration or a horrible end. The past culture is always said to be better, or a "Golden Age".

(3) *Social and cultural changes are progressive:* These believers say that man seeks to attain some goal. Progress is conceived as an increase in man's technical understanding and mastery of nature and the study of man himself, or as the achieving of social, economic and political freedom. The special political institutions, the concepts of various things and the unfolding of man's spiritual potential are the by-products of economic, social and political conflicts and these become implements and vechicles of progress of the society.

(4) *Social and cultural changes are cyclical:* The believers of this say that the same

system of societies and the same sequence of civilisation, follow one another in the endless turns of a cycle.

B. Contemporary schools of thought on the types or theories of social and cultural change

Sociologists differ on the theory of social and cultural change and so have given rise to five contemporary schools of thought. These are (1) Positive Organism, (2) Conflict Theory, (3) Sociological Formalism, (4) Social Behaviourism, and (5) Sociological Functionalism.

(1) *The positive organism:* Social change was conceived as progressive and evolutionary. This theory collapsed when it was demonstrated to have relied on value promises and inadequate methods.

(2) *The conflict theory:* It developed in its early days, as specialised forms of theory of social progresses resting on the mechanism of individual and group conflict rather than on the imminent evolution of organism-like structures. This theory declined because of the lack of proponents rather than any structural defect.

(3) *Sociological formalism:* This was the first school of thought explicitly to renounce its ties with history and to shift the whole theory of social change to an insignificant place in its consideration.

(4) *Social behaviourism:* This has been the most receptive to various theories of social change. The cultural lag theory of the pluralistic behaviourists has attempted to preserve the sense of the old progress formulas by means of its distinction between material and non-material culture. The social action theories have been receptive to a variety of explanations of special social changes without integrating its many ideas on social change into a single consistent form.

(5) *Sociological functionalism:* This has dominated American sociological theory since World War II. It rests on theoretical formula similar to that of positive organism.

Because of such differences sociologists feel that the theory of social and cultural change needs to be re-examined.

Social behaviouristic theory of social and cultural change

Of all the major types of social theories, social behaviourism seems to hold out the maximum promise for a new approach to the theory of social and cultural change.

III. THE APPROACH OF THE CHANGE AGENT TOWARDS PLANNED CHANGE

Every change agent makes the following five assumptions either consciously or unconsciously.

(1) The nature of the client system.

(2) The process by which the client system got into trouble or problems which need solution.

(3) The nature of the trouble.

(4) The process which will lead to the solution of the trouble, and

(5) The ways in which he himself can contribute to bring about the desired change.

The first three are the diagnostic principles of the change agent and fourth and fifth can be called analyses of the functions of the change agent.

A. Diagnostic orientations

This includes—(1) The problem related to internal relationships, (2) the problem of external relationships and (3) motivation of the client system.

(1) *Problems related to internal relationship of the client system:* The change agent will try to help the client system develop a new and more appropriate power structure either (i) by adding new demands to the existing structure, or (ii) by revising the relationship between the existing power structure and the system as a whole. He works with individuals, in small groups, large organisations and communities.

The agent may concentrate on (i) changing the distribution of power within the client system, (ii) altering its characteristic ways of mobilising energy, or (iii) correcting the pattern of communication.

(2) *The problems of external relationship·* The change agent may proceed from three different orientations:

(i) Orientation which looks for the discrepancies between the real and perceived environment and attempts to adjust them by correcting the client system's unrealistic perceptions. (ii) If the value and behavioural goals of the client system are at variance with its own best interests and the client can be led to adopt more appropriate goals and values by undertaking new modes of behaviour and new experiences. (iii) The skills which the client system may use to solve the problems which are presented either by the external environment or by the patterns of human interaction within the system.

(3) *Motivation of the client system:* There are two forces which may increase or decrease the readiness of the client system to face change called change forces and resi.tant forces.

(a) *Change forces:* It has its origin in any aspect of the solution which increases the willingness of the client system to make a proposed change.

(b) *The resistance forces:* It has its origin in any aspect of the solution which reduces the willingness of the system to make a change.

B. Motivations for change

Four types of such motivations have been noticed:

(1) The client system may feel dissatisfaction from patterns associated with the present system.

(2) The dissatisfaction may arise from a perceived discrepancy between what is and what might be. For example the community members may not feel any real dissatisfaction with the working of the village panchayat (council) but when they see the improvement made by the panchayat of some neighbouring village, they may begin to want similar things for their own Panchayat.

(3) The behaviour of the individual may change as he grows older or develops from an infant to adult, with the technological and physiological advancement. This requirement brings pressure for change.

(4) The community may not be satisfied with the growth rate or production rate and then there is pressure for change.

C. Resistance to change

(1) Inability of the community may bring resistance to change. (2) Sometimes the change objective appears to be of doubtful value and the question is whether or not it is safe to experiment. (3) Clinging to existing satisfactions. (4) The client system may be doubtful and suspicious of the value of the help which the change agent has to give. (5) Dissatisfaction with the change agent which occurs later in the change project. (6) Emergent resistance force may be credited when factors in the situation which were unnoticed and unimportant at the beginning of the change process, turn out to be major obstacles to change, *e.g.*, cost of the change project in terms of time, money or energy may turn out to be more than the client system can handle. (7) If the actual diagnostic phase of the project consumes so much time and energy that nothing is felt for the work of changing. (8) The impending end of the relationship with the change agent may set up either change or resistance forces.

D. Role of the change agents

The change agent's role may include the following activities:

(1) *Diagnosing the value of the client system's problem:* The situation has to be diagnosed—what is the trouble? and what is causing the trouble?

(2) *Assessing the client system's motivation and capacity to change:* The change agent must assess the client's readiness to enter into a helping relationship and he must determine whether or not the client possesses sufficient motivation and capacity to hold up its end of the partnership.

(3) *Apprising the agent's own motivation and resources:* It depends upon: why the change agent want to help the client system or what rewards he wants for himself *i.e.*, money, professional advancement, research data etc.?

(4) *Selecting appropriate change objectives*: These may be: (a) different internal balance of power, (b) new pattern of communication, (c) release of additional energy, (d) revaluation of goals, (e) adjustment between external and internal reality or, (f) the development of more effective problem solving procedures.

(5) *Choosing an approach type of helping role:* They may be of five types, namely: (a) Mediating and stimulating new connections within the client; (b) Presenting expert knowledge or procedures. (c) Providing strength from within, (d) Creating a special environment, and (e) Giving support during the process of change.

(6) *Establishing and maintaining the helping relationship with the client system:* It necessitates: (a) The need for adequate sanction or approval of the client system; (b) Clarifying expectations about the change relationship, i.e., the change agent should decide what parts of the client system will be directly involved in the change relationship, and (c) Regulating the intensity and quality of the helping relationship.

(7) *Recognising and guiding the phases of the change process:* The seven phases may be listed as follows:

(a) The client system discovers the need for help, sometimes with the assessment of the situation by the change agent;
(b) A helping relationship is established and defined;
(c) The change problem is identified and clarified;
(d) Alternative possibilities for change are examined, change goals or intentions are established;

(e) Change efforts in the reality situation are attempted;

(f) Change is generalised and established; and

(g) The helping relationship ends or a different type of continuing relationship is defined.

(8) Choosing appropriate, specific techniques and models of behaviour which will be appropriate for each progressive encounter in the change relationship.

(9) Contributing to the development of the basic skills and theories of the profession.

IV. METHODS OF INITIATING PLANNED CHANGE

The researches show that there are considerable differences among change agents in their awareness of the potential choices which can be made in the selection and application of working techniques. Some agents take pride in their professional ingenuity, they are at pains to perfect their choices of particular techniques for use at particular times and with particular client systems. Other agents seem to rely consistently upon the standard techniques, which they acquired in their training or which have worked well in previous situations, and which they assume to be generally applicable. These methods may be given as follows:

(1) The association may start when a change agent perceives a need for help in a particular client system and sets out to try to stimulate the system's awareness of its needs.

(2) The change association may start when a third system connected in some way with both, the change agent and the potential client system, perceives the client system's need for help and takes the initiative in bringing the client system and the change agent together.

(3) The association itself becomes sensitive to its own malfunction and actively seeks help from an outside source.

The last one is the most common type of starting point in work with personality systems though not with larger systems.

Initiation of change sequence

(a) *Cases in which the change sequence is initiated by the change agent*

There may be five methods in this category:

(1) Methods by which change agents make known their availability and readiness to help.

(2) Methods by which change agents stimulate an aspiration for improvement in the client system.

(3) Methods by which change agents heighten or spread sensitivity to specific problems.

(4) Methods by which change agents offer help in solving an acknowledged problem.

(5) Methods by which the change agents create a special social atmosphere in which the accepted standard is to recognise the existence of problems and the need for help.

(b) *Cases in which the change sequence is initiated by a third party*

(1) Clarifying the situation with the third party, i.e., other than the change agent and the client system for example, the shopkeepers or citizens of a particular area of a town may ask a change agent or social agency to make contacts with students who disturb the life of the community.

(2) Using the third party as an aid in giving help.

(c) *Cases in which the change sequence is initiated by the client system stabilising the change relationship*

(1) Assessing the capacity to accept and use help.

(2) Assessing the motivation to accept and use help.

(3) Assessing change agent resources and motivation.

(4) Obtaining a mutuality of expectation for the change relationship.

(5) Clarifying expectations about the kind and amount of work which will be required.

(6) Anticipating difficulties which will emerge in the change relationship.

(7) Defining the influence relationship.

(8) Classification of special goals of the change agent.

V. WORKING TOWARDS ENSURING CHANGE

It covers four aspects (a) Working towards change, (b) Transfer of change, (c) Stabilisation of change and (d) Training the change agents.

A. Working towards change

(1) *Diagnosing the problem/problems:* This is done by obtaining information through direct questionnaire, simple survey procedure and using post-meeting reaction sheets with small groups like:

(a) Self-questioning technique.

(b) Selecting information from neighbouring systems.

(c) Eliciting a demonstration on the problem.

(d) Participating as an observer in the client system's routine activities.

(e) Projective communication.

(2) *Processing information or formulating a diagnosis:* Once the information has been gathered, the change agents make their diagnosis in the following ways:

(a) Diagnosing from assumption of generality of problem,

(b) Diagnosis by change agents acting independently,

(c) Diagnosing by change agents and client systems acting cooperatively,

(d) Self-analysis.

Stimulating understanding and acceptance of diagnostic insights. Imparting diagnosing skills.

(3) *Stabilising goals and intentions of action:* This is done by:

(a) Defining the direction of change.

(b) Arousing and supporting intentions to change.

(c) Providing opportunities for anticipating testing.

(d) Developing and mobilising competence in action.

(4) *Resistance forces in the process of planned change*

(a) Conceptual or intellectual difficulty which arises for both change agent and the client system, in converting diagnostic insights into projections of possible goals and means.

(b) Diagnosis often reveals the need for accustomed pattern behaviour to be changed while the group resists this change.

(c) Conflict between the influence of the change agent and the influence of the client system's 'operating group'. The client system may fear that the changes which seem useful may be really negative, so it resists.

(d) The client system may have a fear that it actually does not possess the strength or skill which is required for contemplated change.

(e) Occasionally the change agent's own behaviour during this stage creates a justified resistance in the client system.

B. Transfer of change

Client's expressions of intent to change and even his ability to grasp new concepts, acquire new skills, are not safe indications that an actual change occurs.

(1) Situational context in which help is given to the client system.

(2) The initiation of change efforts. This depends on: (a) methods of giving direct support to the client system during the initiation of change and (b) methods for developing support within the larger client system for change efforts.

C. Stabilisation of change

(1) *Assessing efforts to change:* The change agents should help their client system to evaluate change by contrasting the conditions before and after change. Has the change corrected the problem which was uncovered in the diagnosis? There should be some self-auditing to assess the progress.

(a) *The momentum of change effort as a stabilising factor:* A changed state of affairs produces changed expectations and satisfactions, and these in turn tend to maintain the change.

(b) New needs of status as a stabilising factor.

(c) Methods of encouraging a spread of change through demonstration.

(d) Methods of helping to allay resistance to spread.

The institutionalisation of change as a stabilising factor: Once a new practice is adopted, or a new pattern of behaviour is fully accepted, forces for the maintenance of the new state of affairs and against additional change begin to arise.

(2) *Achieving a terminal relationship.*

(a) General preparation of changeability.

(b) Methods by which the role of the change agent may be permanently incorporated in the client system.

(c) Conducting periodical examinations.

(d) Learning where and how to ask for further help.

D. Training the change agent

After examining the functions of the change agents, we should develop the course contents of the change agents as regards their need in the scientific and professional areas.

(1) *Conceptual diagnostic training:* The training should include education not only in change concepts but also in the skills of diagnosis techniques, for asking the right questions, for establishing valid patterns of observation or measurement, for using reliable methods to collect, process and interpret data.

(2) Orientation to theories and methods of change.

(3) Orientation to ethical and evaluative functions of the change agent.

(4) Knowledge of the sources of help.

(5) Optional and rational skills.

The problem of training specialists and generalists in planned change

There may be five main dimensions along which specialisation develops. These are:

(1) The specialisation by type of client system. These may be training in psychiatry, clinical psychology, social work, education, industries, group work, etc.

(2) Specialisation in terms of diagnostic orientations and methods.

(3) Specialisation by areas of change objectives.

(4) Specialisation by level of problem.

(5) Specialisation by five type of change methods.

The aspects like training facilities, types of training of change agents, etc., have been given in the Part II of this book: 'Training Of Extension Workers'

AGRICULTURAL TECHNOLOGY AND RURAL SOCIAL CHANGE

The relative advantage of innovations like improved seeds, fertilisers, insecticides, etc., as compared with the old practices constitute a condition affecting acceptance of changes. In economic terms this is the comparison of output per unit of input (in the form of fetilisers, pesticides, improved seeds, etc.) on the relative efficiency of new items. It has been observed that the greater the efficiency of new technology in farming, producing returns in the form of economic or consumption goods, the greater the likelihood of its acceptance. An important qualifying condition of this principle is the relative ease with which the new technique can be demonstrated and the amount of time it takes to do this. This is affected by various socio-economic and cultural factors like: size of holding of the farmer, his educational level, availability of capital, exogenous forces (like transport and communication, change agents like Block staff and subject matter specialists of the Agricultural Universities), social status of the farmer, cultural prejudices, etc.

The adoption of a new practice is the decision of an individual farmer and his family and is influenced by a series of events or[1] activities bearing upon the decision-making process. This is shown in Fig. 20.1

When a developing country launches an Agricultural Development Programme, in the beginning the rate of acceptance is slow, then the commutative effect brings rapid acceptance until almost all the potential adopters have accepted the change. Some of

[1]E.A. Wilkening, "Adoption of Improved Farm practices as Related to Family Factors," *Wisconsin AES Res. Bulletin 185*, 1950.

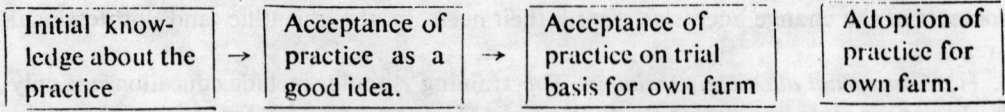

| Initial know-ledge about the practice | → | Acceptance of practice as a good idea. | → | Acceptance of practice on trial basis for own farm | | Adoption of practice for own farm. |

Fig. 20.1 Activities bearing upon the decision-making process

the practices are accepted more quickly than others. In some of these the farmer wants to see the results at other farms. The steps of adoption are given in Fig. 20.2

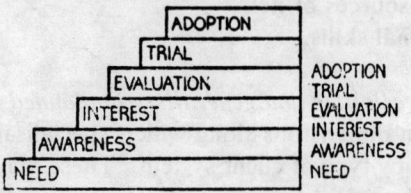

Fig. 20.2. Adoption stages

Effects of technology

(1) *Machine replaces uneconomic use of work animals:* With the acceptance of farm machinery run by friction power or electricity, the need for working animals are reduced. This helps in the completion of farm operations in time, levelling of the land, finishing work in lesser time and with lesser human labour. The growth of this trend in the USA is shown in Table 20.1

Table 20.1
Replacement of work animals by machines in the USA

Year	No. of Tractors in '000	Work stock fig. '000
1910	1	24211
1920	246	25742
1930	920	19124
1940	1545	14478
1950	3615	77781
1953-54	4400	5035

(2) The productivity of farm labour increases and man hours' workload is reduced. Figure 20.3 shows that since 1910 the output per man hour has increased by 200 and the man hours worked have been reduced from 130 to about 55 in 1971. In other terms it can be given that in 1910, 100 hours were required to produce one bushel of maize. This had been reduced to only 7 minutes in 1971 (see Fig. 20.3).

(3) Due to the lesser number of labour units required for producing the same amount of grain, the farm population in the USA declined from 75% in 1950 to 6% in 1971. This rate increased from 2% from 1800 to 1850 to 6% in the decade upto 1875. It came down to 50% in 1920, and went on decreasing as shown in Fig. 20.4.

(4) With the adoption of technology in agriculture the persons supported per farm worker increases. In the USA this figure has increased from 5 in 1850 to 42 in

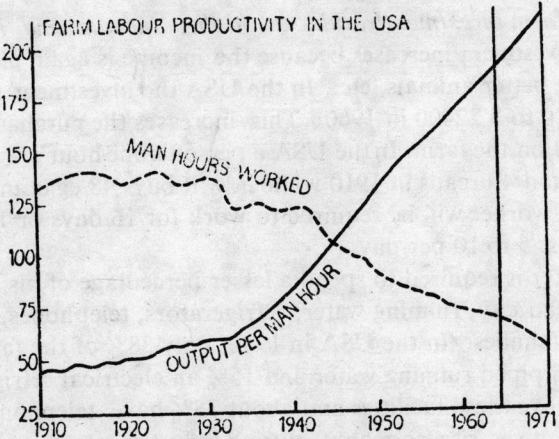

Fig. 20.3. Farm labour productivity in the USA.

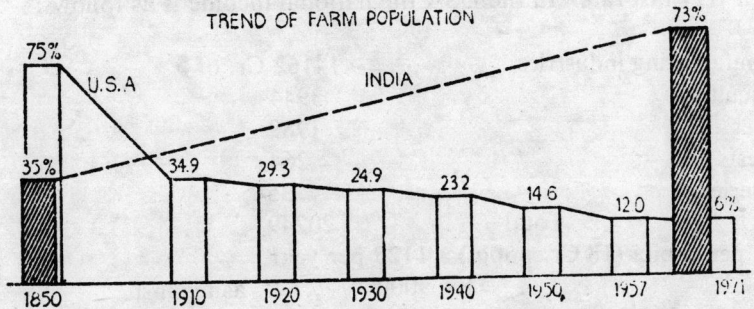

Fig. 20.4. Trend of farm population in India and the USA.

1971, while in India during the same period this figure decreased from 21 in 1850 to 3.5 persons per farm worker upto 1971 (see Fig. 20.5).

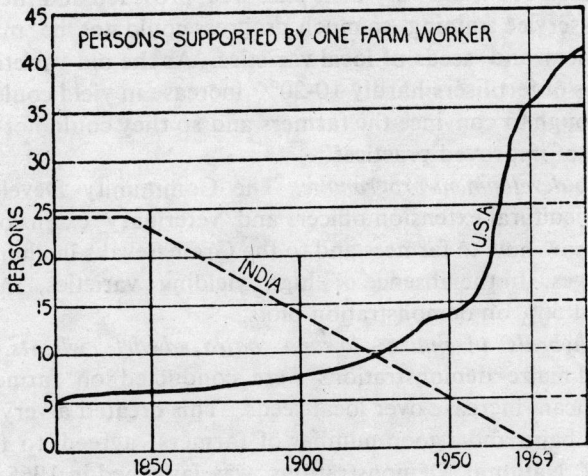

Fig. 20.5. Persons supported by one farm worker in the USA and India.

(5) *Increase in farm investment results in higher income and higher standard of living:* The farm investment increases because the income is again ploughed back in the form of machinery, better animals, etc. In the USA the investment per farm increased from $ 2700 in 1910 to $ 22400 in 1960. This increases the purchasing power per hour of labour employed on the farm. In the USA a person's one hour's wages could purchase 4 oranges, 4 eggs, and 4 breads in 1910 while now it buys 48 eggs and 16 breads. While in India an average worker will be required to work for 16 days or 128 hrs. because he earns only about Rs. 5 to 10 per day.

Because a worker is required to spend a lesser percentage of his income on food the other things like electricity, running water, refrigerators, telephones, etc., can be maintained by the farm families. In the USA in 1940, only 38% of the farm households had electricity, 18% had piped running water and 15% an electrical refrigerator ; while now nearly all farmers have these facilities and about 75% have telephones. This rise in the standard of living gives rise to manufacturing industries, trade, professional services, transport and communication, personal services, etc., and so the national income increases at a very fast rate. In the USA the national income is as follows:

1.	Manufacturing industries	14162 Cr. of $	70.2%
2.	Agriculture	3944	19%
3.	Mines	1789	8.7%
4.	Forests	264	1.3%
5.	Fisheries	35	0.12%
	Total	20249	

Income per capita (18 Cr. popu.) $ 1125 per year.

=Rs. 9000   ,,   as against

Rs. 360 for India i.e., 25 times.

Innovations in Indian agriculture

(1) *Before Independence:* Although the agriculture departments in the States were created as early as in 1904, but very little staff was provided and there was no arrangement for their in-service training, so much progress could not be made except to the supply of fertilisers and seeds of local varieties. As the old varieties were not able to sustain high dozes of fertilisers hardly 10-20% increase in yield could be demonstrated. This was not enough to convince the farmers and so they could not have much interest for the adoption of improved practices.

(2) *Community development programme:* The Community Development Organisation provided agricultural extension officers and veterinary extension officers to provide technical know-how to farmers and to the Gram Sevaks in charge of smaller units of about ten villages. In the absence of high yielding varieties, the yields could be increased to about 50% on demonstration plots.

(3) *Era of hybrids in maize, jowar, bajra, dwarf wheats and paddy:* In 1961 when hybrid maize demonstrations were conducted on farmers holdings, this gave a very significant increase over local seeds. This created a very good platform for hybrid jowar and bajra and a good number of farmers agreed to try these varieties. So a Scheme of National Demonstrations was launched in 1965-66. The results of these are given in Table 20.2

Table 20.2
Scheme of national demonstrations 1965-66

Crop	All India average Q/Ac.	Local seed local practice Q/Ac.	Local seed recommended Q/Ac.	Hybrid seed recommended practices Q/Ac.	%increase over local practice
Maize	3.62	7.50	10.62	17.0	225%
Jowar	1.52	5.68	8.03	13.2	240%
Bajra	1.21	3.04	6.16	8.40	270%
Average of 3 crops	2.14	5.41	8.27	12.88	255%

Returns per rupee invested (see Table 20.3).

Table 20.3
Return per rupee invested

	Increase over local seed local practice	Increase Over Hy. seed Rec. practice
1. Hybrid Maize	Rs. 0.64	4.0
2. Hybrid Bajra	Rs. 0.38	2.35
3. Jowar	Rs. 1.02	2.10
Average of Maize, Bajra, Jowar	0.68	2.10

(4) *Dwarf wheats:* Mexican wheats under the name of Lerma Rojo and Sanora-64 came to farmers' fields in 1964-65, but because of their red colour they fetched lesser price by Rs. 12 per quintal. But in November 1967, when the seeds like S-227 and S-308, were released by the Seed Releasing Committee of the Government of India, the progressive farmer even paid very exorbitant prices. As an illustration it can be given that the Gwalior Dairy Farm Ltd., Gwalior purchased seeds of S-227 and S-308 for Rs. 3500 per quintal, the same varieties were available for Rs. 200 per quintal in *rabi* 1968, while the produce of this crop was sold in May, 1969 at the general wheat price for consumption purposes at Rs. 84 per quintal in the Gwalior open market. This happened because within two years the seed multiplied very rapidly and many farmers had accepted it. In village Rudrapura near Gwalior about 65% of the wheat farmers had the latest varieties In *rabi* 1969 triple dwarf variety of wheat, which was not even released by the Seed Release Committee of the Government of India, was sold at Rs. 800 per kg or Rs. 80,000 per quintal. In 1969-70 the rate of this seed was Rs. 15000 per quintal. This exorbitant rate was because the farmers were convinced that this wheat would give them yields of 100 to 120 q/ha as compared to 40-50 q/ha for other dwarfs like S-227 and S-308, etc., and 10-15 q/ha with local wheat varieties. They are now convinced that because of its dwarfness it does not lodge with high doses of fertilisers, it gives more tillers and more grain per ear· and

also can be sown as late as December end, thus giving chance of taking a *kharif* crop of potatoes and *rabi* crop, or even a summer crop, like Bhindi, Moong, Lobhia, etc.

Dwarf paddy: Taichung Native 1 and IR-8 dwarf varieties created confidence that these varieties give very high yields over local rice varieties and that they could stand higher doses of fertilisers, without lodging, thus resulting in more tillers and higher yields.

It is interesting to note that the high yielding programme of hybrids in maize, jowar, bajra, dwarf wheats and IR-8 paddy has created so much confidence among the farmers and subject-matter specialists of Agricultural Universities that the S.M.S. as well as farmers cooperating in the demonstrations accepted Jaya and Padma varieties of paddy in the *Kharif's* demonstrations in 1969, even when they have not been tried on Jawaharlal Nehru Agricultural University farm in Madhya Pradesh. These crops were introduced in the National Demonstration Programme for the first time at the Jabalpur Campus in 1970 and all paddy demonstrations in this area were of these two varieties.

(4) *Potato:* In potato the new varieties namely Kufri, Chandramukhi, Sinduri, Chamatkar, etc., alongwith the introduction of plant protection measures and use of fertilisers etc. have increased the yields upto 400 quintal per hectare or even more. The example of Farrukhabad district (U.P.), where the farmers have very much specialised give clues that if agro-industries or facilities for cold storage do not develop side by side, the prices fall down to the extent that it becomes uneconomical to grow the crop. The digging charges to be paid to labour at a time in February-March 1969 were more than the total returns from the produce of the field. The capitalist is reluctant to invest his money in cold stores since he is fully convinced that the increase is a normal feature. Since 1970 the cooperatives of warehouses have come out to construct cold stores. This will be a step towards industrialisation after development in agriculture.

(5) *Soybean:* Quantitatively we have almost become self-sufficient in 1971. But the quality of food or diet our people prefer is very poor. Soybean has 40% proteins. In 1970 *kharif* it was planned to cover an area of 1.5 lakhs acres. Its demonstrations for the first time were conducted in *kharif* 1968. Of course it is a good crop and can even replace hybrid maize and groundnut at the present prices. But the farmer has to be convinced that it will have a market and the same price it has now. Side by side attempts are being made to develop industries for extracting its oil for vegetable oil industries and for use of the by-product as antibiotics, protein tablets, etc.

Extension activities of Agricultural Colleges/Universities and their role in the acceleration of acceptance of innovation

The agricultural colleges in India took up extension activities in the surrounding villages through their extension departments for the first time in 1960-61 after the Ford Foundation helped the State Governments in the establishment of extension wings. The USAID (formerly TCM) helped some colleges by way of technical staff who could train their counterparts in such colleges. Later on the Agricultural Universities created separate Directorates of Extension. These Directorates have created teams of subject-matter specialists who provide technical know-how to the farmers adopted by the extension departments at each college or wherever they are needed by the Agricultural Extension Officers of the State Departments of Agriculture. Besides demonstrations on farmer's holdings there is a regular training programme for farmers and personnel of the state departments of agricultural and animal husbandry in technical things such as extension methods, production of literature on improved practices and high yielding crops etc. These universities, which number 22 are now becoming great centres of dissemination of agricultural information through various activities. The results of some demonstrations at Jawaharlal Nehru Krishi Viswa Vidyalaya, Jabalpur Madhya Pradesh for 1968-69, show the economics of high yielding varieties as follows:

Table 20.4
Economics of high yielding varieties (JNKVV, Jabalpur, 1968-69)

	Cost of inputs in Rs.	Grain yields q/ha	Straw per q/ha	Gross returns Rs.	Net returns in Rs. per ha
(1) Dwarf wheats					
1. S-308 Mrs Dubey: Jabalpur	1187.50	45.70	57.25	4959	3762.50
2. S-227 Kulwant Singh	1125.00	56.75	92.00	6100	4970.50
3. K. Sona Mangilal Powarkheda	1175.50	52.19	88.73	5650	4475
Average	1162.60	51.55		5303	4404
Net Profit per rupee spent on inputs = Rs. 2.9					
(2) Dwarf paddy					
1. IR-8 S. L. Sharma, Raipur	1000.00	41.65	68.5	2250	1550
2. IR-8 G. Urkude, Varaseoni	875.00	42.25	80.95	3100	2225
3. IR-8 Shiv Ratan, Jabalpur	1062.00	76.25	139.60	4925	3863
Average	919.03	53.35		3521	2546
Net profit per rupee spent on input = Rs. 2.6					
(3) Potato					
1. Potato 1645-Janki pd. Gwalior.	2125.00	253.00 (Tubers)		12650	10555
2. Potato C-140 Yuvraj	2650	435.00 ,,		21500	17700
Average	2365.00	344.41 ,,		17675	14700
Net profit per rupee spent on inputs = Rs. 6.21.					

IMPACT OF TECHNOLOGY ON RURAL SOCIETY

How the acceptance of technology is bringing about social change in our rural areas has been studied at various campuses of our Agricultural University in Madhya Pradesh. The results may be presented as follows:

Due to the efforts of exogenous forces like community development organisations, the Agricultural Universities or Colleges, means of transportation and communications educational facilities, rural electrification, irrigation facilities and the resultant into increased incomes have brought about a change in the material, possessions and amenities rather than traditions, customs and beliefs.

The study by Parwar, in Rewa district further indicated that the aspirations of the rural people are sufficiently elevated as seen through their opinions with regard to the desired educational accomplishment of their children; the willingness to accept cooperation of lower caste people and to give them equal opportunities in the affairs of the village; the desire to have women participate in various organisations and the family planning.

A study on the impact of C.D. on the rural social system with reference to agriculture by Choudhary[2] revealed

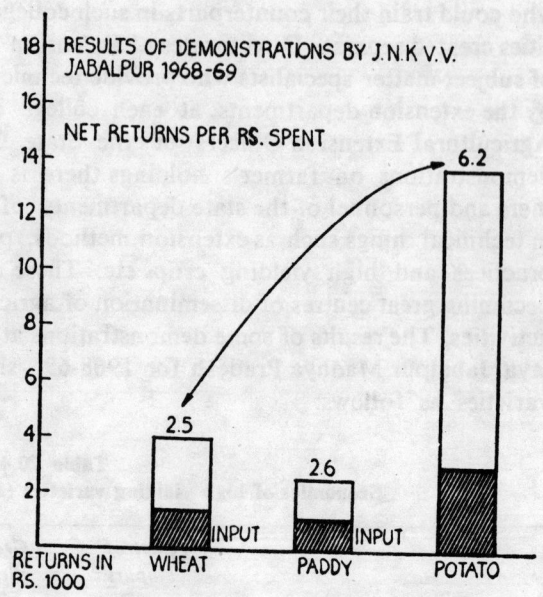

Fig. 20.6. Results of demonstrations by JNKVV, Jabalpur, 1968-69

that a fairly large percentage of farmers has accepted the use of irrigation, fertilisers, improved seeds and implements whereas the practices like use of pesticides, storage in a scientific way, soil conservation and reclamation, green manuring and compost-making have been adopted by a very small percentage of farmers. In other words it can be said that their acceptance is very slow.

Regarding the factors affecting adoption the study further revealed that (1) unawareness and lack of conviction combined with poor economic status and lack of education seem to be the most apparent causes of non-adoption of innovations. (2) Literate farmers show better response in addition of recommended practices. (3) Cultivators with bigger holding have adopted a greater number of practices as compared to small holders.

Goel and Dahama[3] in a study on "the effect of education and transport facilities in bringing social change in rural society of Jabalpur and Sehora block" revealed that in villages where both transport and educational facilities were not available the feeling of untouchability still remains strong. But where education developed, 20.6% respondents reported that their feeling about this superiority or inferiority complex changed. This change was 25.4 per cent in villages where only transport developed. But in villages where both the facilities developed the percentage of respondents who said that they do not have any regard to it was 47.6 per cent. This shows that the development of

[1]Parwar A.K., Extent to Which Exogenous Forces through C.D. Have Brought about Social Changes in Rural Areas of Rewa, M.P., 1967, M. Sc. (Ag. Extn. Thesis).

[2]Chaudhry, C.L., Impact of C.D. on Rural Social System with Special reference to Agriculture Programme in Gwalior (Morar block), M.P., M.Sc. (Agriculture Extn. Thesis), 1967.

[3]Goel, R.B.. "Effect of Education and Transport Facilities in Bringing Social Change in Rural Societies in Jabalpur and Sehora blocks, M.P., (M. Sc. Extn. Thesis, 1966)

education and transport weakens caste rigidity which is a hindrance in the development of society. Similar improvement was indicated in the acceptance of family planning, co-education in village schools and participation by village women in social and organisational activities.

In a study on the "Use of radio as a medium of communication by the farmers of C. D. block Jabalpur, V. D. Saraf found that a significant proportion of farmers now listen to the radio, the daily farm broadcast, and 1/3 occasionally. Agricultural programmes, market rates and news are the most important programmes liked by the respondents.

Farmers belonging to middle caste groups listen to programmes in a larger proportion followed by upper and lower castes. The majority of the farmers like to listen to news regarding improved seeds followed by fertilisers and pesticides, and programmes in which specialists from Agricultural Universities discuss improved practices. It may be mentioned that the JNKVV, sends tapes of talks on important topics which are relayed from All India Radio, Indore and Raipur every Sunday at 7 p. m. Two questions are also relayed to the farmers and for the best replies prizes of Rs. 20 each are given per week. This has proved very interesting and has motivated people to listen to the radio programmes on innovations and technology in agriculture.[1]

In a study on the comparative effectiveness of Agricultural Development programmes of the Package (IADP) Districts and Non-Package Districts of M. P. by R. M. Jaiswal of JNKVV, Jabalpur, it was noted that a large percentage of farmers in Package Districts had adopted more of improved seeds of paddy, wheat, groundnut, manures and fertilisers, insecticides and fungicides and improved implements as compared to Non-Package District.[2]

In a study on "impact of service cooperative societies on increasing agricultural production," conducted at Rewa in M. P. by A. K. Gumasta, it has been found out that due to facilities from the cooperatives the farmers were able to increase their area under cultivation, to use more fertilisers and to adopt high yielding varieties. This shows that more and more of such cooperatives need to to be developed.[3]

Sources of information and their effectiveness in adoption of technology

In a study by Q. A. Rafiq on this subject, it was found that 81% of the farmers of Sehore area were aware of the improved seeds, 88% of new fertiliser and 86% of new plant protection measures. The study further revealed that the important sources of information available to the farmers were: neighbours, friends and relatives (100%) Panchayat members 96%, VLW's 97%, Agriculture Extension Officers 55% and Extension Workers, Agricultural College 32%.

Channels of communication used by extension officers

The study on this topic revealed that the most common channels for information were exhibitions, demonstrations and posters—87%, 64% and 57%, respectively. Other

[1]Saraf, V.D., A Study on Radio as Medium of Communication of Information to Farmers on NES Block, Jabalpur, 1967-68.

[2]Jaiswal, R. M.A., A Comparative Study of Effectiveness of Agriculture Development Programme in the Package and Non-package Districts of Raipur Division.

[3]Gumasta, A. K., Impact of Service Cooperatives on Increasing Agricultural Production in Rewa Block, M.P.

important channels were radio 42%, film shows 29%, literature 21%, meetings 18% and field trips 12%[1] (Reported more than one channel).

Influence of socio-economic characteristics on the utilisation of sources of information

The study indicates that the farmers in the young and middle age-group have generally utilised the SMS of Agricultural Colleges and the Agriculture Extension Officers of the State Agriculture Department more as compared to the farmers of the older age-group. With the increase in the educational level of the respondents, the utilisation

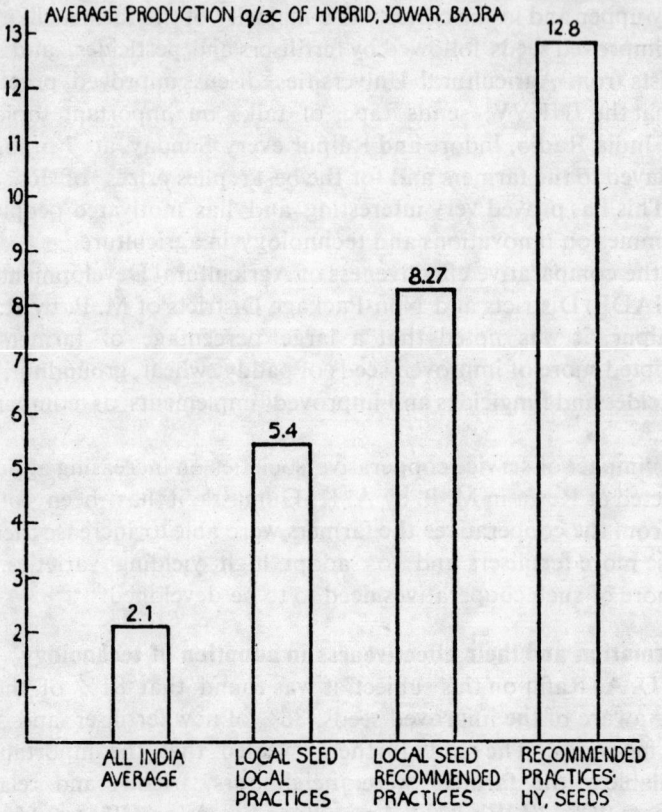

Fig. 20.7. Average production per q/ac of hybrid Maize, Jowar and Bajra.

of the services of Extension Specialists from Agricultural Universities and State Development Departments of Agriculture was more.[1]

[1]Rrfiq. Q. A., Study of Various Agencies Communicating Farm Information Among the Selected Farmers of Schore Block, M.P.

CHAPTER 21

GROUP MOBILISATION
AND LEADERSHIP DEVELOPMENT

In any community, an individual is subjected to many influences. His behaviour, ideas, knowledge are determined by the pattern of culture, status, system, role of authority, etc., and social institutions built up around him. In the community development process, an extension worker aims at bringing about changes in attitudes, knowledge and skills of the people. It is, therefore, necessary to identify the existing group structure for bringing about any change in rural life. The fact is that we find groups everywhere and that they multiply wherever there are human beings. Groups and group-forming are largely a matter of socially transmitted tradition. A newly-born child is socialised by becoming a member of already existing human groups and by adopting the social values.

Definitions of group

(1) It is an aggregation of two or more persons among whom there is an established pattern of interaction. It is recognised as an entity because of its particular type of collective behaviour.

(2) The group is a moving unit of interacting personalities and any group is constituted by the fact that there is some interest which holds its members together.

Occasions for group association

The common situations in which individuals pool their interests and become members of social groups can be:
  (a) Physiological kinship or origin from the same anscestors,
  (b) Marriage,
  (c) Religion,
  (d) Common language,
  (e) Neighbourliness,
  (f) Occupational or economic interests,
  (g) Attainment to some association like school, profession, club, etc.,
  (h) Common danger,
  (i) Mutual aid, and so on.

Nature of the group

Most of the groups we see are based on common habits, ideas, attitudes, wishes, etc. The group is the sum total of the behaviour of its members. If one knows all about the individuals, one knows about the group. Some thinkers are of the opinion that a group is something greater than the sum of its individuals. A group has a life-history, history, traditions, symbols, objectives of its own which stand for all the members as distinguished from the individual, i.e., it has a group mind in a group person.

According to another opinion, the group should not be thought of as a real group person having a group mind, nor is it solely an aggregate of individual behaviour, rather it should be conceived as a set of a common pattern of interaction which results in group behaviour. There is constant interaction among the members as a group and constant movement, striving and interplay of personalities.

It is not for members to follow the leader like sheep. They help one another express divergent ideas about objectives and they advocate different methods for attainment.

To maintain the cohesiveness of group, frequency of interaction should take place among the members and opportunities should be offered to all in group activities.

The group should also have such objectives as may provide direction of movement to a large number of people and a goal which can be attained with the resources of the group and through group effort, or else it may bring frustration.

Type of groups

Rural Sociologists have classified groups in the following broad categories:
  (i) Group, Mass, Public, Crowd.
      Group—ranging from as few as five to fifty persons and at the same place.
      Mass—when the number is very large and they may not be at the same place
          e.g. Mass audience of radio.
      Public—the people of a particular area or region.
      Crowd—A large gathering of people at the same place.
  (ii) Small, medium and large groups.
 (iii) Formal, informal groups.
  (iv) Statutory, non-statutory.
   (v) Functional, defunct.
  (vi) Aggressive, passive.
 (vii) Cohesive, incohesive.
(viii) Democratic, autocratic.
  (ix) Voluntary, involuntary.
   (x) Political, social, religious, caste, income, majority/minority.
  (ix) Primary, secondary, tertiary.
There are other different bases for the classification of groups like:
  (a) *Primary and secondary:* They are distinguished from each other by their type of social contact and degree of formal organisation. In the primary group, there is face-to-face association, the contacts are personal, individuals live close to one another socially and do not need the formal framework of a constitution to achieve their purpose. Member of a family, a neighbourhood, or a friendship circle are good

examples of primary groups. In this type, members are loyal to one another because of personal regard and the sharing of many interests. The secondary group is larger and more formal, specialised and indirect in its contacts. It relies more upon the stability of its social organisation of unity and continuance.

(b) *In-group and out-group:* The second basis of classification centres on the social attitude. We feel the characteristics of persons who belong to the same group and their attitude towards those who are members of an outside group (regarded as strangers, foreigners, etc.).

(c) *Transitory or permanent:* The third type of distinction may be made on the basis of their degree of stability or social relationship. It may vary from a group of momentary interest in a passing event to the relatively permanent interests as in a family.

(d) *Voluntary and involuntary groups:* Voluntary groups are those where one has become a member according to his choice, e.g. clubs, cooperatives, etc., while in the case of involuntary groups, the choice does not rest with the individual members but in factors like race, family, caste, groups, neighbourhood, community, and religion.

Groups in the rural community and methods of approach to them

Village communities in rural India are generally found to be associated with social groups and institutions which determine the pattern of the individual's life in the community. As we are mainly concerned with the group and their mobilisation, we should understand the fundamental difference between groups and institutions. Groups connote the dynamic personal element in association, while in institutions we observe the formal, organised, stable pattern through which dynamic interests are expressed. The following are some of the groups in rural society:

(a) Household

It includes the members of the family and other persons who may be residing there to assist in farming and other household affairs. There is the possibility of a greater degree of interactions among the members of the same household and thus any change adopted or refused will involve the whole group. It is often difficult to introduce a new idea into a large household because of the different personalities. The best way is to start work with smaller households.

(b) Neighbourhood

Households always exist in clusters in our country. The proximity of the families to each other binds them into a strong group. Thus several neighbourhoods constitute a village.

The interaction among the families is greater as there are many things which they share like a common source of water, roads, and open-platform (chabutra), bathing ghats, etc. In a neighbourhood, an individual is exposed to the attention of the others and cannot be easily influenced to decide a thing. The work should start with the help of key persons in the neighbourhood.

(c) Informal group

People with common interest remain together for a longer time. The pattern of interaction of such groups may be informal, personal, intense. In our country, the form of association is mostly informal. Informal groups like friendship groups, mutual aid groups or clique groups may be observed in progress in the villages. In friendship groups, the relationship among members is personal and meetings are more frequent. They may be formed on the caste, age or income basis.

In mutual aid groups, the frequency of help which one renders to another is more. Here also the interaction is more personal.

These groups can be identified by noticing who has visited most frequently for counselling, for sharing joy, for gossip or casual conversation, the structure develops around him. In the development process, to reach such a man and to get his approval amounts to approval of the group. It happens because of the high degree of communication among the members and each member is influenced by the group in the decision-making process.

(d) Formal group

Formal groups have now become quite popular in villages. There are schools, panchayat cooperatives, etc. However, members still need quite a bit of training in the group process to make the functioning of such organisations a success. The Extension worker should work through the office-bearers, as they are the recognised leaders in the community. At times, the task may become difficult if the office-bearers have become a part of group conflicts.

(e) Family group

It is a basic social unit. The oldest member is generally the head of the family. His decisions are final. Any change to be brought about in the way of living or in the method of crop production must have his consent.

(f) Religion

The whole village is structured around a village temple or deity. The significance of the religious structure for extension work is that assemblies of people for religious festivals may be used to impart necessary information and skills about improved implements, seeds, fertilisers, sanitary latrines, etc., by organising exhibitions. It is perhaps more effective to approach through religious persons whose words may have some value.

Caste groups

Caste is both the strength and weakness of the society. Neighbourhoods may be formed on the caste basis thereby reinforcing the solidarity.

Properties of a Group

Important properties of a group are listed below:
  (i) Plurality but not too large.
 (ii) Physical togetherness.
(iii) Common goal or objectives.
 (iv) Activity or actions to achieve the goals.
  (v) Leaders and followers.

   (vi) Internal and external conflicts or differences.

   (vii) Cohesion or unity.

   (viii) Sense of belonging, leading to security/pride/satisfaction.

Group dynamics

Despite a good deal of information now available about the nature, formation, functioning, growth and degeneration of groups, it is admitted that the principles concerning one or the other aspect of the "group" are not only tentative but also full of notable exceptions if not seeming contradictions. It is also true that no two groups are going to be completely identical in all the different aspects like size, composition, goals, programmes, activities, and cohesion. For either of these reasons, the functioning of groups is considered as 'dynamic' and not 'static'. A functioning group (leaving aside the defunct) shall always have some progress through its activities, and encounter problems of varying intensity and nature from within or outside. Man being a social creature likes to be in one or other group and thereby to satisfy the instinct of 'belongingness'. But once within a group he may also come across certain annoying types of experiences.

Principles of working with groups and their mobilisation

For full mobilisation of the members of the group, it is essential that the programme, or activity, should fulfil the basic urges for security, recognition, response and for new experiences which motivate people to work for the attainment of the objectives. Besides, the programme of social action has to be based on the following fundamental principles.

(1) Identification of the leadership pattern in a group is a very important step for its mobilisation.

(2) The leader should draw all his powers from the group itself and not from outside.

(3) To secure the participation of the members of a group it is absolutely necessary to associate them actively in the decision-making process. There must be cooperative decisions.

(4) Once decisions are made, then execution must be the responsibility of all members of the group. All members must participate in its execution. This can be done by delegated responsibility.

(5) Every member should be helped in the execution of his delegated task by all giving the assistance required without injuring his ego.

(5) The leader must accord due recognition to all members in the achievement of groups' goals. He must not take for himself all the credit.

(7) It is the primary duty of a leader to devise methods to sustain the member's continuous interest.

LEADERSHIP FOR DEVELOPMENT

Agricultural production acquired a new emphasis during the Fifth Plan period with the introduction of the new strategy in agriculture. Since then many innovations in agriculture has been introduced in rural areas in order to make the country self-sufficient in food production. It was realised, however, that no substantial improvement could be made without the cooperation of farm leaders in the agricultural production programmes.

The greatest need of the day is, therefore, to effectively educate and communicate the information to the millions of farmers who have to adopt these innovations to modernise agriculture. In spite of our best efforts, the majority of our rural people tend to resist change, being conservative and tradition-bound. They must be made to realise that it is conducive to their own progress and development.

The task of changing the outlook of millions of rural families, acquainting them with the new knowledge and orienting them towards the acceptance of the innovations, is indeed a difficult task which a few extension personnel can hardly achieve. Naturally, they have to take the help of local leaders. The prime need today, therefore, is for 'pragmatic leadership'—a leadership which can assume responsibility in accelerating the new strategy of agricultural production.

It is generally observed that the development personnel have preconceived notions about some fixed characteristics and roles of leaders as a result of which they fail to develop the proper type of leaders for the right type of work. Hence, it is necessary that the right concepts of farm leadership should be properly understood by the extension personnel.

Concepts defined

Leader is a person who has been spontaneously considered, or chosen, as being influential in a specific situation or situations.

Leadership is the process of influencing the behaviour of the individual in a given situation or situations.

Thus leadership is the phenomenon of influencing, guiding and directing the actions and thoughts of the people in the intended direction. The leader of a group must somehow perceive what the group wants. He must contribute something that will move the group closer to that goal and his contribution must be accepted before he can be said to have patterned the behaviour of the group.

Other definitions of leadership are given below:

Leadership means the direct face-to-face contact, between leaders and followers. It is a personal-social contact (Allport).

The leader is the servant of the group. The position of the leaders is an essential mechanism of effective group organisation (Sundarson).

Leaders are persons who are selected by the people because of their special interest or fitness to work on some phase of the local programmes. (J.S. Garg)

A leader is one who helps the members of the group, as an individual he accepts the responsibility for thinking through problems and working out solutions that need to be discovered. (S.N. Singh)

Leadership is a process of mutual stimulation, which by the successful interplay of relevant individual differences controls human energy in pursuit of a common cause. (Paul Pigors)

An individual is a leader in any social situation in which his ideas and actions influence the thoughts and behavionr of others.

A leader is one who, in a social situation, can elicit (stimulate) positive reaction from other members of the group (B.M. Stogdill)

Types of leaders

There are several ways of classifying leaders, some of them are listed as below:

(a) Democratic, autocratic or *laissez-faire* type leaders.

(b) Formal and informal leaders.

(c) A head, ahead and the head of group.

(d) Professional and lay (voluntary) leaders.

(e) Political, religious, social, academic.

(f) Elected, selected or nominated.

(g) Popular and unpopular.

(h) Traditional and progressive leaders.

Theories of leadership

There are four theories that attempt to explain the phenomenon of leadership.

(i) *Trait theory*—A person who possesses certain traits of excellence becomes the leader of the group.

(ii) *Functions*—It is not the mere posssession of some superior generalised traits that enables a person to become a leader for all types of responsibilities. But the ability to perform the functions determines the potentiality of a person to be a leader. A good singer can be the leader of singing party and so would be a player.

(iii) *Situation*—Under certain circumstances, it is the situation that becomes more important in determining whether or not a person will become a leader. When the situation changed from war to peace even Churchill, who was so successful during war, was shifted from the position of leadership.

(iv) *Interaction*—It is now held that it is none of the aforesaid three theories that independently explain the phenomenon of leadership fully. It is the sum total of these three that provide better explanation.

Some principles of democratic leadership

The following principles have been identified in the democratic functioning of leadership.

(i) Leadership is a function of the group and not of any individual.

(ii) It is responsible for establishing the climate of the group.

(iii) It helps in defining the objectives and purposes of the groups.

(iv) It helps the group to organise itself.

(v) It helps in determining procedure.

(vi) Responsibility for decision rests with the group.

(vii) The group examines its problems and increases its efficiency.

(viii) It is sensitive to the feelings and ideas of members.

(ix) It uses both the internally and externally available resources.

(x) It helps the groups to test its own thinking.

Personality dynamics of a leader

Like other individual human beings, a leader carries with him his past experiences, emotional tendencies, goals and needs as well as personal standards. Followers generally rate their leaders on the higher scoring of various personality dynamic factors. In addition to these due to environmental and socio-psycho-interactional processes, a leader acquires a better self concept of himself.

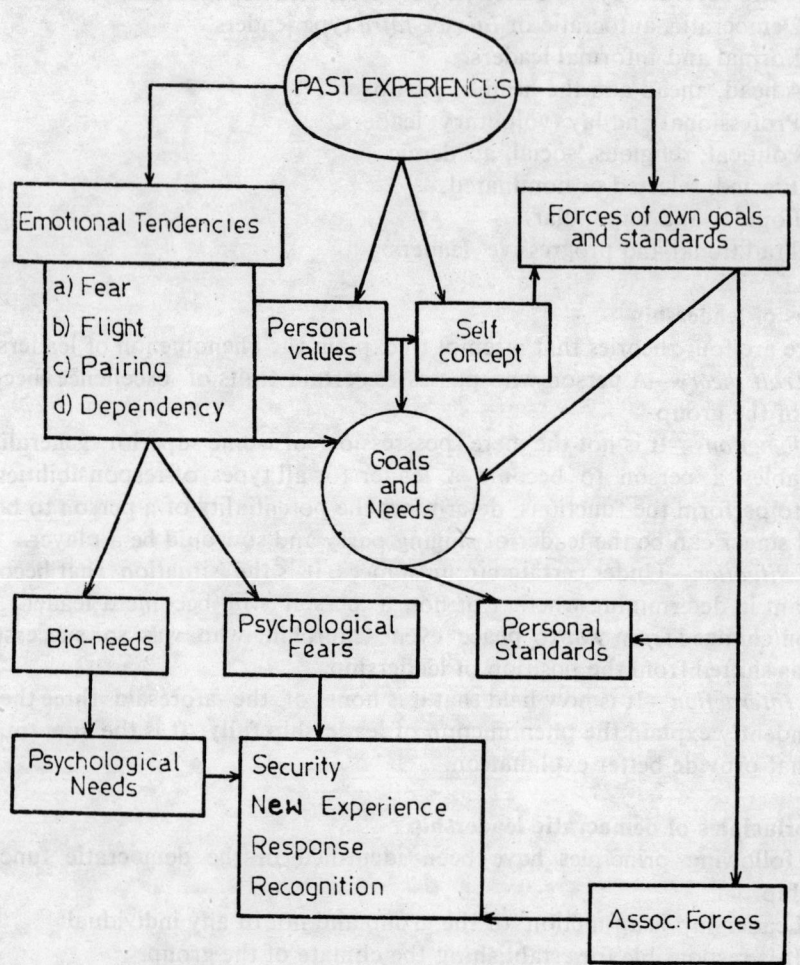

Fig. 21.1. Personality dynamics of a leader

Functions of a leader

The following functions have been identified:

(1) Executive;
(2) Planner;
(3) Policy maker;
(4) Expert—in human relations as well as technical field;
(5) External group representative;
(6) Controller of internal relationships;
(7) Purveyor of reward and punishment;
(8) Arbitrator;
(9) Examplar;

(10) Group symbol;
(11) Surrogate of individual responsibility;
(12) Ideologist;
(13) Father-figure; and
(14) Scape goat.

Determinants of effectiveness in leadership functions—(ten 'A's)

(1) Awareness of the functions of the group.
(2) Ability (self-judgement) in performing the functions.
(3) Achievement of goals—Nowhere—Somewhere—Achieving something.
(4) Assignment of group functions to members.
(5) Appraisal of effects of distribution of functions.
(6) Accomplishment of different purposes under different environments.
(7) Attainment of positive values as a leader.
(8) Attaching a high code of conduct, ethical values and high morale in the group.
(9) Arrangement of communication structures.
(10) Acceptance of failure.

Factors determining effectiveness of a leader

The most important factors identified through researches in relation to effectiveness of leader are listed below:

(1) Need fulfilment.
(2) Prestige.
(3) Valued membership.
(4) Cooperative relationship.
(5) Heightened interaction.
(6) Clarity of goal.
(7) Small units.
(8) Homogeneity
(9) Outside events.
(10) Increased position.
(11) Attacks from environment.

The bases of power for leadership

French and Raven (1938) defined the following five bases of power:

(1) Reward power: These are based on the followers' perception that the leader has the ability to mediate reward for them.

(2) Coercive power: These are based on the followers' perception that their leader has the ability to mediate punishment for them.

(3) Legitimate power: These are based on the perception of the followers that their leader has a legitimate right to prescribe behaviour for them.

(4) Referent power: These powers based on the followers' identification with their leader and perception that the leader has some special knowledge or expertise.

Pattern of farm leadershjp

M.S.K. Reddy (1960) and J. Rao (1966) identified four types of leaders, namely traditional leaders, caste leaders, political leaders and functional leaders.

B.N. Sahay, (1966) identified major patterns of leaders in the Maler and Santhal tribes and Santhal paraganas. According to him the traditional and emergent leaders were found to be very effective in influencing the change in rural areas.[1]

Deshmukh (1966) identified three types of leaders namely; formal, informal and compsite.[2]

J.P. Yadava, et al., (1972) identified agricultural leaders, traditional leaders, political leaders, opinion-making leaders, decision-making leaders and caste leaders, depending on the nature of roles performed by them.

S.V. Reddy, (1972) identified agricultural leaders, social leaders and agro-social leaders. Among the above three categories also, some were found to be informal and the rest composite in nature.

It has been observed that the agro-social composite[3] leaders were found to be quite effective in ushering in technological change in the field of agriculture.

Characteristic of farm leaders

Keeping in view the modern theories of leadership, several characteristics that were associated with farm leadership in rural areas were identified. Researches have shown that farm leadership in a progressive village was characterised by mass media exposure, gregariousness[4] and urban contact; while in a less progressive village it was characterised by farm size, social participation and liberal values. It was also observed in a progressive village that the above three characteristics could predict leadership to the extent of 56.4%, and in a non-progressive village to the extent of 70.2%. Development personnel may keep these characteristics in view while selecting leaders.

Homophily-heterophily between leaders and followers

The importance of the leaders in influencing the followers to adopt innovations has been widely recognised. Logically speaking, the choice of a leader should be based on two considerations: first, he should be in a position to offer better advice than his followers and second, the followers must place a certain amount of credibility in his advice. Besides this, there may be a number of other factors influencing the leader-follower interactions.

Homophily refers to the similarity between a leader and his followers in terms of certain socio-psychological attributes, or traits like knowledge, education, socio-economic status, etc., and heterophily refers to the differences between a leader and his

---

[1]Traditional emergent leaders are those who are traditional leaders keeping themselves uptodate with the current conditions and social institutions.

[2]Composite leaders are those who hold positions in village organisations and at the same time are recognised by villagers as their leaders.

[3]Agro-social composite leaders who are found to be associated both in agricultural and non-agricultural development activities. Besides this, they also hold positions in a village organisation.

[4]Social tendency to associate with others.

follower in terms of certain socio-psychological attributes or traits, like knowledge, education socio-economic status, etc.

In the progressive village, the leader-follower interactions were found to be dependent on their social participation, socio-economic status, knowledge of high yielding varieties, knowledge of credit, knowledge of marketing, knowledge of multiple cropping, farm size, gregariousness, urban contact, cosmopoliteness, mass media exposure, contact with extension agency and innovativeness. Hence one can conclude that leaders and followers were heterophilic with respect to the above traits. On the other hand, the leader-followers interactions were independent of their age, education, conservatism and political affiliation. Hence the leaders and followers were homophilic with respect to these traits.

In the non-progressive village also, heterophily existed with respect to age, education, social participation, socio-economic status, knowledge of high yielding varieties, knowledge of credit, knowledge of multiple cropping, farm size, gregariousness, urban contact, contact with extension agency and innovativeness. On the other hand, it was observed that leaders and followers were homophilic with respect to caste, cosmopoliteness, and political affiliation. Therefore, the developmental agencies could better utilise the existence of homophily and heterophily in order to strengthen the leadership phenomena in general and leader-follower interactions in particular.

Role of farm leaders

The role expectations of farm leaders in view of the new strategy of agricultural production were ascertained form the experts in the field of agricultural extension, i.e., Agricultural Extension Officers and the farmers themselves. By working out the index of the census all the three categories agreed that the following roles are expected to be performed by the farm leaders in view of the new agricultural strategy.

(1) Raising demonstration plots and showing it to others.
(2) Keeping themselves abreast with the latest agricultural technology.
(3) Adopting themselves all the improved agricultural practices.
(4) Organising meetings and other discussions groups.
(5) Serving as marketing advisers.
(6) Supplying the improved seeds to the farmers.
(7) Assisting the farmers in getting credit.
(8) Serving the innovative farmers in the village.
(9) Educating the farmers to grow more than two crops a year.
(10) Acting as liaison officers between the extension workers and the farmers.
(11) Educating the farmers in the latest agricultural technology.
(12) Helping the fellow-farmers in getting the needed agricultural inputs.

It was, however, observed that most of these roles are not performed by the leaders, for the 'concept of self-development' is inhibiting them from doing so. Hence the extension workers should motivate the farm leaders for performing the additional roles enumerated above and for strengthening the new agricultural strategy.

Leaders and group-functioning are inseparably linked with each other. In fact, there is a psycho-dynamics between the two. It is a kind of chicken-egg type of controversy to ask the question whether it is an effective leader who enables a group to function effectively or is it the good group that gives birth to an effective leader. Both of these go hand-in-hand. There cannot be an effective leader unless there is a functional group, that he is leading, and surely a good functional group does provide fertile ground for leadership to appear and develop.

CHAPTER 22

PROBLEMS OF SCHEDULED CASTES, TRIBES AND OTHER BACKWARD CLASSES AND INDIA'S APPROACH TO IT

Due to historical factors, special consideration is being shown to the backward classes. The term backward classes has been used to include scheduled tribes, scheduled castes, notified tribes and other classes that are backward. Due to rigid caste system that prevailed in India, certain sections of the population suffered from distinct social and economic disabilities and came to be known as backward classes.

The policy followed by the Government of India towards the backward classes recognises two distinct implications that these sections are not on par socially, economically and educationally with the rest of the poupulation and that the wide disparities between the backward classes and the rest of the population have to be reduced if the country is to march forward.

Article 46 of the Indian Constitution lays down a directive principle of State policy. It provides "The State shall promote with special care the educational and economic interests of the people and in particular of the scheduled castes and the scheduled tribes, and shall protect them from social injustices and all forms of exploitation."

Scheduled castes and tribes are those castes and tribes who enjoy the various special provisions under the various articles of the Indian Constitution and whose name appears in the schedule of the Indian Constitution.

The term tribal has been described as "territorial communities living in the relative isolation of hills and forests. Their comparative isolation, in some ways has kept them apart from the mainstream of society in the country. Partly because of their isolation and partly because of the limited world view, charaterised by lack of historical depth (resulting from the early merging of history into mythology and an overall traditional orientation) they are integrated in terms of certain themes rooted in the past. These integrative themes, and a special culture focus, gives them a separate cultural identity, and they often possess latent or motivational systems which are remarkably different from those of other people."

It may be mentioned that no precise definition of the term "tribe" has yet been formulated.

SOCIAL PROBLEMS

Although untouchability as such has been abolished under Article 17 of the Constitution, the practice is still observed, in some form or the other, particularly in the rural areas. The persistence of caste distinctions and caste prejudices constitute a challenge to our nation. It is, however, gratifying to note that discrimination based on caste prejudices, though deep-rooted, is gradually weakening. The impact of conditions of modern life in towns tends to remove unsocial habits which have the sanction of custom. In the villages, on the other hand, where till recently there was no stimulation for individuals to overstep the barriers of custom, this evil of untouchability and its resultant disabilities persist, parliament enacted the Untouchability (Offence) Act 1955 which came into force throughout the country on the 1st June, 1955. This social legislation is a major step towards ensuring the scheduled castes their rightful place in society.

The common forms in which 'Untouchability' is manifested in the country are, by denial of:

(a) Drawing water from the public well.

(b) Entry to kitchen, etc.

(c) Service by barbers and dhobis.

(d) Entry into temples.

Another social problem faced by the scheduled castes and other backward classes is that of forced labour. Forced labour, wherever prevalent, is generally practised to the disadvantage of the backward classes Traffic in human beings and beggars and other similar forms of forced labour have been prohibited under Article 23 of the Constitution. In Orissa, this system is known as the 'Gothi System'. In certain parts of M.P. it is known as 'Harwahi Pratha'.

Various approaches to remove the social evils suffered by the scheduled castes and other backward classes have been attempted by social reformers. The classical example of Gandhiji's efforts to remove the disabilities suffered by the Harijans is very well-known. Inspired by Gandhiji, many social reformers and non-official agencies took up the case of these classes. Mention may be made of:

(i) All-India Harijan Sevak Sangh.

(ii) The Bharatiya Depressed Classes League.

(iii) Ishwar Saran Ashram, Allahabad.

In addition to the non-official agencies, the Central and the State Governments have been trying to remove the social and economic disabilities of the Scheduled Castes and other backward classes. Most State Governments have Harijan Welfare Departments and a large amount of money is being spent to solve the problems of these classes. At the Centre, the Ministry of Home Affairs has been given direct responsibility and the Commissioner of Scheduled Castes and Tribes is the agency through which it works. Special provisions have been made in the Indian Constitution relating to certain classes. Article 330 brings out these provisions of Seats in State legislatures and Parliament, Reservation of posts in Government service, for Scheduled Castes and Scheduled Tribes. Seats are also earmarked for scheduled castes in various State educational institutions. The State Governments have been trying to remove the disabilities suffered by these classes in various ways, e.g., Untouchability Acts, Temple

Entry Act. Improving the conditions of scavengers and sweepers, constitution of mixed hostels, mixed colonies, etc. Attempts have been made also to improve educational and economic conditions of the scheduled castes and backward classes. Educational programmes include giving of scholarships and stipends, reservation of seats in techni-cal institutions, relaxation of age for admission to higher and technical education programmes.

The State and Central Governments have been providing legal aid to the scheduled caste persons in civil cases. The Ministry of Information and Broadcasting through the Radio, Press, Films, Middle units, etc., have been trying to mould public opinion against untouchability and other such practices.

ECONOMIC PROBLEMS

In addition to the social problems, the members of the scheduled castes and backward classes have special economic problems of their own. Out of 824 lakhs of people of the scheduled castes mostly engaged in agriculture, a good majority are landless labourers. The scheduled caste agriculturists constitute 26 per cent of the total agricultural classes in the country, but form 33 per cent of the landless labourers. This problem, to a certain extent, has been solved by the Government by providing lands to the landless. This is done with land obtained from cultivable waste lands, land obtain-ed through imposing the ceiling on holdings and land collected through Bhoodan and Gramdan. The State Governments have also obtained legislative and executive measures to provide security of land tenure to the Scheduled Caste.

The scheduled castes have also suffered displacement from their homes due to the construction of large industrial projects. The Government has been trying to rehabili-tate them, and provide loans, ploughs, bullocks, seeds, etc., to many scheduled caste cultivators. Credit and technical know-how have also been provided.

As stated earlier, agriculture and village industries are the mainstay of the scheduled caste. The economy of the backward classes is dependent on cottage industries to a very great extent because their agricultural economy is poor and very unstable. The problems of village industries are poor techniques in production, low income of artisans and inadequate credit and marketing facilities. The Government has undertaken pro-motion of village industries among the backward communities during the last three Five Year Plans.

In addition to all the measures rated above to solve the economic problems of the scheduled castes, the Government has been trying to give them relief by various other measures, such as starting Forest Labour Cooperatives, initiating measures for debt reduction and keeping a check on the activities of money-lenders.

MEDICAL AND PUBLIC HEALTH PROBLEMS

On account of the unhygienic conditions of living, lack of drinking and bathing water facilities, the backward classes suffer from many diseases. The common diseases are malnutrition, leprosy, T.B. and venereal diseases. Nutritional deficiency is a major public health problem of all backward classes. In the Harijan colonies the sanitary con-ditions are deplorable. The houses are ill-ventilated and over-crowded. Unless these problems are solved, the health problem will remain acute. State and Central Governments are attempting to solve these problems. The setting up of dispensaries, hospitals, health and maternity centres, construction of wells and slum clearance are some of the programmes that are being undertaken.

PROBLEM OF HOUSING

Housing conditions of the backward classes are extremely unsatisfactory. The low income of a person of backward class prevents him from improving his housing conditions. The State and Central Governments are providing funds for this purpose. Schemes include village housing projects, urban housing quaters for conservancy staff and slum clearance, rural housing for scheduled castes, etc.

We have attempted in brief to bring out the problems of the scheduled and other backward classes and approaches that have been made to solve their problems.

PROBLEMS OF TRIBES

The tribals in our country have certain special problems which need to be kept in view when planning farming programmes for them. The existence of these special problems has not permitted the application of the general programme drawn up for non-tribal areas. This has been disputed by one school of thought which feels that problems of the tribal areas are a part of the larger rural problems. The problems of the tribal areas can be classified under the following headings:

(1) Economic Problems: (a) Agriculture, (b) Land Tenure, (c) Village Industries, and (d) Indebtedness. (2) Communication, (3) Health and Sanitation, (4) Education, and (5) Problems of Drink.

(1) Economic problems

(a) *Agriculture:* Out of the total population of 19.0 million tribals 17.3 million are engaged in agricultural tasks. The scheduled tribes agriculturist form 7 per cent of the total agricultural classes of India. Some of the important problems of tribal areas are:

Land availability: Land available for agriculture is limited. Soil erosion connected with shifting cultivation, use of primitive agricultural implements, difficulties in the use of fertilisers, lack of improved strain of seeds and lack of irrigation facilities are some of the major agricultural problems. Various attempts have been made to solve these problems: rehabilitation of tribals on better lands, improving methods of shifting cultivation, domination, terrace cultivation, etc. Supply of improved implements, evolving better strains for hilly areas, development of horticulture, consolidation of holdings and provision of irrigation facilities are some of the important programmes.

(b) *Land tenure:* The tribal population in our country has suffered a great deal to loss of land. Most State Governments have adopted legislative and executive measures to provide security of land tenure to the scheduled tribes which have prevented large scale eviction.

(c) *Village industries:* The problems of village industries are poor techniques in production, low income of artisans and inadequate credit and marketing facilities. This has led to general decline in traditional industries and crafts. Programmes to revive and strengthen traditional industries and crafts have been attempted by the Government. Production-cum-training centres were also started and loans and marketing facilities are being made available.

(d) *Indebtedness:* Indebtedness is very high among the tribals. Poverty is the main cause of indebtedness. Even for subsistence requirements the tribals need loans. Because of lack of security their credit worthiness is very low and only the village money-lender is ready to advance loans at exorbitant interest rates. Expenditures on social customs, inherited debts, etc., are the causes of indebtedness. Legislative measures for debt redemption and for checking the activities of money-lenders have been enacted by most of the State Governments. Institutional credit is also being made available.

(2) Communication

In the tribal areas, lack of communication facilities is a great handicap in economic and social advancement. The government is giving its attention to this problem and sufficient amount have been provided for the construction of fair weather roads in the last five Plans. Lack of communication has led to problems of isolation.

(3) Health and sanitation

The tribal people face special problems of health on account of their primitive way of life. Lack of drinking and bathing water facilities, belief in witchcraft and sorcery rather than in medicines, have all combined to bring about accute health problems. They suffer from malnutrition, leprosy, T.B., venereal diseases, etc. The missionaries, the Bharatiya Adimjati Seva Sangh, the Ramakrishna Mission, the Red Cross Society, the Servants of India Society and other non-official and official agencies have been combating the problem.

(4) Education

The percentage of literacy except in those areas where missionaries have worked, is very low. There are areas where it is practically nil. Attempts by official and non-official agencies to tackle the educational problems are being made. Establishment of schools, award of scholarships, reservation of seats, relaxation of age limits for admission, etc., are some of the measures that have been attempted. The problem of textbooks in tribal dialect, the availability of teachers, the scattered nature of villages and the distance to school have also to be considered.

(5) Problems of drink

The use of liquor (rice-beer, etc.) forms an integral part of the social life of tribals. Unfortunately, due to the excise laws which have been enacted, the tribals have become addicted to distilled liquors. This has led to a drain in their economy.

SOLUTION OF THE PROBLEMS

There can be four main approaches to the solution of the problem of tribal people.

(1) The social service approach, (2) Political approach, (3) Religious approach, and (4) Anthropological approach.

1. The social service approach

Voluntary Social Service agencies have done a lot of humanitarian work in tribal areas but their idealism has not been matched by a proper understanding of tribal values and culture. They enter into the tribal areas with an over all solution for all tribal problems. Some of their reforms, though well meant, have led to a handful effects because their frame of reference was different.

2. Political approach

The British Government followed a scheme of creating excluded and partially excluded areas and gave separate political representation to the tribals. The Government of India, after independence, followed to a very great extent the same policy but initiated a programme of directed change.

Another political approach that has recently come into the picture is the demand for political autonomy for tribal areas. This is to be found in the Naga areas and certain parts of Bihar where the demand for separate States has come up.

3. Religious approach

This approach has been followed by the missionaries. This has to be considered in the context of conversion leading to a better life or disorganisation of tribal life and culture.

4. Antropological approach

The main features are: (1) Understanding and respect for tribal organisation, their values and culture. (2) Identifying the problems of different tribes at different economical and cultural levels. (3) Indentifying integrative forces in tribal life. (4) Formulation of tribal welfare plans. (5) Orienting workers for tribal areas.

STATE APPROACH TO THE TRIBALS

The main planks in the approach are:

(1) People should develop along the lines of their own genius and we should avoid imposing anything on them. We should try to encourage in every way their own traditional arts and crafts.

(2) Tribal rights to land and forest should be respected.

(3) We should try to build up a team of their own people to do the work of administration and development. Some technical personnel from outside will, no doubt, be needed, especially in the beginning. But we should avoid introducing too many outsiders into tribal territory.

(4) We should not over-administer these areas or overhelm them with a multiplicity of schemes. We should rather work through and not in rivalry with their own social and cultural institutions.

(5) We should judge the results not by statistics, on the amount of money spent, but by the quality of human character that is evolved. Various approaches that we have seen so far can lead either to: (a) isolation; (b) assimilation and/or (c) integration.

PART IV

COMMUNICATION AND AUDIO-VISUALS
FOR DEVELOPMENT

CHAPTER 23

CONCEPT AND FUNCTIONS OF COMMUNICATION

This chapter gives the definition and meaning of communication, the communication process, its importance to C.D. and extension workers, its scope and purposes, the models of the communication process and the elements of communication.

Communication can best serve in the development and modernising of India if it is treated as a science, an art and indeed as a subject-matter discipline related to the other Social Sciences. It is much more than editing and printing publications, writing news stories, broadcasting radio talks, preparing exhibits and motion pictures, or publicising demonstrations.

DEFINITIONS AND MEANING

The word communication originates from the word 'Communis', which means common. So communication is an act by which a person shares the knowledge, feelings, ideas, information, etc., in ways such that each gains a common understanding of the meaning, intent and use of the message.

The sociologists, the educationists and the psychologists have defined communication in various ways and according to the disciplines to which they belong. A few definitions of these definers are given below:

(1) Leagans says, "it is a process by which two or more people exchange ideas, facts, feelings or impressions in ways that each gains a common understanding of the message. In essence it is the act of getting a sender and a reciever tuned together for a particular message or series of messages."

(2) According to Schramm, "communication occurs when two corresponding systems coupled together through one or more non-corresponding systems assume identical status as a result of a single transfer along the chain, we are trying to establish commonness."

(3) Loomis and Beegle define communication as "the process by which information, decisions and directions pass through a social system and the ways in which knowledge, opinions and attitudes are formed or modified."

(4) Coleman and, Marsh say that in a broad sense, "all educational and action programmes in agriculture are communication."

(5) Howland says that "communication is the force by which an individual communicator transmits stimuli to modify the behaviour of other individuals."

(6) Warren Weaver thinks of communication as—"all the procedures by which one mind can effect another".

(7) Gist says that "when social interaction involves the transmission of meanings through the usage of symbols it is known as communication."

(8) Communication is anything that conveys meaning, that carries a message from one person to another" (Brooker, 1949).

(9) Communication is discriminatory response of an organism to stimulus" (Stevens, 1942).

(10) "Communication is the mutual interchange of ideas by any effective means".

(11) "Communication is the control of behaviour through descriptive and reinforcing stimuli" (Hortman, 1966).

(12) "Communication is the process of effecting an interchange of understanding between two or more people."

(13) "Communication is a purposeful process, which involves sources, messages, channels, and receivers."

(14) Communication is defined as "a process by which an individual, the communicator, transmits (usually verbal symbols) to modify the behaviour of other individuals—Communicators" (Hovland, 1964).

(15) Communication has as its central interest those behavioural situations in which a source transmits a message to (a) receiver, (b) with conscious intent to affect better behaviour (Gerald Miller, 1968).

(16) Communication is the arrangement of environmental stimulus to produce certain desired behaviour on the part of the organism.

(17) Communication is any occurrence involving a minimum of four sequential ingredients: (1) a generator of a (2) sign-symbol system which is (3) projected to (4) at least one receiver who assigns meaning (Robert Goyer, 1967).

(18) Communication is a first principle in philosophy (Woodraw W. Sayre).

(19) Communication does not refer to verbal, explicit and intentional transmission of messages alone . . . . . The concept of communication would include all those processes by which people influence one another.

(20) Communication is the imparting or interchange of thoughts, opinions, or information by speech, writing, or signs (American College Dictionary).

So it can be concluded that communication is a process of social interaction, i.e., in a communication situation two or more individuals interact. They try to tangibly influence the ideas, attitudes, knowledge and behaviour of each other. Communication is an exchange of information, knowledge, ideas or feelings taking place between two individuals. In a face-to-face situation communication is not a mere exchange of information but something more, because in such a situation, along with the information one passes, the gestures, expression, language, the manner of expression and tone—all these combined together, create a sort of impact on both. Some kind of change occurs as a result of interaction. This change may be visible in terms of knowledge and behaviour.

Communication can occur even without uttering words

Communication can occur even without words. Our four senses—audio, visual, touch and smell communicate. The ringing of an alarm clock communicates to us that we are to get up, the peep outside the window i.e,, the visual sense, gives us the indication of weather—rain, snow, fog, storm, etc.; the touch of a pot, whether hot or cold, communicates to us whether it can be handled or not; the sense of smell gives us knowledge whether Halwa, Omlette, Paratha, is being cooked for breakfast.

So when a message is sent from a source to a receiver and produces a specific mental or physical response communication occurs.

Communication—a two-way process

The index of communication may not always be a positive reaction. Therefore, it is essential that the transmission of facts or information is carried in such a manner that the meaning intended and the use of the message is understood by the communicatees, so that it becomes a two-way process.

Communication has many varieties

There are various ways in which people communicate, e.g., the exchange of greetings differs from country to country. It is different even among different religions and groups of people in the same country. We say Namaste with folded hands, or bow and touch the forehead, while saying 'Adabarj', or as among the Sikhs say 'Sata-Shri-Akal' in Punjabi. Simple gestures are an effective tool for communication. So a good communicator is able to find out feelings or reaction through varieties of ways.

Communication process

Communication is the process of transmitting meaning between individuals. This process has been going on ever since the dawn of history. It is vital for the progress of society. Early man communicated through symbols and gestures and later on the spoken word, in the form of language, was used for communication. As technology developed, written words and other media were used, in addition to the symbols, gestures and spoken words. Every symbol and gesture had a meaning in the primitive times and even today they carry meaning and have an important place in the communication process.

ELEMENTS

Communication—complex and mostly indirect

With the development of science and technology the forms and ways of communication have become more specialised. Radio, television, movies and telephone systems are the different methods of communication of recent origin. Earlier communication was mainly oral or written and was direct because the commuicating individuals had a face-to-face contact. However, in the complex societies of today the process is more complex and indirect because of the use of modern gadgets. This type of communication is more of an indirect type as the individuals do not face each other. People in such situations, communicate without coming into close proximity.

IMPORTANCE OF COMMUNICATION IN EXTENSION WORK

Communication has attained great importance in the Community Development and

Extension Programmes. It is through this process that the aims and objectives of the programme are to be widely disseminated to the people and useful information to solve their problems is to be passed on to them. This necessitates that the extension workers should have a thorough understanding of the communication process (see Fig. 23.1).

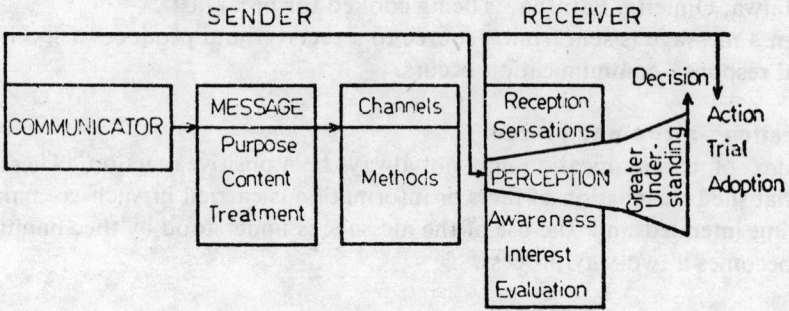

Fig. 23.1. Communication process

The extension worker cannot expect to bring about change unless he is able to communicate effectively. He has to create a conducive situation where information can be transmitted with greater impact on the people. The new knowledge acquired through research has to be disseminated to effect change in the methods of farming or living and in improving them. The central challenge, therefore, to the extension worker is to help people to adopt innovations for increasing the production of crops and livestock, to help homemakers into good homes, children, etc. The better the communication the earlier will be the development of a society.

COMMUNICATION MODELS

Communication takes place when the sender selects a certain message and gives it a special treatment for transmission over a selected channel to a receiver who interprets the message before taking the desired action. This can be represented through a diagram as follows:

$$\boxed{\text{SENDER}} - \boxed{\text{MESSAGE}} - \boxed{\text{TREATMENT}} - \boxed{\text{CHANNEL}} - \boxed{\text{RECEIVER}}$$

Fig. 23.2. Communication Model

These become the elements of communication. The explanation may be given as follows:

(1) The Sender: We may call him the communicator/speaker/source. It is the person or apparatus that puts the process into operation. The sender may be the extension worker/teacher in a meeting or in front of a microphone/radio. He decides what message to send, how to treat it, so that his audience—farmers/students/housewives, youths—can follow it, and what channels radio/newspaper/lecture/film show/slides, photographs/specimens to use and which receivers or audience to reach. If he makes a poor choice his communication is likely to fail.

(2) The message: This is the 'information package', the technical know-how for

improving farming, livestock, home, village sanitation, health, etc., of the people. It may be a single signal—as on poster or complete information through a pamphlet about the 'package of practices', instructions, blue print, etc.

(3) The treatment of the message: It refers to the ways in which the message is handled before it is placed on the channel. Its purpose is to make the message clear, understandable and realistic to the audience.

(4) The channel: It is the avenue of communication, i.e., in a telegram, the wire over which the message is sent, in a radio talk, it is the radio station, studio and wireways, in an article, the newspaper in which our message is to appear.

(5) The receiver/audience: The receiver may be a single person when we write a letter; it may be a group of people who read the message, or the masses who listen to the radio, and see television. The more homogeneous the audience is, the greater are the chances of effective communication.

Other models of the communication process

Some sociologists, educationists, psychologists, anthropologists and rural sociologists have described the process through various models. Their usefulness lies in the manner in which they are used.

(1) *Aristotle's model*

SPEAKER — SPEECH — AUDIENCE

Fig. 23.3. Aristotle's Model

Aristotle says that all these three ingredients or elements are essential for communication. These can be organised to study the process through the person who speaks, the speech he produces and the person/audience who listens. Such communication takes place in a face-to-face situation, or in direct commuication. The speech is either a message, an idea, a thought or a feeling.

(2) *Shammon-Weaver Model*

SOURCE — TRANSMITTER — SIGNAL — RECEIVER — DESTINATION

Fig. 23.4. Shammon-Weaver Model

If we translate the source into speaker, the signal into speech and destination into listener we have the Aristotle's Model plus two mere ingredients: a transmitter which sends out the message and the receiver which catches the message to take it to its destination.

(3) *Westley and Machean Model:* This also have five elements/ingredients on the lines of the Shammon and Weaver's Model. Here, the sender encodes the message which is passed through a channel and is then decoded and its meaning is drawn, after which the message is clear to the receiver.

SENDER — ENCODER — CHANNEL — DECODER — RECEIVER

Fig. 23.5. Westley and Machean Model

(4) *Leagan's Model:* It has six elements.

| COMMUNICATOR | — | MESSAGE | — | CHANNEL | — | TREATMENT |
| AUDIENCE | — | RESPONSE OF AUDIENCE |

Fig. 23.6. Leagan's Model

It is more or less designed on the pattern of the Westley and Machean's Model. Though the terminology is different, most of the elements are common. Audience response is the sixth element about which Leagans says that it is vital to the process especially when it is meant to bring about change in people.

(5) *Berlo Model:* It has also six ingredients.

| SOURCE | → | ENCODER | → | MESSAGE | → | CHANNEL | →
| → | DECODER | → | RECEIVER |

Fig. 23.7. Berlo Model

The difference from the Westley and Machean Model is that Berlo adds message, to his model.

SCOPE OF COMMUNICATION

(1) *Verbal:* The researches show that, on an average, a person spends about 70 per cent of his active time on communicating verbally—listening, speaking, reading and writing. In other words each of us spend about 10 or 11 hours a day on verbal communication. Language is one of the codes we use to express our ideas.

(2) *Non-verbal:* Non-verbal communication includes the gestures, facial expressions, movements of arts, etc., which make our communication more effective.

(3) People communicate on many levels, for many reasons, with many people, and in many ways. A typical man on an average day may communicate in the following ways (the Illustration is of an Agricultural Extension Officer):

(a) He reaches his office and gets his mails—it is written communication.

(b) He receives a peon in the office who conveys to him that the BDO wants him in his office—it is spoken communication.

(c) When the clerk enters his office and greets him with a "Namaste, Sir"— it is spoken communication.

(d) He conducts a meeting of VLWs—it is group-communication.

(e) When he comes back to his office and is engaged in thought about writing the report—it is self-communication.

(f) He goes through the reports from the VLWs—it is written communication again.

(4) The word communication has become popular in management, in industry, in agricultural universities the extension services and advertisements. Newspapers, magazines, oratory, photography, journalism are markets for professional communicators. The market has been increased by the need for advertising and public relations experts, radio, television and film producers, audio-visual experts, etc.

(5) *Communication industry:* Opinion seekers, attitude researchers and marketing researchers, etc., all play their roles in the communication industry. On the basis of researches differentiation can be made between advertisements. The audio-visual experts create the impact of the message on the audience. The use of half-naked photographs of women is a subject of controversy but it pays for the advertisers.

(6) *Communication in management:* In industrial management most of the time of the working day is spent in talking, giving information to subordinates, receiving information from top management and transmitting it to them. Meetings and interviewing increase the efficiency of workers and improve coordination. As automisation develops even the mere machine operator will spend more time in manipulating symbols.

(7) *Communication removes the time-lag:* The accelerated pace of research has made it more difficult for scientific, technical and operating personnel to keep abreast of recent developments. An extension worker in agriculture is outdated if he lacks communication about the latest researches on wheat, paddy, soybean and other crops varieties, the use of fertilisers; and the plant protection measures developed in the last five years. This necessitates in-service training, development of communication centres, extension directorates and other such agencies to keep them up-to-date. Similarly the farmers have to be demonstrated the improved practices, given information through radio-programmes, supplied with literature which they can follow, they have to be given the opportunities of seeing demonstrations, exhibitions, the farms of the progressive farmers or an agricultural colleges, etc. If this gap between the knowledge developed and the technology known to extension workers and farmers is widened, the pace of progress will be slow.

FUNCTIONS OF COMMUNICATION

One of the functions of communication which humanity has developed to their extreme social advantage is that of communicating to some living aspect of the environment (such as a person) in order to establish, maintain, exploit or alter the relationship with that person. According to Lee Thayer the basic functions of communication may be categorised as under:

(1) The information function

The basic elements of adapting oneself to the environment or adapting the environment to oneself is information. We must have some information about going on in our environments to concern ourselves about it. And we must have some information about ourselves, our intentions, goals, etc., in order to have something to be concerned about. So the getting or giving of information thus underlies all communication encounters, either directly or indirectly. Information is basic to all of the other applied functions of communication. Communication is not going to occur unless someone is acquiring and consuming some information about himself or his environment.

Usually, when we speak of informative communication, we refer to 'international' communication. That is, we refer to the consequences of reactions intended or sought by the originator.

(2) Command or instructive functions

Those who are hierarchically superior (in family, business, military, civic or personal life) often initiate communication either for the purpose of informing their subordinates or for the purpose of telling them what to do, how to do, etc.

One of the expectations that properly socialised subordinates bring to their relationships with superiors is that they are obliged to accept certain kinds of orders from certain superiors to do certain kinds of things. When the rules about who can order whom to do what things, are mutually understood, neither the supervisor nor the subordinate expects to engage in a dialogue.

The command and instructive functions of communication are more observable in formal organisations than they are in informal organisations. Individuals who are hierarchically (positionally) superior within an organisational structure are both privileged and obligated to command (and/or to control) certain task-related behaviour of their subordinates.

According to David Barlo, a person can and will accept a communication as authoritative only when the following four conditions are simultaneously obtained:

(1) he can and does understand the communication.

(2) at the time of his decision he believes that it is not inconsistent with the purpose of organisation;

(3) at the time of his decision, he believes it to be compatible with his personal interest as a whole; and

(4) he is able mentally and physically to comply with it.

The command purpose of communication is as pertinent to informal relations as it is to formal relations although in ways which are probably not as apparent.

Informal relations which persist over a time, particularly two person or one person face-to-face encounters, are founded upon mutually understood relationships prescribing certain behaviour towards one another. The participants continuously exercise some permanent or momentary prerogative they have in order to command the behaviour of another person.

Whenever we exercise such a prerogative to order or direct another's behaviour in some way, the communication which occurs is serving the command purpose. Whether being exercised by one person or by an aggregate in some collective way, the command function inevitably underlies much human interaction.

(3) Influence or persuasive functions

According to Berlo (1960), the sole purpose of communication is to influence. We communicate to influence, to effect with intent the behaviour of other person(s).

Aristotle defined the study of rholotic (communication) as the search for all the available means of persuasion. So he clearly implied that the main aim of communication was 'persuasion'.

The purpose of influencing another's comprehending system in some way would be to alter that receiver's general beliefs, understandings, values, orientations, etc., in some desired way By contrast, influencing another's behaviour is typically more action specific and situational.

(4) Integrative functions

The major functions of communication at the interpersonal level is that of self integration or of continuously off setting any disintegration, (i.e. entropy that might otherwise occur).

At the level of formal organisations, larger than face-to-face human groups, integrative functions are provided in part by bureaucratisation, proceduralisation, industrialisation, etc. When a social system exceeds the integrative limits of face-to-face encounters, the necessary integrative mechanisms become embedded in that social systems, literature, art, folklore, mythology, beliefs, mores, orientations, etiquette and institutional practices.

It is important to realise that the integrative functions of communication (as is true for all the functions of communication) are *ephemeral*. Undoubtedly there is some advantage both to the individual and to the organisation in the relative integrity of their prespective structures. But this advantage would hold only if the competencies or capabilities thus created have some value or usefulness to the adaptive or the goal pursuing capabilities of the individual and or the organisation.

In the seventeenth century a school of thought known as *Faculty Psychology* made clear distinction between the 'mind' and 'soul'. This mind-soul dualism was interpreted as a basis for two independent purposes for communication. One purpose was intellectual and the other was emotional. By this theory, one purpose of communication was *informative*, an appeal to mind. A second purpose was persuasive, an appeal to the soul, the emotions. A third purpose was *entertainment*. There has, however, been a tendency to interpret these purposes as exclusive. One is not giving informamation when he is entertaining or entertainining when he is persuading and so on.

Schramm (1949) described the purpose of communication as *immediate reward* and *delayed reward*. He suggested that individuals are rewarded immediately on receiving or producing some kind of message. Both these are *consumatory purposes*. For example, an artist may compose a piece of music and be satisfied in the composing process. As against this, the purpose of communication could be *instrumental*, e.g., the favourable response produced in his audience is instrumental in producing further behaviour on their part.

All communication behaviour has as its purpose, its goals, the production of a response. When we learn to phrase our purpose in terms of specific responses from those attending to our messages, we have taken the first step towards efficient and effective communication. The failure to affect the receiver in ways that were intended can be attributed to one or both of the two causes—*ineficiency* and/or *misperception*.

Dimension of purpose

(a) The 'WHO' of purpose

Any analysis of communication purpose or of success in achieving the response intended needs to raise and answer the question for whom was this intended. When someone writes, another must read it, when someone speaks, another must hear it.

One dimension of any analysis of communicative purpose is the discovery of the intended receiver for the message. The communicator may intend his message for himself or others. Others who receive it may or may not be those for whom it was intended.

In any communication system, there are at least two lots of desired responses, the purpose from the communicator's point of view and from the receiver's point of view. When the communication purposes of the source and receiver are independent or complementary, communication can continue. When the purposes of the source and receiver are incompatible, communication breaks down.

(b) The 'HOW' of purpose

How does the source or receiver intend to effect behaviour, what kind of effect does he want to produce? This question needs to be analysed from at least two point of views, the consumatory and instrumental purposes described earlier.

The source or the communicator can have both consumatory and instrumental purposes. The receiver of a message also can have both primarily consumatory or instrumental purposes in receiving a message is whether the purpose is satisfied by consumption of the message, or is the behaviour produced by the message itself used later as an instrument to elicit further behaviour.

Conclusion

In conclusion, all communication behaviour has a purpose. The main function or the purpose of communication is to change or guide other people's behaviour. To achieve this purpose various approaches can be used. It could be informative, commanding or instructing, influential or persuasive and/or entertaining.

The purpose of communication is designed for a particular person(s). It could be for the communicator himself, or a particular individual, or a group of individuals. Similarly, it can be fulfilled either by immediate reward or delayed reward. It can be both consumatory or instrumental. However, the information-productivity may be seen in Fig. 23.8.

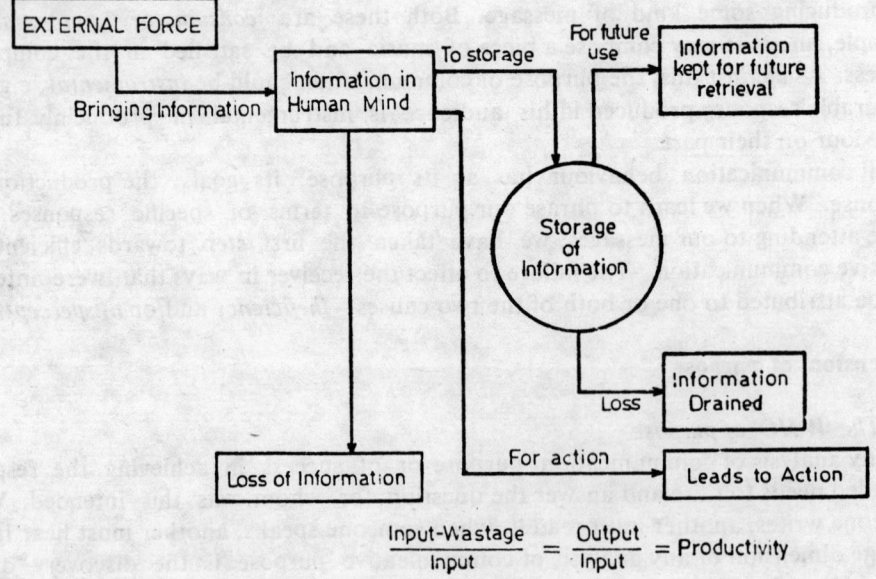

$$\frac{Input-Wastage}{Input} = \frac{Output}{Input} = Productivity$$

Fig. 23.8. Flow of information

COMMUNICATION CHANNELS

Definition

Channels are physical bridges between the sender and the receiver of a message. Channel is a word borrowed from telecommunication and applied to a number of different aspects of the communication process. They are the avenues between a communicator and an audience on which messages travel to and fro. They are the transmission lines used for carrying messages to their destination. A channel may be anything used by a sender of messages to connect him with the intended receivers. The crucial point is that he must get in contact with his audience. The message must get through. Common channels of communication in the extension situation include meetings of all kinds, radio, books, bulletins, letters, newspapers, organised tours and personal contacts. Others may be added to the list such as telephone, television and leaders at work. All of these make it possible for a communicator to transmit his message to the intended audience. Thus channels serve as essential tools of communication.

Dimension of channel

For a clear concept of the channel we need to look at:
(i) The modes of encoding and decoding messages.
(ii) Message—Vehicles.
(iii) Vehicle carriers.

If two persons are talking to each other, their speaking and hearing mechanisms are in motion. The oral message produced by one has to go to the other person through a message vehicle. The oral message is carried out by sound waves. Finally, the sound waves themselves need something to support them, a wave-carrier. Usually, in human communication at least, sound waves are supported by air.

As channels are the connecting links between communicators and receivers, they must effectively join together these two essential elements of the communication process.

Classification of channel

Roger and Shoemaker classified channels as follows:

(1) *Interpersonal and mass media channels*

While interpersonal channels are those which are used for face-to-face communication between two or more people, mass media are mechanical devices through which an individual or a group can reach a relatively larger population in a shorter time. The audience members may be physically separated.

(2) *Localite and cosmopolite channels*

Localite means communication of the same system.

Cosmopolite indicates communication between many cultures, any thing outside the system.

While localite channels originate within the social system of the receiver, cosmopolite channels have their origins outside his immediate social system. For example, interpersonal channels may be cosmopolite or localite depending on the location of service but mass media channels are almost always cosmopolite.

Characteristics of channels

Rogers and Sovenning (1969) have provided the distinguishing characteristics of interpersonal and mass media channels(see Table 24.1).

Table 24.1
Characteristics of channels (Rogers and Sovenning 1969)

Characteristic	Interpersonal channels	Mass media channeles
1. Directions of message flow	Two way	One way
2. Speed to a large audience	Slow	Rapid
3. Message accuracy to a large audience	Low	High
4. Ability to select receiver	High	Low
5. Ability to overcome selectivity process	High	Low
6. Amount of feed back	High	Low
7. Possible effect	Attitude change	Increase of knowledges

The nature of channels

The practical decision which the communicator makes is the choice and combination of channels within a primary group. This decision does not often enter when the other group members are at hand and one can talk to them face-to-face. But when one is separated from the primary group, even by a short business trip out of town, then one often has to make a decision about channels. The choice is relatively simple at this level of communication but when planning communication for larger groups of people the choice is exceedingly complicated, even difficult. Sometimes availability and audience capability help to determine it. For example, where the audience is illiterate one must use pictures and the spoken word. Where the audience does not have radios, obviously one cannot depend on radio channels. But in the most usual situation where radio and print and pictures all reach the intended audience one must make a decision complicated by a number of factors. We can differentiate channels on a number of useful scales. Here are four of these:

(1) *Time-space-time:* Printed materials, still pictures, and art objects are space-organised. A radio broadcast and a telephone conversation are time organised, Face-to-face communication, sound, films, television are time and space organised. In reading, the reader can set his own pace and turn back whenever he wishes to check the relation of one page, paragraph, one sentence to another. In listening, however, he is at the mercy of the communicator. He cannot control the pace or turn back. Because of this difference, the space-organised media appear to offer more favourable conditions for difficult concepts, for masses of detail, for criticism, discrimination and selectivity on the part of the audience. On the other hand, the time-organised media appear to offer some advantages for rote learning of simple material, and for encouraging suggestibility in an audience. Space and time media share the advantages and disadvantages of space media and time media. There are apparently eye-men and ear-men, that is, individuals who are especially skillful in receiving space or time-organised communication.

(2) *Participation:* Centril and Allport have shown that it is possible to characterise the media as to whether they permit much or little participation on the part of the audience. Thus, a media scale might be created running from most participation to least participation, something like this: personal conversation, discussion groups, informal meetings, telephone, formal meetings, sound-motion pictures, television, radio, telegraph, personal correspondence, form letters, newspapers, billboards, magazines and books. A higher degree of social participation tends to create a sense of involvement, a group bond, a circular pattern of influence and decision making. It provides maximum feedback.

(3) *Speed:* Timeliness is maximum in television and radio. There is a considerable sense of timeliness in newspapers, some in magazines, less in motion pictures least in books.

(4) *Permanence:* Books probably give the greatest sense of permanence. Next come motion pictures and magazines. There is but a small amount of permanence in newspapers. Least permanent are radio and television. Deutschmann (1957), suggested a simple classification for communication situations from which we give the following examples:

Communication situations

Private		Public		
Face-to-face	*Interposed*	*Face-to-face*	*Interposed*	
			Assembled	*Non-assembled*
Two people converse at dinner.	Two people converse on telephone.	Public meeting	Movie theatre audience	Viewing televisian at home.

Selection of communication channels

Proper selection and use of channels results in successful communication. Without proper use of channels, the message no matter how important, will not get through to the intended audience. As source-encoders, we have to decide how we will channel messages so that our receiver can decode them: can see, hear, touch and even occasionally taste and smell them. In other words, we can look at channels of communication as the skills possessed by the source and the sensory skills possessed by the receiver.

There are several channels of communication available to the extension workers, the functions of which differ depending upon several factors, especially (i) the purpose of the communication itself, and (ii) the degree to which the recipient of the communication is at present predisposed towards acceptance. There are four objectives which may influence the choice of channels.

(a) To make announcements of meetings, exhibitions and educational activities and to attract attention to organisational programmes and resources.

These announcements are news and usually disseminated through the channels of mass media like radio, television, newspapers, etc. However, studies in India have shown that mass media is not being properly used to play this role.

(b) To disseminate information and to teach skills to persons already interested.

This type of communication would include detailed information about issues of new skills.

(c) To promote acceptance, or adoption of practices being recommended for individuals and families.

It is action-oriented. This means that certain channels which are more extensively used by these particular segments will be utilised by the communicator.

(d) To promote acceptance and adoption of ideas by organisations as such.

While promoting acceptance of new ideas leading up to adoption, many obstructions can enter the channels. These are often referred to as 'noise', that is, some obstruction that prevents the message from being heard by or carried over clearly to the audience. 'Noise' emerges from a wide range of sources and causes.

The following are some of these:

(1) Failure of a channel to reach the intended audience. Usually no one channel will reach an entire audience. Some examples: Meetings—all people cannot or may not attend. Radio—all people do not have access to a receiving set, or may not be tuned in if they did. Written materials—many people cannot read, and others may not.

(2) Failure on the part of a communicator to handle channels skilfully. In a meeting, when everyone cannot hear what is said, and see what is shown, they cannot receive the message.

(3) Failure to select channels appropriate to the objective of a communicator. If the objective were to show a certain group of people how to do something—dig a compost pit, build a sanitary latrine, cook vegetables, etc., radio, circular letters or newspaper could not do the job. The channel needed is a method-demonstration meeting.

(4) Failure to the channels in accordance with the abilities of the audience.

(5) Failure to avoid physical distraction. The physical distractions include people moving in and out, loud noise in or out of the group, heat, lighting, crowded conditions and many other forms of distractions.

(6) Failure of an audience to listen or look carefully.

(7) Failure to use enough channels in parallel. The more channels a communicator uses in parallel at about the same time, the more chances he has for the message getting through and being properly received. No single channel will ordinarily reach all people who need to receive a message.

(8) Use of too many channels in a series. The more the channels used in a series, the less chance a communicator has of getting his message through to the intended audience.

To overcome the above problems one should take the following factors into acconnt:

(1) The specific objective of the message

(2) The nature of the message, degree of directness versus abstractness, level of difficulty, scope, timing, etc.

(3) The audience—size, need, interest, knowledge of the subject, etc.

(4) Channels available that will reach the audience or parts of it.

(5) How channels can be combined and used in parallel.

(6) How channels, that must be used in a series, can be reduced to the minimum and those used made effective without fail.

(7) Relative cost of channels in relation to anticipated effectiveness.

(8) Time available for communicator and audience.

(9) Extent of seeing, hearing or doing that is necessary to get the message through.

CHAPTER 25

COMMUNICATOR-COMMUNICATEE RELATIONSHIPS

Communication is one of the oldest activities of man. Far more stimuli come to us then we are able to attend to. The attention which we pay is selective depending upon the purpose for which we see these objects. The signs of communication have to compete for an audience. As we know communication is a process of getting a sender and a receiver tuned in together for a particular message or a series of messages. The communicator and receiver are the important persons in communication. As the communicator is the person who puts the process of communication into operation, he is the source or originator of messages. He is the sender of messages. He is the first to give expression to messages intended to reach an audience in a manner that results in correct interpretation and desirable response. The communicator may be a Village Level Worker, a Block Development or Panchayat Officer, or any other person. As we have said above the commnicator is the sender of messages. The one to whom he sends the message is the receiver or audience, or listener or communicatee. The following are the communicator and communicatee relationships:

(1) Orientation
(2) Empathy
(3) Feedback
(4) Physical interdependence
(5) Credibility
(6) Interaction
(7) Homophily, Heterophily

(1) Orientation

The term "orientation" is used as equivalent to 'attitude' in its more inclusive sense of referring to both cannotive and cognitive tendencies. The phrase 'simultaneous orientation', itself represents an assumption, namely, that A's orientation towards B's and towards X' are interdependent. That is the certain definable relationship between A and B, between A and X and between B and X are all viewed as interdependent as explained in the following diagram (Fig. 25.1).

(i) A's orientation towards X, including both attitude towards X as an object to be approached and cognitive attributes.

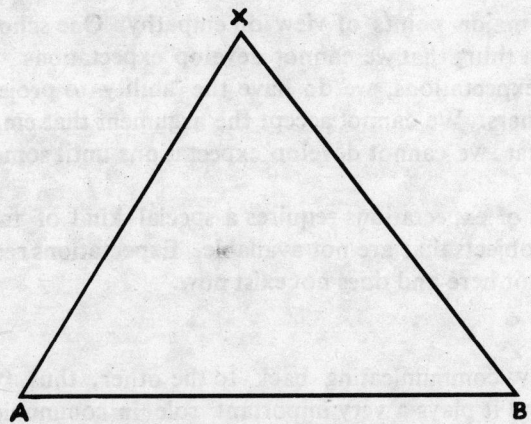

Fig. 25. 1. Simultaneous orientation

(ii) A's orientation towards B in exactly the same sense.

(iii) B's orientation towards X.

(iv) B's orientation towards A.

This very simple system is designed to fit two-person communication.

The assumption that co-orientation is essential to human life is based upon two considerations of complementary value.

(1) The orientation of any A toward any B is rarely, if ever, made in an environmental vacuum. It is not certain that even the most person-oriented communicators are devoid of environmental reference. The more intense one person's concern for another, the more sensitive he is likely to be the other's orientations, to objects in the environment.

(2) The orientation of any A capable of verbal communication with almost any conceivable X is rarely, if ever, made in a social vacuum. There are few, if any, objects so private that one's orientation towards them are uninfluenced by other orientations. This is particularly true with regard to what has been termed social reality.

In short it is an almost constant human necessity to orient one towards objects in the environment and also towards other persons.

(2) Empathy

When we develop expectations, when we make predictions, we are assuming that we have skill in what the psychologists call empathy—the ability to project ourselves into others people's personalities. We can define empathy as the process through which we arrive at expectations and anticipations of the internal psychological states of a man.

As sources and receivers, we carry around images of ourselves and a set of expectations about other people. We use these expectations in encoding, decoding and responding to messages. We take other people into account in framing messages. We frame messages to influence a receiver but our expectations about the receiver influence us and our messages.

There are three major points of view on empathy. One school of thought argues that there is no such thing that we cannot develop expectations.

We do develop expectations, we do have the ability to project ourselves into the internal states of others. We cannot accept the argument that empathy does not have meaning for us, that we cannot develop expectations until some kind of interpretation process occurs.

The development of expectations requires a special kind of talent. We need to be able to think about objects that are not available. Expectations require decisions about the things that are not here and does not exist now.

(3) Feedback

One is constantly communicating back to the other, thus, "the return process is called feedback", and it plays a very important role in communication. Communication often involves an action, reaction and interdependence. The communicator can use the reaction of the receiver as a check for his own effectiveness and a guide to his own future action. The reaction of the receiver is a consequence of the response of the source. As a response consequence, it serves as feedback to the source. When a source receives feedback that is rewarding, he continues to produce the same kind of message. When he gets non-rewarding feedback, he will eventually change his masage.

(4) Physical interdependence

The function of the source and receiver are physically interdependent although the functions may be performed at different points in time and space.

(5) Credibility

Credibility is the degree to which a communication source is perceived as trustworthy and competent by the receiver.

An individuals attitude change is positively related to the credibility with which he perceives the source of a persuasive message. If a client perceives that a change agent possesses relatively higher credibility than various other sources and channels, the client will be more receptive to messages from that change agent.

The credibility is limited to "how to" information and does not usually extend to an ability to persuade the individual to a favourable attitude towards innovation.

(6) Interaction

Interaction is the mutual and reciprocal influencing of each others behaviour. The concept of interaction is central to an understanding of the concept of process in communication. If two individuals make influences about their own roles and take the role of others at the same time and if their communication behaviour depends on the reciprocal taking of roles, then they are communicating by interacting with each other. We can communicate without interaction, however, to the extent we are in an interactional situation. Our effectiveness, our ability to affect and be affected by others, increases. Homophily is a condition of interaction.

(7) Homophily—heterophily

One of the fundamental principles of human communication is that the transfer of ideas most frequently occurs between a source and a receiver who are alike, similar or homophilous.

Homophily is the degree to which the pairs of individuals who interact are similar in certain attributes such as beliefs, values, education, social status and the like. Social relations are much closer between individuals who resemble each other in occupation and education. Why does homophily occur? Because better communication occurs when source and receiver are homophilous. When source and receiver share common meaning, attitudes and beliefs and a mutual language, communication between them is likely to be effective. Most individuals enjoy the comforts of interaction with others who are quite similar. Interaction will be greater when the source and receiver share their beliefs, attitudes, etc. and there will be more communication. For example when the extension worker go to the village people, the response will be better from them and interaction will be more between the communicator and communicatee. Heterophilic interaction is likely to be the cause of cognitive dissonance because the receiver is exposed to messages that may be inconsistent with his existing beliefs and create an uncomfortable psychological state. Homophily and effective communication breed each other. The more communication there is between members of a dyad, the more likely they are to become homophilous. The more homophilous they are, the more likely it is that the communnication will be effective. Individuals who break the homophily boundary and attempt to communicate with others quite different from themselves are beset with the frustration of ineffective communication. Differences in technical competence, social status, attitudes and belief all contribute to heterophily in language and meaning, thereby leaving the message to go unheeded.

But we can not say homophily is more effective than heterophily. In some cases heterophily is more effective than homophily and in some cases homophily is more effective than heterophily. Both have different effects in different situations.

CHAPTER 26

FEEDBACK IN COMMUNICATION

THE FEEDBACK PROCESS

According to Berlo (1960) "if a communication source decodes the message that he encodes, if the message is put back to his system, we have feedback". When an individual communicates with himself, the message he encodes is fed back into his system by his decoding system. In other words, action-reaction interdependence in communication is referred to as feedback. Communication often involves an action-reaction interdependence. The communicator can use the reaction of the receiver as a check of his own effectiveness and a guide to his own future action. When a source receives feedback that is rewarding, he continues to produce the same kind of message. When he gets non-rewarding feedback. he eventually will change his message.

Schramm (1955) points out that each person in the communication process is both an encoder and a decoder. He receives and transmits. However, a person will decode a message and interpret it in accordance with his own experience and then encodes a response accordingly. The same is true of both the receiver and the source. Hence as Schramm (1959) points out, each is constantly communicating back to the other. The return process is called 'feedback' and plays an important part in communication because it tells both the source and the receiver, how their messages are being interpreted.

For effective communication, feedback is of paramount importance. It concerns to and fro communication. This return process is called feedback. It serves to control and correct the signals and go forward. It also serves to realign all the signals within the network in relation to one another. Feedback is an error-correcting mechanism that can overcome noise. It makes persons truly interacting members of a communication system and tells us how our messages are being interpreted. An experienced communicator is attentive to feedback and constantly modifies his message in the light of what he observes in, or hears, from his audience.

We often overlook the power of the feedback to affect the source. We fail to realise the extent to which the receiver affects the communicator. When they indicate that they do not understand, he repeats. In the case of mass media, drastic changes are made as a result of the feedback obtained in the form of opinion polls, attitude surveys, etc.

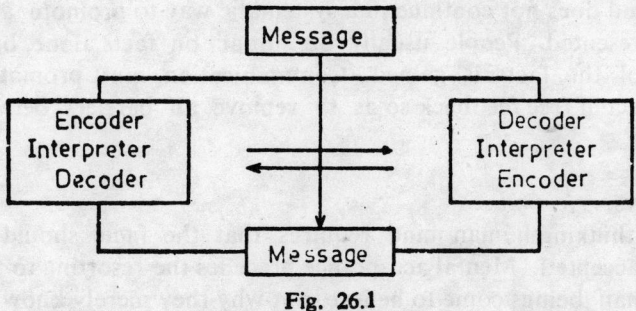

Fig. 26.1

Feedback provides the source with information concerning his success in accomplishing his objective. In doing this, it exerts control over future messages which the source encodes.

Communications research bears testimony that learners perceive better gain, more knowledge and retain longer when opportunities for feedback are provided in a communication situation. Person-to-person communication permits maximum feedback. The source has an opportunity to change his message on the spot as a result of the feedback he gets.

FEEDBACK AS RESOURCE ORIENTATION

The concept of feedback is usually used to reflect a resource orientation, rather than a receiver orientation or a process orientation. When we talk about the receiver's responses as feedback for the source, we are observing a communication situation from the point of view of the source. 'Free flow pattern of feedback' has been found to be most effective in communicating messages to an audience as compared with other levels of feedback on the basis of a knowledge and confidence score. A limited answer pattern of feedback has been proved to be the second best way of disseminating information. Thus it can be concluded that gain in knowledge is directly proportional to the amount of feedback. In other words, gain in knowledge is the function of feedback in the process of communication.

It has also been observed that with every increase in the amount of feedback there was consistently a corresponding increase in confidence among the respondents in their knowledge gain. The gain in confidence is the function of differential feedback in the communication process.

ROLE OF FEEDBACK IN EXTENSION EDUCATION

In extension education, it is not enough merely to deliver the message but it is of paramount importance to see the resultant effect of the transference of the new ideas. The audience-response in the shape of desirable action is needed in the form of free feedback. The following gives an idea of the possible variety in response that may result on receiving a message from a typical farm population.

(1) *Understanding* vs. *knowledge*
Communicative efforts often fail because they stop simply with the laying of facts

before people, and does not continue in a systematic way to promote an understanding of the facts presented. People usually do not act on facts alone, but only when an understanding of the facts is gained. Communication must promote understanding through effective and free feedback so as to remove all barriers between the sender and the receiver

(2) *Acceptance* vs. *rejection*

An alert and thinking human mind requires that the facts should be understood before they are accepted. Mental acceptance precedes the resorting to physical action. It is what human beings come to believe, not why they merely know that determines what they do when they are free to act as they choose. Feedback is most essential to help them act in a right way.

(3) *Remembering* vs. *forgetting*

When opportunity for an action is not immediately available what learned may be forgotten through delayed action. This basic principles has extensive implications for training extension personnel. Transmitting the right message to the right people at the right time is often a crucial factor in successful communication, with the help of free feedback, to an extent it is possible.

(4) *Mental* vs. *physical action*

Change in the mind of a man must always precede change in the action of his hands. A message suggesting physical action could end with the source. So feedback is most essential to remove the mental barrier in the way of actual adoption of farm innovations.

(5) *Right* vs. *wrong*

The intent of communication is to promote desirable action by an audience as determined by the communication and expressed in his objectives. For a variety of reasons, farm people fail to behave precisely according to instructions even when they have understood and accepted them. Whether as individuals or groups, human beings have their own ideas about how to act. This situation can only be corrected through constant free feedback to rectify the transmission errors entering the communication channels. From the above we can say that:

    (i)   Feedback is source oriented.
    (ii) Feedback varies in different communication situations.
    (iii) Feedback affects the source or communicator.
    (iv) Feedback exerts control over future messages.
    (v) Feedback affects communication fidelity.

FEEDBACK IN COMMUNICATION OF INFORMATION

Effective communication is the core of succssful education at all levels and also the key that unlocks the door to human relationships which is to exchange knowledge and thought. Communication refers to the exchange of knowledge, skills and attitudes among persons and the social groupings. In other words, communication implies the movement of knowledge to people in such ways that they act on the knowledge in order to achieve some useful results. Since the objectives of all the programmes is to bring about desirable change in the behaviour complex of the people, the phenomenon of communication is of especially great significance.

Researches have shown that different communication channels perform different functions with varying degrees of success in the transmission of information about farm matters. It is found that a farmer may hear about new ideas through a certain method, learn more about it through another, be influenced to adopt or reject through another and learn the specific information needed to put the ideas into practice through still another.

EFFECT OF FEEDBACK IN COMMUNICATION OF INFORMATION

Levitt and Muller (1951) conducted experiments to investigate the kinds of feedback that existed between a sender and receiver. Some effect of feedback on communication were reported by controlling different kinds of visual and verbal feedback signals. They have classified them in four different amounts of feedback from zero level to full. They found that full feedback has the greatest effect on communication. It increased the accuracy with which the information was transmitted and it seemed to permit the participant to learn a mutual language, which language once learned may obviate the necessity for further feedback.

Arnold Tustin (1952) while giving an introduction to the general principles of cybernetics, high lighted how feedback was the basic mechanism behind the automatic control in thermostat, guided missiles and also in physiology and economics.

Schramm (1956) stated that in the mechanism of feedback the hearer accepts the ideas which are communicated effectively and if they are truely clear. The hearer nods his head either in agreement or disagreement. Schramm further stated that we get feedback from our own messages too, that is, we hear our own voices and most of the time ourselves correct the mispronunciations.

Rosenberg and Hall (1958) conducted further experiments and distinguished between different kinds of human feedback not only in amount and quality but also in original feedback of the sender's own response, of his team responses or both responses. They found that in human communication the least significant feedback was the response from the teammate. Self-response and combined responses were more important controls of the signals sent.

Power, et. al. (1960) formulated a general feedback theory of human behaviours and introduced the concept of open and closed, lower and high orders of systems, positive and negative feedback.

Feedback maintains the stability and equilibrium of a communication system.

CHAPTER 27

ORGANISATIONAL COMMUNICATION IN AGRICULTURAL DEVELOPMENT*

'Organisation' and 'communication', both independently, are omnipresent, universal and crucial penomena influencing our total activities, life and living. When one visualises them together in terms of 'organisational communication', one can get the thrill of a marriage between the two giants which is, of course, existing, complex, at times baffling, but ultimately wholesome and rewarding. Both are, indeed, inhertently interwoven; there cannot be an organisation without its own communication network, while the reverse can be true—communication commonly takes place in a non-organisational context. Communication, no doubt, is the life and blood of any organisation, and, therefore, the performance of any administration can be adjudged on the effectiveness and efficiency of its communication system.

Historically speaking, the existence of the organisation—the social system and communication—and the media of expression, is as old as the evolution of the human race itself, but due cognisance to them as two distinct subjects has been of relatively recent origin and more even lately to the organisational communication. In the context of agricultural administration, this subject has yet to gain currency. Happily, however, a conscious start has now been made in this direction as a subject of immense scope and practical utility as also a curious area for investigation.

Much earlier, Roethlisberger (1941) noted that the executive's environment is largely verbal communication. Thayer (1961) on the same plank, stipulated that "most administrators in most business and industrial organisations, spend at least 75 per cent of their time communicating, and not infrequently as much as 95 per cent of their time communicating to others and being communicated to. We may safely infer from these figures that any improvement in the administrator's ability to communicate would in fact be an improvement in his ability to administrate." As a matter of fact, communication occupies a strategic place in development administration (more so in agriculture) which is characterised by flexibility, decentralisation, constant interactions, intimate relationships and the rapid flow of information to and fro. Figure 27.1 presents

*With the courtesy of Dr. C. Prasad, Assistant Director General (Education), I.C.A.R., New Delhi.

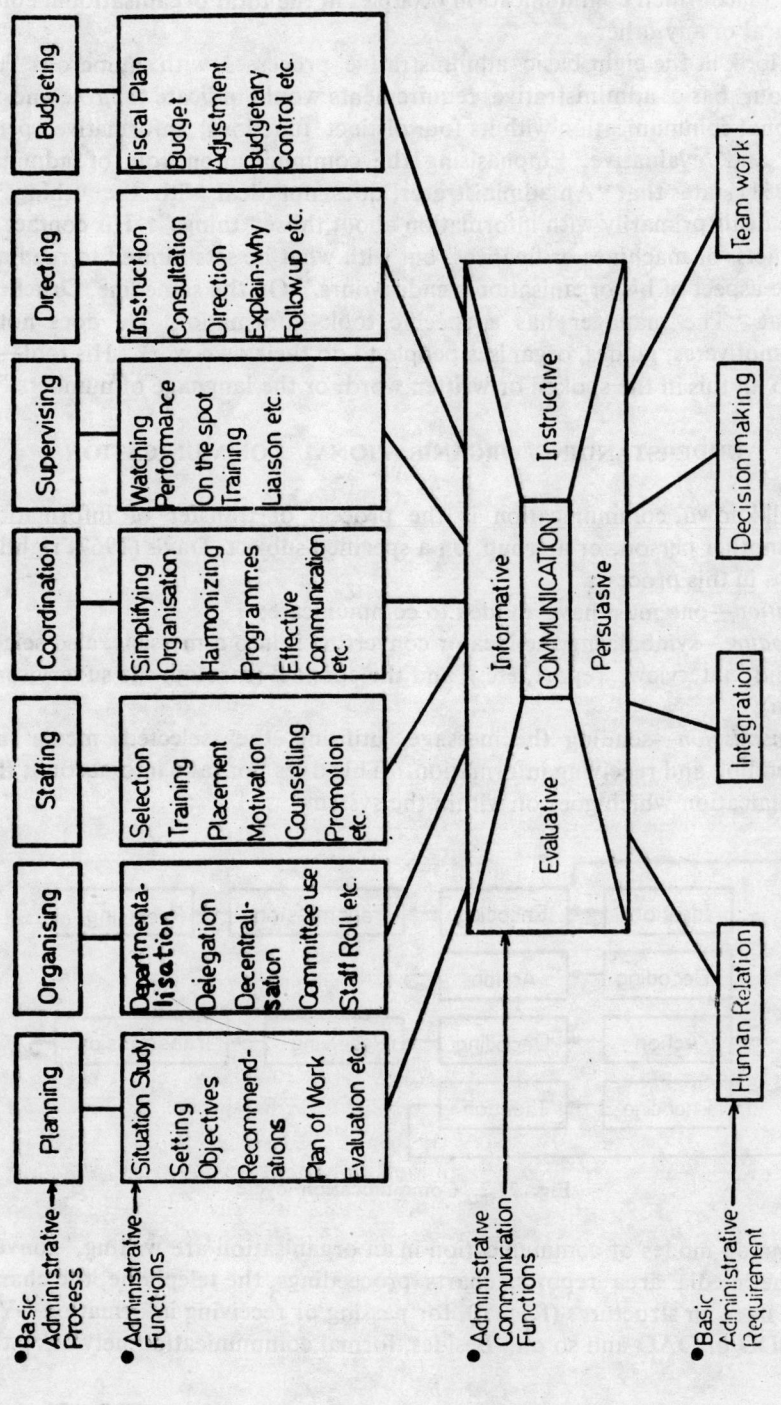

Fig. 27.1. Communication basic to administration

Planning | Organising | Staffing | Coordination | Supervising | Directing | Budgeting

Situation Study
Setting
Objectives
Recommend-
ations
Plan of Work
Evaluation etc.

Departmenta-
lisation
Delegation
Decentrali-
sation
Committee use
Staff Roll etc.

Selection
Training
Placement
Motivation
Counselling
Promotion
etc.

Simplifying
Organisation
Harmonizing
Programmes
Effective
Communication
etc.

Watching
Performance
On the spot
Training
Liaison etc.

Instruction
Consultation
Direction
Explain-why
Follow up etc.

Fiscal Plan
Budget
Adjustment
Budgetary
Control etc.

COMMUNICATION

Informative
Instructive
Persuasive
Evaluative

Team work
Decision making
Integration
Human Relation

• Basic
Administrative→
Process

• Administrative→
Functions

• Administrative
Communication
Functions

• Basic
Administrative
Requirement

the crucial place which communication occupies in the total organisational context, be it agricultural or any other.

A close look at the eight basic administrative processes with numerous functions and the four basic administrative requirements would indicate the role and scope of organisational communication with its four distinct functions; informative, persuasive, instructive and evaluative. Emphasising the communication role of administrator, Thayer (1961) states that "An administrator, does not deal with the "things" of his world. He deals primarily with information about those "things". His contact are not with products or machines or finances, but with what he sets himself to read and hear about these aspect of his organisation's endeavours." On the same line, Drucker (1954) reports that "The manager has a specific tool: information. He does not handle people; he motivates, guides, organises people to do their own work. His tool—his only tool—to do all this in the spoken or written word, or the language of numbers."

UNDERSTANDING ORGANISATIONAL COMMUNICATION

As is well known, communication is the process of transfer of information by a person to another person, or a group, on a specified subject. Davis (1967) rightly points out six steps in this process:

(1) *Ideation*—one must have an idea to communicate;

(2) *Encoding*—symbolising the idea or converting it into a message, also selection of media (radio, interview, report, etc.) and the channel (through the supervisor, or by-passing him);

(3) *Transmission*—sending the message, utilising the selected media and the channel; sending and receiving information. This does not take into account the informal communication which goes on within the system.

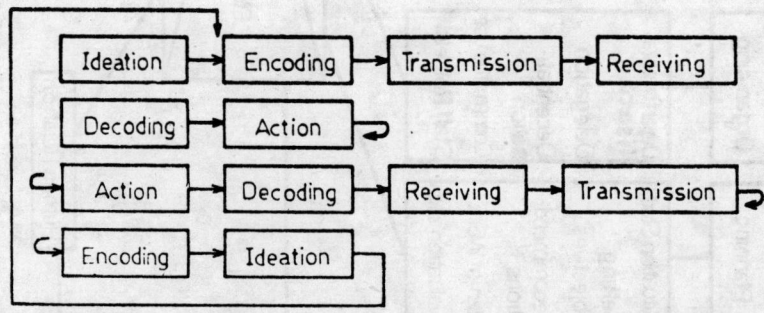

Fig. 27.2. Communication cycle

The common modes of communication in an organisation are writing, conversation, reading, the media area reports, charts proceedings, the telephone, the channels are established lines, or structures (formal), for passing or receiving information—VLWs to AEOs to BDO or DAO and so on. Besides, formal communication networks, there are

VLW=Village Level Worker, AEO=Agricultural Extension Officer, BDO=Block Development Officer, DAO=District Agricultural Officer.

always informal channels in all organisations—friends' circles, coffee counters, tea breaks, etc. In other words, the numerous channels through which messages flow from person to person throughout the administration make up the communication networks. Though omnipresent and active, administrators have hardly learnt to make proper use of the informal channels.

TYPES OF ORGANISATIONAL COMMUNICATION

In communication literature, organisational communication has been classified into first, formal (follow-lines of authority) and informal (grape vine) communication. Whether the authorities wish it or not, informal networks do exist in all organisations. They can be a source of clarity or confusions, of help to the organisation or a problem, depending on how they are veiwed and utilised by the management. The informal channels are more active, at times threatening, if the formal channels do not cater to the employees information needs. Second typology puts it as operational communication—relating to organisational operations; situational communication—dealing with specific situational problems; and institutional communication—all communications with regard to the organisation.

A more practical approach in understanding administrative communication is to conceive it in terms of: (a) Cross-communication; (b) Downward communication; and (c) Upward communication. Some elaboration on these may be helpful.

(a) Cross-communication

Incumbents in any organisation are naturally, as also professionally, required to interact with each other horizontally or diagonally within the administrative structure. Such contacts and relationships are more pronounced in development administration and more seriously in the agricultural production system. This is a basis for healthy cooperation and coordination at present.

Cross-communication, in multi-dimensional subjects like agriculture and its multi-agency involvements becomes the more important. Such communication takes place more at the lower echelons and should be encouraged and utilised by the management. For adequate cross-communication, an effective use of meetings, conferences, newsletters, special bulletins, etc. can be made use of.

In some of the organisations in the USA, the supervisors can dial a specific number to get the latest recorded information. Is it not exciting?

The concept of layering (Newman 1962): delay due to strict and rigid communication networks, and Fayol's bridge (Fayol 1949), by-passing immediate superiors or other higher-ups for first hand and rapid information, are worth nothing. Nevertheless, such communication must be permissible and the bosses must be kept informed about the communication and the outcome.

(b) Downward communication

The flow of information from top to bottom in the organisation is a common feature. The higher-ups would like to send messages in the form of orders, directions or general educational news either written or oral to different levels of the organisation. Timeliness, quality and adequacy (or over-communication) of communication are three important ingredients which must be kept in mind while communicating down below the lines. People can get fed up with too many reports, circulars, instructions, etc., and thus can find less time for work. Besides, it has negative repercussions. Management, therefore, must be judicious and well informed. Employees must not be starved of information nor should they be overfed with it. Proceedings and resolutions must result in improving actions.

It is important to realise that normally there are several links or levels through which the messages have to travel and more of these levels relate to the management group. There are at least four to five levels in the administration before the informrtion can reach the actual users at the operational level. The chances of loss or distortion of information are great and hence communication cannot be taken for granted by the superordinates. In one study (Clark and Abraham; 1960) in the USA, 67 per cent of the verbal communication from the Board Directors was understood by the Vice-Presidents, 56 per cent by the plant managers, and 30 per cent by the foremen. By and large, only about 20 per cent goes to the real workers.

The superordinates and subordinates must have a common frame of reference in order to communicate better. But this is a vulnerable area; most of the higher-ups take it for granted that they know the problems and levels of understanding of the lower personnel. The administrative and managerial staff must deliberately prepare themselves to be effective and efficient communicators.

(c) Upward communication

Two-way communication is an imperative in all types of interaction; the downward communication will be poor, incomplete and ineffective in the absence of proper and timely upward communication for many of the top-down communications are based on upward communications. In the context of the democratic decentralisation concept in action in our rural reconstruction efforts, upward communication occupies a still greater significance. But, unfortunately, upward communication has always been found wanting either due to the weakness of the lower staff, non-availability of facility or the discouragement of the higher-ups.

The process of upward communication is like going up a hill. It is much slower and more difficult than coming down. The upward communication is greately handicapped for several obvious reasons: (a) the higher staff and lower workers function in a cross-cultural situation—the latter suffer from inadequate knowledge, poor language and communication skill, low socio-economic status and prestige, less freedom of expression, no expert advice or guidance, and inadequate communication facility; (b) the superiors wrongly assume that they understand the lower staff—their problems, needs, grievances, etc.; (c) upward communication is slow, delayed, filtered and diluted; and (d) the lower staff due to so many limitations communicate in consistence with the linkings and attitudes of the higher officials. If this principle is not adhered to filtering is much more—the supervisor would not like to forward what he thinks can reflect on him.

The preceding discussion makes it clear that the management of the organisation must have a stronger design to encourage upward communication than the plan for the downward communication. To enhance the upward communication, the administrators, managerial staff and supervisors should encourage counselling services, grievance systems, consultative decisions, opinion surveys, suggestion systems, informal get-to-gethers, formal and informal meetings and so on. Above all, all these devices will work when the superiors have an open door policy—open to facts, criticism and suggestions.

Thayer (1961) classifies administrative communication on the basis of the functions which it serves:

(1) Informative communication—informing someone;

(2) Instructive communication—instructing or directing someone;

(3) Evaluative communication—evaluating someone or something; and

(4) Persuasive communication—influencing the followers, or the workers of the organisation.

A FEW BASIC TIPS

Developing communication skills on the part of administrators, managers, and in fact, all incumbents is a prelude to a good relationship and performance; one cannot do much in want of this in one's career. Some of the basic truths of communication between or among individuals within an organisation or without, are:

(1) *People attach meaning according to their taste and liking, necessarily the communicated messages*

This needs hardly any elaboration. The old adage in Hindi, "Sawad Zihwa (tongue) Me Nahi Hai, Man Me Hota Hai" is so common and well known. Unless the individual is rational and fair, he will not relish even bitter truths, for they don't suit him. A man with integrity, sincerity and devotion, with strong will and desire, can overcome this personality lacuna.

(2) *For effective communication the common frame of reference between the communicator and the receiver is a sine qua non*

This is another well-established truth. This, in fact, is the core of the education system and has been utilised since time immemorial in teaching—learning contexts. In order to communicate with students, the teachers must bring themselves down to the level of knowledge, understanding and comprehension of the students. This is all the more important when one is involved in an adult teaching—learning complex such as in extension education. In order to do a better job of communication with the farmers, one has to be at the grassroot level. From the village level onwards, in all hierarchies in organisation, there naturally exists a gap between the two categaries of personnel (communicator and receiver) in terms of their knowledge, background and understanding, and this must be duly recognised in day-to-day communication relationships.

(3) *A better communicator is one who has respect for the facts and is willing to share them with people who can make good use of those facts*

A successful communicator must have ideas and facts to extend or talk about, otherwise it will be communication without content; it will be empty talk—a waste of time. However, there are also people who have the facts but cannot part with them. Both are indeed miserable. A blending of the two is essential for better utilisation of innovations and ideas for the good of the people and the society at large.

(4) *A well established communication network is not a guarantee of effective communication*

Organisations generally are satisfied with the structural arrangements for giving or receiving information. But such a communication network is nothing better than a building blue print; in fact, it is the cement, bricks, etc., the skilled hands of the workers which will ultimately make the building. So, merely holding frequent conferences and meetings, or sending out so many circulars and reports cannot help the people—their knowledge, attitude and willingness alone can make the communication fail or succeed.

(5) *Informal communication can be a great source for maintaining the health of the administration*

It is a negative approach for administrators to question why someone talked with someone else the way he did. In fact, such information can be utilised by the authorities to examine the background for it and to take the necessary measures to improve relations, and to educate the incumbents or become educated by them. For the coherent and coordinated working of the departments, the higher-ups should look forward to informal communications through recreational get-togethers, picnics, social calls, tea clubs, coffee counters, etc. Much information which can be gathered through informal sources cannot be made available through the formal one.

(6) *A good communicator is a listener too*

Culturally, we are a talkative people; we would like to talk and talk without letting people share their ideas and views or the time to clarify their confusions. As a matter of fact, in order to do justice to the communication cycle, one must develop a habit of listening to others as much as one would like to communicate to them. Listening is a great art and one must have patience for it.

SOME RECENT STUDIES

Sharma (1969) identified ten important components of the working environment and ranked them in the order of their importance as per the responses of the judges. The components of the working environment in order of their relative importance were: communication, decision-making, local leadership, interpersonal relations, team-work, people's participation, family adjustment, supply and service, guidance and supervision and job satisfaction.

The finding showed that VLWs and AHEOs were only somewhat satisfied about the most important component of the working environment—the communication. The VLWs were not well-informed about the extension programmes and they got limited satisfaction from the freedom to exchange their ideas in the organisation, the instructions given to them, the feedback process and use of communication channels. However, they showed satisfaction on one-sub-component—the language of communication. The AEOs and PPS (Plant Protection Supervisors) were found to be sound on the Block Communication System.

Some of the major findings of Haque (1970) in a study on distortion were: The

AHEO = Animal Husbandry Extension Officer.

three messages (use of 2-4-D for weeds control in wheat, foliar spray of urea, and stem borer control in Maize) on agricultural practices were distorted both in terms of knowledge as well as understanding. There was more distortion of the message in understanding. There was more distortion of the message in the IADP districts which did not have a liaison with an Agricultural University or Agricultural Research Institute.

The extent of distortion was more in the 'very new' practice than in 'new' and 'Old' practice, in both the sets of IADP districts. Even in the 'old' and 'simple' practice like 'Use of 2-4-D to control weeds in wheat crops, the distortion occurred to the extent of 24 per cent in the Set I, IADP districts and 34.76 per cent in the Set II, IADP districts.

There was significant difference between the extent of distortion of any two of the messages in all the IADP districts. This significant difference was attributed to the differences in the characteristics of the practices like the 'old' and 'new' and 'simple' and 'complex'. There was significant difference between the district, block and village level workers in terms of the extent of distortion in the three messages. The extent of distortion increased along with an increase in the number of ladders in the hierarchy of the organisation. There was less distortion at the district level, more at the block level and very high at the village level.

Yadava (1971) studied communication patterns and upward communication in CD Block Administration. Some of the salient findings are reported here.

The work related to communication among Block Officials of IADP, IAAP, and the normal CD were more often vertical than horizontal. The upward communication of VLWs with respect to information, instruction and persuasion was relatively fair, but in the case of evaluation the result was extremely poor. Regarding horizontal communication of the VLWs the result was poor in all the four types of communication. The type of communication (up, down and across) of the ADO (Ag) (Agricultural Development Officer) varied from good to poor; and of the BDO both upward and dwnward were extremely poor to zero. The examination of the extent of the formality of communication between VLW to ADO (Ag)/ADO, ADO (Ag) to BDO, and BDO to his superiors with respect to upward communication indicated that the formality of communication in comparison to informality of communication was in the ratio of about 40 to 60. A similar result was recorded with reference to downward communication from BDO to ADO (Ag.)/VLW and ADO (Ag) to VLW.

An analysis of the accuracy of upward communication revealed that the communication in the normal CD Block between VLW—ADO (Ag.) VLW-BDO, and ADO (Ag.)-BDO was relatively better than the IAAP and IADP Blocks. In other words, the accuracy of upward communication was in this order; first normal CD Blocks, second IAAP Blocks; and third, IADP Blocks.

Mathur (1972) in his study in the Delhi Union Territory reported that the official pattern of downward flow of instruction had not been clearly defined in any of the five blocks of Delhi territory. There was overlapping of responsibilities, vis-a-vis issuing instructions to the subordinates at Block and Village Levels. The VLWs received instructions about laying out of demonstrations from the two superiors at a time. Only 32.85 per cent of the VLWs in all the five Blocks preferred to have instructions from their BDOs whereas 67.15 per cent preferred that their AEOs should instruct. About 36.35

per cent of the AEOs in all the five blocks received instructions from the headquarters staff at Delhi and not from the BDOs. In upward communication, short-circuits in communication had been noticed. According to the responses of the AEOs and VLWs, short circuits with reference to technical problems existed to the tune of 34.01 per cent. The AEOs consulted the outside agencies without the knowledge of the BDOs. The BDOs and the AEOs competed to extend solutions of technical problems to the VLWs who themselves were equally divided in showing their preferences on this point. There were short-circuits in communication at the lower level of the block hierarchy as far as solution seeking for the administrative prolems were concerned.

The BDOs totally depended on issuing verbal instructions to their subordinates at meetings. While the AEOs preferred to receive instructions in writing, the VLWs preferred meetings for this purpose. The AEOs who received written instruction from their BDOs passed them on to their VLWs. Written communication was comparatively used more in the case of administrative problem solving than technical problem solving. The AEOs more frequently used individual contacts with the VLWs for solving their problems as compared to the BDOs. Although the AEOs preferred to receive written instructions from their BDOs they wanted to reduce this tendency in administrative problem solving.

Effective communication has been recognised as an important means for mean.ngful coordination. Pelz (1966), however, found out in his study that when district officials were communicating among themselves, they used writing nearly half the times and personal contacts only one-fifth of the time. They, however, used writing and formal meetings twice as often as they thought desirable for communication with each other and they used formal meetings and personal talks only half as much as they preferred to. Not surprisingly, therefore, often a lot of time is wasted in the name of coordination without bringing effective results towards that end.

Conclusion

Administration as a field of specialisation has been relatively neglected and mis-understood. In the technical field like agriculture, its inefficiency has been all the more felt. The Agricultural Administrative Committee (1963—Nalagarh Committee) pointed out that, "Administrative lapses have universally contributed towards shortfalls in implementation of Agricultural Schemes and thereby directly caused shortfalls in production." Organisational communication in agriculture is an important dimension in agricultural administration which requires our attention.

For better understanding, together with several facets of agricultural administration, studies should be made on organisational communication coherently, starting from State to the Village levels. Communication stands for the life of the organisation. How can it be ignored?

CHAPTER 28

COMMUNICATION PLANNERS: ROLE AND TRAINING

An Asian Regional Seminar on the Training of Communication Planners was convened by UNESCO. It met from 16th to 21st December 1974 at the National Broadcasting Training Centre in Kuala Lumpur.

The seminar was held to examine the need for and develop recommendations or guidelines for the training of communication planners. It was UNESCO's first international seminar on the subject and was intended to lead into further work in the area.

The seminar followed a logical path by clarifying the scope and meaning of communication and communication planning, before proceeding to spell out the role, (including his place in the organisation or system of government) of the communication planner. The scope of this report, reflecting the work of the meeting itself, described the role as well as the training of communication planners.

Meaning and scope of communication and communication planning

The term communication is used in a number of different ways. At one extreme, a narrow use is limited to the media of information; at the other, a very wide meaning embraces any means whereby a message passes from one person to another, including face-to-face and even non-verbal communication. The scope of the term was to include anything which might be considered part of national communications, as a resource of the community. This would clearly include radio and television facilities, the press and books, film and cinema and such innovations as video-cassette, CATV and satellite communication. Postal, telephone and telegraph services, if not included as such, could not be omitted entirely especially from long-term planning considerations, where a telecommunication and a broadcasting department might need to agree on the shared use of facilities.

Organised face-to-face communication, such as is involved in rural extension and community development work, was included in the definition. Considerable interest within the region was acknowledged in traditional forms of communication such as puppetry and in the relationship between these and modern means of communication provided by the mass media. Rather than these two being in conflict, possibilities may be explored whereby traditional forms can be preserved and extended through mass media or the film. Since social and cultural diversity are political facts and their encouragement a national objective in many places, the seminar was to include this approach to traditional means of communication within its scope.

Another problem is the tendency while acknowledging that newspapers and periodicals, films and books, are part of the fields of communication, to exclude them from consideration for planning purposes, as they may often lie beyond the reach of government investment and direct control. Radio and television may be under a Ministry or Department of Information or Broadcasting ; film and book production and distribution, if not entirely in the private sector, at least, may answer to a different department.

The tendency to equate communication planning with existing areas of government departmental control, even in situations where political change is rapid and administrative rearrangements frequent and sometimes far-reaching, contributes to a sometimes exaggerated distinction between hardware and software, with concentration on one of these to the virtual exclusion of the other. A distinction is made between the infrastructure which may then be put aside as the responsibility of another department such as Works or Telecommunications, and the subject-matter for broadcasting. Inasmuch as the latter rests with different user departments such as National or Rural Development, Agriculture, Health or Education, this also tends to get omitted from considerations of communication planning. Planning may thus be restricted to radio and television broadcasting, perhaps mainly to programming within limits set by departments providing and owning the infrastructure, and without systematic consultation with the major user departments as to long-term needs. These kinds of communication cannot be omitted simply because they lie outside government control in all or some countries in the region, if comprehensive decisions are to be made as between the various communication media, and scarce resources allocated to those most effective for attaining national objectives underlying communication planning.

Sources of confusion and resistance

Communication planning is not yet a familiar or even a very meaningful idea. In some places, while it is coming to gain acceptance, it is still a novelty. There are several sources of confusion and resistance. To some cultures the very idea of complex integrative, forward planning is an alien, western management technique which sit uneasily on a civilisation with other values and orientations. Even when the principl of systematic planning wins approval, some feel the process to be too much out o harmony with the present style of Government which may depend much more or personal and informal procedures and relationships rather than formal interdepart mental planning, coordination and decision-making.

A second source of resistance was identified as a belief that planning a communica tion system at the national level is either too complicated or politically impracticable Systems approaches to planning might be thought helpful at the programme or projec level within an area of communication, such as expanding radio broadcasting, but th inputs, variables and especially the external, environmental uncertainties become so complex at more general levels that a systems approach may be thought useless. Thi would imply that national level communication planning, if not left to chance and th product of competing pressures and interests, was at least an art rather than a science t be approached systematically and theoretically.

Elements in the planning process

Elements in the planning process were identified as: collection and analysis of basic data about the country; an inventory of present communication resources; analysis of present communication policies; analysis of communication needs; analysis of communication components in National Development Plans and Programmes; analysis of constraints on communication developments; definition of aims of future communication policies; with design of alternative strategies; making choices between strategies in terms of other perceived economic, social, cultural and educational relevance; the phasing of overall communication development.

Another analysis identified the following elements: objectives; environmental factors beyond the scope of planning ; resources available, and comparison of alternative strategies ; evaluation of their probable outcomes, criteria for selection; a dynamic management system for implementation.

Future role of the communication planner

The future role of the communication planner is to prepare the communicator for integrated global planning, taking account of the various media and media mixes required consideration as to whether or not this included increasing complexity of the technology itself. The seminar placed emphasis on the need for any important technology to adapt to the country's needs and situations rather than allowing technology to displace society's needs which must be accorded primacy in the approach of the planner to his task.

The necessity for controlled experimentation did receive attention as part of the essential process of developing continuous assessment, or evaluation of the results of communication planning as it is implemented.

Communication in support of development

This leads to the consideration of the criteria by which its scope might be determined: rather than the media themselves, the criterion selected might be the messages transmitted or the uses to which communication is put; thus communication for development purposes would be distinguished from communication for the sake of entertainment, or commercial advertising or news dissemination. Entertainment-oriented communication also has a powerful social influence and possible effect on the attempt to meet national objectives.

Extension or organised face-to-face communication

Extension or organised face-to-face communication is kept within the scope of planning. Extension provided a form of communication which might be more effective than mass media which was already widely practised but in which duplication and waste might be common, both as between different extension workers and as between extension workers and certain mass forms of communication. Some elements, notably the human receivers, clearly lay beyond the reach of planning control, and others, notably the subject-matter to be transmitted, were easier to control in some countries than others. Thus there remained differences as to the effective scope of planning. An argument for treating communication planning firmly within the framwork of development planning was advanced for a realistic appreciation of the national and regional problems and the differences within developing countries.

It was agreed that communication planning should be taken to embrace the following: (a) infrastructure (economic, technological, organisational/administrative); (b) information processing and transfer systems; (c) media and channels; (d) personnel or human resources: (1) communicators; (2) recipients; (e) supporting communication services : organised interpersonal communication and extension services; (f) contents; (g) purposes or objectives (recognising that they may vary, but that national development goals are usually central). It was recognised that the central focus was on mass communication, and that a multi-media approach with inter-media comparisons, was necessary. It was important to recognise realistically what could not be planned and to acknowledge the different levels of planning, also that planning is forward-looking as well as derivative and day-to-day.

Technological options and problems of planning for future change

One of the most important and difficult tasks confronting any planner working in a modern, complex and rapidly changing society, and particularly in an area such as communication where technological innovations are rapid and may have far reaching implications, is to obtain some appreciation of the variety of changes which are likely to occur and the alternative futures which may thus be opened up.

It is not very difficult to project the present into the future in a linear way and so predict more of whatever now occurs, or is developing. It is more difficult, but very necessary, to be able to conceive the various possible as well as probable futures which might open up, to make judgements about and choices between them and to plan with a view to moving towards whatever is held to be most desirable.

Among the themes central to this presentation, the following may be highlighted:

(1) The need to understand and predict society's communication needs and to exploit both technology and other current resources to meet them.

(2) The emergence of a powerful knowledge of industry and the significance of the linking, for example, of communication facilities to a powerful computer base, thus allowing the emergence, as a "spin-off" of many services for which the communication facilities are merely the channel, not the source; and

(3) The role of the telecommunication engineer and planner which is to explain and display possible technological resources and alternatives so that others responsible for identifying needs and selecting as to priority between them can make appropriate choices.

To predict what society will be doing in the future, the telecommunication planner has to consider the likely activities of people (employment, education, entertainment, social, personal, group, community); the size, shape and location of cities and buildings; the changes which might occur in public and private transportation. All these have an impact on society's communication needs. Hence the development of a long-term plan is a very complex mix of many factors of which engineering is but one. Future planning must consider at least the following: diversity of possible service: market research on non-developed concepts, a large number of network alternatives; social and economic interactions, and long-term planning horizons.

The primacy of needs over technology push is always asserted. Countries should resist being seduced into technological innovation for reasons of fashion and prestige and

without anticipating fully the possible consequences, for instance, of introducing channels of communication (whatever their technological form) before there was adequate
and suitable material for transmission. Examples were given from within the region
both of costly psychological and bureaucratic resistance to timely innovations and of
innovations held to be premature because the software to use the technology was not
available or inappropriate because they represented a diversion from more pressing
areas of need.

ROLE AND TASK OF THE COMMUNICATION PLANNER

In examining the role of the communication planner, it is important to keep in mind
the distinction between the present situation in which communication planning is
practised variably and often scarcely recognised as a necessity, and a more desirable
future state to which countries in the region might move as the planner comes to be recognised and his training prepares him for his work. Planning tends at present to be rather
at the sectoral or departmental level, to project from present situations and needs within
sectors rather than looking across the board at different communication needs and
possibilities and the relations between them. Similarly, there appeared to be little
attempt to argue a case for expansion of communication resources compared with
other aspects of national development. The need for more integrated planning
because of the cost of investment in infrastructure and also inadequate consultation with
others who might wish to use the same facility resulting in inadequate capacity cannot
be overemphasised.

Within the diversity and the lack of regular integrative planning, there emerged
from each country's presentation a clear trend towards providing one or another form
of machinery for consultation, coordination or control in the communication field.

Administrative segregation, and sometimes bureaucratic competition and duplication,
was still the commoner situation and it was stressed that far closer coordination and
shared planning was required with such important user departments as agriculture,
health and especially education. Nowhere, it seemed, was there yet planning for communication as a function and resource of the society, irrespective of which departments
of government were responsible for various hardware or software elements. Even when
national development was agreed to be the overriding purpose for developing communication resources, there could be differences of emphasis: thus communications
might be entirely at the service of government to publicise plans and foster morale; or
there might be more emphasis on such significant supplementary or ancillary objectives as reducing the gap between the rich and poor, the urban and the rural, the
educated and the uneducated. Some of these objectives might have more immediate
significance for communication planning than for some other departments of State;
introducing colour television in response to urban middle class aspirations might be at
the expense of extending an existing communication facility more widely and effectively to the rural population. Even among communication professionals from develop-
ment-conscious countries took part in the seminar, there is some doubt whether
communication is to be developed as a multi-directional community resource or whether the emphasis is to be on a strictly disciplined development of a tool to serve the
communication requirements of the national plan.

Research and evaluation, the essential prerequisites for planning, are generally little recognised and practised although here again there seems to be a significant shift in several countries towards greater allocation of effort and resources to evaluation. The lack of hard research-based information was the most serious shortcoming at present, even more serious than the shortage of money in many countries. Linked to it is the extreme scarcity of qualified personnel competent enough to understand and work in the local situation. The other major constraints relate to the lack of recognition of the role and task of the Planner in this field, and also the anxiety stemming from the highly political, and thus vulnerable character, of the communication sector.

The seminar settled on the following general definition:

Communication planners are persons, or groups of persons, at various levels of responsibility, who, having gathered information about past and current communication needs, activities and resources, and future possibilities, process and integrate them. They then formulate viable alternative plans or programmes to meet anticipated communication needs and promote constructive activities for the total well-being of communities and individuals.

Objectives

Policies and plans should include consideration of, at least, the following areas of possible conflict: (a) the rights of individuals to communicate and to privacy; (b) equality of access between urban and rural areas; (c) openness versus becoming tools of politics, commerce, thus imposing or reflecting values; (d) antipathy through over-communicating; (e) horizontal dialogue versus vertical; and (f) the right to ask questions and receive answers.

Approach to objectives

Policies and plans should include consideration of at least; (a) evaluation of personal and institutional communication needs; (b) human, physical and financial resources; (c) priorities, when resources do not meet needs; (d) maximum utilisation of existing and proposed resources, maximum effectiveness of the media; and (e) economic and social cost-benefit and fullest exploitation of available technology.

A job analysis of the communication planner, produced the following summary (which concentrates on a preferred future role, rather than the specific constraints and applications in different countries today):

(1) The communication planner is at the centre of the communication process; the basic philosophy is that he must serve two masters, government and society.

(2) Because of this position, it is essential that the planner has an understanding of: (i) the broad philosophical notions as to where his society is moving; (ii) a global outlook on the interdependence of various systems; (iii) good understanding of the structure of society, its needs, values, attitudes; and (iv) on a time dimension, knowledge of the past, skills to operate in the present, and a vision for the future.

(3) In a broad sense, therefore, the planners task is to translate society's needs in such a way that administrators can use them, and to translate government policy into plans for social action.

Qualities of a communication planner

(a) Philosophical understanding of development in the country and globally; (b) Theoretical knowledge in such areas as Communication Theory, Social Psychology, etc.; (c) Skills in data-gathering and analysis relating to the present and for future forecasting ; and (d) Ability to understand the past, appreciate the present and plan with vision for the future.

The desirable qualities for communication planners are: (i) political consciousness; practical appreciation of political processes and possibilities; (ii) knowledge of institutional settings (the environment within which his work takes effect); and (iii) On anti-bureaucratic instinct and a sense of social responsibility.

Functions

The functions of the communication planner implying various specific skills include the following: (a) To prepare alternative policies and plans to meet society's future communication needs. This involves exploring the needs of various government departments and of other sectors of society; (b) To identify constraints and obstacles to implementing plans; (c) To prepare contingency plans; (d) To set objectives including promotion both of national goals and values and of appropriate technological innovations; (e) To develop a comprehensive inventory of human and technological resources, and to plan for the fullest possible use of these existing resources; (f) In planning, to keep in sight the components of funds, means (especially technology) and manpower, including both requirements and training strategies; (g) To undertake analyses of the channels of communication and of the audience; (h) To study network design and to study message design; (i) To undertake cost-benefit analyses of programmes prepared to meet policy objectives; and, (j) To ensure that a feedback process is built into the programme for feedback and evaluation which are seen as essential components of planning.

Levels of planning

Five levels were distinguished for which it was possible to discuss communication planning namely : the Planning Commission Level ; the Ministry Level (including e.g. Education, Agriculture, as well as Information) ; the Departmental or Sectional Level (e.g. National Planning of particular media) ; the Regional or Provincial Level ; and the Local Level. The need for rationalisation and coordination at all these levels cannot be over emphasised.

It is felt that communication planning needed to be grounded in the different ministries concerned so as to keep touch with needs and realities. However, since it is and will long remain a very scarce resource, it should not be looked into different ministries, but somehow provided a degree of freedom to permit a cross-functional perspective. Possible machinery suggested or already being employed, included National Communication Policy Councils, a Cabinet Committee on Communication and Information, or a Federal Office of Communication and Information. One important question was the extent to which such a body should be official ; it might be drawn exclusively from relevant ministries and departments or it could include representatives of the community, consumers and the private sector. There was a clear need for communication planners to keep touch with the 'grass roots', but it was less clear whether this should be through a standing committee, be it advisory or charged with planning itself.

The model that found most favour assumed that there was a National Planning Commission (under one name or another) and a number of ministries with an interest in National Development and Communication Resources apart from a Ministry of Information for which this was the sole or main area of responsibility. There should be a sectoral (or sub-sectoral) committee, as a permanent sub-committee of the Planning Commission. Its members would not be full-time but would function as an advisory group, meeting from time to time. They would be serviced by the Secretariat of the Planning Commission which would also have a permanent secretariat-type Communication Planning Cell. The Planning Commission was preferred to a Ministry of Information Location, to secure a wider interdepartmental perspective. Interdepartmental coordination and planning might occur both at the ministerial level (through the sub-committee of the National Planning Commission, or a committee of cabinet ministers, if national traditions lend themselves better to this), and at the level of senior administrators and planners.

TRAINING STRATEGIES AND OPTIONS

Different advantages were quoted for training located in different places:

National training, which may take many forms such as *ad hoc* courses organised by national staff or foreign experts, or courses built into the continuing in-service schemes, or courses which are part of the established educational structure of technical colleges, training colleges, universities, etc., was compared with regional training, i.e., training, especially at the middle and upper levels to meet the needs of a number of countries in a given region. Regional training has the advantages of financial saving, through centralisation of resources; justification for a better and larger staff; a stronger appeal to international aid sources ; and the opportunity to develop regional exchange of experience and materials. The third alternative is foreign training, i.e., training in countries outside the region especially for high level staff. This has a particular function in the development of international standards, the interchange of ideas, and the furthering of a professional concept.

It was noted that foreign training tends to mean training in the technologically more advanced countries; it could however also mean training in some other developing country setting, such as Africa or Latin America.

The seminar considered different subjects that contribute to Communication Planning. Some countries already teach communication studies, while others do not, so that practitioners moving into planning roles may or may not have had any formal academic training in communication. They may on the other hand have had initial or post-experience training in a relevant discipline such as public administration, economics or management. Post-experience training might be by means of a higher degree or diploma or in the form of short courses at a staff college or study tours as part of a Public Service Staff Development Programme.

Training might comprise a mixture of formal theoretical units, supervised work and study on the job, exposure to visiting experts, and study tours including elements of formal instruction within the region or beyond.

The existing training resources and potential in the region as it relates to the future training of communication planners, must be examined carefully. Should these be supplemented and linked one with another so that within the region a number of centres would be developed with modest additional resources which would together meet most of the region's needs for professional preparation and stimulation of communication planners. Such an approach would have to identify the main areas of need as well as the potential growth points and evolve a programme for strengthening selected institutions.

Education and communication need to be coordinated, even integrated more closely than has now occurred, for some elements still refer specifically to educational institutions. The relationship with non-formal education is particularly important.

Introductory units designed to give a brief synthesised overview of the whole field, might be as follows: (a) Philosophy and methodology of planning, generally; (b) Economic needs and communication planning; (c) Socio-cultural needs and communication planning; (d) Psychology related to communication planning; (e) Communication and education structures and communication planning; (f) Education and communication; (g) Politics and communication planning; (h) Regional and local character of communication planning; and (i) Evaluation and communication planning.

The emphasis throughout should be on the application of various disciplines to problems in this field not on their study as an end in itself.

The second phase adopts the ILEP principle of a global planning exercise but includes also a pilot project.

The third part of the course would offer the following complementary units; (a) Economics of communication and need for communication; (b) Organisation, structure and methods of communication; (c) Regional and local problems; and (d) Political structure, administrative organisation and communication planning.

Fourthly, the following more specialised units were suggested; (a) Cost analysis methods; (b) Planning of non-formal education and face-to-face communication; (c) Programming and budgeting techniques; (d) Manpower planning (recruitment and training) for communication; (e) Training of communicators; (f) Team approaches to communication planning; (g) Techniques of evaluating communication programmes; (h) implementation of reforms and innovations (e.g., technological, programming); (i) Management techniques; (j) Data processing and information systems; (k) Technology of communication, and (l) Forecasting techniques.

There would be a preference for in-service sandwich formats over straight-through, full-time study.

The following outline is put forward, recognising that other modules would be added to match other specific needs:

Planning: Economic aspects of communication; management aspects of communication, research design and quantitative methods, methods of forecasting, perspectives on national development communication and planning; systems analysis and planning methods including an introduction to: statistics, computer science, operational management techniques such as PERT, programming, budgeting, critical path analysis.

Communication: Communication theory (mathematics, mass communication, interpersonal); Audience and need analysis: channel analysis and network design, technological innovation in communication; futurology of communication.

Other supporting disciplines: Psychology of communication, sociology of communication; political and legal aspects of communication, organisation, administration and management.

It should be emphasised that each of these modules is to be understood in a practical and applied sense and studied in a regional and national context as well as to provide a theoretical grounding.

CHAPTER 29

PROBLEMS IN COMMUNICATION

Communication is a process. Process is the act of proceeding a series of actions or operations definitely conducting to a desired end. Each episode of communication has at least three phases:

(1) Expression
(2) Interpretation
(3) Response.

These are the crucial points in communication. If the expression is not clear, the interpretation will be inaccurate and the response improper, thus one's effort to communicate will not succeed. In other words if the source does not have adequate or clear information if the message is not encoded fully, accurately, effectively in transmittable signs; if these are not transmitted fast enough and accurately enough, despite interference and competition, to the desired receiver; if the message is not decoded in a pattern that corresponds to the encoding; and finally if the destination is unable to handle the decoded message so as to produce the desired response, then, obviously, the system is working at less than top efficiency.

Main problems in communication

These are:

(1) The problems that the individual has in fulfilling his own goals and adoptive needs—logically they have their origin in the adequacy and the appropriateness of his own strategies or technical communication competence.

(2) At the inter-personal level, communication problems may be sourced in the relative inadequacy or inappropriateness of the communication competence of any, or all, of the participants. That is, any given problem may be attributable to one or the other, or to both persons engaged in a two-person communication encounter.

(3) An originator or a receiver, may fail to achieve his communicative goals or intentions for reasons other than the skill and comprehensibility involved. There are situations in which intercommunication is satisfactorily achieved but the consequences anticipated by the receiver for doing, thinking, or feeling as intended by the originator are so negative as to preclude the fulfilment of the originator's intentions.

(4) A communication system which links two or more people together may be more efficacious, more or less, economical, or both. Often the source of this order of com-

munication problem is in the inappropriate designation of criteria by which the system's progress is to be assessed.

(5) Yet another higher-communication problem of some complexity is the organisational level of analysis. It is at this level of analysis that we should contemplate problems which have their source in the relative incompatibilities of communication systems at their interfaces. Those incompatibilities may emerge at the interfaces of different levels of systems.

These problems of communication process can be classified by various methods. Some of these methods are:

According to phases of communication
Every communication process has at least three phases.

(A) *Relating to the communicator*
(1) *Ineffective environment:* The environment created by the communicator (Extension Worker) influences his effectiveness. The physical facilities, air of friendliness, respect for others' point of view, recognition of accomplishments of others, permissiveness and rapport in general, are all important ingredients of a climate which is conducive to effective communication.

(2) *Disorganised efforts to communicate:* To make sense, the communication effort must be organised according to some specific form or pattern.

(3) *Standard of correctness:* This involves the use of correct words or other symbols correct logic and correct content or facts.

(4) *Standard of social responsibilities:* This infers that when one communicates, one assumes responsibility for the effect of one's communication on the respondents and the society.

(5) *Cultural values and social organisation:* Cultural values and social organisation are determinants of communication. For effective communication, the communicator must possess knowledge of the cultural values of his listeners.

(6) *Inaccurate symbols:* The system of symbols used to represent ideas, objects, or concepts must be accurate and used skilfully. The crucial points in the use of symbols to convey ideas is to select those that accurately represent the idea to be conveyed and are understood by the audience. Symbols are meaningful to a person only when he understands what they stand for.

(7) *Wrong concept of the communication process:* A common mistake committed by the communicator is the identification of the part with the whole or the parts fallacy. Successful communication programmes of rural development is not a single unit. It requires a series of unit acts. The way one thinks about communication will influence its quality.

(B) *Relating to transmission of message*
Many obstructions can enter at the interpretation level. These are often referred to as, 'noise', that is, some obstruction that prevents the message from being heard by or carried over clearly to, the audience. 'Noise' emerges from a wide range of sources and causes which effect the interpretation of the message.

(1) *Wrong handling of the channel:* If a meeting, tour, radio programme, or one of

the other channels, is not used according to the correct procedure and techniques, its potential for carrying a message is dissipated.

(2) *Wrong selection of channels:* All channels are not equally useful in attaining a specific objective. Failure to select channels appropriate to the objectives of a communicator will interrupt the interpretation of the message, in the manner in which it is desired, by the intended audience.

(3) *Physical distraction*: Failure to avoid physical distraction often obstructs successful message-sending.

(4) *Use of inadequate channels in parallel:* The more channels a communicator uses in parallel, or at about the same time, the more chances he has of the message getting through and being properly received.

(C) *Relating to the receiver*

(1) *Attention of the listeners:* There is an unfortunate tendency not to give undivided attention to the communicator. This is a powerful obstruction that prevents the message from reaching its desired destination.

(2) *Problem of cooperation, participation and involvement:* Both the communicator and the receiver must be brought into the act. Hence, the listener must work a little hard. Learning is an active process on the part of the listener and unless the respondent is on the same wave length, the character of what is sent out hardly governs the communication process. Thus it takes two to make communication.

(3) *Problem of Homogeneity:* The more homogeneous an audience, the greater the chances of successful communication. Likewise, the more a communicator knows about his audience and can pin-point its characteristics the more likely he is to make an impact.

(4) *Attitude of the audience towards the communicator:* An important factor in the effectiveness of communication is the attitude of the audience towards the communicator. It is a function of the communicator to make their attitude favourable. Indirect data on this problem come from studies of 'prestige' in which subjects are asked to indicate their agreement or disagreement with statements which are attributed to different individuals.

According to various types of problems

These are (1) Technical problems; (2) Semantic problems; and (3) Influential problems.

(1) *Technical problems:* These are problems concerned with the accuracy of the transference of information from sender to receiver. Certain things that are not intended by the information source are added to the signal. These unwanted additions may be distortions in the shape or shading of a picture or errors in transmission. All these changes in the signal are called 'noise.'

(2) *Semantic problems:* Problems regarding the interpretation of meaning by the receiver as compared to the intended meaning of the sender. This is a very deep and involved situation even if one is dealing only with the relatively simple problems of communication through speech.

(3) *Influential problems:* The problems of influence, or effectiveness are concerned with the success with which the meaning conveyed to the receiver leads to the desired

conduct on his part. It may seem, at first glance, undesirably narrow to imply that the purpose of all communication is to influence the conduct of the receiver.

According to nature of problems

(1) *Physical problems:* The possible disorders affecting communication fall generally into the following categories. Speech and voice defects; anxiety-tension reaction such as those involved in stage fright, or feeling of inferiority, which noticeably affect speech, paralysis, disease or characteristics of physical appearance which interfere with expressive bodily action or which tend to call forth unfavourable reactions on the part of the listeners; lack of skill in the use of background or staging techniques, together with defects, such as radio station in the means and conditions of transmission.

(2) *Psychological:* These psychological difficulties are, in part, a function of the very nature of language; in part, they are due to the emotional characteristics, and mental limitations of human beings. These general considerations concerning the psychological nature of language are the background against which more specific difficulties in communication can be understood. These specific obstacles merit special attention: (i) the failure to refer language to experience and reality, (ii) the inability to transcend personal experience in inter-group communication, (iii) stereotypes, the assimilation of material to familiar frames of reference, (iv) the confusion of precept and concept, ramification and personification.

(3) *Cultural:* Cultural differences pose serious barriers in the communication process. Within this expanding field of activity, we may distinguish three small questions: (i) the way in which communication systems are related in given cultural values, (ii) the particular ethical problems of responsibility raised by our current use of communication systems and (iii) problems of communication when cultural boundaries have to be transcended.

Other classified problems

(1) *Entropy and redundancy:* Information is defined in terms of its ability to reduce the uncertainty or disorganisation of a situation at the receiving end. Entropy simply means the uncertainty or disorganisation of a system, redundancy is the opposite. Entropy will obviously be at its maximum all states of the system are equally probable, that is, when they occur completely at random as when a coin is tossed.

(2) The idea of noise is another information theory concept which intuitively makes sense in the study of communication. Noise is anything in the channel other than what the communicator puts there.

(3) Channel capacity is heranot important concept which is common both to information theory and to massc ommunication. Error can be reduced as much as desired by keeping the rate of transmission below the total capacity of the channel. If the channel is overloaded errors increase very swiftly.

(4) One of the major problems of communication policy and techniques is to find ways of controlling the interpretation which an audience will place upon events and notions.

CHAPTER 30

INTERPERSONAL COMMUNICATION AND THE MASS MEDIA IN DEVELOPING SOCIETIES*

It is assumed that transmission of new ideas through face-to-face communication and through the mass media can prepare a climate that is propitious for the acceleration of change in the desired direction. Besides bringing about attitudinal and value changes, communication is also expected to impart knowledge of new skills and techniques.

Developmental uses of communication

The case for developmental uses of communication has been convincingly argued. First, communication helps to enlarge mental horizons. Second, it can be used to raise levels of aspiration. Third, through communication, attention can be focused on problems having a bearing on the contemporary developmental context. Fourth, it can be effectively employed to build consensus on the new economic and cultural goals and on the instrumentalities of achieving them. Fifth, through imaginative communication, experimentation can be encouraged and knowledge relating to their success and/or failure can be widely diffused. Sixth, it can also be utilised to teach specific skills and techniques. To sum up, communication can play a powerful role in nation building and development and can contribute significantly to bring about social change in the desired direction.

Integration with key sectors of development

Looking back on the experience of the last twenty-five years, we find that many of the high hopes held out by enthusiastic salesmen for communication have been belied. The results of over two decades of communication efforts have fallen far short of the expectations. It is now realised that communication by itself cannot fulfil many of its promises unless it is meaningfully integrated with simultaneous effort in other key sectors of development. It is wrong to assume that mass audiences are eagerly waiting for messages from outside on which they will begin to act enthusiastically. The credibility of the source of information and the medium itself has first to be established. Not much attention appears to have been given to this problem.

*An extract from an article by S.C. Dubey (1975) "Communicator", I.I.M.C., New Delhi.

In the Third World, as well as in the more developed countries, careful analysis of experience shows that educational uses of the mass media, especially radio and TV, succeed more in imparting nuts and bolts type of knowledge and skills, much less in altering deeply ingrained attitudes and values. Except for bringing about minor changes in relatively simple technology and winning acceptance for innovations that are a variation of the established practices, communication has generally contributed to the maintenance of the status quo. The messages sent out through the mass media largely reflect the interests of those who finance, control, and run the media.

Promotion of false sense of optimism

There are reasons to believe that in many contexts the media promote a false sense of optimism: unfulfilled hopes soon give rise to a sense of frustration that is detrimental to the larger developmental aims. One can legitimately suspect that the interests that control the media deliberately utilise them to serve their short-run objectives. This, in the long run, often proves counter-productive. Thus, we arrive at the inescapable conclusion that it is erroneous to claim for communication an independent and autonomous role in developmental change.

Communication has to be geared to wider policy processes that bring about fundamental structural alterations in the society and cause changes in the relationships of production. These are essential to realise the social and economic transformations visualised as the objectives of developmental planning. This calls for a strong political will and resolute administrative action. Communication cannot create these. At best it can only have an anticipatory, preparatory and supportive role. Much of the success of development programmes depends upon the quality and soundness of the planning techniques. The effectiveness of communication links between different agencies involved in developmental planning, especially feedback from grassroots and upwards, can impart a greater degree of realism to the plans.

Supportive role of Media

Communication can also help to diffuse knowledge in respect of the goals of development and prepare people for the roles expected of them. But its own role is essentially supportive; it does not vitally determine the quality either of planning or of implementation which need expertise of different kinds. Developmental effort that needs massive mobilisation and participation of the masses cannot be sustained by ideas and information emanating from remote sources. They can be useful, but they need other essential support, in terms of on-the-spot guidance and necessary supplies, that makes the acceptance of innovations a practical possibility. This necessitates a development-oriented bureaucracy and technocracy as well as strong local organisations.

Communication in developing societies

In the developing societies interpersonal networks of communication continue to be strong. Face-to-face communication carries a considerable volume of messages. In fact the credibility of this channel is the most well-established and the messages conveyed through the non-traditional mass media invariably require its seal of approval. Much of the information in these societies is conveyed in face-to-face interaction. Studies in

India suggest that messages originally received via the mass media get substantial diffusion through the interpersonal networks. These networks are also engaged in a continuous surveillance of the environment.

Their approval/disapproval performs an important control function. Messages carried by the mass media are subject to a critical scrutiny by the interpersonal networks. On the basis of this scrutiny a consensus is gradually built in respect of their desirability and necessity or otherwise.

Alongside of the interpersonal networks the traditional media occupy an important place though modern education and the inroads made by the mass media have diminished their power in some respects. They consist of many folk forms of dance, drama, narrations and entertainment which have hitherto performed two important functions: they have been the principal instruments for the transmission of the cultural heritage and also major providers of entertainment. Except for certain classical forms, where maintenance of purity of style has been rigidly insisted upon, there is considerable variability and flexibility in the form and content of the traditional media.

They permit scope for comment on the contemporary scene and for the transmission of new ideas. In this they often succeed remarkably because of their grasp over the mass mind and the use of an idiom that is familiar to the common people. They can be turned into powerful instruments of mass education and of diffusion of developmental ideas. The Jatra in Bengal, Nautanki and Ras in Uttar Pradesh, Burrakatha in Andhra Pradesh, and Harikatha in western India, for example, have all been put to entertainment uses. Experience suggests that when their entertainment function is not seriously impaired they can be used to reinterpret tradition and to invest new cultural emphasis into them. They can also inject developmental ideas in an understandable and acceptable form.

Mass media are class media

Speaking of the mass media in the developing societies, one can safely assert that what are described as the "Mass Media" are in effect "Class Media". Consider, for example, the role of newspapers and TV in India. Because of low rates of literacy the reach of newspapers is still very limited. Even in relatively literate and politicised States like Kerala, where a newspaper may be read by forty to fifty persons in a coffee house, and where some of the items in print may give rise to heated debates in which even non-literates join, it is difficult to regard the newspaper as a truly mass medium. TV on the other hand, has not been able to become a mass medium for a very different reason. Involving high cost technology, as it does, the country has not been able to establish a network of telecasting stations. Besides the high cost of TV sets makes them out of the purchasing power even of the middle class.

Until two decades back even the radio was a class medium—a status symbol. Thanks to the transistor revolution it is slowly moving to deserve the designation of a mass medium. However, radio is handicapped by a stereotyped image which assigns to it the two primary functions of popular entertainment and transmission of current news. To turn it into a truly instructional medium, imaginative efforts are needed. In certain fields like agricultural (and horticultural) development, and to a limited scale in the field of public health education, it has succeeded in establishing a measure of credibility but this has been most conspicuous where a local organisational base had been created and interpersonal networks were activated to diffuse the developmental messages.

The cinema is fast becoming a truly mass medium but what it offers is generally escapist entertainment. In India, the movies project a dream world in rainbow colours—a world which has little to do with contemporary social reality. The new trend is to use this medium as a forum of creative expression. One wonders when serious efforts will be made to make the cinema an instrument for purposive value change and serious instruction. Several other audio-visual aids have been experimented upon towards developmental ends. Much of this has been gimmicky. By and large, messages conveyed through them consist of a series of exhortations. Their in-depth effects have not been evaluated, but it would be safe to assume that they do not leave a lasting effect.

The total communication effort does not produce the desired pay off because its three components: face-to-face communications, traditional media, and mass media, tend to function independently without any meaningful effort for coordination and integration. The mass media get higher prestige because of their high cost and newness, interpersonal networks and the traditional media get neglected because of their low prestige rating. The mass media are handicapped by their elite bias, sophisticated style, and urban idiom. Proper interfacing between the three media systems could sharpen the power of the mass media and produce the desired results much quicker. Where the mass media have borrowed from the traditional media and have activated interpersonal networks the results have certainly been impressive.

Absence of fit

The absence of fit between face-to-face communication through the mass media creates a number of problems and limits the effectiveness of messages sought to be transmitted through the latter. Communication through the mass media rarely makes a direct impact leading to value or behavioural change, for its messages have to pass through cultural filters built into the network of interpersonal communication. The messages coming through the media are subjected to interpretation and evaluation in the channels of face-to-face communication.

Interpersonal communication explicates the meaning of media messages in the traditional cultural framework and idiom. In the process meanings can change resulting in significant goal transfers. Distortion of meaning can be avoided if the mass media communicators maintain close links with those who occupy key positions in the interpersonal network and try to enlist their support to ensure the fidelity of their messages in the process of communication.

The reach of the mass media being restricted, we find that the interpersonal networks function as an important agency to carry forward their messages. It is well established that these networks diffuse the messages much wider than the media. Thus, it is essential to utilise the conventional communication networks for the widest possible diffusion of what is sought to be communicated through the mass media.

Interpersonal network

The interpersonal networks contribute towards making the messages transmitted by the mass media, the themes of a continuing dialogue. The pros and cons of new ideas and innovations are discussed from diverse angles. This leads to consensus building either in favour or against them. It is important to note that the fate of new ways of thought or alternative techniques is often decided in the debates carried out in face-to-face interaction. The credibility of the media is also built or destroyed through such discussions.

The mass media in the developing societies, as they are organised today, only carry messages from the centre to the periphery. Feedback mechanisms are poorly organised. If the dialogue at the interpersonal networks level can be effectively tapped there would be reasonable assurance of the centre receiving adequate feedback from the grassroots level.

In behavioural change, especially where established modes of behaviour and techniques are sought to be altered, messages from a distant and impersonal medium are not enough. They have to be supplemented with on-the-spot demonstration. People are bound to have some doubts and difficulties. These have to be cleared. Those who are in two minds about the utility of the elements of change have to be convinced. This necessitates a ground-level organisation for communication equipped to take up the task from where the mass media have left off.

The best mix for successful communication, therefore, appears to be a combination of the mass media, local extension organisation with subject-matter specialisation and communication skills and key opinion leaders who can contribute significantly towards moulding the peoples' modes of thought and action. The magic of words and pictures can entertain and inform but it does not produce the preferred behavioural change. Imaginative utilisation of the interpersonal networks supported by a strong extension organisation is essential for making developmental communication effective.

CHAPTER 31

COMMUNICATION APPROACHES AND AUDIO-VISUAL AIDS

COMMUNICATION AND EXTENSION APPROACHES

Communication media and extension methods are the tools of approach as they increase the effectiveness of extension work. An extension worker, must first know "what methods are available to him", secondly, he should know, "when to use a given method, and thirdly, "he should become efficient in using each method."

Extension may be said to be extension approach or technique for reaching the people. The purpose behind the approach is to stirr the people to motivate them to act towards some specified goal. This may be to fire up their imagination for a higher standard of living through higher yields in crops, better animals, better home managements, etc. The approaches may be grouped as shown in Fig. 31.1.

Approaches in Communication and Extension

Individual approach through:	Group approach through	Mass approach through:
1. Personal visits	1. Demonstrations	1. Films and slides
☐(a) Farm units	(a) Method	(a) Farm visits
☐(b) Home visits	(b) Result	(b) Home visits
2. Personal letters	2. Training the leaders	2. Flash-cards
	3. Discussion meetings	3. Printed material
	(a) Group-discussion	4. Models and exhibits
	(b) Panel discussion	5. Radio
	(c) Symposium	6. Recorded talks
	(d) Forum	7. Charts, diagrams, etc.
	(e) Group interview	8. Circular letters
	(f) Dialogue or public	9. Newspaper stories
	conversation	10. Campaigns
	(g) Workshop	11. Television
	4. Field days	
	5. Tours	

Fig. 31. 1. Approaches in communication and extension

Individual approach

For this approach, the extension worker should know about the motivating factors involved in making the life of the individual.

This makes it necessary that the extension worker should know what is of interest to the person he wants to approach.

For this kind of approach, the extension worker is required to keep the following objectives in mind:

(a) to find out the villagers' interests,

(b) to discover to whom the villagers tend to look for leadership and for other purposes.

(c) to find out the villagers' problems and their interest in solving them,

(d) to create learning attitudes among the villagers and himself.

Advantages

(1) It provides first-hand information about village problems and activities. (2) It establishes confidence in the worker. (3) It develops goodwill. (4) It helps the extension worker in the selection of good leaders and establishing of good relations. (5) It stimulates interest. (6) It provides a high ratio of expectation and efforts.

Group approach

This is an approach to two or more people. For it, the extension worker is required to know: (1) type of group he is approaching, (2) leadership patterns, and (3) particular interest of the group.

This approach, as shown in Fig. 31.1 may be through: (1) demonstration results or methods, (2) training the leaders in the techniques of improved agricultural practices so that they may adopt it on their farms and then may help in motivating other villagers to adopt the same, (3) organising discussion meetings so that the farmers are able to discuss their problems and find solutions. In such meetings, the specialists can discuss the various methods and practices.

Mass approach

In this method, the masses are approached through films, slides, film-strips, radio talks, exhibitions, use of flash-cards, etc. It has been estimated that in some communities this method has amounted to 30 per cent of the total approach against 18 per cent in case of individual approach and 25 per cent in group approach. The visual and audio-visual aids help the extension worker to approach and contact the masses.

MOTIVATING OUR AUDIENCE

A. Individuals

Every person has four basic wishes which motivates him. We can communicate in a better way if we know our people well and also know their wishes. These wishes are: (1) security, (2) response, (3) recognition, and (4) new experience.

(1) *The wish for security:* The wish for security motivates some people to accumulate greater wealth with which to have better homes, better clothes, education for the

children and satisfaction of the biological and social needs, so that they are free from worries and wants.

(2) *The wish for response:* All people want to be liked by others, they want to be appreciated and loved, which may be called the wish for response. The desire for response differs from the desire of recognition. With response people do not particularly care whether they are richer or poorer than the next fellow, so long as they are liked and appreciated.

(3) *The wish for recognition:* A farmer who wants to be recognised as the best cultivator or Krishi-Pandit wants stauts in the society. All have this wish and this has to be used by the Extension Workers or communicators.

(4) *The wish for new experience:* Some farmers want some varieties to try for a new experience. The Triple Dwarf Wheats were tried by farmers even when they were not released by the Seed Releasing Committees. They tried them because they wanted to gain new experience.

All persons do not experience all the four motivating forces in the same way. These wishes or motivating forces are to be used in the extension programme to bring a response from the people.

B. Groups

Regardless of why or how, the farmers become group members and within that structure they have a certain status, a particular role to play, certain rights and authorities assigned to them, and they accept designated responsibilities.

(a) Blocks to participation

Logically, it may appear that each farmer or group member would actively participate in the group projects, but this is not so. Each person may have one or more "blocks" that prevent his or her participation. For good communication we as extension workers should identify and eliminate these blocks. The most important ones may be given as follows.[1]

(1) *Fear:* A member may feel that others in the group are smarter than him and that his participation may leave him open to ridicule.

(2) *Insecurity:* Perhaps others in the group may not like him. He may say the wrong thing or his clothes may look shabby.

(3) *Lack of knowledge:* Some member may lack knowledge about the objectives of the group, or may not even know that such a group exists.

(4) *Lack of time:* Somebody's name may be on the membership list but he may not have time to attend meetings.

(5) *Lack of skill:* One may feel that others have more training and experience than he has and so does not participate.

(6) *Vested interests:* A member may have more land and thus he may not participate in the group meeting which is going to decide to have more taxes on big owners.

(7) *Group values:* One may belong to a different political group and his participation in village meeting may put him in an awkward situation.

---

[1]Adapted from Hadley Read, *Communication Hankbook,* University of Illinois.

(8) *Group means:* The objectives may be right but a member may feel that this **was** not the way to get the job done.

(9) *Group demands:* There is always a call for a special meeting or a special drive.

(b) *Ways in which individuals adjust to frustration*

There are eight ways in which individuals adjust to frustrations that block their participation. As extension workers we can reduce their effect on good communication by recognising and understanding them. These are:

(1) *Aggression:* When someone's ideas are not accepted, or are ignored, he may strike back. He refuses to go along with any one else's ideas and may attack the motives of others or he may turn against himself and refuse to say another word throughout the meeting.

(2) *Compensation:* Since someone feels that he is not good at talking in a group he offers to record minutes or arrange for tea, etc.

(3) *Rationalisation:* A member may feel that the idea or the project to be taken up in the village may not be any good in the first place. May be there is no need for the group.

(4) *Identification:* Some members may feel that getting on a friend's side is the best thing to do. He feels that it would be right because that friend whom he has identified with is always right.

(5) *Displacement:* Someone may not like the chairman of the committee so he tries to find faults with the person making the report.

(6) *Conversion:* When a member feels that he cannot get his project accepted by the group, he suddenly tries to find out some excuses to get the meeting postponed and may say that the meeting place was too hot or similar things.

(7) *Idealisation:* Somebody may overvalue his own abilities or the contribution of a close friend and may say that the idea is good because Mr. Such says so and Mr. Such is always right.

(8) *Projection:* When something goes wrong people blame it on an imaginary cause so that they are not required to face the real situation. For example, if the attendence is poor at a meeting we may say it is poor because of rains.

(9) *Regression:* People so seldom 'get their way' that it is best just to go along with the crowd.

COMMUNICATION AND EXTENSION METHODS

Since extension is education and education is the process of bringing about or producing maximum desirable change in human behaviour, there must be some tools to do so. These tools are called 'Extension Teaching Methods' and are popularly called 'Extension Methods'.

They are basic and proven methods of extension teaching for approaching, working with, encouraging and influencing village people to accept and adopt improved practices of all aspects of community development, whether agriculture, health or industry of the village. Thus, they are the methods of contacting and extending "know-how" to the people who live in the villages, by attracting their attention, arousing interest and leading them to have successful experiences with new ways of doing things that are an improvement over traditional practices.

A proper understanding of these methods is essential in successfully carrying out an extension programme. A lack of this understanding resulting in casual employment of methods, leads to the following consequences.

(1) The benefits of the extension programme do not reach as many people as quickly as they should.

(2) Many new practices might not be accepted by the people since they are not properly presented.

(3) The extension worker might develop frustration because of the indifferent responses and people might loose confidence in the extension programmes.

(4) An ineffective extension programme would mean not only enormous wastage of resources but also serious repercussions which would render further welfare work more difficult.

Difference in methods of extension and formal education

The methods of extension education are different in some respects from the formal educational methods:

(1) Extension works with adults and youths in actual life situations while formal education is concerned with children and youth preparing for life.

(2) Participation in extension activities is wholly voluntary.

(3) Extension centres round the recognised needs of the people though it encompasses the entire range of human activity.

(4) Extension teaching is so informal that it becomes difficult at times to distinguish its educational activity from service activity.

(5) Extension education programmes are necessarily cultural change programmes as through them we aim at replacing the old and traditional practices by new and rational practices.

The methods employed have a direct influence on the effectiveness of the job undertaken. It has, rightly been emphasised by Dr. Ensminger in the following lines:

"Extension methods are to the extension workers what machines' wrenches, screwdrivers, vices and hammer, are to the mechanic. An effective mechanic has available and knows how to use the tools required to do a given piece of work. This effectiveness as a mechanic lies in his ability to do many complicated jobs; this in turn, depends on his having access to the required tools and in knowing how to use them properly".[1]

To become efficient in the use of extension methods, we must know what methods are available, when to use each method, and how to use it effectively. In the following pages, attempts have been made to present the more important methods, to discuss the potential use of each method, and give guidance for its application in working with the cultivators of villages, to organise and educate them to the point of accepting and following improved agricultural livestock raising, home management and other practices.

In thinking about and using extension methods, we must always search for those methods which will produce the desired results. Some methods are useful to attract

---

[1]D. Ensminger: A Guide to Gram Sewaks for Agricultural Production, Ministry of C.D., 1959.

attention, e.g., exhibition; some are helpful in opening the minds of the villagers and making them inquisitive, e.g., film-show; some are used to demonstrate new ways of doing things, e.g., method demonstration; some are to test out new methods under village conditions so that the villagers can see for themselves the merits of the new practice, e.g., result demonstration; and, some are to be used in getting village people started in thinking and acting together, e.g., group discussions.

Our success in getting organised for an Agricultural Production Programme and in making the organisation work effectively will depend on our ability to create interest among cultivators in higher living levels, to understand how they can achieve the higher living level by their own efforts and on your ability so help them gain the skill necessary to do so. To carry through this task, we need to use several extension methods. These must be properly selected and used skilfully in relation to each other.

In addition to the above knowledge of extension teaching methods and skills, the extension worker must have a clear understanding of his following as a teacher:

(1) Specific changes in knowledge, understanding, skills or attitudes which are desirable.

(2) How people can be influenced to change.

How people learn?

People are motivated to learn if it can satisfy a basic need—such as a desire for security, new experience, affection, recognition, etc. The extension worker, therefore, must understand these powerful motive forces of learning, both in individuals and in groups. Adults learn best when they have:

(1) A strong desire to learn.

(2) Clear goals before them.

(3) Put forth efforts to learn.

(4) Receive satisfaction from what they have learnt.

People learn through seeing, hearing about, and doing the thing to be learned. Before seeing, hearing or doing can take place, the learner must:

(1) Have the thing to be learned call to his attention.

(2) Have a conscious desire or want.

(3) Have an opportunity to act.

To learn readily from another person, the learner must have confidence in that person. Learning will occur if satisfaction to the learner results from the above steps.

The extension worker will have to organise the activities so that there will be repetition of the desired behaviour. Each repetition of one practice done before in a sequence increases the efficieny in achieving a desired change in behaviour. The following are involved in the process of teaching:

(1) *Attention:* Getting the attention of the people for the change that is desired.

(2) *Desire:* Building the people's interest.

(3) *Conviction:* Convincing the people.

(4) *Action:* Getting the action done by the people.

(5) *Satisfaction:* Making certain that the people who have adopted the changes get satisfaction from their action.

Extension work consists of arranging situations in which the farmer, farm-woman, boy, or girl may see, hear about and do the thing to be learned. The extension worker plans these situations in such a way that the thing to be learned is easily called to the attention and interest is developed, desire is created and the opportunities for action on the part of the learner are at hand.

A review of our teaching situation shows that our class-room is either a Block, village, home of a villager, or a farm. Our students are the men, women, boys and girls within the area in which we work and they may or may not come to the meeting on reading the newsletter, article, etc. Our subject-matter is based upon the finding of the Experimental Farms and Research Institutes, laboratories, or surveys.

Methods of extension teaching

Extension field studies, conducted over a long period of years and in many countries show, that people are influenced by extension education to make changes in proportion to the number of different teaching methods with which they come in contact. As the number of methods of exposure to extension information increases from 1 to 4 the number of farm families changing behaviour increases from 35 to 98 per cent as shown below.

Percentage of familes who change their behaviour:

(1) ....   35 p.c.
(2) ....   64 p.c.
(3) ....   86 p.c.
(4) ....   98 p.c.

The researches show that the more ways through which people are exposed to extension information through meetings, demonstrations, use of bulletins, news stories, radio talks, personal visits and other methods—the larger is the acceptance of recommended practices.

The percentage of families responding increases rapidly as the number of contacts through different methods increases to 5 or 6. If exposed in 5 different ways, approximately 7 out of every 8 families receiving information change their behaviour. Therefore, widespread response is desired, people must be exposed to teaching effort in several different ways. This is but another way of saying that repetition in a variety of ways is exceedingly important to learning an accepted educational practice.

People who have had personal contacts with extension workers have used 4 times as many practices as have people who have had no contact.

Personal group and mass approach

(1) Various teaching methods were responsible in influencing 81 per cent of the changes in practices and only 19 per cent was due to indirect influence. Methods which provide for personal contact between people and extension workers account for about 17 per cent or 18 per cent, out of this 81 per cent of the total influence of all Extension Methods. They also furnish the confidence and information on which recommendations made through owners are based.

Methods through which groups of people are reached produce about 25 per cent of the total influence of all methods. These are general meetings, method demonstration meetings, leader training meetings and study courses meetings. These motivate the people through learning, seeing, hearing, discussing and doing.

(2) Each Block has a small professional staff. This has from 10,000 to 80,000 potential pupils—the rural population of the Block. This means that methods must be used which will enable the extension worker to contact, either directly of indirectly, a large number of people. Such methods, requiring news stories, circular letters, radio, exhibits, bulletins and posters—sometimes referred to as mass media—account for about 38 per cent of the total influence of all methods in use in the USA. In India, this percentage will be much lower because of illiteracy of the people and lack of facilities of mass media.

(3) Indirect influence such as, talking and visiting the neighbours, observing things along the road accounts for about 19 per cent of the total influence in USA. In India, this percentage may be different. Indirect spread of improved practices from one person to another shows the effect of satisfaction and confidence which are good indicators of total extension influence in an area.

(4) Age of the farmers, size of the farm, location of farm, tenure and status of the farm, have little bearing upon the adoption of recommended practices by the farm people in the USA. But in India it is the reverse. Recent investigations in India and our experiences of working with farmers indicate that Indian farmers of the age-groups 30-40 adopt maximum practices. Older farmers, over 40 years age, are very slow in adoption. The bigger the size of the holding more are the chances of adoption, with some limitations. Tenants and sharecroppers are mostly non-adopters, while cultivating owners are better adopters. Similarly, the nearer the farm is to city and roads, better is the rate of adoption due to demand, communication facilities and transportation.

(5) The higher a person's socio-economic level the more likely he or she is to adopt the recommended practices.

HOW TO SELECT TEACHING TOOLS

Since our studies show that the combination of several methods is more effective than one method, we are not concerned with choosing the best, but rather we should know: (1) what all the methods are, (2) what each has to contribute, and (3) what is the best combination of personal, group and mass media for a specific plan of work or educational campaign.

Other considerations also enter into our thinking. Among them are:

(1) The length of time the programme has been under way in the area.

(2) The character and stage of development of the programme, for example, result demonstration may no longer be needed to give proof of practices recommended.

(3) The personality and skills of available workers, both paid and volunteer.

(4) The sex, age, education, motives and other complex human characteristics and customs of the people to be reached.

(5) General local conditions, such as seasonal work, weather conditions, available meeting places, organisation and leadership.

(6) Financial and other resources, including such as equipment and returns per unit of time spent on the method.

This is only a suggested list. It is very important to use right methods and tools in the right proportion at the right time.

For our purposes in extension, we can group extension methods as:
(1) Direct contacts,
(2) Demonstrations,
(3) Handling and use of audio-visual aids,
(4) Conducting meetings, conferences and tours, and
(5) Arranging exhibitions.
Here we will discuss direct contact and demonstrations only.

(1) Direct contact

This is a fact-to-face relationship with village people individually and with Panchayats and other village groups. In the first round of the village, the extension worker, or the extension student in this case, should; (a) be helped to get acquainted with the village people where he will work so that he or they (students of the class) can: (2) be helped (by their teachers) to explain the objectives and methods of their visit to the villagers, (3) be helped to learn village problems and the interest of the village Panchayat in solving these problems.

As the students continue to work in the village assigned to them by their extension wing or teacher, they may make more and more contacts with villagers, through the Panchayats, cooperatives and special interest groups. These group contacts will be for the purpose of arousing villagers' interest in new village problems and to get them thinking that it would be a good thing if they started trying to work out their own solutions to given problems.

Suggestions for making direct contacts more effective:
(1) The teacher should help the students make it clear, by their approach to villagers, that they understand and like village people and that their objects is to help the villagers, while learning.
(2) They should develop the art of listening.
(3) They should be sure of their facts and technical knowledge. If they do not know, they should consult their teachers and other specialists in the subject.
(4) They should use simple language and the talk should be of interest to the village people.
(5) They should avoid arguments.
(6) When the students and staff leave the village they should feel and express genuine friendliness and appreciation so that the village people welcome them and show the desire to have them visit their village again.

Practice: The teacher may demonstrate how to approach and talk to villagers, then, he should give them a chance to handle the villagers, and to develop contacts.

(2) Demonstration

Among the communicational and educational techniques, 'demonstrations' are the oldest, best, and simplest tools for transmitting sophisticated technology in a simple and understandable form.

Historical perspective
"Cooperative Demonstrations" in USA (1903) to the newest innovations of

'National Demonstrations and Farmers Training (1965, 1971) in India have their own history and past. But the main issues involved in the concept of demonstration is first, last and always for educational purposes. It is 'teaching by example'.

Objectives of the demonstrations

(1) It provides the advantages of improved practices.

(2) It brings the research to the doors of users.

(3) It shows the worth, value and potentialities of techniques.

(4) It dramatises by arousing interest, creating desire motivating one to action, and finally to satisfaction.

(5) It fires the imagination and provides convincing results.

(6) It builds confidence in: (i) Scientific facts, (ii) extension workers and (iii) cooperating farmers.

(7) It persuades neighbourers to adopt recommended practices by demonstrating proofs.

(8) It is used as a vital media for communication, dissemination and diffusion of information.

(9) It upholds the principles of 'seeing is believing' and 'learning by doing'.

(10) It develops local leadership.

(11) It provides scientists with a 'field laboratory' and 'problem-solving platform.

(12) It accelerates and provides subject-matter for training in the forms and use of extension methods.

In summary, the demonstration is said to be successful if it changes the knowledge, skill, understanding and attitude of the clientele and can bring desirable changes in their total behaviour pertaining to the use of new practices or adoption of technology.

Demonstrations may be: (A) (i) method demonstration, and (ii) result demonstration, and (B) (i) simple and (ii) composite demonstration.

Method demonstration

In it the extension worker, or the student of extension, demonstrates an improved practice, i.e., how the thing is done. To give an illustration, when he demonstrates the Japanese method of paddy cultivation, he shows how to remove the seedlings from the nursery, how to wash them in water, how to put the seedlings in the soil, and at what distance, so that inter-culture operation by Touchi Gurma is possible. Another part of the same subject of paddy cultivation may be "How to raise a nursery of paddy". In it the demonstrator, i.e., student of extension or the extension worker, shows the farmers on their field, how to measure and lay out the nursery, how to put manures and fertilisers, how to remove empty kernels from seed by soaking it in a bucket of water, how to make the seed disease-free, with what dose of Agrosone G., how to make the seed spread over the nursery, etc. The farmers watch the whole process in this method demonstration and do as the extension worker tells them. Similarly, the worker demonstrates how to castrate a bull, inject animals, prepare mixtures for spray and how to use the sprayer, etc.

There are some points which should be taken into consideration while demonstrating practice. The teacher can help the student in becoming an effective demonstrator by laying emphasis on the points given in the next section.

Phase of demonstrations

An effective demonstration programme involves five essential phases. The first phase is of analysing the situation. This requires a large amount of facts on all aspects of the situation. Information is needed about the people, their interests, education, what they think they need, their customs, habits and physical situation like soil, market, size of farm, corpping systems, communication and the resources, etc.

The second phase is deciding on objectives or goals to be accomplished in conducting a demonstration.

(This must be stated in terms of behavioural changes in people as well as the socio-economic outcomes).

The third phase is the demonstration plan, and execution of demonstration.

The plan includes the three stages or steps, viz. (i) Pre-demonstration stage, (ii) Execution stage and (iii) Follow-up or post-demonstration stages.

The specific steps to be followed as sugggested by Singh (1970) at each stage are mentioned below:

(i) *Pre-demonstration stage:* Deciding the number of demonstrations, planning the crop rotation. selecting the site and farmer, explaining the purpose to the demonstrating farmers and the other farmers.

Getting soil and water tested, deciding the package of practices for each crop, working out input requirements. Making arrangements for inputs well ahead of time. Preparing a written plan and calendar of activities, constituting, in consultation with the farmer, a committee for assessing yields. Deciding the days for conducting the demonstration meetings and inviting village leaders and farmers to witness the demonstration.

(ii) *Execution stage:* Laying out the demonstration by applying the package of practices, taking observations on the demonstration. Bringing the farmers to the site of training. Explaining the practices demonstrated during field days.

Taking an eye estimate of crop yield. Keeping accurate records. Assessing fertility status of soil. Analysing production costs and results, submission of reports.

(iii) *Follow-up stage:* Disseminating results, assessing the inputs of demonstration. Preparation of information material based on results of demonstrations. Enrolling willing farmers for conducting demonstration during the next crop season. Providing technical information to willing farmers and help in planning the corps for their farms. Estimating and arranging the required inputs for them. Visiting such farmers from time to time to give the necessary assistance.

From the above steps it becomes rather obvious that the scientists, specialists, extension workers, other agencies and cooperating farmers have to work 'hand-in-glove', if the demonstration is to be a success. The State Department of Agriculture, Agricultural Universities. Ministry of Food and Agriculture, N.S.C.,[1] F.C.I.[2] and

[1]National Seeds Corporation.
[2]Fertiliser Corporation of India.

Banks can play a significant role along with agencies like Departments of Education, other mass communication media and All India Radio, etc.

The fourth phase is evaluation of the demonstration programme i.e., determining the extent to which the objectives of the demonstration have been achieved. The earliest determination yardstick is to observe whether people have started doing something that they were not doing before. Phases of evaluation should be built into the plan of work during earlier planning with local people.

The fifth phase is reconsidering after evaluation has taken place. It is review of previous efforts and results which reveal a new situation. If this new situation shows the need of repetition then the whole process may begin again, which new or modified objectives. This is a continuous process.

Demonstration bridges the gap between research and adoption. Demonstration has been used to describe a great diversity of activities from basic research done by scientists to the routine operational activities of the farmers. As we know the foundation is laid by exploratory or applied research about the new knowledge, then comes the adaptation (by adaptive research) of the applied research to local conditions.

A good demonstration can be defined as that which provides the greatest acceptance of the best practice in the shortest period of time, or in other words the demonstration which very speedily bridges the gap between research and adoption of new innovation.

Important tips for conducting a good demonstration
These are:

(a) Know your audience well. Whom do you wish to reach? What is their level of knowledge and literacy? What is their sphere of influence?

(b) What are your resources? Do not have ambitious plans and don't plan more than what can be done well.

(c) Remember that changing people's practices is more delicate than surgery. A poor demonstration may be worse than none at all. Do check whether there is sufficient staff, equipment, transport, inputs, etc., before carrying out the demonstration.

(d) Ask yourself if you can freely provide knowledge inputs as and when needed? Because once you change the knowledge it will demand heavy food for thought.

(e) Don't try to show too much. One or two variables are usually all that can be demonstrated at one time. Keep watch and demonstrate the interaction of variables.

(f) Maintain proper checks to illustrate efficincy of the practice.

(g) Plan an information campaign to ensure conact with the target audience.

(h) Choose your cooperators carefully. Be sure the cooperator cooperates with you. Get him involved and keep him informed.

(i) Consider location and accessiblity both for lay farmers and VIPs.

(j) Involve the agencies, individuals and others in all the operations. This lends credibility to the demonstration.

(k) Organise field days, trips and visits of people who may be potential users of the demonstration and its results.

(l) Keep records, prepare talks, charts, photos, slides, news stories, technical bulletins and other aids. Frequently use them.

(m) Evaluate the demonstration programme and note the points of failure or key to successes etc.

To Summarise

(1) The demonstrator should encourage the audience and see that people understand and learn to do what is being demonstrated.

(2) Before starting the actual working, he should tell the audience: What is being demonstrated?

(3) Tell the audience, especially the interested farmers, the importance of the practice being demonstrated.

(4) Help the audience to go through the steps of demonstration so that they can repeat the process themselves without further help.

(5) Invite questions and create an atmosphere that the audience may clarify its doubts.

(6) A demonstrator should be well-prepared in the subject himself, and should take the help of his colleagues and teachers, whenever necessary.

Result demonstration: In such a demonstration, the result of demonstrated practices are shown in comparison to existing practices or control. In this process, the student or extension worker may take the help of audio-visual aids like film, slides, pictures, comparative diagrams, etc., so that the farmers' imagination is fired and they have some idea of how things were done to obtain higher yields. For example, in the Japanese methods of paddy cultivation, the worker may show a film prepared by the Indian Council of Agricultural Research. He may also arrange an exhibition where the results of some previous demonstrations on paddy raised by the Japanese method may be shown through pictures, diagrams, actual plants and the diagrams of the results obtained. When farmers get motivated and are ready to offer one or two plots for demonstration, the extension worker should arrange to raise the nursery, or get the seedling, from his college farm. He should also arrange for the supplies of fertilisers, seeds, implements, etc., at appropriate time. The whole class may be used for transplanting, weeding, etc. On days when weeding or use of Touchi-Gurma is being demonstrated, farmers may be invited to see the operation. The layout may be shown on a board with details of the demonstration, so that villagers may see and read.

Selection of plot: (1) The plot should have average fertility. (2) As far as possible, it should be near the roadside, or a common path. (3) There should not be any tree in the field. (4) It should not be very near to habitation. (5) There should not be any possibility of being grazed by animals and (6) It should not be sloping.

The result demonstration may include the method demonstration also. For example, when we demonstrate Japanese method of paddy cultivation, sometimes we have to show the methods of planting a nursery, transplanting, use of weeder—Touchi-Gurma, etc. At times when we bring the farmers to watch the differences in the fields with improved practices and the control, it becomes the result demonstration of various practices.

Points for consideration in result demonstrations: (1) The students should demonstrate on specific problems of the area-drilling wheat against broadcast, raising paddy by transplanting against seeded, hybrid maize against local variety.

(2) It should be carried out correctly, in detail and must be in sequence.

(3) Better to conduct more than one demonstration in the same village, on the same subject.

(4) Never try to discover new truths, but rather try to improve the adaptability to local situations of those discoveries already made by research specialists in the area.

(5) Emphasis on the quality of demonstrations rather than increasing the number and having a poor quality.

(6) Do not repeat demonstrations repeatedly.

(7) The demonstration should be located by a well-travelled roadside or path.

(8) Demonstrate as soon as results are evident.

(9) Present definite and detailed costs of practices and item of the practices and compare it with the traditional methods or control.

(10) Hold meetings at demonstrations sites to study progress and results and to disseminate the information so that other farmers get convinced, and adopt the practices.

(11) Use audio-visual aids to support the results of demonstrations.

Planning the demonstrations: (1) The plan of demonstrations should be based on the felt needs of the farmers.

(2) Result demonstration should be set up in a manner as to provide comparisons of practices. 33×33 ft. field for each practice is sufficient. This is 1/40th of an acre.

(3) Data regarding cost, dates of treatments and operations, etc., should be maintained in a proforma.

Simple and composite demonstrations: Simple demonstrations show the difference in the control plot and the plot treated with only one practice e.g., difference in the yield due to use of fertiliser or use of plant protection, irrigated and unirrigated, local seed versus improved variety seed.

The composite demonstration includes many improved practices where improved seeds, fertilisers, plant protection, irrigation, improved cultural practices, etc. are all combined together to show the maximum results. In maximisation demonstrations all the package of practices are put together.

Phases of scheme of demonstrations on farmers' holdings

The scheme of demonstrations has passed through stages: (1) 1952-1960, simple demonstration, (2) The era of hybrids in Maize, Jowar and Bajra 1960-64 (3) The era of improved varieties in paddy till the Scheme of National Demonstrations, and (4) National Demonstration Scheme.

(1) *1952-60 Simple demonstration:* In the absence of high yielding varieties in maize, jowar, bajra, wheat and Paddy the demonstrations conducted by the C.D. Block staff included the use of fertilisers, plant protection measures and improved cultural practices. Because old varieties could not give very high yields and these were susceptible to high dozes of Nitrogen and there was danger of lodging, the fertiliser use remained limited to about $\frac{1}{4}$ what we recommend for the high yielding varieties. The yield could be increased to hardly $1\frac{1}{2}$ times or just double. This could not motivate the farmers much to accept our recommended practices.

(2) *Era of Hybrids, in Maize, Jowar and Bajra:* The Ford Foundation helped some of the Agricultural Colleges to establish extension wings in 1960-61. At the same time the hybrids in maize came in under names like Ganga Lal, Deccan, Ranjit. The

Agricultural Colleges and the Block staff took up demonstrations on hybrid maize, which gave 6 to 8 times yield over the control plots i.e., local seed and local practices. This specular difference created the awareness and interest among the farmers that if they adopt the recommended varieties and improved practices they can get these yields under their conditions also.

CHAPTER 32

VISUAL AIDS

VISUALS IN INFORMATION AND COMMUNICATION

A Visual is what can be seen. Visual helps one to communicate more effectively. Out of the five physical senses through which we learn, the eye is the most helpful in learning. Words are not enough for communicating an idea. The same word may even mean different things to different people. We speak different languages and so many times communication becomes difficult. We use audio-visual aids to provide our audience with a situation near to reality, so that they get the ideas readily. For this purpose we use demonstrations, pictures, photographs, slides, graphs, charts, display material on bulletin boards, black boards, models, specimens, film-strips, flannelgraphs, puppet shows, drama, motion pictures and television, etc. These aids help in making the spoken words clear because the ideas are put across through more than one of the senses. Researches have shown that people learn 25 per cent to 30 per cent more when visual aids are used in teaching; as compared to simple talking. The aids help in holding attention, when visual aids they motivate to take action, create interest, increase permanency of learning and make our job of teaching or communication easier. In the adoption process we are required to use individuals, aids and methods in combination. If we use some slides related to the topic or specimen together with a film or film-strip and provide reading and discussion opportunities, we shall be more effective.

Choice of visuals

In using teaching aids we have to be selective and also have to take into consideration the stage of the adoption process and also the audience. A poster, for example, may not be of much help in the awareness stage, an exhibition may be an ideal medium to enthuse our audience for adoption of the practice at the trial or testing stage. Similarly puppet show may not be of much use if the farmers are facing an epidemic in their cattle. An epidemic calls for immediate action and we have to organise a practical demonstration of the control measures together with repeated broadcast of the message on the radio to be effective.

Teaching aids have to be used in support of a talk to bring out the salient features which we want the audience to learn. They are only aids to verbal words and the words depend on the teaching aids asmuch as the teaching aids depend on the words.

Planning for use of visuals

While planning for use of our visuals we should think of: objectives, audience, media, resource and technique.

(a) *Objective:* We should be clear in our mind as to what essential points are of concerns our audience and what can be the barriers to our audience in learning the same.

(b) *Audience:* Who are they? What are they? and Where are they?

(c) *Media:* In teaching certain media are well-suited for certain jobs. If we want to communicate the idea of different parts of a machine we may prefer to use a model, if we want to show the operation involving a number of factors we use still pictures, charts, slides, but if we want to show a flying bird, or moving tractor we use film. So we have to decide which aid will help in teaching our audience in a better way. The decision is also on whether to use a single aid or in a combination.

(d) *Resources:* While planning for the use of aids we have to see our resources of finance, or equipment and facilities for making and using them. We may have a film projector and films but may not have electricity or a generator for a film show in a village. Even though we may not have an artist we can use visuals prepared from cut-out pictures from journals, magazines, etc.

(e) *The technique:* When taking about a photograph, the use of a camera is not the only technique we are required to know, but also the direction from which picture is to be taken, the distance, and the face of the object. While taking photographs for slides we have to take into consideration, what each slide should show.

(f) *Preparation:* Preparation of most of the visuals calls for a thorough understanding of the subject-matter on which we are preparing our aid or aids. Different visuals call for different treatment of the message. We have to find a way how best to depict the message for easy understanding by the audience. A good layout needs pictures, photographs, words and colour. The important points of consideration may be local interest, technical correctness, logical correctness of the sequence of ideas, a card index for logical sequence, and jotting down points on separate cards for every visual, rehearsal before using the aids, and faith on the utility of visuals in the communication process.

Selecting a theme for visuals

The subject-matter of a visual is picked up after establishing the objectives of the visual. Once the objective is established make a rough outline of what to present? Collect enough information about the subject and then: (1) sort out the different relevant points, arrange them in a logical manner and discard unimportant points (2) Spell out these points clearly for the visuals and translate the verbal symbols into' pictures. This is visualisation. It can be done by a 'storyboard' technique. Take a few sheets of paper and divide each sheet into half vertically. On the left hand side of the sheet, write briefly the points you need to bring out in the visuals. For each point of the theme you must have separate sheet. Fill in each sheet according to the number of points you have to illustrate. If you want photographs to be taken or models or other visuals to be made indicate clearly, either on the top of the sheet or at the bottom, as per your requirements.

If necessary take the help of an artist to make rough drawings on the right hand side of the sheet. In this way the ideas are transferred and when these sheets are ready the artist of photographer or both can do the job.

Layout and design of visual aids

Layout is the disposition of various elements—display, illustration, ornamentation, the white space in a pattern that is pleasant and attractive to the eye and makes reading easy and convenient, as experience has shown.

Principles of layout

(1) It should be well balanced, i.e., it is laid out in such a way that there are equal attractions on each side of the centre. This balancing can be: (a) formal, and (b) informal. Formal balance is when weights are placed at equal distances from the centre. Informal is when unequal weights are placed at such distance from the centre that balance is obtained.

(2) It should be rhythmic, i.e., there should be movement from part to part in a design.

(3) There should be unity in all elements.

(4) There should be variety in the design which relieves monotony and sameness.

(5) There should be emphasis so that the eye is carried first to the most important point.

(6) Subordination, i.e., the minimisation of certain parts of the design.

(7) Contrast—It causes thing to stand out and makes them instantly and strikingly apparent.

Colours

Colour makes our designs attractive. Light travels in waves at different rates of speed, and these waves produce in the eye the sensation which we call as colour. The colour of an object is determined by the wavelengths it does not absorb.

The primary colours of pigments used in our art and printing are: red, blue and yellow. All colours may be obtained by mixing various proportions of these colours. The secondary colours like orange, green and purple are got by mixing red and yellow, yellow with blue and blue with red respectively. Black and white are not classed as colours. Black is the absence and white is the presence of all colours. They are called neutral or achromatic colours. All other colours are called chromatic.

Dimensions of colours: These are the properties or qualities which differentiate colours. They are:

(a) The *hue* or warmth and coolness.

(b) The *value* of the colour and the lightness or darkness.

(c) The *intensity* or chroma, or brightness and dullness of the colours.

Hue is the term used to indicate name of the colour such as red, blue or green. Just as soon as green turns bluish *it has changed its hue* and is called blue-green instead of green. The quality of warmth and coolness is the most important thing to remember about hues. Cool and warm colours are alien to each other. They contrast rather than harmonise.

Value describes the light and darkness of a colour. White is the highest value and no hue can be as light as white. Black is the lowest valve, and no hue can be as dark.

Intensity shows how bright or dull a particular colour is.

Visual aids can broadly be divided into (1) projected, and (2) non-projected aids. The projected aids are again of two types—(a) projected-still aids like film strips, slides, opaque projected material etc. (b) projected movie pictures, which are shown through movie projectors. The non-projected visuals like black board, pictures, posters, charts, flash cards, flip books, flip charts, flannelgraphs, picture strips, exhibits hoardings, etc do not require any equipment, like a projector, for their display. These aids are very easy to make, easy to carry and can be made with locally available inexpensive material. The projected material requires electricity, or a power generator, which may not be available to many extension workers in interior villages in countries like India.

VISUAL AIDS—NON-PROJECTED

The non-projected aids can be divided into: (a) teaching aids and (b) display type.

(a) Teaching aids

The teaching aids which are non-projected visuals and can be prepared and used by teachers or extension workers are: (1) chalk board, (2) Pictures, including photographs and hand drawn pictures, (3) Flash cards, (4) Flip books—similar to a set of flash cards but bound at the top in the form of a calendar, (5) Flip Charts—few charts on a particular theme put together and bound together at the top, and (6) Flannelgraph.

(b) Display visuals

These include posters, hoardings, charts and exhibits. Once they are displayed they stand on their legs and convey the message to whosoever sees them. There is no necessity for any one to stand by their side and explain.

(1) Posters

A poster helps the extension workers to get across one idea to the audience. It is a visual which has to catch the attention of the audience and pass on to them a simple message at a glance. The audience should become aware of the event, practice or idea you want to communicate.

A poster has to be bold in design, simple to understand and attractive in colour. Its components may be: (a) picture or illustration, (b) the words, (c) colour and (d) space.

(a) *Illustration or picture:* It should be such as to bring out the message clearly at a glance. If it is a drawing, the actual thing to be shown should be brought out in bold relief. Avoid unnecessary details so that the viewer's attention is not confused If you use a photograph, avoid unwanted surroundings and bring out the point prominently. While preparing illustrations keep in mind the experience of the audience and use objects familiar to them. (Fig. 32.1)

(b) *Caption in words:* As small as possible. A five word caption is the best. Never write the caption vertically as it creates difficulty in reading. Do not break the caption.

(c) *Colour:* Use bright attractive colours. The centre core can be highlighted with a more prominent colour. Even in the caption some prominent word can be given a

Fig. 32.1 Posters

different colour. Do not use more than three colours, otherwise it may be confusing. Do not use odd combinations of colours.

(d) *Space:* If a poster is loaded with pictures and words the viewer gets lost. So provide adequate space.

(e) *Layout:* It should be well balanced so that the veiwer's eyes can travel smoothly and quickly through the caption and illustration. It should hold his attention and clearly bring out the message to the viewer.

(f) *Check:* After the rough layout is complete show is to some people of the level of your audience. If there is any misconception or ambiguity, remove it.

The poster should recommend action. It should be placed where people pass or gather. It should give only one idea and details should be given through other media.

Diagrams

Charts and graphs

(a) *A diagram* is able to illustrate a process or an object which cannot be brought to a class room or meeting. We can draw a picture of any specimen like goat, cow, building plan, sketch of a machine, etc.

(b) *A chart* contains a series of ideas. While a poster is generally used in the awareness stage, a chart is used in the later stages especially in the testing stage either alone or in combination with other aids. Charts can be: (i) Pictorial, (ii) Organisational, (iii) Flow Chart, Suspense Chart or Strip Tease Chart, and (iv) Tree or Stream Chart.

(i) *Pictorial chart.* A chart may contain pictures suitably coloured and written matter. It may also contain a graph or may be a combination of pictures and graphs. Pictorial charts depicting the important steps of package of practices of any crop, or the how-to-do type of things, with brief captions are very effective in communicating technical information to a lowly literate audience.

(ii) *Organisational chart:* This shows the structure of an organisation, say **State** Department, Agricultural University, Development Department, etc. (Fig. 32.2).

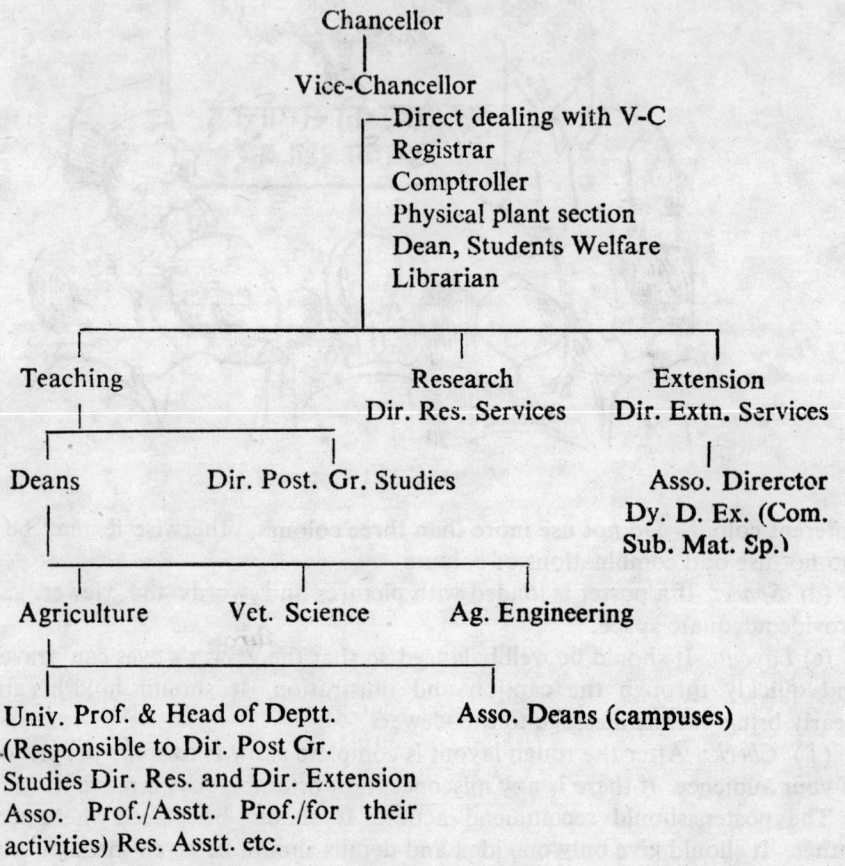

Fig. 32.2. Organisational chart of JNKVV, Jabalpur.

(iii) *Flow chart:* When we try to tell a story of how a product is obtained as a result of series of processes, we can depict it in the form of a flow chart.

(iv) *Tree or stream chart:* In it the divisions and sub-divisions are represented by: a trunk of a tree with branches and sub-branches, or a stream (river) with its tributaries or sub-tributaries.

(v) *Suspense chart or strip tease chart:* The full story is depicted in writing or in a picture, and is kept covered with strips of paper. As we talk we remove the strips of paper as we proceed in our talk. These are fixed with tape so that they can be removed easily (Fig. 32.3).

Planning for charts: We have to decide as to: (i) what can we communicate through charts, (ii) who is audience, and (iii) where we can use charts.

Time chart or table chart: Anything that is recorded or presented in a tabular form is a Table chart. It may be illustrated as in Table 32.1 showing yield of maize Cobs in mounds from various demonstrations conducted by the extension wing, agricultural college, Jabalpur, 1962.

Graphs

Getting a precise idea or drawing a comparison or conclusion from numerals or statistical data needs presentation of data through graphs. Different types of graphs are used for different purposes. These are:

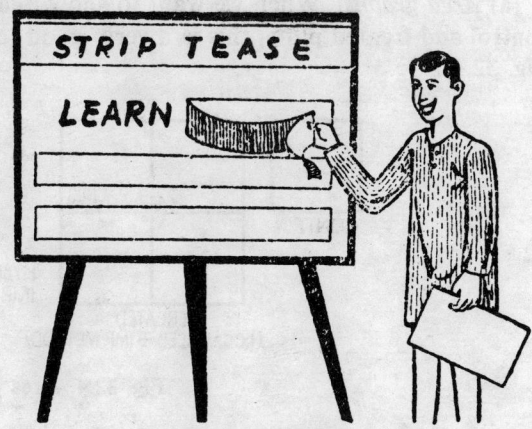

Fig. 32.3 Strip tease chart.

Table 32.1
Time chart or table chart

Place	Hybrid maize local seed		Hybrid maize with improved practice	
	Local practice	Improved practice	Deccan	Ganga 101
Shahpura	13.4	25.8	96 4	99.0
Lakhapateri	7.6	40.6	109.0	114.0
Kundan	3.2	4.6	128.0	96.0
Vet. Col. farm	21.0	26.4	86.4	90.8
Ag. Col. farm	7.0	34.4	66.3	72.0
Sagada	4.4	8.6	23.2	28.0
Burghi	7.0	23.0	40.0	42.0
Sihora	5.0	8.2	29.4	28.0
Rampur	—	32 4	74.2	78.3
Kudan	150	24.4	81.2	95.6
Average	9.3	22.9	73.9	74.2
Index No.	100.0	254.4	800.0	802.2

(1) *Line graphs:* With this we show the trends of prices, farm production, etc. This is plotted on a linear graph.

(2) *Tree or stream chart:* In it, the divisions or sub-divisions are represented by: trunk of a tree with branches and sub-branches, or a stream of river and its tributaries.

(3) *Graphs:* Graphs are quite effective in conveying complicated facts and showing comparisons and contrasts. These may be: (a) Area Graphs, (b) Bar Graphs, (c) Pie Graphs, (d) Line Graphs, and (e) Pictograph.

(a) *Area graphs:* When we want to show figures like yield from one acre of land in control and treated plots, this is a very good aid for representing the figures (see Fig. 32.4).

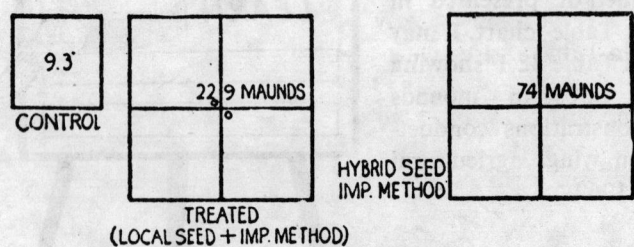

Fig. 32.4. Area graph.

Yield in mounds in control and treated plots as given in Table 32.1 (Area in each block should correspond with the ratio of figures.)

(b) *Bar graphs:* These can be: (1) Multiple Bar Graphs, and Divided Bar Graphs.

(1) *Multiple bar graph:* It compares two or more bars with a numbered scale to show the desired information. The bars can either be vertical or horizontal depending upon the size of the graph paper and contents of the data to be graphed (Fig. 32.5).

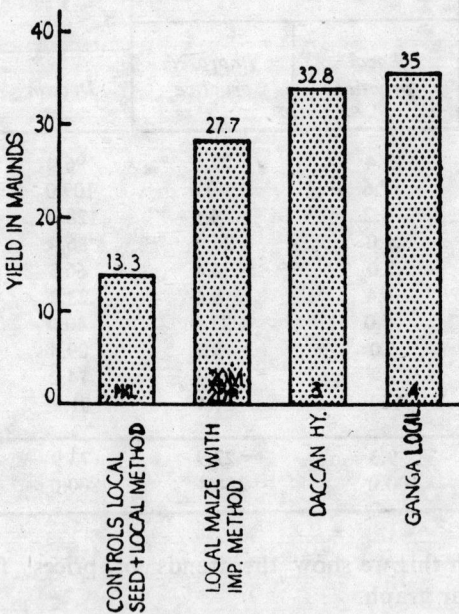

Fig. 32.5. Multiple graph.

Bars showing the yield of maize in cobs as shown in Table 32.1.

(2) *Divided bar graph:* Each bar has sub-divisions to indicate the respective

divisions. These sub-divisions may be represented with different colours or different types of lines or signs. These can be illustrated in the following way in case of a family expenditure, Table 32.2 and Fig. 32.6.

(c) *Pie graph:* In making such a graph, a circle is divided into segments to indicate different parts of a whole.

Table 32.2
Family budget

Items of expenditure	Amt. Rs.	% of total
1. Food	250	50
2. Clothing	50	10
3. Education	50	10
4. Heat and Light	50	10
5. Miscellaneous	25	5
6. Servicing	75	15
Total	500	100

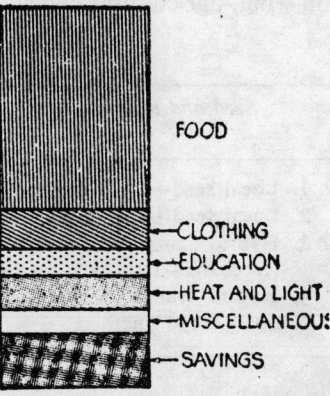

Fig. 32.6. Divided bar graph

Illustration: Amount provided in the III Five Year Plan, as given in Table 32.3, may be represented in the circle as follows (Fig. 32.7)

Table 32.3
Plan allocations: Third Five Year Plan

Items	Amt. in Rs. crores	Degrees out of 360 in circle
1. Agri. & C.D.	1068	50
2. Irrigation	659	
3. Power	1012	
4. Vill. & small indus.	264	
5. Industries and mines	1520	
6. Transport & communication	1456	
7. Social Services	1300	
8. Inventories	200	
Total	7500	360

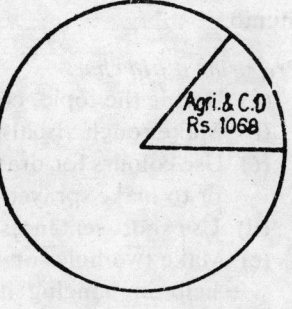

Fig. 32.7. Pie graph only for agriculture budget.

How to work out the degrees:

Out of Rs. 7500 crores exp. on item 1 is: 1068 crores

$$\frac{1068 \times 360}{7500} = 50 \text{ degrees}$$

Out of 360 degrees, the angle will be $\frac{1068 \times 360}{7500} = 50$ degrees

(d) *Line graph:* It can show the growth, trend or frequency of a factor. This is graphic transaction of the numerical or statistical data. Many things can be shown b lines or dotted lines or lines of different colours or types.

(c) *Pictograph:* This is a pictorial graph. It uses actual symbols or figures to indicate the proportionate amounts as given in a numerical table. In place of figures, actual figures of say milk bottles when we show consumption or production of milk, bags of wheat production, cobs of maize, figures of men or women when we show population given in ratio.

Illustration: Production of maize in ten demonstration plots conducted by extention wing, agricultural college, Jabalpur, 1962 (Table 32.4).

Table 32.4

Seed and method	Yield in cobs in mds.	Index No	Figs of cobs (No.) or bags of grain
1. Local seed + local method	9.3		1
2. Local seed + Improved method		100	
3. Hybrid maize (Deccan) + Improved method	22.9	254	2.5
4. Hybird Ganga	73.9	800	8
101 + Impd. method	74.2	800.2	8

Flip chart

It is like an album of drawings, pictures, charts. It is an aid and assists an extension worker or a teacher to tell a story. Its advantages are that it is handy and can be carried easily, and can be prepared with a few simple tools. We can prepare it ourselves because it requires two pieces of cardboards of about 15" to 20", sheets of paper, colour pencil or ink and brush, some cuttings of pictures or stencils over which ink can be sprayed with the help of an old toothbrush by running over the hairs our thumb.

Preparing a flip chart
   (a) Decide the topic, collect relevent facts, and select important points.
   (b) Make rough visuals, make drawings simple.
   (c) Use colours for drawings, or use bold photographs. Use stencils to draw lines or to make sprayed pictures.
   (d) Use short sentences.
   (e) Make two holes on the upper side and tie a string which hangs loose and can help in hanging it on a stand or a black board. The stand should be like "V" upside down.
   (f) The script describing the pictures or sketches should be written on the back side of the previous page or on a separate sheet from which to talk while using the illustrations.
   (g) Rehearse well before presentation (see Table 32.4).
Presentation: (1) All members of the audience should be able to see the person who presents; (2) select a suitable spot; (3) introduce your subject, develop the topic and summarise the main points; and (4) invite questions and answers in a friendly way.
Picture books: Picture books can substitute for film-strips. A commentry to accompany each poster can be written on the back of the previous one. The person who turns the pages can read aloud the appropriate text.

Flash cards

These are the series of cards which when presented before the audience in proper sequence, tell a complete story. Each card is of about 10″ to 12″ in size and contains a picture or diagram. Each individual card is "flashed" before the audience accompanied by the verbal commentary. The extension worker or the student who wants to use them, holds them in hand and flashes the card one after another.

Preparation of flash cards

A brief story should be written. The story should end with suggestions or a morale that leads to action. A suitable title should be selected for the story. The story should be divided into a number of scenes which are to be presented in a number of individual cards.

Different scenes which remain abstract in the preceding stage appear in appealing visual forms. Art paper is cut into pieces of 10″ × 12″. The figures may be: (1) "Jetman" or (2) Matchstick, Flash cards using "Jetman" are called "Jet Series". Other categories may have photographs, drawings, pictures and diagrams.

Fig. 32.8. Flash card—how to use it?

The cards are numbered in sequence. Every set of cards should have a title. There should be a commentary written on the reverse of each card so that the person who presents it to the audience can easily read the commentary from the reverse. Attractive lettering increases the effectiveness of the flash cards.

How to use a flash card: (1) The story should be familiar to the student or person who presents the card.

(2) He should use simple words and local expressions.

(3) He must hold cards in a way that the audience can see clearly, better against the body—and should point out the pictures on the cards.

(4) He must bring local names of the people or villages.

(5) Some important points may be jotted down by the back side of the cards to help in the telling of story.

(6) The cards should be stacked in order, as one card is finished it may be slid behind the other. In this way, they will remain in order for the next time (Fig. 32.8).

Felt-boards, flannelgraphs or khaddargraphs

This is a board with a surface of felt, flannel or khaddar cloth which is used for fixing pictures or parts of material on the back of which there is piece of sandpaper to stick.

How to use a flannelboard: Pre-planning should include answers to the following:

(1) What is going to be presented?

(2) Are the cut-out materials prepared and ready for use?

(3) Why is the flannelboard going to be used?

(4) How is the information going to be presented?

(5) What will the audience get out of it?

Fig. 32.9. An extension worker explaining something to farmers with the help of flannelgraph.

The Flannelgraph (Khaddargraph or Feltgraph) can be designated as a picture-drama. Its pictures, board and background are equivalent to actors, stage and background scenes respectively in a drama. It not only saves time in the class but creates interest in the class room or village meeting, thus helping the audience to learn better (Fig. 32.9).

The story should be simple and should not involve too many characters. It should have a good beginning, the subject-matter and an ending with definite suggestions.

Place the board high on a firm table or stand so that it can be seen easily by everyone in the audience. Number the several objects and place them in order. If there are several groups or parts, place each separately numbered in easy to open folders or envelopes and number the envelopes consecutively.

To aid memory, make brief notes on a piece of paper and identify it on the pictures or material to be put on the flannelboard.

Do not block the view and give sufficient time to the audience to see and understand each part. Have someone to help you in fixing the illustrations.

(a) Chalk board

It is called blackboard also. This is helpful in meetings and group discussions. For village programmes, the extension wings may have a folding chalk board made from rexin cloth or chalk board made from plywood about 30″ × 40″ in size. This can be painted with black or green chalk board paint. It can be in two pieces with hinges in the middle, with a small strip of wood attached to the inside of the fold so that it can be slid across the board after it is opened and can make the board firm. It requires a chalk and a eraser.

Increasing the effectiveness of the board.
(1) Do not crowd the board with too much material at a time.
(2) Write in bold letters.
(3) Do not talk as you write.
(4) Face group after writing and continue discussion.
(5) The lighting arrangement should not cause glaze.
(6) Yellow chalk on a green board gives better results in night meetings.
(7) All unnecessary and unrelated material should be erased.
(8) If possible, keep pointer and stand on one side of the board.

(b) Bulletin board

It is a board with a background of coloured cloth. It can be covered with glass, netting or a plane board (Fig. 32.10).

Fig. 32.10. Bulletin board.

The material for display may be news sheets, announcements, booklets, bulletins, circular letters, newspaper cuttings, cartoons, pictures, charts, posters, maps, graphs, subject outlines, etc.

This is a good medium for displaying the creative work of the students. Such boards should be fixed in colleges, in the villages of the extension wing or those covered by an extension programme.

How to use it: (1) The students or extension worker should collect suitable illustrations and other display material connected with the extension programme in advance; (2) they should classify it and file it; (3) they should display it in an interesting manner; (4) each item should have a title followed by a brief description; (5) the material should correlate with the extension as regards extension work; and (6) it should tell a complete story.

Location and type of material and colour: The board should be at a place where it will be seen by most of the people for whom it is meant. The board should be fixed at eye-level and should have a work surface or something similar on which the material to be displayed can be attached with drawing pins

Classwork: Divide the students in groups. Each group may be put in charge of a bulletin board. Those who display in a better way throughout the year should be given due credit and appreciation by way of grades in the sessional work and a certificate for good work.

(c) Exhibitions

Exhibition is one of the best programmes of extension which the extension wings or extension workers can arrange successfully. An exhibition can show actual things practices, results of demonstrations, programmes in progress through charts, diagrams, displays, layouts, models, etc. These can be arranged on a big scale just like the one at the Gwalior Fair in December-January every year. At such fairs, agriculture takes one section of the whole exhibition. Small-scale exhibitions may be arranged for village meetings, film shows, etc.

Layout of agricultural exhibitions on a large-scale: In such exhibitions a gate, which depicts village life, may be prepared with material available in the village. The exhibits may be grouped in sections like—agricultural information, agricultural implements, soil conservation, crops, dairy, horticulture, flower show, entomology, plant pathology, agricultural economics, extension, etc. Some agencies like firms dealing with insecticides, machines and bodies like I.C.A.R., etc., may be invited to display their material. Space should be provided for film-shows, meetings, shops for tea, etc.

Exhibitions in villages on a small-scale: For arranging exhibitions in villages, the extension wings may have their own charts, diagrams, models, purchased or prepared in the extension wings. Some of the things can be borrowed from sections of the college, or from sections of Research or Extension (District Agricultural Officer, etc.) Information, etc. An Agricultural Exhibition Committee, including the villagers, students, etc., may also be organised, if necessary.

Display: Exhibits should be displayed and planned so as to be easily seen. Photographs, charts and posters should be prominently placed at eye-level.

Material for stands, etc.: As far as possible, use material available in the villages. Stands of bamboo, or wood, woven with Newar, Kana, Chatai, Sutli, etc., may be prepared for permanent use. Cardboard folders, or folders of plywood, or hardboard, may also be prepared. Even charpais, arranged in a U-shape, can serve this purpose.

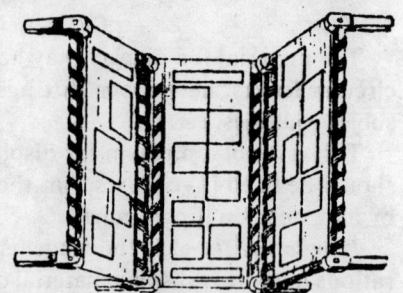

Fig. 32.11. Using charpais (cots) for a stand.

Framing: For framing, we can paste pictures on cardboard and put bamboo or wooden frames. Frames which are replaceable with catches at the back can be made. The pictures or diagrams may be framed in glass and put in wooden crates so that they are not damaged in transport.

Exhibits, specimen and models: Good exhibits tells a story without the need of an attendant. While planning to prepare an exhibit, limit it to one idea and make it simple and large. It should be timely, durable and attractive having bold letters and few items. All parts which need explanation should be labelled (Fig. 32.12).

VISUAL AIDS—PROJECTED

Such aids include slides, film-strips and films. Slides are projected by slide projectors or magic lanterns, film-strips by film-strip projectors or slide projectors with the film arrangement, and film by movie projectors. Slides can also be projected by overhead projectors. The projection of these aids involves various types of equipment beginning from the simple magic lantern to the complicated sound film projectors.

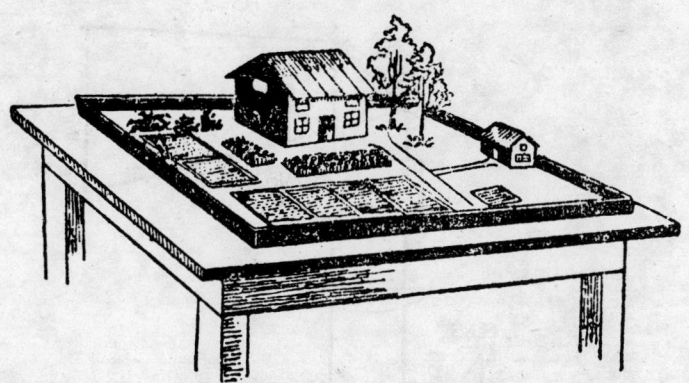

Fig. 32.12. Specimen and model.

Types of projection

Projection can be of three types: (1) Direct projection, (2) Indirect projection and (3) Reflected projection.

(1) *Direct projection*

The slide projector, film-strip projector and the film projectors are based on direct projection. In such projection, the rays of light directly come from the projection lamp or some other source of light, pass through the condenser lens, the object (slide, film-strips or film), the objective lens and finally the enlarged image appears on the screen. The loss of light in this projection is very negligible (Fig. 32.13).

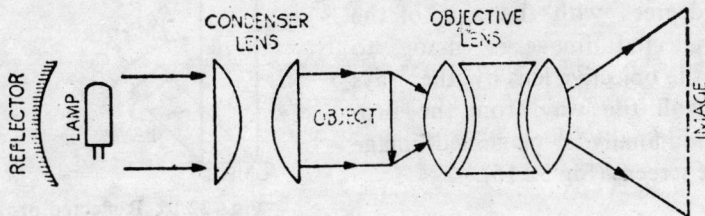

Fig. 32.13. Direct projection.

(2) *Indirect projection*

This principle is used in the overhead projector. The rays of light come from a projection lamp, (Fig. 32.14) enter one element of a condenser lens unit and are reflected by a plane mirror placed at an angle of 45° with either of the axes of this condenser lens unit. The reflected rays enter the other element of the condenser unit, pass through the slide, or the transparency, enter the objective lens and are again reflected by another plane mirror, placed at an angle of 45° with the axis of the objective lens to form an enlarged image of the material on the screen. The source of light in this case is considered to be indirect, so this method is called "indirect projection". The loss of light in this case is more as compared to direct projection.

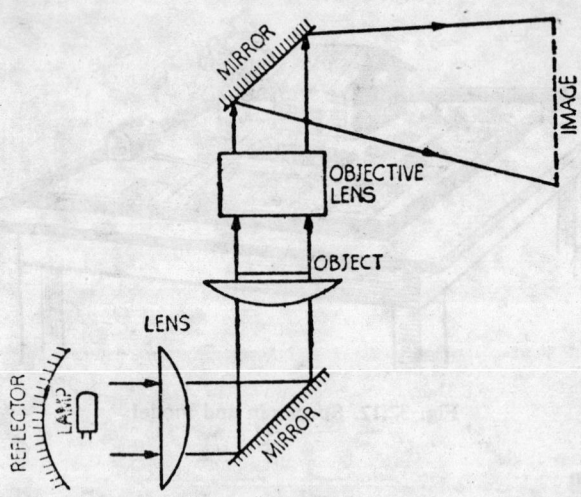

Fig. 32.14. Indirect projection.

(3) *Reflected projection*

Opaque projectors are based on this system. In it the light indirectly coming from the lamp hits the surface of the picture (object to be projected) at an angle and consequently the image of the object is reflected on a large mirror fitted at an angle of 45 degrees with the axis of the object. The reflected image is made to pass through the objective lens by the rays of light coming all the way from the projection lamp, and finally a magnified image appears on the screen (Fig 32.15).

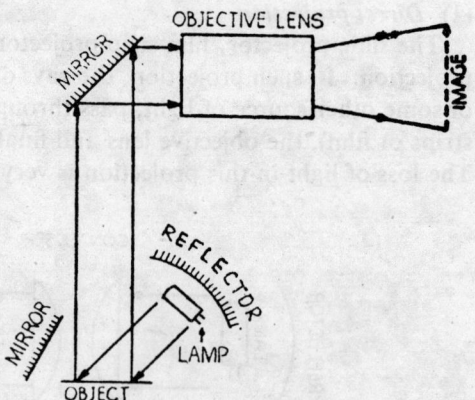

Fig. 32.15. Reflected projection.

Projectors

(1) *Opaque projectors*

In India and England, opaque projector is also called as Epidiascope. The word "epi" means upon or at and "scope" means a machine for a looking upon. It projects opaque pictures. The Americans call it "Spencer Delineascope or Baloptician." It uses two systems of projection: (1) direct system to project transparent materials, and (2) reflected system to project opaque materials. It is a combination of a slide projector and an opaque projector. It is fitted with two different objective lenses (Fig. 32.16).

In the epidiascope, the projection lamp is fitted as to allow movement in the desired inclination. Change of epidiascope (reflected) to diascope (direct) projection is done by levers.

Use of epidiascope: The object (picture, diagram or a page of book) is placed on the platform, which is brilliantly illuminated by a bright projection lamp. A reflector is used to concentrate the light on the material being projected. The projection lamp, which is usually of 1000 watts, produces heat so there is a fan for cooling. The large mirror placed at an angle of 45 degrees above the object being projected, reflects it and sends an image through the objective lens to the screen.

Fig. 32.16. An Epidiascope.

Materials: Pictures, cartoons, drawings, magazines, illustrations, etc., which are to be projected, can be arranged on a strip of paper which can be rolled or mounted on cloth-strips or on card board.

To prepare folder card sets:

(1) Assemble a group of individually mounted pictures in the desired order. Use 8×8 inches mounts for folded card sets.

(2) Lay pictures out on table in order from right to left facing you.

(3) Attach each mount to the next one with a piece of 3/4 of an inch cloth-binding tape on the back.

(4) Leave a small space about 1/16 or 1/8 inches between mounts to allow for the folding.

(5) Place topic, unit or subject and other identification on the back of the first mount to facilitate filing. These pictures will fold into a small compact unit and as each mount is pushed through the projector it refolds in the same order.

To make a rolled paper base: (1) Arrange related illustration in the desired order; (2) secure ordinary rolled wrapping paper, if necessary trim to 8 inches width; (3) paste the materials in the centre of the paper facing you, allowing 6 inches for each picture; (4) work from right to left and leave at least 1 inch between pictures; (5) roll the complete unit and fasten with a rubber band or string; and (6) identify material on outside of roll for filing.

Parts of epidiascope: (1) Epi and dia projection adjusting lever. (2) Platform adjusting lever. (3) Knob to adjust diaobjective lens. (4) Knob to adjust the level of epidiascope. (5) Epi-object lens. (6) Terminal. (7) Switch. (8) Knob to open chamber. (9) Film-strip and film-slide adjustment.

Operating an opaque projector: (1) Set up projector and insert plug in electric outlet. (2) Turn on lamp. (3) Turn on motor for cooling system. (4) **Place picture** on model tray or "plate" and bring housing into place with lever. The bottom of the picture should face the front of the machine. (5) Bring image to sharp focus by turning lens left or right. (6) If the pictures are of post card size, or smaller **use the** card-holder which is in the slot under the model tray. (7) If using a newspaper, **maga**zine of textbook or actual object, adjust the lens for each. Turn blower to fuller speed. (8) After showing material, turn off blower and lamp. Hold up extension cord, cover projector and return the machine to storage.

(2) *Slide projectors*

Slide projectors are based on principle of direct projection. The classification of such projectors may be:

(1) $3\frac{1}{4} \times 3\frac{1}{4}$ *Inches slide projector:* It requires either an electric lamp or petromax lantern for illumination. It is called Magic Lantern or Projection Lantern. The petromax lantern is lighted and placed inside the projection chamber.

(2) *Dual purpose projection lantern* (Fig. 32.17): It can project $3\frac{1}{4} \times 3$ inches and 2×2 inches slides. It has a lens on sliding girdles with sufficient extensions which gives a pin-sharp picture. It has a heat-proof, crystalline enamelled body. Accetylene gas as well as an electric lamp can be used in it.

(3) *Multi-purpose projector:* This can also be of two types: (a) petromax, and (b) electric. These are suitable for displaying $3\frac{1}{4} \times 3\frac{1}{4}$ slides or $2 \times 2''$ slides, or 35 mm film-strips.

(4) 2×2 *Inches slide projectors:* Its operation. (1) Carefully remove the **projector** from the case and place on a table or any table stand.

(2) Insert projector plug in electric outlet of proper voltage.

(3) Adjust screen in front of the projector.

(4) Insert slide carrier in its holder. Check it for centring and secure it by tightening the set screw.

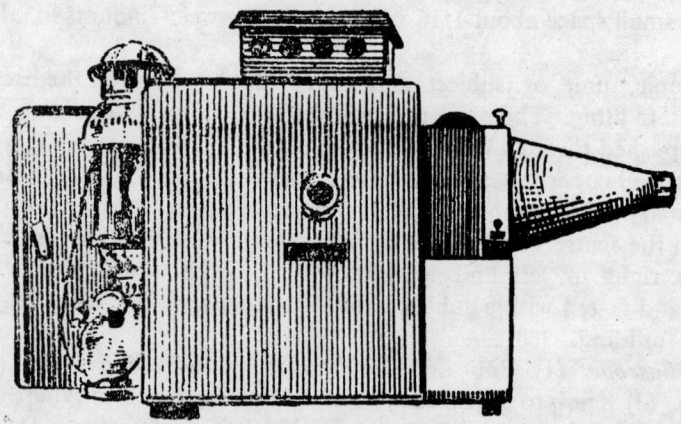

Fig. 32. 17. Dual projection lantern.

(5) Place a test-slide in the right hand side of the carrier and gently push the frame

over to the centre.

(6) Turn on projector light.

(7) Focus image on screen by turning the objective lens backward or forward.

(8) To change height on the screen, adjust wing nut at the base of the projector or put something like a hook under the projector face.

Automatic slide projection: When a series of 2×2 inches slides are to be exhibited, it is convenient to use an automatic projector such as the ARGUS Automatic Slide Changer or Golde Nu-manumatic Slide Projector, the Selectroslide the Airequipt Automatic Slide Changer or the Kodaslide Ready Mount Changer. This equipment makes it possible to store 20 to 50 slides in a carrier, or magazine, and then to feed them automatically into the projector by means of a cable release or a remote punch-button control.

Attaching the changer: (in Aurgus Automatic Slide Changer). To attach the changer, take a position behind the projector, holding the changer with its operating handle to your right, and the mounting rails facing away from you. Engage the mounting rails over the two sides of the square mounting bracket on the projector, and slide the changer down until the stop plugs at the top come to rest.

Put slides 2×2 inches size in the frames and then in the magazine. If it has an arrangement where the frames on the slides are not to be put, put slides in your magazine as such. Pull the operating handle all the way out. Insert the loaded magazine from the rear with the index card up and its Argus name plate to your right. Be sure you insert it under the rail at the top edge of the vertical guide plate on the changer. Slide the magazine forward until it engages the ratchet device which controls its automatic forward movement. Now slide the magazine forward or backward until No. 1 on the index card is opposite the indexing notch in the top guide rail. The changer is then ready for automatic projection.

To project your slides, simply push the operating handle to the left as far as it will go. This inward motion selects each frame or slide and moves it into position for viewing. Pulling the operating handle out to the right as far as it will go, return the slide to the magazine and advance the next one into position for the inward stroke.

Showing slides: The Argus projector can be used for slide-cum-film. It costs about Rs. 1,500. It has a bulb house and a fan to cool the machine. Bulbs ranging from 300 to 1000 watts can be used in it. A lever is provided at bottom to bring the projector upward and downward.

Slides can be shown on a slide-holder as well as an automatic slide-changer. Only 35 mm. slides can be shown on this.

Slide-viewer: There are many types of inexpensive viewers which can help in arranging the slides. We can see these before we want to use them on the projectors and so can arrange them in the order we want to show.

Film-strip arrangement on slide projectors: Some film projectors have dual arrangements for slides as well as film-strips. The film-strip is a continuous strip of film consisting of individual frames or pictures arranged in sequence, usually with explanatory titles. Each strip may contain about 20 or more pictures.

In sound slide-film, explanations are given audibly through a recording which is synchronised with the pictures.

Operating a film-strip arrangement: (1) Hold film-strip so that first picture or title frame is right side-up an printing can be read in a normal manner. The surface of the film towards you when viewed should always be on the outside of the roll.

(2) Hold film so that unrolled end is away from you (printing now reads backwards). Raise spindle and place film so that the spindle is in the centre of the rolled film. Lower film and spindle to film track.

(3) Gently pull out 6 to 8 inches of film and insert film end into channel immediately behind film track. Push film into channel far enough to engage the sprocket and then turn knob clockwise.

(4) Turn switch to fan, then to lamp. Turn objective lens out counter-clockwise about 1½ inches. Advance film to first picture and complete focussing by turning lens until image is sharp.

(5) So that parts of two pictures may not appear on the screen, turn the framing control in a clockwise direction until one picture is centred on the screen.

(3) Overhead projector

This equipment uses the principle of indirect projection. Making use of a lens of short focal length and two mirrors to reflect the picture on the screen, the overhead projector can be placed in front of the group. The extension worker or the teacher can face the class or group while projecting standard lantern slides or large size transparencies with this projector. It can project different varieties of teaching aids, such as the charts, graphs, drawings, diagrams, maps and work-sheets, which are prepared in transparent materials. The transparency to be projected is placed on the horizontal platform of the projector. Sheets of plastic or cellophane paper are suitable for use on it. We can write or draw sketches on them with a special type of ceramic pencil or crayon available for the purpose. We can write directly on the transparency while the same is being presented to a group. The transparency to be projected on a large size screen should be of 10×10 inches.

Some overhead projectors like Master Vu-Graph can project 35 mm film strips and lantern slides when fitted with a special attachment. This projector has F/3-5 projection anastigmat lens, whose diameter and focal length are 4″ and 4″ respectively. It has a 500 W medium pre-focus projection lamp giving clear and bright screen images (Fig. 32.18).

(4) Movie projectors

Movie projectors may be classified on the basis of size of film: (a) 35 mm film projectors are used in commercial cinema-houses, (b) 16 mm film projectors used in extension wings or block programme, etc., and (c) 8 mm projectors. This classification is on the width of the film in millimetres. There may be silent, sound or silent-cum-sound film projectors. The basic principles of projection are similar in all types.

Some of the well-known projectors are: R.C.A. (Radio Corporation of America), Victor, Ampro, Bell & Howell and Kodak, etc. There is some difference in their design and assembly of different knobs and switches, but they are similar in operation. In each case, the film starts from a loaded reel, passes through the first sprocket wheel film-gate, second sprocket wheel, sound drum (if a sound projector) and ends in an empty take-up reel.

Threading the film

Place the spool loaded with film on the top spool arm spindle with the perforation owards the operator and the empty (take up) spool on the rear spindle. Press them firmly on the spindle until the small retaining spring balls lock the spool on the spindle. Pull off about 5 inches of leader film for threading. The film, if correctly bound, should feed from the spool with the perforated edge, towards the operator. Slip the film into the slit of the base of the spool arm over roller. Lead the film below first sprocket, slide the film as far towards the machine as it will go. Holding the film slightly, press on the top to open the guard. Pull gently on the film until the perforation sets over the sprocket. Then release the tab, looking the film over the sprocket swing lever upwards (this lever is beyond the projector lens). This movement will open the film gate from the first loop following the loop outline, on the side of the gear-case. Place the film into the channel behind the lens, being certain that it is fully seated in this channel. Then close the gate by pressing down lever as far as it will go. From the second loop,

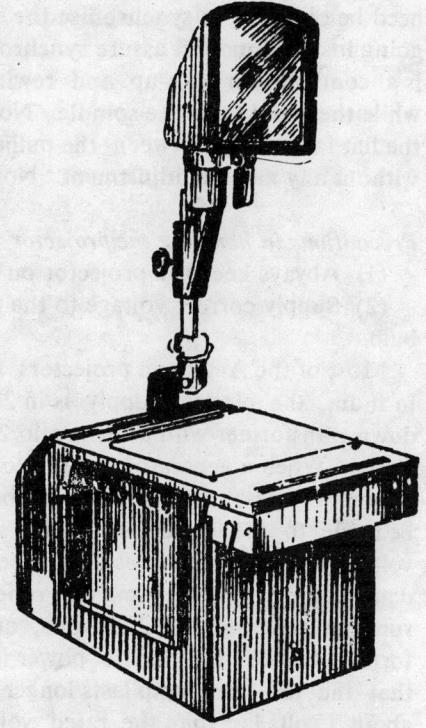

Fig. 32.18. Master Vu-graph overhead projector.

conform to the outline on the gear-case and slip the film over the second sprocket. Again, press the film as far towards the projector as it will go and while maintaining the correct loop size, lock the film. Now turn the hand setting knob, several times in a clockwise direction. This will engage the film with the shutter teeth. If the lower slides upward, continue to turn the hand setting knob until the shutters are withdrawn, when the film may be pulled down to reset the loop to the lot-line on the gear-case. It is not possible to move the film downward through the gate unless, the shutter teeth are withdrawn.

Again, test the threading with the hand-setting knob. Lead the film from the second sprocket, under the top roller of the oscillatory stabiliser, around the sound drum, under the bottom of stabiliser roller, and over the third sprocket. Press the film as far towards the projection end as it will go over the sproket, when the oscillator stabiliser is moved to its extreme position by the tension on the film. Open the film guard by pressing on tab. Then free the film just sufficiently to permit the oscillatory stabiliser to pull it back to the first available set of perforations. Release the tab, permitting the guard to lock the film in place on the third sprocket. Press the film under the snubber roller, and the guide roller, and then to the take-up spool. The film must be inserted in the slot in the case and over the roller on its path to the take up spool. The film should pass around the bottom of the take-up spool. Remove the film-stake before starting the projector by revolving the take-up spool clockwise. No special precaution need be observed to synchronise the sound to the picture, since adherence to the foregoing instructions will assure synchronisation. The mechanism on the rear spool arm is a combination take-up and rewind device. Set this for take-up, pressing the lever while the spool is on the spindle. No adjustment is necessary for various films since the flat fabric belt between the pullies provides complete and automatic compensation without any manual adjustment. Now the projector is ready for operation.

Precautions in handling the projector

(1) Always keep the projector on a film base.

(2) Supply correct voltage to the projector. Too great a voltage will fuse out the bulb.

Most of the American projectors run on 110 volts A.C. (Alternating Currrent) and in India, the electric supply is in 220 Volts, so it is necessary to use 1500 Watt step-down transformer with a turn ratio 2 : 1. A variable voltage transformer is always preferred. When a generator is used to supply electricity to the 110 volts Projector, the output voltage of the generator can be adjusted to 110 volts, and then connections may be made to the projector. Such a situation presents difficulties when the generating voltage suddenly fluctuates and if the fluctuated voltage is more than 110 volts, it can damage the projection lamp and other electronic tubes of the projector. So it is safe to run the generator at 220 volts, and step down the voltage to 110 volts by a transformer, before the electric power is fed into the projector. It is seen from experience that the projector lamp lasts longer if the projector is operated at a voltage which is about 5 volts less than the rated voltage. It is, therefore, necessary to run generator at 210 volts and then stepdown the voltage to 105 volts so that the projector can be operated at this voltage. A generator, producing 115 volts, A.C. current can be adjusted to run at 105 or 107 volts before the projector unit is connected to it. In this case, a transformer is not necessary unless the voltage is required to be stepped up to 220 volts to run 200 volts projector.

In case of 220 volts D.C. current, the way is to change the wiring of the projector so that a 220 volts bulb can be used from the main supply. An invertor or vibrator will be necessary to change the 220 V. D. C. to 110 V. A. C. so that the amplifier of the 110 volts projector can work:

(a) So see the correct current A. C. or D. C. as is required in your equipment.

(b) Use transformer if A.C. supply is more than 110 volts.

(c) All connections in the projector should be in the off position.

(d) The transformer taping or the resistance or converter should be set to the voltage of the main supply before making any connection to the projector.

(e) It is important that the equipment is earthened by connecting the third lead in the main cable to the earthern pin on the wall plug or other suitable points.

(3) Before threading the film, examine the film and see that there is no breakage. If broken during projection, then join by cement by cutting it at suitable point and pressing.

(4) Examine the hand winding knob to be sure the film is correctly laced.

(5) See that the loops in the film are of correct size.

(6) Never touch the film lens or condenser, or any other glass part with oily or dirty hands. These parts should be thoroughly cleaned with the lens-cleaning tissue

paper. Never use a dry or wet piece of cloth.

(7) Lubricate the projector at regular intervals.

(8) Always put the switch in the following order.

(a) Amplifier (will take $\frac{1}{2}$ minute to warm up);

(b) Projector switch;

(c) Projector lamp switch.

(9) Always keep spare parts, e.g., spring belt, exciter lamp fuse, projector lamp.

(10) Never take the projector bulb out immediately after it has been used.

(11) Before actually starting the projector, see that the correct speed is chosen for silent or sound film. If the switch is in the forward direction, the projector is switched on.

(12) Never attempt to remove or adjust the lens of the sound optical system, as it requires special training.

(13) The pilot light should always be off when projector is in operation.

Oiling (see Table 32.5)

Table 32.5
Oiling

Name of oil cup	Silent speed	Sound speed
Oil cup A	1 drop of projector oil after 8 hrs. operation.	1 drop after each 4 hrs. operation.
Oil cup B	1 drop after 32 hrs. use	1 drop after each 16 hrs.
Oil cup at the sprocket	saturated felt reservoir every 6 months.	saturated felt reservoir after every 3 months.

Operation

In case of sound projector:

(1) Unless the speaker and projector form one single unit, the cable must be plugged into an amplifier outlet.

(2) Locate the speaker near the screen and off the floor. Check the sound system.

(3) Warm up the amplifier several minutes before starting the projector.

(4) After starting the projector, turn up volume. It should not be too much.

(5) To obtain clear sound, adjust tone control.

(6) Before stopping the picture, turn down the volume.

(7) Put the projector on stand (its own) or any other good stand, or table,

(8) Fix up its screen at a distance of twice its width from the projector.

(9) Open the projector, fit up the reel arms into the projector, and supply the proper spring belts to the reel arms.

(10) Connect the speaker cord to the projector.

(11) Check up the electric supply and see that you get the rated voltage for your projector.

(12) Connect the projector to the power supply by means of "power cord" provided with the projector.

(13) Switch on the amplifier and advance the volume control a little. Inserting the

microphone plug into socket in the projector, test the loudspeaker. The microphone can be removed after this test.

(14) Switch on the exciter lamp and put the speed switch in "sound" position. Advance the volmue control a little. If a piece of paper is moved in between the sound lens and the sound drum, you can hear the sound effect in the loudspeaker. This test confirms that the optical sound system of the amplifier is functioning. The exciter lamp can be switched off after this test.

(15) Switch on the motor and then switch on the projection lamp. In some projectors, such as Victor, the two operations are controlled by one switch. If the lamp is switched on first, it will be overloaded with current and be fused. Focus the light on the screen and adjust the tilting screw to bring the rectangualar area of light to the centre of the screen.

(16) Thread the fiim as described previously. Check up your threading by rotating the threading knob. If the threaded film moves as the threading knob is rotated, then it has been threaded correctly.

(17) Be sure that the speed switch is in "sound" position if you have threaded film having sound. Switch on the motor. Operate the projection lever on knob, as the case may be, and let the film start moving.

(18) Switch on the projection lamp and refocus the image on the screen. As the time is pre-focussed it will not take time to focus the image sharply. It may be necessary to frame picture on the screen by adjusting a knob.

(19) Switch on the exciter lamp and adjust the volume and tone controls for a pleasing and loud sound.

(20) Stop projection when the "End" appears on the screen and remove the take-up reel from the arm. Let the motor be on to cool the projector.

(21) After the show, disconnect all electrical connections, and put everything in order as you want them for the next show.

Screen for projectors

White wall, white bed sheet, a beaded screen, matte screen, aluminium or silver-colour painted rasin cloth , or engineer's tracing cloth, can be used as a screen.

The beaded screen is covered with minute glass beads which serve as a reflecting surface for the projected picture. It is useful only in long narrow rooms. It can be used in a place 40 to 50 feet wide.

The matte screen has a smooth white surface which does not reflect as much light as the beaded screen does. This is quite suitable for use in wide rooms. Members who sit on outer lines of the centre line can have a better view than with the beaded screen.

The aluminium or silver screen is used while showing three dimensional pictures because it gives a better illusion of depth than other surfaces.

The beaded screen on tripod, which is portable, is good for showing pictures in the villages. For class room, we can hang bigger screens on the wall and have black curtains for shows in the day-time.

Formula for working out the size and distance of screen from projector:

$$\frac{w \times d}{f} = W, \text{ or } w \times d = w \times f$$

Were w = width of the projector in inches.

d = distance of the projector from the screen in feet.

f = focal length of the lens in inches.

W = width of the screen in feet.

Aperture width and focal length of the lens of a projector can be easily ascertained and when the two values are known it is possible to calculate "w" when "d" is known and vice-versa. Each type of projector has a standard aperture size as given in Table 32.6.

Table 32.6
Aperture sizes of projectors

		Aperture width—"w"	Aperture height
1.	8 mm Projector	0.772″	0.129″
2.	16 mm Projector	0.380″	0.284″
3.	35 mm Projector	0.825″	0.600″
4.	35 mm Still projector (single frame)	0.900″	0.680″
5.	2″ × 2″ Slide projector	1.300″	0.900″

Example. (a) Distance at which screen should be placed: A 16 mm projector using an objective lens of focal length of 2″ is to project a film on to a screen of 6′ × 8′. Find out the distance at which the screen should be placed

Here f = 2″, w = 0.38 and W = 8′. "d" can be easily calculated

$$w \times d = w \times f \text{ or } \frac{W \times f}{w} = d$$

therefore, $d = \frac{8 \times 2}{0.38} = \frac{16}{0.38} = 42.1$ feet

Example. (b) Size of the screen in width: A 16 mm projector is having an objective lens of focal length of 1″ and is to be placed at a distance of 13 feet from the screen. Find out the width of the screen you will require for showing the film show.
Here   d = 13, w = 0.38″, f = 7″

$$W = \frac{w \times d}{f} = \frac{0.38 \times 13}{1} = 4.94', \text{ or roughly 5 feet should be the width of the screen.}$$

Example. (c) Height of the screen: The ratio of width and height should be 4 : 3. In example (b) above, where the width of the screen is 5 feet or 60 inches, its height shall be 3.9 feet or roughly 4 feet or 45 inches.

PHOTOGRAPHIC EQUIPMENT AND PHOTOGRAPHY

There is nothing more interesting to people than to see themselves in pictures. Picture-taking of the various stages in getting a demonstration established, for example, can be used effectively in showing large groups of villagers, many of whom may be in the pictures. For groups of people, numbering about fifteen, slides, film-strips or movies are most effective.

Care should be taken, therefore, to insure that every picture tells a story or teaches a lesson.

Cameras

The types of cameras are;

(i) *Miniature cameras:* Such cameras are very small. Simple types are used by children. Some special purpose cameras are: (1) *Spy camera*—which can fit into the palm of a hand. It is used for pictures taken secretly. (2) *Wrist camera*—It is no bigger than a wrist watch and can be strapped to the hand just like a wrist watch.

(ii) *Box camera:* This is the simplest of all cameras. At one end it has a large hole covered by a simple planner type of lens, the aperture of which cannot be varied. Some box cameras have a reflex type of view-finder.

(iii) *Folding cameras:* These types of cameras are: (a) *View cameras*—Such cameras are used by professional photographers to take pictures for advertising. The "saw-toothed bellow", a cloth box between front and back, can be squeezed or pulled out, twisted and turned. Sheet films or plates are fit into the back. The front has a movable holder for different lenses. When in use, this camera is attached to a tripod, that holds it steady. (b) *Press camera*—This is a kind of view camera built specially for newspaper photography and is built very ruggedly to endure rough handling, yet it always give good pictures. (c) *Studio camera*—This is an oversize camera. It is put on a tripod which may even be wheeled. This is generally used in the portrait photo-grapher's studio

(iv) *Twin lens reflex:* "Upstairs" lens focusses an image in the finder corresponding exactly to the one that the lower lens focusses on the film. One side of the camera is open to show how it is built.

(v) *Aerial camera:* This camera has an enormous lens. When aimed straight down from the plane, it photographs miles and miles of a country. Such cameras are used in making maps.

(vi) *Movie camera:* This is driven by a spring or an electric motor and the film moves through the camera. The tiny claw, automatically inserted into holes along the sides of the films, pulls the film through a channel the "filmgate". Thers is a spring in the gate just opposite the lens of the camera. Here the film stops for an instant while the shutter opens just long enough for an exposure. When the shutter closes, the film lets in light and the claw pulls fresh film into position for the exposure of another frame. This happens many times every second. The usual rate of speed is 16 frames per second (Fig. 32.19).

Parts of a camera—lens, diaphragm and shutters

The photographer, before taking a picture, should ensure that the lens is correctly focussed, that the shutter is set for correct timing and that the diaphragm is adjusted to the correct opening before taking a picture. These settings depend on whether the light on the subject (of which the picture is being taken) is bright or dim. The light can be measured by an exposure meter.

A complex shutter can be set so that when it is set it will remain open exactly as long as photographer wants. To catch the action of a rapidly moving object this shutter can be set to open for only 1/800th of a second. For a still object, the photographer can set the shutter for one "full shutter" or for a time exposure.

Diaphragm: The diaphragm opening can also be made larger or smaller to suit the photographer's needs. The larger the opening, the more light will pass through and strike the film. The various diaphragm openings are called "stops". Stops are shown by symbol "f" followed by such numbers as: f/6.5, f/8, f/11, f/16 and f/32. These show that the larger the number, the smaller the stop. A box camera is set to take pictures at a diaphragm opening of f/16 and a shutter speed of about 1/25 second.

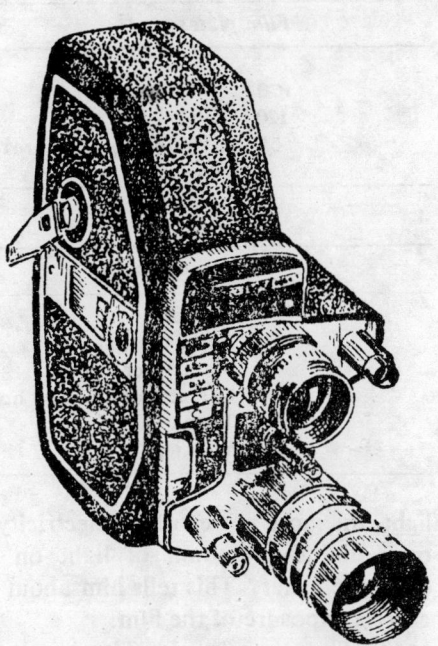

Fig. 32.19. Moive camera.

Lens: A lens designed to let in more light is called a falter lens.

Shutter: This is a chopper of light. There are two types of shutters.

(1) *Irish shutter:* An Irish shutter is a plane with a definite hole sizes. It may be (a) Plate type, (b) Circular shutter, and (c) The modern type Irish shutter. The Circular shutter has different sizes of circular holes on a circular plate which can be rotated and the holes are adjusted over the lens. The Irish shutter consists of several iron plates which cover one another. It is situated near the lens.

(2) *Focal plane shutter:* The shutter moves at the focal plane. As it moves over the film or plate, it does not check the light. This is adjusted over the film and moves when the shutter is released. The shutter moves all over the film. The opening, in constant movement, is finished within a short time of e.g., 1/100 of a second and illuminated all parts of film (Table 32.7).

Point to be remembered. There is one word SAFER which will help in remembering all the precautions.

(1) The camera should not be shaken—hold your breath and press. The subject must be at a standstill.

(2) Do not obstruct the lens.

(3) Do not move the camera up and down.

(4) Do not take pictures against the sun.

(5) Wind the film after each exposure.

Accessories to the camera

The accessories of a camera are:

(1) *Exposure meter:* Exposure meters are of many types, but inside all there is a photo-electronic cell in which electrical energy is generated by light. The brighter the

Table 32.7
Film size and shutter speed

Film plates		Film size
620	8 exposures	$3\frac{1}{4} \times 2\frac{1}{4}$ inches
120	12	$2\frac{1}{4} \times 2\frac{1}{4}$,,
35 mm	36 or 20 exposures	24×36 mm

Shutter speed	Per second
Aircraft	1/600
Express train	1/500
Horse race	1/250
Car at 40 miles per hour	1/300
Tonga	1/100
Walking	1/50

light, the more powerful the electricity. A moving needle, electrically controlled, shows on a dial the amount of light on the subject at which the photographer aims the exposure meter. This tells him about the shutter time and diaphragm stop to use for correct exposure of the film.

(2) *Flash attachment:* There are two types of flashes: (a) battery-operated, and (b) electronic flashes. These flashes help in taking pictures where there is insufficient light.

(a) *Battery-operated flashes:* In the battery-operated flashes, the flash bulbs are used which go off when the camera is clicked. These bulbs are attached to the flash gun which has batteries and a reflector. A new bulb is fitted for every snap. This is synchronised or timed to go off just at the instant the button is pressed to take a picture. The flash gun holds the batteries. The flash gun is fitted in the camera at the place provided. When the button is pushed, the electrical connection between the batteries and the flash bulb sets off the bulb. After taking the picture, flip the lower lever at the back of the flash gun and the bulb pops out, or it can be lifted out. After that, wind the film, insert another bulb and get ready for the next picture.

Some flash guns have a printed table at the back of the reflector. On this list is the type of bulbs to be used for different distances. For coloured film, use blue coloured bulbs which may cost about Rs. 5.00. Ordinary bulbs are available at about Rs. 3.50 each.

(b) *Electronic flash guns:* These are operated by electronics. In this case, there is no need to use bulbs which may go off for each picture exposed. One electronic flash gun of Hopt may cost about Rs. 520. It lasts for many years without any running cost except ordinary torch batteries, when electricity is not used[1] (Fig. 32.20).

Automatic picture taking
Some cameras have an automatic arrangement. In these, the photographer himself

[1]Hopt type by Libert Industries, Hyderabad, India.

can adjust the camera with distance, light, timing, etc., on the tripod stand. After making this setting, he comes to the place at which he set or joins the group of which the picture is being taken. The camera takes about nine seconds to click itself and expose the film.

Handling the movie camera

(G.B. & Howell 6-27 16 mm Cine Camera)

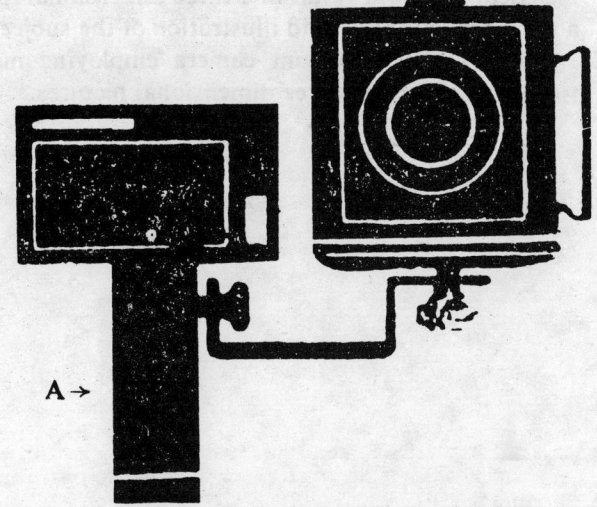

- (a) Before filming the footage indicator is to be set at zero.
- (b) Wind the motor key.
- (c) Remove the lens cap and clean the lens with lens-cleaning tissue or linen.
- (d) Ascertain the required lens aperture by means of an exposure meter.

A →

Fig. 32.20. Electronic flash gun (Hopt) A.

- (e) Adjust the lens aperture.
- (f) Focus the lens of camera if not a fixed focus one.
- (g) Looking through the view-finder, compose the scene nicely.
- (h) Set the camera to the required speed say 24 frames per second.
- (i) Press the release button.

Angle of filming

Do not shoot only horizontally or on the eye-level of the subject. But find new and interesting angles, sometimes taking downwards and upwards shots. The subjects appear taller when the shots are taken upwards and shorter when taken downwards. Take the majority of the shots from near the subject. If the camera has a close-up lens, better take close-ups. Use tripod for steady filming.

Length of scenes

Eight to ten scenes are considered to be sufficient for scenes for every-day life. This time may be reduced to 5 to 6 seconds for taking close ups such as head and shoulders. For shooting an action 13-15 seconds are sufficient. Do not turn the camera from one point to another while picture is being taken.

Editing the film

In editing, all inferior shots should be discarded and the shots rearranged in sequence in the film. Titles should be arranged and inserted in the appropriate places.

Three dimensional pictures

Such pictutres may be obtained with the use of stereorgraphs and the stereoscopes. The stereograph is a card containing two pictures usually photographed by a camera with twin lenses. This is a simple device with two separate lenses and facilities for holding the stereograph. Adjust the position of the stereograph until it is properly focussed. This will result in a three dimensional picture. A third dimension provides a more realistic and vivid illustration of the subject.

Stereo-realist a 35 mm camera employing matched lenses and producing twin transparencies takes three dimensional pictures.

CHAPTER 33

AUDIO-AIDS RECORDING

There are three ways of recording the sound: (1) Mechanical, (2) Magnetic process and (3) Optical process. Disc recording is done by the mechanical process. Tape and Wire recording is done by the magnetic process and recording of sound on a movie film by the optical process.

DISC RECORDING

In the discs or Gramophone records, discs of lac and plastic are usually used. In broadcasting transcriptions lacquer coated discs of glass and metal are used. They are embossed and engraved. They can be used for teaching, group meetings, entertainments, etc. The rates of revolutions per minute of the disc are 78, 45 or $33\frac{1}{3}$. The $33\frac{1}{3}$ r.p.m. records are long playing (L.P.), having 16 inches diameter and taking 15 minutes for each side, or 33 minutes from both. The common gramphone records revolve at 78 revolutions per minute and take approximately 3 minutes for one side. A disc with 45 r.p.m. takes about 5 minutes. The recording time depends upon the size of the disc per inch when the speed of the revolution remains constant.

The disc recordings require an electric turnable with pick-up attachment or a spring turnable (Gramophone) with sound box attachment to be played back. The gramophone consists of one turnable to be rotated by spring mechanism and a sound box. The turnable rotates the record at the rated speed and the sound box produces sound. The sound box with its pin is placed slowly on the rotating record and the fine point of the pin or needle is made to vibrate by the grooves cut on the record. These mechanical vibrations are transmitted to the diaphragm of the sound box and cause vibrations in it. These vibrations come to the ears of the listeners as the original sound recorded on the disc.

The modern equipment known as the record player contains a turn-table, a pick-up, an amplifier and a speaker, all in one unit. On it can be used all the three types of record discs having different speeds, it can be made to rotate at a particular speed by means of a sliding lever. The latest models of record players are fitted with automatic record changers by which 10 to 50 records can be played one after another, on one side only. After one side is played, they can be reversed. This saves time and the labour for changing the record every time.

Operating a record player: (1) Read the manual of the manufacturer and ascertain the rated voltage and frequency of the record player.

(2) Varify the electricity requirement and your current supply. Some American models operate on 110 V. AC-60 cycles supply. In this case, a step-down transformer is required. So plug in the record player only when you are sure that the rated voltage is available.

(3) Switch on the record player. Its amplifier takes a minute or two to warm up. Advance the volume control and hear if there is the typical howling sound coming from the speakers. The sound indicates that the electric circuit of the equipment is in order.

(4) See that the pick-up has good needle. Some costly needles are now available which can be used for years.

(5) Set the turn-table speed to the proper value depending upon the specification of the record to be played.

(6) Place the record on the turn-table. If the record player incorporates an Automatic record changer, place a set of records in position. Just press the button of the record changer and the turn-table will start functioning.

(7) Adjust the volume and tone controls.

(8) After removing all the records, switch off the record player and remove the plug from the line supply.

WIRE RECORDING

The wire employed for this purpose is a steel wire which has diameter of four to five mils, (1 mil= 1/1000th of an inch). The process of magnetic recording on this wire is based on the working principle of an electro-magnet. When the microphone of the wire recorder picks up the sound to be recorded, feeble electric currents are generated in the coils of the microphone. The alternating electric currents are amplified by an amplifier incorporated in the recorder and are fed into the coils of the recording head, which is an electro-magnet. When the recording wire passes through the recording head it is influenced by the magnetic field lying across recording head, and a series of magnetic fields remain throughout the length of the recording wire. These magnetic fields vary from one another depending upon the pattern of sound waves picked up by the microphone.

In the process of playback, the reverse process takes, i.e., the magnetised wire passing through the playing head of the wire recorder induces alternating electric current in the coils of the playing head which, when amplified and fed into the speaker, produces the sound orignally recorded. The recording head is also used as the playing head in playback.

This wire is available in spools which are of three types: (1) lasting for 15 minutes, (2) $\frac{1}{2}$ hour, and (3) one hour. Erasing can also be done. So the same wire can be used again and again.

TAPE RECORDING

Using the principle of magnetic recording, recording can be done on tapes made of paper, plastic or metal. The plastic and paper tapes are very thin, having a width of

1/4 inch. These have an ultra thin coating of iron oxide on one of their sides. The metal tape is incorporated in the tape recorder itself as a continuous belt for recording. The plastic or paper tapes are wound in spools. The tape recorder accommodates two spools, one empty take-up spool and the other containing tape for recording or play-back as the case may be. It operates on the same principle as the wire recorder. In it we use iron oxide coated tape in place of steel wire. Old recordings can be erased, and splicing at broken tape is possible by using Scotch Tape. Such tapes are light, compact and can be stored for a long time.

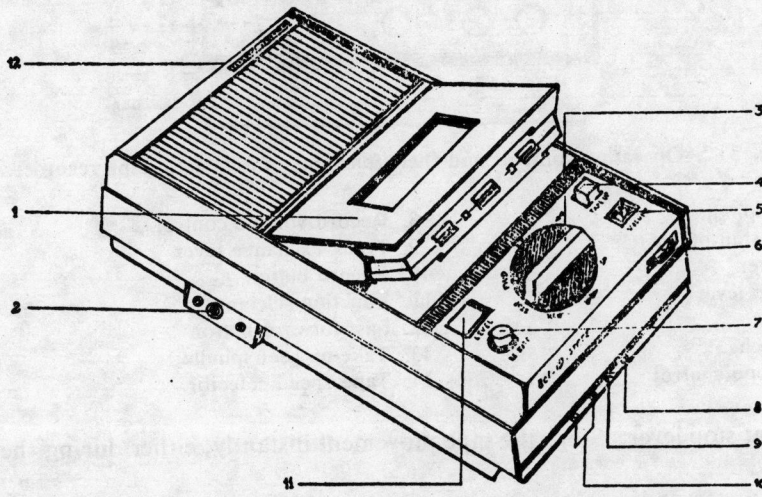

Fig. 33.1. Cassette tape recorder.

Functions of seven important controls and connectors (Fig. 33.1):
(1) Cassette compartment—for inserting cassette.
(2) A.C. adapter jack—for A.C. operation.
(3) Functions selector—Controls the functions of fast forward, rewind, play and stop. By turning it to the respective place the desired effect can be obtained.
(4) Tape-up button—For lifting cassette compartment.
(5) Volume indicator—For visual checking of volume level.
(6) Volume control—For adjusting the volume during playback.
(7) Recording button—To be used along with functions selector for recording.

How to operate a tape recorder (Fig. 33.2)

Various types of tape recorders are: R.C.A., Philips, Ferrograph, Amro, Magnetape, Revere, Grundig and Ekotape. Their principles are generally the same. However the manufactures manual should be studied when the tape recorder to be used for the first time by the user.
(1) Feed reel spindle: Carries the reel with tape.
(2) Automatic shut-off switch: Automatically stop the machine when the tape breaks or runs out.
(3) Tape counter is also known as position indicator. It helps to locate individual recordings.

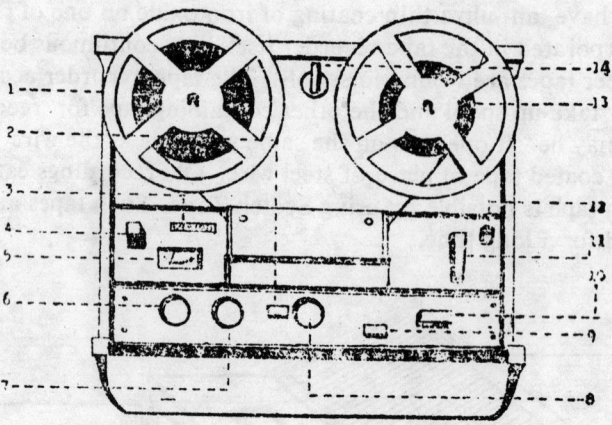

Fig. 33.2. Operating controls and their functions in a cassette tape recorder.

1. Feed reel spindle
2. Automatic shut-off switch
3. Tape counter
4. Instant stop lever
5. Level meter
6. Power switch
7. Playback tone control
8. Record volume control
9. Track exchange lever
10. Record button
11. Function selector
12. Fast forward button
13. Take-up reel spindle
14. Tape speed selector.

(4) Instant stop lever: Stops the tape movement instantly, either during the recording or replay.

(5) Level meter: Indicates the current in the recording head. Too little current will have an unsatisfactory signal to noise creation. If there is too much noise the result is distortion.

(6) Power switch: Function is on and off and volume control.

(7) Playback tone control: Adjusts the playback tone quality.

(8) Record volume control: Helps in adjusting the level of sound during recording.

(9) Track exchange lever: Selects tape tracks for recording or replay.

(10) Record button: For recording, this button should be pressed first and then the function selector should be moved to forward position.

(11) Function selector: Selects all tape functions like rewind, stop, forward, etc.

(12) Fast forward button: To move the tape forward rapidly.

(13) Take-up reel spindle: Carries empty reel.

(14) Tape speed selector: To select the desired tape speed.

Useful hints for the operator

(1) Know your recorder thoroughly. If it is to run off 60 cycles, get a 50 cycles adopter for it on 50 cycles supply in India.

(2) If it runs on 110 volts, use a transformer.

(3) Plug in the tape recorder to the socket of the electric supply line when the correct voltage supply is available.

(4) Switch on the recorder and allow the amplifier to take a couple of minutes to

warm up. Advance the volume control a little till you hear the typical howling sound from the speaker. This means that the electric circuit of the recorder is in order.

Recording a programme—loading the machine

(1) Turn selector switch to wind on.

(2) Load reel on left spindle with free end of the tape in front and with coated side of the tape inside.

(3) Take free end of empty reel on the right. Attach it and wind a few turns by hand.

(4) Draw more tape in front of small peg on the right side of the cover.

(5) Start motor and wind on.

(6) See that the tape is in front of small peg on right side of the recorder.

(7) Do not touch main selector switch when tape is running.

Selection of speed

On the recorder, there is a knob marked L and H meaning Low and High. L is 3 inches per second. Turn this knob only when the machine is stopped. Some recorders have additional speeds of 1-7/8 inches and 15 inches per second. The speed indicates the rate of movement of the tape over the recording head per second. The speed of 15″ per second is very good for recording music, orchestras, etc. Speech can be recorded at $3\frac{1}{4}″$ per second. The speed of $7\frac{1}{2}″$ per second is quite alright for recording music. So adjust the speed by selector switch.

(1) To begin recording, press the recording button of the recorder and simutaneously advance the volume control to see that the over-load lamp of the recorder does not glow, while the recording lamp fluctuates when recording goes on.

(2) Watch the recording lamp always. If fluctutions do not appear in the recording lamp, just advance the volume control a little till the fluctuations appear in the recording lamp. But take care that the overload lamp does not glow.

(3) When the programme is over, press the button marked "STOP".

Rewinding of the recorded talk

When you want to hear what you have recorded, return the volume control to minimum and press the rewinding button. After rewinding, press the "STOP" button to stop the machine. At this stage, the talk is recorded, and it can be reporduced or played back.

To play back recorded matter

(1) Place the spool containing the recorded tape on the left spindle and let the tape pass through the recording head (here playback head or playing head) to the empty spool placed in the right spindle.

Press the playing button and adjust the volume and tone controls. Here you get the recordings played back. Press the "STOP" button when you want to stop the machine.

Push button

Five buttons allow automatic operation of the recorders as follows:

(a) Fast: For rapidly rewinding the tapes which has been recorded or played.

(b)	Record:	For making a tape recording, or for automatically erasing the previous one.
(c)	Stop:	For stopping, without shutting-off the main power switch.
(d)	Play:	For listening to a tape which contains recorded materials.
(e)	Fast:	For advancing the tape at an especially fast rate in order to play back or begin recording at some inside spot on the reel or tape.

Erasing

Erasing of a recorded talk, etc., can be done in two ways. To erase a recording from a particular portion of the tape just let the portion of it pass through the recording head when the recording button is pressed. This simple operation is enough to erase the recording from the tape. The alternative method is to use a recorded tape for recording when the new recording is impressed on the tape, the old recording automatically vanishes. The second method is used for editing a complete recording when additions and alterations are necessary. So recording requires careful handling.

Uses of tape recorder

A tape recorder can be used for many purposes. The uses mostly depend upon the imagination of the teacher and the taught. The following are some of the more important uses:

(1) It helps the teacher and student alike to hear the recording of their voices and makes them much more critical of their own speech; thereby it provides an effective means of self-instruction.

(2) It enables the extension worker to be in more than one place at a time.

(3) It facilitates editing of sounds—shortening, eliminating, or adding of materials from many different sources.

(4) It helps in preservation of sounds for future use.

(5) It can be used for evaluation of sounds.

(6) It helps transportation of sounds from one place to another.

(7) It is used for duplication of sounds.

(8) It helps in synchronisation of sound with pictures.

(9) It is of great help in the teaching and learning of foreign languages

(10) It is used in the learning and teaching of music.

(11) It helps the practice of public speaking.

(12) It is used for rectifying defective speech.

(13) It can be used for recording radio plays, dialogues, group discussions, symposia, role-playing, interviews and songs by extension workers. Thus recorded tapes can be used in different teaching situations.

(14) It is of immense help in drama rehearsals and various extension education programmes.

The uses outlined in the foregoing paragraph are only a few of the possible uses of the magnetic recorder available to the resourceful teacher either in the class or outside the class room.

Ten features to look for in a tape recorder

(1) *Simplicity:* Most of the tape recorders are easy to operate. You should choose one which has the minimum number of buttons and knobs. The 'cassette' tape is the simplest of all.

(2) *Protability:* The recording equipment should be as light as possible. Specially the one which is intended to be used exclusively in extension field activities. Generally the recorders are classified into four types. Each type is appropriate for a specific situation.

(i) Heavy-duty class room unit—The largest recorder built for class room use, it weights about 15 kg. A trolly is usually necessary to move it from room to room but it is most often mounted permanently at one place.

(ii) Portable class room unit—Weighing about 11 kg, can easily be carried from room to room.

(iii) Tape deck unit—Used in a fixed location e.g., information recording studios, language laboratories and radio recording stations, etc.

(iv) Light weight portable—This model weighs less and is battery powered, but can also be used on AC or DC current. For outside class room use, these are very useful. The cassette recorders belong to this category.

(3) *Cost:* The amount of money available should be carefully considered before purchasing the equipment. Secondly, the selection should not be based only on the cost of the equipment. Generally expensive equipment is durable and as a result it may prove cheaper in the long run.

(4) *Construction:* Strong construction is very important because generally the tape recorders are portable in nature and have to be moved from place to place, especially the ones which run on batteries should be as strong as possible.

(5) *Speed:* The higher the speed used, the better will be the quality. If you want to record good music with the utmost fidelity, one of the recorders that operates at 15 I.P.S. will be useful. If you want it mainly to listen to recordings of classical music $7\frac{1}{2}$ I.P.S. is the best speed for it gives excellent reproduction.

If you only want to record a speech, and economy is more important than fidelity, the slow speed of 1-7/8 or even 15/16 I.P.S. may be alright. Many people find a happy compromise by purchasing a machine with two speeds usually $7\frac{1}{2}$ and $3\frac{3}{4}$ I.P.S. In case the equipment is to be used for a variety of purposes and in a variety of places, it should have several speeds such as 1-7/8, $3\frac{3}{4}$, $7\frac{1}{2}$ and 15 I.P.S. The faster the playing speed, the more tape you will use to record a given piece of music or speech.

(6) *Size of the tape reels:* Different machine will use different sizes. Some use 3″ diameter reels; many models use 5″ or $5\frac{3}{4}$″ reels. There is a greater advantage in using 7″ or even $8\frac{1}{4}$″ reels. 64 minutes of recording, or replay, can be done if a 5″ reel is used at $7\frac{1}{2}$ I.P.S. speed on a double track machine. But if it is a 7″ reel, the duration of recording or replay will be double.

(7) *Recording tracks:* The tape recorders can be classified according to the nature of the recording and replay heads fitted to it. Some have single track recording, some others have double track, four tracks and more. The important point to be understood here is, each time you double the number of recording tracks, you halve the width of the tape.

On a four track recording machine you will get twice as much material on to a given spool of tape as with two tracks. For recording long speeches and to play lengthy uninterrupted music, the four track tape recorder is very economical. However, it will be wise to spend your money on a good basic quality rather than the dispensable 'extras'.

(8) *Frequency range:* In fact one of the most important points to be considered in making the selection is the sound frequency range of the equipment, and the programmes you plan to record. Every sound has a frequency range expressed in term of cycles per second. The male voice usually has a range between 100 and 8,300 cycles per second, and the female voice usually between 170 and 10,000 cycles per second. But many musical instruments have a much wider frequency range varying from 30 to 16,000 cycles per second. For high fidelity recording, the frequency range of the equipment should be similar to the frequency range of the sounds in the programme.

(9) *Company and dealer:* You should choose this carefully. It is always better if you choose tape recorders from well known companies and reputed dealers. Preference should be given to a local dealer who can service the equipment.

(10) *Performance:* You should operate the various controls by yourself in the dealers shop itself to make sure that everything is alright.

PUBLIC ADDRESS EQUIPMENT

These include: microphone, amplifier and loudspeaker. A pick-up with an electric turn-table or spring turn-table is used in the public address equipments when recordings are played. The microphone and the pick-ups are connected to the inputs terminals of the amplifier, and the loudspeaker is connected to the output terminals. The microphone converts sound waves into alternating electric currents which are fed into the amplifier. The amplifier is an electronic device to amplify these electric currents. The amplified electric currents fluctuate in accordance with the vibrations of the sound waves. When these amplified electric currents are fed into the loudspeaker, it converts them into sound waves and we hear the loud voice of the speaker. All these processes take no time to be completed and so the sound picked up by the microphone is reproduced simultaneously by the loudspeaker (Fig. 33.3).

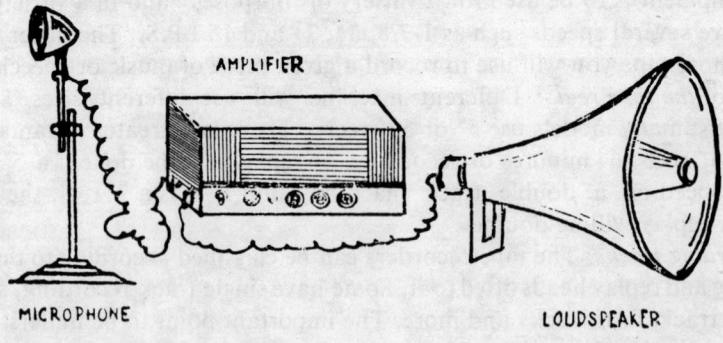

Fig. 33.3. Public address equipment.

An amplifier requires electricity which may come from dry battery, wet battery or A.C./D.C. power supply.

Operating the public address equipment

(1) Note the special characteristics of the microphone, the amplifier, the pick-up and the loudspeaker, if any, and ascertain the voltage necessary to run the amplifier.

(2) Connect the microphone into the proper input terminals of the amplifier and, if necessary, connect the pick-up into the input marked "Phono".

(3) Connect the loudspeaker to the proper output terminals of the amplifier. A loudspeaker connected to the improper output terminals of the amplifier is mismatched and so produces distortion in sound. An amplifier has many output terminals, but the pair suited to the particular speaker should be selected,

(4) Connect the amplifier to the proper power supply. Use a step-down transformer if the amplifier runs on 110 volts supply and the power supply is 220 volts. If you are using a generator, adjust its voltage.

(5) Switch on the amplifier and see that its pilot lamp glows. If the pilot lamp does not glow, it means that electricity is not fed into the amplifier, or the lamp is defective. Try to locate the defect in the connecting wires, electric supply, plug point or the pilot lamp. It takes some time to warm up and a typical sound is produced on advancing the volume control a little. Some amplifiers use more than one microphone in addition to the pick-up and separate volume controls for each of the microphones and the pick-ups in use. The volume control which is in the circuit of the microphone or the pick-up used should be operated, and other unused volume controls should be kept at their minimum.

(6) To test the microphone, repeat some word like "Testing". Never blow air from your mouth, it is moist and will damage the sensitive microphone. If testing is not successful, locate the fault in the connections, or in any other circuit of the system.

(7) Place the microphone at a distance of about 10 inches from the speaker. When your test shows that the microphone is picking up sound, advance the volume control and adjust the tone control to get the volume of the desired sound.

(8) When you use a pick-up to play a recording, bring all volume controls to zero and advance the volume control of the pick-up circuit to the desired extent.

(9) It is better to have a highly directional microphone because it is pick-up sound only from one direction, and so does not produce feedback, i. e., the howling sound coming from the speaker when the microphone faces it. If you do not have a microphone having "highly directional properties" you can avoid the feedback by placing the speaker at a considerable distance from the microphone.

RADIO

Radio is a good source of communication of ideas to the rural people especially in a country like India. It carries news bulletins and special programmes for rural people, housewives and children. This is a good source of dissemination of agricultural information to farmers. Forums are now organised under the joint auspices of All India Radio and the State Community Development Departments. The All India Radio stations publish a Journal *Akashvani* which gives the metres and frequency in kilo cycles on medium and short waves.

Handling a radio set

The radio receiving set receives only one selected programme at a time, and conveys the same through its speaker. The station is selected by a tuner of the receiving set which tunes the set to the frequency of the station. The movement of the tuner over the dial of the radio set is controlled by rotating the tuning knob located on the cabinet. The entire broadcast frequency range is divided into a number of bands, each band including a small range of frequencies or wave-lengths. A band selector switch or knob is incorporated in the cabinet of the radio. There is also an on and off switch, a volume control and a tone control to the radio. In most of the radios, the on and off switch and the volume control are incorporated in a single knob. Many costly radios have sockets to accommodate the pick-up jacks of the turn-tables when the recordings are amplified by the amplifying circuit of the radio and reproduced through its speaker or any other external speaker connected into the terminals and the output transferer.

Power for radios

A radio can be operated by dry battery, wet battery, alternating current (A.C.) or direct current (D.C.). For rural areas with no electricity, dry battery sets should be used. In case of wet battery sets, the charging creates a problem.

Installing a radio

Aerial and Earthing is very necessary for better functioning of the radios.

(1) *Aerials:* Aerials can be outdoor as well as indoor. An outdoor aerial is better. It can be "T" type or "L" type (Inverted). "T" type is said to be better. While fixing the outdoor aerial, use two bamboos. You should never use a stud on iron pole for it. In case of a portable radio, there is no necessity for an outside aerial because it has a built-in aerial. In a transistor set, there is no necessity for an aerial.

(2) *Earth connection:* It can be done by burying the end of the wire at least one foot deep underground. In case of a portable radio, just connect a small length of wire to the "earth" lead chassis.

Operating a radio

(1) Plug in the radio to the power socket.

(2) Switch it on. It will take some time to warm up. The transistor set does not require time to warm up.

(3) Advance the volume control a little.

(4) If the radio has a "magic eye" do not advance the volume control.

(5) Tune the radio to the frequency of the desired station by rotating the tuning knob.

(6) When you have caught the station as indicated by the magic eye, advance the volume control and adjust the tone control or the base-treble selector switch. In tuning a radio which has no magic eye advance the volume control and be sure that the desired station is caught.

(7) Never move the tuner when the volume control is considerably advanced because by doing so the speaker gets damaged.

(8) The radio should face the group and the group can be seated in a semi-circle.

Nature of the medium

Radio is a spoken means of communication. The broadcaster has to get and hold the attention of the audience, otherwise the message is lost. Radio is transient and fleeting. Its impression is quick and faint. It is one-way communication. The message should be simple and clear so that people can understand it and act.

Radio, a "mass communication" tool, can:

Inform;

Stimulate curiosity;

Arouse and build interest;

Create the desire to learn, see, hear and act;

Widen horizons and mental outlook, break down prejudices, and bring enlightenment;

Promote favourable attitudes and influence emotions:

Inspire to some form of action;

Interpret policies.

Guide listeners' interest; and

Help them grasp the significance of new ideas and thoughts.

Use

Radio is a very fast medium. It is popular, pleasing, even exciting. However, it cannot be used to convey heavy, detailed knowledge.

It can be used for:

Announcement—meetings, demonstration, etc.,

Intimation or information—regarding availability of materials, prices, places, etc.;

Warnings—relating to weather, outbreaks of diseases, pests;

Seasonal hints;

News stories;

News reviews—about farmers, etc.,

Interviews;

Questions and answers;

Short talks;

Plays, skits, ballads, burrakatha, etc.;

Features; and

Documentaries.

Advantages

The radio:

Can reach more people more quickly than any other means of communication;

Can disseminate timely and urgent information;

Is relatively cheap.

Can reach illiterates; and

Builds enthusiasm and maintains interest.

Limitations

Some severe limitations to the use of radio are:

Broadcasting facilities are available only in limited places:

Time assigned to extension is limited;
Frequently losses out in competition with entertainment;
Difficult to check on results;
Requires a special technique;
Not enough sets in rural areas; and
Influence is limited to people who can listen intelligently.

CHAPTER 34

OTHER TEACHING AIDS

NON-PROJECTED AUDIO-VISUALS

(1) Puppets

Puppets can be interesting aids for telling stories to the village people. The puppets may be: (1) Glove or hand puppets, (2) String puppets, (3) Rod puppets, and (4) Shadow puppets. A glove or hand puppet is simple to handle for the students and they can prepare some stories which can be shown with the help of these puppets. Such puppets can also be prepared by the students in the class or at homes.

Glove or hand puppets

This is like a three-fingered glove which fits on the hand. The first finger is inserted inside the head and moves it, when we tell a story. The middle finger and thumb fit in the hands and move them. (Fig. 34.1)

How to prepare a hand puppet. Material required: A used post card, old newspaper, glue, two pieces of string, Indian ink, colour box, pins and brushes, scraps of coloured cloth, a pair of scissors, needle and thread.

Procedure: (1) Roll the piece of used post card around your finger. Glue it into a firm tube which fits the finger.

(2) Crumple a piece of paper into a ball of the size of your finger, press this ball over and around the tube on your finger, and give it the shape of a head.

(3) Tie a piece of plain paper and use Indian ink to put on eyes, hair, nose, lips, etc., and put red and black colours as needed to give it an attractive appearance.

Fig. 34.1. Puppets

(4) Take a piece of bright coloured cloth and sew it into a long tube and tie the cloth on the neck and then turn it.

(5) Some puppets may be prepared to play roles of females, some of males or children. They may have moustaches, turbans, salwars, kurtas, etc., depicting the life and characters you want to show to the audience.

(6) The stage for the show of puppets can be prepared by using a wooden frame,

two chairs, one cot, two pillars of verandah, two charpoys.

(7) The puppets should not be seen with the hands or body of the puppeteers. Songs or speech from the back or recorded talk are used. Usually, two puppeteers are behind the stage and so only four characters can be on the stage at a time. The actual voices of men, women and children can be imitated (Fig 34.2).

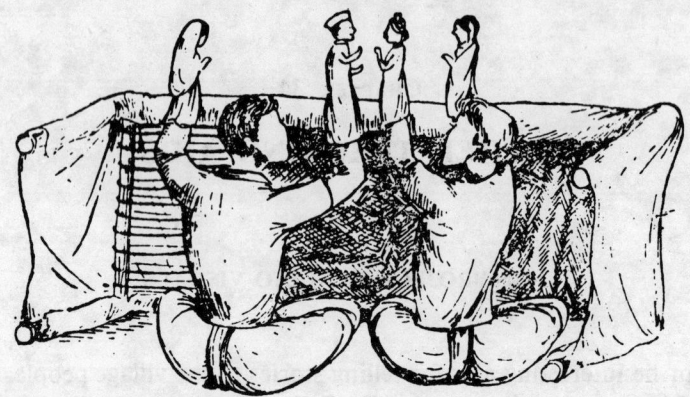

Fig. 34.2. Stage and how to show a puppet.

(8) Before the show, a brief description of the dialogue is given. There should not be silent pauses. The dialogue should be quick, and speeches and scenes should be short. There should be lot of actions, wit and humour.

(9) Everyday people and familiar situations should be used which have relationship with village problems.

(2) Drama

The students of the extension wings of Agricultural or Veterinary Colleges with the help of their teachers, teachers of village schools, VLW's and villagers, can arrange to produce dramas in their villages. This is a good source of entertainment and education for the villagers. One-act plays, depicting the village life, its problems and solutions, can be written and prepared with simple themes. The school building or any such place, which has a stage and some place for the village audience to sit can be used for it. A curtain, if possible, with village pictures printed on it may be used as a backdrop. Petromax or lantern or electricity, either from power line or generator, can provide the lighting (Fig. 34.3.

Fig. 34.3. Staging a drama in a village (Kurki by money-lender).

The subjects for drama stories may be: (1) Poor yields and role of demonstrations on improved practices, (2) Working and organisation of the C.D. programme, (3) Role of democratic decentralisation through village leaders, (4) Youth, Mahila and Krishak Mandals, (5) How to handle village problems like purdah, child marriage, waste of money through ceremonies, etc., (6) Dowry, a big evil, (7) Solving problems of education, health, sanitation, credit, middlemen etc., (8) Role of cooperatives, etc., and (9) The extension wing and how villagers can be benefited from it, etc.

(3) Folk songs and folk dances

The village have a great fascination for their folk songs and dances. We go closer to them if we participate with them and organise such functions, at times exhibitions, meetings, film-shows, drama, etc. Songs connected with the development programmes and practices in local dialects can be composed by some student or villager and sung with the help of Harmonium, Tabla, Sarangi, Jhanj, Chimta, etc. This is a good way of conveying the information to the villagers. Competitions for songs and dances can be arranged and even some prizes given, if possible. The Block staff has some funds for such programmes.

USE OF TALKS, MEETINGS, CONFERENCES, TOURS, CAMPAIGNS, CAMPS, ETC., FOR EXTENSION

Talks

Public speaking

A good speaker can influence people. Confidence and courage are necessary for making a good speech. Fear and discouragement create obstacles. Doing things, which one fears to do, can remove fear from the speaker. Better preparation may develop confidence. This preparation means assembling of thoughts, ideas, conventions, experience and urges. It requires concentration and thinking. Speaking in a class will prepare the student of extension for making speeches in the villages. The student should be motivated to speak by assigning some marks of the practical work for speeches in the class and villages.

Preparation: (1) Choose the topic of speech at least seven days before the talk.

(2) Do not try to cover a large ground.

(3) Talk about the topic.

(4) Converse on the topic with your friends.

(5) Think of your experience for illustrations.

(6) Think of your audience, what they want and what can be of interest to them.

(7) Read, and find out what others think about the subject.

(8) Select and arrange the material which you have gained through the above process.

(9) Assemble your thoughts, take those which are desirable and which are tuned to the audience requirements and discard the undesirable.

(10) Read extensively to have reserve information.

(11) Plan your speech.

(12) Write the speech and rewrite after polishing it.

(13) Read but do not memorise.

(14) Remember the main points. If necessary, write them on a card or slip of paper.

How to win the interest of the audience: (1) Tell something new and of interest to the audience.

(2) Introduce the topic to the audience.

(3) Use general illustrations.

(4) Be natural.

(5) Talk in a conversational way.

(6) Emphasise important words.

(7) Talk with specific points.

(8) Secure goodwill, by smiling and other humorous ways.

(9) Crowd your audience together.

(10) Check the physical arrangement like proper light, ventilation, as far as possible. Do not keep other members on the platform.

(11) Do not roam on the platform.

How to open your talk: The speech should have three parts: introduction, body and conclusion. The introduction should be such that it appeals directly and quickly. Never begin with an apology. Arouse curiosity by giving some factual statement. Begin with an illustration. Shocking facts have great power to make people attentive.

How to capture an audience: (1) Eradicate all ill-feelings.

(2) Get a *yes* response from your audience.

(3) Do not challenge.

(4) Present the facts and let the audience form their own opinion.

How to close: In any speech, the beginning and the end are very mportant. Closing is most :mportant because the final words are remembered longer. Closing should have smoothness. Summarise your points and appeal for action. Give sincere compliments. Close with humour, if possible. Close with practical quotations, if possible.

How to make meaning clear and be impressive: (1) As far as possible, avoid the use of technical terms.

(2) Illustrate your ideas, if possible through visual aids.

(3) Re-state your ideas in different words.

(4) Be convincing and have good suggestions.

(5) Try to avoid contradictory ideas.

(6) State the ideas with enthusiasm and conviction.

(7) If necessary, make small things very large and large things small.

(8) Quote authority to support your statements.

How to get action: The greatest power that a man can have is the power to influence people for action. For this: (1) draw the attention of the people, (2) gain confidence, (3) be earnest, and (4) motivate them to act.

Radio talk

Previously, we have discussed how to handle the radio as listeners. Here we are concerned with how we, as extension workers, can help the country in producing good programmes and effective radio talks for our rural people.

(1) Radio is a device with which the whole mass can be contacted at a time, efficiently and economically. Nowadays, with the increase in rural electrification, the number of radio sets in India is increasing greatly. Moreover, people are purchasing battery sets and they have realised that it is a good thing to have one in the house. Radio sets have been provided in the common meeting places by the C.D. Organisation. Therefore, it is a useful tool for extension work in rural areas. Radio can be depended

upon as an extension tool because the majority of our rural people are illiterates.

(2) Many villages lie in the interior and the means of communication and facilities for them are very few to enjoy in their leisure period. Radio can give them recreation and information, etc.

(3) Speeches of great leaders, agricultural experts, educators, etc., can be transmitted to them by means of radio.

(4) News regarding important information can be conveyed to a large number of people at a low price.

(5) A greater number of people can be approached as it has got a greater appeal.

(6) People's participation in extension programmes can be stimulated and then attitudes can be changed.

(7) Above all, education can be harmoniously blended with entertainment.

(8) Since agricultural conditions differ from place to place, more and more radio stations are necessary to give regional information to the farmers.

Broadcasting time in radio: The best time for broadcasts for the rural people is the evening time between 6 p.m. and 8 p.m. At this time, majority of them are free to listen, and usually assemble at their meeting places. Duration of programme may be half an hour. To make the programme successful, it is necessary that:

(1) It should be based on the needs of the people,

(2) It should be presented in an interesting way,

(3) It should be educative, and

(4) It must have clarity.

Topics of broadcast for rural people: The subjects for rural people in India can be:

(1) Weather forecasts.

(2) Current market reports.

(3) Farming information on improved varieties of seeds, fertilisers, tools, etc., and the time and manner or their use.

(4) Contagious diseases in animals and their protection.

(5) Legislation, and the changes in policy regarding agriculture.

(6) Facilities like credit for purchase of animals, fertilisers, seeds, repair and construction of wells, etc., available to farmers through the C.D. programme and other agencies.

(7) The best time of certain farm operations, application of fertilisers, green manuring, control of pests, diseases, etc.

(8) Information about exhibitions, crop competitions being organised by the Central Ministry of Agriculture or State Department of Agriculture and district exhibitions.

(9) Information regarding useful implements, their use, price, place from where they can be purchased, etc.

(10) Information on fruit preservation, etc.

Presentation of talks in an interesting way: There are two styles of presentation (a) with the help of a script, and (b) with the help of discussion.

The type of presentation is decided by the time available for broadcast, the subject and persons involved, e.g., certain subjects can be best handled as straight talks. Other may be done by a two-way interview, or discussion and some other rough presentation to the farmers and their families. Straight talks should not exceed 5 to 6 minutes duration; a dialogue will hold interest for about 10 minutes. The opening should attract attention.

To maintain the interest, there should be variety in the programme. There may be different segments each connecting with the other smoothly. Emphasise the right points.

It should be remembered that the style of communication through this medium is essentially conversational. Its purpose is to communicate ideas.

There should be clarity of organisation and a logical step-by-step relation of ideas. In presenting information, start with a known fact and relate it with your subject, point by point, with each point leading to the next. Go from known to the unknown. Simple organisation of a talk allows the listener to follow every word. If the listener misses some part he thinks over it, and while thinking he misses the rest of the broadcast.

Basic principles of broadcasting: These can be summarised in three parts: (1) clarity, (2) vividness, and (3) variety.

Short, simple sentences, familiar words, straightforward ideas, repetition of important facts, examples and illustrations, and not too many ideas will make the talk more effective. Only those facts which you understand well enough should be included in the talk. Do not use difficult terms and words, because the purpose of your talk is to convey an idea, or its meaning to rural people who are illiterates or have a small vocabulary in their language.

To attract and hold the listener's attention, use graphic, concrete picture words, fresh approaches, e.g., illustrations and anecdotes (stories from real experience).

Appropriate humour, exclamations, variety in the pitch and delivering the talk in an interesting way will impress the people.

Preparing the script: It should be so prepared that to the listener it should sound as though someone were talking to him in a friendly, informal style.

First, collect the materials from your experiences, visit places like farms, the library, etc. Then arrange it in the proper order. Trim it to the exact size, leaving some material unused, which can be taken up in case you finish earlier. Do not fail to include supporting, or illustrative facts, to back up the main points and lastly, do not try to tell all that you know about the subject. Time is limited and you have to emphasise one idea at a time. Try to make sure that the listening public understands what you mean. Repeat, wherever necessary. Be sincere and friendly. Talk on personal—I, you or we basis.

In a dialogue, never use statistical tables. In an interview, do not frame such questions to which the audience knows the answers. Do not follow an answer with an unrelated question. Do not hesitate to stop or repeat, if necessary. At the end, summarise the points which you want your listeners to remember and act upon.

Other points of importance: (1) The script should be written legibly, i.e., in bold type.

(2) Keep your voice at the room level.

(3) Speed should be normal.

(4) When the mike is to be moved and you need a change in the arrangements, take the permission of the studio in-charge or ask him to do it.

(5) Do not whisper or talk while someone is broadcasting.

(6) Try to find out the defects and shortcomings of your pronunciation. Correct them next time, but do not bother about them while actually broadcasting.

(7) If you have a cough, signal the operator, so that he will keep the mike off the air for a while.

(8) Keep the broadcast slightly flexible so that you can extend or cut short, as required.

(9) Be at ease before the mike.

Score card for judging: The students may be given practice of broadcasting stories on agricultural problems and learn how to judge the talks according to the following points (Table 34.1).

Table 34.1
Judging the script

Item	Marks allotted	Obtained	Remarks
1. Timeliness of the broadcast			
2. Appropriateness:			
(a) Applicability to the region of the listener			
(b) Use in practical life situation			
3. Script:			
(a) Clarity			
(b) Language and organisation			
(c) Vividness—familiarity, attractiveness, humour, end, etc.			
(d) Subject-matter			
(e) Variety			
4. Delivery:			
(a) Unhesitating Fluent, but slow and steady			
(b) Raising and lowering the pitch, wherever necessary			
(c) Avoiding unnecessary noises			
(d) Timings			
5. Overall impression			

Meetings

Stages in a meeting

A. *Planning:* (1) Selection of topic, (2) Timing, (3) Selection of place, (4) Selection of speaker and chairman, (5) Advertising and publicity, and (6) Physical arrangements.

B. *Conducting the meeting:* (1) Programme procedure, and (2) Audience participation,

C. *Follow-up of meeting:* (1) Summaries, (2) Press reports, (3) Displays. (4) Other methods, and (5) Evaluation.

Discussion meetings

Main Types: (1) Lecture forum or discussion forum.

(2) Panel discussion.

(3) Symposium.

(4) Group interview.

(5) Form dialogue or public conversation.

(6) Debate discussion.

(7) Workshops.

The points under each head given here may serve as an illustration on how to prepare short notes from lessons. The teacher may demonstrate the organisation, sitting procedure and conducting of such meetings by dividing the class into groups.

(1) *Lecture forum or discussion forum:* (a) Speaker-audience technique; where two or more persons present talks.

(b) Subject is controversial.

(c) Speakers do not tear each others' cases.

(d) Followed by question-answer period.

Duties of chairman. Tell the audience their part in the forum.

Introduce the topic himself.

Introduce the speakers.

Supervise questions and answers.

Duties of speaker (basic principles to be followed).

Talk to the entire audience when answering questions.

Stand up when answering the questions.

Do not make personal remarks.

Keep the answers to the point.

Keep the answers brief.

Do not try to bluff when you do not know the answer.

(2) *Panel discussion:* (a) Four to six members sit in a semicircle facing the audience.

(b) Carry on discussion on given topic among themselves,

(c) Leader introduces speakers and encourages less talkative speakers.

(d) Audience speaks when their turn comes.

(e) Panel members are selected from better informed persons.

Environmental set-up for conducting the panel discussion

(i) Functions of chairman.

(ii) Functions of panel members.

(3) *Symposium:* (a) Short series of lectures usually by two to five speakers each with different viewpoints.

(b) Audience encouraged to address questions and comments.

(4) *Group interview:* (a) Leader interviews persons on a platform.

(b) Leader-dominated panel discussion.

(c) Excellent for getting information from experts.

(5) *Forum dialogue:* (public conversation).

(a) Usually, two volunteers selected from audience.

(b) Discuss a question on which they may or may not have opposite views.

(c) Followed by discussion.

(6) *Debate discussion:* (a) Teams of usually two or three persons discuss controversial subjects.

(b) Each speaker speaks for the allotted time.

(c) After debate, audience also invited to join the discussion.

(d) It encourages the speaker to colour information and suppress facts not favourable to his side.

(7) *Workshop:* (a) A special type of working conference of a week or of more duration.

(b) There are lectures, individual conferences, and emphasis on working groups.

(c) Work sessions arranged under the guidance of consultants.

(d) Participants can work on a special problem either individually or as members of groups.

(e) Mostly used for professional improvement and in-service training.

(f) Success depends on having well-defined objectives and a homogeneous group vitally concerned with objectives.

(g) Problems for discussion are brought in by participants.

(h) Managed through a steering committee.

(i) Elements of workshop:

  (i) Lectures by staff members.

  (ii) Group meetings, with groups selected according to interest.

  (iii) Individual consultation and study.

  (iv) Informal discussion at odd times.

  (v) Inspirational or social events.

  (vi) Library and other resources for study.

Conferences

We can participate in conferences more effectively by keeping the following tips into consideration:

(1) Have something to say of interest to the groups. Find out what kind of an audience you will be addressing and direct your talk to their interests, not to your own.

(2) Have a series of specific points to follow. Tell the audience in advance how many points you intend to make and specify when you come to each of these points.

(3) Think through in advance what it is you want these people to take away with them after they have heard your speech. Be convinced that what you say can be of help to the listeners. Do not apologise for your limitations and shortcomings. They will find them out soon enough for themselves.

(4) Talk "to" not "at" the people. Look at them, not at the ceiling or out the windows.

(5) Be confident that you can do a good job. This necessitates proper preparation. Don't worry about nervousness. It is necessary.

(6) Speak naturally, in a loud, clear, but not a shouting voice. Don't try to use a lot of unnatural gesticulations which you read about in some book. Be yourself.

(7) Have a neat, well-groomed appearance, don't overdress and don't fuss with your tie or hair in front of the audience.

(8) Have the lights on over the audience to whom you are speaking. Observe their faces for approval, interest, boredom, etc. Their expressions are the best indicator of your success.

(9) If possible, put an outline of points on a blackboard, or chart, before commencing and refer to them as you progress.

(10) Give an eye-catching title to your talk. Illustrate particular instances with your own experiences. But don't over do this.

(11) Never memorise a speech! Use only brief references and notes if possible; avoid reading it. Rehearse your speech befor :i. and, present it to yourself, or to any friend, as a practice technique.

(12) Try to relax a tense group. If the situation permits, speak to some of the audience members personally. This relaxes them, and spreads throughout the group. Humorous stories or anecdotes at the outset often help to relax the group. But be careful with stories. Most people are unable to tell one properly. If in doubt, as to whether the story is appropriate, forget it. Nothing is less humorous than an out-of-place or off-colour story which falls flat on its face.

(13) Don't try to talk to the lowest mental level present. This is an insult to those of average intelligence (the majority), who feel that you are talking down to them. People are generally a lot smarter than we give them credit for (especially other people).

(14) Never try to play down a member of the audience, or to embarrass a questioner by implying that his question is stupid (even if it is).

(15) Try not to get angry, even if the provocation is extreme and unfair. If you do get angry, avoid showing it (if you can).

(16) If a question period is to follow the talk, let the audience know this, so they can be gathering points.

(17) When asking questions, use questions which provoke thought among the whole audience, not just one or two persons or sectors of it. When initiating a question period, don't ask "are there any question"?; the silence can be very embarrassing. Instead ask "Now, who has got the first question?"

(18) When you ask the audience, a question ask it generally to all of the group, then single out a respondent and identify him. This causes everyone to listen and think about it; if you say, "Mr. Sharma, what do you think about such and such?" Everyone else will relax and watch Mr. Sharma try to get himself off the spot. But if you say, "What do you think about such and such . . . (then) Mr. Sharma?"; all the audience will think about the question just in case you call on them and not on Mr. Sharma.

(19) Stop a question period before people run out of questions. Don't keep asking for questions. Here, again, the resulting silence can be very embarrassing and may take the wind out of what has already been said.

(20) Avoid giving a talk right after a meal. Mental capacity is at its lowest after eating., "A full belly makes a dull brain."

(21) Keep your speech as short as possible without its becoming meaningless. Better to stop while their interest is still aroused then to keep on until they get restless and become tired and bored.

(22) Don't try to summarise your whole speech at the end. By doing so, you merely prove to the audience that you can actually say in five or ten minutes what it has taken you forty or fifty minutes to say.

(23) If possible, hand out a manuscript or summary of your talk after, not before or

during the talk. Nothing is more distracting than to have people consulting papers and reading them while you are talking. If they must be handed out, other than at the end, take time out from your presentation to distribute them, and to let the audience look them over. Then resume.

(24) Above all, be interested in what you are saying, and show it. Enthusiasm generates enthusiasm. If you are genuinely interested in your topic, and in sharing your viewpoints with the audience, then they will automatically detect that interest, and will immediately acquire a similar enthusiasm.

(25) Take every possible opportunity to speak. Practice leads to perfection.

Tours

A tour is essentially a visit to demonstrations, plots, farms of progressive farmers, poultry, dairy, orchard, model house, etc.

(A) A technique of group contact:

(1) May be a day visit to one demonstration site, college farm, etc.
(2) May be a whole day visit to several nearby demonstrations.
(3) May involve a week or more time and visits to distant projects arranged by the Block programme as a "Bharat Yatra".

(B) A tour is the most expensive extension method. It involves time, transportation and facilities and a number of preparations.

(C) The concept upon which the tour is based may be psychological or sociological:

(1) Preparation of an idea comes to an individual through sensory organs.
   (a) First, it is heard—simple ideas are perceived, more complex ideas require more sensory stimulation.
   (b) Words alone are often inadequate, but reinforcement by seeing the process, or its results, may enable one to perceive the total.
(2) Observation of results, or the process in action, also may overcome anxiety resulting from the prospect of change from the fortable "old" to the unknown "new".
(3) Communities often gain in cohesiveness and initiative when they realise that neighbouring groups have attained certain goals—the spirit of competition also works within an individual.

Purpose of tour

(1) To see the results of a new practice.
(2) To see a new practice demonstrated.
(3) To see the operation of a new implement or tool, etc.
(4) To see the accomplishments of other villages, college farms, etc.

Plan for your tour

The student of extension or extension worker in charge of the village should take into consideration:

(1) To help the villagers recognise the problems of low yields or unscientific practices followed by them.

(2) To create interest to get what others are getting.
(3) To generate discussion to satisfy or remove their doubts.
(4) To provoke action.

Before the start of a tour decide
(1) What the villagers are to see and learn?
(2) What equipment, tools, etc., shall be needed?
(3) Who will guide the tour and who shall assist him?
(4) The date, time, place of assembling from where they are to be taken.
(5) Arrangements for transport, water, refreshments, etc.

Evaluation of the tour
After the tour evaluate whether:
(1) Everyone could see what was desired.
(2) Time for questions and answers was given.
(3) People asked questions.
(4) People did not get tired.
(5) Interest created for future action.
(6) To have follow-up programme.

Campaigns

Importance
India's population is growing fast and this has created food shortage. If production of food is not raised by 5 per cent per year, this problem may continue. This increase is possible only if *Rabi* and *Kharif* campaigns are carried out, and farmers are helped in raising better crops and increasing their yields by the use of improved seeds, plant protection measures, fertilisers, weedicides, etc.

What is required for these campaigns?
(1) Cooperation and coordination of various agencies engaged in development of agriculture and improvement of villages.
(2) Planning of activities, meetings, etc., at District, Block and VLW circle levels.
(3) Involvement of farmers and agencies in the campaign.
(4) Timely taking up of operations.
(5) Provision of supplies like improved seeds, fertilisers, implements, insecticides weedicides, etc. before time.
(6) Use of irrigation facilities, if available, to their maximum.
(7) Use of compost and other village resources for manuring.
(8) Provision of Takkavi loans and right use of such loans.
(9) Dissemination of usable technical information and demonstration of improved practices.
(10) Evaluation of campaign and corrections in the new starts.

How farmers respond?
Farmers respond to the educational process, if:

(1) They are aware of the need and the way to improve.

(2) They are given information on how to use a better practice.

(3) They are helped in securing supplies in good time and are shown how to use them.

(4) They are taught in detail how to prepare the soil, transplant, fertilise and keep weeds and insects out.

Any campaign, to get new practices adopted, e.g., Japanese method of paddy cultivation, takes preparation and constant encouragement for at least a 4 months' period, upto and including planting.

Stages in a campaign

First stage: The holding of (1) village leader's meeting and (2) community meeting to give all farmers an awareness of the need for the programme and what each can do to cooperate. The leaders' meeting is in preparation for holding a mass meeting in each village to secure interest and concern.

In the mass or community meetings, the farmers will learn of the opportunity to enrol in the project, i.e., to offer cooperation in the use of improved methods for the *Kharif* or *Rabi* season. The village leaders will get the names of the farmers who are willing to cooperate, they will then be enrolled.

Second stage: The "enrollees" will be called to a second meeting. At this meeting, they should be given detailed instructions as to what will be expected of them, as *co-operators*—to agree to use improved practices, and as *demonstrators*—so as to set aside a field on which a demonstration can be carried out under the supervision of the staff of the extension wing or block. The number of *enrollees* may be limited. Those farmers, who enrol as "sign ups" should be given preference in the distribution of seeds, fertilisers, credit, and technical advice.

Third stage: After the cooperators and demonstrators have committed themselves, individual farm plans of operation should be worked out, in which each enrolles' will locate and outline the area to be used, indicate the method to be used, get detailed instructions as to how to prepare, fertilise, plant and take care of the improved crops.

Fourth stage: Actual demonstration of a practice is in the field. For it, the technicians, supplies etc., should be ready. Other farmers should be invited to watch the method demonstration. This is to be followed through till harvesting, collection of data, etc.

Village camps

For intensive work and proper training under field conditions, it is necessary that camps in the villages be organised during vacations or the trimester or semester break. This is possible for about 15 days during winter vacations (Dussehra-Diwali), and 15-20 days in the summer vacations in May and June under the traditional system. During the winter vacation camp, the students will be able to participate in the harvesting of *Kharif* crops and sowing of wheat. If there are Veterinary, Home Science or Agricultural Engineering Colleges in the same campus the camps should be combined. These are more effective.

Objectives

(1) The students will be able to apply the principles of extension they learnt in the class room to real field situations and gain first-hand experience thereby.

(2) They will see the functioning of the N. E. S. Organisation, Applied Nutrition Programme, Family Planning work, Educational system, Panchayats, Co-operatives etc.

(3) The coordination of various activities by their extension wing through various development agencies.

(4) Develop the skill for making apt choices and use of various extension methods while working with villagers, both with the individual and with groups.

(5) They will conduct socio-economic surveys and collect first-hand information on various aspects of village life.

(6) They will develop the technique of studying village situations, analysing problems, finding out potential solutions and planning multi-phased village programmes, and develop a plan of action and its implementation.

(7) It will teach them listing of village problems, giving them priorities and assessing the 'felt' needs of the villagers.

(8) It will teach them planning and preparation of individual farm production plans, and following these plans in terms of credit and supplies and needed technical information, wherever possible.

(9) They will get training in the procedures and techniques, employed for carrying out simple evaluation of extension work.

Preparation for the camps

The staff of the extension wing should plan in advance the programme of the camps: location of camps; villages in which to work, Block and other officials to be contacted; supplies like food, fertilisers, insecticides, seeds, implements, cots, transport arrangements; expenses to be met; officials required for orientation in the camps; orientation in the villages; visitors to be invited in the camps; staff to accompany the students, etc.

Programme schedule

The following may present an idea on programme schedule (Table 34.2).

Table 34.2
Programmes Schedule

Date...................

(1) Orientation : (i) at the campus (from...................to...........................)

(ii) in the village (from...................to...........................)

(2) Practical work in villages (from...................to...........................)

(3) Review session (date...........................place.......................................)

(4) Evaluation session on the campus (date..)

(a) *Programme of Orientation at the Campus* (Table 34.3)

Table 34.3
Orientation Campus

Date	Time	Item	Name of teacher official/specialist speaker
First day	7.30 A.M.	Registration	
	8.00 ,,	Training objectives and programme outline	Prof. of Extension
	8.30 ,,	About the places where camps will work	B.D.O. or...........
	9.00 ,,	Training plan and Physical arrangements	Name................
	9.00 ,,	Choice and use of Extension Methods	Name................
	10.30 ,,	Soil sampling	Agrl. Chemist Name................
	11.30 ,,	Chlorination of wells	Sanitary man/
	12.30 ,,	Baiting of house rats	Entomologist
Second day:	7.30 A.M.	Individual crop production plans, purpose and procedure	...
	8.15 ,,	Poultry farming	...
	9.00 ,, to 1 P.M.	Demonstration and technical information on;	

(a) Solar energy treatment of wheat seed
(b) Agrosan/ceresan treatment of groundnuts.
(c) Rat baiting in fields
(d) Control of pests
(e) Control of stored grain pests
(f) Weed eradication (what weed)
(g) Kitchen gardening
(h) Soil conservation methods
(i) Planting of fruit trees
(j) Castration of animals
(k) Artificial insemination in animals
(l) Making soak-pits
(m) Preparation of compost
(n) Sanitary latrines for rural homes

Date	Time	Item	Name of speaker
		(o) Poultry, Home Management, Fruit Preservation, Implements for Farmers	
Third day, if necessary:		Village situation studies Evaluation projects Holding of meetings and use of audio-visual aids Daily work schedule Code of conduct Joint session with B.D.O...... and allocation of Headquarters.	

(b) *Orientation in the village:* After they have been oriented in the campus and have reached their respective villages, they will devote a day or two as required in getting acquainted with the day to day work of the VLW's and AEO's. They will hold discussions with field staff about the functional set-up of the organisation, and the working approach. Here, they will use the information given in the chapter on Organisation of Community Development. They will visit and observe some projects completed by the Block staff and the projects in progress.

(c) *Practical work in the villages:* The staff of the campus, the Block staff and other officials of the development departments, in consultation with village leaders and students, will plan a schedule of day to day work—first day schedule, second day, third day, fourth day and so on (Table 34.4).

Table 34.4
Practical work in the village

Date	Time	Item
First day:	6.00 P.M. onwards	Contact village officials and leaders and explain the programme Prepare a list of farming families with the headman, if not yet collected Divide the families in convenient groups, according to Patti or Mohalla, so as to contacting one such group each day Associate one or more such villages every day, select a suitable place for mass meetings in consultation with village leaders

Date	Time	Item
		Plan seating, lighting, exhibition, etc.
		Visit each family personally
	8.00 P.M.	Hold mass meeting, finalise next day's schedule with village leaders, and decide demonstrations to be conducted and the arrangement of supplies
Second day in village:		
	7.00 A.M.	Reach the village and contact village leaders, Concentrate on one Patti if the village is large
	7.30 A.M.	Make individual contacts with families and arrange method demonstrations. If it is sowing time of wheat, then demonstrate Soaking of seed for solar energy treatment. Demonstrate other practices as planned
	1.00 P.M. to 3 P.M.	Lunch and rest
	3 P.M. to 6 P.M.	Demonstrations and project with housewives, Poultry farmers, kitchen gardens, shramdan with villagers and school children
	7 P.M. to 10 P.M.	Group meetings with village leaders for assessing the day's experiences and planning next day's programme, recreation, film show, etc.
Third day and after:		
	7.30 A.M. to 1 P.M.	Morning shift as arranged previously—demonstrations, poultry, veterinary home management
	1 P.M. to 3 P.M.	Lunch and rest
	3 P.M. to 7 P.M.	Village survey and exhibition, Home Science projects, kitchen gardens, school projects
	7 P.M. to 8 P.M.	Supper
	8. P.M. to 10 P.M.	Film shows, recreational programme, group meetings, etc.

(d) *Code of conduct:* The success of the field training through such camps should be judged as much, may be by the understanding of village problems and the skill in tackling them, as by the appreciation earned from the villagers with whom the students work. For it our participants need to display a high standard of behaviour and conduct in their villages. The following points may help in this regard:

(1) Display a desirable standard of behaviour during your stay in the villages as worthy students of your institution and citizens of India.

(2) Exhibit politeness in your approach and dealings with the people.

(3) Win their confidence by showing sincere interest in their problems.

(4) Display a high standard of moral character as judged by the values of the people in the villages.

(5) Always maintain an impartial status in case you happen to be drawn temporarily into some controversial issue.

(6) Fully adjust yourself with the level of comforts and conveniences available in the village.

(7) Do not contravene any of the social customs and particularly those about which the villagers are sensitive.

(8) Do not let your stay in the villages be exploited by any individual or group of people for personal or sectional ends.

(9) Do not make purchases on credit.

(10) Do not pose to know the solutions of all the problems presented to you when you are not sure in your own mind.

(11) Do not make any commitments which you cannot honour.

(12) Do not stare at people in the village.

(13) Do not ridicule people and their opinions, respect their views and always keep your promise.

Evaluation of the camp work

One day before the completion of the camp, a meeting of the participants may be organised, where the students may be helped to complete their schedules and to discuss problems met with during the camp. After it, the students will be required to wind up the camp, collect things and move back to the campus. A report of the work, statement of expenses, completion of stock books, etc., should be done.

In the campus, while they are in their classes, they should be asked to fill up some proforma whereby they may evaluate the programme in term of its planning, organisation, execution and the experiences gained. They should be asked to complete their reports for the examination.

JOURNALISM IN EXTENSION WORK

Journalism exists to perform a service, but the service it performs is conditioned by the ideology of the society it serves. Social philosophers classify ideologies into some categories, but men everywhere know that actually there are only two concepts of what men's relations should be with one another.

Some contend that every man should be his own master; others insist that a few men should be the masters of all. There lies the difference between democracy and totalitarianism.

Democracy is more than a design for government, it is a dynamic social philosophy which puts human values first. Democracy is an altruistic mode of living which makes the pursuit of happiness more than a persuit. It is the cooperative process of social adjustments by means of which free men, as equals, build a just and human civilisation. It is a way of life for the brotherhood of man.

To democratise life, we must democratise knowledge. To give direction to the ethical and scientific principles of democracy, freedom of expression and freedom of action must be based upon free access to truth. A truth itself may remain undiscovered unless channels and media of communication provide all men with an unrestricted flow of public information and public opinion. In a free society, a free press is as essential as the legislature, judicial and executive branches of a government. It is truely a weapon of democracy.

How does journalism serve this purpose in a democratic society? The definition of journalism will provide the answer. According to Welsely and Campbell, "Journalism is the systematic and reliable dissemination of public information, public opinion and entertainment by modern mass media of communication."

Scope

The scope of journalism can be discussed in terms of the perspective of mass media of communication as follows:

(1) Men run to and fro for knowledge.
(2) Men are hungry for the knowledge of past.
(3) Men seek knowledge for the present.
(4) Modern men are voracious newspaper readers.
(5) Modern men read periodicals.
(6) The spoken word is a factor in mass communication.

Functions of journalism

Explorers of journalism have discovered that the media of mass communication have from one to three purposes.

(1) They may inform, disseminate news and miscellaneous non-news items.
(2) They may influence, giving the public either a social or commercial message.
(3) They may be entertaining, presenting features, fiction, humour, comics and similar matters.

Unless the media perform at least one of the following basic functions successfully, they are unlikely to be a profitable business enterprise. The basic functions are:

(1) *The news function:* The primary function of the press today is to inform. A Newspaper should be just. Arther Robb has said "Factual information of the days news is the elementary function."

But what is the days news? Examining the glut of public occurrences, ideas and situations, newspapermen must determine which will interest the public. How ? By measuring these occurrences, ideas, and situations in terms of their immediacy and proximity to, their magnitude and significance for the community that they are to serve. Yet, factual presentation of the days news is not enough. Complex situations require interpretation and explanation. Background information must be provided to supplement the news. To provide this material and to enrich his news story, the reporter may have to serve as a historian or a geographer.

Mass news dissemination, therefore, should stress interpretative as well as objective reporting. Such news gatherings may be colourful but not coloured. Only thus can the public be provided with accurate and significant data with which to approach reality scientifically and to make decisions intelligently.

(2) *The opinion function:* Modern man frequently finds himself in the midst of conflict and confusion. As a citizen, he may feel it his duty to vote at every election; yet

often he goes to the polls bewildered, for he sometimes is asked to vote on measures that he does not understand. He wants and needs a medium of communication that will help him to act on the basis of logical arguments, not emotional appeals.

Thus the modern press has to be both a daily teacher and a daily tribune (popular leader). To influence a public, the newspaper may educate, counsel, advise as well as exhort, expose and excoriate (urge, exhibit, remind). For that reason, the editorial is the only means of building public opinion.

Significant in helping people to build good judgement and good taste are the critical articles that some newspapers publish. Reviews of motion pictures, musical events, art exhibits, radio programmes, records and books stimulate interest in these art forms.

Supplementing editorials are reviews, the well-rounded newspaper today provides articles and columns of guidance and personal services. Legal, financial, educational, medical, parental and beauty problems receive attention as well as do the heartaches of the lovelorn. Of somewhat similar nature is some of the miscellaneous non-news material.

Actually, the newspaper influences the public more through its advertisements than through its editorials. Unquestionably, both display and classified advertisements are read, for the public interested in commercial messages outlining the nature, scope and quality of various goods and services.

(3) *The entertainment function:* Features are the apple pie on the newspaper daily bill of fare. They top off a somewhat heavy portion of sirloin steak and French fried potatoes, the news and opinion on the menu. They give the reader a balanced diet, so that he can finish his intellectual intake with a pleasant taste in his mouth and no fear of indigestion.

Entertainment is where you find it. It pops up in human interest stories and news features. It sparkles in bright columns and gay interviews. It smiles through home-spun verse and light essays. It bursts out boisterously in the comics some of which are most uncomic.

Entertaining the public is a business too. Since it is too big a job for the local staff, newspaper rely upon syndicated material.

Public interest in various features, comics in particular, sometimes determine the choice of a newspaper—a fact, about which every circulation manager as well as editor is aware of. Subjected to the critical scrutiny of educators and sociologists, the entertainment matter in newspaper sometimes evokes disapproval.

CHAPTER 35

COMMUNICATION THROUGH WRITTEN WORDS

It is playing a great part in communicating with farm people, home makers, etc. Newspaper stories, magazine articles, leaflets, pamphlets, bulletins, circular letters, wall newspapers and radio scripts are increasingly being written by the extension staff and read or listened to. The written word is helping make advisory work with farm people more interesting.

Spoken words are forgotten after some time. The written word can be put up for reading another time, and it can be referred to. The written word is regarded as more authentic. The written word has power. If written well it convinces and motivates people. The purpose in writing for farmers and homemakers, etc., is to attract their attention, interest them, make them understand and remember. These techniques help one in becoming a good writer for farm people, homemakers or the client system. For writing the following replies are to be given—why do you write, whom of writing, what of writing, where, when and how.

(1) *The why of writing:* To give your audience information which they do not have to explain and give further information.

(2) *Whom of writing:* For whom are you going to write i.e., for crop raisers, vegetable growers, fruit growers, cattle breeders, poultry farmers, homemakers or whom ? Keep your eyes and ears focussed on your audience or client system, to what he or she or they want to know.

(3) *The what of writing:* Choose your subject with care. Think what of they already know about it. Mark the boundaries of the subject and confine yourself to it. See how much of the subject your reader can take without getting tired of it. Do not give an overdose.

(4) *The where of writing:* Where to publish, i.e., the newspapers, magazines, leaflets, bulletins, reports, resumes, etc.

(5) *The when of writing:* It should be timely. It should have seasonableness.

(6) *The how of writing:* Writing should be brief, specific, accurate, convincing. Do not talk down to the readers. No one likes super attitudes or preaching. Be practical. Avoid exaggeration. Introduce a human element in it. Make it personal and lively, entertaining and interesting. Use common words, which are familiar to your readers. Be specific and concrete. In place of 'tilling' the soil better use the word 'ploughing'. Address the reader direct (Active voice).

Sentences: One sentence should have one idea. It should follow logically and should lead to the sentence that follows it. Use short sentences.

Paragraph: It is a group of related ideas. Make your paragraphs short. They give a pause to the readers, and make your writing look attractive. Each paragraph should contain a group of sub-ideas related to the main idea. Thus, though separate from other paragraphs, it never stands by itself. A paragraph leans to the paragraph that precedes.

Need for news to our client system

The farm people or homemakers, etc., have a curiosity for news. News may be defined as:

(1) Any new idea, event, situation or development, of interest to a large number of people, is news.

(2) It is a report of any event, containing timely and hitherto unknown information which has been accurately gathered and written for the purpose of serving a reader or listener.

So an event is not news, only when reported it does become a news.

The value of news is only;
(1) When it is timely;
(2) Read with interest by people;
(3) It is unusual;
(4) It is important from a reader's point of view;
(5) The shorter the distance from the event, the more the interest of the reader in the news.

Pyramid structure of news writing:
This may be seen in Fig. 35.1.

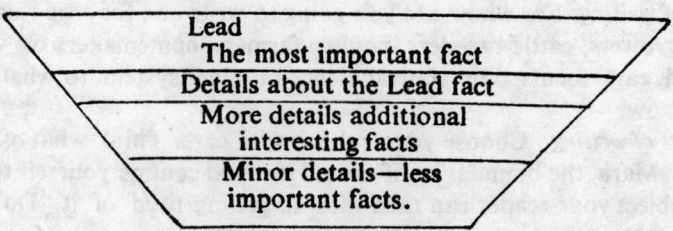

Fig. 35.1. Pyramid structure of news writing.

When you have collected all the facts you want to write them down in order of their importance. Then pick up your most important or interesting fact for the LEAD point. Spend some time in carefully wording it, write the story next, weighing each fact as you write it.

To make your story good, economise on words; use the most effective words you can think of, keeping in mind the reader farmer, i.e., homemaker, etc.

Illustrations of lead

'Soils Need Fertiliser' (JNKVV News).

Jabalpur dated July 7, 1972

"About 18.4 million tonnes of nutrients are removed from the soil every year by different crops in the country, according to agricultural experts.

Writing in *The Handbook of Agriculture*, brought out by the ICAR., the experts point out that in terms of fertilisers the removal rate is 4.2 million tonnes of Nitrogen, 2.4 million tonnes of Phosphate and 7.3 million tonnes of Potash and 4.8 million tonnes of lime.

Production of larger yields through improved varieties of crops and intensive cultivation increases nutrient removal further and they warn that unless the soil is given sufficient doses of chemical fertilisers and other nutrients, the drain of manurial supplies will continue to make the soils poorer."

Interviewing experts to gather information for writing

The expert may be a subject-matter specialist in Agriculture/Animal Husbandry/Home Science/Medical man etc.

Before interview: Looking to the need for the best person for your interview, decide person, fix time and place. Familiarise yourself with the subject of the interview and the person to be interviewed. Jot down some questions to be asked at the interview. Phrase the questions in such a way that the interviewee's interest is aroused.

The interview: Do not straight way start shooting the questions at him. Put him at ease. Begin with less important questions. Be enthusiastic. Some respondents may give exaggerated figures of production. You have to be on guard against all this and find ways to check. There may be some other persons present at the time of interview, and they may also throw some light on this subject. Jot down. Go over your notes and re-check the information. You may like to give some photographs or illustrations.

After interview: Decide which things you will retain. Then think of a LEAD and style of writing. Give prominence to the person you have interviewed. Sprinkle quotations.

Writing for Newspapers

Writing a column in a newspaper is a good way of communicating with the client system in a regular and friendly manner.

Your personal column is a two-way bridge between you and the reader. Give him information and ask for his comments, problems and questions.

Use the 'I' way of writing as: I saw, I hear, I think and so on. The 'fiction' style or human interest style is also a good approach. Begin with good, catchy headings like: "Farm News", "Farm Home", "Better Homes", "Farmers' Notebook", "Our Agriculture", "For Farmers". Give photographs on some occasions. (Fig. 35.2)

Illustration

FARM NEWS

By. . . . .

Headings:

Planning the sample

Soil Testing Lab
Tobacco Damp is off
Digested Bone Meal
OUR HOME
By
Tej Ratan Singh
Simple Food Tips
Weaving of Spare Time.

Fig. 35.2. Newspaper for farmers.

Feature stories

(1) The feature story explores the background, the birth and the growth of ideas or events and provides a glance at the future too. It conveys to the writer what the readers think about the idea or event.

(2) It has appeal to the reader's imagination.

(3) Feature is more a personal, "chat" with the reader. It can be written in first, second or third person.

(4) In it the writer has freedom.

(5) Only unvarnished truth is presented in it.

Types of feature stories

(1) *News features:* More details about the news of a farmer who wins a prize in a crop competition, etc.

(2) *Utility feature story:* How to do a definite piece of work. Process story.

(3) General information feature.

(4) *Experience feature:* It may be: (a) personal experience story, (b) the confession story, and (c) third person experience story.

Considerations for feature stories

(1) Subject should be new,

(2) Subject should have seasonableness,

(3) Subject should not be of use only to a small section of the readers,

(4) There should be enough material for it,

(5) Subject should be specific,

(6) Prepare your plan in accordance with:

    (a) What the magazine wants,

    (b) What the reader wants from you,

    (c) What kind of readers this magazine caters to their standard of understanding the language.

Practical examples

Mastitis

(1) *Outline:* The disease: (a) A disease of the udder, (b) Cattle affected in India.

(2) *How is it caused.*

(3) *Symptoms.*

(4) *Precaution.*

(5) *Control.*

Spend some time on preparing the outline. It will help the flow of ideas.

Smoothen your transition from one sentence to another, and from one paragraph to another.

Think of the title, the lead, the body and conclusion.

The title attracts the attention of the reader. The LEAD takes over control from the title. It has to create interest in the mind of the reader. A well-written lead tickles the curiosity of the reader to want to know more about what you are saying, and invites him to go ahead and read it.

The succeeding paragraphs of the main body continue to hold the reader's interest throughout, so that he grabs at the several ideas narrated as he goes along.

Then conclusion. He makes up his mind what action should be taken. Emphasise the main theme.

Importance of pictures in stories

(1) Pictures tell us more than words can ever do.

(2) It draws the viewer's attention and arouses interest in the subject-matter.

(3) It helps cut down the length of the writing.

(4) The layout of a page looks more interesting with pictures.

Type of photograph for a story

(1) It should fit with the story,

(2) Type out the heading on the back of the story.

Writing captions on the pictures: Give caption in present tense. But if the reference is to some past action, then give it in past tense.

Wall Newspapers

Now, Indian Council of Agricultural Research, New Delhi and the Ministry of Community Development, Government of India are producing big posters with illustrations and information which can serve as wall newspapers for our villagers. Similar posters and wall newspapers can be prepared by the students of extension wings using simple writing and coloured pictures. For effective use of such wall newspapers, the student of extension should take these points into consideration.

(1) Paste them in conspicuous places throughout the village i.e.,

(a) places where people gather.

(b) places where people pass through.

(c) places that are protected from wind and rain.

(2) Call attention to the paper.

(3) Arrange so that such papers are read by literates to illiterates.

(4) Important points which have already been discussed under posters should be ta into consideration for wall newspa (Fig. 35.3).

Fig. 35.3. A wall newspaper.

Leaflet, pamphlet and bulletins

Leaflet contains 4-12 pages stitched or stapled at the centre. Pamphlet varies in size from 12 to 24 pages and a bulletin is a bulkier publication with 24-48 or more pages.

A bulletin is normally on a subject that requires detailed treatment. When you want to write about a crop on which a large number of research results are available and you want to give all the details you have collected, you write a bulletin on it.

If you want to write about only one important aspect, you choose the shorter and more specific leaflet form e.g., control of pests and diseases.

An extension bulletin is formal and is meant to give information on the practical side of the problem.

Leaflets are mostly for giving a 'how to do' or process story, a set of improved practices to be followed in growing a crop, or the steps to be followed in solving a home or farm problem.

Illustrations play a bigger role in leaflets than they do in a magazine story.

A good use of colour adds to the attractiveness of the leaflet and gets more readers.

Stages in preparation

There are three stages: (1) planning, (2) writing, and (3) review.

After you have completed the writing, go over it once again. Better do it after a few hours. If possible show it to someone else.

Illustration: Making the Bordeaux Mixture.

Circular letters

It is a quick and cheap method of communication and proves very effective if done well. This is a letter which is reproduced and sent with the same information to many people. Receiving such mail from the extension wing or the office connected with the extension work will have great influence on the village people. A good circular letter should :

(a) Be brief.
(b) Be simple, so as to be understood by poorly literate people.
(c) Have a single purpose.
(d) Be part of our programme in the village or the campaign.
(e) Be clear.
(f) Have complete information.
(g) Lead to action.

Fig. 35.4. A farmer reading a circular letter from an extension wing.

Circular letters can teach villagers and also save them the time taken to come to the extension wing or block office or even the VLW. They are inexpensive. It can be cyclostyled or if this help is not available, the help of the school teacher can be obtained in using the students to copy it (Fig. 35.4).

Such letters must have:

(1) A personal touch, and
(2) Short sentences and short paragraphs.

The personal touch arouses interest and makes the letter popular. Such letters should be weekly or fortnightly depending on the need of time and the facilities available. The contents should be news and announcements as well as how-to-do-it stories. The cost should not be much, and distribution must be fast. Use the local language or, at least, a common medium.

Illustration: A letter from a student of extension wing M.Sc. (Ag.) Final to a villager in village Tikeria, Sehora Block, District Jabalpur.

Extension Department   2nd Sept. 1971
J. N. Krishi Viswavidyalaya, Jabalpur.

Shriman Pradhan Rohini Pd. Ji,

A Farmers' Day has been arranged in our Extension Department on September 15, 1971. The AEO, Sehora has agreed to provide transport facilities to farmers of your village. They will be brought in the buses to the College farm to see the various demonstrations on paddy conducted by the M. Sc. students of Agronomy of our College. The buses will leave from the Primary school building Tikeria at 7.30 a.m. All the farmers of your village are very cordially invited to take advantage of this guided tour. The farmers will be received by our Dr. O. P. Dahama, Head of Extension Department at the Farm Gate, Adhartal. Dr. Chaubey, Professor of Agronomy, his staff and students of M.Sc., will give us a round and explain the details of their experiments. Hope you will bring other friends with you. With regards.

Sincerely yours,
R. L. Agrawal, M. Sc. Student

Writing for a radio talk

Use the radio to inform, alert, suggest, direct, interest, stimulate and motivate people.

Its limitations: It cannot teach, cannot go into details and cannot specify. People must listen when you are talking. They cannot put off listening as with printed matter. There may be many interruptions and distractions. If they miss some of your words, they cannot ask you to repeat them.

You cannot make use of your smile or frown. You cannot gesticulate or use visuals, as you would do when talking to them in person. You cannot even see how your listener is taking it in.

Strong points

(1) It can stimulate and motivate, and so can persuade.
(2) It has a good place because most of our people are illiterate.
(3) You can give timely reminders about some project or practice.
(4) You can rouse the interest of those who otherwise would not be interested.
(5) You can report farm news.

Writing the news: The news for the radio has to suit the ear and not the eye. It has to be short, simple and direct, with familiar words and simple sentences. This has to be done because it is a 'Voice to ear method'.

Script for the talk

(1) Select a topic,

(2) A five minute talk is ideal—120 words per minute, 600 words for the talk plus 50-100 words as stand-by,

(3) Select only one phase of the talk,

(4) Write out the central fact,

(5) Write the script,

(6) Make your script clear and convincing and your arguments logical so that it stimulates and maintains enough interest in the listener, and

(7) Summarise clearly what you have said.

CHAPTER 36

COMMUNICATION THROUGH SATELLITE

With the evolution, revolution and breakthrough in the use of electronic-communication system, the world today has gone far ahead in developing Satellite Communication System. A quantum leap in communication technology has brought the world nearer to each other and the messages are flashed in seconds just after their origin to the destination of their users through satellites. These satellites are an artifical object put into orbit around Earth. These are small planets that move through space around the Earth or another planets.

In the developing country like India, tremendous amount of diversities in culture, agriculture, agro-climatic variations, languages and demographic-cum-ecological imbalances exists, hence, the major thrust is to provide fastest communication system that provide unity among diversities and simultaneously operate for the 'location—specific-programmes' through messages coated with local language and culture for higher and quick acceptability. As such, in the India's space programme the primary aim is the application of space science and technology to further national development objectives through mass communication and education via satellites. The organisation entrusted with the realsation of these aims is the Space Commission, backed by the Department of Space, with Bangalore being the headquarters of both. The Indian Space Research Organisation (ISRO) is responsible for the planning, execution and management of research activities and space application programmes. The ISRO Satellite Centre (ISAC) at Bangalore is responsible for the design, fabrication and integration of space craft and the development of satellite technology.

The first Indian Satellite *Aryabhata* named after the famous ancient Indian astronomer and mathematician was launched in April, 1975. With the launching of *Aryabhata*, India has acquired indigeneous capability in Satellite Technology. The second Indian Satellite, *Bhaskara*, was launched in June, 1979 from a Soviet cosmodrome for earth observations, useful in the fields of forestry, hydrology, snowcover and snowmelt, geology, soils, land use and ocean surface studies. An improved version of *Bhaskara* satellite, called *Bhaskara* II with a wider scaling range, was launched in November, 1981.

Rohini Satellite (RS-1), developed at ISAC, was the first Indian satellite launched from the home base using indigenous satellite launch vehicle (July, 1980) followed by Rohini series, RS-D-1 (May, 1981) and RS-D-II (April, 1983). All these satellites were launched for experimental observations providing needed firm data-base and remote sensing of national resources being one of the major goals of ISRO. Efforts are under-way to develop an Indian Remote Sensing Satellite (IRS) by mid-eighties by the Space Application Centre.

Space Application Centre (SAC) is also engaged in the planning and execution of the space application projects of ISRO. It's objective is to apply space science and technology to practical uses. To achieve this goal, SAC has taken up work in telecommunications and television (TV) broadcasting and reception via satellites, use of remote sensing techniques to survey natural and renewable earth sources, studies in space meteorology and satellite geodesy.

SITE: In an year-long (August 1975 to July 1976) experiment, the SAC conducted and organised direct broadcast of television programmes via, the National Aeronautical Space Agency (NASA) Satellite ATS-6, popularly called as Satellite Instructional Television Experiment (SITE). During the experiment community TV sets were installed in 2,400 villages in Rajasthan, Bihar, Orissa, Madhya Pradesh, Karnataka and Andhra Pradesh. The instructional pro-grammes in agriculture, health, education, industries, medicine, recreation and several other areas were beamed directly via the satellite. Large number of academic institutions, universities and governmental organisations were identified and encou-raged by ISRO to undertake research and development studies in space science, space technology and space applications relevant to Indian Space Programme. Even the Planning Commission conducted an independent study of SITE and observed that the television did play an important role as a reinforcing agent in the adoption of agricul-tural innovations and raised the level of aspirations, which could be further channe-lised productivity towards the attainment of people's participation in nation building. It successfully transmitted messages in health and medicine, economic affairs, social changes etc. It also provided experience in the development, management and testing of a satellite based instructional television system in rural areas. It significantly enhanced Indian capability in the design, development, manufacture and operation of direct reception sets.

STEP: SITE (1975-76) was followed by Satellite Telecommunications Experiments Project (STEP), a joint project using the Franco-German Symphonics satellite in 1977-79, conceived as sequel to SITE, STEP was for telecommunications what SITE had been for television. Under STEP experiments in remote area communications using transportable terminals, radio-net-working, emergency communications, digital communications, multiple access, integration of satellite circuits into terrestrial net-work and multiple audio-video transmission were conducted. The project was mainly aimed at providing a system test of geo-synchronons communication satellite and to sharpen India's expertise in the design development, fabrication and operation of communication systems involving geo-stationary satellite.

INSAT: The SITE experiment was so successful in demonstrating the potential of communications satellite for development of the country that the GOI decided as early as in November, 1975—when SITE was only four months old—to use satellite for domestic communications. This gave a green signal for INSAT System. The INSAT system is a multi-purpose operational space system providing telecommuni-cations, meteorology and television services from a common satellite in geo-stationary orbit. It provides long-distance telephoning, communication in the remote areas and islands as well as emergency communications. The meteorological capability includes 24-hour observation of weather system, data collection and relay from remote, unattended plateforms and a disaster warning. Television capability relates both to direct TV broadcasting from satellite to community TV sets in rural areas to radio networking.

The first generation Indian National Satellite (INSAT-1A) was launched in April, 1982 from Cape Canaveral, Florida, U.S.A., and parked at 74°E longitude position. Unfortunately, the INSAT-1A was burnt in the month of September, 1982, just after five months of operation and was therefore, abandoned. After 18 months INSAT-1B was launched into space on August 30, 1983 and parked at 94°E position. This unique three-in-one satellite developed a serious snag just after launching, when it failed to deploy solar array to its final configuration, which was overcome very successfully on September 10, 1983. This satellite is going to help bring television facilities to thousands of rural homes and opens up the prospects of educating villagers in the remotest areas, in the affairs of the nation and associating them in the task of development, along with creating wider vision of the world.

The user system has already alerted for developing suitable soft-ware for the satellite communication. Accordingly, the University Grants Commission has already started harnessing the INSAT-1B for a programme of students engaged in higher studies and the educated public at large. Initially 5,000 colleges all over the country have been asked to buy TV sets in addition to supply of sets to various academic institutions by the UGC. The UGC has a plan to use the satellite to link up top class teachers in various institutions through tele-link, for simultaneous teaching classes, not only to improve teaching standards but also to give big boost to modernisation of education. In this linkages local teachers will answer some of the questions the students may ask, while major questions could be referred to the teacher for answer at latter teleconferences.

Similarly, the Ministry of Agriculture through its' Directorate of Extension have plans to disseminate information on crop-production, crop-protection and cropping system sequences by involving specialists who will communicate directly to the farmers and on getting feed-back, the follow-up action are also being planned. The Indian Council of Agricultural Research while associating itself with the Directorate of Extension Programmes, will also use satellite in importing knowledge about innovations, results of researches, applicability of such results on the farmers fields based on outcome of adaptive, operational and other coordinated researches. ICAR in collaboration with agricultural universities (24) and its specialised stations/Institutes (34 with more than hundred sub-stations) developing plan to provide location-specific and field and farmers-oriented problem-solving messages along with feed-back and follow-up systems. The use of satellite by the ICAR through the two important national projects viz., NARP and NAEP will be geared up in a joint broadcast of relevant, specific and need-based topics with special responsibility in their agro-climatic zones. The plant protection and weather forecast will be a routine matter along with emergent messages on epidemics or calamities or pests diseases—prevention and control.

The other areas like animal husbandry, animal health, medicine, fisheries (inland

and marine), poultry and other avians, agro and social forestry, mixed farming systems, home management, farming systems, dairying, horticulture and engineering etc., will also be covered suitably either as a direct message and/or coated with some cultural and recreational components.

A programme of training the trainers, trainees and target beneficiaries for almost all the user ministries and departments will be a regular feature of telecast from the satellite. This will be linked with the knowledge of services and organisations helping the cause of development and working with common objectives.

Ministries and Departments, viz., Health and Family Welfare in collaboration with ICMR, Social Welfare with ICSSR, ICCR, Science and Technology with IITs, CSIR, Polytechnics, Rural Development with CART and NIRD, Industry with large network of Industries and Industrial Institutes, Labour with Labour Institutes, Civil Supplies and Cooperation etc., are developing their intensive capsule messages for their ultimate users leading up to the grass-root level.

Both nationalised and other banks went to use INSAT-1B to transmit cheque facsimiles for certain outstation branches so that outstation cheque could be cashed instantaneously. They also want the facility to transmit foreign exchange data and check their inter-branch accounts. Similarly, newspapers want the INSAT-1B facility so that they could start multi-edition papers using facsimile transmission. The NTPC, the fertiliser companies, the NHPC etc., want the facility to remain in constant touch with their far flung plants most of them situated in being inaccessible areas.

In short with INSAT system, india is taking quantum leap in education and communication technology and over a period of time several communication media-mix will be developed, revolving round the application and utilisation of INSAT, in transferring, translocation and transmitting the development messages to the remotest parts in the country and providing audio-visual system for illiterate population. The literacy, mass education, mass communication and family welfare programmes are the high priority areas in the INSAT system.

Part V

PROGRAMME PLANNING AND FIVE-YEAR PLANS

PROGRAMME PLANNING

MEANING AND PRINCIPLES OF PROGRAMME PLANNING

Programme planning is a procedure of working with the people in an effort to recognise unsatisfactory situations or problems, and to determine possible solutions, or objectives and goals. This is a conscious effort to meet the needs, interests and wants of the people for whom the programme is intended. The elements of people's needs becomes a central concern of planners for rural development.

Extension programme

According to Kelsey and Hearne (1949) "an extension programme is a statement of situation, objectives, problems and solutions."

USDA (1956) defined "an extension programme, which is arrived at cooperativel by the local people and the Extension Staff and includes a statement of: (1) the situation in which the people are located, (ii) the problems that are a part of the loca situation, (iii) the objectives and goals of the local people in relation to those problems; and (iv) the recommendations or solutions to reach these objectives on a long-term basis (may be several years) or on a short term basis (may be one year or less)."

Lawrence (1965) says that "an extension programme is the sum total of all the activities and understanding of a County Extension Service. It includes (i) The programme planning process, (ii) Written programme statements, (iii) Plan of work, (iv) Programme execution, (v) Results and (vi) Evaluation" (Fig. 37.1).

In drawing up a programme, the following questions give key-orientation and justification: What needs do people have? How can needs be identified? What plans of priority should be set up for meeting the people's needs? What resources are necessary to meet the people's needs? How should resources be organised and directed to help people meet their needs?

In programme planning, we are required to know where we are now, and where we ought to go, so that we may better judge what to do and how to do it? It gives meaning and system to action. It prepares the basis for a course of future action. It is an intentional effort carefully designed to attain certain specific and predetermined goals assumed to be important.

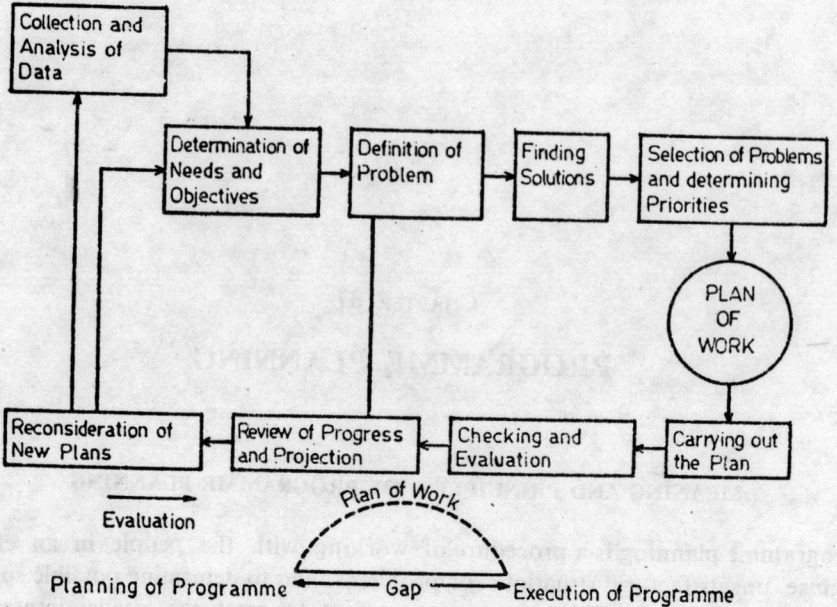

Fig. 37.1. Developing a plan of work.

Components of programme planning

The components of programme planning are complex. These are: People—their needs, their interests, useful technology, the educational process, analysing situations, making decisions about what should be done, determining action, projecting the desired shape of things into the future, etc. It involves the study and use of facts and principles, knowledge, imagination and reasoning ability. Often it requires a mastery of skills and techniques of research, the ability to synthesise facts and value judgements in a process of sound decision-making about the objectives which the programme seek to attain.

PRINCIPLES OF PROGRAMME PLANNING AS APPLIED TO EXTENSION PROGRAMMES

To develop a useful and effective programme, the following principles should be kept in mind as suggested by Kelsey and Hearne (1955):

(1) Extension programme planning is based on an analysis of the facts of the situation.
(2) Extension programme planning selects problems based on the needs and interests of the local people.
(3) Extension programme planning determines priorities; defines objectives and solutions which offer satisfaction.
(4) Extension programme planning has performance with flexibility.
(5) Extension programme planning has balance with emphasis.
(6) Extension programme planning has a definite plan of work.
(7) Extension programme planning is an educational process.

(8) Extension programme planning is a continuous process.

(9) Extension programme planning is a coordinating process.

(10) Extension programme planning involves local people and their institutions.

(11) Extension programme planning provides for evaluation of results.

BASIC PRINCIPLES USED IN EDUCATIONAL PLANNING

(1) Clear and significant objectives: Programme objectives designate directions of movement. Since that is so, objectives properly becomes the focus of primary material and human resources for attaining change. Maximum progress may be possible only when the objectives are clear and full commitment of resources is made to achieving them, and effective use is made of the resources. A good programme objective is one that provides possible direction for large number of people to move some distance in the direction in which they want and need to go.

(2) Planning at the top and lower levels: To achieve the broad purposes of Community Development requires planning at the top level and also at the lower levels, i.e., at national, state, district, block and village. If the statement of purposes at higher levels is to be realistic and useful in guiding the programme at lower levels, it must be reformulated at each lower level to align it with varying situations.

(3) Crucial questions taken into consideration: A number of crucial questions about programme planning need to be asked and their answers taken into account in the planning process. Their proper answer will improve the preciseness with which programmes are developed. These questions may be: To whom and to how many people is the programme important? In what way is the programme significant to the people—economically, socially, aesthetically or morally? What is the relative importance of the programme objectives? Who thinks the programme is important, i.e., the nation, state, block or village? Who arrived at programme objectives? On what amounts is the programme based? Does the programme reflect the significant needs and interests of large numbers of people? Who is acquainted with the programme and its purpose? How clearly conceived and understood is the programme by those who are to participate in its execution? What would be the likely consequences in one, five or ten years, if work on certain parts of the programme is not carried out.

(4) General agreement among various levels—National, state, district, block and village: For planning an effective programme, the village level workers and those at higher levels need to agree on three points: (a) a basic philosophy regarding programme development, (b) a clear policy that reflects the basic philosophy, and (c) a workable procedure that gives general direction but provides ample latitude for the adjustments needed to meet local situations. Such questions may serve as guidelines: What is the relative importance of programme development as a step in the rural development process? Who should participate in the programme development and in what way? How much time should be allotted to the task of planning? In which villages and blocks or districts should such programmes be developed? Upon what kinds, and amounts, of factual information should the programme be based, and how should this be collected? To what extent should procedures provide for participation of the people of the village and block level? Should the different phases of Block Programme be organised into a single overall unified programme? What will be the role of the

technical specialist in programme development? To what extent should village leaders be involved in the programme development and how should they be involved?

(5) Programmes should be based on adequate and current facts pertaining to local, regional and national situations: Facts about the local situation and others affecting it are the foundation upon which the official and non-official bodies at various levels should build to carry out an effective programme. These facts should reflecte local needs and the enlightened desires of the people. They show not only what people think they want but also what is best for them. Facts about the local situation help to identify problems and needs with which the people are concerned, by pointing out the gaps between what is and what should be, by indicating shortages and drawing attention to undesirable trends. To have adequate facts, data on the following four categories need to be obtained; (a) current trends and outlook, (b) the people themselves—their needs, interest, knowledge, social organisation, etc., (c) physical factors about agriculture, industry, health sanitation, etc., and (d) community problems—communication, education, etc.

(6) A small number of the most significant needs should receive major attention.

(7) Skilful involvement of progressive village leaders.

(8) Long range programmes are more effective: The important needs of people cannot be met in the short period of one or two years. Changing what people believe, what they do, is a slow process. Long and constant effort is usually needed to accomplish important community development objectives. Care should be taken in the planning process to provide assurance that the short period interests of people are also their long-term advantages.

(9) An integrated approach to problems of farm, home and the community is more sound and effective. The primary way to achieve coordination and integration in programmes is through common understanding among officials. This can be attained through joint participation in appropriate phases of the planning process.

(10) Cultural values and the social system must be taken into account. Cultural values reflect what people generally think is important. The social system tends to maintain adherence to the scale of established values. In traditional cultures, the social system and prevailing cultural values tend to serve as forces working against social and economic reform. Even in advanced societies they have influence. So people's values and their social system must be understood and taken into account by the planners of rural development programmes.

(11) Programme content must be determined with care and precision.

(12) The interpretation of the programmes to officials and non-officials and to the general public is an essential step in successful programme planning.

ABILITIES NEEDED BY PLANNERS

(1) To understand the nature and role of the Extension Service Organisation, it requires knowledge of: (a) Development, present scope, philosophy and objectives of community development; (b) Organisation and administration of the agency at the national, state, block and village levels; (c) The role of various categories of

personnel at various levels in the hierarchy; and (d) Responsibility and opportunity of the agency in a developing country. Knowledge about these is very necessary for an extension worker. Effective professional leadership requires competence in these areas on the part of the extension workers.

(2) Knowledge and understanding of technology related to subjects with which the programme is to deal: Adequate knowledge and understanding of technology appropriate to one's professional job requires: (a) thorough knowledge of current technology, (b) acquaintance with current technology, (c) knowledge of reliable sources of technology, (d) understanding of how technology relates to specific problems, and (e) continuous study.

(3) Ability to clarify objectives of a programme and state them so that they are useful in guiding its execution. The ability to clarify and state objectives for one's work includes: (a) an understanding of the nature, purpose, and the role of objectives, (b) knowledge of levels and interrelation of objectives, and (c) skill in stating and using objectives to guide educational activity. The importance of clarifying objectives and goals, is found in two major truths: (a) subject-matter and methods necessary to attain educational goals can be wisely selected only when the objectives are specific and clearly stated; (b) evidence of the effectiveness of community development work can be collected only in the light of specific and clearly defined objectives.

(4) Ability to organise people and things: It requires the understanding of: (a) the nature and function of organisation; (b) principles of organisation; (c) techniques of organisation; and (d) the nature and role of coordination and integration of programmes. Good organisation is that which generates group activities, ideas, facts, materials or persons so as to get the best performance with the least effort. The ability for good organisation is shown by definite regularity, and predictability in the everyday performance, of persons or groups doing the job expected of them. The act of organisation requires coordination and procedure analysis, actions, their proper perspective—to unify designated effort into an integrated whole. Under procedure analysis, important facts upon which the success of a procedure rests is discovered. These are the facts which are of much importance and need consideration in the design of procedure.

(5) Skill in seeing the relationship between principle and practice. This involves the knowledge and understanding of (a) the nature and role of principles related to community development and extension work; (b) the nature and role of techniques and procedures for carrying out programmes; (c) the inseparable interdependence of principle and practice in the extension educational process.

The extension worker must understand the principle lying behind his technique in order to make the technique most effective. The term practical here suggests that whatever technique works well in a situation, regardless of its complexity, is practical. Principles give meaning to technique. Techniques give application to principles.

(6) Skill at inquiry. This ability requires the skills of (a) identifying their problems; (b) discovering focal points of concern; (c) determining alternative solutions; and (d) evaluating possible solutions and making decisions about them.

(7) Skill in human relations: Human relations are concerned with how people

get along with one another. Extension workers are required to discover how to get people to act in the ways they want them to do.

PROGRAMME PROJECTION

Programme projection is long range programme planning. It involves the logical analysis of all available information and the setting up of long range goals and objectives for the people to work. According to Nieder Frank (1960) "programme projection means improved programme planning by looking more broadly, looking more deeply, looking longer, or farther ahead and with the involvement of more people." Thus the programme projection is an expanded concept of extension programme planning.

Objectives of programme projection

The major objectives of programme projection as enlisted in the *Extension Service Review* (1956) are:

(1) Helping rural people to better apprise and understand the adjustments which they should make in view of the rapidly developing agricultural technology, thereby to improve their standards of farming and living.

(2) Developing, with local people, significant long-range programmes designed to meet the interests, needs and major problems of the area.

(3) Helping extension workers to reorient and redirect their educational programmes and services and make efforts in the light of what the farm people want.

Programme planning and programme projection

According to Lawrence (1962), programme projection differs from the ordinary type of programme planning in the following ways:

(1) Programme projection is long-range planning and is broader in scope. It is a more complete and a more balanced approach.

(2) It involves the collection and interpretation of pertinent background information from local, state and central sources.

(3) It is much more thorough in the study and analysis of local problems. It is a more intensive kind of programme planning.

(4) It usually involves more local people with a wider range of interests.

(5) It makes greater efforts to determine the kind of extension assistance that local people want in helping them solve problems and to attain their goals.

CHAPTER 38

DEVELOPING A PLAN OF WORK

Extension education is of a voluntary nature. It purports to aid people in solving problems. In so doing the widespread participation of people in planning and conducting these informal educational efforts is stressed.

To accomplish the above functions requires deliberate and careful forethought, if maximum efficiency of operation is to be achieved. Normally two documents are produced as the result, the programme and the plan of work.

This chapter is planned to give the details about developing a Plan of Work.

DEFINITION AND ANALYSIS OF THE CONCEPT

Kelsey and Hearne have defined the plan of work as "an outline procedure so arranged, as to enable efficient execution of the entire programme. It is the answer to what, where, when and how the job will be done."

A.H. Maunder terms it as, "a listing of activities by which the objectives already decided upon shall be achieved."

Lynn L. Pesson refers to it as, "an annual document that outlines the activities to be conducted with people in order to accomplish the objectives of the programme. It describes the efforts that they will expand with people. When properly designed it should be based primarily on helping people to achieve these objectives."

A.T. Mosher, says that it is: "a decision as to which teaching activities are to be employed and with what frequency, with respect to each of the objectives of an extension programme within a given period of time."

To summarise the above definitions, it is clear that a plan of work contains:

(1) Listing of activities for a season, preferably a year.
(2) These activities are detail outlines of predetermined objectives.
(3) They are immediate goals to be achieved.
(4) It is an outline of action to be taken namely:
   Where it is to be done;
   What is to be done;
   How it is to be done;
   Who is to be reached; and
   How results might be measured.

Here each change agent develops specific projects to carry out recommendations expressed in the programme. Edger J. Boone, rightly emphasised that, "educational jobs listed in the plan must be related to the general objectives in the programme as planned." He further says, "included in the plan of work are such things as:

> The specific jobs that need to be done;
> The subject-matter that is needed;
> The people who are reached;
> How each job will be done;
> Where each job will be done; and
> Who will do each job."

Thus the plan of work becomes a teaching plan. It is a guide for daily action. It dictates direction in the selection of learning experiences and teaching tools and methods.

Why have a plan of work?—Importance and scope in extension

Jalihal K.A. (1970) has pointed out the importance of a plan of work. He says, "in extension teaching, it is needless to mention that the teaching should be designed to organise learning experiences so as to bring about learning, resulting in the desired change of people's behaviour in order to solve their day-to-day problems based on their needs and interest."

The plan of work starts the extension teaching process by assisting people to come out with some of their objectives for their learning, based on their felt needs and resources, so as to help them solve their problems.

When this plan of work has been agreed upon, it should be recorded in concise but understandable terms, and copies distributed to all organisations and persons who are concerned with its implementation. Unless this is done even those participating in the decisions will soon disagree as to what was proposed to be done.

This will contribute to uniformity of presentation, ensure attention to necessary details and facilitate comparison and coordination of plans at the various levels and in the areas involved.

It is the function of the Village, Block and District Programme Committees, in consultations with the extension agencies and workers, to determine the number and kind of activities to be carried out, and where necessary to appoint committees or designate local organisation with the responsibility for their implementation. This is only possible when we develop a plan of work, at each level and for each projects.

PLAN OF WORK—A FORMAT OR A MODEL

Dickson and Dotson of the University of Tennessee developed the following contents for an annual written country plan of work:

(A) *Forward*.
(1) The purpose
(2) The procedure
    (i) Development
    (ii) Writing

(B) *Priority programme objectives selected for emphasis.*
(C) *The working objectives.*
(1) Brief statement of the current gap or problem.
(2) A limited number of working objectives for each programme objective selected.
(D) *Scheduling* (a) Learning experiences, situations, who, where, when, and (b) Teaching methods; who, where, when.
(1) How—The methods to be used.
(2) The objective sought.
(3) Who—is to be responsible, and who will be available as a resource person.
(4) When will teaching be done? What methods will be used in teaching?
(5) Where will teaching take place? What methods will be used.
(E) *Internal staff objectives*
(1) Planning and reporting.
(2) Attending annual events.
(3) Preparing for teaching.
(4) Professional improvement.
(F) *Calendar.*
(1) A general month-by-month summary statement or major events including both scheduling and internal staff objectives.

Elements of the plan of work

The extension plan of work is structured into two basic parts: One is the educational activities to be undertaken with a specific clientele group. This part is composed of a series of teaching plans. Each teaching plan is designed to accomplish a specific educational objective. The second part is organisational. It refers to those activities necessary to a successful educational programme that will be conducted during the year.

A well-developed plan of work will focus on the important educational objectives that are to be reached.

For each teaching plan that is developed the specific parts that should be included are:

(1) Educational objectives: Who is to be reached? i.e., audience.
What subject-matter is to be used? i.e., subject-matter.
What behavioural change is expected? i.e., behavioural changes in the knowledge, skills, attitude and goals.
(2) Educational tasks: For the subject-matter content of each objective, there are specific tasks that must be identified in the plan.
(3) Clientele to be reached—must be identified in the plan.
(4) Methods to be used.
(5) Location of teaching.
(6) Calendar of teaching objectives.
(7) The teacher.
(8) Evaluation.

Tayler suggests five principles for consideration in selecting learning experiences:

(a) The learners must have experiences that give him an opportunity to practise the behaviour implied in the objective.

(b) These learning experiences must be structured so that the learners get satisfaction from the behaviour implied in the objective.

(c) The behavioural changes expected are within the realm of possibility for the student.

(d) For one educational objective there are many educational experiences that can be offered.

(e) From the same learning experiences, several outcomes can result among different students.

Prerequisites for developing a plan of work

The following are the prerequisites:

(1) A clear concept of the extension teaching process.

(2) An adequate insight into the fundamental principles of learning and their implications for extension education programme development.

(3) Specific understanding about the method of extension programme development.

(4) Acquaintance with the situation faced by the extension clientele.

(5) Knowledge of technical subject-matter and extension teaching methods.

(6) Able guidance in conducting discussions so as to avoid dissipating energy in direction other than creative thinking.

A model:

Steps in developing a plan of work for agriculture

Steps	*Responsibility*
(1) Prepare a summary of the current agricultural situation calling attention to economic factors and national policy considerations.	State, or National, Extension Service and Ministry of Agriculture.
(2) Review progress and accomplishments to date in relation to long-time programme, indicating those projects that should be continued and those to be completed.	Extension Advisors and Programme Committees, local leaders of groups.
(3) Make minor adjustments.	Extension Advisors and Programme Committees, local leaders of groups.
(4) Select problems for intensive action in current year and set goals for accomplishments.	—do—
(5) Designate local leaders for each problem or project.	Community Groups.
(6) Prepare action programme indicating: (a) Methods to be employed in demonstrations, exhibitions, leader training, meetings, farm tours and publicity, etc. (b) Number of activities. (c) Where they have to be conducted. (d) When is to be held.	Extension Advisor in consultation with Extension Specialists, Community Groups, leaders and Programme Committees.

(e) Person responsible.

(f) Demonstration material required.

(g) Specialists' help needed.

(7) Prepare calendar of activities and adjust for   Extension Worker.
efficient use of time.

(8) Give publicity to plan of work indicating leaders   —do—
responsible for each project.

(9) Provide for evaluation through adequate records   —do—
of methods used and results achieved.

FARM AND VILLAGE AGRICULTURAL PRODUCTION PLANS

Farm planning

Meaning of farm planning: It is a tool for optimum utilisation of the available resources in the maximisation of the attainable income of the farmer. It is a process of ascertaining the weaknesses and bottlenecks in the actual raising of crops and live-stock of an individual farmer and then arriving at some alternative plan best suited to his farm for obtaining maximum and continuous profits. It is designed to put farm resources to the most profitable use.

Need in India

Yield per acre and per animal is very low in India. People need a balanced diet. There is diversity in climate and other resources, so different regions and farmers need different farm plans. There is a low standard of living due to low production. The average per capita income is Rs. 70 per month and 60 per cent people earn less than Rs. 50 per month. So we need farm planning, and for doing that, we have to prepare village production plans.

Prerequisites for farm planning

(1) It should be accepted by our people that farm planning is a challenge to their technical and managerial ability to assist the cultivators in developing new plan.

(2) It should be accepted that it seeks to educate the farmer in problem-solving and changing his attitudes.

(3) It is accepted that it wants to bring a change in the farmer's way of doing things through educational techniques—extension methods based on "Seeing is believing", which involves:

(a) To provide farmers with an opportunity to learn something new and profitable in farming and livestock raising.

(b) To stimulate the mental and physical activities of the farmers so as to attain optimum production from the available resources.

(c) To conserve the available resources for their profitable use in future.

Phases of farm planning

The six phases may be: (1) Analysing the present situation; (2) Raising social and economic conditions with better returns; (3) Developing alternative plans; (4) Convincing the farmers to adopt new plans; (5) Adoption of new plans; (6) Evaluation of the results of new plans and reconsideration by maintaining records.

How to demonstrate the usefulness of farm planning?

(1) *Demonstrate a good farm organisation:* Utilising the land properly by cropping systems, planting orchards, raising fodder, use of capital, proper adjustment with irrigation resources, manure and fertiliser supply, control of pests and diseases, utilisation of labour, etc.

(2) *Demonstrating improved farm practices:* This can be through method demonstrations on practices like: preparation of better seed beds, proper seedling, transplanting, use of fertiliser, raising better calves and chickens, use of plant protection measures and disease control in animals, birds, etc.

(3) *Demonstrating results:* Result of improved yields with controlled practices are shown in comparison, e.g., different dozes of fertilisers compared with no fertiliser, better fed calves, use of insecticides on control plots. The result may be presented through charts or diagrams or photographs, slides, film-strips, etc.

Objectives behind farm planning

(1) To help farmers in increasing the food production of the country.

(2) To develop interest for optimum use of resources.

(3) To create subject-matter for extension workers.

(4) To make the farmers 'plan-minded'.

Preparing a farm plan

Preparation of the following information:

(1) Map of the plots of the farmer.

(2) Particulars of household and farm labours.

    (a) Household.

    (b) Annual farm servants.

(3) Inventory; real estate: area . . . . developing houses . . . . farm buildings. implement-shed . . . . machines and implements . . . livestock (a) . . . . (b) . . . . (c) . . . (d) . . . .

(4) Owned land and operated area: particulars of cultivated plots.

(5) Present plan:

Crops produced	Season	Area			Produce			Remarks
		Irri.	Unirri.	Main	By-products values			
				Quantity	Value	Value	Quantity	

(6) Weaknesses in the present Plan:

Items	Details of measures suggested	Remarks

Operational weakness.

Weakness in the resources.

(7) Alternative plan:

Area		Area and expected produce				Remarks
Crops	Others	Main		By-products		
		Quantity	Price	Quantity	Price	
(1)						
(2)						
(3)						
(4)						
(5)						
Total						

(8) Estimated additional expenditure and additional returns (on account of improvements envisaged in the alternative plan).

(a) Cultural practices:

        (1)

        (2)

        (3)

(b) Manurial practices (1)   (2)   (3)   (4)

(c) Additional fertilisers: Type, method and time of application.

(d) New varieties of seed: (1)   (2)   (3)   (4)

(e) Plant protection measures:

(f) Improvement in irrigation:

(g) Others:

(h) Labour and manurial utilisation:

    (a) Family and bullock labour.

    (b) Manures and fertilisers.

Present plan	Alternative plan	Additional yield	Remarks

(10) Actually implemented plan:

Crop production	Area under crops	Production		Improvements affected	Remarks
		Main	By-product		

(11) Food requirements to be furnished by the farm.

Items	Present plan		Alternate plan		Actually affected	
	Quantity	Value	Quantity	Value	Quantity	Value
(1) For family						
(2) For livestock						
(3) Others						

(12) Measures of profit under the present and alternative plan.

Enterprise	Present plan	Alternate plan	Actually implemented	Remarks

(A) *Crops programme*
   (a) Intensity of crop.
   (b) Total expenditure.
   (c) Gross income.
   (d) Returns to owned capital.
   (e) Interest on owned capital at . . . %
   (f) Returns to family labour used.
   (g) Total male work days.
   (h) Returns per male work days.
   (i) Value of home-consumed labour.

(B) *Other enterprises*
   (1) Enterprise first:
      (a) Implements.
      (b) Total expenses.
      (c) Gross income.
      (d) Returns to owned fixed capital, family labour and management.
      (e) Interest on owned fixed capital, family labour and management at . . . .%.

(f) Returns to family labour and management.
(g) Total of man working days used.
(h) Returns per man work days (Rs.)
(i) Value of profits consumed at home:
   Enterprise I.
   Enterprise II and so on.

Village agricultural production plan

A Village production plan is an outline of activities so arranged as to enable efficient execution of the agricultural production programme of the village. It answers questions like: What is to be produced? Why is it necessary to produce? How can it be produced? When to produce? Where to produce? and, to whom the allotment is to be made? Its basic function is to provide a guide for use in carrying on production work in agriculture and animal raising in a systematic manner for sometime.

Prerequisites for such plan

(1) Background information about sources like type of soil, temperature, irrigation facilities, crops raised, marketing facilities, animal-breeds, subsidiary occupations, supply functions, facilities for banking, supply of capital, etc.

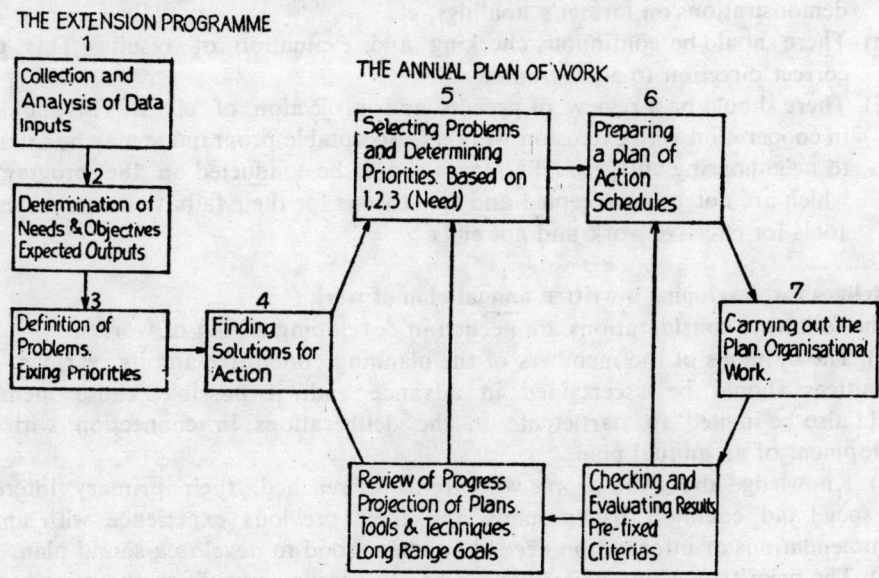

Fig. 38.1 Village Agricultural production plan

(2) About people, leadership, etc.
(3) Involvement of people in preparing a village production plan.
(4) Supply of labour.
(5) Possibilities of organising cooperative societies and farmers organisations.
(6) Preparation and execution of programme of agriculture production.

(a) Collection and analysis of data. This requires collection of data on: (1) Basic information about village—population, number of families, number of farm families, other main occupations of the village, medical aid, drinking water, attitudes and beliefs of the village population, social classes, formal and informal groups, local leaders, etc., (2) Nutritional situation, (3) Information about farm management and programmes: total area under cultivation, size of average agricultural holding, soil types and quality of crops grown, cattle-feeds and fodder, agricultural machinery, irrigation resources, financial position of farmers and their credit needs.

(b) Determination of objectives. This is to be decided by active members of participating families or the panchayat.

(c) Definition of problem: (1) Problems which can be solved by villagers with their own resources. (2) Problems that need community cooperation without outside assistance, e.g., approach road by Shramdan. (3) Problems that require outside help, e.g., plant protection services, etc.

(d) Finding solution: The VLW, AEO and Veterinary Extension Officer must have clear understanding of and offer solutions to the village problems.

(e) There should be programme committees at different levels.

(f) The annual plan of work should be drawn up.

(g) For carrying out the plan, there should be programme to train the leaders, demonstrations on farmer's holdings, etc.

(h) There should be continuous checking and evaluation of results. This gives correct direction to a programme.

(i) There should be a review of process and projection of plans. This should be in cooperation with extension workers. Acceptable programme may be extended to neighbouring villages and research should be conducted on the programmes which are not being accepted and the reasons for their failure. Programmes are tools for effective work and not ends.

Guidelines for developing a written annual plan of work

The following considerations are needed in developing a plan of work:

(1) The opinions of the members of the planning committee and its various sub-committees should be ascertained in advance and, if possible, those members should also be invited to participate in the deliberations in connection with the development of an annual plan.

(2) Knowledge about the people who are to be reached, their primary interests, their social and common backgrounds and their previous experience with similar recommendations or information needed be understood to develop a sound plan.

(3) The priority working objectives need to be drawn out from the priority programme objectives for considering the development of an annual plan and a mention of the same must briefly be made.

(4) All the different personnel should have a common conference to discuss the development of the annual plan.

(5) The previous annual plans and the annual reports should be thoroughly studied by the different personnel, and wherever possible, a summary of the previous work should be in the possession of each.

(6) The priority based on short-time objective when drawn from the programme objectives need to be classified according to major areas of programme emphasis.

(7) Each of the subject-matter specialists should state the number of teaching objectives with reference to each short-time programme objectives.

(8) The teaching objective needs to be started in a manner specifying the behaviour as desired and the context in which the behaviour is believed to be appropriate and the people, or group, who are expected to change.

(9) The names of the key personnel whose position, business, reputation or skills can be utilised should be included in the committee, while developing the plan of work.

(10) The methods to be used to create a learning experience in relation to each teaching objective has to be prepared.

(11) While listing the methods, the time when teaching has to be carried out should be noted, and the whole arranged chronologically. This will enable the agent to judge whether the activities are too many in some months and with low in other months. By taking into consideration the alternatives, the activities could be arranged more or less uniformly throughout the year.

(12) Along with the teaching activities, other activities like meeting with the superviser, attending any conference and many other known activities must also be listed so as to arrange the teaching activities without clashing with these.

(13) All the agents should try to get over duplications of activities in the plan of each by discussing their plans jointly.

(14) The assistance needed from specialists in different months should be visualised and included in that month's schedule of activities. Details regarding what work will be expected of him, what he needs to bring in term of supplies and teaching materials, what relation a particular activity is to the whole Block Programme, wha follow-up is needed, etc., have to be noted, so as to enable the agent to correspond with the specialist or arrange for a conference. This will also enable him to write for their services well in advance in many instances months earlier.

(15) At least 5 per cent of the time in each month should have flexible arrangement, so as to accommodate any unforeseen changes without causing a major setback to the planned teaching activities.

(16) The places where the teaching activities are expected to be carried out should be tentatively determined on the information already known to the agents. Immediate steps should be tal. .n to finalise the same after contacting the person or persons involved.

(17) While working out the details of the teaching activities and methods, plans for evaluation should be built in as a part of the activities.

(18) The assistance that is needed from other organisations and the local available resources, must be taken into account while listing the activities in order to make them workable.

Selecting methods and structuring learning experiences

When the effectiveness of extension teaching is considered and the plan of work is reviewed several requirements stands out as primary factors to consider in planning (Fig 38.2). These include:

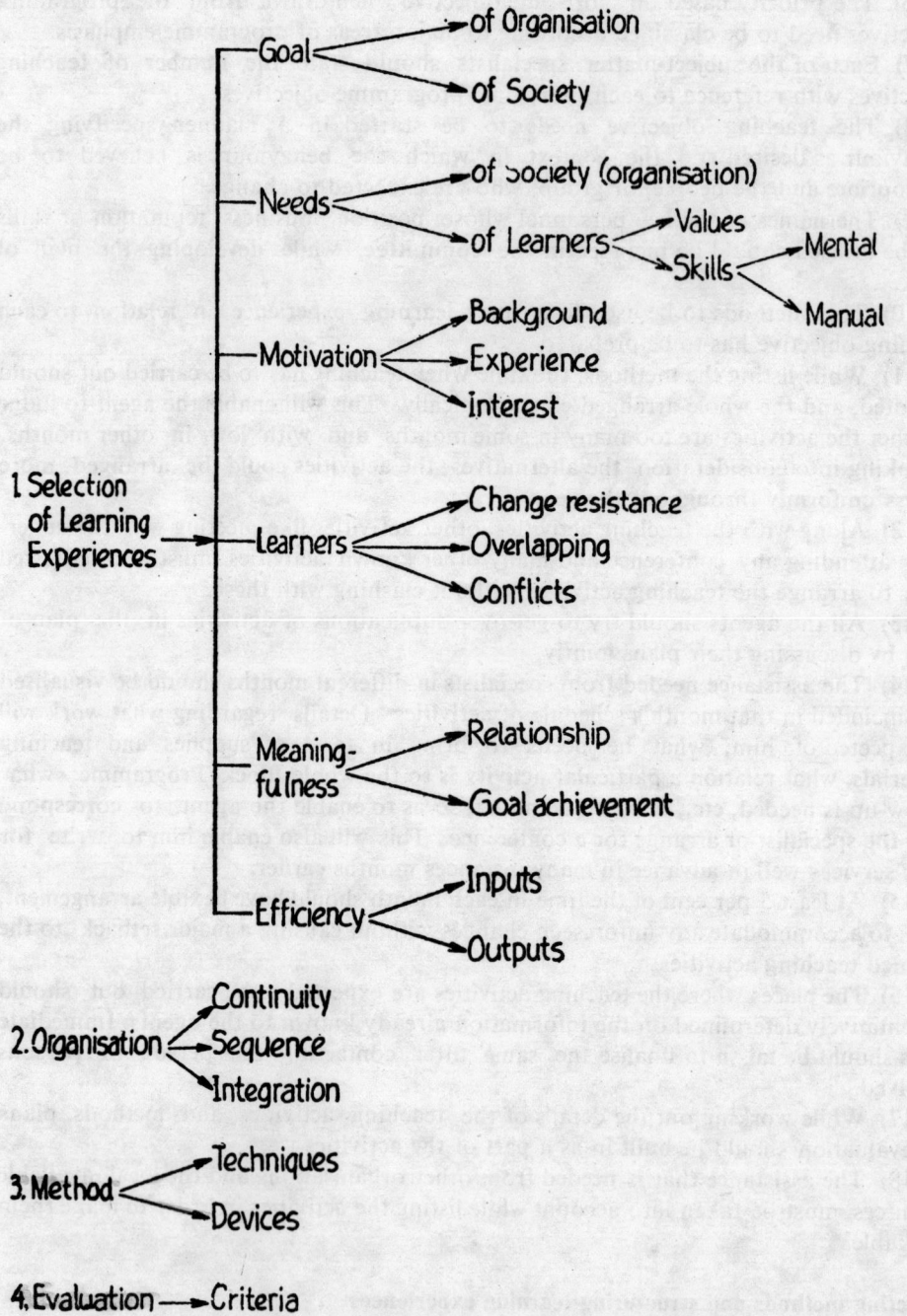

Fig. 38.2 A schematic outline of learning experiences.

(a) Thorough knowledge of the audience;

(b) Cognisance of the factors affecting the acceptance of change by people;

(c) The application of sound educational techniques in structuring learning situations; and

(d) Fixing teaching objectives.

(a) *Knowledge of audience*

The following information is needed:

(i) Collect social, economic and technological information.

(ii) Analyse each group of clientele as a basis for planning the facts collected (i).

(iii) Develop programme objectives from (i) and (ii)

(iv) Use. (i), (ii), (iii) as a guide in selecting learning experiences.

(v) The selection of learning situations depends upon the following valuable data.

(i) *Personal characteristics:* Such as age, educational status, income, size of operation, family status, and psychological characteristics.

(ii) *Values and attitudes:* These have a profound influence on the acceptance of extension teaching. Cultural influence are dominant in shaping values and attitudes. Lionberger comments that culture can hinder or speed up change.

(iii) *Socialisation patterns:* Lionberger comments that the neighbourhood and the social clique exert much influence upon the adoption behaviour of the people. Brunner observe that the lower the socio-economic status of the area, the higher the proportion of persons who wanted adult educational activities to be located within their neighbourhood.

(iv) *Economic situations:* Trends in recent years have indicated that agriculture in the future will contain fewer but more specialised, more efficient and larger farm units. These units will be highly mechanised with high capitalisation needs. The other low-income farmers generally offer more resistance to change. Economic consideration touch all the areas of life. Recent emphasis on resource development indicates that this area should receive consideration.

(v) *Technological situation:* People must use the latest technology. Extension workers need to keep abreast of these and other changes that continually take place. In addition, unfelt needs must be ferreted out along with the needs and expressed interests of the potential clientele. The data on these must be judged by the latest extension recommendations based on the latest research findings and/or standards jointly developed by the people and extension workers.

(vi) *Stages in the diffusion process:* Beal and Bohlen have described these steps as follows:

(i) Awareness: (ii) interest; (iii) evaluation; (iv) trial; and

(iv) adoption. Consideration of these stages are plan of work.

(vii) *Individual differences in adoption:* At any given point in the teaching process, the extension worker may find members of a group in all five stages of the diffusion process. The point at which the majority are located is a major determining factor in the type of learning situation that should be structured for that group.

(viii) *Indirect influence:* The extension programme objectives imply change. When broken down into teachable units, these objectives usually involve specific practices and/or ideas that specific audiences could adopt.

Changes occurs gradually through, what some rural sociologists call, the "trickle-down process". According to Lippit, Watson and Westley, there are three possible starting points:

  (i) a change agent (such as extension worker) perceives a need;

  (ii) the client system (an audience) itself becomes sensitive and actively seeks help; and

  (iii) a third party starts the process—possibly by getting the change agent and the client system together.

(b) *Factors affecting acceptance of change*

Beale and Bohlen have identified four important sources of information; these are:

  (i) Neighbours and friends.

  (ii) The agricultural agencies (including extension system).

  (iii) Salesman and commercial leaders.

  (iv) Mass media.

(c) *Structuring the learning situation*

In the process of structuring the learning situation, the following four points serves as education guidelines: (i) Motivational forces; (ii) Educational objectives; (iii) Methods and techniques; and (iv) Evaluation.

While structuring the learning situation, the priority emphasis should be given to the subject-matter which may be as follows:

Classification of subject-matter: Subject-matter is selected and taught in order to develop interest, knowledge or understanding, skills or attitudes. These outcomes are interwoven and are dependent upon each other.

It would be a long job to teach and draw a plan of work for everything that is known about any one problem and it would not be necessary. But a plan of teaching must fulfil a need.

The needs of a learner are different from the needs of his teacher or extension workers. On the basis of need we can divide subject-matter into the following categories (Fig. 38.3).

  (i) Vital subject-matter: That which is absolutely essential for the accomplishment of the objective.

  (ii) Important subject-matter: That which is included for the purpose of giving the learner a basic understanding.

  (iii) Helpful subject-matter: That which is related to the problem and gives a broader sense of understanding on which to build.

  (iv) Superfluous subject-matter: That which has such a small bearing on the needs of the learner, that it serves no useful purpose in helping him to do his job.

Subject-matter and the learner's needs

The problem of a teacher is to select the bits of knowledge or subject-matter that the learner must know in order to accomplish their objectives. Time and other factors permitting, subject-matter which is desirable to know might be taught. It is rarely

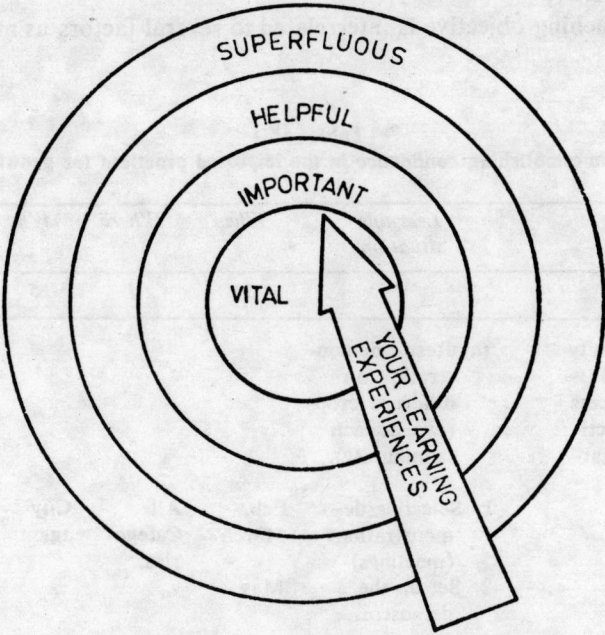

Fig. 38.3 Subject-matter and the learners' needs.

worth the effort to teach things which are just nice to know or which are superfluous to the needs of the learner.

Selection of the subject-matter

Each problem in the programme will have its objectives stated in terms of what the the learners want and need to know to be able to do or accomplish. These general objectives will have to be analysed into the behaviour change relative to specific vital subject-matter.

The prime sources of information which will help in the selection of the proper subject-matter will need be surveyed. The starting point in the selection of subject-matter is at the learning or teaching level of the learners. The subject-matter which will be vital will be dependent upon the previously determined objectives and the present level of the learners.

If one of the specific objectives is interest development, the subject-matter that has real interest-building qualities will need be selected and will be vital. The goals need be established and the subject-matter that will help to do this job will be vital to learners, and to this problem. Subject-matter that will aid in bringing about the desired understanding will also be vital. Subject-matter that is not needed to realise desired objectives will be eliminated as superfluous to the immediate needs of the learners. If time is strictly limited, it may be necessary to cut short instruction in the important subject-matter and even the vital information.

(d) *Teaching objective*

Selection of teaching objective is interrelated to several factors as may be seen from Table 38.1

Table 38.1

To help learners in establishing confidence in the improved practices for growing garden crops

Learning experience to be provided	Learning situation	When	Where	Who	Assisted by
1	2	3	4	5	6
(1) Provide opportunity to establish local proof of the success of improved practices in growing garden crop.	(a) Result demonstration on different crops (two in each community).				
	1. Selecting demonstrations (meetings)	Feb. March	All Categories.	City agent	Community agent
	2. Set up the demonstrations.	May	,,	,,	Ext. Agronomist.
	3. Supervise the demonstrations.	July August Sept.	,,	,,	Ext. Horti. & others.
	4. Result demonstrations meeting.	Aug. Sept.	,,	,,	Supervisor Ext. Agro. Ext. Hort.
	5. Collect data	Sept. Oct.	,,	,,	
(2) Have the people observe the quality of produce from successful gardens.	(b) Exhibits	Sept.	,,	City fair	Community agent.
	(c) Photographs of demonstrators in the plot.	Aug. Sept.	News paper Comm. club Comm. fair	,,	
(3) Let them get an opportunity to study the production records of demonstrators and discuss the same.	(d) Farm & home visits.				
	(e) Community meetings.	Oct. Nov.	All comm.	City agent.	Community agent.

A schematic outline of learning experiences should take into consideration the important components of personal, organisational, methodological and evalution criteria (as may be observed from Fig. 38.2).

Plan of work and calendar of events—annual plan of work

Formulation of the work plan is part of programme planning. It takes the programme topics which local people have participated in choosing and decides what teaching activities to employ and with what frequency. But an additional question needs to be asked. Is the necessary knowledge and the necessary materials available? To get answers to this and hosts of other queries, we end up with the following; for working out the details with respect to each objective listed below:

First: Proposed topics of objectives are listed.

Second: Knowledge and supplies—amount and services available.

Third: Primary teaching activities—most useful for particular topic are listed.

Fourth: Subsidiary teaching activities—includes news releases, etc., are planned.

Fifth: Frequency—number of increases of repetitions of each activity felt to be necessary for effective teaching.

Sixth: Within what time—indicates time when each of these activities ought to be carried out.

A paradigm of plan of work gives the various details as shown in Fig. 38.4

(a) *Preparation of a calendar of events*

An extension worker, to be efficient, needs a calendar of events. Like so many processes and techniques, this matter of putting a work-plan on paper, figuring out what activities need to be conducted with respect to each proposed objective, making up a calendar of events which sums up these activities for each week, and charting the consequences of these in terms of the time required to carry them through, can become quite a useful document for smoothening the enthusiastic, spontaneous teaching activities which are the "acting" role in the extension drama.

Just as local participation is essential in one phase of programme planning, so local extension agents needs to be those who develop work plans and a calendar of activities.

(b) *A guideline*

The following outline and form is used, with variations, in many states in the USA as a guide for the preparation of Annual County Extension Plan of Work:

(1) Brief review of situation in relation to objectives stated in the long time extension programme, including reasons for selection of problems designated for attack in current plan of work.

(2) List of selected problems, proposed solutions and goals.

Examples:

Problem	Solutions	Goals
Low milk production	Improvement of winter feeding (a) Greater use of protein concentrates (b) More ample supply of grass sileage.	Increase average daily production per cow during winter months from 8 litres to 10 litres.

(3) Procedure and methods for each major projects:

Activity	Responsibility
(a) Use of protein cnoncentration	Deptt. of Nutrition/Chemistry
(b) Supply of grass saleage	Deptt. of Agrostology/Biochemistry
(c) Supply of equipments required	Deptt. of Stores/Workshop.
(d) Audio-visual materials to be prepared	Communications Centre/Deptt. of Audio-visual Aids
(e) Assistance required from extesion specialists	Directorate of Extension Education

Within the local community, a simplified plan of work may be adopted in consultation with local committees or organisations. It will include the district-wise activities in which the community is involved and other activities of a local nature that are not of interest to the country or district as a whole. Local youth groups and homemakers clubs, control of local weed problems, development of local markets, solving of drainage problems in small areas, are such examples.

In laying out an Annual Plan of Work careful consideration should be given to resources and facilities available; the experience of farm people and staff in cooperative action; progress already achieved on various problems; and acute current problems demanding attention.

Attempting to work on too many problems at once results in dissipation of the efforts of the staff, and division of interests among the individuals and group.

(c) *Annual plan of work: a format*
Name of County/Block....................Programme Division............Major Area of work......... Situation......
Long-term objectives:

The Programme		The Plan of Action			The Evaluation
Specific problem	Teaching objectives	Methods & learning experiences	When required (specify days)	Agent responsible	How to measure results.

Criteria for judging the plan of work

(1) Could the staff justify the plan of work to members of the Block Programme Planning Committee in view of an up-to-date programme statement?

(2) Is there evidence that the working objectives are means towards obtaining the programme objectives?

(3) Are the objectives (programmes and working) realistic in view of the Block situation?

(4) Are the long range working objectives related to the current years teaching objectives?

(5) Is there a brief situational statement to orientate the plan of work?

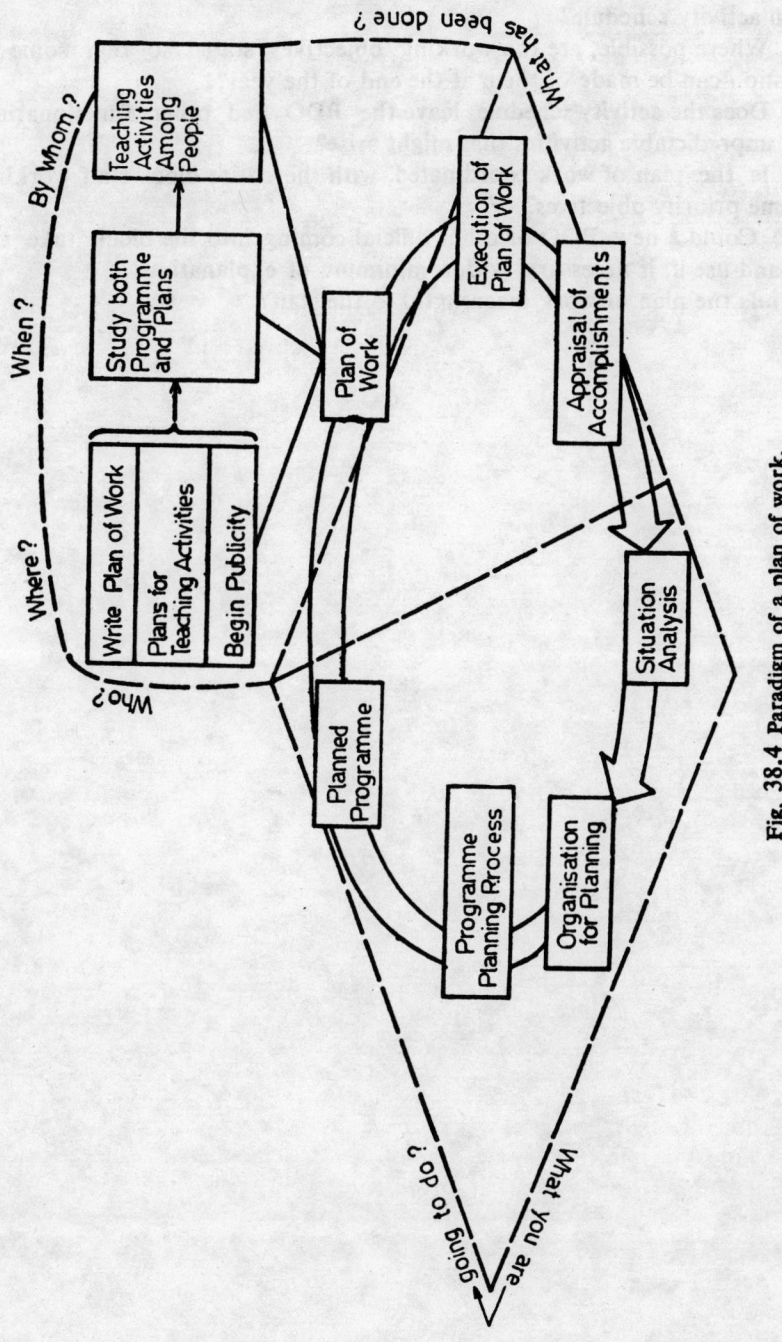

Fig. 38.4 Paradigm of a plan of work.

(6) Are the working objectives clearly, specifically and consciously stated and not just an activity schedule?

(7) Where possible, are the working objectives stated so that some measurable evaluation can be made of them at the end of the year?

(8) Does the activity schedule leave the BDO and other functionaries, free for extra, unpredictable activities that might arise?

(9) Is the plan of work coordinated, with the entire block staff working towards the same priority objectives?

(10) Could a new BDO or other official coming into the block take the plan of work and use it, if necessary, with a minimum of explanation?

(11) Is the plan of work meaningful to the staff?

CHAPTER 39

A PLAN FOR IMPROVED PROCEDURES OF PROGRAMME DEVELOPMENT IN INDIA

Programme planning, as it is defined,[1] is a procedure of working with the people in an effort to recognise unsatisfactory situations, i.e., the problems, and determine possible solutions to meet the objectives and goals. According to Mueller,[2] "conscious effort should be made to meet the needs, interests and wants of the people for whom the programme is intended."

Steps

In developing a programme for extension work, the following steps should be involved:

(1) Study the situation; (a) the people, their habits, attitudes and values, (b) the physical conditions, and (c) collect background information.

(2) Identify the local leaders and obtain their support. These leaders may be the formal and informal, the organisation and different interest groups, and their leaders.

(3) A planning committee should be set up with designated persons representing broader important interests in the community, or area. The designated leaders should be asked to choose representatives of various groups and organisations in the area. The responsibility should be distributed by forming the sub-committee for planning.

(4) Determination may be made up of: (a) the important needs and interests of the people, (b) how research findings will meet these needs and interests, and (c) the help to be given by the Government should also be taken into consideration.

(5) Setting up objectives, i.e., in what direction and to what extent the existing situation should be changed. The objectives should touch the largest proportion of the people of the village or region. Existing customs and values of the people must be taken into consideration.

(6) A system of priority for taking up the problems should be set up.

[1] K.A. Venugopal, *Eassay Development of a Course of Study in Extension Education for Under-graduates at the Osmania Ag. College*, Hyderabad, India, 1957, pp. 119.

[2] A.D. Mueller, *Principles and Methods in Adults Education*, New York, Printice-Hall, Inc., 1937.

(7) The decided teaching objectives and teaching methods should be worked out.

(8) A periodical review of the situation and reconsideration of the plan for setting up revised objectives should be done.

These steps can be represented diagrammatically as in Fig 38.1.

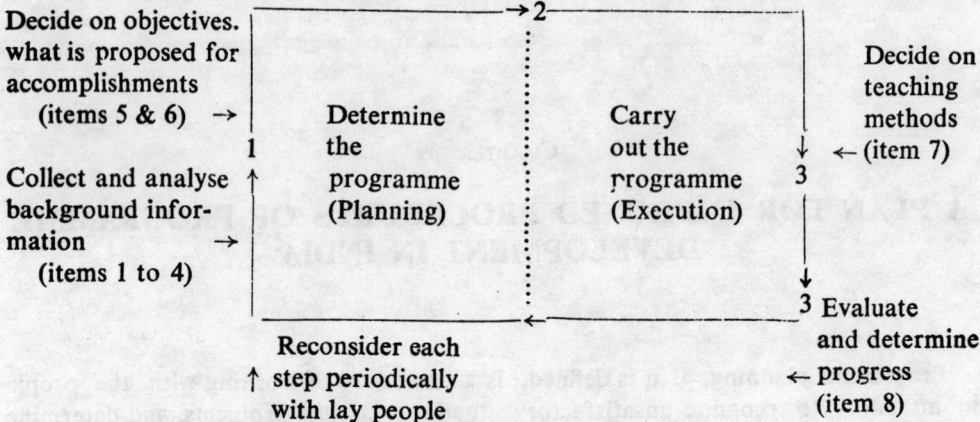

Fig. 39.1 Steps in developing a programme for extension work.

Note: This concept is intended only to clarify the steps in planning the programme. They are not separate from each other. They take place continuously, in varying degrees throughout all phases of programme planning.

So our plan of work must include:

(1) What is to be done?
(2) Who is to do it?
(3) How it is to be done?
(4) When it is to be done?
(5) Whom it is to be served and reached?
(6) How results might be measured?

Who is to build the extension programme?

The rural people and the professional workers are to build the programme. The participation of the village people for whom the programme is to be made is very essential because[1] the extension programme should be planned with and not for the people. Participation of local people results in making the programme go smoothly and with greater momentum and develops personality in participants.

The professionals are required to help the people in giving background information, in recognising the needs, framing the objectives, suggesting the solutions, evaluating the programmes, building up public opinion by propaganda and revising the planned programme.

So the village level worker, the extension specialist and the BDO have to play their part by supplying information, by guidance and also by actually working as secretaries of various committies.

[1]Edmund Des Brunner and Hsin Pio E. Yang, *Rural American and the Extn. Service*, New York, Bureau of Publications, Columbia University, 1949.

A survey of the existing conditions

Before making any programme, a survey of the existing conditions and situation is called for:

(1) Finding out whom to contact in the village for discussion and to gain new ideas about the village.

(2) To know the decision-making groups and to trace the channels of communication which carry the decisions to the individuals in community.

(3) Kowing the opposing forces working in the community and also the institutional and prestige groups.

(4) Knowing the history and culture of the people and the physical conditions.

(1) *The study of the physical situation of the village, includes*
  (a) The soil—climate complex.
  (b) The means of transportation.
  (c) Size of holdings, fragmentation, etc.
  (d) Livestock, fodder, farm buildings, etc.
  (e) Houses, etc.
  (f) Farm and other equipment.
  (g) Occupational distribution, caste structure, etc.
  (h) Land tenures.
  (i) Credit facilities, etc.

For obtaining such information about the village, the census reports, revenue records and actual visits to the village and talks with the villagers will help.

(2) *Problems affecting groups of people*
  (a) Drinking water supply.
  (b) Medical aid and health facilities.
  (c) Village roads, back-yards, etc.
  (d) School facilities.
  (e) Cropping facilities.

This data can be obtained by an actual survey of the local conditions through leading persons of the villages.

(3) *Survey regarding improvements in agriculture and animal husbandry and village industries for getting increased production*
  (a) What improvements are needed regarding soil conservation and crop rotation.
  (b) What improved strains of crops can be introduced.
  (c) What manures and fertilisers, etc., are necessary and how to get them.
  (d) What cultivation practices need change.
  (e) What horticultural improvements are essential.
  (f) What vegetable improvements are necessary.
  (g) What measures are necessary for control pests and diseases.
  (h) What improvements in the existing marketing systems are necessary.
  (i) How to improve the cattle breeds, their feeding, breeding, etc.
  (j) Which cattle diseases need to be controlled.

(k) Which village industries need to be revived.

(l) What subsidiary occupations can be introduced, or improved, for balancing the farming system.

(4) *Study of social conditions of social structure*

To collect data under this head, the following survey is necessary.

(a) *Special or locality groups:* (1) household, (2) neighbourhood, (3) village, (4) community, (5) trade centres, and (6) region.

(b) *Interest groups:* These are both formal and informal.

(1) Friendship groups.

(2) Neighbourhood groups.

(3) Special interest groups like sports, drama, etc.

(c) *Institutional groups:* These are:

(1) *Family:* Joint families are likely to be less receptive than nuclear families. In a traditional society like that in India, the oldest members especially males, make decisions. The ladies are the custodians of custom and tradition. Changes cannot be initiated without the sanction of the elderly man in the family.

(2) *Religion:* Religious recitations, songs and festivals can be used to get the people together.

(3) *Caste:* Caste reinforces neighbourhood solidarity. Single caste villages have a rigid authoritarian leadership. In a multiple-caste village, an intercaste structure develops out of mutual dependence.

(4) *Economic:* In India, usually, the parental profession is followed by the sons. The recent laws of land reform, credit, marketing, etc., are changing this structure. This may increase the receptivity of people to adopt change.

(5) *Education:* Primary school teachers live in the villages and develop family relations and attain wide influence.

(6) *Government:* The Gram Panchayat will be a decision-making institution in many respects henceforth on account of the powers and responsibilities delegated to it.

(7) *Prestige groups:* In India, vertical movement in the society is very slow. Status is determined by caste, family history, financial condition, personality traits and age of the person. It is always better to approach the lowest group through the leaders for the acceptance of change by the community.

CONSTITUTING A PROGRAMME BUILDING COMMITTEE

The constitution of the village committee is just a formality. The real representatives and the leaders are not much involved in it The people generally feel that it is imposed over them. The local leaders are not taken into confidence and delegated with responsibility. All groups and interests in the village should get representation through their leaders. Sub-committees should be formed to share responsibility. The participation of the people develops in them the feeling of that "it is their programme" and so gives momentum to the programme.

Setting up objectives

The criteria for setting up the objectives should be that:

(1) They should be within the reach of the people economically, socially and educationally.

(2) They should be based on the genuine needs and interests of the people.

(3) They should contribute to the fundamental aim of extension, i.e., a better life.

The extension worker can help in setting up the objectives in the following ways:

(a) He should hold formal talks and ascertain genuine needs of the people.

(b) He should bring all local leaders together and get them to discuss problems for better understanding.

(c) He should supply background information and make suggestions concerning the technical matters.

(d) He can suggest solutions of the problems.

The lay leaders can play the following part:

(i) They should consult people and ascertain genuine needs and interests.

(ii) They should educate the people in their own groups.

(iii) They should study the background information and then fix up priorities for the projects to be taken up.

Plan for carrying out the programme

As given in the structure of the organisation, the carrying out of the programme is primarily the responsibility of the Block Development Officer or any Extension Officer acting in his place, as in M. P., who is concerned with the administration of the programme after it has been finalised through various stages. This requires effective delegation of authority to require action of the others and also of function in the nature of services to be rendered to other staff members. Such delegation in order to be effective requires:

(a) A good basic organisation.

(b) Courage on the part of the administrator.

(c) Faith in the associates.

(d) Granting of authority commensurate with the responsibility which the staff members will have.

(e) The authority or function delegated must be clearly understood.

(f) Avoid conflicting or overlapping delegation.

(g) Be sure that all staff members concerned are aware of the delegation.

(h) Encourage, on the part of staff members, a desire for responsibility.

In addition to extension staff, local leaders for various parts of the programme should be found, trained to assume responsibility and guided to work which they are interested in.

Regular staff meetings should be held at which time the plans for the immediate future should be laid out; the demonstrations to be held, the priority to be given to various works, who shall be on tour for a particular period, what inspections shall be made of work in progress, what supplies are needed for carrying out the work, what equipment and cooperation is needed from other departments, how can they do best the jobs required, etc.

Problem regarding fixing of the targets

A considerable number of people, as we mentioned in the previous pages, are not involved when the information is gathered from the community.

Cases are common where at the time of getting information from the local people, some of the BDOs or extension staff at block level and VLWs do not take pains even to go to the villages and gather information about their needs and interests. The community development workers generally approach two or three persons in that community and receive information from them about the needs of the community as a whole. Sometimes, one or two persons are invited to the block headquarters, and reports are completed according to their information. After this, these reports reach the National Planning Commission at the national level. Sometimes, it happens that the information gathered about the needs of the village is not based upon the community needs but the needs of one segment of the community. This is a sort of misrepresentation of the community problems.

Autocratic community development organisation procedures

Most of the powers in the area of programme planning are concentrated at the national level, in the hands of the NPC[1] There lies no doubt that this body formulates broad policies for the working of the community development organisation and extension people at all leveis hesitate to make some changes. Funds are sanctioned under various heads to be spent in a given time and the BDO or Extension Officer in the Block has less authority to spend these for other purposes even if they feel the need to do so.

Consequences of the above problem

In a situation like this, where there is less individual decision-making and powers are mostly concentrated at the higher level, the following consequences can be noticed:

(1) *People consider it as a Governmental programme:* People take it as a Governmental programme because they are not involved in making the analysis of the situation and then planning a programme. They think it as just like other programmes, imposed by the Government for implementation. This is the reason that they do not make sacrifices to make this programme a successful and useful one. Sometimes, the NPC assumes that it knows the needs of the people, and plans the programme according to that impression. But it is difficult for the NPC, or other levels of the organisation in the State, to estimate the needs of the people when the communication sources between the Government officers and people at the village level are poor. In other words, we can say that this programme fails to meet the felt needs and interests of the people. In such cases, people feel frustrated and sometimes develop quite prejudiced ideas against the existing system of government machinery.

(2) *To achieve the physical targets become the objective of the Community Development Organisation:* All efforts of the VLWs are concerned to achieve the physical targets fixed by the higher authorities. Sometimes, the basic needs of the people are ignored at the cost of achieving these physical targets. The result of this procedure is that the village level worker does not care to change the outlook of the people through the educational process but he just wants to attain his own goals. People

1 National Planning Commission.

may achieve these physical targets under some kind of pressure. There is doubt if they will be able to continue this programme in the absence of community development workers.

(3) *Underestimation of capacities and abilities of the local people:* The higher authorities in the organisation think that people are not able to plan their own programme, so it is better to sell a programme to them, at this stage. No doubt, villagers are ignorant, illiterate and poor, but opportunities should be provided to train people for the programme planning and evaluation. To underestimate their abilities is not the objective of this organisation, which is based upon the principle of people's programme with Government participation. It is difficult to sell the ideas, objectives and principles of this organisation until and unless people are ready to receive the same. This is the reason that people expect too much from the Government and do not like to take the initiative themselves. People have tremendous abilities but the proper type of opportunities are not provided to develop them.

(4) *Problems that affects the coordination between the specialists of various departments at all levels:* In India, we have different Ministries for different services like health, education, industries, etc., and all these departments have their own targets to achieve at the block level. The block specialist tries to achieve these targets individually and there is lack of coordination.

No doubt, it is an improvement of rural life by different agencies but the approach is not integrated. As we have seen the community life is not divided into different segments, so the approach to improve the rural life should be comprehensive and total.

"At the block level, some subject-matter specialists feel the strain of divided loyalties. Although the formula is that they are administratively responsible to the block development officer and technically responsible to their subject-matter departments. This is more easily said than done. Especially, since the lack of smooth coordination at the state level is not secret and is reflected at the lower level of administration."[1]

If the targets can be adjusted easily, according to the felt needs of the local people, and programmes are planned by the people themselves, then there can be less possibility of any kind of rivalry among the specialists of various departments.

(5) *It affects the morale of community development workers:* Last, but not least, an important consequence of this problem is that it affects the morale of the extension worker. As there are less powers at all lower levels for independent decision-making, instead of planning, there is simply a tendency to receive, interpret and hand down orders from one level to another. These officers are all aware of the problems and difficulties of their own subordinates but they feel helpless due to the general lack of appreciation on the part of their own supervisors.

If the extension workers feels that he is not able to achieve these targets in time due to some unfavourable circumstances he tries to produce some false reports for the bosses. When these reports reach the national level, they think that lot of improvements is going on through the community development programmes but actually this improvement in some cases is limited to files only.

[1]*Community Development Review*, September 1959, Vol. 4, No. 5, p. 57.

Similarly, when some minister or big officer happens to visit the communities, lot of artificial improvements are shown to make him satisfied. Community development workers spend a major part of their time doing this sort of thing rather than on doing some job for the village people.

Suggestions to solve the problem

The following suggestions may be noted:

(1) *Decentralisation of powers:* The first step to solve this problem is to change the administrative set up of C.D. Organisation. By this change, we mean that powers should be decentralised and individual decision-making should be encouraged. The officers at the higher level should be trained in the basic objectives and principles of Community Development Organisation. They should have considerable knowledge of how to deal with their subordinates in such a way that they can achieve the real purpose of this organisation. This is an educational programme and no place to enforce anything upon the people against their wishes. There should be clear definitions of the roles of each and mutual understanding of the responsibilities of extension and C.D. workers and the people at village level.

Decentralisation of power is one answer to this problem. At present, officers hesitate to take the initiative and they always depend upon their immediate bosses. For example, in any block Rs. 10,000 is sanctioned for education. In that area almost all communities have Elementary Schools and students can go to other communities to attend the Higher Secondary Schools. At the same time, people being poor and uneducated, do not value education. In such a situation, education is not their felt need. Suppose, there are heavy floods in an area where people are doing farming on subsistence basis. Due to this calamity crops are distroyed, houses are damaged and now the felt need of the people is to repair their houses, to get food to eat, to get seed to plant and to get some fodder for livestock. The people will approach the BDO to help them in their distress. He has no authority to reappropriate the money sanctioned for education. He has to seek permission from the District Collector and then the Collector has to ask the Development Commissioner for the same. This procedure will take four or five months. Villagers are suffering now but they will receive the aid after five months. There is wastage of money, energy and time in this centralised type of procedure. If the powers are distributed at all levels, then timely problems can be solved and the confidence of the people can be won easily.

According to Mosher, "The over-centralisation of programme building is always a danger. This danger is never out-grown because administrators and extension agents are human beings, and each one always tends to feel that he knows best what the programme should be. Administrators are in a strongest position to push their views becase of powers which they yield with respect to budget and employment.[1]

Of course, this has been inherited from the British rule and now the government is moving towards a new direction under Article 40 of the Constitution of India. The Government launched a scheme of democratic decentralisation in October 1959. Under

---

[1]"Establishing a Young Extension Service", Cornell University, Ithaca, N.Y., Mimeo Release No. 1, July, 1959.

this scheme, the implementation of rural development plans is the responsibility of the Panchayat (Village Council), the Government providing only assistance and guidance. This decentralisation of the administration pattern has now made people their own masters. It is they who decide how they should be governed by officials who are there to help them.

(2) *To involve the administrators, C. D and Extension Workers (at all levels) and local people in programme planning:* The goal of C.D. and Extension Organisation in India is (1) to raise the level of agricultural production, (2) to raise the level of living of rural masses, and (3) to strengthen the position of the nation as a whole.

According to Mosher, "What we are really trying is a process which results in full information about the interests and needs of local people, which capitalise on their interest and secure their participation in thinking about what the objectives of the programme ought to be and which also takes into account of, factors which are better known to administrators and subject-matter specialists."[1]

In a country like India, where we have so many problems to solve through this Organisation and people are not accustomed to these types of programme planning, it is difficult to give full authority to the village people. Even within the villages there are some factions and it is equally possible that those groups dominate in planning programmes according to their needs and interests. That type of programme will not represent the needs of the people. The village people need technical and financial help from Community Development Organisation because their problems are numerous and it is difficult to slove them with community resources.

It is equally dangerous if we give full authority to the administrators to plan a programme for the people because the administrators are also not be able to diagnose the problems of rural life without involving local people. Situations differ from State to State and from Village to Village and at the same time, needs and problems changes quickly. The assumption that these administrators know all the needs of local people has no weight.

So the proper way of fixing the targets is to involve local people in programme planning and provide opportunities for them to make independent decisions. At the same time, to make them feel that they have to consider the national targets while planning a programme for the community.

(3) *To maintain systematic linkage:* In India there are three types of system of programme planning:

(a) Government (administrative body, i.e., the NPC).
(b) Community Development Organisation (including C.D. and all other national-development departments).
(c) The Community (at Village Level).

To attain the true purpose of C.D. it is necessary that all these social systems should be linked together. Their cooperation is necessary for its success. So now let us see how we can provide systematic linkage between them. To make adjusment between national targets and local goals is a technique of reconciling. Every social system has some aims and objectives which it wants to achieve by one way or other. The job of the village level worker is to provide a link between these social

[1]Ibid.

systems at the village level. He has some targets from the national level and at the same time, he is aware of the felt needs and interests of the local people. He should approach the community not with a bundle of targets but with an intention to diagnose the situation. After some time, when he feels that people have started to accept him and have some faith in his recommendations, it is wise to make the people feel that he is not going to sell the ideas of the Agency, it all depends upon the people, whether they accept these ideas or not. He should not commit them to any improvement beforehand, but he should lead the people at a level where they themselves become aware about their needs and ready to take some actions to fulfil them. He should create a learning situation instead of imposing anything upon the people. He has in his mind the targets which he received from his boss, but he should not tell them about these targets. He should tactfully create such an atmosphere in the community, that people take the national targets for their own goals and interests, and put out efforts to achieve the same. He should draw out idea from the people and lead them to some action.

Suppose, there is a target set by the national government that three should be a 20 per cent increase in wheat production in the next year. The VLW has this target to achieve. With the help of local potential leaders he should organise surveys of the resources like the land, irrigation facilities, capital of farmers, etc. He should also consider what kinds of other felt needs this community has. What are their values towards the increase in agriculture production and so on.

If he feels that the situation is favourable and there are possibilities for achieving this type of target, then he should involve the people in this project and make them feel that the increase in wheat production will help them to raise their standard of living and, at the same time, it will solve our national problem of food shortage. This is the stage where he should organise some demonstration plots to show the results of the best varieties of wheat. This is the procedure where he can achieve the national targets while taking care of the people's interests.

At this stage, we can conclude how this adjustment can be made between national targets and community goals. At first, a considerable number of people should be involved, when the information is gathered from the community before planning a programme. The second step is that broad policies of a tentative nature should be fixed by the National Commission and there should be reasonable flexibility in the targets so that the community development extension workers and local people can make the adjustment according to the situation. This point will lead to the encouragement of independent decision-making at all levels.

When these targets reach the community, the Villge Council is the best organisation to make an adjustment in these targets and fix local goals. There should be perfect autonomy at the village level and frequent interaction between the Village Council and the Block Planning Committee.

It is quite clear that the development of the community is more important than the development of the targets. Achieving targets is not the only aim of this organisation. But its goal is to produce self-reliant personalities who can transform the socio-economic conditions for their own communities through their own efforts and contribute to solve the national problem also.

The main aim of the organisation is to change the outlook of the people while changing their behaviour (ideas, attitudes and skills), so this organisation should create opportunities for the local people where they can plan their own programme while considering national needs and interests.

COORDINATION OF VARIOUS SERVICES IN COMMUNITY DEVELOPMENT AND EXTENSION

Important aspects of coordination

(1) *Communication:* Initial task in coordinating the programme of rural development is that of establishing clear channels of communication among agencies. Communication is an important factor in linking one agency with another when there is an objective common to all. It should be recognised that communication is a two-way process built upon the principle of mutual dependence.

(2) *Role system:* The second aspect is the need for making the role system clear. The rights and duties assigned to any agency occupying a certain position in the social system should be clearly defined. Coordination develops when the role of one agency is made clear and is understood by other agencies with complementary roles. This is a fundamental factor in coordinating different patterns of agency behaviour. Deviation in the role behaviour of one agency contributes to confusion in the entire social system.

(3) *Ends and objectives of related programme:* Community Development Programmes have been established in many countries as a means of channelising the work of various technical agencies or departmments into a unified effort in rural development. As stated in the *Community Development Handbook:*

"Success in keeping the programme going well depend on how far Community Development Work is geared to the overall development programme both in the planning stage and in the field ·············The aim should be to build up an integrated team approach with field staff, including technical officers and Community Development Workers, operating in a partnership which should join hands with local leaders and local oganisations."

This is an important aspect and it also helps to avoid overlapping in programmes and functions.

Another important task of community development is to make its ends and objectives clear to all related agencies. The specific duties to be performed should be made known and understood by all agencies and departments. Means should be provided for each agency to meet together for the purpose of knowing and understanding what is expected of each of them, so that they will be in a better position to help and support each other. This procedure will strengthen communication and help to avoid some of the problems incurred because of lack of coordination. In countries where community development is newly established, both the government and staff in-charge should try to emphasise its importance so as to give it status with the agencies with which it has to work. This would assist in securing coordination generally, and specially across the levels within related agencies.

(4) *Orientation of personnel:* Since community development must obviously carry the major responsibility of the programme and its coordination, it should see that agencies and departments on whom it must depend are oriented as to its importance,

objectives and programme. Coordination should not be considered a matter of theory, but of reality. Depending upon the specific circumstances and situation, orientation may be done in the following ways: (1) Seminars, (2) Conferences, (3) Lectures and talks, (4) Mass media, (5) Audio-visual aids, (6) Demonstration, and (7) Socio-drama.

(5) *Administrative control:* (a) *Interpreting an transmitting policy:* The community development agency should see that the policy formulated at the highest level of the government is transmitted to all levels in the sub-system, and that there is no by-passing of its directives. Similarly, it should follow the same procedure with respect to other agencies and departments coordinated with community development in rural development. When coordination countinues across the level of similar roles among the agencies, all policies governing the operation of community development and its related agencies would be known and understood. Likewise, policies would be passed down the lines to all whose work may be affected. Where such policies can be interpreted as being conducive to or aiding coordination, the agencies will be able to make effective use of the provisions enacted with respect to the work.

(b) *Budgeting control:* The budget is an important factor in the administration of community development programmes. No work can progress without an adequate budget. Through it, control can be effected in such a way as to regulate operation in conformance with set producers. From this point, a downward scale of relationships with authority should exist at all levels, until it reaches the area of actual operations. Coordination could reasonably be effected at each of these levels in descending scale. It is necessary for all persons of authority from the source of its provision down to the line of actual operation, be responsible for seeing that a coordinated approach to the work provides results warranting the amount of expenditure to maintain the agencies.

(c) *Technical personnel:* Following the line of authority, the services of technical personnel should be so arranged that they should be made available within the requirements of the Community Development Programme. The officers in charge of areas would be responsible for working together to determine at what time, and during what stages of the project, specialised skills are required. Necessary requisitions could be made accordingly to meet the prevailing needs.

(d) *Coordinating committees at all levels:* This committee is formulated in the community development programme by having an advisory committee at each level of the Government. The Government official at each level works as secretary. "These advisory committees should be the policy-making and coordinating structures of the Community Development Programme."[1]

(e) *Personnel selection:* Maximum care should be taken in selecting suitable workers who feel themselves to be servants of the public and not officers. Each staff member should be willing to forego any credit for departmental achievement, for the goal of the people and the programme. The agency staff should be comprised of persons who will not be agency-centred, but who are prepared to work along with other agencies towards the achievement of common objectives and to coordinate their efforts.

(f) *Where coordination is required in India's programmes:* In the Community Development and Extension Programme of India, as in many developing countries, coordination is required at three levels:

---

[1]James W. Green, *Community Development Review*, No. 6, Washington D.C., ICA, Sept., 1959, p. 49.

(i) Coordination between community development organisations and other departments or agencies engaged in rural development work.

(ii) Coordination between the various branches of the same department, e.g., coordination of agricultural research, education and extension branches of the agricultural department.

(iii) Coordination between Foreign Aid Advisors, counterparts and agencies in host country.

How coordination is available to community development organisation in India?

As shown in the organisational chart, the services are well coordinated from Federal Level to Village Level. The services of various development departments are at the disposal of BDO, the District Collector and the Development Commissioner and also to the Ministry of Community Development at the Centre. But coordination is lacking in between the agencies of the same department, specially in the three branches of the Department of Agriculture—Teaching, Research and Extension. Till now the three services could not be integrated and have no coordination, which was so much needed. In nearly all the states, they were working in watertight compartments having no or very little connection with each other. The teachers seldom saw the results of the researches done at Research Stations of their States or Regions, as there was no direct connection between the two services. Similarly, research people had no direct touch with the problems and needs of the farmers. The extension staff below directorate level, i.e., the Deputy Director of Agriculture, the District Agriculture Officer or Assistant Director of Agriculture, Extension Specialist attached to the Development Block, had no connection with the teachers of Agriculture Colleges or research workers at Agricultural Research Institutes. Under this situation, the research done at research station was not on the problems of the farmers and the technical knowledge spread by the extension specialists was not what should have come from a research station. This required itegration of teaching, research and extension in agriculture.

How a National Programme is developed

The development of a Five Year Plan Programme has to pass through various levels of its organisation, i.e., the village to block, district, the state and the national level and then to the Planning Commission of India. After the finalisation and fixing of various targets and financial outlay it comes back via the opposite direction, i.e., national, State, district, the block and village levels for reappropriation and necessary adjustments in the previous targets and money demands.

About a year or more in advance, a Five Year Plan of the country is developed, all the different levels of organisation are sent the necessary instructions for developing their plans and the programmes for C.D. and extension.

At the village level, the VLW with the advice of the Village Advisory Committee and other such helping hands, collects the data and information regarding the available and expected resources from the village, in the form of labour, material and money and the expected outside help keeping these in view the immediate and long-term development plans of the village. The Village Advisory Committee works out the village plan, from year to year. The priority is also fixed and the various items of development under each head are given in detail in a proforma provided by the

Planning Commission of India. When it is finalised by the authorities concerned and discussed by the participants to their satisfaction, it is sent to the BDO for further compilation.

The BDO with the help of the Advisory Committee scrutinises the village plans of his Block and after making necessary adjustments, compiles the Block Plan which is submitted to the Collector for its inclusion in the District plan.

The District Officer, with the advice of the District Advisory Committee compiles a similar plan for the whole district, after making scrutiny and adjustments in the Block Plans, and then submits it to the Development Commissioner of the State.

The Development Commissioner with the advice of the State Advisory Committee keeping in view the State resources, outside aid, the items of priority at the state level scrutinises plan and finalises the State Plan for further transmission to the Ministry of C.D. and National Extension Service.

The Central Ministry of C.D. and Cooperation prepares a national plan and submits it to the Planning Commission of India.

The National Planning Commission reviews the data critically for planning a programme for the nation. They take into consideration the following three factors:

(1) The data which they receive from various State Governments.

(2) The funds available for the plan from national, state and outside aids, etc.

The Planning Commission after finalising their scrutiny calls a meeting of all the State and Central Ministers for C.D. and Cooperation along with the State Development Commissioners. The State plans are discussed with the State representatives and when some agreement is achieved, the plans are sent back to the state for reconsideration.

When the plan is received back, the Development Commissioner of each State calls a meeting of the Collectors and BDOs. of the State and discusses with each the necessary adjustment needed in the plans at each level. The Collectors and the BDOs discuss their plans with the advisory committees at the appropriate level and make necessary adjustments and reappropriation. After the required scrutiny, the plan is again submitted through the previous route, i.e., from village to block, district, State and national levels and then to the Planning Commission. After that, it is finalised and the State Governments are authorised to proceed with their work. In the same way, the various authorities at different levels are assigned with their responsibilities and ask to go ahead with the sanctioned programmes and to submit periodical reports of their progress. From time to time information is collected, evaluations are made and necesssary directions and instructions are issued for reappropriation and desired progress.

During plan period: During the plan period, when the programme is in action, timely reports keep the Government, at various levels, and the Planning Commission well informed about their achievements and the hurdles.

Programme evaluation organisation of the Planning Commission on the working of community projects and N.E.S. Blocks: Another unique thing in the extension and C.D. programmes of India is the Programme Evaluation Organisation. It is an independent body functioning under the Planning Commission which undertakes periodical assessment of community projects and N.E.S. blocks and ensures that the objectives and the approach of the programme are being adhered to in implementation.

For evaluation, the country has been divided into three regions of East, South and Central, with headquarters at Delhi, Calcutta and Bombay. A team of evaluation officers is maintained for investigations into the working Projects. A permanent evaluation assistant is posted at each block for regular evaluation and reporting to the P.E.O... for sample surveys, a number of Blocks (about 20) is selected in each region for critical study. The evaluation officers stay in the selected blocks and collect data on the proforma provided by the head office. The organisation publishes its annual report with recommendations on the improvement and working of Extension and C.D. services in the country.

NATIONAL PLANS IN INDIA

The need for planning in India was felt long ago. The struggle for political independence was the struggle for planning. The leaders of India raised a voice against the exploitation of the policy of not allowing any development. When the so-called developed nations of today were developing their resources, India was losing its time. In the absence of planning, the country became the backward as the British used to call it, or the 'Under developed' or 'Low Income' country, which India's supporters call it now. It had poverty, ignorance and disease. These still are there though, of course, not to the same extent. Due to their policy, India became an agricultural country. Its industries, transport and communications remained undeveloped. Farm holdings divided. Farmers were not given any extension service or technical advice. The agricultural occupations became uneconomic and risky.

Basic plans in India

In spite of the exploiting policy of the British colonial rulers, the people of India made efforts for planning the resources. They made their plans and schemes even during the 1940's. But the foreign rulers did not pay any heed. These plans which were formulated before independence were: (1) the Bombay Plan, (2) the People's Plan, (3) the Visvesvaraya Plan, and (4) the Gandhian Plan.

(1) *The Bombay Plan:* This was called "A plan of economic development of India" It was prepared by eight businessmen of Bombay in 1945. The main objective of this plan was to double up the per capita income within the period of 15 years. It was divided into three stages of five years each. The plan embodied essential objectives in the field of balanced diet, textile requirements, house construction medical comforts, promotion of education, etc. The proposed total outlay on it was Rs. 10,000 crores. Out of which Rs. 4,480 crores was to be spent on industry, Rs. 1,240 crores on agriculture, Rs. 940 crores on communication, Rs. 490 crores on education, Rs. 450 crores on health, Rs. 2,200 crores on housing, and Rs. 200 crores on miscellaneous items. For financing, they estimated to get Rs. 2,600 crores from external sources, Rs. 4,000 crores from government savings, and Rs. 3,400 crores from credit.

(2) *The People's Plan:* It was prepared by Shri M.N. Roy in 1944. Its guiding principle was, "production for use as distinct from production for exchange". The estimated total expenditure was Rs. 15,000 crores, divided as follows: agriculture Rs. 2,450 crores, industry Rs. 5,600 crores, communication Rs. 500 crores, health

Rs. 760 crores, education Rs. 1,040 crores, and housing Rs. 3,150 crores.

(3) *Visvesvaraya Plan:* This was prepared by Shri M. Visvesvaraya and accepted by the All-India Manufacturers' Organisation, in 1944. Its primary object was to raise the country's economic efficiency to a level at which the average citizen would be able to find employment and to earn a livelihood. It was a 15-year plan costing Rs. 10,000 crores divided over Agriculture Rs. 1,240 crores, Industry Rs. 1,240 crores, Communication Rs. 940 crores, Education Rs. 490 crores, Health Rs. 450 crores, Housing Rs. 2,200 crores and Miscellaneous Rs. 200 crores.

(4) *Gandhian Plan:* It was prepared by Prof. S.N. Agarwal, based on Gandhian ideas. Its objective was to raise the material as well as the cultural level of the masses to a basic standard of living within a period of 10 years. Total expenditure was, estimated at Rs. 3,500 crores. Out of Rs. 1,175 crores was laid out for Agriculture, Rs. 350 crores for Rural Industries, Rs. 1,000 crores for Large-scale Industries Rs. 20 crores for Research, Rs. 400 crores for Transport and Rs. 260 crores for Health.

National Planning Committee

A National Planning Committee was appointed by the Congress Working Committee of India in 1938, with Shri Jawaharlal Nehru as its chairman. The Committee laid out certain guidelines so as to realise planned advancement from year to year. The report of this Committee stated that the State should own key industries and services, natural resources, railways, waterways and other means of public transport. In 1942, when the Government of India established development departments, the National Planning Committee appointed 20 sub-committees to coordinate the work of planning. These sub-committees were on separate subjects like, manufacturing industries, land policies, agriculture, finance, etc. Separate reports were published which became the basis for Government planning in future.

Government planning in India

In 1944, the Central Government of India set up a Planning Department under the charge of the late Shri Ardeshar Dalal. The Department appointed several committees to report on various aspects of planning.

After India achieved political independence, the Congress Working Committee passed a comprehensive resolution on 19th January, 1950 on "Planned Economy" for the country and appointed a Planning Commission.

The planning machinery and method of making plans

The nature of the planning machinery in India and the different planning procedures and techniques which have evolved since 1951 have been largely determined by the fact that India is a Federal Democratic State with a mixed economy striving for a progressively socialistic pattern of society.

Both as the machinery and in procedure of planning, the Planning Commission occupies a pivotal position. Its main functions are advisory and coordination. It is a structure and system between administrative departments which are too closely involved in day-to-day problems and establishes coordination between them

Planning Commission

The Planning Commission is a multi-member body including full-time members who are prominent public men, administrators, or technical experts, as well as some part-time members who are important Cabinet Ministers.

The Prime Minister of India is the Chairman of the Planning Commission since its inception. The Minister for Finance is the Member-in-charge of Finance in the Commission in an ex-officio capacity. These arrangements ensure coordination between the Commission and the Central Ministries. The Commission in its day-to-day work functions through a series of Divisions and Sections each headed by a senior officer. The various Divisions may broadly be divided into two categories—(i) General Divisions which are concerned with special aspects of the entire economy; and (ii) Subject Divisions which are concerned with specified fields of development.

Members, Advisors (Programme Administration) and other senior officers of the Commission carry out special inspections and investigations from time to time. The Plan Coordination Section of the Commission also collects all key data about the progress of various programmes and projects. Moreover, there are two special bodies for evaluating the actual working of the various programmes and projects, included in the Plan. These are the Programme Evaluation Organisations which evaluate the current problems of the Rural Economy, and the Committee on Plan Projects which undertakes important problem-oriented studies. The Research Programme Committee initiates research in economic, administrative and social problems related to planned development.

The National Plan evolves gradually in a series of stages wherein the different Ministries, State Governments, experts—official and non-official and public are consulted. The finally considered Plan is submitted to the Cabinet, the National Development Council and Parliament. The Plan, as approved by Parliament, goes back to all the concerned authorities for implementation of their respective programmes and projects.

At the initial stage of formulation of a Plan, a number of working groups are set up comprising selected administrators, economists and technicians from various Central Ministries and Divisions of the Planning Commission, as a means of coordinating the work of the Ministries in formulating realistic and acceptable plans for different sectors of the economy.

A number of standing bodies variously known as Panels, Advisory Committees or Consultative Committees are also set up to take into account the views of other knowledgeable people, especially non-official experts on different aspects of planning. The most important advisory bodies are: (1) Consultative Committee of Members of Parliament for the Planning Commission, and (2) Prime Minister's Informal Consultative Committee for Planning.

Each Five Year Plan fixes the broad targets and operational decisions. Budgetary allocations are normally made in terms of annual plans. Work on the annual plans precedes the annual budgets. Around September each year, the Planning Commission indicates to the State Governments the more important objectives, the amount of Central assistance they could reckon for their annual plans and asks for the draft proposals. The proposals of the States are discussed in detail during November and

December, the Central Ministries participating in the deliberations. A similar examination is undertaken in the preparation of the capital budget. The allocations agreed upon with the Ministries and the State Governments become the basis of budgetary provisions for the following year and are thus the main operational instruments for the Five-Year Plan.

The Central Ministries are closely associated with the work of the communication, not only through the working groups, but also through their various executive departments, research institutions and advisory committees on many of which the Planning Commission is represented. Of all the ministries, the Ministry of Finance has naturally the closest relation with the Commission of Finance which plays a most important role in planning. Apart from the Central Ministries, there are two official organisations, viz., the Reserve Bank of India and the Central Statistical Organisation which are closely associated with the work of the Commission.

In its relation with the States, the Planning Commission deals with the Chief Ministers on matters affecting detailed administrative co-ordination at the State level, and on specific issues with the State Departments or the Ministers directly concerned. Coordination is also sought to be achieved through the National Development Council consisting of the Prime Minister, Chief Ministers of the States and members of the Commission. Advisors of the Commission, and Advisors (Programme Administration), are also instrumental in providing an effective link between the Commission and the different State Governments.

At the State level, there is a Planning Department generally directly under the Chief Minister. It coordinates the work of other departments for the preparation of development plans and presents reports on the fulfilment of the State Plan. It usually works through the system of Working Groups. It is supported by the State Statistical Bureau. The Plan formulated by it is put up to the Council of Ministers of the States. Proposals for strengthening the planning machinery at the State level through the setting up of Planning Boards was under consideration for sometime, and now all the States, except Madras and Kerala, have State Planning Boards. The composition of these Boards, however, differs from State to State.

Planning machinery (Fig. 38.2)

Planning at the district level and the block level has normally been done jointly by the officers of the various development departments working at their respective levels, and the members of District Councils or Block Councils and non-official representatives.

The District Collectors and Block Development Officers have been responsible for the necessary coordination at the district and block levels respectively. An attempt has been made to carry the process of planning down to the village level but it has not yet become an integral part of the planning process in the country.

On the basis of the recommendations of the Balwant Rai Mehta Committee's report, the State Government have undertaken legislation for reorganisation of the district administration by providing for a popular planning organisation between the village and State levels. Panchayat Raj is now under implementation in most states in the country. In Madhya Pradesh also Panchayat Raj is being implemented shortly. With the establishment of Panchayat Raj as a tool of area planning in most of the

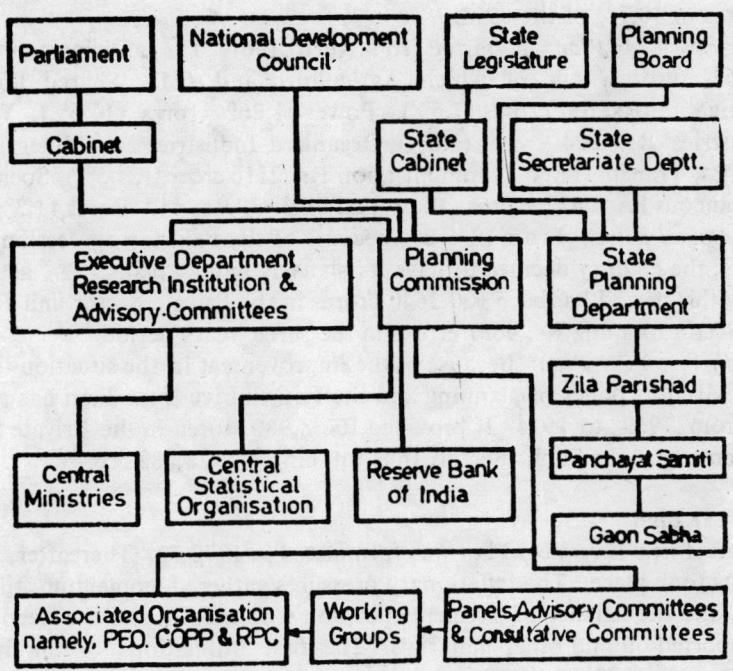

Fig. 39.2 Planning machinery.

States, Panchayat Raj has now come to reality. Under Panchayat Raj legislation, detailed provisions have been made about the functions of Panchayat Raj bodies at different levels in the matter of preparation of plans, mobilisation of resources and implementation of plans in the district.

Five Year and Annual Plans

All planning was brought under Five Year Plans from July 1, 1951. The outlay under each plan can be seen as follows:

(1) *First Five Year Plan:* It started from July, 1951. It envisaged a total outlay of Rs. 2,069 crores in the Public Sector and Rs. 1,700 crores in the Private Sector. The distribution of expenditure in the Pubic Sector was: Agriculture and Community development Rs. 369.43 crores or 17.4% of the total outlay, Irrigation and Power 540.41 crores or 27.2%, Transport and Communication Rs. 497 crores or 24%, industry Rs. 173 crores or 8.4% Social Services Rs. 340 crores or 16.4%, Rehabilitation Rs. 85 crores or 4.1% and Miscellaneous 52 crores or 2.5%.

(2) *Second Five Year Plan:* It started from April 1, 1956. The total outlay was Rs. 4,600 crores. The total outlay on various heads in the Public Sector was: Agriculture and Minor Irrigation Rs. 320 crores or 7% of the total, Community Development and Cooperation Rs. 459 crores or 9.8%, Power Rs. 410 crores or 8.9%, Village and Small industries Rs. 180 crores or 3.9%, Industry and Minerals Rs. 880 crores or 19.1%, Transport and Communication Rs. 1,290 crores, or 29.1%, and Social Services

Rs. 860 crores or 18.7% of the total.

(3) *Third Five Year Plan:* It started from April 1961. The anticipated expenditure was Rs. 8,631 crores, out of which Agriculture and C.D. Shared 1,760 crores (20.4%), Irrigation Rs. 657 crores (7.6%), Power 1,262 crores (14.6%), Village and Small Industries Rs. 224 crores (2.6%), Organised Industries and Minerals Rs. 1735 crores (20.1%), Transport and Communication Rs. 2116 crores (24.5%), Social Services and Miscellaneous Rs. 1,422 crores (16.5%) and others Rs. 112 crores (1.3%).

(4) *The Annual Plans:* From 1966-69, because of the Pakistan aggression and then the droughts, the country decided to have its plans as annual plans. The actual investment during this period has been Rs. 3640 crores in the Private Sector and Rs. 5817 in the Public Sector totalling Rs. 9657 crores in the three years period.

(5) *Fourth Five Year Plan:* Because of the improvement in the situation the country has again revived its policy of planning and the Fourth Five Year Plan has again been executed from 1969 to 1974. It provided Rs. 8,980 crores in the Private Sector and Rs. 15,402 crores in the Public Sector, thus totalling Rs. 24,582 crores.

Fifth Five Year Plan

The Draft Fifth Five-Year Plan was formulated in 1972-73. Thereafter, two major developments took place. The inflationary pressures gathered momentum till September, 1974, and the balance of payments position worsened due to the steep rise in the prices of imported oil and other materials. The first intimations of the inflationary pressures came in 1972-73, thereafter these pressures gathered strength in 1973-74 and continued unabated right upto September, 1974.

The Annual Plan 1974-75 was formulated at a time when the inflation rate was quite high. It was, therefore, designed mainly to control inflation and increase production particularly in the key sectors. The Plan outlays had to be kept at a modest level. Yet care was taken to ensure adequate provisions for Agriculture, including Irrigation and fertilisers, energy (power, coal and oil), ongoing projects in steel, non-ferrous Metals, and certain basic consumer goods industries. Emphasis was on fuller utilisation of the unutilised capacities. The provision for social services was restrained but kept at a reasonable level.

Having achieved a certain measure of price stability by the end of 1974-75, the Annual Plan for 1975-76 aimed at growth under conditions of price stability. Agriculture, irrigation, power, coal, oil and fertilisers therefore continued to receive, priority. Projects capable of yielding quick results were received special attention. Labour discipline and sustained anti-hoarding/smuggling operations created an appropriate climate. An excellent harvest gave timely vigour and push. The national income estimated to have increased by 6 to 6.5 per cent during 1975-76—agricultural production by about 10 per cent and industrial output by 5.7 per cent. Procurement of nearly 13 million tonnes of foodgrains in 1975-76, alongwith imports, enabled the build-up of a high level of stocks of foodgrains (17 million tonnes).

Agricultural sector

This is the most vital sector. Gross domestic production at 1960-61 prices from the agricultural and allied sectors, increased at an annual compound trend rate of 2.07 per cent during the period from 1961-62 to 1973-74.

Demand for foodgrains

Based on the realised levels of growth of income upto 1975-76, the target of 5.2 per cent per annum of compound income growth in the remaining years of the Fifth Five Year Plan and the estimated relationships between purchase of foodgrains and growth in total consumption expenditure per capita, the demand for foodgrains in 1978-79 was estimated at 127.69 million tonnes. The targets of income growth presently postulated for the Sixth and the Seventh Plan periods lead to estimates of the demand for foodgrains at 150.9 million tonnes and 178.2 million tonnes respectively, provided the elasticity of demand of foodgrains to consumption expenditure remains constant. These projections are consistent, both methodologically and in quantities, with the upper limit of requirements of foodgrains in 1985 estimates by the National Commission on Agriculture to be within a range of 150 million tonnes to 163 million tonnes.

Non-foodgrain crops

The expected rate of growth in the non-foodgrains crop is presently estimated at 3.94 per cent per annum in the Fifth Plan period, rising to 4.96 per cent per annum in the Seventh Plan period. Given the growth rates in the animal husbandry, fishing and forestry sectors, the rate of growth of the Agricultural Sector as a whole is postulated at 3.94 per cent in the Fifth Plan period and at approximately 4.30 per cent through the Sixth and Seventh Plan periods.

Fertilisers

The estimation of fertiliser demand is sensitive to the increase in irrigation facilities and the spread of new technologies. The demand is estimated in terms of nutrients at 4.80 millions tonnes in 1978-79 and approximately 8 million tonnes in 1983-84. Suitable investment decisions in relationship to these fertiliser demands are being made in the area of nitrogenous and phosphatic fertilisers. Still there will be some area of uncertainty in estimation of demand arising both from the lack of fully disaggregated data and relationship of fertiliser application to behavioural responses. Any spurt in demand may, therefore, have to be met from imports. The requirements of potassic fertilisers will continue to be met substantially out of imports.

Forestry

The forestry sector has to play an important role in the economic development of the country. Forests occupy about 23 per cent of the area and their contribution in the net domestic product at 1960-61 prices is 1.4 per cent. The targets of demand for industrial wood for the prospective period are consistent with the projections of the National Commission on Agriculture. The problems relating to the forestry sector are mainly organisational. In view of the tight land balance being anticipated, coverage by forests has to be integrated with the land utilisation plan. Development of communications is also necessary in relation to the optimal exploitation of the available forest wealth in inaccessible areas.

The energy sector

Given the non-enewable resources base of the economy, the main emphasis is on coal, electricity and crude oil, and the substitution of imported sources of energy wherever possible. These three leading sectors of energy accounted for 3.96 per cent of the gross value added in the non-agricultural sector in 1973-74. This share is expected to go up to 5 per cent by the end of the Fifth Plan period and 5.56 per cent by the end of the Sixth Plan. The revised production estimate for the coal sector is placed at 124.0 million tonnes in 1978-79 and is estimated to go up to 185 million tonnes in 1983-84. Long-term rates of growth of between 7 to 8 per cent compound per annual for this sector are expected to be sustained through the Seventh Plan period also.

Demographic profile

The National Population Policy lays down a target for birth rate of 25 per thousand and a population growth rate of 1.4 per cent by the end of the Sixth Plan period. The policy envisages a series of fundamental measures including raising of the minimum age for marriage, female education, spread of population values and the small family norm, strengthening of research in reproductive biology and contraception, incentives for individuals, groups and communities. The targets laid down in the National Population Policy correspond to those laid down in the Draft Fifth Plan for achievement by the end of the Sixth Plan, and are expected to be reached. For period 1986-91, the population growth rate is estimated at 1.1 per cent. The population is estimated at 725.4 million by 1988-89 and at 744.8 million by 1991. The rural population is estimated at 545.1 million by 1988-89 and the urban population at 180.3 million.

Financial resources

The resources for the Fifth Plan were re-assessed in consultation with the Ministry of Finance, State Governments and Union Territory Administrations. For the public sector these were estimated at Rs. 19396 crores for the first three years of the plan, and at Rs. 19907 crores for the next two years, making a total of Rs. 39303 crores for the five-year period. The estimates for 1974-75 were at current prices, while those for the subsequent years were at 1975-76 prices. The total for five years went a slight change and the resources for 1974-75 were also re-computed in terms of 1975-76 prices.

Briefly, the revised plan outlays were as follows :

		(Rs. crores)
(1)	Central Sector	19954.10
(2)	States	18265.08
(3)	Union Territories	634.06
(4)	Hill and Tribal Areas	450.00
	Total	39303.24

(A) Objective of different plans

I Plan (1951-56): (1) To curb the inflationary situation and rectify food shortage in the country.

II Plan (1956-61): (1) Rapid growth of the country's economy; (2) (Rapid industrialisation with particular emphasis on development of basic and heavy industries;

(3) A large expansion of employment opportunities ; and (4) Reduction of inequalities in income and wealth and a more even distribution of economic power.

III Plan (*1961-66*)*:* To secure an increase in the national income of over 5 per cent per annum; (2) To achieve self-sufficiency in foodgrains and to increase agricultural production; (3) To expand basic industries and to establish machine building capacity; (4) To ensure substantial expansion in employment opportunities; and (5) To establish greater equality of opportunity and bring about reduction in disparities in income.

IV Plan (*1969-73-74*)*:* (1) To increase economic growth with stability; (2) To bring about greater economic self-reliance; (3) To ensure safeguards against uncertainties; (4) To ensure social justice to weaker sections and to prevent concentration of economic power, and (5) To create more employment opportunities.

V Plan (*1974-79*)*:* The objectives in view were removal of poverty, achievement of self-reliance and outlining strategies which had helped to overcome the constraints in achieving the objectives. The strategies relate to growth in the three leading sectors, viz., Agriculture, Energy and Critical Intermediates, and the creation of additional employment opportunities.

(B) Strategy of the plans

The *First* Five Year Plan was modest and its main objective was Agriculture and Irrigation. The *Second* Plan aimed at strengthening the capital base of the economy; at the same time the employment criterion and the development of small scale industries together with the development of heavy industries were emphasised. The Third Plan provided equal priority to Agriculture and Industry. The *Three Annual Plans* aimed at consolidating the gains achieved in the previous three plans. The *Fourth Plan* reiterated the need for self-reliance and aimed at achieving equitable distribution of benefits. Agriculture still enjoyed the priority in this plan.

Achievements during plans

The First Plan prepared the ground for economic acceleration. The Second Plan faced two problems : (1) foreign exchange crises and (2) the balance of payments difficulties and the inflationary trend in the economy. During the Third Plan emergency created by Chinese and Pakistani aggressions gave rise to the need to mobilise resources, both for Defence and Development. A marked rise in the production goods for Defence indirectly led to further rise in prices. Together with this, the end of the Third Plan period witnessed some tendency towards recession in the industrial field. After 1966, the annual plans aimed at placing the economy on a stable footing. The beginning of the Fourth Plan has shown signs of industrial recovery, which was expected to be followed by a rapid rate of growth.

During 1950-51 and 1967-68 the national income has increased by about 80 per cent, crop production by 70 per cent, and industrial output by 170 per cent. The per capita income, if we take 1960-61 as the base year, has increased from Rs. 269 in 1950-51, to 291 in 1955-56, Rs. 309 in 1960-61, Rs. 315 in 1965-66 and Rs. 336 in 1967-68 (Fig. 38.3).

The foodgrain production increased from 50.8 million tonnes in 1950-51 to 66.8 million tonnes in 1955-56, 82 million tonnes in 1960-61, fell down to 72 million tonnes

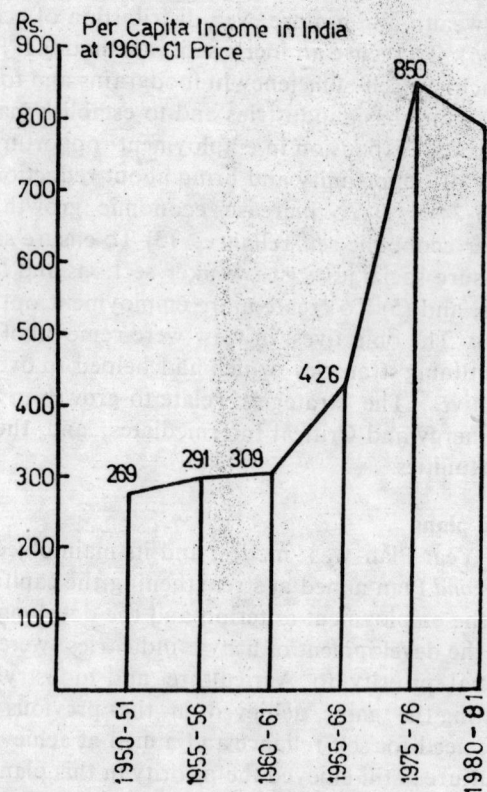

Fig. 39.3 Per capita income in India.

in 1965-66, 98 million tonnes in 1968-69, 105 million tonnes in 1970-71 and 118 million tonnes in 1975-76. (Fig. 38.4)

Agricultural transformation: With the introduction of high yielding varieties of foodgrains and modernised methods of production, as recommended by the extension service of the Agricultural Universities, the country has achieved a breakthrough in agriculture. The alacrity with which our farmers in Punjab, U. P., Andhra Pradesh, Mysore and even in M. P. and Rajasthan etc. accepted the new farming techniques, and the avidity which they have shown for inputs, like high yielding variety seeds, fertilisers and insecticides has exploded the myth that our farmers are backwards, ignorant and impervious to innovations and modernism. Farmers have purchased seeds of new wheat varieties in 1967-68 at the rate of Rs. 35 per kg. They have accepted new rice varieties even without conducting demonstration. They accepted Triple Dwarf wheats even before the varieties were released by the Seed Releasing Committees of the States. With this success and conviction, large numbers of people who are not traditional farmers are inclined to take up agriculture as a business and industry. Around cities like Jabalpur, Ludhiana, Hyderabad, etc. we find that the businessmen have purchased land for setting up farms, and they are themselves coming to the extension and subject-matter specialists of these Universities for advice. Retired military personnel and also from the other services have purchased land and are deve-

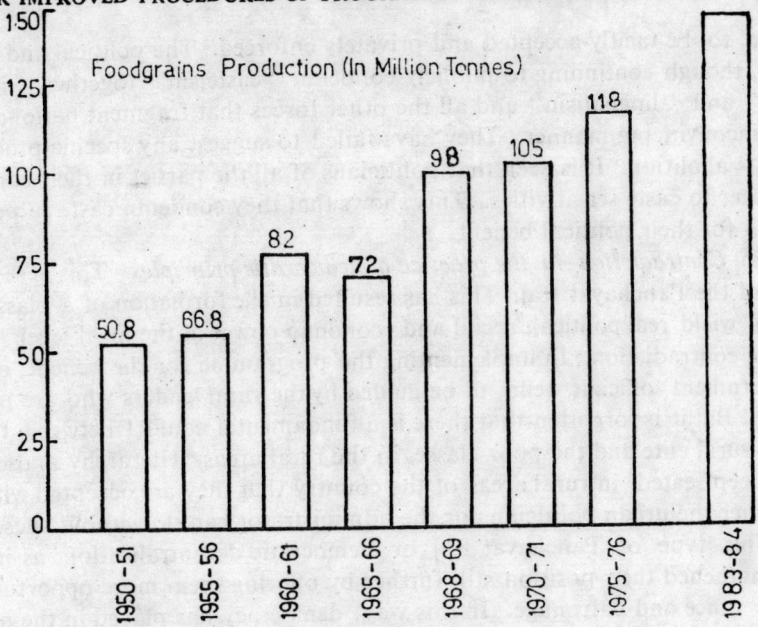

Fig. 39.4 Foodgrains production.

loping their mixed farms by keeping dairy herds, poultry units and vegetable crops. This is the result of planned development.

Industrial transformation: Due to planning, the traditional stagnant economy of the country has been transformed into a growing economy with a strong industrial base. It has not only increased its production in traditional items like jute, cotton or tea, but also in non-traditional industries like steel, basic metals, machine tools, heavy machine building equipment, railway coaches, electric, steam and diesel locomotives, shipbuilding etc. It's growth is remarkable in heavy and light electrical equipment.

Weaknesses in our planned programme

(1) *Dichotomy between ideals and reality:* The political parties and the conflicts in them have created this situation. Those who had been in the forefront of the struggle for independence stepped into political offices, as Members of Parliament or State Assemblies and some achieved ministerial status. The leaders of the Centre held more say over policy than those in the States. But it was the conservative element in the Congress which gained an initial advantage from the imperative need in the face of so many urgent problems to stabilise the political order. This was the beginning of the split in the ranks of the newly formed political elite. A few zealous members of the Congress defected to the Communist Party and many others left to form new left-wing parties like: PSP., BKD, etc. But the Congress continued to remain in power.

(2) *Divergence of precept and practice:* The persistence of the caste structure is a striking example of it. Caste was outlawed in the Constitution of India. A Bill was adopted by Parliament in 1955 which made the practice of untouchability a criminal offence. A number of policy measures have also been legislated to help the so-called Backward Classes, yet we find that nothing has changed. Caste is coming more and

more to be tacitly accepted and privately enforced. The political and intellectual leaders, though continuing to publicly condemn "casteism" together with "communaism" and "lingualism" and all the other forces that fragment national life, do so in an unconvincing manner. They have failed to suggest any specific practical measures for its abolition. It is seen that politicians of all the parties in their campaigns patently cater to caste sensitivities. This shows that they condemn caste in public and then use it for their political benefit.

(3) *Contradiction in the practice of democratic principles:* This is seen in the working of the Panchayat Raj. This has resulted in the formation of a 'class of rural elite', who wield real political, social and economic power at the local level. Thus there is a basic contradiction. In implementing the programme for the benefit of rural areas, government officials tend to be guided by the rural leaders who are part of the rural elite. But it is forgotten that there is a fundamental conflict between the interests of the rural elite and the poor classes in the rural areas. Hierarchy and exploitation are so deep-seated in rural areas of the country that they are accepted without question. Neither the urban politician nor the administrator can do without these rural leaders.

This type of Panchayat Raj or democratic decentralisation, as it is called, has strengthened their position still further by offering them more opportunities for political office and patronage. In this way, democracy has played in the hands of a petty plutocracy which has become the major hurdle in the successful implementation of democratic planning for the welfare of the people of the country. This shows that social revolution should precede economic revolution.

(4) *Evasive land reforms:* The Land Reforms have been ambiguous in enactment and evasive in implementation. They have brought little justice to the village poor. The Tenancy Acts, intended to make the tiller of the soil its owner, have failed to achieve the desired result and likewise the Ceiling Acts which aimed at equitable distribution of land have also failed in their objective. The programmes of aid with their accent on status and property are more beneficial to the richer classes, and the delays and complexities of the administration likewise favour the privileged.

(5) *Mounting prices:* The spiralling prices of essential commodities during the Fifth Plan, and even after the devaluation of the Rupee, despite Government's assurances to the contrary have broken the back of the common man. The market price of essential commodities, particularly of industrial goods, has no relevance to the cost of production. The exorbitant profits earned by businessmen and heavy taxes on essential commodities have aggravated the situation.

Suggestions

(1) *Planning at base and not at apex:* The district administration, which is close to the people and has a democratic foundation, should be the principal unit of economic planning. Under its direction, integrated Land Reforms must be implemented as time-bound programmes. It should be closely connected with development plans, so that there is effective coordination between the reforms and the reorganisation. Credit and technical assistance should proceed hand in hand. Credit should be governed by the needs as well as by the expanding capacity to use, not by status and property. In development activities, the panchayats ought to play a significant role and should be the organs of service and authority.

(2) *Sixth Plan must concentrate on public sector:* The management of public sector industries has been very scandalous, inefficient and mismanaged. The puclic sector can be successful provided: (1) the right type of persons are chosen for the higher echelons ; (2) they are equipped with sufficient authority and free from ministerial interference, and (3) they are made accountable for the failure of projects in their charge. The Administrative Reforms Commission in their report on public sector undertakings made recommendations in this regard but they have been ignored.

Part VI

DEVELOPMENT PROGRAMMES

CHAPTER 40

COMMUNITY DEVELOPMENT PROGRAMME

This Chapter will describe the problems of the world which needs community development and organisation. It will define the terms Community Development and Community Organisation. It will also show the elements involved in community work, the objectives of community development work and the philosophy behind the work.

The problem

About 80 per cent of the world population lives in the economically underdeveloped areas. These lie in South-East Asia, the Middle East or the Far East. The foreign rulers, or their own emperors, or kings and their agents, like landlords, exploited these people. Due to exploitation and the suppressive policies of such rulers, these countries became poor or remained undeveloped or underdeveloped. They could not develop their resources for their betterment and they had malnutrition, illiteracy, ignorance and ill-health. Some of these countries, like India, had to undertake long struggles to get political freedom from the foreign rulers. The aim behind political freedom was to bring economic and social freedom to the poor masses.

The Governments of these countries, who have made themselves free from foreign bondage, have assumed wider responsibilities for the promotion of economic development and human welfare. They have found in their rural communities their most primitive and traditional ways of doing things through the administrative machinery which worked under foreign rule; the lack of financial resources at their disposal, the increasing population exerting high pressure on existing resources of land, necessitated the undertaking of development programmes and planning. Besides the problems in underdeveloped countries, the developed countries or the urban areas of underdeveloped countries also require to take care of their communities from problems of disorganisation, disintegration, decline, insecurity, breakdown, instability, etc., which are the results of industrialisation and urbanisation. Such developed countries, or parts of underdeveloped countries, also need social welfare programme or organisational work.

Community development is an exclusive term. It is frequently used to encompass any and every effort towards the advance of community interests. A variety of interpretations are therefore easily available. Community development is a compound term. It is useful, therefore, to consider its components, to start with.

The community

(1) A community is a group of people, who live in a geographical area and have an interest in each other for the purpose of making a living.

(2) It is a form of social organisation existing between the family and state.

(3) A community, is a locus for social systems of a particular kind composed of interacting social institutions which meet the basic human needs, through the function of which people have developed a sense of belongingness and a potential ability to act together as an entity.

A community, while in itself consisting of several parts, is also a part of a larger social system. It is a dynamic social unit which is subject to change of internal or external origin. Some of the important characteristics of the community are (1) Communities are close-knit entities (2) Their customs are interrelated, (3) These communities are complexes of sub-group relationship and (4) There is a discernible leadership within the community.

Development

The term development connotes growth or maturation. It implies gradual and sequential phases of change. MacIver uses the word 'development' to signify an upward course in a process "that is, of increasing differentiation". Beskoff refers to the term 'social development as social evaluation' and 'social progress'. Speaking after Hobhouse, he states that the term 'social development' comprehends some overall movement towards greater efficiency and complexity but with the recognition of the concomitant problems.

With this understanding attention may now be turned to the varieties of community work.

Community work

The community unit is, in some instances, a geographical area, or a community of interests, or association of interests. In either case, the problem of concern is how the members of these communities may come to be identified with and share responsibility for the development of a community and the larger society of which it is part, by utilising the riches which the Humanities and Sciences have made available to modern man.

Community work involves: (1) self-determination, (2) community pace, (3) growth in community capacity, and (4) the will to change. In this chapter, attempt will be made to explain these conceptions.

(1) Self-determination

People in a local community may not always recognise "the emergency", or the nature of the problem seen by the community development worker, who is an outsider. Due to it the community may resent action taken by the change agent. The community development worker is at an initial disadvantage, when he tries to put over to the local people new methods of cultivation of crops or raising livestock, etc.

"This disadvantage is based on the fact", says Margaret Read, "that he does not know how the local people regard their traditional practices, nor what they think of his new ones." The change agent or worker is sure that he is right in what he is advocating and he cannot see why in view of their sickness, or lack of water, they do not see his point of view and at least try it. He who, in our modern age, has been brought up with an almost blind faith in anything called scientific, does not easily realise that the farmer has a sense of security in his very insecurity. We think he must want to know how to solve food shortages, how to reduce the death rate, etc., but that insecurity is the thing he knows and he understands it is so far as he has always lived with it and adjusted his practices and his ideas in relation to it.

For bringing a change in the ways of doing things, there can be two ways: (1) either use force to change or (2) motivate people to change. As regards force, experience shows that there may be reaction of suspicion, hostility, or increased insecurity and apathy. Thus, many of those who are looking up towards meaningful change, and the more capable communities, are resisting trying to press or "sell" people techniques, services or projects which are conceived or developed by experts or small groups organised for planning.

Before any programme is introduced, there is need for frequent staff meetings of the community development workers themselves in which village practices should be discussed and in which assumptions and value judgements of workers should be questioned by the in-charge of the team of change agents. The Philosophy behind a programme should be why certain practices are being done by some national groups in a community and how these practices fit in with their culture. Secondly, there should not be any attempt to impose new standards on these people—to challenge existing beliefs and practices, rather an attempt is made to create a situation in which a free interaction of community development workers and village people takes place. This interaction between the change agents and client system will lead to an exchange of ideas and it is expected from it will arise a need in villagers for change in some of the practices they are following. People will change only when they feel ready for change and this requires creating readiness for accepting the new ways and practices of doing things.

Because it is not possible to consult all members of the community regarding full details of the programme, it seems necessary that ways and means must be found to provide the average citizen with some sense of participation and control over his changing environment.

(2) Community pace

There is general recognition now that most of the communities have their own techniques and pace for carrying on several works. They cannot be changed radically without disrupting the life of the people. The problem of change is not simply writing on a blackboard our technical ways of doing things but it is to recognise the fact that different people have a different language for social action and indeed have set attitudes on social action for solving their problems. These aptitudes need to be further developed in the historic setting of their past to meet the requirements of the present and future.

The change agent coming from outside may feel that the pace of development in the community where he works is slow, yet this deliberate pace permits adaptation both to the change introduced and to the many-sided effects arising from the change.

(3) Growth in community capacity

Experience has shown that successful working on one problem increases the capacity of the community to deal with other problems which the community has to make up later for its development. This is because the community develops problem-solving techniques in dealing with one problem which may help them with new problems. It is also being recognised that the community that can become involved in a process by which it deals with one of its common problems may also become involved in a process of self-understanding and integration that will make it possible for this community to extend the range and scope of the problems with which it can deal successfully.

(4) The will to change

Experience shows that the will and desire of people for a given change facilitates the work for bringing about a change in the community many times, when a change is pushed ahead in a community, there is not much in the programme. If ideas of techniques or projects are imposed on the community when there is no desire to adopting these, the idea or technique may be accepted, but the community does not grow under such a situation. It grows and develops the capacity only when it develops a will and desire to grow; only when it makes a struggle and strives or makes hard attempts to overcome its difficulties and only when it gathers sufficient strength to overcome its problems.

Major divisions of community works

The major divisions are community development, community relations and community organisation. These represent different situations or "settings" for work, but there are fundamental similarities in the work being attempted. These may be explained as follows:

(1) *Community development*

Community development designates the utilisation under one single programme of approaches and techniques which rely upon local communities as units of action and attempts to combine outside assistance with organised local self-determination and effort and which correspondingly seek to stimulate local initiative and leadership as the primary instrument of change.[1]

In agricultural and underdeveloped countries like India, emphasis is placed upon those activities which aim at promoting the improvement of the basic living conditions of the village communities including the satisfaction of some of the non-material needs.

The objectives and methods in such programmes are:

(1) Programme implanted by external agent: The extension agent—VLW or BDO or AEO etc., secures acceptance and implants work by:

---

[1]U.N. Document of E/CN. 5/291 Programme of Concerted Action.

(a) Diagnosing the community's need for his services. He prescribes a programme and seeks to establish this programme.

(b) The extension worker needs not only to prescribe, but to persuade and by a variety of "sales methods" convinces the community to use it.

(c) He discusses with people the need for such projects or programmes as he has in mind by: giving literature, showing films, slides photographs etc., of work done at other places, and organising meetings, etc.

(2) *Multi-purpose approach:* A team of experts, as posted at our Block headquarters in India, seeks to provide a variety of services—agriculture, education, health, industries etc.

(3) *Inner-resource approach:* In such a programme, the extension or community development worker encourages people to identify their needs and work cooperatively to satisfy them.

(2) Community relation

It implies the methods by which an agency, association or council relates itself to the geographic community. It includes:

(1) *Public relations*: Attempts of an organisation or agency to enhance is prestige, position or product in the community at large. It is a careful study of employees, consumers of the services of the organisation or extension service and the community at large, so that there is awareness within the organisation of the strength and weaknesses of its own position in the community.

(2) *Community services*: Provision of services to group in the community or to the community as a whole.

(3) *Community participation:* Such participation may stem from the following motives:

(a) Keeping the agency or association related to other important groups in the community.
(b) Maintaining contact with new developments.
(c) Keeping some control over plans for future developments in the community.
(d) Coordinating services with those of other services, or agencies.
(e) Supporting cooperative planning and development of new services in the community.

(3) Community organisation

It is a *process* by which the *community* idenitifies its needs or objectives, orders (or ranks these needs or objectives, develops the confidence and will to work at these needs or objectives, finds the resources (internal or external) to deal with these needs or objectives, takes action in respect of them, and in so doing, extends and develops cooperative and collaborative attitudes and practices in the community[1]. It can be analysed as:

(1) *Process:* The word process, which we have used in the definition, means simply the conscious or unconscious voluntary movement from identification of a

[1]G. Ross Murray, *Community Organisation: Theory and Practice*, Harper and Brothers, New York.

problem to solution or attainment of the objectives in the community. So the job of the extension worker is to help, initiate, nourish and develop this process.

(2) *Community:* This term we have used in the above definition, for:

(a) a village, block, village-group, district or State, i.e., a geographical area.

(b) groups of people, who share some common interest or function which may be development of agriculture, education, health or any welfare programme.

(3) *Objective:* (a) To create a welfare community, i.e., bring into significant association those persons who are part of the social organisation:

(b) To make plans to meet general needs; and

(c) To win support of the community.

(4) Identifying needs or objectives of the community where we want to work.

(5) To rank the needs by priority in the development programme.

(6) Finding resources for completing the projects or programmes.

(7) Take action in respect of the needs; and

(8) Develop cooperative and collaborative attitudes and practices.

It requires people who can endure, welcome and move comfortably with diversity, intension and purpose to serve the community to achieve its goal.

Preference for the term of community development

Now more and more people use the term community development in place of the other two: community organisation and community relations. According to Sanders, there may be two reasons for this; first, the health and welfare field has studied and published the techniques and procedures of community organisation to the point where this term has taken on a social work connotation with many people. Where this has happened, those who were thinking in broader terms than the social welfare field found some other term more appealing. Second, development has a more popular appeal than organisation and certainly fits much better with the economic approaches whose sponsors think of themselves as being involved in community development. Community development provides a larger umbrella under which all the people engaged in such work of community organisation, community relations, etc., can gather in a better way.

ANALYSIS OF THE TERM—COMMUNITY DEVELOPMENT

(1) Community development is bringing forth the potential abilities and qualities of group of people who live together in a common territory and who have an interdependent relationship with each other.

(2) It is a continuous process of social action by which the people of a community:

(a) Define their common and group needs;

(b) Organise themselves formally and informally for democratic planning and action;

(c) Make group and individual plans to meet their needs and solve their problems;

(d) Execute their plans with maximum reliance upon their own resources; and

(e) Supplement their resources from outside the community, when necessary, with services and material.

(3) According to Carl Taylor, Community Development is a method by which

people in villages are involved in helping to improve their own economic and social conditions and thereby they become effective working groups in the programme of their national development. This carries the assumption that people become dynamic if they are permitted to make their own decisions and are helped to carry on the programme.[1]

(4) The Community Development Division of I.C.A., defines it as a process of social action in which the people of a community organise themselves for planning and action; define their common and individual needs and problems; make group and individual plans to meet their needs and solve their problems, execute these plans with a maximum reliance upon community resources; and, supplement these resources, when necessary, with the services and materials from Governmental agencies outside the community.

(5) The Cambridge Conference defining it said that "It is a movement designed to promote better living for the whole community and if possible on the initiative of the community." But if this initiative is not forthcoming spontaneously, then by the use of techniques for arousing and stimulating it in order to secure its active and enthusiastic response to the movement.

(6) The United Nations defines Community Development as, "A process of change by which the efforts of the people themselves are united with those of Government authorities to improve the economic, social and cultural conditions of communities in the life of the nation and to enable them to contribute fully to a national programme."

So from the above definitions it can be concluded that:

(a) Community Development is a process of change from the traditional way of living to progressive ways of living.

(b) It is a method by which people can be assisted to develop themselves with their own capacity and resources.

(c) It is a programme for accomplishing certain activities in fields and concerning rural people.

(d) It is a movement for progress.

When viewed as a process the emphasis is on change that takes place in people socially and psychologically. When viewed as a method the emphasis is on activities like: development of health, education, agriculture, etc., and when viewed as a movement, the emphasis is on the emotional content or ideology behind the programme.

Essential elements of community development

The successful Community Development Programme stresses the following basic elements:

(a) Activities undertaken must correspond to the basic needs of the community. The first projects should be initiated in response to the expressed needs of people.

(b) There should be concerted action and the establishment of multi-purpose programmes.

(c) Change in the attitudes of the people is as important as the material achievement through Community Development during the initial stages of development.

---

[1]C. Taylor, *A Critical Analysis of India's C. D. Programme*, 1956 (Adapted).

(d) Community Development aims at increased and better participation of the people in community affairs, revitalisation of existing forms of Local Government and transition towards effective local administration where it is not yet functioning.

(e) The identification, encouragement and training of local leadership should be a basic objective in any programme.

(f) Greater reliance on the participation of women and youth in community projects invigorates development programmes, establishes them on a wide basis and secures long-range expansion.

(g) To be fully effective, community self-help projects require both internal and external assistance from the Government.

(h) Implementation of a Community Development Programme on a national scale requires adoption of consistent policies, specific administrative arrangement, recruitment and training of personnel, mobilisation of local and national resources and organisation of research, experimentation and evaluation.

(i) The resources of the voluntary non-governmental organisations should be fully utilised in Community Development Programmes at the local, national and international level.

(j) Economic and social progress at the local level necessitates parallel development on a wider national scale.

Faiths behind community development

(1) Community Development is based on the faith that rural people have the capacity to improve, if helped. The State should create favourable conditions and give direction through self-exerted leadership and group effort. It is based on villagers' needs and the community has to be the basic unit.

(2) People's participation is significant. The people should regard all aspects of Community Development as their concern, and develop their capacity and faith in themselves and in the capacity of their own co-operative action to solve their local problems. This requires their fullest participation and the programme should fully involve them in the process of improving themselves through their own efforts.

(3) It has to be organised on a small community-unit basis. This gives the advantage of mutual helpfulness, intimate relationships and mutual confidence.

(4) It has faith in the democratic approach, i.e., belief in the dignity of man, respect for the individual, his freedom of choice and his right of free expression of opinion.

(5) It has faith in science and technology. Development of agriculture, health, sanitation, housing, transport, etc., requires the application of science and technology.

(6) It has faith in social justice. It must help all classes of rural society, otherwise community solidarity and cooperative action cannot be achieved. It should give particular attention to weaker sections of the society. It must promote cohesion in the community.

Objectives of the community development programme

In any programme, the objective is to raise the economic and social level of its people, e.g., in India, the objective behind the Community Development Programme is to develop the resources of the people numbering about 640 millions who form the rural population. The elements of develodment are:

(1) *General:* Farm, home, public service and village community.

(2) *Specific:* To bring improvement in the production of crops and animals, living conditions, health and education of the people.

(3) *Elements who need change are:* People—men, women and youth.

(4) *Change agents:* The change agents are:

(1) *Voluntary local leaders*—Members of Panchayats, Village and Block Advisory Committees, etc.

(2) *Professional community development workers*—village level workers, extension officers, block development officers, etc.

Philosophy behind community development programme

The philosophies on which the community development programme should be based are as follows:

(1) *Work based on "felt needs":* The programme should help the community to solve some of the problems which it feels are existent.

(2) *Work based on assumption that people want to be free from poverty and pain:* It is assumed that the members of the community want a standard of living that allows them to be free from pain caused by lack of sufficient food, lack of sanitary conditions lack of clothing and shelter. On the social side it is assumed that the people have four basic wishes: (a) security, (b) recognition, (c) response, and (d) new experience.

(3) It is assumed that people wish to have freedom in controlling their own lines and deciding the forms of economic, religious, educational and political institutions, under which they will live.

(4) *People's values given due consideration:* It is presumed that cooperation, group decision-making, self-initiative, social responsibility, leadership, trustworthiness and ability to work are included in the programme.

(5) *Self-Help:* The people actually plan and work on the solution of their problems themselves. If the problems of the community are entirely ameliorated through the efforts of some outside agency, then the development of such things as group decision-making, self-initiative, self-reliance, leadership, etc., will not be forthcoming and it cannot be said that the community is developing.

(6) *People are the greatest resource:* It is by getting the participation of the people in improvement activities that they become developed.

(7) The programme involves a change in attitudes, habits, ways of thinking, relationships among people in the level of knowledge and intellectual advancement of people, changes in their skills, i.e., practices of agriculture, health, etc.

APPROACH TO RURAL DEVELOPMENT IN A DEMOCRATIC SOCIETY[1]

Rural development in a democratic society is not a matter only of plans and stati-

[1]Based on the talk by Dr. J. Paul Leagans, Ford Foundation Consultant on Extension Education at Central Institute of Study and Research in Community Development, Mussoorie (India), Dec. 1958.

stics, targets and budgets technology and methods, material aid, professional staff organisations and the machinery to administer them, but one of using these mechanisms skilfully as a means for changing the mind, heart and actions of the people in ways that result in improvements educationally, socially, economically and morally. Hence, the process is of working with people, not for them; of helping people to become self-reliant, not dependent on others; of making people the central actors in the drama, not the stage hands or spectators.

So the key to rural development in a free society is the human element, not material aid. The central means is education of the people in ways of improving their farms, home and community. This change must emerge from the people's own decisions to act, result from their own efforts and utilise their own resources to the maximum. To progress along these lines requires careful mobilisation of the resources for promoting advancement and sharp focusing of them on changing the minds of people educationally.

This process of educating the rural people is a complex one because its major components are complex. It includes the people, the educational process, democratic procedures and technology.

This is the democratic way of rural development and India's National Extension Service and C. D. Programme has chosen this way. So it becomes the duty of all workers from top to bottom to have this philosophy and action in mind while directing the programme.

The central challenge then, before the extension workers, is to have the philosophy, approach and to remain aware that the work is tough.

Major elements involved in India's community development and extension process[1]

The major elements constituting the foundation of the N.E.S. and Community Development Programme in India are:

(1) *The objective:* i.e., to raise the economic and social level of 580 million villagers of India.

(2) *General elements requiring change:* Farm, home, public services and the village community.

(3) *Specific elements requiring change:* Crops, livestock, living conditions, services like health, education, cooperatives, organisation, developing leadership, etc.

(4) *Elements who need change:* The people, i.e., men, women and youth living in villages.

(5) *Change agents:* (a) Voluntary local leaders, (b) Professional: village level workers and extension specialists.

(6) *Professional and material resources:* The staff of Blocks, District, State and National levels with their resources, now engaged in the programme.

For achieving progress in the work these elements engaged in each of these has to undergo a change or has to promote a change in the desired direction. So each one has to be viewed as an essential element, each one has to be viewed as a part of the whole scheme. They have to be viewed as a single, unified and coordinated set of

[1]Based on the talk by Dr. J. Paul Leagans, Ford Foundation Consultant on Extension Education to practicants in the 2nd Orientation Course, Oct. 1958.

units so that each one is able to contribute its maximum in the development programme.

Basic principles useful in understanding the role of these elements

(1) To make progress towards the central objective, the elements like farm, home public services, community, the people and the local leaders, all should undergo change. This change must be felt by the people to be important and must be related to the primary needs of the village.

(2) Change in farm, home, public services, etc., must be kept balanced and simultaneous.

(3) The people must first be changed educationally in order to bring about change in their farming, home-making, health and community.

(4) All these elements are interrelated perpendicularly and each is influenced by all the others.

(5) The change agents, voluntary and professional need to be properly selected, trained and used.

(6) The professional change agents must assume responsibility for all professional leadership and joint responsibility for the success of the programme along with the people of the villages. They must be real servants, educators and professional leaders, not merely administrators. They must derive satisfaction from the progress in their work.

(7) The primary professional and material support must be available in time and adequately to the village workers and other agents of change so that they do not lose their confidence and are able to get resources in time.

(8) Each of these elements described must be viewed as having a highly significant place in the whole organisation and programme. Aided self-help through education and cooperation is the principle on which our programme rests.

TYPES OF COMMUNITY DEVELOPMENT PROGRAMMES

According to their geographic scope, emphasis on development or on community organisation as the main objective and the effect on the prevailing structure, development programmes can be classified into 3 categories, (1) Integrative type, (2) Adaptive type, and (3) Project type.

(1) Integrative type

This type of programme is countrywide in scope. It emphasises on development and the coordination of technical services. In the early years it involves substantial changes in the administrative organisation and functioning of the Government. It has a readily identifiable organisation which is designed to marshal and coordinate, at each level, the efforts of the Government and Non-Government agencies which can make a contribution to community development. In some cases, new administrative areas are created within the traditional ones in order to coordinate technical services at a point closer to the people. Substantial technical and financial resources are channelled through this organisation to achieve centrally planned development goals.

India's programme is of this type. It was the fore runner of similarly designed programmes in Afghanistan, Indonesia, Iran, Pakistan, Philippines, Thailand and Vietnam. The spread of such a programme is attributable not only to the desire for integral development of rural areas but also to the influence of the Indian example and to the tendency of some of the technical assistance experts in community development under both international and bilateral programmes to recommend this type of programme.

Common characteristics: This type of programme has the following characteristics:

(a) An agency, attached to a central planning office of the President or Prime Minister, which has operating responsibility for the programme. Another possibility is to have a neutral ministry of federal level to take primary responsibility for the programme. Neutral ministry refers to a ministry which is devoted to such matters as local government or finance, which is not identified with any of the principal technical services. This is better for obtaining the cooperation of the several technical services than a functional ministry. This term, 'Functional Ministry' refers to a ministry which is responsible for technical services, e.g., Ministry of Agriculture, C.D. Cooperation, Education and Health.

(b) A cabinet level committee presided over by the Prime Minister or the President with the head of Community Development Organisation as the Secretary. This gives policy guidance and leadership to the programme.

(c) An interdepartmental committee, presided over by the head of the community development organisation, either in addition to the Cabinet Level Committee or in place of it.

(d) A development committee at the State level, district level, block and village level, with the chief executive of the respective unit as chairman and a community development officer as secretary. There are also representatives of local legislative and private welfare organisations.

(e) Where there are no small divisions of districts, units like Blocks, as in India, are created.

(f) Workers like VLW's in India, are appointed to provide a link between villagers and the Government's technical services.

(g) Grant-in-Aid and other inducements are provided not only to spur self-help efforts but also to channel such efforts to establish goals.

(2) Adaptive type

This type of programme is designed to be countrywide in scope. It lays emphasis on community organisation and self-help and involves little change in administrative organisation of government. It is designed primarily to stimulate self-help community effort toward locally determined goals and to attract the support of the technical departments thereto. These are called adaptive type because they can be attached to almost any department and adapted to the prevailing administrative organisation of Government. Most of the Community Development Programme in Africa, like Ghana, and the Caribbean are of such type. Some of these programmes have as their objectives the improvement of interdepartmental coordination and a better relationship between national measures and community development activities. For the most part, however, they utilise existing machinery and informal methods for this purpose. Very seldom there are interdepartmental committees at each level of goverment or new administrative areas or sub-areas established especially for community development purposes. There is wide diversity in the structure of this type of programme because of the adaptations.

Responsibility may be vested in one of the functional ministry like Agriculture, Education, Social Welfare, or in a ministry of Local Government, or in rare cases, as in Kenya, in a separate ministry of Community Development. The field organisation will take one or the other of two basic patterns depending on whether there are administrative districts where the field activities of different departments may be coordinated.

Where such districts do not exist, field contacts with the technical services are arranged largely on an informal basis. This is the case, in Puerto Rico where the group organisers of Community Education Division, Department of Education do not have formal ties in the field with representatives of technical departments.

Where administrative districts exist, community development personnel are integrated into the prevailing field organisation. For example, in the former British territories in Africa, a typical arrangement for community development officers was to serve as members of district or provincial team which is composed of administrative and technical officers and representative members of local communities, with the senior administrative officer presiding. There are, however, diverse forms of organisation in these territories. Because of the common policy of adapting the existing administrative framework to the purposes and methods of community development, in Northern Rhodesia, the General Administrative Officer is the Chief Community Development Officer. Although some characteristics of programmes cited as examples are like those of the integrative type, they are included in the adaptive category because they serve as a channel of planned development and involve little change in the organisation of Government.

(3) Project type

This is a multi-functional but limited by geographical scope to certain parts of the country, and usually emphasises development. It predominates in Latin America and is also common in many other countries. Its forms may be: (a) Inter-Ministerial in character; with primary responsibility for administration resting in a Functional Ministry, e.g., Rio-Coco Project under the Ministry of Education in Nicaragua, (b) In an autonomous agency under the general direction of an official appointed by the President and a council composed of representatives of Ministers and other Government and private institutions, e.g., the Projects of the National Indian Institute of Mexico and the Indian Economic Development Service of Guatemala, or (c) Multifunctional with responsibility for both policy and administration vested in a single department, e.g., cultural missions of the Department of Education of Mexico.

The structures of these types are such that they cannot be extended on a nationwide basis without interfering with the operations of other Governmental agencies. However this is not necessarily a characteristic of this type of programme. For example, an interministerial regional project might develop a pattern which is applicable elsewhere. Also, a project type programme like the National Indian Institute of Mexico or Economic Development Service of Guatemala might be designed to establish

services in remote areas for which the regular ministries would initially provide technical support and later assume responsibility.

Changing nature of programmes: Of course, there are three categories as described
above, but the programmes within each category differ substantially in purpose,
organisation and method of administration. In certain cases, it is difficult to decide in
which category the programme should be placed. The programmes in Burma, Ceylon,
Ghana, Jamaica and Uganda exhibit characteristics of both the integrative and
adaptive types. Further programmes in the these categories may be highly unstable.
The starting point and method of progression differ according to circumstances in the
countries concerned. The present integrative type programme in the Egyptian region
and the Philippines for example, evolved from a situation such as that exists in Mexico
today. The effort in Ghana to accelerate the pace of development through increasing
use of campaigns is producing evidence of the integrative type in a programme which
could be classified as adaptive. The integrative type of programme in India was
launched straight away, with only some experimentation beforehand on a pilot project
basis. However, this and other integrative type programmes will, in due course, take
on the characteristic of the adaptive type as the organisation of the programmes and
the methods of relating community self-help to Government effort become more stable.

PRINCIPLES OF COMMUNITY DEVELOPMENT AND
COMMUNITY ORGANISATION

Based on the philosophy behind the programme, the following principles can be
listed for the community development and organisation work:

(1) Creating discontent with existing conditions and standard of living among the
village people or the members of the community. This will create a common feeling of
importance for the development programme. The needs imply conditions including
necessity, requirement, urgency, vacancy, scarcity and lack of something.

The needs can be identified by the programme planning process, i.e., by showing
the village people their actual situation and what they should have, and showing them
the gap between the two situations. Unless they know what they can be, or what their
standard of living should be, they cannot aspire for the higher standard of living
(Fig. 39.1).

If they know this situation, they will have discontent or dissatisfaction from their
present standard and will aspire for the higher success through hard work.

(2) Discontent must be focused and channelled into organisation of the village
communities, planning their programme and taking action to satisfy their needs, i.e.,
specific problems. To provide motivation for action, discontent must be focused on
something specific, i.e., construction of a road, establishing a school, increase in the
yield of crops, etc.

(3) The discontent which initiates community organisation must be widely shared
in the community and should be properly channelised.

(4) Village organisation, which is supposed to initiate the development work on
the village problems, must involve village leaders who may be formal (Patel, Sarpanch,
Patwari, VLW, etc.) and informal leaders. These leaders should be accepted by the
major sub-groups of the village.

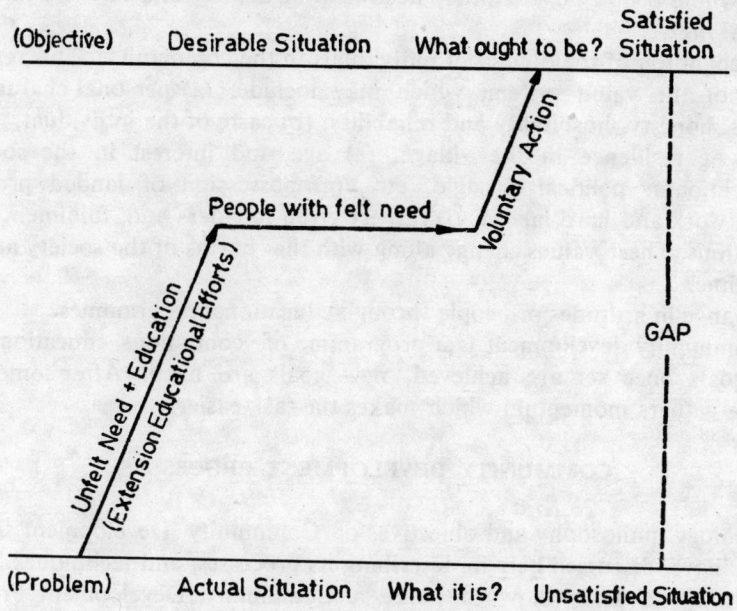

Fig. 40.1 Concept of need.

(5) The village organisation—Panchayat, Advisory committee at block or district or higher levels which plans to undertake community work must have goals and methods of high acceptability.

(6) There should be some emotional involvement in the programme when it is started. People should feel motivated by this project or programme of their village which may give them a higher standard or solve some of their problems.

(7) The latent potentialities and resources of the village people should be utilised for this work.

(8) The village organisation, which is meant to take up development work in the village, should develop active and effective lines of communication within their active members and between the organisation and the village people. All should know what are they going to do and what is being done and what will be their plan and also should know how they were doing, etc.

(9) The village organisation should support and strengthen the groups which cooperate in the development programme of the village.

(10) The organisation should be flexible in the organisational procedures without disrupting its regular decision-making routines.

(11) There should be arrangement for the development of effective village leadership through training and guidance.

(12) Understanding the community and its social structure. The structure includes: (i) the organisation of the community, i.e., division of population into farmers, businessmen, administrators, etc., (ii) the groups in the village or community—religious or political, etc., and (iii) pattern influencing social structure—under it the worker is required to know: (a) who makes important decisions in the commu-

nity, (b) to whom people go when they need help or advice, and (c) who influence the decision-making.

(13) Recognition of the dignity of individuals in the community. This requires the knowledge of the value system, which may include: (a) personal characteristics—truthfulness, honesty, hospitality and reliability, (b) caste of the individual, (c) wealth, (d) length of residence in the village, (e) age and interest in the social works, (f) participation in political struggle, etc., (g) possession of landed property, (h) sincerity in work and hard labour, (i) respect given to elders and fulfilment of duties and obligations. These values change along with the norms of the society and also the change of time.

(14) Change in attitudes of people through educational programmes.

(15) Community development is a programme of continuous education. It never ends. If goals once set are achieved, new goals are fixed. After some years, the programme gathers momentum which makes the task easier.

COMMUNITY DEVELOPMENT PROCESSES

The ideology, philosophy and objectives of Community Development Programme which we have discussed help in describing its processes, and techniques. These processes help us to know how to make a Community Development Programme a success. The C.D. Programme, as Carl Taylor says, has to combine all the elements of organised activity, which are needed to achieve effective cooperation between organised community groups and organised sources of technical, economic and local assistance which local groups must receive. The method of community development has two broad divisions:

(1) Extension education, and (2) Community organisation.

(1) Extension education

Extension education aims at improving the quality of the human being as a member of his community and to improve his/her knowledge and skill as a crop grower, dairy-man, homemaker, artisan, health-seeker, etc.

So extension can be: (a) Agricultural extension dealing with crop raising or improved ways; (b) Animal husbandry and veterinary extension dealing with the raising of livestock in a better and improved ways; (c) Home Science extension—dealing with improved ways of keeping a home, cooking food, decorating a house, raising children, keeping a house clean and free from mosquitoes, flios, rats, preserving fruits, kitchen gardening; extension of knowledge about nutrition, family planning, etc. There can be other similar branches in other areas of improving the life of people living in villages and cities.

(2) Community organisation

Under the process of organising the community, the working of the three basic institutions connected with village life namely: the Panchayat, the Cooperative and the School, and the organisations like farmers' organisations, women organisations and youth organisations, has to be improved and made effective, so that the C.D. work goes on smoothly and progresses well.

The process which the C.D. programme has to undergo can be listed as:
  (i) Establishing rapport in the community;
 (ii) Appraising the situation—identifying problems and needs;
(iii) Planning the programme and projects;
 (iv) Selecting initial projects and long range projects;
  (v) Securing participation of the people and involving them;
 (vi) Developing effective communication channels;
(vii) Development and use of organisation channels—Panchayats, Farmers' Organisations, Women's Organisations, Youth Organisations, involving village people in the District Committees, Block Committees, Village Committees, etc., for different activities related to Village Development Programmes; and,
(viii) Developing adequate community leadership.

I. Establishing rapport in the community

Rapport is a condition of mental responsiveness between the change agent (C.D. worker) and the client system (the community or the village people) with whom the work is done, in a way that both parties are capable of responding and with apparent spontaneity to each other This requires that the C.D. worker is able to create confidence among the community. This requires the knowledge of the groups, knowledge of the dynamics of planned change and the ways of motivating the village people.

II. Appraising the situation—Identifying problems and needs

For any programme of community development, a study of the present situation of the people, their problems and needs is necessary. The people should say what are their felt needs and what should be the priority in taking up the problems for solution. The needs of the people constitute the core around which a successful C.D. programme can be built. Needs imply conditions, including necessity, requirement, urgency, prerequisites, vacancy, scarcity, lack and indispensability.

Basic aspect of a concept of need[1]

Following are the basic aspects of a concept of need.

(1) *Man is an independent living system surrounded by an environment with which he constantly interrelates.* The well-being of man depends on keeping a balance between the internal forces produced by the energy resulting from the food intake and the external conditions produced by the environment. To keep the human system in equilibrium with the external forces, it is necessary that certain needs be met. In this sense, every person is continuously meeting his needs—trying to attain those conditions of living that give satisfaction.

(2) *Peoples needs are to be identified by finding through the programme planning process: the actual, the possible, and the valuable:* Here, by the word actual means What Is, by possible means What Could Be. For making a programme it is necessary to analyse the present situation and to decide which is most valuable. Thus, it becomes the objective of the programme to change people and the present conditions in which

[1]Government of India, Directorate of Extension, Ministry of Food & Agriculture., *Extension Education in Community Development*, pp. 100-105 (Adapted).

they live to the most valuable and possible conditions. Making the analysis and decisions necessary in this context, is the essence of Programme Planning to meet the needs of the community.

(3) *Needs of the community may be the difference between what is, what could be, and what ought to be*

(4) People have to recognise the gap between the actual, the possible, and the desirable, and place value on attaining the desirable conditions before they will become motivated to change in a desirable direction.

(5) The needs of the people may be (*a*) *Physical needs*—food, clothing, housing, etc., (*b*) *Social needs*—group status, affection, belongingness, etc. (*c*) *Integrative needs*—the need to relate oneself to something larger and beyond oneself, a philosophy of life, etc.

III. Planning the programme and projects

This process includes the following four major elements that are generally viewed as important:

(a) A plan for involving local people in the planning process.

(b) Procedure in programme planning.

(c) The programme—the product of planning.

(d) The annual plan of work.

These have been discussed elsewhere in this book. Here let it suffice to say that "planning is the formation of major economic decisions: what and how much to produce, how, when and where to be produced and to whom it is to be allocated by the conscious decisions of an accepted authority on the basis of a comprehensive survey of the economic system as a whole." In the case of C.D. programme it may be Farm Planning, Village Planning and preparing plans for VLW circle or block and so on.

IV. Selecting initial projects and long-range projects

The initial projects may be included under short-term planning: In this planning, immediate problems, economic and social, receive the attention of the planners. It mainly takes the shape of partial planning, emergency planning or accidental planning.

Long-term planning: It has wider range and scope. It may be structural and functional. Structural planning aims at revolutionising the whole economic structure of the society and thus paving way for an essentially new order to come. It concentrates on basic problems facing the community or even country. It proves greatly beneficial to the country as a whole unless the party in power completely loses confidence in the mid-stream of planning.

Functional planning can only deal imperfectly. This is because the problems have to undergo day-to-day changes thereby calling for an adjustable type of planning.

V. Securing participation of the people and involving them

Decisions about programme objectives are usually best when made both by the officials and the community or their representatives. This involvement or participation can be obtained possibly through some organised efforts or approaches. If we organise the village people into farmers organisations, youth clubs or women's associations, etc., people will be involved in programme planning and its execution. The following criteria, which are usually met when local people contribute in the programme planning are:

(1) Organise representative committees of non-officials, which should function on a continuing basis in developing and maintaining a current programme of development in the community.

(2) The members should represent major interest groups—social, economic and different strata and other important elements in the community.

(3) Each member of such an organisation should understand three things: (a) the purpose of the community or committee, (b) how the committee can function in attaining its purpose, and (c) the member's role in his individual capacity.

(4) The selection of such members of the committee should be made by democratic way.

(5) To maintain a continuity, certain number of members should be replaced every year and the committee should be of a permanent type.

If people are selected in such a way, they will feel responsibility, and if anybody does not take part in the meeting, there can be some action taken, e.g , a member, if he is absent for three meetings continuously, he will be replaced through a new election.

VI. Developing effective communication channels

Well developed communication channels help in the Community Development Programme. These channels may be: (1) transport facility, so that the people come in contact with the outside world and become aware of the progressive ways of doing things and living in a progressive way. (2) The radio if it is available in the village, helps the villagers to listen to new things which otherwise they would have not been able to hear. Many rural programmes regarding agricultural development, veterinary and animal husbandry, Home Science and other technical things can be heard if there are radios in the villages. (3) If the workers of the Community Development Organisations, Agricultural Universities, Agricultural Department, Home Science Colleges, etc., come to the villages and communicate with the people living there—talk to them, show films, arrange exhibitions, the people become aware of the innovations. They may even agree to have demonstrations of new practices in their fields or homes and then may adopt these. The researches by L.N. Sharma and R.M. Goel, conducted at Agricultural University, Jabalpur and the studies at the National Institute of Community Development, Hyderabad, and others have revealed that the development of communication channels helps in the adoption of innovations. So such channels have to be developed if the pace of development is to be increased.

Communication is a conscious attempt to share information, ideas, attitudes, etc. It is the act of getting a sender of information tuned to the receiver. In Community Development or extension work the worker is the sender of information and the villager or farmer is the receiver. It includes the worker, the message or content, the channels of communication, the treatment of message, the audience (villagers or farmers or community), and the response of the audience. The C.D. workers' ability to influence others is closely linked with his ability to communicate his ideas. Good communication does not consist in simply giving orders, but in creating understanding.

It also does not consist of merely imparting knowledge, but of helping people to gain a clear view of the meaning of the things we want to communicate. Villagers or farmers will learn things if they are communicated useful ideas effectively, the present need of our village people is more people saying the right things, at the right time, in the right way, to the right people the on right occassion, obtaining right results in right direction.

Communication problems

According to J. Paul Leagans, each episode of communication has at least three phases: (1) expression, (2) interpretation, and (3) response. If expression is not clear, the interpretation inaccurate and the response improper, one's effort to communicate will not succeed. It is easy to control what one's expressions say or mean, but difficult to control how an audience or community or group interpets, responds to, and acts upon them.

Factors making communication more effective

The factors that make communication more effective are:

(1) *Communication is limited by one's concept of the communication process:* Different people think differently about communication: the speech-makers, leaders in group dynamics, the artists, the social scientists, the administrators have different ways of communication. Successful communication in a C.D. programme is not a single unit act, but requires a series of unit acts planned to assure effective sequence and integration. It starts with the recognition of needs which new ideas can help to meet and proceed within until people have acted upon them. So in C.D. programme, the workers should combine the unit acts into an integrated whole.

(2) *Communication is a two-way process* and involves interaction between the C.D. workers or teachers and the receivers, i.e., the community, village people or trainees.

It is not enough just to tell or demonstrate a practice. The C.D. worker has to make the persons or audience understand clearly what is to be learned and what the audience should do about it. Comments and questions from the side of receivers will serve as feedback to give an idea whether the thing has really been communicated. Direct questioning by the communicator, establishing a friendly environment and permissive climate in the meeting or class room are other methods for aiding effective learning. The two-way process is necessary to ensure that information presented by the C.D. worker is interpreted as intended.

(3) *The C.D. worker must have ideas before he can communicate to an audience:* It is not enough that a C.D. worker must have ideas but he should also know how to organise and present them clearly, forcefully, accurately and adequately. In this work, the C.D. worker should not cling always to what he knows, but he should pay attention to what the client system or the receivers of ideas think because they are the public opinion.

(4) *The system of symbols used to represent ideas, objects or concepts must be accurate and used skilfully:* To convey the meaning of a thing, man invented symbols. For example, to say something about cow it is not proper and practical to bring a cow into the class room or meeting, but to name this thing as: *cow, Gai, Gow,* or whatever it may be called in any language. The word cow, etc., is symbol for writing as well as for speech. These words became language, and language is communication of ideas. More recently, people have created visual and audio-visual aids, which are symbols for

expressing ideas more effectively; it may express ideas or feelings through sound, shape, colour or motion of a thing. The important point is to convey ideas by selecting the things that make our ideas become impressive and effective. The symbols are meaningful to a person only when he understands what they stand for.

(5) *Cultural values and social organisation are determinants of communication:* These differ from one culture to another and also within the same culture. Hence, knowledge of ideas and action which the value system will accept, and which it will reject, along with the channels of communication established by the particular social organisation in a community are very necessary to effective communication for C.D. programme.

(6) The environment created by the communicator including the physical facilities, friendliness, rapport, recognition of the accomplishment of others, all affect the communication.

(7) For effective communication, cooperation, participation and involvement of people with whom we work are essential.

(8) Standards of communication influence its success. These standards can be effectiveness, keeping the contents compatible with the social code of the society, correctness of words or symbols and social responsibility.

(9) Evaluation of the programmes and projects for further improvement in the use of communication.

Elements of communication

The important elements of communication are:

(1) *The communicator:* The qualities of a good communicator are:

(a) What he knows: These include his objectives, the needs of his audience, their interests and abilities; his message—its contents, validity, usefulness and importance in the C.D. programme: his channels of communication; his professional abilities and limitations;

(b) What is his interest in his audience and its welfare, his message and how it can help the community, the results of evaluation of communication, interest in the communication process, interest in the use of communication channels and interest in improving his method of communication:

(c) His preparation; and

(d) His skills in selecting the message, treating the message, expression, selection and use of channels, understanding his audience, and collecting data.

(2) *The message:* A message is the information the C.D. worker or the communicator wishes his audience, or the village people, or community to receive, understand or accept and act upon. The message may be scientific information about agriculture, homemaking, livestock raising, etc. A good message should be in line with the objective to be attained by the C.D. programme. It should be clear and understandable by the audience. It should be in line with the mental, social, economic and physical capabilities of the audience or the community and the economic, social or aesthetical significance to the needs, interests, and values of the community. It should be specific, simple, accurate, timely, supported by facts, appropriate to the channel selected; appealing and attractive to the community; and applicable, adequate and manageable within their resources.

(3) *Channels of communication:* Channels are the connecting links between the communicators or C.D. workers and receivers or the community. For effective work, the C.D. worker should take the following factors into consideration: The specific objective of the message; the nature of the message; the size of the audience; its needs, interests, knowledge of the subject; channels of communication available; relative cost of channels; time available to the communicator and audience; the extent of seeing, hearing or doing a thing, etc.

(4) *Treatment of message:* Treatment of a message relates to the technique or manner of performance necessary in presenting the message. Its purpose is to make the message clear, understandable and realistic to the community. It requires original thinking, deep insight into the principles of human behaviour and skill in creating and using improved techniques of presentation of a message. This makes an effective teacher, extension worker, C.D. worker or a communicator. Three ways of treating the message can be:

(a) *Matters of general organisation:* These include, repetition of ideas; contrast of ideas,—chronological compared to logical or psychological; starting with strong arguments compared to saving them until the end of presentation; inductive compared to deductive, proceeding from general to specific and drawing of conclusions.

(b) *Matters of speaking and acting:* The communicator should limit himself to a few ideas, should strive to be clear, he should know the facts, he should not read the speech, he should know the audience, he should not talk down to people or over their heads, he should decide on the dramatic effect desired and should quit in time.

(c) *Matters of symbol variation and devices for representing ideas:* Making a speech, use of real objects or models, specimens, photographs, graphs, charts, motion pictures, slides, dramas, puppets, songs, flash cards, flannelgraphs, etc.

(5) *The audience:* The audience is compared of the intended respondents, or members of the community in the C.D. work, who are to gain economically, socially or in other ways by the message or information given by the change agents or the C.D. worker. It may consist of one person or more: male, female, adults or children or youth formed in occupational groups or interest groups. The more homogeneous an audience, the greater the chances of successful communication.

Types of audience: The audience can be: (a) the potential audience, (b) the available audience, and (c) the action audience, physical and psychological audience. At the primary level, there are only two audiences: (i) the audience which the communicator intends to teach—intended audience, and (ii) the unintended audience, i.e., all others in the geographical area.

The intended audience may have the following four groups: (1) listeners who act on the message, (2) listeners who do not act, (3) listeners or attenders, and (4) non-listeners or non-attenders.

How to know the nature of audience: (1) Communication channels established by the community; (2) the system of values held by the community or audience, i.e., what they think as important; (3) forces influencing the community conformity, i.e., its customs, traditions, etc.; (4) individual personality factors—susceptibility to change, etc.; (5) the native and acquired abilities in the community; (6) the educational, social and economic levels in the community; (7) pressure of occupational responsibility, i.e., how busy or concerned the community is; (8) the community needs as the community sees them and as the C.D. worker sees them; (9) why the community is in need of changed ways of thinking, feeling and doing things; and (10) how the community or audience views the situation.

(6) *Audience response:* If we assume that through the means of planned communication, an intended audience or community has received a useful message, that it has understood the meaning and intent of the message, interpreted it properly and that it has generally accepted the message, the question remains: did the community or audience act in response to the message? If so what kind of action took place, by whom and to what extent? Until the desired action results in the community, the development programmes do not achieve their essential objective. So in evaluating the effectiveness, the important criterion or standard of judging is the nature and extent of action taken by the people who needed to act.

The message in C.D. programme is intended for action now, for adoption now and not for use sometime later. The response largely depends on:

(a) *Understanding* vs. *knowledge:* Understanding of a thing is attained only when one is able to attach meaning to facts, see the relationship of facts to each other and to the whole of the proposition, and the relationship of the total body of facts to the problem under consideration. People only act when an understanding of facts is gained. So communication must promote understanding in the members of the community.

(b) *Acceptance* vs. *rejection:* Before taking any action it requires mental acceptance of the thing.

(c) *Remembering* vs. *forgetting.* For example, the action is delayed in getting started. Transmitting the message to the right people at the right time is often a crucial factor in successful communication.

(d) *Mental* vs. *physical action:* As J. Paul Leagans says: Change in the mind of man must always precede change in the action of his hands. So, for physical action, mental preparedness in the community members is necessary.

(e) *Right* vs. *wrong:* For many reasons, people often fail to behave precisely according to instructions, even when they understand and accept them. In this case, action will be wrong.

VII. Development and use of organisation channels

Organisation channels here mean the organisation of male or female adults and youth according to their interests in occupational, recreational or interest groups. These may be farmers' organisations, women organisations, youth organisations called by various names. If the work in C.D. is undertaken through these organisations, the participation and involvement of the community members increases.

A village without its own organisation and institutions cannot think, plan or act as a village unit. The C.D. workers, if they are not able to help village organisations, cannot assist the community in gaining experience in doing their own things themselves under their own leadership. These organisations should be developed in the initial stages when people think of developing their community.

The voluntary village organisations should not be looked upon as a link in the Government bureaucracy. Voluntary organisations cannot be assigned tasks by the

C.D. staff. They can, however, be aided and encouraged by the official C.D. workers to assume responsibility for village programmes which are in their interest. For balanced village development, village organisations are expected to be responsible for certain types of action which are important. When the village community recognises the importance of its own organisations, there is better work.

The voluntary organisations should be people's organisations, created by the people and led by them. These organisations can be formed by the C.D. workers through Village Panchayats in formal groups, engaging the people's attention in such problems as youth, recreation, women welfare, etc. As the people gain experience in discussing their problems in these informal groups, they can and will gradually become interested in wanting to work together to solve their problems.

(1) *Using village panchayat for community development work*

Panchayat literally means a council of five elders chosen to look after the welfare of a village. In former times the village in India was more or less a self-supporting, miniature republic. It produced its own food and clothing, managed its own affairs and provided justice to the satisfaction of the community. It was responsible for the all-round development of the village, and for peace, order and happiness. All accepted the decisions of the Panches. Under the British rule, the Panchayat lost its power and prestige. Administration and justice became centralised and localised in urban areas. After the achievement of Independence in India, the Panchayats were again revived. Article 40 of the Constitution of India provided that: The State shall take steps to organise Village Panchayats and endow them with such powers and activity as may be necessary to enable them to function as units of self-government.

For improving the working of the C.D. Projects, the Government of India set up a Study Team on Community Development which submitted a report in 1957 and recommended democratic decentralisation by the establishment of Panchayat Raj. On January 12, 1958, the National Development Council endorsed the recommendation of the study team called Mehta Committee, because it was under the chairmanship of the late Shri Balwantrai Mehta. On the broad principles recommended by the Mehta Committee, Panchayat Raj has been established in Andhra Pradesh, Assam, Madras, Maharashtra, Mysore, Orissa, Punjab, Rajasthan and U.P. Now the Panchayats, the Cooperatives and the Schools are the basic institutions at the village level for carrying out the Programme. The elected Panchayat has charge of all development programmes in its jurisdiction. The Cooperatives function in the economic sphere. The village school is being developed as the community centre to undertake work in educational, cultural, recreational and other allied fields. Associate organisations such as women's and youth organisations, farmers' associations, etc., functioning in their respective areas, are linked up with the Panchayat in its development activities and are helped by the Panchayat in their working.

Organisation under Panchayat Raj System: All the adult members (above 18 years) in village or a group of villages, as decided by the Collector of the district, having a population of about 1000 form a Gaon Sabha. The village, or the group of villages, is divided into 10-15 constituencies. Each constituency elects one member as their representative to the Panchayat. These elected members form the Village Panchayat. Each Panchayat has one President (Pradhan) and a Vice-President (*Up-Pradhan*). Some work committees are formed in each Panchayat. Some members are co-opted from women's organisations, youth organisations, farmers' organisations, cooperatives, etc.

All the Presidents of Village Panchayats in a block form *The Block Panchayat Samiti*. In addition, the Block Panchayat Samiti co-opts the M.L.A.s or M.P.s of the block. Each Block Samiti elects its president and vice-president and divides itself into various committees.

The presidents of all Block Panchayat Samities in a district form *Zila Parishad*. The M.P.s and M.L.A.s and some other special members are also included in the Zila Parishad. The Zila Parishad sets up special committees to deal with the specialised fields of development as: agriculture, education, health, youth, work, women's programmes, etc.

The VLW works as secretary to the Village Panchayat, the BDO as secretary to Block Panchayat Samiti and a Gazetted Class II Officer is provided to act as secretary to the Zila Parishad.

Organisation of Panchayats which are still on the old pattern: In States, where Panchayat Raj has not yet been adopted the Village Panchayat is elected as in the above case, but there is no such organisational set up at the block and district level. Over five Panchayats there is one Nyaya Panchayat for deciding petty cases. The Nyaya Panchayat conducts preliminary hearing of cases and can impose a fine.

Functions of Panchayat: The Village Panchayat plans village production programmes, frames the budget for village development, serves as a channel through which government assistance may reach the villagers, develops common lands, constructs repairs and maintains common village buildings like Chaupals, Panchayatghars, wells, roads, schools, etc., organises Shramdan (voluntary labour), promotes village societies, maintains the village library, garden, maternity and health centres. These functions are supervised and aided by the Block Samities, and Zila Parishads.

Financing of Panchayat: The Village Panchayat gets aid from the block budget, collects taxes from village people as house tax, duty on commercial goods, etc.

Role of Panchayat: The C.D. programme was originally conceived to promote programme planning, execution and evaluation at the village and block levels. Panchayat Raj now formally places the responsibility with the people. There is considerable progress in involving the village people in the planning process. The larger task is now for the C.D. workers of District and Block and village level to develop and maintain appropriate working relations with the Zila Parishad and Block Panchayat Samiti. For all such C.D. staff it is necessary to develop positive attitudes about the following points:[1]

(1) The Block staff must understand that Block Panchayat Samiti and the Village Panchayat must now become social institutions in India, having their ultimate objective guiding the villagers in the democratic development of village life and being the guardians of a village programme for village development.

(2) The Block staff must understand that while it is in fact taking its direction from the Panchayat Samiti, it has a continuous responsibility to educate and guide.

---

[1]Government of India, *A Guide to Community Development*, 1962, p. 127.

(3) The Block Samiti must gain competence in learning how to blend the knowledge of science with the knowledge of Rural Sociology of the Indian village.

Panchayat samiti sub-committees: For effective working, such sub-committees are necessary. Individual members should feel that they are being requested to help in an important way, and that through their participation on the sub-committees they will contribute in a tangible way to the rapid and effective involvement of village people in planning and development. This can and will happen only when the Block staff recognises the important role the panchayat samiti sub-committee can play in creating widespread villager participation in village and block development programmes.

How the C.D. workers can develop effective relations with Panchayat Samiti? (1) The C.D. workers at the Block level must from time to time, have thorough discussions with the Panchayat Samiti on the objectives and methods of the C.D. programme. The Block Panchayat Samiti and the Village Panchayat should be visualised as having a permanent place as an institution, assigned with guiding the democratic development in the village, in which village leaders and village organisations and institutions assume responsibility for continuous planning and execution of balanced village development programmes.

(2) The C.D. Staff at the Block and the Panchayat Samiti should work hard and make attempts to reach a working understanding about the village problems which the group would identify as being block-wide in nature, and the emphasis they feel should be placed on solving the problems. Both parties, the change agents and the client system, should understand that the primary objectives must be to create an interest among the villagers in the development of their village, knowing the needs of the people, which of the problems the villagers want to solve immediately and to look to the Village Panchayat as the village institution responsible for the all-sided development of the village.

(3) Systematic village visits, which involve the Sarpanches, the Gram Sewaks and the technical staff at the block level should be organised in the villages. This will develop team work between the C.D. workers, the village people and the Panchayat.

(4) The Block Samiti and the C.D. workers at the Block level should reach an agreement that systematic village plans should be developed by the Village Panchayat under the leadership of the sarpanches and with the assistance of Gram Sewaks and the technical staff.

(5) The Block Panchayat Samiti, following the systematic Village Panchayat discussions with the Gram Sewak and the technical staff, should meet with each Gram Sewak and give approval for the development of individual plans of work on all the villages. The meeting should produce a meeting of minds on the part of the Panchayat Samiti and the Block staff about the following:

(a) The immediate emphasis that each Village Panchayat wishes the C.D. workers to give in the development of plans of work of each village and in getting each Village Panchayat actively engaged in the C.D. work.

(b) The problems which are wider in geographic scope and which require the cooperation of several villages should be clearly defined and the plans of work agreed to by the Block Panchayat Samiti.

(c) Plans of work for the Block Panchayat Samiti should be clearly defined and understood, so that the Block staff effectively and fully meets its responsibility by helping the Village Panchayats when and where help from the staff has been scheduled, in the Village and Block Plans of work.

In this way a draft plan should be developed for the block which should have three things: (1) Statement of the objectives and methods of work of the C.D. programme. (2) Individual Village Panchayat Plans, and (3) Block Smiti Plans of Work. This should be signed by all members of the Block Panchayat Samiti and all members of the Block staff.

This type of programme require training of the Sarpanch, and the Gram Sewak, who are required to act as stimulator, motivator, educator and the link between science, the knowledge and experience being used in the village.

(2) *Role of cooperatives in community development work and how to make cooperatives effective village institutions?*

Under the present organisation, just like the Panchayat a statutory administrative institution for planning and execution of all developmental activities, the cooperatives are responsible for the economic development of the village. A cooperative society has to be registered with the Registrar of Cooperative Societies through the Cooperative Extension Officer placed at the Block level. A fee of Rs. 50 has to be deposited in the Treasury. A minimum of 10 members are necessary for any primary society. The fields can be arrangement of supplies, credit, marketing, cooperative farming, etc. The society develops its own constitution and by-laws.

By-laws: An illustration of by-laws of a village cooperative society may be as follows:

(1) *Name of the society:* The name of the Cooperative Society shall be: ....
....

(2) *Area of operation:* The registered address and the area of operation of the society shall be: ....village...........................P.O. Tehsil
...................................district...................................

(3) *Objectives:* The objectives of the society shall be: to increase production in agriculture and to raise the standard of living of its members. For these aims, the society shall undertake:

  (a) To receive money from members and non-members for granting loans to members for achieving the objectives of the society.

  (b) To arrange for the agricultural implements and heavy machinery and give them on hire to members. Arranging supplies of fertilisers, etc.

  (c) To run a Cooperative Consumers' Store for supplies required in the village.

  (d) To arrange for the sale of members' produce of their farms.

  (e) To help in irrigation projects, National Saving Schemes, encourage local industries, provide warehousing facilities, help farmers to learn improved agricultural practices, and develop relationships with the other villages, etc.

(4) *Working area:* Name of the village.

(5) *Membership:* To be limited to those who fulfil the desired conditions.

(6) *Nomination of members:* Each member will nominate his successor with two witnesses.

(7) *Ceasing of membership:* When the member becomes mentally invalid, withdraws his share money or becomes bankrupt or is expelled by the Society.

(8) *Transfer of share:* No share shall be transferred or sold.

(9) *Removal from membership:* The managing committee can remove a member who does not pay arrears, disobeys by-laws, or shows unsatisfactory behaviour towards the Society.

(10) *General meetings:* The General Body is the supreme authority. It generally meets after the preparation of an Annual Audit Report. The meeting of this body, can be called after taking the special permission from the Assistant Registrar, Cooperative Societies.

(11) *Quorum:* At least half the members should be present.

(12) *Work of the General Body:* Election of the President and Vice-Presidents. Suspension or dismissal of an office-bearer, to consider the Annual Report and Budget, sanction of loans, fixing interest, etc.

(13) *Managing Body:* It will consist of seven members including the President and Vice-President. It will work for one year. The election shall be held at the time of the meeting of the General Body.

(14) *Qualifications for membership:* A person must purchase at least one share, and should fulfil other conditions.

(15) *Meetings of the Managing Committee:* Meetings of this Body should be held at least once a month. For a quorum 4 members should be present.

(16) *Powers and duties of the Managing Body:* It will see that the by-laws are followed. It shall arrange for the maintenance of records, profit and loss account, audit of accounts, admission of new members, issuing new shares, removal of the members who are undesired, calling the meetings of the General Body, recovery of loans, fixing interests, taking securities, control over recurring and non-recurring expenditure, appointment of cashier and other employees if needed, purchase of supplies, machines, etc.

(17) *Objectives of loans:* Loans shall be accorded for: (1) purchase of seeds, fertilisers, implements, cattle-feeds, improvement of land, repair of house, cattlesheds, etc., educational improvement, development of mixed farming, etc.

Some more items may be added or some may be left out from these, for the better working of the Society.

Making cooperatives effective: Service Cooperatives are more useful in the present circumstances. This is because after the farmer has been educated in using fertiliser, improved seeds and implements for improved farming, he needs these things in his village at the right time and at reasonable prices. The Cooperative is the only solution for such supplies. Because India has about 6 lakhs villages and it is impossible to have Cooperatives in each village we should group villages to assure the required minimum population for a society. All villages so grouped should be represented on the Cooperative Board so that each village participates in the Service Cooperative, a village should have its own unit which can meet regularly ensuring that these Cooperatives have solid roots in the village. The main job of the C.D. workers is to educate the members to effectively meet their responsibility to the Cooperative Societies. The members of these Cooperatives need training. The managers and accountants should also be given some specialised training during service period.

(3) *Developing the village school as a community centre*

To develop a village school as an effective institution capable of playing an important role in the village development, the village teacher needs to be better-trained, better paid, better housed and raised to a higher social position, so that he is respected in the village society. This will attract enthusiastic persons to join teaching profession. It requires that the

(1) C. D. workers should patiently and persistently guide village people to see the educational problem as it should be seen. They should emphasise the need for a good teacher who is well trained, has the right attitudes motivated and can provide better education;

(2) It should be emphasised that the building is not very necessary but teacher should be the first priority. The villages can raise the standard of education by:

  (a) Giving the teacher proper recognition and respect, providing him good house, good salary, giving him a plot for vegetable growing, etc.

  (b) Providing a good and sufficient building which will provide the required accommodation.

(3) The Village School teacher should be expected to play an important role in village development. He should be trained as a social educator. This needs organisation of camps for the school teachers at Block Level.

The points to be emphasised in a Teachers' Training Camp for better participation in the C.D. work can be:

  (a) To change the outlook of the teacher and help him to persuade villagers towards a progressive village life;

  (b) To help and guide the teacher to adapt himself to the village with humility and absence of snobbishness;

  (c) To infuse in him the dignity of labour;

  (d) To train him in a democratic co-operative way of life;

  (e) To train him to help villagers recognise their problems and plan together steps towards solution of these problems;

  (f) To train him to assume a role of leadership in village life; and

  (g) To give the teacher a background of a rural culture and to show him how it can be effectively used in village improvement work.

Such knowledge will help the teacher to live with the villagers as one of them. Once he is thoroughly integrated into village life, he can help the villagers by working with the Gram Sewak and Village Panchayats in all the developmental activities of the village.

(4) *Youth organisation on lines of the 4-H Club*

The working and organisation of 4-H Club in the USA has been given elsewhere in this book. The purpose of organising such youth clubs in the villages is to develop young people into better farmers and citizens by equipping them with the best skills attitudes, habits and values of life so as to make them intelligent, well-informed and productive citizens of the community.

The Rural Youth Programme in India was first organised in the villages around

Santiniketan by the workers of Vishwa Bharati in West Bengal. In 1953-54, experiments were initiated in certain parts of the country to organise such clubs on the lines of the 4-H Clubs of the USA.

Objective of youth clubs: Broadly, the objectives of the rural youth clubs are to develop physical, mental, moral and social standards in youth. The specific objectives are:

(1) Developing the qualities and skills of leadership so that they may be helpful in the development of the community.

(2) Providing them opportunities for building up their character and health.

(3) Providing them with technical information about improved practices in agriculture, home economics, etc., so that they may become leaders for others.

(4) Teaching them the value of research and developing in them the scientific attitudes towards the problems of farm, home and village.

(5) Training them in cooperative and community work so that they are able to solve their own and group problems.

(6) Teaching them the dignity of labour.

(7) Joining with friends for work, fun and fellowship.

(8) Developing talents for greater usefulness

These objectives are to be achieved on the principle of learning by doing and earning while learning. For this purpose, they take up some projects according to their aptitude and ability.

The Social Education Organiser guides the working of youth clubs in the Block. The VLW organises such clubs in the villages of his circle.

Points of importance for organising youth clubs: (1) The C.D. worker should make contacts with the village leaders and parents of youth.

Discussion with village leaders and specially with parents of the youth are necessary. These persons should be told the objectives of such clubs. The village school teacher should also be approached.

(1) He can make a valuable contribution to such clubs.

(2) In the beginning, only interested youth who are willing to join should be enrolled.

(3) Some potential voluntary leaders should also be associated.

(4) In the meetings of the club, some interesting programmes like film shows, use of flannelgraphs and flash cards on interesting topics should also be arranged. At such meetings, the youth club members should be given a broad understanding of the economic and socio-recreational projects.

(5) It is better to initiate sports and cultural programmes.

(6) If some projects for the youth are selected and training is provided to run such projects on a voluntary basis, this would encourage participation.

(7) The C. D. worker should assist the youth members in planning their projects like vegetable growing, poultry raising, etc., and keeping the records.

(8) The projects of the youth should be evaluated and the results should be presented in the meetings as encouragement to others.

How to constitute a youth club: The model constitution of a rural youth club can have the following things :

(1) *Name of the Club and Village:* like, Yuvak Mandal, Bela village.

(2) *Membership:* Voluntary, age-group (18-25), Subscription (Rs......)

(3) *General Body:* This body will have full power to lay down policies, plans and programme of work. The budget will be placed before this body for approval and accounts passed in (month......) every year.

(4) *Office-bearers*: The executive will comprise: President, Vice-President, Secretary and Treasurer.

(5) *Functions of the Executive Committee:* The committee will regulate admission to the club and draw up programmes. The Executive Committee shall meet at least once in a month. It will promote inter-club visits, competitions, celebrations of National Days, talks by outsiders, demonstrations of improved practices, etc.

Duties of the office-bearers: The duties of the President, Vice-President and other office-bearers can be laid out as follows:

(a) *President:* To conduct meeting on parliamentary lines, to keep the speakers on the subject, to maintain and improve the working of the club.

(b) *Vice-President:* Preside over meetings in the absence of the President.

(c) *Secretary*: To record the proceedings of the meetings, maintain the records of the club, call the rolls, and read minutes, attend to official correspondence, circulate notices, count and record votes when taken, prepare Annual Reports, read communications, if any, at the meeting, plan programmes, guide members in all their activities and send useful notes on the club for publicity.

(d) *Treasurer:* Receive club funds and act as its custodian, collect dues, maintain regular accounts, assist in preparing an Annual Budget, prepare financial statements and reports.

Club pledge: Each member should take a pledge which can be worded thus: "I solemnly declare that I shall be an active member of the Club, shall abide by its rules and serve my village and the community through the Club to the best of my ability."

Funds: The funds can be raised through: membership fees, donations from individuals and institutions, Government aid through the Block or otherwise, aid from local bodies.

Similar mention can be made about: Control of funds, expenditure, withdrawal of funds, audit of accounts, etc.

Objective: As laid in the early part.

Motto: It can be:

Work is worship, Plan your work and work your plan, united we stand and divided we fall, work and not luck is the basis of hope, etc.

Meetings: Members may meet twice a week, Executive once a month, and General Body once a year.

Activities of the Club: Group projects, afforestation in village, building paths and roads, crop protection campaigns, etc.

(1) *Individual projects:* Sowing of crops, vegetables, planting fruit trees, poultry, bee-keeping, etc.

(2) *Recreational projects*: Races, sports, tours, training camps, running a library.

(3) *Affiliation:* Just like the club in each village, there can be Block organisation, District organisation and State organisation and so on.

(4) *Project registers:* Registers for projects can be maintained with columns like:

Name of member, project undertaken, individual or group, area sown, yield, value on yield, cost of seed, etc., net profit.

(5) *Evaluation*: An Annual Evaluation report should be prepared by the Secretary so that members may take advantage of it.

Making club programme interesting for the youth: To create interest among the youth, study tours to places like Agricultural Colleges or Universities, Extension Training Centres, farms of progressive farmers, agricultural exhibitions, etc., are necessary. There should be competitions and youth rallies, etc.

(5) *Farmers' organisations*

The farmers' organisations like Farmers' Forum of India, Bharat Krishak Samaj, Tonnage Club of M.P., etc., come under this heading. In the villages, the farmers can be convinced to have branches of such organisations, if these do not exist. As an illustration, the Constitution of the Bharat Krishak Samaj is given as under:

(a) *Bharat Krishak Samaj*

(1) *Objectives:* The main objectives of this organisation are:

(i) To study the problems of farmers.

(ii) To protect, advance and promote the social, economic and cultural interests and activities of the agricultural producers, farm youth and farm women in the country.

(iii) To undertake propaganda, training and education of the agricultural producers and farm families, and cooperate with Government and other agencies for the uplift and amelioration of the farming community and rapid progress of agriculture so as to raise it to the level of an efficient industry in India.

(iv) To assist in formulating national and international agricultural policies and progress in the interest of farmers, and to collaborate and cooperate with similar organisations of agricultural producers in India and abroad for the furtherance of the said objectives; and

(v) To collect funds, hold meetings, conferences, send representations, deputations, memoranda, etc., to fulfil the above.

The Forum shall be a non-political, non-sectarian association of agricultural producers and all those who are interested in the promotion of their welfare.

Its Headquarters are located in New Delhi. There is a Chairman and a General Secretary to supervise and coordinate the activities. There are state, district, block and village level units of the organisation.

(2) *Membership:* There are 8 types of members, namely:

(i) *Ordinary Members:* They are required to pay Rs. 1 as admission fee, Rs. 3 as annual fee or Rs. 15 for five years.

(ii) *Life Members:* Admission fee for such members is Rs. 10 and subscription of Rs. 100 for whole life.

(iii) *Family Life Members:* Admission fee Rs. 10 and subscription for life time Rs. 140. One or more family member can be nominated by such a member at Rs. 40 extra than life members.

(iv) *Corporate Members:* Any corporate body or concern can become a member by paying Rs. 100 as admission fee and Rs. 100 as annual or Rs. 1000 as life membership.

(v) *Institutional Member:* Admission fee Rs. 50 and annual subscription Rs. 100 or Institutional Life Membership Rs. 1000.

(vi) *Associate Member:* An official of a State Government Agriculture, Veterinary or Forest Department or Community Development can become a member by paying Re. 1 as admission fee or Rs. 5 as annual subscription or Rs. 100 for life membership.

(vii) *Honorary Member:* A person who renders some valuable service to the Samaj.

(viii) *Patron Member:* National leaders and other such persons; organisations or firms rendering valuable service may be accepted as Patron Members of the Samaj by the Governing Body.

All India Farmers' Council

(1) This is the policy making body of the Samaj and it is constituted of:

(a) All members of the Governing Body of the Samaj.

(b) Representatives of the States.

(c) Representatives of other organisations.

(d) Agricultural experts, Project Development and other officers.

(e) Representatives of the Ministry of Food and Agriculture, Ministy of Information and Broadcasting, Indian Council of Agricultural Research and Agricultural Universities.

(f) Representatives of Life Members, Corporate, Institutional and Associate Members.

(g) All Patrons and Honorary Members.

(e) The President who shall be the Minister in-charge of Food and Agriculture, Government of India or any other such person selected as President.

(i) The President's nominees upto a maximum of five.

(2) The Development Commissioners, Directors of Agriculture and Animal Husbandry and Registrars of Cooperative Societies and Principals of Agricultural and Veterinary Colleges in the various States shall be ex-officio members of the Council.

(3) The Council shall meet at least once in a year, or as often as desired by the Governing Body, or on a joint requisition given by one fourth of the members of the Council.

(4) Sixty members of the Council shall form the quorum for the meeting.

(5) The tenure of the Council shall be 5 years.

The Governing Body: It is constituted of the Chairman, Vice-Chairman: Secretary General; members to represent each State and the Union Territories out of the panels submitted by the State proportionate to their membership on the basis of one representative for every 300; Life Members; Government experts and representatives of other organisations nominated by the Chairman. Its members shall not exceed 51. In addition, the President, Chairman of State Krishak Samaj or the State Secretary, the Ministers of Agriculture, Cooperation and Animal Husbandry at the Centre and in the States shall be ex-officio members of the Governing Body.

The Governing Body carries out the policies of the Samaj, collects funds and administers them, appoints committees, can remove any member from the Council on grounds of misbehaviour or for working against the interests of the Samaj. It meets at least twice a year. The quorum for the meeting of the Governing Body is 11. The tenure is 3 years.

Standing Committee: This is constituted by the Chairman of the Samaj, out of the members of the Governing Body. It has 11 members, including Chairman, 4 Vice-chairmen, and Secretary General. It meets occasionally and looks after the day-to-day work of the Samaj. The quorum is of 4.

Pradesh Executive Committee: Ordinarily the Minister in-charge of Agriculture, or the Lt. Governor in the Union Territories, or Chief Commissioner, is requested to be the President of it. There are 15 members including a non-official Chairman, 3 Vice-Chairmen.

Pradesh Krishak Parishad: It has all the members of the Pradesh Executive Committee, Presidents and Secretaries of the Samaj in the Districts, Heads of Departments of Agricultural, Veterinary and Animal Husbandry, Cooperatives and Community Development, Director of All India Radio from the Capital of the State, Rural Economists, Principals of Agricultural, Veterinary and Animal Husbandry and Home Science Colleges, or Heads of Agricultural Research Institutes or Stations in the State, representatives of Women's Organisations and representatives of Life Members, Ordinary, Corporate, Institutional and Associate Members in the Samaj. The Parishad deals with all matters affecting the interests of agricultural producers in the State and shall supervise and direct the functioning of the Samaj in the districts. It should meet at least once a year. Its tenure is 3 years. One-fifth of the total members forms a quorum.

District Krishak Committee: All Presidents, Chairmen and Secretaries of the Sub-Division, Taluk, or Block Krishak Samaj, and representatives of the members of the Samaj constitute it. It elects a President and Chairman and Vice-Chairman.

The Secretary should be as far as possible a whole-time or part-time employee appointed by the Committee. It deals with all matters affecting the interests of the agricultural produce of the district and supervises and regulates the formation and functioning of the Samaj in the district. One-third of the members is required to form the quorum and its tenure is 3 years.

Sub-Divisional, Taluk, Tehsil or Block Krishak Committee: All conveners of the Village Samaj in the sub-division and representatives of the members of the Samaj constitute it. It elects a President, Chairman, Vice-Chairman and a Secretary, and deals with all matters affecting the interests of the farmers in the sub-division. One-third of the members form the quorum and tenure is 3 years.

Gaon Krishak Samaj: (Krishak Samaj in villages): Seven or more members should be enrolled in the village where it is formed. They elect a convener who will convene the meetings and shall keep the accounts. It is the backbone of the farmers in the district. The funds are kept in a Post Office account.

VIII. Developing adequate community leadership

In the C.D. programme, leaders are expected to initiate action which helps the community to adopt improved practices. So the qualities to look for in a leader for C.D. work are not the personal traits, which are acquired by a few but mostly come by birth in a family, but the requirement consists of the skills which can be learned

and improved upon. For C.D. work, the leadership is expected to initiate and coordinate activities of members of various groups for the development of the village.

Types of leadership existing in rural areas

The following types of leadership exist in rural areas:

Hereditary type of leadership: This category includes the village landlords, village
headman, the Patel or Lambardar and the village priest.

(2) *Type based on occupational pattern:* This is not so prominent or obvious but it
exists in functional groups. This may be governed by the caste structure. Their
influence is not widespread but restricted to a particular group of persons in the
community.

(3) *Personal leadership:* Such leaders are respected because of their knowledge and
skills in a particular field. This type really leads the people. Such leaders are educated
youth who return to the village and engage themselves in some occupation, retired
persons who maintain close contact with their home village.

(4) *Political and social type leadership:* During the movement to achieve political
freedom in India, some persons even without big names, influential families, or even
without education, got chance of showing their interest in the country and its people.
They are respected because they showed their interest in social development. These
persons many times are of good help in the C.D. programme.

After achieving Independence there has been a gradual change in the rural leadership. The traditional leaders are being replaced. Of course, if the traditional leaders
have changed themselves and adjusted themselves according to the new role, they still
continue to occupy the place of leadership. But the caste or communal leadership has
vanished to a great extent.

For community development leaders, the important thing is to recognise the
traditional leaders. But such leaders should not be assigned work where action is
required because they may involve the C.D. workers in occupations of favouritism to
big persons.

The job of the C.D. worker is to identify the potential leaders. He is required to
know some of the techniques useful in the process of selection of leaders.

How to identify leaders for community development work

While identifying leaders it is important to know: What job is to be done, what
characteristics and skills the job requires, where to find the person possessing
the needed qualifications, what group will support or follow this person, which
qualities can be improved by training and which may not be changed, how he can be
induced to work for the community.

The following are the methods whereby potential leaders may be given chances to
participate with other villagers and the C.D. worker can *locate such* leaders:

(1) *Discussion methods:* Discussion gives encouragement and assurance to the
potential leaders to express themselves, and, over a period of time may make him
more confident in accepting some position of leadership. So the villagers should be
involved in meetings where group discussions can be arranged.

(2) *Workshop method:* In this method, a large group is broken into smaller groups,
where people discuss and make decisions and present their decisions. The C.D.

worker acts like a consultant and observes the deliberations. This will give him a chance of locating the leaders.

(3) *The questionnaire or socio-metric method:* This requires interviews of the villagers, or the community members, according to a prepared questionnaire or schedule. This may have questions like: Whom they ordinarily consult for advice on farming, advice on home affairs, advice for village problems, who maks decisions about community affairs in the village and so on.

(4) *Seniority and past experience:* In some communities, the oldest person is supposed to have the most knowledge and experience and normally can add stability to the group. But this may not be a proper way of locating a leader.

Developing leadership

In any leadership development programme, training is necessary. In this training, the aim of the C.D. workers should be to give a clear concept to the leaders of what they are expected to do and why. So the psychology of adult learning should be understood and observed. Interest and enthusiasm needs to be developed and maintained. The objectives of training the leaders may be as follows:

(1) Mastering functional concepts that would serve as a framework for understanding and interpreting group behaviour, social learning and cultural differences.

(2) Methods of identifying and analysing problems. The ability to see the problems in perspective.

(3) Develop competence in group processes: Cooperative thinking, exchange and analysis of ideas, facts and teaching, processes of converting discussion into consensus, ability and disposition to conceive group goals, respect for and understanding of others.

(4) Acquire technical skills necessary to carry out a job, diagnose situations, learn how to approach problems, plan appropriate educational procedures, learn skills in handling appropriate diagnostic techniques, conduct open discussions, learn team work with other leaders, etc.

Methods of training the leaders

There can be: (1) Informal method, and (2) Formal method of training.

(1) *Informal method:* It may be (a) observation, i.e., noticing how others have performed. This may be a visit to other farmers' holdings, (b) reading the printed literature, circular letters from C.D. workers, and (c) talking with other leaders or progressive farmers or others in the field of interest.

(2) *Formal method:* (a) Lecture. It may be supplemented with other formal methods, (b) Discussion and workshop, (c) Forum, panel, or symposium, (d) Audio-visual aids, (e) Field-trips, (f) Apprenticeship—learning things by staying with others who have adopted improved practices, (g) Training groups—formal leader training camps, (h) Direct assistance from experts, (i) Buzz group—discussion by all in the group of less than 7 persons for a duration of about 6 minutes, and (j) Giving responsibility to local leaders so that they develop self-confidence.

Developing desire for change in local leaders

To get new practices adopted, a desire to change has to be created among the leaders. Some methods useful in this respect may be:[1]

(1) Show them new practices and their results to create an awareness.

(2) Arrange tours to demonstrations and farms of progressive farmers.

(3) Evaluate the results of new practices and present the results in the meetings of these leaders.

(4) Bring in specialists, e.g., in meetings of farmers, bring in an entomologist, plant pathologist, agronomist, social scientist and a chemist, etc.

Expectations from rural leaders

The training and development of the rural leaders should be based on the expected role he has to play. The expectations may be: (a) assistance to the community in identifying its needs, (b) help to the community by setting some examples of achievement before them, (c) helping the community to move towards goals, (d) encouraging interaction among members of the community, (e) keeping the members of the community together, (f) acting as the resource person for the community. These processes discussed in the Chapter, will help the C.D. workers in the community development prog. amme.

SCOPE OF COMMUNITY DEVELOPMENT

Due to the long presence of foreign rulers in India, the country remained uncared for as regards the development of its people and it has always been exploited only for the use and benefit of foreign rulers. Its own people were not allowed to take up any programme which could bring it to the level of nations which were developing themselves in the past decades. The foreign rulers exploited it to enrich themselves. The worst part of it has been that it was turned into a raw material producing country for the industries of Britain and a consuming market for their manufactured goods. When the so-called 'developed' nations of today were making headway in industry and development of their resources. India was being exploited and was struggling for its political independence. In the absense of its own popular government, resulting in the absence of development programmes and proper and timely planning, it became what the world calls it, 'An Underdeveloped Country'' and it is a symbol of it because it has poverty, disease, hunger and ignorance.

Thanks to the long struggle of non-violence which changed the hearts of the foreign rulers, they left on August 15, 1947. But they left it in a situation that created more problems because they partitioned it into Pakistan and India. This was a big test: "whether the people were able to be called citizens of free nation". The new problem was the biggest of all, to rehabilitate 9 millions of refugees was the gigantic problem. Within four years the country could find a way of solving the other problems for which the struggle for independence was undertaken. The blue-print of future India came in the shape of its First Five Year Plan. On April 1951, the country launched its First Plan. On October 2, came the Community Development and the Extension Programme because this was the real need for developing its people and its resources, as the nation was underdeveloped.

[1]Hilda Taba, *Leadership Training in Inter-Group Education*, American Council of Education, 1953.

An underdeveloped community

An underdeveloped community is one which is unsuccessful in reaching its goals because it is not making full use of its resources. From the viewpoint, this value decisions concerning what goals and what abilities become important because a community may be more or less developed in relation to any particular goal. That is, a community may be well developed in achieving one goal but uuderdeveloped in achieving others. Of course, one goal affects the other, e.g., development of education may bring certain techniques and the community may become developed, but on the other hand, if a high standard of living is not achieved then in relation to this goal the community is underdeveloped. But if a community is working and trying to solve its problems it may be spoken of as a developing community.

India's resources are very rich. It has good soil, sunshine, sufficient irrigation water, diversity in climate which gives chances of raising crops throughout the year, it has manpower, which is one-fifth of the world human population and it has one-fourth of the cattle population of the world. It has good mineral resources and fair chances of industrialisation. But when it became independent, only 8 per cent of the population was able to read and write. Milk consumption was only 3 ounces per capita per day. Food was inadequate not only in quality but also in quantity. Its farming was very primitive and still the same implements and appliances are in use which we find in the Farmers' Museum in Coopers's Town in N.Y. State, USA kept there for showing to people how the farmers and homemakers were doing things hundred years back.

The bureaucratic system of government, which the country inherited from its rulers, became a hindrance in the way of illiterate farmer who has always been afraid of Sahibs (bosses), Rajas and Maharajas (kings). He has seen the furious eyes of Tehsildars, the white-collared agricultural officers, the grain procurement officers, the tax collectors and the zamindars (landlords), etc. The Great Depression Period 1929-34, the Second World War, the great famine of India in 1943, the suppression of the Independence Movement in 1942 by the British regime, etc, led the farmers to feel that there was no government or any organisation which would think of their development. The colleges of Agriculture were teaching what was not the agriculture in Indian villages, the research workers in Agricultural Research Stations were not concerned with village problems, the extension staff was not in any way related with the agricultural researchers and staff of agricultural colleges. There was no coordination at any level. Different departments were going in different directions.

Speciality of farming occupation

The farmer's occupation is a multipurpose activity. This is more critical in India. He being a small holder cultivating only two or three acres of land, has to engage in diversified farming and so has to act as an agronomist, horticulturist, animal husbandryman, a soil scientist, plant protection-man, a labourer and a manager, all as one. So his life becomes a complex one. The natural calamities like floods, droughts, attacks of pests and diseases, locust invasions and fluctuation in prices of his produce, make his occupation very risky. This type of life, under the organisation of 1940's, i.e., before community development was organised, where there were so many agencies dealing with different works, the red tapism or delay in work and the bribery, annoyed him. When he was not given any help in an easy way, the farmer decided not to depend on the so-called development activities of those days.

The psychology of a defeatist farmer, who had never been given attention and help, is still a hindrance in the extension and community work. He is still afraid of untested persons called extension specialists and their technical methods and practices. The old extension specialists who graduated from agricultural colleges before 1956, were given no training in techniques and methods of extension. Even today the courses offered at many Agricultural and Veterinary Colleges are not what they should be for extension specialists. The approach, the background of rural sociology the knowledge of the psychology of villagers, acquaintance with village problems, and working under village conditions are still lacking and make our extension specialist feels that he has been given work which does not fit in with his taste. The village conditions are not able to provide him a living atmosphere, as there is no proper schooling facility for his children, and his wife does not get the housing conditions to which she is accustomed. All these make him a new man, a different person from the villagers. Under such circumstances, he loses his zeal, interest and enthusiasm.

The villagers are still being exploited by the money-lenders and are still wasting their hard-earned money on many useless ceremonies.

Thus the extension worker has to face the task of bringing out the villagers from the vicious circle. He has to help them in getting the services, provided by various departments nearer to them. He has to help and guide them in adopting the scientific methods of farming, in reducing their uneconomic expenditure in making farm and family plans for them and thus help them to raise their standard of living and make their lives prosperous. The extension education teachers have to teach in such a way that their clients become real extension workers, the authorities responsible for running the Agriculture Colleges and Training Centres, have to provide the atmosphere and facilities so that the teachers are able to use the ways which are helpful in preparing good extension workers. The universities have to change their old system and revise the syllabus and curricula by adopting the advanced systems of modern education for extension workers from countries like the USA which have been tested and have made their extension workers successful persons in their job. This whole field for opening schools, providing health and sanitary facilities, good living conditions along with development of agriculture and village industries, etc., is a tremendous field and has vast scope for the extension workers, as also for those in charge of any work related with the country's development.

Limitations

(1) Most of the people are still illiterate and it is a difficult task to train about 640 million people living in about 6 lakh villages. For such a population the Extension Methods like demonstration, individual approaches, exhibitions, group meetings and training classes require thousands of extension workers.

(2) Lack of communication channels and specially mass media—absence of television, one or two broadcasting radio stations in each State covering vast areas, lack of radio sets and transistors, lack of roads, lack of vehicles like jeeps, motor cycles, etc., are the major limitations in the C.D. Programme.

(3) Limitations of funds and staff for training farmers. In some backward states

like Madhya Pradesh, where the villages are small and far away from each other, the Agricultural Extension Officers, the Veterinarians, etc., have to act as technical advisers for about 180 villages—the size of a Block area. Besides their extension activities in villages the extension workers are required to do some administrative and clerical jobs also, and this reduces their working day. So to educate the people of about 180 villages in the 150 days left for such work, i.e., one day per village and that too in villages where for about 4 months in the rainy season it is difficult to reach, is a difficult and rather impossible task.

(4) A traditional society, with old ways and practices does not want to take risk unless it sees the results. Because change creates insecurity and uncertainty so there was resistance in the early years.

(5) In an illiterate, traditional society the real leadership could not come forward. People with vested interests tried to get advantage by fooling the real client system, and the extension agency.

(6) Preaching to rural people and educating them in new practices requires very careful handling and needs highly skilled workers who have knowledge of "how change takes place" and the skill to induce them. It is very difficult to produce a large number of such workers.

(7) In the beginning, such limitations may not have been realised and objectivities were very vaguely formulated. Thus, when goals are not fulfilled, to the extent they were formulated, there is public criticism which leads to further weakening the support to community development.

(8) The change-over from an attitude of heavy dependence on the Government to one of self-dependence takes place very slowly, and since there is lack of properly trained personnel and weaknesses in the supply line in the initial stages there is disappointment among the people.

WEAKNESSES IN THE COMMUNITY DEVELOPMENT PROGRAMME AND SUGGESTIONS FOR IMPROVEMENT

A critical anlysis of the programme with regard to the objectives shows that the programme has some weaknesses. These can be given as:

(1) The Programme has remained largely a Government administered programme with people's participation and has not yet become a people's programme with assistance from Government agencies. Of course, no single agency operating in the field is responsible for this weakness. The complementary role of the people and the Government agency has to be realised in the operation of the Community Development Programme. Therefore, attempts by all the agencies concerned in changing their approach to the Programme, both by Governmental agencies on one hand and the people, their leaders and their representative on the other are necessary.

(2) There has been too much emphasis on end-results and less emphasis in following the correct methods and process to bring about change in the attitudes of the people, or what we call social change.

(3) Due to lack of understanding of the objectives of the C. D. programme there has often been lack of adherence to the real objectives f the C.D. programme. There has not been much concentration on essential items.

(4) The achievements, whatever they have been, have not been used to restore and revive the confidence of the people in themselves, in the Government machinery and in the Programme as a whole. This was an integral part of the Total Development Programme of the country which is going through the Five-Year Plans and which has three major objectives—economic development, social justice and democratic growth. These must be interrelated and support each other.

(5) Extension education methods, which are so essential for a democratic approach, remained mostly as a claim.

(6) Lack of uniform understanding about the concept, principles, methods, role, functions, etc., at all levels from village to national level.

(7) Lack of proper and adequate supervision and guidance, both administrative and technical at various levels.

(8) Establishment of superiority by providing democratic leadership is very much lacking to replace autocratic authority.

(9) The C.D. workers feel unhappy at all levels. Their moral is not very high: Unhappy workers or change agents cannot make a good organisation. The weaknesses are:

(a) Many of the workers were brorowed from their parent departments, which were working on a different approach and in the traditional ways left behind by the foreign British Government, the new atmosphere of working conditions created by the introduction of C.D. programmes require the traditional Government servant to change himself completely to function as an effective C.D. worker. The new approach in the C.D. programme calls for a big transformation in the role of Government. It's instrument, the administration, has to be transformed from one which maintain law and order and directs the people to one which helps the people and works with the people, educating them, organising them and developing in them initiative, a sense of responsibility, and capacity to undertake tasks for themselves. This needs a change in the attitudes of the public servants and in the methods of their working. The will, wish and notions of a community development worker have to be subordinated to to the needs, convictions and decisions of the people. To be efficient and effective, he has to get himself accepted by the people before he can make people accept and adopt improvements advocated by him for better living. Our C.D. worker is working under two pressures, the ambitious targets from the Government authorities at higher level on the one hand, and comparatively inadequate measure-preparedness of the the people in terms of their recognising needs, willingness to put in additional efforts, and resources to satisfy such needs, non-availability of resources, problems of mobilising their resources, natural and situational handicaps, etc., on the other. It is therefore, a much more difficult job to be a successful Government servant in other sectors of governmental organisations like, Revenue Department, P.W.D., etc. This is perhaps one of the important reasons that a large number of the workers in the C.D. programme appear to be anxious to get back to the departmental set up, if any, or choose an alternative position elsewhere, if possible.

(b) There exist certain traditions and conventions about the "code of conduct", with reference to vertical and horizontal relationships between the functionaries working at various levels in the administrative hierarchy. These continue as a legacy of the past. While there is apparently very little difference in the form and structure of the administrative machinery in the pre-Independence and that in the post-Independence periods, in the operational details a great many changes are envisaged, to enable the instrument of Government to undertake and discharge the new responsibilities in the context of changed purpose, policy, requirements and emphasis. "Although the Community Development Programme has to be a people's programme, it has also to be organised and directed by the administration; and yet it cannot be completely directed from the top by a set of rules and procedures", as Dr. Carl Taylor rightly pointed out. New traditions and conventions of working with colleagues, extending assistance, offering guidance, assisting people to take dicisions, respecting decisions taken by people, etc, through self-example or, in other words, by democratic leadership, in place of autocratic authority, and to set requirements of a changed situation have become imminent. Supervision and inspections also must have different meanings, purposes, methods and procedures. They need to be more problem-centred and situation-oriented, attempting in consequence to assist the field workers overcome difficulties and solve problems faced by them in the field. Introduction and adoption of these reforms in the day-to-day functioning of the admininistrative machinery, particularly at the levels responsible for supervision and guidance, brook no delay. But have things happened this way during the last ten years? Most of the persons working both in the administrative machinery as well as in people's organisations—practically at all levels—appear to suffer from the usual weakness of clinging to tradition-bound ways of working without permitting adequate changes warranted by new requirements, the old tradition of "direction" from above and "obedience" below seems to continue without much change. Even problems and difficulties presented as arising from peculiarities hardly receive due consideration. Effective supervision and guidance rendering "on the spot" assistance to the field workers to solve their difficulties and overcome their problems, are also very rare. Consequently, there is a peculiar atmosphere prevailing in regard to the mutual relationship between community development workers at various levels; among themselves on the one hand and between official and non-official agencies on the other. Community development workers, especially at the field levels, therefore, experience a feeling of suffocation and embarrassment.

(c) There appears to be an appalling lack of perception about the community development and Panchayat Raj movements. The natural consequence, therefore, is that there are several misgiving and erroneous notions about the whole programme, its suitability, effectiveness, expectations in the initial stages and the like. In the field, supervisory agencies and social workers are hardly seen to make any effort to bring about conviction and promote faith in the programme. It will not be an exaggeration to suspect whether the agencies accept this as an obligation in the discharge of their functions related to promotion of rural development activities. The Head of the US Mission of the International Cooperative Administration in one of his reports said that "the greatest single obstacle in initiating an effective Programme is the suspicion and indifference of the very people, the development programmes are designed to help." The community development workers are operating in a very peculiar situation. Recognition and sympathy are some of the best forms of incentives to workers. Use of proper methods of measuring progress and judging performance of individuals is very much lacking universally. Consequently, it is difficult to discern between "real efforts" and "make-believe efforts" in the implementation of the Programme. There are, therefore, instances and occasions when the latter scores over the former, The ultimate result of all this is that many of the field workers in the Community Development Programme feel depressed and dissatisfied.

(d) Normally, a person working in a government organisation regards public service as a means of livelihood and a career-making enterprise. There is nothing wrong in this. However, a spirit of service to the nation and to the people at large is essential, in addition. It is this special attitude that will build in him the strength that a worker should have to enable him to apply himself devotedly to the cause of Community Development Programme. Preparedness for hard work and sacrifice, which are the pillars of planned development in a developing country like ours, follow faith and devotion to the cause. Observations and studies in the field, however, indicate trends to the contrary. Efforts to promote the same by creating an atmosphere of sympathy, humane approach, personal example, on the spot guidance and real democratic leadership do not seem to be coming forth in adequate measures from the agencies concerned. Secondly, some of the workers responsible for directing the operation of the Community Development Programme are saddled with manifold, connected and unconnected responsibilities. This is particularly so at the district level and above. As such functions, which require immediate attention to avoid conspicuous far-reaching effects in public life, claim the maximum time and energy, it permits only luke-warm, if not indifferent, treatment to the Community Development Programme. Imagination and originality are the backbone of a growing programme, and experience may be used as the most trusted guide and an eye-opener. The routine nature of functioning in this programme does not permit adequate contribution to promote the same. Lack of time, lack of spirit, lack of understanding, lack of perception and above all, lack of appreciation of the one's own role and functions, result in a very unhappy situation. Finding fault with others, accusing agencies, other than oneself for failures and the inability to establish superiority by real merits as against authority, very often lead to disappointment, frustration and dissatisfaction among the workers in the field.

(e) Rural development in a democratic society is not a matter only of plans and statistics, targets and budgets, technology and methods, material aid and professional staff, agencies and organisations to administer them, but also of using these mechanism skilfully, as educational means for changing the mind, heart and actions of people to attain improvements economically, socially, politically and morally. Man is endowed with the internal desire for improvement. He needs only to be shown the paths clearly and convincingly and provided with the necessary resources and help. In an organised programme to promote rural development through community development and Panchayat Raj movements, the workers of the National Extension Service Organisation constitute the connecting link between the people and the institutions created to promote their economic, social and political development. Hence, upon the character, quality, training and skill of the workers largely rests the success of the programme. Proper training of these functionaries has been accepted as the heart and nerve centre of the entire movement. Arrangements have been made and are being strengthened further for the training of functionaries associated with the operation of the Community Development Programme at all levels. The principal objectives and contents of such training programmes are to (a) develop and intelligent understanding about the concept, principles, objectives, methods, etc., of the Community Development Programme; (b) give information about the processess, methods and content of the programme; (c) make the functionaries recognise their role, responsibilities and functions; and (d) to create a suitable outlook in the workers. In other words, the training programme makes an attempt to bring awareness about "what the programme has to be along with what has to be the role of each category of worker." It also tries to relate "what the programme actually is in the field", thereby pointing out the weaknesses, shortcomings, problems and difficulties. Attempts made from time to time to recognise efforts of the agencies concerned to remedy unfolded weaknesses and overcome shortcomings are also considered. The changed role of each class of functionary at various levels from the village upto the National, does not escape consideration in the training programmes. Community development workers, particularly upto the Block Level not only appreciate the ideas and practices but they begin to advocate them in their writings, papers, discussions, talks, etc. But when they go back to the field the majority of them, about a year or so after their return from training, begin to complain that there is very little by way of "on the spot guidance" to correct mistakes and wrong methods of working. On the contrary, what is insisted upon is that the job expected should 'anyhow' be done and compliance reported. There, thus appears a very wide gap between "what the programme has to be" and "what it is in the field". The community development workers then feel lost and begin to harbour a feeling that all they had heard, read, or written, was of no use and begun to advocate out of conviction was nice at the training centre only. This inconsistency, or a very wide gap between principles and practice, perhaps, is one of the most serious factors shaking even the honest, sincere and devoted workers.

(f) It may be very interesting to note a question that is very commonly asked at the various training centres by the community development personnel working at various levels. "What is the use of training us as long as our superiors responsible to guide, supervise and evaluate our performance and progress of achievements do not have a clear understanding about the concept, processes and methods of the Community Development Programme together with our role, functions, problems, handicaps, etc"? Some of the functionaries, particularly those working at the district level and above, see training as 'theoretical and not practical'. It is, thus evident that the working conditions obtaining in the field are very peculiar. The ultimate result, therefore, is that even the trained community development workers find themselves unable to use most of their training in the implementation of the community development programme. The problem baffling community development workers in this situation appears to be a conflict between implementation of the community development programme to achieve results through 'universally accepted processes and methods' on the one hand and achieving results 'anyhow' on the other. As a result, workers find themselves in a dilemma.

(g) While writing about the four 'faiths' essential for the success of community development, B. Mukherjee in his book on Community Development in India states, "Community Development must have faith in science and technology, that these can contribute to the betterment of the rural people and that accelerated economic and material progress is possible without producing and adverse effects." He further pointed out that, "the rural people's capacity to take advantage of science and technology is very limited. It is for the Community Development Programme to provide the processes and techniques through which the rural people can take advantage of science and technology." Thus, welfare of the people is attempted to be promoted by making them accept and adopt new, beneficial and improved practices in the conduct of their life activities, recommended by use of science and technology as against the traditional ones. This is a very difficult task. Harmonious traffic and communication between the needs of the people, their capacity, resources and preparedness on the one hand, and substantially beneficial practices having possibilities of being adopted under the life and living conditions of the people on the other, must have a close relationship of mutual adjustment. Instances may be drawn from the various facets of the Commmunity Development Programme like raising of agricultural production, improving health and sanitation, improving village cattle wealth and others. To implement programme relating to these items, a worker must have a list of extension recommendations under the given set of conditions obtaining in the area. This list may be prepared (jointly by the Gram Sewak (VLW), extension officer, and the specialists in the subject at various levels. The list of improvements or new practices to be recommended should contain such items as will meet the requirements of a very large section of the population. Adoption, non-adoption and reversion of improved practices, among other factors, very much depend upon the proof of benefits in a given situation. Conditions vary very widely from region to region. It is therefore, felt that a network of recognisation, to test the reflectiveness of the new practices recommended, is highly essential. Modifications to general recommendations also could be worked out through such institutions or research centres. At present, however, our workers in the Community Development Programme appear to have been mostly left to themselves. When we look to the list of recommendations or items of improvements included in a District or a Block Programme, it appears, to be a very long one. But when we go to a village, the list becomes so small, in many cases, that there is hardly any material for the 'programme content' of the village. Secondly, whatever items of improvements are considered useful for being advocated are very general and not specific, relating to the situation of the village and its surroundings. Consequently, there are several cases of non-adoptions and reversions of improvements advocated. Success leads to success and promotes growth of initiative and ambition. Whereas failures lead to disappointment and frustration. The community development workers in the field, in spite of their best efforts under all the limitations of their working, meet with such failures and do not get "on the spot guidance" and assistance to solve the technological problems raised by them. Consequently they are disheartened and this results in a slackening of effort.

(h) The position as indicated in the foregoing paragraphs by way of illustrations, is very delicate and at the same time difficult to be recognised and appreciated. In our attempts to create a favourable atmosphere for the operation of development programmes, lot of time, energy and resources are being observed in neutralising the negative forces. Introduction of Panchayat Raj is designed to create a more favourable situation and suitable atmosphere for the operation of the Community Development Programme. A change in the form and structure of the people's organisations and those of Government is envisaged with the fundamental approach of putting in

united efforts of both the agencies to promote rural welfare. Facilities for the training of all those associated with the Community Development Programme—officials and
non-officials, at all levels from the village up to the national level have also been
created. This, however, does not mean that Panchayat Raj and training of workers
at all levels are panacea for all the problems of community development
workers in the field. With appropriate people's organisation in Panchayat Raj and
elaborate training programmes for all concerned, a time has, perhaps, come when we
should very seriously consider the need and problems of effective supervision and
guidance to the community development workers in the field. Organised efforts to
dispassionately locate the factors responsible for making community development
workers feel unhappy need to be undertaken. Studies through scientific enquiries by
specialists in the fields of Social Science, Political Science, Public Administration
and Administrative Intelligence will be very helpful in revealing realities in terms of
depth and dimensions of the problems on the one hand and causes responsible for the
same on the other. The findings of such studies will be able to help in recognising
our efforts, in some of the details like supervision, guidance, methods of measuring
progress of achievements, performance of workers, involvement of people, etc.,
to promote and strengthen operation of the Community Development Programme.
This in turn will inspire community development workers to plunge themselves
headlong into the movement, striving for its utmost success, both under normal conditions as well as in the present situation of an urgency to achieve self-sufficiency in
various production programmes.

Abolition and revival of posts of BDOs in Madhya Pradesh

Because of the weakness in keeping a non-technical officer as Block Development Officer to supervise and coordinate the activities of the technical Extension
Officers in agriculture, veterinary, etc., the Government of Madhya Pradesh abolished the posts of BDO's. in 1966. Formerly they wanted to post Agricultural Graduates or Veterinarians to this post. But, because of the political pressures the
BDOs posts have again been revived from April 1969. Researches have shown
that the agricultural graduates and specially those with M. Sc. (Agri.) Degree in
extension education proved better extension workers. The former Development
Commissioner of M. P. was convinced that such graduates did a better job but the
authorities revived their decision of keeping the same non-technical people who gave
the development work a shape which was in every department as regards their
approach of work which had red-tapism, delay and hindrances for illiterate farmers.
This has hampered the work.

The challenges to the scientists

(1) *Varieties for rainfed areas:* The varieties evolved for wheat, paddy, soybeans,
potato, have given high yields in irrigated areas only. What about the 80 per cent unirrigated or rainfed area? In some States like M.P. we have only 7 per cent area under
irrigation. The work at Agricultural University Jabalpur, on triticale (a cross between
rye and wheat), and the work on gram varieties, *arhar* (where we need a short duration
variety which can be harvested before wheat is sown), sunflower (Sep./Dec. flower)
lentil, may be solutions in dry areas. In evolving these our scientists have accepted the

challenge. The farmers in places like Narsingpur and Jabalpur, where Haveli system is followed have already adopted new wheat varieties with 40 lbs. of N, and 30 lbs of K, in rainfed areas, and the crop was good. This would certainly give 15 to 20 mds per acre in place of 5-8 mds per hectare.

(2) *Adjustment in crop patterns:* The economists have to be vigilant about the shifts in the crop pattern. In U.P. the farmers have already realised that sugar cane is not a crop for their area. Some farmers harvested sugarcane earlier and grew wheat. With wheat they can take at least two crops more but sugarcane gives only one in the year. The gram varieties give about 4 times the yield and their prices have gone up by about three times. Sugar cane did not get higher prices and the varieties also do not give 4 times the yields they got in 1965-66.

(3) Difficulty in convincing the farmer to spend his *increased income* on production items like manures and fertilisers, plant protection, fencing, layout and levelling, irrigation, and not on consumption items, or on marriages and other such social ceremonies. For a few years this money has to be *invested in the farm itself*. The whole farm has to be brought under high yielding varieties and should properly be developed.

(4) *Banking facilities:* Now the banks have come forward to help the farmers, hence the farmer should take advantage of it for the purchase of pumps, seed-cum fertilisers, drills, power threshers or even small tractors or bigger ones according to the need. Mechanisation is bound to come and the earlier it comes it is better.

(5) The concept of dual purpose breed in cows has to change, if the country is going to have mechanisation we have to look for cattle breeds which give higher yields. It may be by importing some animals or by a cross-breeding programme. But it has to be swift. Artificial insemination is the only solution. If we stick to our old breeds which do not have the capacity to produce more milk and are uneconomical, we cannot make progress.

(6) *The supply side to be strengthened:* The Cooperatives and private agencies dealing in fertilisers, insecticides, improved seeds, farm-machinery, etc., have to be e ncouraged, so that the farmer gets the right thing at right time and nearer to his place. The Government agencies cannot provide such facilities as being done by businessmen.

(7) *Expectations from agricultural universities:* Now we have agricultural universities in almost all states, their contribution can be:

(a) In providing the right type of extension agents, in-service training and providing the right type of literature and information through radio talks, exhibitions etc.

(b) Research on regional problems through the regional stations, keeping in view the soil types, problem of salinity, and even socio-economic problems like the one in the dacoity areas of Bhind, Morena, Dholpur, Agra. Why these dacoits? What makes them do it? How can their children be prevented from this vice? How to motivate these frustrated and furious people to settle as good citizens? All these need answers.

(c) Providing plant protection education to farmers. New varieties pose new problems.

(d) Guidance on purity of seed.

(e) Providing implements which are suited to our local soil and other conditions.

(f) Providing fruit trees and research on horticulture and helping farmers to have plantations in areas which are lying uncultivated.

(g) Research on marketing and price stabilisation.

(h) Research on social changes due to adoption of technology by rural people. How people accept new ideas? How to motivate people to adopt new practices. What type of training is needed by our extension agents, and how the extension worker should be motivated to work hard and with zeal for the development of the people.

In this way, if we can encourage our workers to dedicate themselves to the improvement necessary for agricultural development and can watch the developments with sharp eyes so as to give guidance in the right direction, the development work will be accelerated.

Expert views on the weaknesses of the community development programme

The studies at FAO, and other institutions have revealed that the greatest impediment to C.D. are social, economic and psychological, and some times organisational constraints, rather than technological problems. The majority of these researches have emphasised vital institutional changes as a pre-requisite to revolutionary attitudinal improvements on the parts of clientale as well as change agents. Some of the specific findings are summarised below:

(1) Taylor observed that some people conveyed to him that instead of it being a Community Development Extension Programme, it had become a construction programme, an amenities programme and finally an administrators programme.

(2) According to Raman, three mistakes have been made in the past in the mplementation of the programme. The first was quick changes in emphasis on specific action programmes—specially those with an economic bias which left little time to consolidate the steady progress towards acceptance of new ideas. The second mistake was to extend the C.D. programme throughout the country in a great hurry towards the later stage at the cost of adequately trained personnel and social education. Lastly the C.D. was lost in short-term target and forgot the basic objectives.

(3) Vepa indicated that there was an increasing trend of disillusionment and dissatisfaction with the progress of the programme, particularly in relation to the Panchayat Raj pattern which has been associated with C.D. He raised a basic question about whether there is a rural community in India which could be developed? Answering this question himself he revealed that there are greater disputes and divisions within the village today than ever before. He further elaborated that the Panchayat Raj, instead of providing new motivation has intensified these disputes and the elections for this institution were fought on a communal basis.

Raising another point on the quantum of people's participation he said that it was only fictitious paper participation rather than functional participation in the C.D. programmes.

Several other eminent leaders in the political, social, economic and administrative fields and sciences including Shri Jaya Prakash Narayan, Vinoba Bhave, B.R. Sen, Saxena and Sirohi have raised the various problems of the working of C.D. and pointedly emphasised that in these programmes the rich are getting richer and the poor poorer. They have spoken out about the technical competence of the workers and the low level of morale, as well as the problem of coordination at various levels.

To summarise the above, there seems to be "stage jumping" in the implementation of C.D., as the new and old. C.D. Blocks were treated on par.

The visiting foreign experts including Carl C. Taylor, D. Ensminger, J. Paul Leagans and several others have criticised the way the programmes were implemented in the C.D. Blocks.

Several reports have commented on the weaknesses of the programme. An important one, "India's food crisis and the steps to meet it" was utilised by the Government of India, to revise the C.D. programme and introduce the intensive agricultural development programme.

SIMILARITIES AND DISSIMILARITIES BETWEEN C.D. AND EXTENSION EDUCATION

The differences between extension and community development, as revealed by the various statements of objectives, processes, forms and principles, have been subjected to a detailed study at Cornell University in the United States of America. The following information, taken from the publication 'Differences between Extension Education and Community Development' (*Comparative Extension Publication No. 5, New York State College of Agriculture at Cornell University, 1958*) by Rudramurthy, B. (1964), shows the current thinking in some countries in respect of extension education and community development. We see clearly that there are more similarities than dissimilarities between these two concepts:

Objectives

DISSIMILARITIES

Extension Education	*Community Development*
(1) Emphasis on the individual.	(1) Emphasis on cooperation.
(2) Education aimed at individual development to obtain economic and social improvement.	(2) Education aimed at groups of individuals to work collectively to obtain economic and social improvement.
(3) Has as its main theme the individual's needs.	(3) Has as its main theme the communities needs.
(4) Emphasises decision-making for change by individuals and families.	(4) Emphasises decision-making by groups and representatives of groups.

SIMILARITIES

(1) To improve social and economic development.
(2) Tackles the problem at the people's level.
(3) Basically an educational approach.
(4) Recognises that people need help if they are to help themselves.
(5) Designed to extend knowledge to rural people.
(6) Aimed at bringing about change.

Process

DISSIMILARITIES

In reading about the process of extension education and community development, no dissimilarity seems to exist.

SIMILARITIES

(1) Both are educational processes.
(2) Both are democratic processes.
(3) Both are involvement processes—involvement of rural people.
(4) Perhaps we can add that extension education and community development being educational, democratic, involvement processes, of necessity are relatively slow processes.

Form

DISSIMILARITIES

Extension Education

(1) Extension is an educational arm of Government, usually through educational institutions or other Government departments.

(2) Emphasises an organisation that either carries out educational services directly or transmits knowledge from other resources to people.

(3) Usually represents a transfer of responsibility from administering Government organisation to another "Educational Group".

(4) Permits cooperation between departments and agencies.

(5) Essentially a "Branch" of the Department of Agriculture.

(6) Not directly involved in promotion of local Units of the Government.

Community Development

(1) Community Development is usually a direct Government approach to straight line organisation.

(2) Emphasises the coordination of service agencies by a working team made up of representatives of different services.

(3) Usually a tight control held by a Government administering agency to cut across participating Governmental departments.
   (a) To recognise and include the various departments that must provide service.
   (b) To eliminate departmental reluctance to participate.

(4) Forces departments and agencies to participate.

(5) Essentially a branch of Government serving several departments of the Government.

(6) Tied into promotion of local units of the Government.

SIMILARITIES

(1) A Government sponsored and supported organisation.
(2) An organisation emphasising cooperation.
(3) Permits a great flexibility in types of organisation to do the job.

CULTURAL FACTORS IN COMMUNITY DEVELOPMENT

Culture is the continuously changing pattern of learned behaviour and the products of learned behaviour (including attitudes, values, knowledge and material objects) which are shared by and transmitted among members of society. The culture of the people of a community or society is dynamic. It continuously changes because of internal as well as external forces or stimuli. Community development work aims at bringing a change in the culture of the rural people in a country. It is a planned programme for the promotion of cultural change among the rural people towards desired goals. So the scientific understanding of the people among whom the community development or extension worker operates is basic to his effective performance. The greater the scientific understanding of the culture of the client system (the people with whom community development works), the greater will be the effectiveness with which the development programme can be planned and executed.

For successful community development or extension work, the worker must study the factors that will facilitate his efforts and also those that will stand as obstacles in his way. Those factors can be of two types: (1) physical or tangible factors—natural, physical or man-made resources, and (2) cultural or intangible factors such as: attitudes of people, their habits, traditions and beliefs. The cultural factors are the components of the social structure of a community. These can be listed as follows:

(1) Institution:
  (a) Government,
  (b) Family,
  (c) Religion,
  (d) Education, and
  (e) Economic system.
(2) Groups.
(3) Organisations.
(4) Patterns of Influence
(5) Value system.
(6) Media of communication.

How the knowledge of these factors affects community development work

(1) *Institutions*

The social institutions are certain well-established ways of acting together, which are stable and permanent and are found universally throughout the world. The village people develop these social institutions in their interaction with one another. These include the government, family, religion, the educational system, and the economic system.

(a) *Government:* In any country, there may be some institutions to control and direct people's affairs at village level. In India, Panchayat is such an institution. This institution stands as an important component of the village structure through which democratic action can be made effective. The community development worker has to recognise such an institution for his effective approach and work. So he should strengthen local confidence and trust in the Panchayat, which he can do by recognising it and channellising activities through it. Further, he should act as a consultant to the Panchayat members, whenever necessary.

The community development worker should recognise and live up to his role of a non-party man, because sometimes there may be an old Panchayat as well as a new Panchayat formed under the new scheme of the Government. At the time of elections of Panchayats, he should encourage people to think carefully about the selection of candidates, but should refrain from indicating whom they vote.

(b) *Family:* In a family, different members have different roles of behaviour and action. Matters like child-rearing, cooking can be changed through the extension work with women. Agricultural development is possible through male heads of the family. An attempt to bring about a change in the cooking habits in a joint family by approaching the wife of the youngest son would normally be incorrect, if her mother-in-law or wives of the elder brothers of her husband are alive. So knowledge and understanding of the structure of the village family and family life will enable the community development worker to plan his course of action to facilitate the acceptance of changes.

(c) *Religion:* There are certain practices or things that are prohibited in certain religions, and some religions have prejudices against some practices or occupations. Pig-rearing for increased income among Muslims or Jews is prohibited by religion. So any programme of community development by adopting this vocation in a Muslim or Jewish village will be a wrong approach. Similarly, some castes have pre-judices—some Brahmins cannot keep poultry. If the community development worker knows that the Ahirs will be more interested in dairying, and Khatiks will accept improvements in the main occupation of sheep-raising, then he will arouse interest in his client system to cooperate in the projects undertaken by him.

So the community development workers must first study the existing situation from the point of view of accepted beliefs and convictions of the rural people. By using this knowledge, he can promote the desired change. By this knowledge, he can make use of the religious Melas, festivals and community gatherings. In Melas, where women gather in some temples on a festival, the Home Economics worker can demonstrate practices of bringing-up children, home improvement, fruit preserva-tion, etc. The festival of Diwali provides a good opportunity for the promotion of home decoration, cleanliness, etc.

(d) *Education:* The village school can be an effective channel for community development. Now the contents of the education imparted in village schools have been revised so as to gear it more closely to village occupations. The students can be taught through project in kitchen gardens, or their own homes or barns. This will give better training and help the community development work through the children of today.

(e) *Economic system:* Every society organises its relationships into a pattern that forms the physical means of livelihood. This pattern meets the economic needs. This includes the land tenure system as property and the occupational pattern. This system as prevalent in India in the form of division of labour through caste system, or Jajmani system, or even exchange of services, provides a good illustration. Some of the occupations have become the occupations of certain castes. The community development worker will benefit from this knowledge.

(2) *Groups*

A group, in a society, is defined as two or more people in reciprocal communication. An individual needs group participation because he has grown up in a group, and has acquired wants that can only be satisfied indirectly by other persons. Some groups that have common interests, others have divergent interests. The community development worker needs this information about groups in the village to gain their rapport in disseminating information, and for other aspects of his work. These groups like women at the drinking water well, men sitting at blacksmith's shop or in hukka groups, social status groups, neighbourhood groups, recreation groups, may not be formally organised, but are important in decision-making. The community development worker is required to know about these groups and should plan the strategy of his approach in accordance with the influence of these groups. This does not mean that we should underestimate the influence of the formal groups, like caste groups. But it is doubtless that the informal groups play a major role on the functioning of normal groups.

(3) *Organisations*

Organisations are formalised groups, systematically arranged units of people with the object of achieving some common goal in which the role of each person it specifically prescribed. The examples may be Ramlila or Kirtan Mandal, Poultry Keepers' Association, Milk Producers' Association, etc. The community development worker must understand that in his approach to an organisation, he is dealing with systematically organised groups of people, who are organised to achieve a common purpose and, where each member has specified roles and functions. He has to know whether the change he is going to bring is in conflict with the common interests or purposes of the organisation. Does it conflict with the prescribed roles of any member of the organisation?

The community development worker has to think how he can use the existing organisation for his work, e.g., Ramlila Mandal for developing artistic talents, Akhara for developing physical culture and rural recreation, Veopari Mandal as a channel of supply of commodities to villagers, etc.

(4) *Patterns of influence*

This means the leadership structure, or power structure, of the village. This is linked to an invisible network connecting and influencing village life in its various aspects. The leadership may be formal or informal. It is important that the community development worker understands how to identify villagers who play each of these roles embodied in leaders. It is not difficult to identify formal leaders, but it is not simple job to identify informal leaders. It requires a careful study of the patterns of influence, leadership and structure in the village. The community development worker needs to know: to whom villagers go when they need advice or when they are in trouble, or who helps them to take decisions and how to act. The important factors that give influence and prestige vary from place to place and community to community. But generally, these may be: (1) Ability to handle a situation and get matters settled at Tehsil or District levels, (2) Caste position, (3) Wealth, (4) Formal education, and (5) Personal characteristics—honesty, trustworthiness, reliability, etc.

(5) *Value system*

A society places different values on the various items which form part of village life, and these differing values go together to form the value system. This value system forms the basis for decision and choice-making in society. These values may be personal values and social values. Many social problems arise out of a clash of values, where one group attaches high values to certain things which are not important to another group. People will accept things easily which fit in their value system and which give them prestige. Some examples of these factors may be: personal characteristics, truthfulness, honesty, etc.; caste of the individual; term of residence: age, possession of land and type of tenure; wealth and economic position, sincerity in work, etc.

This requires establishing a rapport with the elders in the village and to know the things which are desirable for the members of their society.

(6) *Media of communication*

These are the means by which information or knowledge is passed from one group or individual to another. These may be available within the village, or there may be a separate media of communication from one village to another and to the outside world. This may be through gossip groups, hukka groups or through leaders, but mostly it is by web of word of mouth. These disseminators may vary from community to community, so the change agent is required to study these carefully, and also to know channels like newspapers, the radio, web of word of mouth, tradesmen, government officials, or block staff, marriage parties, melas, etc.

ROLE OF THE COMMUNITY DEVELOPMENT WORKER

The role of the professional community development worker can be divided into four groups: (1) Guide, (2) Enabler, (3) Expert, and (4) Therapist.

(1) Role as a guide

In the capacity of a guide for the client system, the change agent or the community development worker is required to: (a) help the community (the client system) to establish and find means of achieving its goals: (b) take initiative in working with the people; (c) be objective about conditions in the community; (d) associate with the community as a whole; (e) accept and be comfortable in his role and learn to interpret his role so that it is understood in the community.

(a) *Help the community to establish and find means of achieving its goals:* For this role, the community development worker is required to be a devotee, helping the community move effectively towards its goals. He has a responsibility to help the community choose the direction and goals intelligently. These goals are to be fixed by the villagers and the methods of achieving these goals are also to be chosen by the villagers, but under the guidance of the worker. For this role he has to have knowledge to identify the needs of the people, the programme planning process and discussion meetings of the members of the community.

(b) *Take initiative in working with people:* Many of the communities in underdeveloped countries as in India are content or satisfied with the status quo or the situation in which they are. They resist the possibility of change with a strong and rigid defence structure. Here he faces the difficult task of stimulating the sense of need for better standard of living. Under such circumstances, he is required to take the initiative in creating discontent or dissatisfaction with the present standard and in suggesting other alternative conditions which may give higher yields or higher profits resulting in a higher standard of living. This requires creating awareness in the people of better ways of doing things so that they aspire for the higher standard and are motivated to achieve the thing in the absence of which they have pain. As an illustration, we can say that the worker shows up the defects in the present farm plans and helps them to have a better farm plan which has given better results to another farmer, or farmers.

This initiative for stirring discontent or dissatisfaction with the existing conditions requires a knowledge of the people, awareness of their potentialities and some concept of what their future could be if they adopt the new techniques, as recommended by the technicians.

(c) *Be objective about conditions in the community:* The change agent works consistently towards his objective of involving members of the community in a process of working towards solving the problems of the community. As his understanding of the community grows, he identifies the problems which he feels may be raised for discussion, and areas which need encouragement and support. For this role, he acts like a medical doctor who recognises the symptoms and expresses difficulties, shows the casual factors and the treatment of these in approving or disapproving certain symptomatic behaviour. Without being satisfied with the present conditions, the change agent can accept the situation as it is. He should not criticise or make comparisons but should understand the ignorance of the people, their vested interests, rigid beliefs and customs, aggression and hostility, etc., that are found in every underdeveloped community.

In the beginning of his work, he neither praises nor blames the village people about conditions in the community, because this may strike at the sensitive spots in the community. But as he proceeds in his work and knows people, he may come to know for his own use: (1) aspects which he must simply accept and not discuss, e.g., deep-rooted religious controversy, (2) weak and blind spots in which he can raise topics for discussion, e.g., change in the cropping pattern, concentration of leadership in few people, (3) characteristics of community life which deserve praise, e.g., successful cooperative projects of the past, goodwill and willingness of the people to participate, and (4) groups or efforts in the community which require his support.

(d) *Associate with the community as a whole:* The community development worker should associate or identify himself with the whole community and not with any group in it. He should resist being captured by any one group, higher or lower class, or left or right wing, or some private enterprise. He should identify with democratic methods of discussion, with problems and projects. His main task should be helping people discover and use the process by which cooperative decisions are made. He acts as a resourceful person, presents facts or results of demonstrations at other places. He should not insist on a particular course of action. In the beginning, he has to establish process and procedures by which the community can make a collective decision. He brings diverse groups together, clarifies issues and enlarges the area of common concern. He should act as an advocate of certain community processes, methods of community work and types of community association. In this way, he associates himself with the community.

(e) *Accept and be comfortable in the role:* Many times, the community development worker faces a situation where members of the community ask questions: "What should be the projects for us this year, or what is the most important thing for us to do now ?" and he is tempted to give his opinion or say to the people what is wrong or what is right. But this is a mistake. He may provide them information, may point out the implications of different ways of doing things, may even suggest alternative ways, but he should never recommend a particular course of action. The members of the community must struggle to make such decisions. By giving a suggestion, he deprives the community of the validity of the process, and growth. Many times the community has to send a delegation to higher authorities and they want to include the professional community worker in it. He should refuse to participate in this way. He may help them to prepare the application, or collect facts, but he should not identify himself as a member of the delegation.

(f) *Learn to interpret the role:* The community development worker has to explain his role as a professional change agent: Why he cannot be "the leader" or make decisions, or recommend the right way of doing a piece of work. He should indicate the importance of the community assuming the responsibility for making decisions and taking action. He should tell them that his role is to assist them. If he talks in this way and operates likewise, he can develop a frame of reference in which he and the community can work comfortably.

(2) Role as an enabler

The role of the community development worker as an enabler is simply to facilitate the community development process. This can be sub-divided as: (a) Focussing discontent about community conditions; (b) encouraging organisation; (c) nourishing good interpersonal relations; (d) emphasising common objectives.

(a) *Focussing discontent about community conditions:* The professional community development worker assists the people by awakening and focussing discontent about community conditions. In some people, this discontent is deeply buried and it requires great skill and patience to facilitate expression; in some people, there is hostility towards some minority group, others there may have some personal problems. Many of these people remain withdrawn, but they can be brought to express their discontent if the worker handles them skilfully. In the beginning, he should listen patiently and encourage verbalisation by interrogation. His role at this point is that of a catalystic agent. He should not work as a salesman of a plan to the people, or tell them a way of attaining a plan, but he should help people to probe their deepest feelings about community life. He should encourage verbalisation of such feelings and should nourish the hope that something can be done by collective efforts. He should not encourage undue optimism about quick and easy success. As an enabler, he is supposed to help people, see the nature of their discontent to overcome the community problems.

(b) *Encouraging organisation:* The first important work of the change agent, as an enabler, is to initiate and facilitate the process by which the discontent of the people is identified. He shall seek to establish meaningful communication so that peoples from various groups may come together to rank there discontent and begin to organise to deal with their problems or discontent. But still there will be some fears, lack of confidence, and feelings that the new association or plan will thereaten their established ways of life. People will move only when they are assured or motivated to proceed in the desirable ways. This requires healthy discussions which they are directed to feel that "something is required to be done about this and this..." It will be fatal or wrong for the community worker to push, to accelerate the pace, minimise difficulties. So it is necessary to review previous discussions, to raise original questions and to encourage verbalisation about all the points discussed previously. The role of the community development worker, as an enabler, requires judgement as to how much encouragement can be given, how much anxiety relieved and how much support provided. But the responsibility for action must lie with the community through its organisation.

(c) *Nourishing good interpersonal relations:* The professional community development worker needs to be a warm, friendly person, who is sensitive to the deeper feelings of the people and interested in the things that are important in the lives of the members of the community. He should be interested in holding meetings in which people feel comfortable, enjoy themselves and feel free to verbalise. So he is not only interested in making arrangements for the meetings and making introductions, etc., but sensitive to the process of interaction which goes on in the group and knows when and how to ask that question which will catch and focus the interest of the group. He also knows when to praise. If the professional community development worker is accepted, liked, and trusted, persons identify with him. They will attend meetings and will accept other people whom he accepts. They will cooperate with others because he approves of such cooperation. Thus, he removes the blocks in the cooperative way of approach to things. As part of his work, he must seek to understand the intergroup tensions and conflicts, vested interests, class differences which stand in his way of work or prevent cooperative work.

(d) *Emphasising common objectives:* The community development worker tries to help the community in way that the process consistency is maintained, with the objectives of developing both: (1) effective planning, and (2) community capacity. He does this usually by asking certain questions like: Why do you disagree? Will it affect this and that thing if we do not do this thing? and so on. He must maintain his objectivity and must remind the group of long-term goals, what time is to be given to a project, and the relationship and content of a programme. He should know the whole community, the whole project and the whole process.

He should consistently work at freeing the community, through its leaders, to realise its potentialities and strengths in cooperative work. Firstly, it is oriented in the direction of helping to express their concerns about their social problems, to find common ground with their fellows in the community, and to achieve satisfaction in cooperative work. He seeks to facilitate the process of community work through listening and questioning, identifying the group leaders and by encouraging persons who show interest in common problems. He does not lead but facilitates local efforts. He does not provide answers but has questions which stimulate insight. He does not carry the burden of responsibility for organisation and action in the community, he provides encouragement and support for those who do this work.

(3) Role as an expert

In the capacity of an expert, the community development worker's role is to provide data and direct advice in a number of areas, about which he may speak with authority. He provides research data, technical experience, resource material, advice on methods which community organisation may need and require in its operation. His functions for such role may be: (a) to diagnose the community, (b) to provide skill for research, (c) to provide information about other communities, (d) advise on methods, (e) to provide technical information, and (f) to evaluate.

(a) *To diagnose the community:* Most of the communities do not understand their own structure or organisation. Under such circumstances, he is required to point out certain characteristics of the community, or the neglected areas, e.g., informal social organisations, forces which separate section and groups in the community, significance of certain rituals, etc. So if cooperative work is to be secured, this has to be found out.

(b) *To provide skill for research:* This knowledge of research methods will enable him to carry out studies on his own and to formulate research policy.

(c) *To provide information about other communities:* The community is required to learn from others. So he should know what others are doing, and how their findings or principles could be used in their work.

(d) *Advice on methods:* He is required to have expert knowledge of methods of organisation and procedure. Of course, the local customs will govern practices at this point to a considerable degree, but the community development worker can provide a good deal of useful advice on selecting leaders, and representation of sub-groups.

(e) *To provide technical information:* He should have technical knowledge at his command. He should know from where such knowledge is to be got. He should be able to bridge the gap between the technical knowledge available and the technical knowledge being used by the people, or needed by the community.

(f) *To evaluate:* He should be able to evaluate and interpret to the community or groups.

(4) Role as a therapist

It implies diagnosis and treatment of the community as a whole. This treatment should be carried through the leaders of groups. The areas in which this treatment is required are: taboos, ideas, traditional attitudes, which create tension and separate the groups. If the community is able to recognise these deep-rooted ideas and practices, verbalise about them and begin to cope with them, it may develop a capacity to function more effectively. He is required to know the origin and history of the community, as is required by a therapist or doctor, in separate parts, social roots of many of the present beliefs and customs, the association of briefs and practices, the power structure in the community, the roles and the relationships between the roles established in the community. His diagnosis must provide the community with some understanding of its nature and character. His treatment must involve the community in a process in which self-understanding relieves tension and moves blocks to cooperative work. The difference in an average worker and a therapist is the depth and thoroughness of the analysis and treatment. He deals with those deep-lying and often unconscious forces which threaten to disrupt the community organisation process.

Difference between an extension worker and a community development worker

The community extension worker may be a technician in his own right, he is not a technician in the subject-matter of the introduced change. He is a technician in the process of change. However, in order to carry on his functions, he must have a general understanding of what the technicians are trying to get accepted and consequently, he must be given general training in all of the subjects which are to be presented to the community. Only in this way he can adequately prepare the ground for the intensified work of the subject-matter technician.

The community extension worker must receive training in the field of agriculture, health, economics, sociology, psychology, engineering and social change. When he has all this he become a generalist, he is ready to enter the field and go to work. But as mentioned above, his work is dependent upon the ability and willingness of the subject-matter technicians to help him. If he succeeds in mobilising a community for change and then cannot carry it through due to lack of technical support, more harm can be done than good.

The reasons for adopting this method of C. D. and extension are economical, psychological and ecological. From the economic viewpoint it is more efficient to have one man working in a community who can call on the services of the other technicians than it is to have one technician from each ministry located in each community. If ten villages are taken as an example and if the ministries or departments of; Agriculture, Education, Health and Home, etc., all have a man stationed in each village, then it will take forty men to cover the area. However, if a community extension worker is responsible for these ten villages and can call on the other ministries or departments for help, these ten villages can be covered with one full-time man and ten part-time technicians. In this way, the technicians can spread their services to many villages rather than limit their full attention to only one, as is being done in India, where one village worker has been put over ten villages and about eight specialists over one Block of hundred villages to help in the technical fields.

Again, from the economic viewpoint, it is more efficient to have a community worker to perform the function of stimulation and perpetuation than it is for the other technicians to attempt to do this job as well as their own. If the technician attempts this it will take him a good deal longer to be effective because of the time period involved in adequately performing these and other functions. Thus, here again, by employing a community worker, more time is given to the other technicians to cover more villages.

From the psychological standpoint, it is less confusing to community members if they have one person to contact rather than several. When several people present independent programmes to a community, either concurrently or separately, the community members find it difficult to separate each person's function into distinct categories. Community life is an integrated whole and the Government worker, who renders assistance, is looked upon as a general service worker who can help to solve problems in any field.

CHAPTER 41

CASE STUDIES OF COMMUNITY DEVELOPMENT PROGRAMMES OF DIFFERENT COUNTRIES

C.D. IN INDIA: PROGRESS AND PROSPECTS

The Community Development Programme, launched on 2nd October 1952, aims at bringing about an integrated development of rural India, covering the social, cultural and economic aspects of community life. This is sought to be achieved through the fullest development of available human and material resources on an area basis, thereby to raise the rural community to higher levels of living with the active participation and on the initiative of the people themselves. The highest priority in the programme is accorded to agriculture, the mainstay of about seventy per cent of the rural population. Other important sectors include improvement of communications, health, sanitation, housing, education, rural employment, welfare of women and children and cottage and small-scale industries.

The basic objective of the programme has not undergone any significant change during the Five Year Plans, though in the process of working there have been some variations in the emphasis in the programme aspect. In keeping with the objective of achieving growth with social justice, the Fifth Five Year Plan has stressed the need to orientate integrated rural development towards more employment and a better production base.

At the beginning of the Fourth Plan, there were 5,265 Community Development Blocks in the country. Following reorganisation in many States, the number came down to 5,123 on 2nd April 1974. This included 483 trial development blocks.

Programme pattern

Initially a community development block covered an area of about 1,300 sq km with about 300 villages and a population of about 2,00,000. The pattern was revised from 1st April 1958. A block now covers an area of about 620 sq km with 110 villages and a population of about 92,000. A Block has two active stages of operation. Stage I of five years, followed by Stage II of another five years. At the end of ten years, the Block enter the post-Stage II phase.

On 2 April 1974, out of 4,177 blocks for which a stagewise break-up was available, 22 were in Stage I, 498 in Stage II and 3,657 in the post-Stage II phase. For implementing the programme in the blocks, there is a schematic budget provision of Rs. 12 lakhs for Stage I and Rs. 5 lakhs for Stage II. Supply of funds for the Blocks remained mainly the responsibility of the Central Government till the end of the Third Plan (1966). But from the begining of the Fourth Plan (April 1969), the financial arrangements became the responsibility of the State.

Table 40.1 gives details of the coverage and Statewise distribution of Community Development Blocks.

Table 41.1
Coverage and distribution of community development blocks

State/Union Territory	Number of allotted blocks	Population covered (lakhs)	Villages covered ('00)
1	2	3	4
Andhra Pradesh	324	380	271
Assam	130	142	208
Gujarat	218	218	186
Bihar	582	527	677
Haryana	87	94	71
Himachal Pradesh	69	33	117
Jammu and Kashmir	73	38	66
Karnataka	175	240	264
Kerala	144	194	16
Madhya Pradesh	457	368	704
Maharashtra	443	383	359
Manipur	14	9.3	19
Meghalaya	24	9.4	49
Nagaland	21	4.9	8
Orissa	314	201	465
Punjab	116	115	129
Rajasthan	232	226	322
Sikkim	N.A	N.A	N.A
Tamil Nadu	374	330	141
Tripura	17	15	49
Uttar Pradesh	875	773	1,126
West Bengal	335	358	385
Andaman and Nicobar Islands	5	1.2	4
Arunachal Pradesh	43	4.5	22
Chandigarh	1	0.2	N.A.
Dadra and Nagar Haveli	2	0.7	1
Delhi	5	4.2	3
Goa, Daman and Diu	10	8.0	2.5
Lakshadweep	4	0.3	N.A.
Mizoram	20	23.2	—
Pondicherry	4	4.5	4
All India	5,123	4,712.4	5,668.5

N.A.—Not available

Finance

The total resources available for integrated development are much more than the nucleus budget provided for the programme. These are supplemented by resources of substantive development departments like agriculture, health and Education. Besides, there are mobilisation efforts by Panchayats and voluntary contributions by the people.

Expenditure under the plans

The expenditure on community development in the first three Five Year Plans was Rs. 501 crores. From 1967-68 to 1973-74, it was Rs. 172.38 crores. The expenditure in 1973-74 was Rs. 34.83 crores. The Fifth Plan outlay for community development was Rs. 161 crores.

Policy

The Department of Rural Development in the Ministry of Agriculture lays down policy relating to the community development programme and also formulates the pattern of expenditure to be incurred in the blocks. The responsibility for the execution of the programme is that of the State Government.

Advisory body

To advise the Central Government on the twin programmes of community development and Panchayat Raj, a joint consultative council was constituted in 1971. Till then there were two separate councils, one each for community development and Panchayat Raj.

Organisation

A Development Commissioner is in charge of the community development programme in every state. He also coordinate the policies and programmes of different State departments connected with rural development. In some States, however, there is an integrated Department of Agricultural Production and Rural Development under a secretary called the Agricultural Production Commissioner. He is in charge of agriculture in its wider sense, including Community Development, Panchayat Raj and Cooperation.

At the district level, the Zila Parishad is responsible for the coordination and implementation of the programme. The Parishad consists of elected representatives of the people, including the Presidents of the Block Panchayat Samitis, Members of Parliament and Members of Legislative Assemblies from the concerned districts.

At the block level, the Panchayat samiti is responsible for the programme. Its members include elected Sarpanchs (Presidents of Village Panchayats) and a few coopted persons representing women, scheduled castes and scheduled tribes. The administrative personnel, consisting of a Block Development Officer and eight Extension Officers, who are experts in different fields such as Agriculture, Cooperation and Animal husbandry, work under the direction of the Samiti. Voluntary associate organisations like youth clubs, farmers' forums and mahila mandals, supplement the work of the Panchayats. At the village level, while the Panchayat is in overall control of the programme they are helped by associate organisations and the Gram Sewak assists these acts as a multipurpose extension agent having about ten villages in his charge.

Community development in the Philippines

Objectives

(1) To assist in the development of self-government.

(2) To increase the productvity and the income of the rural population through self-help projects in agriculture and industry

(3) To facilitate construction, largely on a self-help basis, of roads which will connect barrios (villages) with principal highways.

(4) To provide governmental services to barrios (villages).

(5) To provide better coordination of governmental services at all administrative levels.

(6) To provide facilities for education, water supply, irrigation, health, sanitation, housing and recreation through a maximum use of self-help.

(7) To arouse the citizen to honour the State legislation.

(8) To improve moral participation in the economic life of the nation.

Set-up and working

The community development programme in the Philippines aims at improving the standard of living in the barrio. The Philippines programme combines some features of India's programme. It also contains certain aspects of the specialised agency approach of the United States and Canada. The barrio community development worker is one of several governmental agents contacting the Filipino villager. The Philippines development plan takes into consideration the numerous Governmental agencies with established programmes. The Barrio Council holds the responsibility of development work at the local level just like the Village Panchayat under the new Panchayat Raj system in India. The C.D. worker is primarily a facilitator and stimulator.

The Philippines C.D. Programme lays more emphasis on promoting barrio-living through the institutionalisation of democratic processes. The movement seeks to stimulate local initiative and leadership as the primary instrument of change. The Bureau of Agricultural Extension, Health Units, Municipal Community Development Council and Barrio Councils have their integrated and coordinated plans for rural reconstruction. The C.D. workers encourage barrio people to do all they can for themselves rather than to be dependent and helpless.

Community development in Egypt

The programmes for rural development in Egypt are carried on through Rural Social Centres. Such centres are under the direction of the Follah Department in the Ministry of Social Affairs. The Ministry of Agriculture also channels its services through these rural centres. Each centre has a staff of a director and a midwife who live in the centre. These directors, in addition to their agricultural graduation, are given 4-6 months special training in C.D. and Social Work. Part-time services are provided by a worker partially trained in handicrafts. The director motivates the people to work in cooperation to solve their problems. The midwife provides maternal and child-health services and maintains a small clinical hospital. She guides the womenfolk in organising themselves for their betterment and welfare. The Government has established elected village councils at the local level which are responsible for making decisions and taking action with the help and guidance of trained technicians.

Community development in Iran

The Iranian-United States C.D. programme was initiated primarily to support a decree, increasing the Iranian peasants' share of crops. The decree also provides that the landlords shall pay a portion of their returns to Village Councils. The Village Council consists of elected members of the farmers, and other members nominated by the landlords and the Government of Iran. These Village Councils are responsible for guiding and promoting the development activities in the villages.

The main objective behind the C.D. programme in Iran was to strengthen village organisation to provide farmers help for initiating and carrying on development projects at the local level and to improve the social, economic and political integration of Iran. In the light of this objective, it is believed that an economically independent and stable agricultural population would develop in the country with the help of local leaders and outside techno-financial assistance.

On an experimental basis, some pilot projects had been started to symbolise an institution of the development activities to popularise the movement and to bring about a socio-economic revolution in the countryside. The results and experiences of these demonstrations and projects could be useful for getting the people's participation in the expansion of the movement.

Community development in Formosa

The Joint Commission on Rural Reconstruction (J.C.R.R.) was created in Formosa at a time when the hold of the National Government of China on the mainlands was crumbling. The situation demanded technical aid and guidance to form an organisation which would support and encourage the local governments, private groups, farmers' associations and Government bodies, such as agricultural experimental stations, which could undertake localised Rural Development Programmes.

J.C.R.R. serves the three objectives, namely:
(a) increase in the agricultural production;
(b) promotion of rural welfare; and
(c) encouragement for good administration.

J.C.R.R. is represented by both the American and the Chinese members. It channelises its support directly to the Governmental agencies wherever they occur. In their absence it may support local initiative and participation on a self-help basis. The development programmes are submitted to the Joint Commission by the Government or private agency. Subject-matter specialists, associated with J.C.R.R., and having close contacts with the local groups, recommend their case for financial assistance if it is at all needed. They study the local problems and put proportional weights on them for financial grants. In emergencies, a direct approach to J.C.R.R. for financial grants is also possible by individuals or local organisations. After the approval of the project by J.C.R.R., the sponsoring organisation is responsible for its proper execution.

Community development in Puerto-Rico

To start an intensive educational programme and creating in the people a felt need for improvements, and a conscious desire to take cooperative action, the C.D. programme was started in this country. The educational process, which consists of dissemination of information and the creation of positive attitudes, is accomplished through audio-visual aids. It is the material that educates the group organiser. The posters and pamphlets are used to give information and pose problems. Film shows are organised, as to educate people how to solve rural problems. A domestic Service Agency prepares useful bulletins and pamphlets in the local dialects.

The community organisers never tell the people that they should take common action to solve their problems, but in time the people spontaneously take joint action. It is at this point that the group organiser assists the people to organise and then to seek whatever help from outside they need. Sometimes it takes years of steady exposure to the educational material before the people realise that "If others have solved problems by common action, why can't we?" Thus, they develop a will to do the things through self-help and outside assistance necessary to get better houses, pure water supplies, sanitary equipment, milk stations, school lunch rooms, cooperative stores, etc.

Although the above benefits are the financial rewards, they are not the objectives of the Community Programme. What they intended for is to educate the rural masses, to create a new type of democratic community which will spontaneously express the needs and find suitable means to meet them. The rest will come in order.

Community development in Pakistan

Just like India, Pakistan had problems of transport, communication, a great number of dialects and many socio-political and socio-economical problems. To solve these, the National Development Schemes were formulated to raise the economic standard of living of the farmers and give them a fuller and richer life. The National Development Organisation is a responsible body formed to carry out the development activities at diffirent levels in close coordination with several Ministries. The administrative set up of the Development Organisation in Pakistan is as follows:

National Development Organisation,
Chief Administrator (Central Level),
Administrator (Provincial Level),
Directors (N.D.O.) (Divisional Level),
Deputy Directors (N.D.O.) (District Level),
Development Officers (Tehsil or Thana Level),
Supervisors—3 in each development area.
Village workers, 30 males and 5 females per development area.

Each development area covers 100-150 villages and has a population of about 1,00,000-1,50,000.

Each village has one Village Council and for every 3-8 villages there is one Union Council. Their functions encompass the whole field of development.

Main functions

The main functions include: (1) Maintenance of public ways and streets. (2) Plantation and preservation of trees. (3) Collection and disposal of street sweepings. (4) Maintenance of water works. (5) Organisation of fairs and exhibitions. (6) Provision of relief measures during natural calamities. (7) Welfare of widows and orphans. (8) Agricultural and industrial development on cooperative lines.

An extension wing is attached with the Ministry of Agriculture to disseminate agricultural information through extension methods. For publicity work, there is a Directorate of Publicity in the National Development Organisation.

For youth organisation work, there are Chand Tara Clubs on the lines of 4H Clubs in the USA. These are organised under the guidance of village A.I.D. workers. There are separate clubs for male and female youth, which take up youth activities such as the Yuvak Dals in India. Women's Clubs have also been organised. There are lady development officers, and lady workers in the field. They conduct classes in arts and crafts, vegetable growing, curing common diseases, etc.

Community development in Thailand

Thailand started a Community Development Programme in 1956. The programme aims at improving the standard of living of rural people socially, economically and culturally, in order to promote stable and self-reliant communities with an assured sense of social and political responsibility.

Objectives: (1) Acceleration of production and increase in familly income from agriculture and village industries.

(2) Improvement and construction of public facilities with active participation of the people.

(3) Improvement of health and sanitation.

(4) Promotion of education, and juvenile training.

(5) Promotion of village culture.

(6) Fostering local government.

Organisation and working: To achieve the aims and objectives of the programme, all ministries and departments concerned jointly frame the development policies at various levels, National and Provincial, with a priority focus on the aim of Village Development.

To provide effective, prompt and timely assistance in community development technical matters, provinces have been grouped into regions called "The Community Development Technical Assistance Centres". There are nine such centres, set up according to a scale of priority. So far two C.D.T.A.C. have been set up—one in the north-east and the other in the South of Thailand.

There are Women's Associations called Smakom Satree, Youth Organisations called Yovakasikorn 4H Clubs and Farmers' Organisations to help in the working of community development.

At the village level, there is a Village Council (Muban Council). Over five villages, there is a committee of five representatives from each village (Tambol), over 15 such centres there is a District called Ampur. In each centre, there is provision for Extension Agents in Agriculture, Veterinary, Health, etc. Each province is called a Chomgvad.

Community development in Taiwan

Taiwan has about 14,000 sq miles of area and a population of 12 million. This gives a density of 860 persons per sq mile of area, which is more than two and a half times that of India. The rapid progress made by this country since 1948 gives an illustration how an under developed country can make strides in agricultural production through intensive extension efforts and planning.

J.C.R.R.—The Joint Commission of Rural Reconstruction created by the Government of Republic of China and the USA in 1948 is mainly responsible for this rapid growth. The development of agriculture has been the main focus of the J.C.R.R. activities, but it also operates in such related fields as marketing and rural public health. Though the Agricultural Five Year Plans are drafted at the Centre, they are revised in consultation with Farmers' Associations and local governments. The typical pattern is that a period of study is followed by an action programme managed by the J.C.R.R. or the Central Government, then the farmers take over full or partial management. The Rat Control Programme, for example, was studied for 3 years (1950-52), launched in 1953, managed from the Centre until 1959, and is now managed locally. Other examples are programmes of renewing rice seed, nursery improvement, introduction of machinery and implements, all of which are partially managed by farmers. All public health programmes including family planning is conducted in partnership with local institutions. The prime burden of extension work has been assumed by the Farmers' themselves. Extension agents are hired by the Farmers' Association, which bears two-thirds of its cost, the rest is paid by the Government and the J.C.R.R. The Extensive Farmers' Cooperatives employ about 13,000 persons, many of them trained by the J.C.R.R.

The lesson of Taiwan and J.C.R.R. is that agriculture is capable of rapid growth, but only if all the necessary factors are present. This underlines the importance to governments of underdeveloped countries and aid-giving nations alike of investing in the physical and human infrastructure that made Taiwan's success possible.

Natural resources of Taiwan: The climate is sub-tropical. The Island is mountainous with less than one-third area arable. Of the 9 lakh hectares of the cultivated land 5.4 lakhs are paddy fields and the remaining are dry lands. The yearly rainfall is between 80-100 inches. Most of the lands are sloping and much water cannot be retained.

Multiple cropping: It is common for the farmers to take four crops in the year, from the same plot—two of rice and one catch crop harvested before each transplanting of rice seedlings. Tobacco, rape seed, flax, maize, jute, sweetpotato, peamelon, sorghum, soybean and a number of vegetables are also raised.

Sugar and rice were the predominant products in 1952, making up 81 per cent of the total production. Products for export now include bananas, canned vegetables, and fresh preserved fruits. Cash crops accounted for 76 per cent of the total value of agricultural exports in 1968.

If we take 1911-15 as the base year, the index number of crop production has gone to 396 in total agricultural production in 1961-65. In crops this figure was 386 and in livestock 386 (1911-15=100). From 1951-55 to 1961-65 the annual growth rate of crop production thus has beeen three times faster than the annual growth rate in land area. During this period the annual growth rate of crop production per cultivated hactare was 3.5 per cent.

IMPACT OF COMMUNITY DEVELOPMENT PROGRAMME
ON RURAL LIFE IN INDIA

The community development programme has under the new approach since 1952, completed 18 years. There may be some weaknesses but it is true that it has created an awareness among rural people and they are now discontended and dissatisfied with their present ways of living and ways of farming. They want more and more facilities. Most of the people know improved practices and a good percentage has already adopted it. Many villages have educational facilities, health centres, veterinary aid, cooperative societies. New people take interest in the elections of their Panchayats, they want leaders who are elected by them and there is some form of modernisation in the villages. The studies conducted by the National Institute of Community Development, and studies at Indian Agricultural Research Institute, New Delhi, and at Agricultural Universities, Jabalpur, Ludhiana, Pantnagar (U.P.) Udaipur, I.A.D.P. Raipur support that there has been an improvement. Some results can be presented as follows:

1. Awareness of community development programme

The studies indicated that about 87 per cent people now know that there is some Community Development Programme, 47 per cent of these include those who said that they have knowledge about some Block Development Programmes and Panchayats only, 21 per cent said that they have heard about the C.D. Programme and Panchayat Raj. Of the total respondents 15 per cent said that they have never heard about such a programme.

In reply to a question whether they knew their village level workers, 61 per cent said that they knew. About 34 per cent of these said that they knew their VLW's even by name and more intimately, 37 per cent said that they did not know their VLW's.

Contacts with block staff: The study indicated that 14 per cent of the respondents did not know their Cooperative Extension Officers, 12.7 per cent said that they did not know their Agricultural Extension Officers, 8.7 per cent said that they did not know their medical doctors in the Block, 7.3 per cent said that they did not know their BDOs and 4.6 per cent said that they did not know their VLW's. The frequency of the villagers contacts with various change agents can be seen in Table **41.2**

(2) Adoption of improved practices

(a) *Agricultural fertilisers:* On the question of adoption of fertilisers 47.2 per cent respondents said that they have heard, were interested in their use, they have even tried and then have adopted also, 17.2 per cent said that they have not yet heard about any such thing. Under improved seeds and improved implements, the figures are as follows:

---

[1]Data based mainly on the survey, *Awareness of C.D. in Village India, Preliminary Report*, Lalit K. Sen and P. Roy, conducted by National Institute of Community Development Hyderabad, 1965-66.

Table 41.2
Frequency of the contacts of the villagers with various change agents

Respondents who said that they:	BDO %	AEO %	Coop. Extn. Officer	Doctor %	VLW %
1. have never spoken with	57.6	62.4	63.4	52.4	41.4
2. have spoken only 1 to 10 times	21.0	11.9	10.2	28.1	22.4
3. have spoken more than 10 times	9.1	7.3	5.5	9.2	28.6
4. do not know	7.3	12.7	14.1	8.7	4.6

Table 41.3
Adoption of improved seeds and implements

	Imp. seeds	Imp. implements	Insecticides
Not heard	24.4%	34.5%	41%
Heard, interested, tried and adopted	36.4%	31.3%	18.7%

(b) *Improved health practices:* Of the total 51.8 per cent of respondents said that they have heard, were interested, have tried and have adopted it. In the case of small-pox vaccination, the use was 78.2 per cent.

In the case of family planning, only 5.2 per cent respondents said that they have not heard about it. On the question of family planning methods 51.6 per cent respondents said that they approve it, 23.7 per cent said that they disapprove it, and 13.8 per cent said that they do not know anything about it.

3. Communication with the outside world

The distance of a village from the means of communication is directly related to its level of modernisation. Better communications through bus services, railway facilities, post offices, distances from town, facilitate visits to urban areas and helps in creating awareness about new and modern ways of living and doing things.

The survey by the National Institue of Community Development disclosed that out of 365 villages they selected on all-India basis, 46 per cent are either on a pukka road, which is usable in all weathers, or are very close to such roads. About 33 per cent villages were within one mile to 5 miles of such roads, 10.5 per cent villages were within 5-10 miles from the roads, and 11 per cent were quite far. There is a bus stand in about every third village, and about 41 per cent villages are located 1-5 miles from the nearest bus stand. Twenty-eight per cent of the villages are beyond 5 miles from the nearest bus stand. About 55 per cent villages had post offices and 35 percent had these within five miles. About 56 per cent of the villages were 10 miles or more from the nearest railway station. Only 6.3 per cent had stations located in the village. As compared to other countries, we may be backward in this respect but if we compare with our conditions in 1952, we have made a good progress.

Influence from urban centres: About 70 per cent of the villages are still outside the immediate influence of urban centres, 7 per cent are within 5 miles and 22.5 per cent within 10 miles of these centres. About 30 per cent of the villagers did not visit a city during 1965 and 57 per cent had some contact with cities. Cities in general, and specially in India, are playing important role in modernising rural communities.

Papers, radio and movies. About 78 per cent of villagers said that they did not read newspapers, about 58 per cent said that they listen to the radio. It was found out that the nearest movie hall was beyond 10 miles for 59.5 per cent of the villagers, about 24.4 per cent are between 5-10 miles and 13.2 per cent are within 1-5 miles, and 3 per cent are within one mile of a movie hall.

4. Institutional development

With the introduction of political stablity, commercialisation of our economy and the growth of a new socio-political ethos the Jajmani, and other traditional systems have become obsolete. In the present-day context, the new institutions are natural replacements of the old ones, as the normative and operational framework for community action and individual behaviour. Our villages, in the past, were more or less sufficient in all the basic needs of the individual, and the community could be satisfied by the traditional institutions. The temple, the caste, the Jajmans, the traditional Panchayat, the Tol (old Gurukul or School) and the joint-family were enough to provide guidelines for individual and community behaviour. With time, some of these have disappeared or have been permanently weakened. New institutions to replace these have not grown rapidly, the functional boundaries have, therefore, widened.

Educational institutions: About 91 per cent of the villages had primary schools, 23 per cent had middle schools (VI to VIII), and 16 per cent of the villages had high schools. About 84 per cent villages had middle schools within 5 miles of their area, about 61 per cent had high schools within a radius of five miles, 23 per cent villages had high schools within 10 miles.

Cooperatives: Sixty-nine per cent of the villages had cooperative societies in their boundary, another 24 per cent had these within 5 miles. About 21 per cent of the villages either had a godown in village or within one mile of the village. An additional 36 per cent had godown facilities within five miles. For 23 per cent villages these facilities were within 5-10 miles.

Panchayats: About 69 per cent villages had Panchayat offices located in the village or within one mile of the village, about 25 per cent were between 1-5 miles of the Panchayat office. For the Panchayat elections, 79 per cent people voted. Under the new Panchayat system the hereditary leadership has been replaced by a democratic leadership. About 56 per cent people said that they prefer unanimous elections. Twenty-one to twenty-five per cent said that they perfer contested elections.

Libraries: Forty-five per cent of villages now have library facilities. Twenty-three per cent are located within 5 miles and 13 per cent are between 5-10 miles and 18 per cent beyond 10 miles of the library.

Extension Officer: About 37 per cent of the villages were found beyond 10 miles of Block headquarters, 7.7 per cent had these within one mile. About 42 per cent of the villages have VLW offices and 47 per cent are within 5 miles of a VLW office. Fifty-four per cent of the villages are within 5 miles of a veterinary stockmen centre and another 31 per cent with 10 miles. Only 16 per cent had such a facility in their own area.

5. Leadership development

The survey revealed that out of 7,225 villagers under study, about 25 per cent had leadership positions. The analysis of these indicated that 55.4 per cent of these were either Brahmins by caste or belonged to higher castes, 33.6 per cent completed their middle school or received higher education, 63.5 per cent completed only primary school, 23.7 per cent were illiterates. Of the total 87 per cent were farmers and 0.9 per cent were agricultural labourers. It may be noted that out of the total sample 2,435 were females.

In reply to a question on the preference of leader in their work, 45.7 per cent villagers said that they will prefer elected leaders, 15 per cent said Government officers, 5 per cent political leaders 3.5 per cent landlords, 8.6 per cent favoured traditional leaders.

Of the total of 1,416, 30 per cent said that they have talked quite often to their BDOs, 25.7 per cent to AEOs, 20.1 per cent to Cooperative Extension Officers, 20.2 per cent to Block Doctors and 61.2 per cent to VLWs. Of these 1,414 leaders 76.4 per cent have adopted the use of chemical fertilisers, 67.5 per cent use of improved seeds, 58.2 per cent insecticides, 41.8 per cent improved plough 85.5 per cent got small-pox vaccinations, 66.3 per cent have used TABC, and 10.1 per cent have used family planning methods.

CHAPTER 42

OTHER RURAL DEVELOPMENT PROGRAMMES IN INDIA

AGRICULTURAL DEVELOPMENT PROGRAMMES

Under the new strategy for agricultural development adopted in 1966-67, the development programmes have been revised to meet the needs of the farmer. Arrangements for the production and supply of improved seeds, particularly of the high yielding varieties, have been strengthened. Efforts are being made to bring science and technology closer to the farmer. The supply of inputs and institutional credit for agricultural requirements are being constantly stepped up. Since growth with social justice is one of the important objectives of the planned development, special emphasis has been laid on programmes for the uplift of the weaker sections of the rural population, particularly the small and marginal farmers and agricultural labourers. The targets and achievements of principal agricultural development programmes are dealt with briefly in the following paragraphs.

Intensive Agricultural District Programme

The Intensive Agricultural District Programme (IADP), popularly known as the Package Programme, was started on a pilot basis in 1961 in seven selected districts. The programme aims at combining technical know-how, credit and production supplies for stepping up agricultural production. During 1973-74, the Programme was in operation in 30.1 thousand villages in 15 selected districts of the country. During 1974-75, 15 more districts—2 each in Bihar and Karnataka, 4 in Punjab and 7 in Madhya Pradesh have been covered by this approach. The operation of IADP has contributed to a significant improvement in the use of critical inputs like improved seeds, fertilisers and plant protection measures.

High Yielding Varieties Programme (HYVP)

The cultivation of high yielding varieties since 1966-67 has resulted in a substantial increase in foodgrains production. Wheat production has been more than doubled. Rice production has also increased through not as much as in the case of wheat. Bajra production has registered some increase but the progress under maize and Jowar is relatively slow.

A major development in rice cultivation was the launching of the Minikit Programme from 1971-72. For optimising the yields of the available high yielding varieties of rice, it has been found necessary to advance their sowing time. Efforts were directed to educate the farmers to raise rice nurseries in advance of the main kharif season. A special programme for timely supply of seedlings, by raising community nurseries at tube-well points and on government farms, was undertaken in three command areas in Bihar. This programme has given encouraging results and is being extended to Assam, Uttar Pradesh, Madhya Pradesh, Bihar, Orissa and West Bengal during 1975 *kharif*. As in the case of rice, Minikit Programmes for wheat, maize, jowar and bajra have also been launched from 1974-75. A special scheme was undertaken this year for the replacement of rust-susceptible wheat varieties in the North-southern hill areas.

The target of coverage of 2.5 crore hectares of area under high yielding varieties of cereals and millets under the Fourth Plan has been exceeded. The coverage was of the order of 2.6 crore hectares. The coverage in 1974-75 was around 3.19 crores and the target for 1978-79 has been fixed at 4.20 crore hectares. The Fifth Plan target of coverage of the high yielding varieties was four crore hectares.

Drought Prone Areas Programme (DPAP)

The Drought Prone Areas Programme, formerly known as Rural Works Programme, was initiated in 1970-71 as a Non-Central Sector Scheme. Seventy-four districts have been identified as drought prone and they have been grouped under 54 units. The programme aimed at mitigating the severity of scarcity conditions by executing rural works to generate employment.

In the Fifth Plan, the main thrust is to restore the proper ecological balance in the drought prone areas. Some of the important elements envisaged in this integrated approach are changes in agronomical practices, restructuring of the cropping pattern, and pasture development through proper management of small and marginal farmers and agricultural labourers. An allocation of Rs. 203.9 crores was made in the Fifth Plan. Six districts, one each in Andhra Pradesh and Karnataka and two each in Maharashtra and Rajasthan, are covered under the programme with World Bank assistance. Project reports on the basis of the new strategy of development have been received from these districts.

During the Fifth Plan, Rs. 203.9 crores were spent on the programme. Of the total expenditure, about 55 per cent was on irrigation works, 14 per cent on soil conservation and afforestation, 26 per cent or road-building and the balance on drinking water. Schemes costing about Rs. 123.64 crores were sanctioned during 1977-78.

Whole Village Development Programme (WVDP)

For both special and functional integration of all programmes connected with agricultural production and reduction of unemployment and underemployment, a new programme called the Whole Village Development Programme was implemented in the Fifth Plan period. To start with bench-mark surveys were undertaken in Bihar, Orissa, Tamil Nadu and Uttar Pradesh. Basic component of the programme are consolidation of holdings, over all Land Development Planning through irrigation, support and restructuring of the cropping pattern. The Fifth Plan outlay for the new scheme is ₹ 5 crores.

SECTORAL DEVELOPMENT PROGRAMMES

Tribal Development Blocks (TDB)

For the development of the tribal areas, 483 Tribal Developmental Blocks were functioning on 31st March 1974 after reorganisation of the 'T.D.' Blocks in Mizoram. A sum of Rs. 120 crores were provided for these block during the Fifth Plan period.

In the Medium Term, Plan (1978-83), Rs. 350 crores have been provided for this programme. The stress will be on Integrated Area Development Plans which will combine the activities of Tribal Development Blocks with Tribal Development Agencies, and other projects launched by the Central Government in the States.

Pilot Project for Tribal Development (PPTD)

A special programme called the Pilot Project for Tribal Development was launched in 1972-73 for the development of six selected tribal areas in Andhra Pradesh, Bihar, Madhya Pradesh and Orissa. Under this programme, the special Tribal Development Agencies are studying in depth the problems of tribal areas relating to communications, administration, social services and economic development, especially agriculture. This programme will, for the present, continue till 1983-84. Two more projects similar to the existing six, have been taken up as part of the Fifth Plan Programme. An amount of Rs. 12 crores was allocated in the Fifth Plan for all the eight TDA projects. During 1977-78, a provision of Rs. 2.47 crores was made. The total grains-in-aid given to these projects since their inception is Rs. 12.03 crores upto the end of June 1977.

Hill Areas Development Programmes (HADP)

For all-round development of agriculture and improvement in the living conditions of the farmers in the hilly areas, some pioneering projects were taken up in Himachal Pradesh, Tamil Nadu and Uttar Pradesh under the Indo-German assistance programme. Based on the encouraging results achieved in these projects, two more such projects in Manipur and Uttar Pradesh were taken up in the last year of the Fourth Plan, financed entirely out of domestic resources. These projects continued in the Fifth Plan and Rs. 2.9 crores was allocated for the purpose. During 1978-79, a sum of Rs. 100 lakhs had been provided.

ANIMAL HUSBANDRY

Cattle and Dairy Development (CDD)

The programmes for the development of animal husbandry and dairying aim at augmenting the supply of nutritive foods like milk, eggs and meat, and helping the small and marginal farmers to diversify their economic activities.

Cross-breeding of indigenous cows with bulls of exotic dairy breeds is encouraged for augmenting milk production. Programmes for selective breeding in recognised breeding tracts, and for upgrading of non-descript animals with recognised dairy breeds are being continued. To support the cross-breeding programme, about 500 exotic dairy cattle of Jersey and Friesian breeds were imported during 1974-75. Five Central Cattle Breeding Farms have been established for raising high quality bulls of Red Sindhi, Tharparkar and Jersey breeds and Murrah and Surti breeds of buffalo. One more Exotic Cattle Breeding Farm at Andesh Nagar (Uttar Pradesh) was established.

To locate superior germ plasm of important national breeds and their utilisation for improvement, a Central Herd Registration Scheme is in operation at State Live-stock Farms and breeding tracts of milch breeds. A central Frozen Semen Bank has been established at Hessarghatta (Bangalore) for the production of frozen semen from high quality bulls of exotic and indigenous breeds. In addition, establishment of Frozen Semen Stations, as a Centrally-sponsored programme, has also been taken up at five Intensive Cattle Development Projects areas at Amritsar, Bangalore, Bhopal, Gurgaon and Lucknow.

Under the Intensive Cattle Development Programme being implemented since 1964-65, seventy projects have been set up in different parts of the country. Another important Cattle Development Scheme is the Key Village Scheme. At present, there are 640 Key Village Blocks.

Owing to drought conditions in most of the States, and large scale diversion of milk for manufacturing milk products like baby food, milk powder and ghee, the average daily output of milk of all dairy plants during 1974 was 27.30 lakh litres as against 28.8 lakh litres during the previous year. The number of dairy plants in operation increased from 141 units in the previous year to 186 units in 1977, compris-ing 92 liquid milk plants, 26 factories for milk products and 68 Pilot Milk Schemes and Rural Dairy Centres.

Sheep Development (SD)

The Central Sheep Breeding Farms set up at Hissar with Australian assistance for Corriedale breed of sheep has a flock strength of over 3,500 Corriedale sheep. Corriedale rams are supplied to various States, to the Haryana Agricultural University and to the Indian Veterinary Research Institute, Izatnagar, for breeding trials. During 1974-75, Australia supplied 1950 Corriedale ewes and 50 Corriedale rams. Short-term training courses for State Sheep Husbandry Officers and Sheep Rearing Training Course are being organised since 1972-73.

Under a Centrally-sponsored scheme, establishment of five large sheep-breeding farms one each in Andhra Pradesh, Jammu and Kashmir, Karnataka, Rajasthan, Uttar Pradesh, Bihar and Madhya Pradesh were started under the Fourth Plan. These farms were fully established during the Fifth Plan.

In order to produce exotic germ plasm for sheep improvement work in the States, 1,302 Merino sheep from USSR were imported during 1974-75.

Poultry Development (PD)

Poultry Development Programmes are continuing both in the public and private sectors. The estimated production of eggs in 1973-74 totalled 770 crores as against the Fourth Plan target of 800 crores. The poultry industry has made a major break-through in attaining self-sufficiency in respect of genetically superior chicks. The three central poultry breeding farms distributed 3.76 lakh chicks for breeding purposes to the States and private poultry farms during 1974-75. Intensification of the scientific

Poultry Breeding Programme at Government farms has enabled the production of strain crosses which have given performance comparable to, and in many cases better than, the exotic hybrids available in the country.

Piggery Development (Pig. D)

All the eight modern bacon factories and pork processing plants established during the Third and Fourth Plan period have been increasingly utilising their capacity for production of pork and pork products. Some of these factories have diversified their products and are handling different types of meat in addition to pork and pork products.

The regional pig breeding stations supply pure breeding stocks of exotic pigs to the farmers for further multiplication and the surplus stock for slaughter in bacon factories. The Model Piggery at Gannavaram (Andhra Pradesh) is supplying piggery stocks of exotic pigs to other States, universities and institutions for taking up pig breeding programmes.

Efforts are being made to import pigs from abroad to introduce economic production units in the existing breeding stock. Special efforts are being made to take up piggery programmes in the north-eastern States.

Fisheries Development (Fr. D.)

Development of fisheries has been assigned a high priority under the Fifth Five Year Plan in view of its vast potential for raising the nutritional levels of the protien deficient Indian diet and as an earner of much needed foreign exchange. The Sixth Five Year Plan aims at achieving a production level of 34 lakh tonnes of fish which would earn for the country foreign exchange worth Rs. 400 crores through export of marine products by 1983-84.

INTEGRATED RURAL DEVELOPMENT PROGRAMME (IRD)

The deliberations of the Indian Science Congress at its session held at Waltair (Andhra Pradesh) in January, 1976, were centred around the theme "Science and Integrated Rural Development—an Agenda for Action".

The papers gave details of a rural development programme directed towards making optimum use of available local resources through purposive inputs of science and technology for the benefit of the rural poor. As a result of this initiative it was decided to make a start with an *ad hoc* provision of Rs. 15 crores in the Union Budget for funding Pilot Projects in Integrated Rural Development.

Criteria for selection of district

A working group consisting of representatives of the departments of Rural Development, Agricultural Research and Eeducation (DARE), Science and Technology (DST), the Planning Commission and the Council of Scientific and Industrial Research (CSIR) was set up in May, 1976, to select at least one district in each State in which to initiate an Integrated Rural Development Project. Initially, twenty districts have been selected as listed in Annexure A. The choice of a District was based on certain criteria, such as:

(a) Economically-backward districts that have considerable development potential;

(b) Districts in which problems of rural unemployment and underemployment are acute;

(c) Districts that already have a certain basic development infrastructure; and

(d) Districts in which scientific and technical institutions have already begun working.

The guidelines for action

Action Plans are being drawn up on the basis of the following guidelines:

(a) The programme must provide gainful employment and increase the purchasing power of the rural poor, in particular, marginal farmers (with holdings of less than 1 hectare), landless labour, artisans, women and children; (Women as a group have generally been by-passed by most programmes for training and technology upgrading. Children are often diverted by economic consideration from the class room to income-earning tasks, and their special needs will require to be met by providing relevant education);

(b) These job opportunities must be provided through the application of science and technology in making optimum use of existing local resources—human, animal, plant, soil, water, mineral and other resources; and

(c) The programme should be simple enough to operate and be economically viable so as to ensure that it is quickly capable of achieving self-reliance and self-replication under similar or varying conditions.

Within the framework of these broad guidelines the programme will have no rigid structure instead, each action plan will be tailored to suit local needs, resources and priorities.

The planning phase

The planning phase has been thought of in terms of the following steps:

Step 1: Compilation of an Integrated Resource Inventory on the basis of data available from a variety of sources. This Resource Inventory will include:

(a) compilation of biological, physical, ecological and other resources of the district;

(b) compilation of data on the quantitative and qualitative aspects of rural poverty, in order to identify the persons drawn from the rural poor who will participate and thereby benefit from the programme; and

(c) listing of individuals/agencies that make up the existing developmental infrastructure of the district and can serve as a useful spring board for action, i.e.,

Official Development Programmes being implemented by the Departments of Rural Development, Social Welfare, Tribal Welfare, Agriculture, Industries, etc.;

Voluntary Development Programmes being conducted by Social Welfare Organisations, Chambers of Commerce and Industry, Scouts and Guides, etc.;

Educational and technical training facilities being provided by schools, colleges, technical/vocational training institutes and industrial units; medical and public health facilities being provided by medical colleges, hospitals, dispensaries, public health centres under official or voluntary auspices; and

credit, crop insurance and marketing facilities being provided by banks cooperative societies, insurance companies, etc.

Step 2: Drafting of a Malady-Remedy-Analysis that will serve to pin-point specific constraints that affect the life and work of the rural poor and to indicate the appropriate way by which these constraints could be overcome and optimum use made of local resources.

Step 3: Vetting the Draft Action Plan will be done through field visits undertaken by interdisciplinary teams in order to secure the comments and suggestions of random groups of the local community, and in particular of the following groups:

(a) Social Action Groups consisting of random groups of participants (i.e., marginal farmers, landless labourers, artisans, women, etc.); local selected representatives (Panchayat Members), Voluntary Social Workers; committee members of local Women's Organisations (Mahila Mandal); Scouts and Guides, etc.

(b) Educators and Scientists groups including Head Masters/Principals of local schools/colleges; and

(c) Administrative and Commercial group including District Magistrate, Bank Manager, Secretary of the Cooperative Society, etc.

Providing an operational base

It is with a certain measure of realism that it has been decided to set up a Rural Science and Technology Complex in a carefully chosen village in the project area. This will serve as the base from which several of the key operations will be conducted. The Complex will provide some of the following basic components:

(a) A Permanent Training Centre (Krishi-cum-Udyog-Vigyan Kendra) for imparting certain agricultural/industrial/technological/marketing skills with provision for demonstration plots; the content of the training programme will be tailored to meet the needs of the project and the method of training will be "learning by doing".

(b) A Mobile Training-cum-Demonstration Unit that would reach out, according to a regular schedule of visits, to train individuals/groups, especially women, that could not be conveniently brought to the complex; and to provide certain repair and maintenance service facilities for agricultural and industrial machinery;

(c) A Rural Service Society supported by the District Lead Bank to provide credit facilities in terms of agricultural inputs such as, seeds, planting, material, farm animals, fish seed, animal feed, fertilisers, farm implements, equipment for cottage industries, etc. The Society will undertake custom hiring of farm equipment and other appropriate machinery. Credit facilities must be based on proven technology, and a modest begining can be made with a system of credit insurance.

(d) A Marketing-cum-Warehousing Component that will provide safe storage and efficient marketing and also ensure that primary producers get a legitimate share of the profit;

(e) An Agro-Meteorological Centre equipped with a basic weather kit to give timely advice to farmers on crop-weather relationships during production and post-harvest operations;

(f) A Forest Nursery with provision for introduction of rapid propagation techniques for the planting of fruit, fuel and forest trees.

(g) A Development School where the children can spend a part of the day in regular class room education, and the rest can be spent on carefully designed projects such as animal husbandry, fisheries, horticulture and handicrafts. These work projects should lay stress on "earning while learning" and the Developmental Schools can help in developing a cadre of self-employed human, animal, plant and soil, healh care workers; and

(h) A Residential Component which will provide basic housing facilities for both married and unmarried scientists, technologists, teachers and student volunteers working in the Project Area.

Task adoption at planning phase

To begin with, several Central Scientific and Educational Agencies have taken on the tasks mentioned below:

(i) Indian Council of Agricultural Research (ICAR), Preparation of Integrated Resource Inventories for the 20 districts in collaboration with all other Central and State scientific agencies, Survey of India: Botanical, Zoological and other surveys, agricultural and general universities and banks and other organisations;

(ii) Council of Scientific and Industrial Research (CSIR)
Developing designs for the Rural Science and Technology Complex;

(iii) Development of Space
Developing the infrastructure necessary for the Mobile Training Units;

(iv) Department of Science and Technology (DST), assisting in the preparation of the Integrated Resource Inventories;

(v) Indian Council of Medical Research (ICMR), developing the Health Care and Nutrition Education Programme;

(vi) Indian Meteorological Department (IMD), setting up agro-meteorological centres;

(vii) National Council of Educational Research and Training (NCERT)
Assisting in the establishment of the Developmental Schools; and

(viii) Indian Council of Social Science Research (ICSSR)
Assisting in the socio-economic analysis of the Programme and developing guidelines for monitoring the progress in reducing rural poverty and unemployment.

This project has thus become a valuable exercise in inter-agency cooperation.

Programme implementation, coordination and monitoring

The entire Programme of Integrated Rural Development is based upon the twin principles of optimum resource utilisation and task adoption by the most appropriate agency. Each agency and institution, both official and non-official, will be able to measure its individual contribution and achievements in fairly precise quantitative and qualitative terms. Thus, it will be necessary to provide a suitable coordinating and monitoring agency to assign tasks to different agencies within a "time-frame" to keep track of progress achieved in implementing these tasks; to assist in removing bottle-necks to progress; and to assess the general impact of the Programme on the economic and social well being of the rural poor.

The District Collector/Magistrate will liaise with a large number of specialised scientists and technological agencies, both official and non-official, providing the District Collector or Magistrate with the help of an experienced and enthusiastic Principal Coordinating Officer. This Officer would work with a District Coordinating and Monitoring Committee consisting of representatives of agencies that have adopt-ed specific tasks and with representatives of the rural poor participating in the programme. At the Village Level, similar coordinating and monitoring groups will be set up to keep track of the Programme.

Self-replicating model of rural development

A basic question is whether it is possible to develop a self-replicating model of rural development by marrying certain universal principles of growth with social justice and ecological balance to the unique socio-economic and cultural conditions of each project area? The answer to this question has been given by Mahatma Gandhi a long time ago. If every action-plan is designed deliberately to benefit the poorest man, then we would have developed a growth model which would confer on human communities, the same uniquiness which the DNA molecule has conferred on heredi-tary mechanisms in Man.

Some neglected Factors in Integrated Rural Development.

V.K.R.V. Rao (1977), in his Convocation Address to the Indian Agricultural Research Institute, observed that "there is an accent in the use of science and techno-logy for rural development. This integrated rural development has become a national slogan and science and technology the main instrument proposed for its implementation". According to him the main factors neglected in this programme are:

(1) In the integrated rural development, the village has been treated as a homo-geneous concept and as a unit of development which is not there. Thus there is a serious problem of uneconomic and non-viable village size for full develop-ment. This requires the possibility for the restructuring of villages to form them into viable villages or rural settlements that can form a more economically efficient base for integrated rural development.

(2) No attempt was made to consider the policy of distribution of land or for more equitable distribution pattern and revitalising the possessing of other productive assets in the rural areas by limiting size of individual units.

(3) Inability of science and technology to solve, by itself, the problem of rural poverty.

The foregoing description relates to only a few development programme which have gained some significance in the past decade or so. A comprehensive list of pro-grammes located in various States and districts is given in Annexure A. First a list of abbreviations for the different programmes is presented. It is followed by listing of these programmes by States and districts.

DISTRICT RURAL DEVELOPMENT AGENCY (DRDA)

In 1980 the Integrated Rural Development Programme was extended to all the development blocks of the country. The target set for IRDP was to assist on an average 600 families in a block from the identified target group, in a year and to assist at least 3,000 families during the Sixth Plan period. Following this, it was decided that there should be a single agency which will be responsible for implementation of all programmes, viz., IRD, DPAP, DDP, TRYSEM Special Livestock Production Programmes and Programme for women and children, etc., so as to minimise administrative expenditure and result in better utilisation of inputs including the personnel. This agency established at the district level named as the District Rural Development Agency (DRDA)/Society. The agency is headed by the Collector/Deputy Commissioner or CEO Zila Parishad in States where he is of the same status. The agency have full time executive officer with the staffing pattern as shown in the chart.

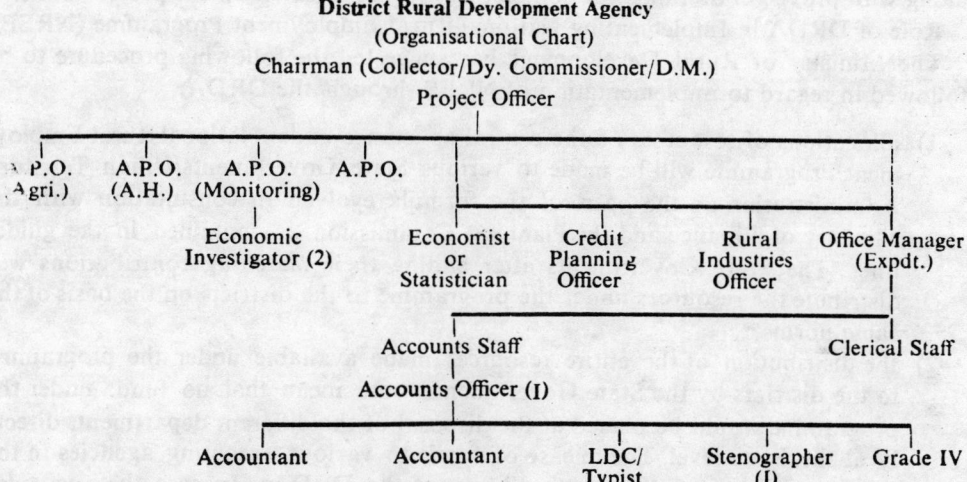

District Rural Development Agency
(Organisational Chart)
Chairman (Collector/Dy. Commissioner/D.M.)
Project Officer

The above pattern is subjected to change as per local requirements. The District Rural Development Agency has a governing body headed by Collector/Deputy Commissioner. Broadly the membership of the governing body of DRDA is as follows:

Chairman	.. Collector
A representative of the State Government	.. Member
A representative of the Central Co-operative Bank	.. Member
One representative of the Land Development Bank	.. Member
Chairman of Zila Parishad or his representative	.. Member
Senior most officer of the Lead Bank	.. Member
General Manager, DTC	.. Member
Two representative of the weaker sections; one of whom may be drawn from scheduled castes and scheduled tribes	.. Member
One representative of rural women	.. Memher
MPs and MLAs	.. Member
Project Officer	.. Member-Secretary

The membership of the agency can be enlarged if considered necessary. Representation may also be given to other major commercial banks where they provide sizeable credit support to the programme. The non-official nominees must be residents of the districts in which the agency is located.

The governing body meets at least once in a quarter. At the initial stages, it may be necessary to meet more often. Emergent meetings being called, as and when necessary, to discuss urgent matters.

DRDAs constitute several functional committees for various specific purposes and tasks. In addition to members of governing body representatives of various other organisations and specialised agencies, viz., industrial and business houses, voluntary agencies, rotary and lions clubs, academic and research institutions and other such bodies may also be invited in such committees on the basis of the relevance of their experiences. It is rather imperative and essential to measure the impact of such IRDP efforts and for doing an inbuilt-system of evaluation and monitoring has been provided along with provision of funds for conducting specific research on the project basis.

Role of DRDA in Implementing National Rural Employment Programme (NREP): The Ministry of Rural Development has suggested the following procedure to be followed in regard to implementation of NREP through the DRDA:

1) allocations of resources of the central assistance under National Rural Employment Programme will be made to various State Governments/Union Territory Administration on the basis of the formula evolved in consultation with the Ministry of Finance and the Planning Commission as contained in the guidelines. The State Governments after adding their matching contributions will distribute the resources under the programme to the districts on the basis of the same norms;

2) the distribution of the entire resources made available under the programme to the districts by the State Government would mean that no funds under the programme would be placed at the disposal of the different departments directly at the State level. The release of funds to various executing agencies in the districts will be the sole responsibility of the DRDAs. In case they consider that any of the works under the Programme should be entrusted for execution to any of the departments other than the panchayatiraj institutions; requisite funds will be made to the officer incharge of that department in the district;

3) the DRDAs will ensure that the shelf of Projects for all the blocks in the district are prepared in time and that no works outside that shelf of projects are taken up for execution under National Rural Employment Programme in the District. They should also ensure that the priorities on the basis of which the works should be taken for execution are decided in consultation with the gram panchayats of the villages in each block;

4) based on the predetermined priorities, District Rural Development Agencies will select the works out of the shelf of projects to be executed under the programme during a particular year in the beginning of the year itself. These works will finally be cleared by the DRDA taking into account the capability of such works to meet the twin objectives of providing wage employment locally and creating durable community assets that will improve the standard of living and the quality life of the local community;

5) while normally most of the works under the programme will be entrusted for execution to panchayatiraj institutions like zila parishads, panchayat samity and gram panchayats, some works could be entrusted to the regular department concerned if the nature of these works is such that the panchayatiraj institutions will not be able to execute them properly;

6) the DRDAs also have the overall responsibility for monitoring the implementation of the programme for which suitable system will have to be evolved by them. They will also be accountable to the State Government to ensure that the returns/reports in respect of all the works taken up for execution in the district are furnished in time; and

7) it is at the level of the District Rural Development Agency that suitable linkages in the implementation of National Rural Employment Programme works will have to be developed. The implementation of the NREP will have to be organised in such a way it gives infrastructural support to the implementation of programmes like Integrated Rural Development and TRYSEM etc. This will reduce the need for creating infrastructural assets out of IRD funds.

General framework

The Central Government provides additional finances for strengthening of administrative machinery or creating a cell at the State level for supervision and guidance to DRDAs in the formulation, implementation, monitoring and evaluation of the IRD Programmes.

DRDAs are expected to take adequate steps in arranging knowledge and physical inputs, supplies and services, credits and other physical assets needed by the target beneficiaries. The Agency liaise with other development department in the district to ensure the provision for improvement of the infrastructure required for the successful implementation of IRDP schemes. To perform these tasks, DRDAs try to draw upon the expertise locally available in the scientific and research institutions viz., ICAR, Agricultural Universities, Regional Research Laboratories, Krishi Vigyan Kendras, Community Polytechnics, Indian Institute of Science and Technology, CSIR Laboratories etc. It is a mutual beneficial relation and helps both parties in accelerating their programmes as per their common objectives. The Agency particularly charged with the responsibility of all round development in the blocks and villages under its influence and see that a village plan register indicating details of all the identified families and the development programmes drawn up for each one of them under IRDP are being maintained in each village.

COUNCIL FOR ADVANCEMENT OF RURAL TECHNOLOGY (CART)

As a result of large scale infrastructural development for conducting research in both farm and non-farm sectors, the quantum of technology evolved by these institutions could not be transferred to the users, which became a serious problem. Though in the farm sector sustained efforts were made for ensuring dissemination and defusion of technologies developed by agricultural universities (24) and ICAR Institutes (40), as a result of that the country made a substantial progress in the field of agriculture and its allied activities. To hasten this process a new project, viz., National Agricultural

Research Project was launched in the year 1979 by the ICAR with the support of IDA for strengthening permanently the capability of state agricultural universities in conducting location-specific, production-oriented, researches in the agro-climatic zones, identified in their service areas. These institutions have an inbuilt system of communication, dissemination and to some extent transfer of technology to the identified target groups.

However, in the non-farm sector, the institutions like IITs, Polytechnics, CSIR Institutions and a large number of voluntary and other organisation evolved technology which could not even cross the fences of the institutions and mostly remained in the laboratories for want of proper mechanism of transferring the same to the users. Hence, a new institution with the name of Council for Advancement of Rural Technology (CART) was established in the year 1982 under the Ministry of Rural Development. The CART which is registered as a Society has the following objectives:

1) To act as the national nodal point for coordination of all efforts at development and dissemination of technology relevant for rural areas for sectors other than these covered by ICAR and its sister bodies;

2) To act as a catalyst for development of technology, appropriate for the rural areas, by identifying the crucial problems encountered by the rural people and funding research and development efforts by different organisations;

3) To strengthen existing institutions of research and develop or set up institutions, so that national level institutions on matters of purely or largely rural interest are built up;

4) To act as a clearing house of information and a data bank;

5) To disseminate knowledge on rural technology to manufacturers of machinery, tools, equipment and spare-parts so that large scale production of technically improved machinery etc., is carried out in the private, corporate and public sectors;

6) To act as a conduit for transfer of appropriate technology to Government departments, public sector undertakings and members of the public;

7) To conduct or sponsor training programmes to trainers so that improved technology is passed on to the beneficiaries in the rural areas;

8) To carry out research studies, surveys, evaluation etc., on the use of appropriate technology; and

9) To do all other such things as the society may consider necessary, incidental or conducive to the attainment of the above subjects.

The CART as a coordinating agency will act as a watch dog for the entire field of rural development. It will advise the government on the requirement of public policies enabling the existing village industries and rural artisans to flourish and expand their activities in the non-farm sector. The requirement of supporting services for supply of raw material, marketing, transportation, standardisation of designs and quality control, etc., will also be looked by this organisation.

Earlier efforts made by the Ministry of Rural Development and other development departments and agencies will be further consolidated and geared up both in terms of training the trainers and directly benefiting the research and extension organisations, by the CART. This will be achieved by building up necessary infrastructure and needed facilities at the national level, state-level and finally reaching up to the village-level. The funding and the procedure of implementation of various projects are being finalised and the organisation has started functioning as per objectives listed above.

NATIONAL AGRICULTURAL RESEARCH AND EXTENSION PROJECTS

With the experience of past thirty years in agricultural research, teaching (training also) and extension education in India, starting from C.D. (1952) and establishment of chain of agricultural universities (since 1960), it was realised that though the technology development was excellent but the technology sustenance and technology transfer remained quite weak and irrelevant for vast majority of area as well as clientele. The infrastructure developed and the manpower created through such efforts remained confined to some pockets or the main campuses of the agricultural universities and/or their research stations. Similarly, the extension also remained quite weak and in spite of evolutions and expansion it could not reach the majority of the farmers.

Hence, to accelerate the pace of agricultural development as a whole and to consolidate the isolated efforts made through launching several programmes, projects and schemes so far, and to bridge the gap between research and extension addressed to overcoming the specific localised and problem-oriented approaches, the Government of India launched two specified projects with the financial and technical assistance from the International Development Bank (IDA) viz., (i) National Agricultural Research Project (NARP); and (ii) National Agricultural Extension Project (NAEP).

I. National Agricultural Research Project (NARP)

The NARP is the first major effort of the Indian Council of Agricultural Research (ICAR) to upgrade and strengthen the regional research capability of the State Agricultural Universities (SAUs). The project is designed to fill the gaps in research and also to meet the needs of extension services and farmers as far as new and proven technologies generated through applied research addressed to specific localised constraints in agricultural production are concerned. The project was launched in January, 1979 and is funded by the ICAR and by IBRD, the soft loan affiliate of the World Bank.

The genesis of the project is that agricultural universities, which have a state-wise mandates for teaching, research and extension education did not possess a strong base for agricultural research at regional level. They were also constrained by shortage of funds to intensify their efforts in this direction. The research programme also had been developed by and large in an *ad hoc* manner based on isolated projects and schemes. The research efforts of the University often were not focussed on local research needs. In many cases, available resources in terms of research scientists and physical facilities were not optimally utilised.*

Hence, the NARP has been launched to remedy the above situation and aims at strengthening regional research centres selected on the basis of specified local needs

---

*ICAR (1982) National Agricultural Research Project (ICAR-IBRD) Manual, ICAR, Krishi Bhawan, New Delhi, India.

in a given agro-climatic situation and strengthening and/or establishing research with available research and extension education facilities and infrastructure. The other aims are:

(a) rationalisation of University research programmes, research organisation and research needs to conduct location-specific research; and (b) strengthening the capability of the agricultural university to undertake such researches by filling the identified gaps in terms of manpower, equipments, laboratories and residential facilities etc., (c) linking research service with extension service in the areas of influence or jurisdiction of the regional research stations developed under the project, and finally (d) application and transfer of research results by conducting field trials, workshops, farmers days, exhibitions, demonstrations and continuous training and visits for the extension workers as well as the farmers in their vicinity, together communicating success stories and needed information by utilising group and mass media of communication for multiplier effects.

II. National Agricultural Extension Project (NAEP)

Based on the remarkable success of NARP project as a result of viable impact in their influence area and realising the further widening of gaps in the extension services, the NAEP project is being launched by the Government of India, so that an effective and efficient transfer of technology is assured. The links established between NARP, IRD and T & V system together produced the desired results.

NAEP is being launched with the help of IBRD-World Bank affiliate, to overcome the various constraints (including organisational and functional) identified earlier and will rectify many of them. The NAEP will further strengthen the capabilities of the State Department of Agriculture (SDA) in the context of overall developmental activities or programmes and will be a remedial measures for rectifying earlier mistakes. The project will assist the state governments for a period of five year with additional assistance to fulfil the gaps so identified and after this period the state governments will run the show with their resources.

To make the project very comprehensive the GOI has issued the following guidelines for preparation of such projects under NAEP:

1) In-depth review of the existing agricultural extension system, including identification of constraints to effective professional extension in the state and specific proposals to overcome these constraints. This will include: (a) a review of the structure, programme and resources of Department of Agriculture and their interrelation with extension activities, (b) a statement of the Department's specific objective and of the extension service, and of means to be followed to obtain these and (c) review of the Department's administrative and staffing procedures as may affect extension.

2) Statement on existing resources of Department of Agriculture and other departments that may be redeployed to further strengthen agricultural extension.

3) Review of links with supporting services (input, credit etc.) and of coordination between the extension service, Department of Agriculture and related departments.

4) Review of extension/research linkage.

5) Review of adoptive research (if any) under the Department of Agriculture and linkage with University research.

6) Review of training for extension workers, institutions involved, type of training and duration of course organised and future need.

7) Review of physical facilities provided in the form of accommodation, incentives to extension workers. Type of mobility available to senior and field level extension workers.

8) Review on manner in which an agency maintaining basic crop estimates, production etc. Crop cutting experiments conducted etc.

Part VII

EXTENSION ADMINISTRATION AND TRAINING

CHAPTER 43

ADMINISTRATION

ADMINISTRATION: TRENDS

As compared pre-independence efforts in providing educational facilities to the masses, the post-independence period has seen a tremendous expansion which has had no parallel in the history of the developing countries. This unprecedented phenomenon of change through educational means and methods can hardly be put in words and shows the great contribution of extension administration. Now, the extension administrators have to prepare themselves to respond to this challenging task. They have to be ready for a comprehensive transformation of the extension educational system so as it keep to continually relevant to the needs and aspirations of the people. Moreover, the forward looking administrators are conscious of shifting the emphasis from 'Maintenance' to 'Extension' or 'Development' Administration. This shift in administration has led to further evolution of extension educational concepts, principles, philosophies and applications. Several researches, studies and other contributions have shown a new trend in extension administration in the recent past. which have been summarised below:

Past practices	Present trends
(1) Traditionalism	Social dynamics and scienticism
(2) Job-task hierarchy	Special processes of social communication
(3) Efficiency as a mechanical process	Efficiency as a human process
(4) Organisation as 'bureaucratic structure'	Organisation as a social institution
(5) Control through command	Control through communication and motivation
(6) Authority from top-down	Authority from the group
(7) Leadership by authority	Leadership by consent
(8) Decision as an individual, highly centralised act	Decision as a collective responsibility and highly decentralised act
(9) Regimented work environment	Demonstration work environment
(10) Technological changes by fiat	Technological changes by consultations

(11)	Based on social or financial punishments	Based on social and/or financial incentives
(12)	Planning preceding the crisis situation	Planning as an inbuilt formalised and continuing process
(13)	Job was rated for subsistence	Job as satisfying experience
(14)	Incomplete and delayed information	Complete and current information as and when required
(15)	Policy and administration dichotomy	Policy and administrative continuum
(16)	Profit with buccaneering	Profit with social responsibility
(17)	'Executive' administration	'Extension' Administration

PUBLIC ADMINISTRATION

The career-student in the field of education administration as applicable to extension has to acquire both understanding and skill about the basic concepts of the manner in which the educational system acquires greater relevance, comprehensiveness, dynamism, basic to the development of the 'whole individual', 'community' and the nation. This chapter will deal with the elements and processes involved in the Development Administration, including Public Administration, Personnel Administration and Teaching, and Training.

CONCEPTS IN PUBLIC ADMINISTRATION

This involves the 'public' and the 'administration'. The word Public pertains to people as a whole and is opposite to 'Private Administration', this word 'public' means 'Government Administration in getting things done', or is concerned with the 'What' and the 'How' of Government. The 'what' is the subject-matter, the technical knowledge of a field, which enables the administrator to perform his duties regarding his extension or any programme. The 'how' is the technique management, the principles according to which the programmes are carried on successfuly. So both are necessary for administration of the programmes.

According to Luther Gullick, "Public Administration is that part of the science of administration which has to do with Government, and thus concerns itself primarily with the executive branch where the work of Government is done, though there are obviously problems also in connection with Legislative and the Judicial branches.

According to L.D. White "Public Administration consists of all those operations having for their purpose the fulfilment or enforcement of public policy as declared by competent authority." Simon, says that Public Administration in common usage, is the activities of the executive branches of the National, State or Local Government.

According to Pfiffner and Presthus, "Public Administration consists of getting the work of Government done by coordinating the efforts of people so that they can work together to accomplish their set tasks. Administration embraces activities which may be highly technical or specialised such as public health and building of bridges. It also involves managing, directing and supervising the activities of workers so that some order or efficiency may result from their efforts.

PUBLIC AND PRIVATE ADMINISTRATION

(1) *Points of similarity:* (a) Many of the skills like clerical, accounting, statistical and managerial required in both are the same. Many times, there is an interchange of personnel between the two. Some retired Government servants are employed by some industrial concerns or some Secretaries or Deputy Secretaries from Government are appointed administrators of the industries like Heavy Electricals, Bhopal, Bhilai Projects, etc. (b) During the past few years, business practices and standards have increasingly influenced the methods of public administration, specially in matters like office management and conduct of the economic and industrial undertakings. The idea of Government Corporations is to import management. (c) Business and Industrial Adminisration has been remarkably creative in the efforts to adjust itself to the changing conditions of our times and public administration cannot ignore the results of its experiments with newer techniques of management.

(2) *Points of dissimilarity:* (a) Public administration is bureaucratic and private administration is business-like. (b) Public administration is political while private administration is non-political. (c) Public administration is characterised by red-tape while private administration is free from it. (d) In conformity with rules and precedents, public administration must be uniform in its application to individuals and classes and must not show preference for, or discrimination against them. If it is there, the discontent and severe criticism follows. In business, they do not bother for uniformity and give favoured treatment to particular categories of their customers without incurring blame. (e) In public administration, finance is in the hands of the legislature while in private administration finance is in the hands of few individuals. (f) Profit motive is the ruling motive of business while it is absent in public administration. (g) Public administration is more closely regulated by law and rules than private administration. In public administration, if an administrator acts in excess of powers legally conferred on him, his action is liable to be challenged before the courts and declared void. (h) The codes of ethics for public and private administration are different, e.g. advertisement of Government Services is not done just like a businessman can do. Government propaganda is looked upon with suspicion and hostility by the public. (i) People in Government Service feel it is more wrong or dangerous to oppose the Government than those in business concerns.

Nature of public administration

Under it we discuss whether public administration is a science or not. Before doing this, we have to know what is science. Exactness and predictability are regarded as the two indispensable characteristics of science and the principle physical sciences seem to possess these characteristics. The scientific character of any study depends upon its methodology, rather than the exactness or certainty to which it can attain. Any subject to which we can apply a scientific method can be called a science. Public administration is a science just like any Social Science. The difference between a social science and physical science is only one of degree rather than of kind. For example, if we study the behaviour of human beings and generalise our findings, these generalisations may not have a cent per cent validity like a formula or the theorems of physical sciences, but the generalisations are useful as probabilities.

In public administration, we are concerned with two things: (a) with the under-standing of how people in an organisation behave, and (b) with practical recommen-dations as to how best to run an administration. With our increasing understanding through research data on administration, we can develop material how our extension administrators can be effective. If administrative decisions are fully recorded, like judicial decisions, with a statement of the circumstances and reasons that led to them, they can become valuable precepts for administrative action, just as judicial precedents are for administration of justice. So, if we collect data on various ways of motivating the subordinate workers of an administrator, ways of better supervision, coordination, etc., in any branch of development work and our approach is scientific and methodological, our field becomes science. So public administration, when based on such findings is a Social Science.

Characteristics of public administration as a social science

(1) Public administration is primarily a science of observation rather than of experiment. It is true with all social sciences, because one cannot conduct laboratory-type experiments in the social sciences and cannot produce artificial conditions for testing. In a certain sense, every new policy applied is a social experiment, results of which can be watched, but here it is not possible to isolate these results from opera-tion of the numerous disturbing factors and to establish unmistakable causal relations, e.g., the operation of a law forbidding child marriages (Sharda Act), may be followed by a reduced infant mortality rate, but we cannot definitely say that the latter is the effect of the former because a number of other causes like increased medical aid, better nutrition, etc., may be simultaneously working.

(2) Like many other social sciences, public administration is a positive and normative science. It is concerned with: What is? and also what should be? We want good administration for a certain end—this end may be an effective extension programme and thus it makes it a normative science. There should be coordinated approach for effective extension work. So what it means is—the slackness, lack of enthusiasm, red-tapism, lack of morale, lack of training, etc., in the extension workers; What should be—morale among the subordinates, informal approach, zeal, missionary work, interest, technical knowledge, etc.—For what?—effectiveness in the extension programme.

(3) Public administration is a progressive science where the generalisations or principles require constant revision retesting and relating the new discoveries. They are never final.

Therefore it is a social science.

Purposes of public administration

The functions of administrative authorities include: Executive, Legislative and Judicial. They have various methods appropriate to different types of functions. For these functions, the activities are divided into various departments or sections. Run-ning these departments involves various functions. These functions have behind them the purposes of the administration. The purpose may be community development through extension education, or law and order, controlling the finance, adminis-tration of transport, industries, etc. The principal categories of administration may be: (1) Planning, (2) Organisation, (3) Command, (4) Coordination, and (5) Control.

Whenever a purpose has to be accomplished, the first step is to collect data, through enquiry or research, regarding the problem we want to solve so that we may define the exact objective and then find out the possible means for realising it. The forecast of these leads to a definite plan for the future action. This plan requires the necessary organisation (of men and material) the object of which is coordination, i.e., producing team work geared to the objective. Coordination leads to coherent command which finally keeps issues in control. These give rise to the understanding of scope of public administration which will be discussed below.

Scope of public administration

The scope of administration consists of the study of three factors namely—men, material and methods.

(1) *Principle has its process and effect:* (1) Investigation (enquiry into facts of what has to be done), (2) Forecasting of the future activity in the light of the investigation and, (3) Planning, i.e., knitting the forecasts together into a well-articulated plan.

(2) *Forecasting has its principle in:* (1) Appropriateness, i.e., to see that the human and material organisation are suitable for the object in hand, (2) Organisation, that is, forecasting the process of oganisation.

(3) *Planning has its principle in:* (1) Order, that is, ensuring material and human order, (2) Command, that is, planning in process, and (3) Central, this is the effect of command.

Willoughby divided the principles of public administration into five major sections: (1) General or overhead administration (including allocation of functions, directions, supervision and control), (2) Organisation, i.e., building up of administrative structure, (3) Personnel, management, material and supply, and (5) Finance.

Posdcorb view: Luther Gullick denoted the fuctional elements by the letters 'POSDCORB' wherein:

P. stands for Planning, i.e., working out in broad outline the things to be done and the methods to be adopted for accomplishing the purpose in hand;

O. stands for Organisation, i.e., building up the structure of authority through which the entire work to be done is arranged into well-defined sub-divisions and coordination;

S. stands for Staffing, i.e., appointing suitable persons to the various posts under the organisation, and the whole of personnel management;

D. stands for Directing, i.e., making decision, and issuing orders and instructions embodying them for the guidance of the staff;

Co. stands for Coordination, i.e., interrelating the various parts of the work and eliminating overlapping of the conflict;

R. stands for Reporting, i.e., keeping both the superiors and subordinates informed of what is going on, and arranging for collection of such information through inspection, research and records.

B. stands for Budgeting, i.e., financial administration.

Subject-matter view: Besides, the common housekeeping activities, or tools or administration, covered by the Posdcorb view, there are various line of functions produced for people like law and order, education, public health, agriculture, public works, social security, justice, defence, etc. Some of these can be grouped under programmes like community development. These programmes, or services, have important and specialised techniques of their own. They are not covered by the POSDCORB activities. In public administration, there are various ways of detecting crime, prevention of breaches of peace, control of goondas, but in community development or extension work the techniques have to be different. Organisation in the Military Services has to be different than that of education.

So both views have to be combined to describe the scope of public administration. Just as the human body has both an anatomy and a psychology of its own, so also administration has common techniques of POSDCORB as its skeleton and the specialised methods of various programmes has its muscles and sinews. Without either of them it cannot function like a body.

Functions of public administration

Applied administration has to be studied country-wise, department or function-wise, Government level-wise, historically and internationally. The main functions of public administration may be: (1) Political, including Executive-Legislative relation-ship; Politics—administrative activities of the Cabinet or Ministry; the Ministry—permanent official relationship. (2) Legislative—not merely Delegated Legislation, but the preparatory work done by the administrative officials and departments in connection with the drawing up of a Bill to be introduced in the Legislature and its passage through that body. (3) Financial—preparation of the budget; its execution, accounting, auditing, treasury management, etc. (4) Defensive—covering military administration. (5) Educational. (6) Social administration. (7) Economic adminis-tration—activities relating to the protection and encouragement of industries and agriculture; securing a prosperous and stable economy, encouragement and promotion of Foreign Trade and Commerce; running of public utilities and enterprises by Government. (8) Foreign administration—conducting foreign affairs, diplomacy, international cooperation, administration of international agencies. (9) Local admi-nistration—activities of local bodies.

CHAPTER 44

ADMINISTRATION AND ORGANISATION

Administration generally involves cooperative effort by the people who form part of the organisation, to achieve the purpose or goal of the organisation. This requires a plan of action and this is called organisation. Organisation comes prior to all administration.

MEANING OF ORGANISATION

The term, organisation is used in three different situations: (1) The act of designing the administrative structure; (2) Building the structure, i.e., appointing suitable personnel to it; and (3) The resulting administrative structure itself.

According to Luther Gullick, 'Organisation is the formal structure of authority through which work sub-divisions are arranged, defined and coordinated for the defined objective."[1]

According to J. William Schulze, "An organisation is a combination of the necessary human beings, materials, tools, equipment, working space and apparatus brought together in systematic and effective coordination to accomplish some desired object."[2]

According to Milward, "Organisation by itself does nothing, it is the staff making up the organisation who do the work."[3]

Origination of organisations[4]

Organisations are for the attainment of some purpose. Some people feel that a new organisation is needed for getting something important done and they set about the task of establishing it. Of course, every new need or task does not necessarily result in the establishment of a new organisation. In public administration, when some new work has to be done, it has usually to be seen whether it can be assigned to one of the existing departments or units. If the task is too big, a new department is created. As new departments, according to the social change or progress or emergency, keep on arising, many old departments occasionally disappear. Some organi-

[1]Luther Gullick, "Notes on the Theory of Organisation," *Papers of Sc. of Adm.*, p. 13.
[2]J. William Schulze, *Bulletin of Taylor Society*, June 1919, Vol. 4. p. 22.
[3]Milward, *Approach to Management*, p. 30.
[4]M. P. Sharma, *Public Administration in Theory and Practice*, p. 82 (Adapted).

sations which are created for work of a temporary nature, are usually closed down, e.g., Food Procurement Department of 1940's in U. P. was closed, because of decontrol. Similarly, a Rehabilitation Department may be closed when there is no problem of rehabilitation of refugees.

CONCEPT OF ORGANISATION

There are two concepts or approaches of organisation—mechanistic and humanistic.

Mechanistic: According to it, organisation is regarded as a machine constructed and operated so as to express and apply a central controlling will. The staff is regarded as the parts of the machine. The formal design may be drawn up by the experts according to certain well-understood principles, like the plan for a building prepared by an architect, according to the principles of mechanical science. After the plan is ready, the staff is appointed. It is based on two assumptions: (a) The basic principles and patterns of organisation are so well-known, that it is possible for experts to draw up a plan to suit the requirements of the purpose. (b) The staff has to be suited to the requirements of the plan rather than *vice-versa*.

Humanistic: In about 90 per cent cases it is not possible to start with a clean slate as a requirement of the mechanistic concept. The organiser cannot get the human material according to the need. He cannot change the men to suit the jobs. The best possible use of the human material is to be made. For changing the attitudes, training has to be devised and modified. We have to adapt the organisation to the requirements of the case and put men on proper jobs. This human element is felt not only in the drawing up of the organising pattern, or constructing according to it, but also in its day-to-day working, once it is established.

Formal and informal organisations

A formal organisation is deliberately planned, designed and duly sanctioned by a competent authority. There may be a chart of the organisational set-up or a manual for the departmental working, roles, responsibilities, duties, etc., like fundamental rules, financial code, manual for different departments, statutes of agricultural universities, blue prints of organisations, etc.

In some cases, even in the formal organisation, there may be dominant personalities, or influential connections of the subordinate with higher authorities which may twist the complex of formal relationships of the organisation. A domineering head may work in such a way that he may reduce his subordinates by centralising all powers of sanction and control. Thus, the concept of organisation highlights the influence of personalities on organisation. Sometimes, the formal organisation has actually to be modified or expanded in order to accommodate a person whose services are considered extraordinarily valuable. Informal organisation may have some of the above elements with all kinds of flexibility.

Units of organisation

In administration, the term unit is used to indicate not only the smallest subdivision of organisation but also the highest and larger formations, such as the section, the division, the branch, the bureau, and even the department. The units may differ from one another in two respects: (1) in kind or quality, and (2) in size or comprehensiveness. Difference of kind among units arises from differences of function or organisational relationships, and those of size from the higher or lower position in the organisational hierarchy (Fig. 44.1).

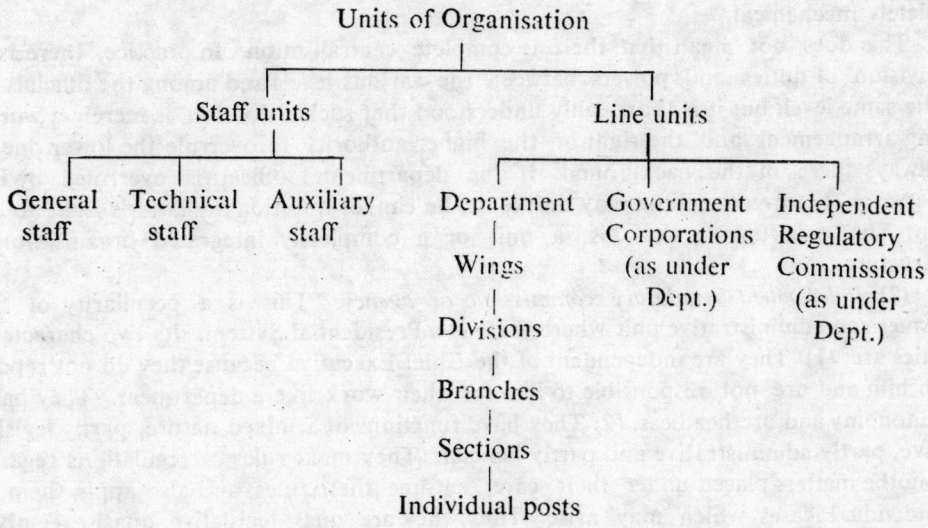

Fig. 44.1 Units of organisation.

Line and staff

The line units are executive, i.e., concerned with the operating or producing of the various services which the administration has to provide for the people. The staff units are those that advise or assist the line units in the performance of their work. Line units command while staff units only advise and help through planning, research, coordination, supervision, etc. Each of the Ministries at the Central Government level in India like Health, Education, Defence, Home, Agriculture, Community Development and Cooperation, etc., is a line unit, or a combination of serveral line units. Besides these ministries, there are also bodies like the Cabinet Secretariat, the Prime Minister's Secretariat, the Planning Commission, etc., which are staff agencies, because their primary duty is not to administer some service or department, but to advise and assist the Cabinet, the Prime Minister and the line department in various ways.

Varieties of line units

As shown in the chart above, there are three varieties of line units—the Department, the Government Corporation and the independent Regulatory Commissions. These arise not from functional but from structural and relational differences among line units, and are qualitative distinctions.

(1) *The department:* It is the first and the largest sub-division of the administrative structure. It is one step below the Chief Executive—the Cabinet in parliamentary countries, or the President in presidential. Its chief characteristic is its complete subordination to the Chief Executive. Under it the line of authority runs unbroken,

link by link from the chief executive at the top to the lowest employee at the bottom. Neither the department nor any of its sub-units or officers can claim any degree of autonomy or authority in their own right. Whatever authority belongs to them, comes from the Chief Executive through delegation. This absoluteness and continuty of control from top to bottom facilities the maximum of unification and it is completely mechanical.

This does not mean that there is complete centralisation. In practice, there is a division of duties and powers between the various levels and among the officials at the same level, but it is thoroughly understood that such a division is merely a working arrangement and the right of the higher authority to overrule the lower one is always there in the background. If the departmental officer is overruled by his superior, however much he may dislike it, he cannot question the latter's right to do so. The department, thus, is a unit of a completely integrated organisational structure.

(2) *Independent regulatory commission or agency:* This is a peculiarity of the American administrative unit where there is a Presidential System. Its two characteristics are: (1) They are independent of the Chief Executive because they do not report to him and are not responsible to him for their work like a department. They have autonomy and are headless. (2) They have functions of a mixed nature, partly legislative, partly administrative and partly judicial. They make rules or regulations regarding the matters placed under their care, enforce these rules, and also apply them to individual cases which may arise. Thus, they are quasi-legislative, quasi-executive, and quasi-judicial bodies. Their work is to regulate and control the property and activities of the private citizens in order to safeguard the social interests. There are nine Regulatory Commissions in the USA like the Inter-State Commerce Commission; Board of the Governors of the Federal Reserve System; The Federal Trade Commission; The Federal Communication Commission; The Federal Power Commission, The Securities and Exchange Commission; The National Labour Relations Board; etc. This was done in the USA because executive power is vested in a single functionary, the President, who is not responsible to the Legislature. There may be fear that if new functions are entrusted to the President, he may become too powerful which may be dangerous to democracy.

In parliamentary countries like India, where the Executive (the Cabinet) is not a single person, but is plural and is responsible to the Legislature, there is no fear of Executive Absolutism, thus no necessity has been felt for such commissions. Of course, the higher courts, universities, local bodies, professional bodies like the Medical and Bar Councils, etc., are there but there is a vast difference between these and the American Regulatory Commissions.

(3) *Government corporation:* To give more freedom and to make some branches less subject to rigid rules in matters of personnel and financial management this has brought a new approach where government enterprises have been thought to run efficiently. These differ from departments in two points: (1) They have a certain amount of autonomy in their internal management, of course, this autonomy is not so complete as in the case of Regulatory Commissions. This is because the corporations are placed under some department to which they are responsible. (2) Corporations are free to hire and fire personnel as they think best. They have considerable

budgetary and financial freedom and often have their own independent funds or means of revenue. Their accounts are subject to commercial audit and not Governmental audit. In India, the first government corporation was the Reserve Bank of India established in 1935, now there are The Damodar Valley Corporation, The Industrial Finance Corporation, Airlines Corporation, Life Insurance Corporation, Municipal Corporation, etc.

Sub-divisions of the department: The department is sub-divided into smaller units at several levels. In India the immediate sub-divisions of the department are called divisions. Some of the larger department are divided first into wings and then each wing sub-divided into divisions. The divisions are split up into branches, the branches into sections and sections into individual posts. In the USA, the first division of the department is bureau, bureaus are divided into divisions and divisions into sections. In India, we have Press Information Bureau under the Ministry of Information and Broadcasting, Plant Protection Bureau under the Ministry of Food and Agriculture. Intelligence Bureau under the Home Ministry. In U.P., they have an Information Bureau under the Department of Agriculture.

The individual post or position is the smallest unit of an organisation. An organisation is a pattern of interrelated posts. The actual work of administration is done by the incumbents of the serveal posts, high or low, which constitute it. The post comes into existence and the duties and responsibilities of the incumbents are attached to it. A post may lie vacant. Absence of an incumbent does not terminate it.

The hierarchy

Meaning

Hierarchy is the rule of control of the higher over the lower. It is a graded organisation of several successive steps or levels, in which each of the lower levels is immediately subordinate to the next higher one, and through it to the higher steps right up to the top. In such organisation authority, command and control descend from the top downwards, step by step, to the bottom. Just as ascending up or descending down a ladder, the foot must be placed on the step immediately above or below and no intermediate step can be jumped over without the danger of stumbling or falling, in administrative hierarchy the role of "Through the Proper Channel" is supreme. All communications to an employee or officer must come through his immediate superior or subordinate, according to their direction upward or downward.

The scalar principle or process

The hierarchical principle is called the scalar principle or process. The word 'scalar' is derived from 'scale' which means ladder with several steps.

Advantages: (1) It is an instrument of organisational integration and coherence. It is like mortar or cement to the building. (2) Scalar chain serves as a channel of communication upwards and downwards. (3) As the communication is through the proper channel, so everyone knows about the action proposed or taken at various levels. (4) Matters of less importance are decided at lower levels which prevent congestion in the flow of business. (5) It helps to clarify and define the relative position and responsibilities of each post in the organisation.

Disadvantages: (1) Delay in the disposal of work.

Here A is the head of the organisation. B is A's immediate subordinate, C is B's immediate subordinate to A through B. D is immediately subordinate to C, but immediately also to B and A. In the same way A's immediate subordination is through D to C and B to A. Finally, F is immediately under E, but immediately also under EDCB and A. If A issues an order affecting F, it must descend to F through B, C, D and E. Similarly, if F addresses a communication to A, it must travel up the line to A through EDC and B. The second arm of the Department is GHIJK. If F of one branch, e.g., Agriculture wants to communicate with K in the other branch, e.g., Animal Husbandry, in Agriculture and Animal Husbandry Department of M.P. State, he will move up through EDCB to A and then descend through GHIJ to K.

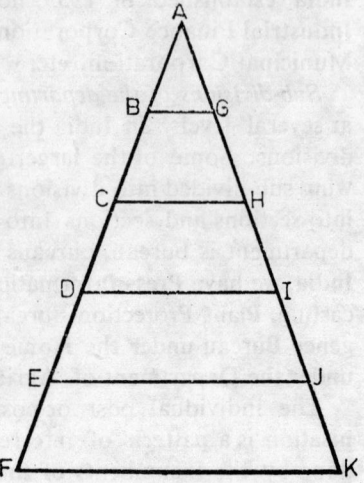

Fig. **44.2** The scalar principle.

In actual practice, however, short-cuts are found out without violating the essential principle of hierarchy. There are two ways: (1) if the immediate superiors say E and J over F and K in two branches agree to such an arrangement, but F and K should keep their bosses informed. (2) A may deal direct with C, if C or A himself keep B informed of what transpires and C enjoys the confidence of A.

Span of control

By span of control, we mean the number of subordinates an officer can effectively supervise. There is a limit to the span of control of every officer. This span of control is related to the psychological problem of 'span of attention'. No one can attend to more than a certain number of things at the same time. The number to which one person can so attend is his 'span of attention'. Span of control is the span of attention applied to the work of supervision and control of subordinates. The span of control varies with: function, personality, time and space. Function means the type of work to be supervised; personality means competence of the superiors and the subordinates; time means the age of the organisation concerned, i.e., how old the organisation is, in set organisations more work can be supervised; space implies the jurisdiction, or the area, to be supervised. If the area is too wide as in M.P. it is difficult to reach interior places, so often. The second point which affects the span is that the individuals are concerned with numerous permutations and combinations of their mutual relationships.

Delegation of authority

Meaning: Delegation is the conferring of specified authority by a higher authority. It is devotion of authority by a person to his agent or subordinate, subject to his right of supervision and control. *De jure* the delegated authority still belongs to the principle, but its *De facto* exercise is allowed to the subordinate.

Delegation is the essence of the scalar principle. The problem of the head of an organisation is to make authority in necessary measure available to his subordinates, without parting with it finally. Delegation enables the head to effect a division of labour and transfer of powers and duties to his assistants, without losing the ultimate power of revision, supervision and control himself. Delegation involves dual responsibility, i.e., (a) that of the subordinates to do the job, and (b) that of the delegating superior to get the job done.

Need for delegation: Delegation is required because of two reasons: (1) the head cannot exercise all the powers legally vested in him, (2) without delegation, the subordinates would not be able to do their work, for responsibility for doing a thing implies the authority or the power to do it.

Types of delegation: (1) There may be full delegation or partial delegation. Full, means complete conferment of the boss's powers on the subordinate.

(2) Conditional or unconditional. Unconditional delegation is free from reservation, while conditional is subject to the boss's right to confirm or revise the action by the subordinate.

(3) Formal or informal. When it is not formally written it is informal delegation, otherwise it is written and called formal.

(4) Downward, upward and outward. When the superior officer delegates to a subordinate it is downward. Delegation upward occurs where the delegator delegates authority over himself to a representative, e.g., delegation of authority by the electorate to a President to rule over it. Delegation outward means delegation to some outside organisation. In Agricultural Universities, there is a selection body from outside, or in Bhoodan, Vinoba Bhave has appointed *ad hoc* committees for distribution of land.

(5) Direct (immediate) or indirect (mediate): In direct delegation, no third person or intermediary intervenes between the two parties to the delegation. In case of indirect delegation, delegation is made through some third person or intermediate link. This is so in the Vatican, in the election of the Pope in which the Council of Cardinals intervenes between the Congregation and the Pope.

Power and authority: Power is the ability or competence to do something. Authority is the right to require or order action by others. An employee at the bottom of the organisation with no subordinates under him has, therefore, no authority, but he has the power to perform his own duties.

Limits of delegation: A superior officer is not allowed to delegate all his authority otherwise he will be superfluous. So the limits are:[1]

(1) Supervision of the work of the first line, or immediate subordinates.

(2) General financial supervision and the power to sanction expenditure above a specified amount.

(3) Power to sanction new policies and plans, and departures from established policy or precedents.

(4) Rule-making power where it is vested in the delegating officer.

(5) Making of the specified higher appointments.

(6) Hearing of appeals from the decisions of at least the immediate subordinates.

[1]M.P. Sharma, *Public Administration in Theory and Practice*, 1963, p. 155.

Integration vs. disintegration

In administration this term, integration, means connecting one or more of hitherto independent organisations with the rest of the organised structure of the country, by placing them under the Chief Executive directly, or through some department or other agency under the control of the Chief Executive. Integration involves the abolition of the independent status of agencies, like the independent Regulatory Commissions, or administrative bodies, or officials directly elected by and responsible to the people.

The integrated system: It is one in which all parts are connected together through a common ultimate subordination to the Chief Executive. In such a system, the line of authority runs unbroken from the Chief Executive through various levels to all the parts of the system, so that there are no loose ends.

A disintegrated system: It has got a number of loose ends in the shape of independent establishments or directly elected officials, at which or before whom the line of authority from the chief authority stops short and is broken.

No country has a completely integrated administrative system. *In India, the Government system is largely an integrated one:* There are three Government levels— Union or Central, State and Local. The latter two are independent of the former and of each other, to a substantial extent, though not wholly. At the Union level, the administrative structure is divided into a number of ministries or departments everyone of which is under the control of the Union Cabinet (or technically the President) which is our Chief Executive. Of course, there are certain agencies and officials like the Union Public Service Commission, the Government Corporations, the Comptroller and Auditor-General who are independent of the Cabinet, in respect of their tenure but they are not independent of the Executive altogether, in the sense in which the American Regulatory Commissions are. They have to abide by the rules and policies issued by the Union Government and make reports to it. Their members are appointed, and subject to necessary safeguards, are removable (except the Comptroller and Auditor-General) by the Union Government. The same is true at State and local levels.

Britain and countries of continental Europe also have an integrated system of administration. The American system is largely a disintegrated one: They have at least five different kinds of independent establishments, namely: (1) the Regulatory Commissions, (2) the Government Corporations, (3) Professional Service Agencies, e.g., those concerned with education or social work, (4) at the State Level, an elected official such as Treasurer and the Attorney-General, and (5) the Auditors. At the Federal Level in the USA, the authority of the President stops short of the nine great Regulatory Commissions. There are also many agencies like the Tennesee Valley Authority which are largely autonomous. At the State Level, there are numerous Boards, Commissions and directly elected officials owing no responsibility or subordination to the State Governor. At the local level, the city departments are often headed by persons or boards directly elected by people. In the counties, the County Board consists of officials elected without any Head Executive over them.

An integrated system facilitates coordination and without coordination there can be no sound public management. The opponents of this system say that there is the possibility of dictatorship by the President, if a large increase were made in his powers, by placing the independent establishments under him. This would be imperil democracy and individual liberty. But in India, there should not be any fear of it. Since we have a parliamentary type of Government and there are autonomous institutions like Universities, Public Service Commissions and certain professionl bodies.

Centralisation vs. decentralisation

Centralised system

In a centralised system, most of the power of decision is vested in the top level or levels so that the lower ones have to refer most problems to the head of the organisation or his immediate subordinates for decision.

Decentralised system

In this system, the lower levels are allowed the discretion to decide most of the matters which come up reserving a comparatively few bigger and more important problems only for those higher up. Decentralisation has two administrative, one political, one geographical and one functional aspects, namely:

Administrative: (1) Delegation of authority in such a way that large areas of discretion are entrusted to subordinate officers and comparatively few questions are referred to the chief at the apex.

(2) Broad grant of power to individual component parts of the organisation and retention of only certain essential powers of control in the head of office.

(3) Political. Much power in the hands of elective bodies and considerable popular participation in administration.

(4) Geographical. Freedom to the field units or agencies away from headquarters and near to the people.

(5) Functional. Functional autonomy to the various departments in respect of their several functions.[1]

Thus, the issue of centralisation vs. decentralisation arises between the superior and subordinate officers within an organisation, between the head office and the component parts of the organisation, between the official and non-official elements, between the headquarters and the field offices, and between the Chief Executive and the functional departments or agencies.[2]

The difference between the two is of degree rather than of kind, because no organisation can be completely centralised or decentralised. The issue of centralisation or decentralisation relates to the point where the balance between the two should be struck. According to White, vesting of much authority in the hands of elected local bodies makes the admintstrative system decentralised, while vesting much authority in the hands of the officials of the central government makes it centralised.

(a) *Territorial decentralisation:* It arises when the field agencies and officials of the Government, scattered all over the country, are allowed to decide most of the problems on the spot, or when local bodies are given large powers to cater to the needs of their local population.

(b) *Functional decentralisation:* It is leaving powers of decision in respect of tech-

[1]Mark, *Elements of Public Administration*, pp. 149-150.
[2]M.P. Sharma, *Public Administration in Theory and Practice*, pp. 120.

nical or professional matters largely to the appropriate technical or professional units of the organisation; educational questions to the universities or board of education; agricultural questions to the agriculture departments of agricultural universities.

Factors responsible for centralisation and decentralisation: These are:

(1) *Responsibility.* The factor of responsibility acts as a deterrent to decentralisation and favours centralisation. Because, the head of any organisation is held ultimately responsible for everything within his organisation, he is naturally unwilling to decentralise and wants to keep important matters in his own hands.

(2) *Administrative:* Administrative factors may be: (a) Age of agency. In an old agency procedure and precedents become more crystalised than in the newer organisations, so it is easier to decentralise; (b) Stability of policy facilitates decentralisation; (c) Competence of the field personnel helps in decentralisation.

(3) *Functional:* If a department has many functions, and all of a technical nature, it is bound to decentralise, because the head of the organisation will not have the time or necessary technical competence to manage all of these directly.

(4) *External factors:* If popular or local support for a programme is desired, e.g., in the Community Development Programme, decentralisation is necessary because without local support, the Village Development Programme will not be a people's programme.

Favourable points for centralisation: These points are:

(1) Swift means of communication have made centralisation possible.

(2) In a centralised administration it is possible to keep experienced and efficient personnel and it becomes economical.

(3) Under modern conditions, jurisdictions smaller than the central government are found to be financially inadequate. The State and local administration has always to depend on central grants-in-aid.

(4) The needs for modern defence and economic planning helps in centralisation.

(5) The desire to emphasise urgency, or importance, of a particular activity by placing it under the charge of central government; the need for uniformity, the attempts of overheads units to gather more and more power, favour centralisation.

Points against centralisation: These points are:

(1) It results in the congestion of business at the higher level of the administrative ladder creates bottlenecks and causes delays in the making of decisions and putting them into effect.

(2) The central authorities, far removed from the people, cannot have adequate knowledge of local conditions and problems which vary from place to place.

(3) It reduces the opportunities for popular initiative and participation in administration and thus tends to weaken democracy.

(4) If proper care can be taken in a decentralised system, than centralisation is not economical.

So neither centralisation nor decentralisation can be accepted as an absolute principle of good organisation. It can be said that while policy-making should be centralised, its administration should be decentralised. Field authorities instead of referring matters for decision to the central authority should have the power of decision themselves, but the central authority should post-audit these decisions to test their conformity to the policy and standards laid down by it.

COORDINATION

Meaning: Its aim is to secure cooperation and team work among the employees engaged in the work of the organisation. Negatively, it is the removal of conflicts, working at cross-purposes, and overlapping in administration. Coordination is the first principle of organisation and includes within itself all other principles which are subordinate to it and through which it operates.

Need of coordination: This is required because the members of any large organisation, when left to themselves, have a tendency to drift away in different directions, thus giving rise to conflicts. The causes of conflicts may be:

(1) Due to ignorance of one another's activities which may result in duplication of work.

(2) There is a tendency among workers in charge of different functions to attach so much importance to their own work as to be unmindful of the needs of others, and thus make encroachments on the latter's sphere. They refuse to see their particular charge as the part of a larger whole to which it must be duly subordinate.

(3) Greed for power and importance, which the heads of some organisations have.

Achieving coordination: Coordination may be achieved in two ways: (1) automatically or, by (2) deliberate process. The mechanism of coordination by the automatic way requires that one individual, the highest authority is made responsible for knowing all the activities and happenings in the organisation, and for relating them into a coherent whole. This is possible in a small organisation, but it is not possible in large-scale organisation because there is a limit to the individual's span of attention and control. In large organisations, coordination has, therefore, to be deliberately planned and achieved. Coordination is a continuing problem which has no final or once and for all solution.

Techniques of deliberate coordination: It can be achieved in two ways: (a) Coercive or compulsory coordination, and (b) Voluntary coordination.

(a) *Coercive or compulsory coordination:* It is achieved through the mechanism of the organisational hierarchy. If there is conflict between two sections of the same department, it is referred to a common official supervisor and his decision has to be accepted by the disputing units lower down. This creates unpleasantness in one of the two quarters. In issuing such orders one has to secure the greatest possible amount of agreement of those to whom the orders apply. If this is not done, the orders will be unworkable.

(b) *Voluntary coordination:* The bulk of coordination in any organisation is secured voluntarily, by mutual agreement and adjustment. The following techniques and methods can be used:

(1) By reference, consultation and clearance with all concerned so that no conflict or duplication may arise. Every proposal or policy which is likely to affect other departments must be circulated to them, to obtain their agreement before being sent higher up for a decision. Questions involving financial aspects must be cleared with the Finance Department. Besides, the lateral or horizontal reference and clearance between departments or sub-units of the same departments,there is also vertical reference and clearance upwards and downwards within the organisational hierarchy. So 'Through Proper Channel', action is necessary.

This action involves delay and this is one of the causes why wheels of Public Administration, says Dr. Sharma, do not move as quickly as they should. Such delay is, however, the price which has to be paid for securing unity of action. This delay can be greatly reduced though, of course, not altogether eliminated by circulation of numerous copies of the letter in place of moving the one file from office to office, and also through oral consultations over the telephone, personal meetings, direct lateral contacts in place of 'through proper channel'.

(2) Conferences. Inter-department or intra-departmental, including even the non-officials, are useful if the issue has a number of parties to be consulted; the matter for discussion is an issue of policy requiring the cooperation of many agencies; or, some new policy or proposal to be explained. The agenda of such conferences needs to be carefully planned so that there may be discussion on certain proposals or solutions. Freedom of discussion and putting forward of suggestions is essential, particulary in inter-departmental conferences where higher officers and their subordinates meet around a table.

(3) Organisational devices. Coordination may be secured by appointing inter-departmental committees, coordination officers, planning committies and Boards. These bodies are outside the organisational hierarchy, though they are attached to it. They secure coordination not through reference to a common superior, but through consulation and exchange of ideas, and thus reprsent the technique of consulative rather than authoritarian coordination. Organisational devices are better where the need for consultation and discussion among many agencies is of a standing and continuous nature. An inter-departmental committee is useful if two or more departments have overlapping spheres of activity. Single Coordination Officers are better for coordination of field activities in the region. Planning Committee or Committees secure coordination through a central plan or programme, which is prepared in close collaboration with the agencies which have to implement it. Such devices are better for organisation of policy and planning and not in routine work. Because they are costly and dilatory, they should be sparingly used.

(4) Standardisation of procedures and methods. It facilitates comparison and measurement of results. Common budget and accounting procedures and procurement of supplies procedures help in checking confusion, misappropriation and wastefulness. It ensures that every worker in the organisation will act in the same way under similar circumstance.

(5) Decentralisation of activities. Each functional unit may be made independent and the central authority nothing more than a kind of holding company. In business enterprises, with varied and complicated activities, this method is possible. Because the whole purpose and outlook of the Government differ from that of a business organisation, the Government Central Cabinet does not want to reduce itself to the position of the Holding Company. This is because:

(a) In Government, there is only one Board of Directors, i.e., the Legislature, to which responsibility is owned;
(b) The inter-relations between the departments are many;
(c) In matters like finance and personnel, the government has to maintain a uniform standard;

(d) In Government, there is no simple yardstick like profit to judge the success in operating departments and thorough supervision is necessary.

(6) Coordination by means of ideas and leadership. Where the central purpose of the organisation is known, understood and considered to be worthwhile by the workers, it binds them together as a coherent group and unifies their separate efforts into common endeavour to realise the goal. Stimulating leadership can create enthusiasm among the workers for the common cause, and spur them to overcome difficulties.

Machinery for coordination: Effective coordination can be secured if there is either a single individual (like the President) or a small group (Cabinet or Committee) entrusted with the duty. A group coordination body is preferable, when the work is extension and large questions of policy viewed from many angles have to be dealt with. Whatever the machinery, with clear directions and rules of procedure issued from time to time, the parties to be coordinated can play a large part in securing coordination. Adequate communication produces coordination automatically.

Coordination requires constant watchfulness on the part of those entrusted with it, and it is a continuous function of the administrator.

Important aspects of coordination: The aspects of coordination are:

(1) *Communication:* The initial task in coordinating the programme of rural development is that of establishing clear channels of communication among agencies. Communication is an important factor in linking one agency with another, when there is an objective common to all. It should be recognised that communication is a two-way process built upon the principle of mutual dependence.

(2) *Role system:* The second aspect is the need for making the role system clear. The rights and duties assigned to any agency occupying a certain position in the social system should be clearly defined. Coordination develops when the role of one agency is made clear and is understood by other agencies with complementary roles. This is a fundamental factor in coordinating different patterns of agency behaviour. Deviation in the role behaviour of one agency contributes to confusion in the entire social system.

(3) *Ends and objectives of related programmes:* Community development programmes have been established in many countries as a means of channeling the work of various technical agencies or departments into a unified effort in rural development. As stated in the *Community Development Handbook.*

"Success in keeping the programme going well depends on how far community development work is geared to the overall development programme, both in the planning stage and in the field. . . . The aim should be to build up an integrated team approach, with field staff, including officers and community development workers, operating in a partnership which should join hands with local leaders and local organisations."[1]

This is an important aspect and it also helps to avoid overlapping of programmes and functions.

Another important task of community development is to make its ends and objectives clear to all related agencies. The specific duties to be performed should be

---

[1] G.W. Green, *Sociology*, Cornell University USA, September 1960 (Mimeo), pp. 1.

made known and understood by all agencies and departments. Means should be provided for each agency to meet together for the purpose of knowing and understanding what is expected of each of them so that they will be in a better position to help and support each other. The procedure will strengthen communication and help to avoid some of the problems incurred because of a lack of coordination. In countries, where community development is newly established, both the Government and staff in charge should try to emphasise the importance so as to give it status with the agencies with which it has to work. This would assist in securing coordination generally and specially across the levels within related agencies.

(4) *Orientation of personnel*: Since community development must obviously carry the major responsibility of the programme and coordination, it should see that agencies and departments on whom it must depend are oriented as to its importance, objectives and programme. Coordination should not be considered as a matter of theory but of reality. Depending upon the specific circumstances and situation, orientation may be done in the following ways: (1) seminars, (2) conferences, (3) lectures and talks, (4) mass media, (5) audio-visual aids, (6) demonstration, and (7) socio-drama.

ADMINISTRATIVE CONTROL

Interpreting and transmitting policy: The community development agency should see that the policy formulated at the highest level of Government is transmitted to all levels in the sub-system, and that there is no by-passing of its directives. Similarly, it should follow the same procedure with respect to other agencies and departments coordinated with community development in rural development. When coordination continues across the level of similar roles among the agencies, all policies governing the operation of community development and its related agencies would be known and understood. Likewise, policies would be passed down the lines to all whose work may be affected. When such policies can be interpreted as being conducive to or aiding coordination, the agencies will be able to make effective use of the provisions enacted with respect to the work.

Budgeting control: The budget is an important factor in the administration of community development programmes. No work can progress without an adequate budget. By its control can be effected in such a way as to regulate operations in confirmation with set procedures. From this point, a downward scale of relationship with authority should exist at all levels, until it reaches the area of actual operations. Coordination could reasonably be effected at each of these levels in descending scale, with those connected with community development and related agencies to be accounted for in terms of justifiable expenditure. It is necessary for all persons of authority from the source of its provision down to the line of actual operation, to be held responsible for seeing that a coordinated approach to the work provides results warranting the amount of expenditure to maintain the agencies.

Technical personnel: Following the line of authority, the services of technical personnel should be so arranged that they can be made available within the requirements of the community development programme. The officers in charge of areas would be responsible for working together to determine at what time and during what stages of the project specialised skills are required. Necessary requisition could be made accordingly to meet prevailing needs.

Coordinating committees at all levels. This committee is formulated in the community development programme by having an Advisory Committee at each level of the Government. The Government official at each level works as Secretary. "These Advisory Committees should be the policy-making and coordinating structures of the community development programmes."

Personnel selection. Maximum care should be taken in selecting suitable workers who feel themselves to be servants of the public, and not officers. Each member should be willing to forego any credit for departmental achievements for the good of the people and the programme. The agency staff should be comprised of persons who will not be agency deterred but who are prepared to work along with other agencies towards the achievement of common objectives and to coordinate their efforts.

Factors influencing coordination

In their study, M.P. Singh, et al. have reported the following factors affecting coordination:

(1) Common agreement on objective, procedures and responsibilities;
(2) Willingness to work together;
(3) Faith in the programme for the success of which personnel are responsible;
(4) Personality, i.e., personal attributes;
(5) Social relationships among personnel;
(6) Existence of machinery for coordination and planned administrative procedures;
(7) Knowledge of own duties and how to perform them;
(8) Status difference;
(9) Concept of the programme possessed by personnel;
(10) Communication among personnel;
(11) Satisfaction with job;
(12) Training basis on the job and orientation;
(13) Periodical appraisal of objectives and procedures;
(14) Social forces— traditions, customs, moral standards and professional ethics; and
(15) Law—rules, regulations, etc.

Building an organisation

The process of building up an organisation is like the making of a coat by a tailor. As an illustration, if we organise an agriculture department in a State, we appoint a Director of Agriculture, divide his functions and appoint Joint Directors, then Deputy Directors and District Agriculture Officers. Then Deputy Directors are assigned different jobs—Marketing, Soil Conservation, Horticulture and so on. This division is like cutting the coat from the total cloth. To prevent disintegration of the Department, these divisional heads are to be interlinked or sewed up by being placed under the supervision and control of the Head of the Department, from whom they derive their authority and to whom they are responsible. So step by step, we reach downwards, like in a Development Department, to the Village Level Worker.

The building up of organisation creates some problems like:

(1) What should be the basis of division and of grouping up work together; (2) At how many levels is the sub-divisions of the work to be done, and how are these steps to be linked; (3) What are the principal units, or organisation; resulting from the division of work; (4) How should authority be distributed and centrally organised; and (5) How to secure team work by the various units of the organisation.

Organisation of the development department (Fig. 44.3)

At the central level, there is the Ministry of Agriculture, Community Development, Cooperatives and Panchayats. At the State levels, there is the Development Minister. There are official as well as non-official organisations at Village, Block, District, State and National levels. These can be given as follows:

(a) *Central level:* On the official side, there is the Ministry of Agriculture, Community Development, Cooperatives and Panchayats with Minister, Secretary and Deputies and Assistant Secretaries. On the non-official side, there is a Central Committee consisting of members of the Planning Commission and Minister for Food and Agriculture, Community Development and Cooperatives and the Prime Minister as Chairman. Coordination with allied ministries is secured through special committees. The matters of policy go before the Central Committee.

(b) *State level:* On the official side, the executive head is the Development Commissioner. He coordinates the activities of all Development Departments. He helps the Development Minister of the State as Secretary to Development. On the non-official side, there is the State Development Committee. This committee consists of: (1) Chief Minister (as Chairman), (2) The Ministers of Development Departments— Agriculture, Health, Education and Public Works Department (P. W. D.). The Development Commissioner acts as Secretary to this Committee.

(c) *District level:* (1) Where Panchayat Raj has been adopted: In such districts, the Zila Parishad is responsible for the programme in the district. This Parishad consists of elected representatives of the people (a) Presidents of the Block, Panchayat Samitis; and (b) M.P's. and M.L.As of the district. On the official side, a Class II gazetted officer has been given to act as Secretary.

(2) Where Panchayat Raj has not been adopted: In such districts, the Collector is in charge of the work and the district officials of the Development Departments and the Block Development Officers work under his supervision and guidance.

(d) *Block level:* In States where Panchayat Raj has been adopted, the official staff is: (1) One Block Development Officer (BDO), a Member of Parliament and a Block Development Administrator, who administers the programme and coordinates the activities of the extension officers under him; (2) Eight extension officers who work in their special fields of agriculture, animal husbandry and veterinary, cooperation, health, social education, cottage industries, panchayats, and public Works.

On the non-official side, there is the Block Panchayat Samiti. Its members are Sarpanches (Presidents of the Village Panchayats) and co-opted members from women and the Scheduled Classes. Voluntary associate organisations like Youth Clubs (Yuvak Dal), Farmers' Forums and Women's Organisations (Mahila Mandal), etc., supplement the work of the Panchayats in their respective functional sphere.

(e) *Village level:* On the Government or official side, the Village Level Worker

(VLW) or Gramsewak works as a multi-purpose agent. On the non-official side, the Panchayat is in overall control of the programme, helped by associate organisations.

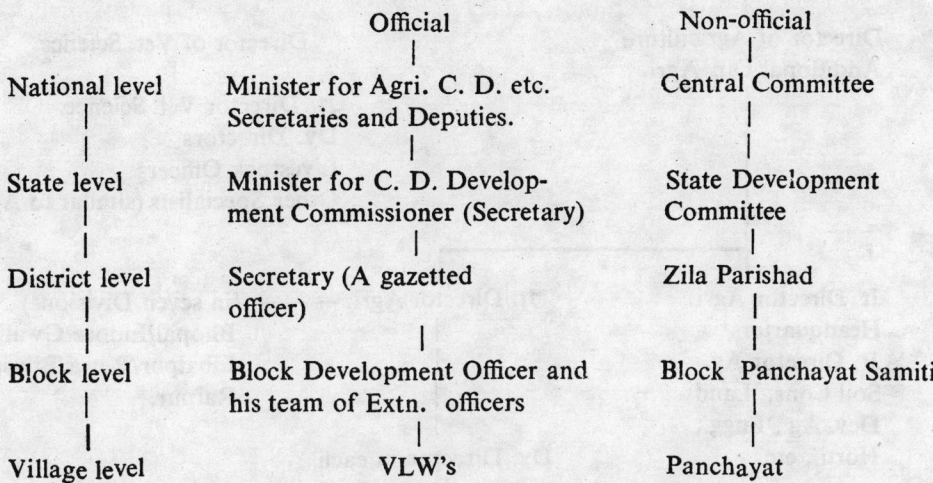

	Official	Non-official
National level	Minister for Agri. C. D. etc. Secretaries and Deputies.	Central Committee
State level	Minister for C. D. Development Commissioner (Secretary)	State Development Committee
District level	Secretary (A gazetted officer)	Zila Parishad
Block level	Block Development Officer and his team of Extn. officers	Block Panchayat Samiti
Village level	VLW's	Panchayat

Fig. 44.3 Organisation of the Development Department.

Organisation of agriculture department in Madhya Pradesh

The set up of the agriculture department varies from State to State. In Madhya Pradesh, the teaching and research branches of the department have been transferred with effect from 31st December, 1964, to Jawaharlal Nehru Krishi Vishwa Vidyalaya, Jabalpur. The extension services are with the department. The organisational chart is given in Fig. 44.4.

PROBLEMS OF PUBLIC ADMINISTRATION

(1) Basis of organisation (Doctrine of Unity)

Organisation precedes the breaking-up of tasks into convenient units and sub-units and linking them up again to secure team work. This raises the problem of the basis on which one should divide the work and regroup it into convenient units. The work of each unit has to be characterised by some similarity or unity. This unity may relate to four things: (1) function or purpose; (2) process; (3) clientele or persons served (farmers in extension); and (4) area or place. This is called Doctrine of Unity.

(a) *Function:* By it we mean main purpose to be achieved, or service to be rendered. These services under community development are agriculture, health, sanitation, education, housing, improvement in diet. The state departments are organised on a functional basis. Major functions may be divided or made up into minor functions, e.g., agricultural development includes, marketing, educating the farmers in plant protection, use of fertilisers, soil testing, weed control, etc. The set-up may vary according to the practice. usage and the political climate in different countries or states.

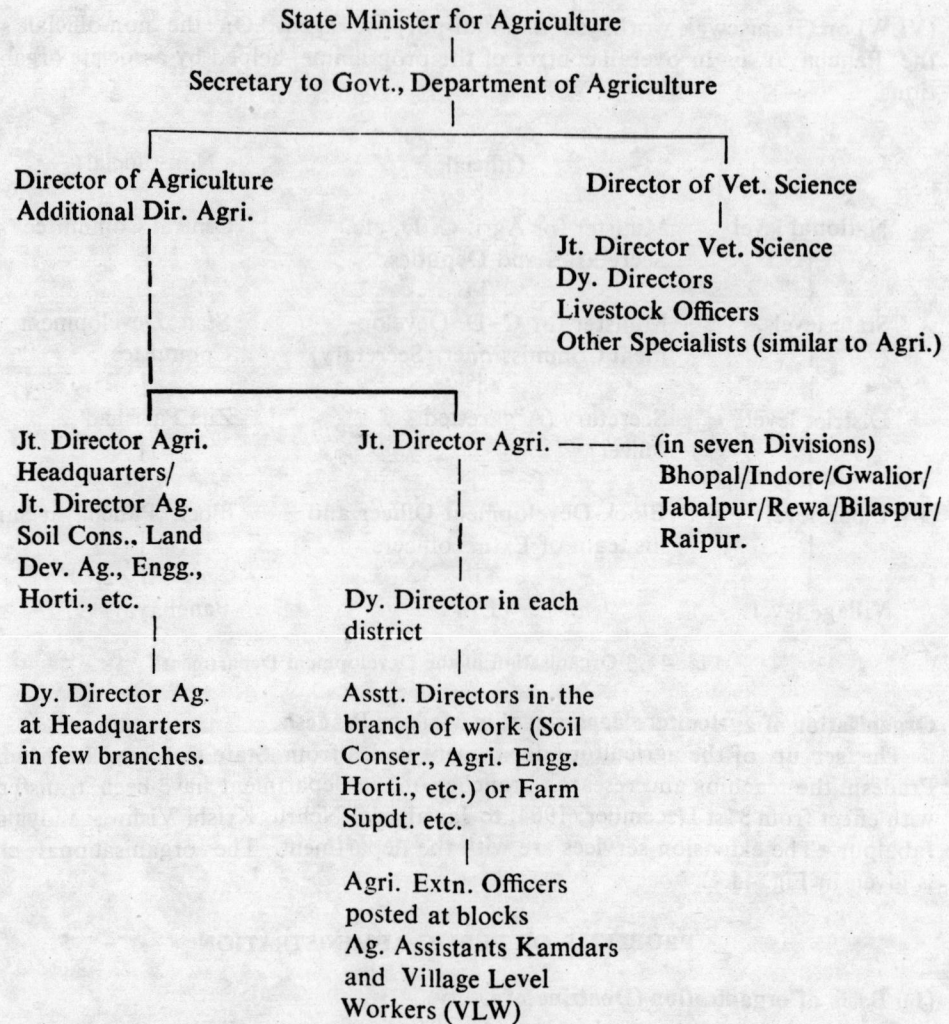

State Minister for Agriculture
|
Secretary to Govt., Department of Agriculture

Director of Agriculture
Additional Dir. Agri.

Director of Vet. Science
|
Jt. Director Vet. Science
Dy. Directors
Livestock Officers
Other Specialists (similar to Agri.)

Jt. Director Agri.
Headquarters/
Jt. Director Ag.
Soil Cons.. Land
Dev. Ag., Engg.,
Horti., etc.

Jt. Director Agri. ——— (in seven Divisions)
Bhopal/Indore/Gwalior/
Jabalpur/Rewa/Bilaspur/
Raipur.

Dy. Director in each
district

Dy. Director Ag.
at Headquarters
in few branches.

Asstt. Directors in the
branch of work (Soil
Conser., Agri. Engg.
Horti., etc.) or Farm
Supdt. etc.

Agri. Extn. Officers
posted at blocks
Ag. Assistants Kamdars
and Village Level
Workers (VLW)

Fig. 44.4 Organisation of Agriculture Department in Madhya Pradesh.

(b) *Process:* This is a technique, or primary skill, more or less of a specialised kind. Engineering, stenography, medical care, legal advice are the processes. In India at the central level, some process departments are: Accounts, Public Works and Law. In the states of India, the Public Works Department (PWD), Medical Department and Local Body Departments like Fire Brigade, Electricity, Accounts are based on process. Process can be defined as a function or activity which cuts horizontally across the various line departments, i.e., is common to all of them, such as, legal advice, finance, accounting, construction and repair.

CHAPTER 45

PERSONNEL ADMINISTRATION

DEFINITION

It is the planning, supervision, direction and coordination of those activities of an organisation (e.g., Community Development) with a minimum of human effort and friction, with maximum cooperation and with proper regard for the genuine well-being of the organisation.

We may use the term 'Personnel Management' also. Management consists of getting others—other job-holders, to do work. The very basis of personnel management is: (a) organisation planning; (b) organisational staffing; and (c) policy formation.

Organisation

It is a term that describes a process and structure. It is a tool of management. It is the process by means of which the combination of factors of production is affected, i.e., highest possible efficiency in this combination.

Organising

It is the process of creating a systematic whole, composed of inter-department pacts.

PROBLEMS OF PERSONNEL ADMINISTRATION

The important problems of personnel administration in extension and community development in rural areas of India are: recruitment, selection and certification of appointment, classification or cadres, determination of pay-scales and other conditions of service, promotion, conduct and discipline, training of employees, superannuation arrangements and employee-employer relations.

Recruitment of extension workers

Recruitment in the field of administration means attracting the proper and suitable types of candidates for the various categories of posts. The extension service has several types of posts—the Gramsewaks or village level workers are to be trained for two years for their job. They should have a bias for village work and the villagers, and also should have an aptitude for this type of job. Unlike this, the job of the various extension workers at the Block level—e.g., Agricultural Extension Officers (AEOs), Veterinary Extension Officers, etc., is technical and requires persons trained in that field upto a graduate or undergraduate level. There are certain posts of extension officers like Extension Officers in cooperatives, panchayats, social education, etc., who can be promoted from the village level workers also in addition to direct recruitment.

Types of recruitment

Types of recruitment are the following:

(1) *Positive recruitment:* When the employing agency attracts the right type of candidates, it is called positive recruitment. For technical posts, there is need of such recruitment. We are still short of graduates in agriculture, veterinary science, engineering, medical science, etc., and for these, advertisements are placed in newspapers, circulars to various Universities, etc., are sent. In case of arts graduates or graduates with degrees in commerce or even in science, there is unemployment and the graduates themselves apply to various agencies.

The method of positive recruitment may be: (1) The attractions of the service may be brought to the notice of the candidates in a telling and picturesque way through publicity, that is, posters, folders, illustrated advertisements in papers and magazines and on the screen, circulars to educational institutions. But in the extension service, the medium is advertisement in newspapers only.

(2) *Passive or ordinary type recruitment:* When it is just a help 'wanted' or 'situations vacant' advertisement, it is a passive type recruitment. For it special or multifarious media is not used. The war-time recruitments are of the above type while the present method in extension service is of ordinary type.

(3) *Direct recruitment* vs. *recruitment by promotion:* Generally, for lower posts, recruitment is made by the direct method while some of the higher posts may be filled by promotion of suitable candidates. In extension service, the VLWs may be promoted to posts of Social Education Organisers. If some candidates happen to have passed the Diploma in Agriculture from Agricultural schools like that at Gwalior and Naugaon in M.P. State, at Bulandshahar and Ghazipur in U.P. or those with Intermediate in Agriculture, they can be promoted as AEOs. Otherwise posts of Panchayat EOs Cooperative EOs etc., are filled by promotion. The BDOs are promotees from Extension Officers. The District Agriculture Officers are chosen from graduates of Agriculture with experience in the post of BDO. Generally, the promotion is according to the classification of cadres in the same branch of work. VLWs are Class III servants, they may be promoted to State service, Class II in the lowest grade of Rs. 425-900, then to Class I higher grade of Rs. 680-1150. These grades may vary from State to State, or even in the same cadre in the same State.

Merits of direct recruitment: In the direct method, the recruitment criteria may be on merit in which (1) All qualified persons can have equal opportunity for public office. (2) By this method, we can tap a much wider source of supply and so can have better talents. (3) It results in constant infusion of new blood into the service. (4) The older employees cannot have the same initiative, quickness, and vigour as the younger officers directly recruited. (5) In the direct recruitment by merit, the young, able men passing out of the universities can find attractive jobs so they will not go to private firms or companies. (6) In technical and personnel fields like extension and community development work, development of new techniques requires new employees to provide leadership in the adoption of those techniques. (7) Competition from outside the service spurs the employees to keep abreast of new development in their several fields, lest they are found inferior in competition for higher posts.

Demerits of direct recruitment: (1) Direct recruitment brings into the service persons without previous administrative experience and prolonged training has to be given to them before they can be entrusted with the responsibilities of a substantive post. This is costly. (2) Direct recruitment reduces incentive to good work among the lower cadres. They feel that their excellence will give them no benefit for promotion to higher posts. (3) When younger persons are placed over older persons, there is jealousy and heart-burning, which is not good for the community development organisation. (4) Even if service people are allowed to compete in the open competition, they find themselves at a disadvantage on the basis of theoretical knowledge of university subjects of study.

So compromise between the two principles is effective. In the Community Development Programme and Agricultural Services upto Class II, there is direct recruitment, then it is by promotion. Even BDOs post (now restored in M.P.) is a promotion post.

SELECTION

The organisation lays down some broad principles including advertisement, qualifications, experience, etc., required in the persons to be engaged. This is given in the *job description*. This job description includes a job summary, an outline of work performed, necessary training, occupational tests, physical activities, working conditions, etc. This may even mention age, height, weight, sex, strength, aptitude for village work, appearance, recognised mental characteristics, intelligence, division attained in the examination. There may be consideration of cultural qualities, education, family background, special skills, moral character, honesty, integrity and reliability. The sequence for selection may be:

(1) Filling out application forms.
(2) Scrutinising the applications and preparation of abstract.
(3) Arrangement for interviews, calling the candidates, informing members of the Selection Board.
(4) Testing aptitude and preparation of merit list.
(5) Physical test.
(6) Medical examination.
(7) Issuing appointment orders.

The basis of selection may involve: (1) Skills to coordinate mind and body in performing certain operations, (2) Experience, (3) Age, (4) Sex, (5) Education and training, (6) Physical characteristics—strength, vision, hearing, (7) Appearance, (8) Initiative, ingenuity and mental alertness, (9) Aptitude, (10) Stability and responsibility, (11) Attitude towards employment, (12) Personality.

Selecting instrument and devices: (a) Interviewing, (b) testing, (c) observational—one eye, hard of hearing, Kahira (whitish eyed) (d) screening devices—photographs, service book, (e) application blank, (f) references to persons who are his previous employers, or those connected with the candidate's education. This may be through written letter, or telephone, and (g) letters of recommendation.

Interviewing: This is to distinguish between those believed likely to prove satisfactory. In interview, the interviewing persons should have a setting so that the interviewee acts as naturally as possible. The interviewers should know the jobs for which they are selecting and they should be aware of their prejudices and tendencies. In interviewing, the following should be covered: work history, family background, educational background, stability, attitudes, personality, health and apparent physical characteristics, integrity, whether trouble-maker or agitator, potential, has his own transport or not.

The interview may be by a panel of experts and they may have a checklist (Fig. 45.1)

	Ratings				
Items	very poor	poor	good	excellent	overall attitude

Fig. 45.1 Interviewers checklist.

Interview may be: (1) Patterned—where interview is carefully directed to give attention to each of the considerations; (2) through diagnostic interviews—this includes specific questions to be asked with respect to work, family, social and personal history.

Testing in selection: This helps in forming a sharper and more precise estimate of particular personal traits. The written examination does not reveal the personality of the candidate. A person who may do well in a written examination may yet lack coolness, initiative, presence of mind, the power of decision and drive, etc., which are so vital in an administrator. The oral test is intended to test the personality of the candidate and thus serve as a corrective of the estimate arrived at by written examination.

The tests can be: (1) on vocational interests, (2) mental ability, (3) proficiency, skills and performance, (4) personality and temperament and (5) attitude.

Their types may be:

(1) Ability tests—indicating what the individual can presently do.

(2) Trade tests—measuring trade knowledge and perhaps the skills in trade.

(3) Intelligence test—test of learning ability and special class of aptitudes.

(4) Aptitude tests—mechanical aptitude or interest in village development work.

(5) Interest tests.

(6) Tests of emotional stability—for indicating the basic temperament of the candidate and appraising what may be described as his characteristic mood.

Types of interviews: (1) Selection board procedure, (2) viva-voce, (3) written paper-cum-viva, (4) weeding interview—in it the purpose is rejection or elimination rather than selection, (5) group discussions among candidates for five minutes or more.

Appointing authorities: Appointing authorities in India are linked with the classification of service. For special posts, Central Class I, Class II, the Union Public Commission selects the candidates and the department concerned in the Central

Government issues the appointment orders Lower posts are filled by the Department through selection boards. There is a Public Service Commission (PSC) in each State. The Department prepares the draft of an advertisement and sends it to the PSC. The PSC advertises the posts in the local and important national newspapers. Posts upto Class II are filled through the PSC. In some cases, the Department appoints through selection boards but concurrence of the PSC is necessary. For lower posts, the appointments are made by the selection boards appointed by the department concerned. For posts of VLWs the Development Commissioner of the State appoints selection boards. The candidates are interviewed and given performance and other tests. For AEOs the Department of Agriculture selects through selection committees consisting of Director of Agriculture, Additional Director and some members. Promotions from VLWs or others posts can be made. For posts of Extension Officer in other departments like veterinary, cooperatives, panchayats etc., (where they exist) the selection is made just like for the AEOs. Post of BDOs are generally filled by promotion from the Extension Officers. Higher posts are filled through promotions.

CLASSIFICATION OF POSITIONS

Meaning: In personnel administration, classification means grouping together of posts into broad classes on the basis of the duties and responsibilities. Posts to which similar duties and responsibilities are attached are put into one class regardless of the department in which they actually exist.

Principal categories of classification: The categories are: (1) Service, (2) Class and the grade. The service may be administrative, Foreign Service, Indian Audit or Account Service, the Secretariate Service, etc. Within these services, there n ay be Senior or Junior Service or Lower Upper grade. M.P. Class I service has the same grade for professors as to the Joint Directors, etc. In the Agricultural University, this grade had been provided for specialists also.

Factors determining classification: (1) The subject-matter or field of activity—engineering, medical, administrative, etc.; (2) the degree or kind of supervision; (3) the supervision, or authority flowing from the post downwards—the more of it there is, the higher is the class to which the post is to be assigned; (4) responsibility other than supervisory if any, ease or difficulty or simplicity or complexity of work: (5) qualification required for the post; (6) availability of persons in the subject.

The classification of service in India at central level is governed by the Civil Service (Classification, Control and Appeal) Rules, 1930, as amended from time to time. At present it is as follows:

(1) The All-India Service.
(2) The Central (Union) Service Class I.
(3) The Central (Union) Class II.
(4) The Provincial (State) Services.
(5) The Specialist Services.
(6) The Central Services Class III.
(7) The Central Services Class IV.
(8) The Central Secretariate Service Class I, II, III and IV.

Within these classes, there may be various subject-matter fields. In All-India Service, there is: Indian Administrative Service, Indian Foreign Service, and Indian Police Service. Within the State Service also, the classification is first into Class I, II, III and IV and then subject-matterwise within the class. The Central Service Class I are at present 24 in number like: (1) Indian Audit and Accounts, (2) Indian Defence Accounts Service, (3) Central Engineering Service Class I, (4) Indian Customs Service, and so on.

Advantages of classification: (1) It systematises and simplifies the administration. Members of these classes are recruited by the same procedure, have same minimum qualifications and scales of pay, and same duties and responsibilities. Thus common treatment of large number of employees is made possible. Whenever a new post needs to be created, its specifications are easily ascertained and reference is made to the class it belongs.

(2) By classification of posts, the estimates of salary and other recurring expenditure in respect of them can easily be prepared. It also facilitate the regulation of other conditions of service because these can be uniformly laid down for each class. Government accounting follows the budgetary heads and sub-heads, the budgeting facilities created by classification are therefore, helpful in account keeping.

(3) It is a safeguard against arbitrariness and favouritism in fixing the pay-scales for particular posts. Each post has a salary according to the class. It also ensures equal pay for equal work.

(4) Lines of promotion for each employee are marked out, and he can know in advance what to expect in due course.

(5) It fosters the growth of corporate consciousness, pride and self-respect within each class. This improves the morale of the services.

(6) It results in a proper definition of duties and responsibilities of each post and thus objective standards of job performance are set.

(7) The adequate classification with duties and responsibilities and lines of promotion of each post clearly laid down facilitates the preparation of organisational charts.

Limitations and disadvantages of position classification

(1) *Disadvantage:* It promotes class consciousness among the services and is likely to prove detrimental to democratic equality, unity and goodwill. The class develops a superiority complex among senior officers and inferiority complex among junior employees.

(2) *Difficulties and limitations:* (a) There is the problem of the marginal groups, which try to be placed in the next higher class, thus the top man in Class II try to get included in Class I on the ground that he is seniormost. (b) Many times there is political pressure on the persons in charge of promotions. (c) There are always some posts whose work is of such an unusual or mixed character, that they cannot be fitted into any one of the classes.

MAINTENANCE OF EFFICIENCY AND MORALE

After the candidates have been selected to particular positions the problem of personnel administration is how to maintain efficiency and high morale so that they are able to devote their maximum to the organisation. The methods employed include: (a) Orientation of new workers, (b) Training of the workers, (c) Providing stimulus and incentives through better pay-scales, pension or contributory Provident Fund, leave, fringe benefits—medical aid, housing facilities, transport and communication, chances of promotion etc. (d) Code of ethics, conduct and discipline. (e) Supervision, (f) Appreciation of good workers through rewards, awards, promotion, etc.

(a) Orientation of new entrants

The worker, after he joins, should be oriented to the staff, philosophy behind the organisation of community development and extension, scope, purpose and objectives of the organisation, traditions and culture of the people for whom they are to work, i.e., the villagers and the farmers where they have to do the extension work, understanding of personnel policies and regulations, code of professional ethics, knowledge and skill in applying the broad principles of extension education, basic understanding of the organisational structure and the workers' role in the organisation. He should know how to supervise and coordinate the extension activities with that of other agencies and resources. He should be oriented into the maintenance of office records, way of writing letters, reports, etc., rules recording use of government funds. This orientation will differ according to the job the extension worker is required to do.

(b) Training of extension workers

The pre-service training the worker received before joining may not be sufficient for the extension job. To improve the ability of the extension worker, he requires in addition to the orientation we have discussed, induction training, job training, short courses and participation in meetings and conferences.

(1) *Induction training:* This is just like orientation of the workers. Some institutes have designed training where extension workers can be given knowledge of the working and organisation of community development and extension service, his place of work and his place in the work team. This is now a formal training given through orientation and training centres.

(2) *Job training:* Extension workers need training about their job. They are given opportunities to visit villages and to learn new techniques. This is a continuous process and is planned to meet the needs of extension workers to help them become better qualified for the responsibilities of their job.

(3) *Short range courses:* The Directorate of Extension, Ministry of Agriculture, Government of India organises a one and a half month's training course for the agriculture extension officers and veterinary extension officers of the blocks in technical subject as well as in methods of extension, at an Agricultural University.

(4) *Periodical meetings and conferences:* The *rabi* and *kharif* season meetings at Agriculture Universities, Colleges or Government Headquarters come under this category.

There are regular training centres and courses being offered at Agricultural Colleges and other centres.

Meeting training needs: The following list of major steps involved in planning and conducting training may serve as a planning guide, and as a check for the plans made for training for some organisations.

Major steps in planning and conducting training: These are as follows:

(1) *State the general purpose and the specific objectives of the training to be given.*

If possible, indicate the direction and extent to which trainees' knowledge, skills, or attitudes are to be developed.

(2) *Decide on the approach to be taken in introducing training:* A safe rule to remember that the top management is not likely to approve training, other line officials are not likely to support it, and trainees are not likely to apply it on the job unless each of them sees the training as a means of doing something *they* want to be done in a way *they* think will succeed, *without too serious a conflict with other demands important for them.*

(3) *Organise and plan for training:* Decide who will do the actual training and be sure that they can do it adequately. Decide whether training will be on or of the job, individual or group; if group, whether seminar, workshop, conference, class, institute, etc. Decide whether committees will be used, who should be on them, whether they will be advisory, directing or operating. Provide for follow-up to encourage on the job application of training.

(4) *Determine who is to be trained:* How many people, of what age, sex, special characteristics, general background, occupations, grade levels, training needs and interests, relationship to each other? Consider carefully how all of this is likely to affect the training.

(5) *Decide on, develop and organise training content:* Sort out established needs into related groups. Select and develop content appropriate to meet these needs, using such sources as supervisors and employees; manuals and other written instructions, pertinent literature, research findings, work materials, job analyses. Arrange this material and other materials in coherent order for learning purposes.

(6) *Choose the training methods to be used:* Use, in balanced variety, those methods that will satisfactorily achieve the desired purpose with the greatest simplicity and economy.

To increase *knowledge*, consider especially: assigned readings, lectures, guided discussions, observation tours, case studies, self-tests. To improve *skills*, consider especially: role-playing, demonstrations, skits, case studies, problem-solving conferences, job rotation, supervised practice on or off the job. To influence *attitudes*, consider especially: role playing, demonstration, case studies, problem-centred conferences, job rotation, movies, inspirational talks (provided your speaker is skilled enough).

For any, or all, these purposes, supplement basic methods with appropriate visual aids or devices and with follow-up discussion.

(7) *Prepare instructional materials or guides, and appropriate time schedules:* See that all persons who are to give training are properly briefed and that they plan and prepare in advance.

(8) *Make clear and detailed arrangements:* Arrange for trainees' attendance. Get space and equipment lined up, making sure that it is ample, well-arranged and as comfortable as circumstances permit. Be sure that everybody will be able to see and hear. Arrange for appropriate publicity records and reports, recognition of trainees, etc.

(9) *Giving training:* Start and stop on time. Make sure discussion is in terms the trainees can understand. Relate what is being taught to what trainees are interested in. Encourage their participation. Allow few, if any, "sit-and-talk" sessions to run longer than an hour or an hour and a half. Get trainees' reactions and suggestions, and those of discussion leaders or instructors.

(10) *See that training is evaluated:* Evaluate training to obtain better information on

which to base decisions and guide efforts to improve. Evaluate in terms of specific objective of training. Use objective evidence and measures and *supports* for evaluation, but do not allow them to substitute for judgement.

(c) *Stimulus and incentives*

The function of incentives is to tap motives and to change attitudes which in turn predict efforts and modify behaviour of the extension workers. Some important incentives under Indian conditions, may be:

(1) *Pay scales:* (a) Pay scales need to be related to achievement. It should be on par with other technical services like Medical, Engineering etc. (b) The Government should act as model employer i.e., the Government should be ahead of private employers. (c) The Government, should pay what is necessary to recruit and retain efficient workers. (d) The pay should be related to the cost of living. As the prices increase above a certain limit, the pay should also increase. (e) Pay scales should be related to the mean or per capita income of the country. The salary of the lower posts, under a democratic principle of equality, should be raised and those of higher posts lowered down. (f) There should be equal pay for equal work and equitable relationship between salaries for different kinds of jobs so that the higher type of work should be paid at a higher scale than the lower one.

The scale of pay varies from State to State and even within the State. The staff employed in the education department get University Grants Commission grades.

(2) *Dearness allowance:* Dearness or compensatory cost of living allowance, which is linked up with a scale is also given.

(3) *Grades and time scales:* As the service of an employee grows more and more valuable because he gains increased experiences as he becomes older, a provision for periodic grade system and time scale should be made.

(a) Grades. In the grade system within each class of service, there are a number of grades, each upper grade carrying a higher salary than the one immediately lower. As vacancies in the upper grades occur, employees from lower grades are promoted.

This system existed in India before the Report to the Islinton Commission. It had the following disadvantages: (1) Prospects of increased salary for the personnel depended upon vacancies occurring in the higher grades. Such vacancies do not occur at regular intervals, so there was an element of chance in the system.

(b) Time scale: The system provides for annual increase of salary by stated amounts upto the maximum of the scale fixed. Sometimes, there are efficiency bars. In it the problem is of : (1) the length of the scale; (2) the promotion between the minimum and maximum salaries of the scale; (3) amounts and the intervals between increments; (4) the expediency of one, or more than one, time scale for the same grade or class, and (5) the efficiency bars.

The proportion in maximum and minimum may be two and a half to three times. Regarding the amounts of, and intervals between, increments there are three alternatives: (a) To give larger increments in the beginning and smaller later. In this case, the idea is that if the starting salary is not substantial, the employee is able to receive a larger remuneration at as early a date as possible; (b) Smaller in the beginning and larger later. It enables the employee to meet the growing expenditure. Amounts of increments smaller in the initial as well as in the closing years of service, and larger during the middle years. The favourable point is that the employee is then at the peak of his ability and his usefulness to the Government or employer is positive.

(4) *Fringe benefits:* These allowances may be: (1) Housing or house rent allowance. (2) Children's education allowance; This is not being given to extension staff; (3) Medical aid. This is free to all staff in extension, provided the treatment is under a Government Doctor and bills are certified by the District Civil Surgeon. Only few medicines are reimbursed. (4) Travelling allowance; This is given to all staff if the journey is performed with the permission of the competent authority and payment is made according to the rules applicable from time to time in M.P. or the Agricultural University, Jabalpur. Officers are entitled as follows :Officers drawing upto Rs. 400 per month. Class II Ticket plus D.A. if there is halt for a full day. If the same day is of arrival or departure then $\frac{1}{2}$ Daily allowance. Out of state the D.A. is double. In case of journey by bus, actual bus fare plus one D.A. for the working day—half for the day of arrival, full for the of day halt and half for the day of departure. For officers drawing Rs. 750. First Class railway fare, plus Rs. 10 D.A. for one day. For bus journey, the above rule also applies. For officials drawing above Rs. 1000 the D.A. is Rs. 15 as the maximum other rules are the same as in case of officers.

(5) *Leave benefits:* Thirteen days casual leave per year starting form January 1 which can be combined with other holidays. On 11 months' service 1 month's earned leave which can be accumulated upto 180 days. Two months medical leave on full pay, next 6 month on half pay, next one year without pay.

(6) *Pension:* A life-long pension according to a graduated scale is given to an employee of extension service in M.P. State, after his retirement at the age of 58 years. It is calculated in this way.

Average pay drawn in the last 16 months before retirement, number of years of qualifying service, upon 80.

(7) *Retirement gratuity:* It is given to all extension workers : $\frac{10}{20} \times$ number of years of qualifying service $\times$ pay last drawn at the time of retirement.

(8) *Family pension:* After even one year's service, if an employee of the extension service of M.P. State dies, the family gets a pension for 5 years.

Different States have some variations regarding these rules but all provide such facilities. In M. P. it is according to the Tarachand Commission Report.

(9) *Hours of work:* All employees are 24 hours servants, but the usual working hours are eight hours per day.

(10) *Promotions:* From the point of view of an employee, promotion is an advancement from a lower grade or class of service to a higher one, carrying a larger salary and higher duties and responsibilities. From the point of view of the employer it means filling up the higher posts by the selection of the fittest persons from within the service. Actually, the promotions made should not leave an impression of injustice or unfairness among the employees, this lowers down the morale. There may be dissatisfaction and frustration among the extension workers in the development departments of the States regarding their chances of promotion. The qualifications of VLWs are such that they cannot be promoted to the posts of extension officers of the next higher grade which is the grade of extension officers at the Block level, because

they are not graduates. Because of this limitation, many of the VLWs have continued to be kept in the same grade even after 16 years of service. The Extension Officers are employees of their parent Extension Department: Agriculture, Animal Husbandry and Veterinary, Cooperative, Health, etc. They cannot be promoted to posts higher than the Block Development Officers (which too was abolished in M.P.) because the Development Department does not have any higher post than this. Their parent Departments many times do not consider them as their employees. So good workers do not want to come to the Development Services. There are cases where BDOs who were borrowed from the Agriculture Department as AEOs in 1952 continued to be BDOs (till 1964) and many junior persons to them in their parent department got promotions.

The Agricultural Universities were approached by the Directorate of Extension, Government of India to provide a special three years' course for VLWs to get B.Sc. (Ag.) Degree. Some of them have agreed and they will have now a chance of becoming graduates and get promoted to BDO's or AEOs, District Agriculture Officers, etc.

In promotion, the following criteria should be followed:

(a) In promotion to the higher posts, merit should be the only consideration to the total exclusion of seniority,

(b) In promotion to the middle posts, merit should be the determining factor and seniority a secondray one, and

(c) In promotion to lower cadre posts, seniority should carry weight, but care should be taken to ensure that exceptional merit is rewarded by quick promotion.

How merit should be determined: Merit is the rival of principle of seniority. It can be determined in three ways : (a) written examination, with or without interview, (b) determination by the head of department in his discretion on the basis of his personal knowledge of the employee and his work, and (c) determination by the head of the department on the basis of service rating and records.

Rating: The employee's appraisal can be through such performance: Name of the employee.........Period covered by the evaluation. (Tables **45.1** and **45.2**)

Instruction for filling the ratings given in the Tables **45.1** and **45.2** by encircling the number in each item.

Instructions. Put mark (×) in the appropriate column under one factor then encircle one figure under rating. (Table 44.2)

Security of job: There should be independence and self-expression.

Working conditions and atmosphere: (a) creating conditions that will generate active and willing collaboration among all members of the organisation, i.e., the conditions which will lead people to want to direct their effort towards the objectives of the Community Development Programme.

(b) A sense of belonging: This can be achieved through cooperative relations on the job, satisfying social relations with one's colleagues, and feeling that others are interested in the individual's welfare, problem and ideas, is an incentive to all workers. Work needs to be comfortable, enjoyable and congenial.

(c) Delegation of authority commensurate with responsibility.

Table 45.1

Employee Rating

Name. . . . .   From . . . . to . . . .

A. Personal qualities	Rating				
1. Industry	1	2	3	4	5
2. Dependability	1	2	3	4	5
3. Judgement	1	2	3	4	5
4. Initiative	1	2	3	4	5
5. Resourcefulness	1	2	3	4	5
6. Forcefulness	1	2	3	4	5
7. Decisiveness	1	2	3	4	5
8. Adaptability	1	2	3	4	5
9. General usefulness	1	2	3	4	5
10. Cooperativeness	1	2	3	4	5
11. Tactfulness	1	2	3	4	5
12. Conduct	1	2	3	4	5
13. Good manners and politeness	1	2	3	4	5
14. Patience	1	2	3	4	5
15. Ability to get along	1	2	3	4	5
16. Sense of humour	1	2	3	4	5
17. Other qualities (Specify) (a) (b)	1	2	3	4	5

Table 45.2

Employee Rating

B. Other factors	Not observed	Not pertinent	Not important	Rating
1. Technical competence				1 2 3 4 5
2. Knowledge of administrative practice				1 2 3 4 5
3. Insight into objectives of own programme				1 2 3 4 5
4. Knowledge and understanding of overall programme				1 2 3 4 5
5. Understanding of the economic factors				1 2 3 4 5
6. Effectiveness in applying regulations				1 2 3 4 5
7. Thoroughness & accuracy of observations				1 2 3 4 5
8. Power and accuracy of observations				1 2 3 4 5
9. Effectiveness of written expression				1 2 3 4 5
10. Effectiveness of oral expression				1 2 3 4 5
11. Negotiating ability				1 2 3 4 5
12. Effectiveness as a supervisor				1 2 3 4 5
13 Managerial effectiveness				1 2 3 4 5
14. Cost consciousness				1 2 3 4 5
15. Security consciousness				1 2 3 4 5
16. Coordinating ability				1 2 3 4 5

Recognition and appreciation: The authorities should recognise the good workers and there should be appreciation so that the workers feel satisfied, take pride in their achievements and others also strive for it. Some reward in the form of a pat on the back, a certificate, grant of some advance increments, publicity in papers or circular letters, promotion to higher post, etc., is required.

Physical working conditions: (a) Good office with equipment, stationary, typing facilities, etc., (b) Residential accommodation, (c) facilities of education for children, (d) Medical aid to family, (e) Study leave, and (g) Scholarships for higher studies.

DEVELOPMENT OF CODE OF ETHICS

India, because it has been under colonial rule for a long time and its principles and practices in the services were laid down with different aims, needs to set a code of ethics for the extension workers. These principles should be such as to motivate them to give their maximum to the cause of the nation in general and the village in particular.

Such code should lay down the *faith* which may create a sense of devotion in them. It can be like this:

"I believe in village life and that it can be rich and wholesome.

I believe in village people; in their ability to solve their own problems and in their power to develop their own lives.

Therefore.

I shall with sincerity of purpose, work, with village men, women and children for better family living, by helping them to make their fields and livestock more productive, their homes more comfortable and beautiful, and their community more satisfying."[1]

This code can be adapted for the village level workers and a similar code can be laid down for personnel administrators.

Code for personnel administrators:[2] "We who share responsibility for personnel administration pledge to;

(1) Place respect for human dignity above all other considerations.

(2) Discharge our duties with a high sense of responsibility to the organisation, its personnel, the community and the home.

(3) Aid in the development of each employee's potentiality and help place them in the position by which he is best fitted.

(4) Hold confidential information in inviolable trust.

(5) Be truthful and objective in all recommendations. Never obscure the facts for the sake of expediency or temporise with difficult personnel problems.

(6) Encourage supervisors to discuss with employees all changes that affect them.

(7) Represent, with full loyalty to both, the employees' interests to management and management's interests to employees; try to show how the interests of one group is essentially the true interest of the other.

(8) Teach, by example, how every member of the organisation is responsible for making himself as efficient as possible, maintaining the highest standards of quality and quantity in his daily work and striving constantly to improve his work methods.

(9) In discharging personnel duties, bear in mind that supervisors have primary responsibility for personnel administration.

(10) Recognise that the overall objective of personnel administration is to protect the just interests of all who are served by the organisation.

[1]Used by Allahabad Agriculture Institute, Allahabad for Gaon Sathi.
[2]Boris Blai: Jr., *Civilian Personnel Officer* (Mimeographed),

(11) Constantly develop and adopt improved methods of personnel administration.
(12) Exemplify in the personnel office those standards of personnel management which are recommended to the supervisors.

Principles to be included in code of ethics

(1) Recognise the need to coordinate activities in which more than one branch of extension service is involved.
(2) Recognise the obligation to develop an appreciation and understanding of the basic principles of the extension service and to uphold them; refrain from using one's selfish objectives.
(3) Prevent disparagement of fellow-workers and predecessors and feel proud of the profession.
(4) Maintain good health—both mental and physical.
(5) Transact all official business through proper channels and hold all inviolate confidential information.
(6) Give due notice in fair time all appointments, resignations or terminations of service, etc.
(7) Be impartial in all relationship with others avoid personal bias or prejudice.
(8) Highly respect the hidden potentialities of with whom one works and do everything feasible to promote one's development.
(9) Be able to make an impartial of the work of an individual in the profession. Expect and welcome it for oneself.
(10) Continue personal development through study, travel, participation in professional and community life and through wholesome human relationships.
(11) Be fair in determining salary schedules in the organisation.
(12) Always maintain friendliness, tolerance, patience, unselfishness, sympathy and cooperation in the relationships with colleagues.
(13) Remember that this is a profession and that its duties require long hours of service, without regard to personal wishes and convenience.
(14) Be diligent and conscientious in conveying the ideals of the profession, namely "To help people help themselves".
(15) Regard as of the highest value the greatest good of the person or person with whom one works, and avoid using another merely as a means to an end.

SUPERVISION

Supervision is generally defined as the art of directing the activities of human beings. Accordingly, supervision can be defined as follows:

"Supervision...is selecting the right person for each job; arousing in person an interest in his work and teaching him how to do it. Measuring and rating performance to be sure that teaching has been fully effective; administering correction where this is found to be necessary and transferring to more suitable work or dismissing those for whom this proves ineffective; commending whatever praise is merited, rewarding for good work, and finally fitting each person harmoniously into the working group—all done fairly, patiently and tactfully, so that each person is caused to do his work skilfully, accurately and completely".[1]

By good supervision, we can motivate people to do better extension work, and this is the aim of defining the term supervision so that we may be able to enlist a few factors that improve supervision in the light of helping extension workers to motivate. As people differ in their attitudes and behaviour, the supervisor has to try many factors so that the persons whom he supervises may be handled in a better way. These factors can be listed as follows;

(1) Supervision is a cooperative activity. It takes place through shared ideas, efforts and experience of all the staff members. Cooperation provides opportunity for the growth of the supervisor as well as the growth of the employee.

(2) Supervision is creative and not prescriptive. It provides opportunity for orginality and self-expression.

(3) Supervision substitutes leadership for authority—opportunities are provided for cooperative formulation of policies, plans and goals.

(4) The supervisor should maximise responsibility and minimise authority.

(5) The supervisor should not try to impose his own work, habits, style or tempo on the workers under his supervision. He must have a 'feel' for the behaviour of the people.

(6) The supervisor should be sensitive to the opinions of others. He should think 'with' rather than 'for' the workers. Discussion should pass up through the line of communication.

(7) The supervisor should inform the worker under him about changes in work affecting him.

(8) The supervisor should try to develop the abilities and skills of those under his supervision.

(9) The supervisor should give clear but general instruction. He should seek to tell extension agents, in a clear and concise fashion, what is expected of them and then let them work out details.

(10) The supervisor should be consultative in his approach—"What do you think about this? rather than a "do this" approach.

(11) The supervisor should provide a sense of security and an opportunity for mutual understanding.

(12) The supervisor should avoid favouritism.

(13) The supervisor should avoid reprimanding or checking the workers in public.

(14) The supervisor should work with the worker in helping him to overcome a particular weakness. This develops self-confidence in him.

By using these factors, the supervisor will be able to motivate the extension workers under him. He can get more and better work by adopting these.

Factors over which the supervisor or administrator has control and which affect the morale of extension workers

(1) He should let each extension worker under him know how he is doing.

(2) He should give credit for work well done and achievements.

[1]Halsey G.D., *Supervising People* Harper and Brothers, N. Y. 1946, p. 6.

(3) He should utilise each worker to his full capacity.

(4) He should give them the chance of self-realisation.

(5) He should tell his assistants in advance about changes affecting him or the group.

(6) He should be fair and should avoid all favouritism.

(7) For increasing job satisfaction, he should:

    (a) Treat each employee with respect.

    (b) Give credit when it is due.

    (c) When correction is needed, do it promptly and tactfully.

    (d) Take prompt action on grievances sympathetically.

(8) Besides all these, he should infuse in his staff the spirit and enthusiasm of the code of conduct which is behind the programme and according to which they are expected to act. The following is an example of it:

The supervisor should repeat time and again.[1]

(1) The villager is one of our important teachers. He is our supervisor in many ways. He manages to live under conditions which most of us could not endure. He has had many years' experience in his occupation. We can learn much from him.

(2) We must be humble in our approach. We must be willing to work side by side with him in his field sincerely and honestly.

(3) We must not assume the role of an expert. We must observe more, listen more and talk less.

(4) We must show appreciation for the villager's achievements, opinions and his knowledge.

(5) We must observe and record the reactions of the villager to our efforts to gain his confidence.

(6) We must use our initiative and resourcefulness in doing constructive work to help the villagers in any way he needs.

(7) We must be patient and tolerant.

(8) We must be persistent in our efforts to win the confidence of the villagers.

(9) In his office, and also near the work-place of his staff, the administrator should hang photographs of leaders like Mahatma Gandhi and Jawahar Lal Nehru, Lal Bahadur Shastri, etc., and should fix on wall pictures or slogans or sayings which will motivate workers towards patriotism and national feeling and towards the need of their service to the nation.

The slogans or sayings can be:

(1) "Salvation of India lies in cottages." —*M.K. Gandhi (Bapu)*

(2) Thus spoke the Mahatma: (Fig. 45.2)

"I would say that if the village perishes, India will perish soon. India will be no more India. Her own mission in the world will get lost. The revival of the village is possible only when it is no more exploited. . . . . ." —*M.K.Gandhi*

(3) The village work frightens us. We who are town-bred find it trying to take to the village life. Our bodies in many cases do not respond to the hard life. But

[1]Adopted from: Government of West Bengal, Development Centre, *Community Development Project*, p. 62.

it is a difficulty, which we have to face boldly, even heroically, if our desire is to establish Swaraj (Independence) for the people, not substitute one class rule by another, which may be even worse......"
—*M.K. Gandhi*

"The Community Development Projects appear to me to be something of vital importance not only in the national achievement that they would bring about but much more so because they seek to build up the community, individual, and to make the latter to build up his own village centre and India in a larger sense." —*Jawahar Lal Nehru*

Fig. **45.2** Mahatma Gandhi

Responsibilities and principles of extension supervisors. Those who happen to work as supervisers in the extension programme can improve the working by adopting the following responsibilities and principles.

(1) Make a job analysis and develop a job description for each position.

(2) Help employees to develop a feeling of responsibility toward the job.

(3) Make the job as meaningful as possible so that it challenges each employee to develop and use his potential capacities.

(4) Develop methods for making work easier without lowering the standards of the organisation.

(5) Make vivid and to the employee the important reason why a given standard needs to be met.

(6) Provide induction and in-service training for employees.

(7) Introduce new employees to fellow-workers.

(a) Give consideration to assignment of a "sponsor" with whom the new employee may feel freer to talk and ask questions.

(8) Introduce new employees to supervisers in the department under whom he will work.

(9) Provide a sense of security and an opportunity for mutual understanding.

(10) Help develop employees as individuals and set up conditions that favour team-work.

(11) Rely on the self-discipline of responsible employees and such self-regulation as inevitably develops in effective team-work.

(12) Recognise and act on the fact that employees need to have some part in establishing good human relations in the organisation.

(13) Provide for employee participation in decision-making.

(14) Be employee-centred.

(15) Use the consultative in approach—"What do you think about this"? rather than the "do this" approach.

(16) Allow for individual differences and self-expression.

(17) Try to understand each employee.

(18) Make effective use of employee differences.

(19) Respect the dignity of each employee.

(20) Give consideration to the human needs of all employees as well as to the technical requirements of the job.

(21) Take time to listen to what each employee has to say.

(22) Find out what the employee means even if he hesitates to say all that he would like to say.

(23) Consider group relations.

(24) Avoid favouritism.

(25) Never encourage employees to talk unfavourably about each other.

(26) Help employees to get a perspective on personal claims by seeing them in relation to situational needs, and the objectives and policy of the organisation.

(27) Make changes as gradually as possible and make only a few changes at a time.

(28) Give clear, precise, timely and acceptable orders.

(29) Give orders that correspond to the employees' development and that match the level of his sense of responsibility.

(30) Give constructive criticism to employees at regular intervals.

(31) Avoid indiscriminate blame.

(32) Avoid reprimanding an employee in public.

(33) Show confidence, when possible, in the employee's good intentions and his capacity to improve in the future.

(34) Encourage the employee to give his reasons for sub-standard work and performance.

(35) Inform employee of disciplinary policy.

(36) Place less direct emphasis upon production as the ultimate goal.

(37) Give a dissatisfied employee an opportunity to express his complaint without the fear of retaliation.

(38) Work with an employee in helping him to overcome a particular weakness.

(39) Settle complaints, as soon as possible, so that they do not become grievances.

(40) Handle complaints or grievances so as to bring out their full significance to the employee who is directly involved.

(41) Handle complaints or grievances with a sense of satisfactory adjustment in regard to the specific problem.

(42) Have frequent contacts with employees.

(43) Think of functions and not only of functionaries.

(44) Think of both function and personnel in relation to the objectives of the organisation.

(45) Take the long view and not just meet each situation as though it existed only for the present.

A supervisor's rating scale: A supervisor may rate himself as regards his ability to supervise his subordinates, on these points:

(1) *Forcefulness*

    (a) Do I give orders properly and see that they are followed out, maintaining a business-like attitude constantly?

(b) Do I keep in touch with the efforts of my men so that I know how well each is working?

(c) Do I preserve the right balance between being too stern and showing too much familiarity?

(2) *Ability to inspire confidence*
(a) Do I show respect for my men and myself?
(b) Am I impartial, or do I play at favourites?
(c) Do I exercise self-control, or do I allow my temper frequently to get the better of me?

(3) *Ability to take a personal interest in the men*
(a) Do I talk to the men as men rather than as inferiors?
(b) Do I give them personal training and discuss their work with them?
(c) Do I get things for them which they would be unable to get without my assistance?
(d) Do I help them to realise their ambitions?

(4) *Ability to get the work done correctly*
(a) Do I give instructions so clearly that no one can misunderstand what is wanted?
(b) Do I check upon my men to see that my orders are followed out exactly?

(5) *Ability to get and use the ideas*
(a) Am I successful in getting suggestions from the men?
(b) Do I use these suggestions when get them?
(c) Do I give credit to the man who gives me an idea when I am talking about it to my supervisors and colleagues?

(6) *Ability to be one of the men*
(a) Do I work with them rather than over them?

(7) *Ability to lead rather than boss over the men*
(a) Do I show the men how they can work more efficiently, rather than order them about showing them how?
(b) Do I train them in better methods?
(c) Do I set the example by being as hard on myself as I am on any of my subordinates?

(8) *Ability to develop team-work*
(a) Am I careful to plan ahead?
(b) Is the mechanical equipment for which I am responsible always ready for work?
(c) Do I place the right men in the right positions?
(d) Do I allocate responsibility for results so that my men know what they have to do?
(e) Does the spirit of team-work exist among my men?

(9) *Ability to show kindliness without being considered easy*
   (a) Do I remember that my men are human beings and treat them with common courtesy?
   (b) Do I work for the inrerests of my men?
   (c) Do I know how to keep the men from imposing on my good nature?
   (d) Can I properly balance praise and censure?

(10) *Ability to reprimand properly*
   (a) Do I always make sure of my case before I reprimand?
   (b) Do I give reprimands in private, except in unusual cases?
   (c) Do I reprimand in a straightforward manner, or do I merely nag.
   (d) Do I give the reasons for my reprimands?
   (e) Do I follow up the reprimand?

(11) *Ability to keep from worrying*
   (a) Do I worry too much about myself, my home, or my job?

(12) *Ability to delegate work properly*
   (a) Do I entrust responsibility to my men, allowing them to make some mistakes?
   (b) Do I train them on the job so that they can take over that I ought to give them?
   (c) Am I willing to delegate work, or do I feel that I want to do everything myself?

(13) *Ability to call forth the best efforts of the men*
   (a) Can I develop enthusiasm in my men?
   (b) Do I know how to prevent idling and carelessness?

(14) *Ability to train men on the job*
   (a) Do I know how to analyse a job before teaching it to a beginner?
   (b) Do I show him carefully how to do it?
   (c) Do I let him try it while I watch?
   (d) Do I correct his mistakes?
   (e) Am I in the habit of keeping my eye on a beginner until he is able to do the job well?

(15) *Ability to make a new man feel at home*
   (a) Do I indroduce the new man to the older men around him?
   (b) Do I show personal interest in him?
   (c) Do I make it easy for him to ask questions?

(16) *Self-confidence*
   (a) Am I sure of myself on the job, or am I afraid of it?
   (b) Do I help my subordinate to overcome self-consciousness?
   (c) Do I show him that he is better than he thinks he is?

(17) *Accident prevention*

(a) Do I believe in safety and accident prevention while working with projectors, electric generators, etc.

(b) Do I know that most of the men working for me have never had to do the kind of work they are doing today or have not heard of a safety programme for electricity, motor-cycle, jeep, etc.

(c) Do I wait for an accident to happen before correcting an unsafe condition or do I *plan ahead*?

(d) Do I read safety bulletins and explain them to my men?

(e) Do I just *tell* my men to "be careful", or do I *show* them the safe way and explain why?

(f) Do I assume the responsibility for safety conditions on my job, or do I "pass the buck" along to the engineer or someone else?

ADMINISTRATIVE AREAS AND FIELD SERVICES

The headquarters and the field

The Government and the administration of any large community cannot be efficiently conducted from a single centre. The people to whose needs the government and administration cater are spread all over the country and more important services have to be carried to their very door. It will not do to have a single big post office or huge school at Delhi and to ask the people of India outside that city to get their post or to send their children to that school or post office. Therefore, numerous sub-centres of government and administration, each to serve the needs of a convenient area attached in administration resulting from the division of the work functionwise for managing the work at field level is essential.

The central place of a given area, where its highest government or administration authority and office is located and from which administrative direction and control fan out over the entire area is known as 'Headquarters' and the rest of the area is called the 'field'. In the indigenous system of India these are known as 'Sadar' and 'Mofussil' respectively. Both the terms are relative to the area we have in mind. When we think of the whole of India, New Delhi is the headquarters, and the rest of the country, including the state capitals are thought of as the field. When we refer to the States, the State Capitals are thought of as headquarters instead of being considered mere field stations of the centre. In the same way the principal cities of districts, tehsils and lesser areas are their respective headquarters, though in relation to bigger administrative areas and their headquarters higher up they are mere field stations.

The field organisation, both in respect of area and authority, is often multi-level. More than one tier or level intervenes between the highest headquarters and the field where the citizen dwells. Thus a villager in India finds himself under no fewer than four governing areas and jurisdictions, namely, of his Village Panchayat, the District Board, the State Government and the National Government. Between the Directorate General of the Post Office at Delhi and the village, six postal areas and centres intervene—the village post office area, the sub-post office area, the postal district, the division and the postal circle, and usually the States.

Governmental and administrative areas

In this connection a distinction should be made between Governmental and Administrative areas. Sometimes the same area is both governmental and administrative, but this is not always. While a government area is usually an administrative one also, the opposite is not true. India as whole, the various States, municipalities, districts, village panchayats are government as well as administrative areas, but the railway zones are only administrative. Distinctions between these areas are:

(1) Government area has its separate constitutional organisation consisting of an elective body called Legislative, Municipal, District Board. Whatever its name, the governmental organisation of such an area is constituted by an exercise of the vote of the people and not by the nomination or appointment of a higher authority.

(2) The governmental area has always an autonomous sphere of activity allotted to it by law or charter. The amount of autonomy may be large or small, but the area always has it in its own right and not on sufferance of some higher authority.

(3) Government area has its separate corporate existence and function. The district in India is an administrative subdivision of the State, but in most States it is also a governmental area, because it has its elected District Board, separate from district office of the Collector, who is main officer of the State Government in charge of it as an administrative subdivision.

(4) The governing body of a governmental area has the power of raising revenue by means of taxation, while no such power belongs to an administrative area or unit. The district as an administrative unit in India, for example, has no power of taxation. Its office in-charge, the Collector or the Deputy Commissioner, cannot raise even a paise by way of taxation, except in pursuance of some law of the State Legislature. The district as an area of local self-government, however, has such power as is vested in its District Board.

Factors determining the formation of governmental areas

The factors which determine the boundaries of the governmental areas are:

(1) *Historical:* In every country many of the Governmental areas are the result of historical accident rather than design. This is largely so in case of the present States in India, Madras, Bengal and Bombay Presidencies grew round the principal commercial settlements which the East India Company established in the early days of its career.

(2) *Geographical:* In a country broken by hills and other natural barriers, geography determines many Governmental boundaries. Punjab and the Uttar Pradesh have been separate units, because they are divided by a watershed.

(3) *Political:* The political factor is related to the considerations of the State policy, or the wishes and the sentiments of the people.

(4) *Financial:* The financial factor may lead to the amalgamation of financially inadequate units with their larger neighbours.

(5) Legal considerations prevent the incorporation of an area under foreign jurisdiction into its neighbouring unit, even when its exclusion is inconvenient in a number of ways. The French and the Portuguese settlements in India could not be merged into the States within whose boundaries they were situated for this reason.

Criteria of the suitability of governmental and administrative areas

(1) The area should be financially adequate, i.e., it should have sufficient revenues to meet the cost of a separate system of government and administration and provide an adequate margin of resources for its development. Each new governmental unit involves additional overhead charges by way of the salaries and expenses of the Governor, the Ministers, the Members of the Legislature, the Secretariat, the High Court and the rest of the paraphernalia of the governmental machinery required. If an inordinately large proportion of the revenues of the area are consumed in meeting these costs, too little would be left for purposes of development and welfare activities. In these circumstances, either a subsidy from the Centre would be required, or the area would remain backward. Considerations of economy require that one overhead system of government and administration should cater the needs of as large an area as possible, consistently with the needs of span of control and efficiency.

(2) It should have an adequate population. The revenue of an area largely depends upon its population, but even apart from this, a certain size of population is required to provide an adequate clientele for services offered. Otherwise, they would become uneconomical and wasteful. A school requires an appurtenant population with children to fill its classes. Otherwise the school cannot run.

(3) The size of the area also depends on the means of transport available.

(4) Many of the services have their own geographical scope and the units of their administration have to correspond to that in extent. Thus the railways, and trunkroads are national in scope.

In case of purely administrative areas, two things are required: first, the area must have population enough to provide work for a wholetime staff. Secondly, it should not be so large as to make its headquarters difficult of access to people living at its extremities.

Field organisation

By field services, or organisation of an administrative agency we mean the personnel stationed away from its headquarters in the country, to carry on its work from the numerous subdivisions within easy reach of the people. It is only through the field personnel that the administration can reach the people. The staff stationed in the field is usually much larger than at the headquarters. Field services are required not only by big jurisdictions like the National Government but also by smaller ones like States, districts, municipalities. It is only through them the individual citizen scattered over large areas can be reached. The staff is not only operational but also supervisory. Where the number of field workers is large, they cannot be effectively supervised and controlled from the headquarters and it becomes necessary to station field supervisors amongst them.

Various patterns of field organisation

Willoughby distinguishes two types of field organisation.

Unitary type: Under unitary type, the various functional departments or units at headquarters do not deal with their opposite numbers located in the field directly, but through a Regional Chief Administrator under whose general supervision the various field services are placed and to whom they report. The system is called unitary because under it there is a single line of command running from the headquarters to the Regional Chief, and it is from the latter that different lines of command and communication to various functional field units branch off. Whatever the headquarters people have to say or order, is said or ordered through the Regional Chief, who then communicates the information or instructions to the field unit concerned. The best example of this type of organisation is found in France and in India. In India the District Collector is the principal chief whois expected to keep his eyes on the whole of the district.

Multiple type: Under the multiple type of field organisation the line of command runs directly from the functional units at headquarters to their respective staff in the field. Here there is no intervention of a middle office in overall control of the regional offices. Each service may, of course, have its own regional headquarters, supervisory officers, but there is no single person controlling the activities in the field.

Luther Gullick distinguishes three types of organisation.

All-fingers: Under the all-fingers pattern the central headquarters office deals direct with the field units without the intervention of any geographical or regional subdivisions anywhere.

Short arms and long fingers: In this type there are geographical divisions or units, but they are located in the central office itself and not in field. This is usually the case with the foreign office or department.

Long arms and short fingers: In this type the geographical sub-divisions are located away from the headquarters in the field itself like the district office in India. In this metaphorical description arms stand for the regional or geographical offices while fingers mean the lines of communication reaching to the lowest field units at the firing line.

The implications of this type may be made clear by an example of hievarchy Police organisation in our State—At present the policemen at various police stations report to the District Superintendent of Police which has his office at the district centre, and he in turn to the Inspector General at the State capital. This is a long arm-short fingers organisation, because S.P.'s office is away from State capital in the field. If the District Superintendent's offices are removed to the State capital and because there are so many regional units of the IG office, the police stations would report to the S.P. for their district, but now functioning from the State instead of the district headquarters. He would now be farther from them and nearer to his own chief than before. This would be the short arm-long finger arrangement. If, however, the District Superintendent of Police and their offices were altogether scrapped so that each police station report to the IG office at State headquarters the all-finger arrangement would obtain.

Reasons for the growth of field organisation

(1) The need to get the particular functions performed because; as we noted, it is only through the field employees scattered all over the country that administration can hope to reach the people.

(2) Development of field agencies may take place with a view to centralisation or decentralisation. In this connection it should be carefully noted that the establishment of field organisation does not in itself involve either centralisation or decentralisation. It can be an instrument of either of them. If the purpose of field organisation is to tighten the central supervision and control over autonomous local government through

the agents stationed at the spot, the rest is centralisation. If on the other hand, field offices of a central agency are created to permit administrative adaptations to local conditions, then a good deal of initiative and power of decision has to be left in the hands of those offices and the result is decentralisation.

(3) Technological progress has also necessitated and encouraged the growth of field organisation in two ways (a) The growth of science and (b) technological development which has revealed important aspects of functions like health, agriculture, education, etc.

PERSONNEL ADMINISTRATION

the agents stationed at the spot and the rest is good situation. Even the other handicaps ... confines of a central agency has created to permit administrative subordination to local ... conditioned than a good deal of initiative and powerful division has to .... 14 hands of those offices as a top trend is acceptable and ....

(4) T chronological progress is also recognised and recognised the growth of field ... organisation is own as ... (6) The growth of science and (b)recognisational development which has regulated particular aspects of the tion. Ike health, agriculture, education, etc.

CHAPTER 46

TRAINING PRINCIPLES AND PRACTICES

MEANING OF TRAINING

Training means to educate a person so as to be fitted, qualified, proficient in doing some job. For an extension worker, training includes education which aims at bringing a desirable change in the behaviour of the trainee, or the learner. This change requires a change in his knowledge, skills, attitudes, values, beliefs and understandings, so that he fits in his job and become qualified and proficient in communicating the desirable knowledge to his client system, i.e., the farmers, animal breeders, home-makers, etc.

Training of employees has been defined by Milton Hall as "the process of aiding employees to gain effectiveness in their present or future work through the development of appropriate habits of thought and action, skills, knowledge and attitudes." It consists mainly of telling, showing and guiding people in the performance of tasks and then in checking the results. Training is not only the idea of knowledge received, but that of such knowledge digested through application, drill and discipline. It means getting a man to do a job correctly, effectively and conscientiously—correctly, so that he can do or apply what he has learnt effectively, so that he can produce the desired results, conscientiously so that his underlying attitudes, convictions and enthusiasms provide the discipline he needs to keep on doing the right things in the right way and thus contribute to the welfare of the organisation.

According to Collins, training must include the instruction, and other learning experiences, which purport to fit the worker into the service so that he competently meets the demands of his job, as determined by the changing leadership needs of people. It has the characteristics of: (a) concern with skill; (b) concern with whole learning, (c) concern with practice, and (d) concern with safe experimentation.

It is an overt process, a sequence of experiences, a series of opportunities to learn, in which the trainee is exposed in some more or less systematic way to certain materials or events. Training is what done to the trainee and it exists to bring about learning in the training.

Lynton and Pareek discussed the relationship of training to other related areas such as education and learning. According to them, education is primarily concerned with opening out the world to the student so that he can choose his interests and mode of living and also his career. Training on the other hand is primarily concerned with preparing the participant for certain lines of action which are delineated by technology and by the organisation in which he works and which also improves his performance in it. Education deals mostly with knowledge and understanding whereas training deals mostly with understanding and skill.

EDUCATION VERSUS TRAINING

According to Sohal (1975), it is possible, although according to some it is not desirable, to differentiate 'Training' from 'Education'. There is in fact, far too much in common between them so that there could only be some hair-splitting differences of academic interest. In a restricted sense 'training' may be taken to connote the acquisition of knowledge, skills or attitudes needed specifically for performing a particular job, whereas 'education' may refer to all sorts of acquisitions, with or without a pre-specified purpose or job, to be performed. Education, is, therefore, inclusive of training as well. But the concept of 'education' in the present day is not merely confined to whatsoever is taking place in the formal seats of learning like schools, colleges, or universities. Any acquisition or change by way of addition in the behaviour complex of homosapiens, taking place at any time of his life from birth to death and from any source or manner, is aptly considered as "education".[1]

Graig and Bittel stated that; "The word 'training' despite the efforts of some to take it a semantic shipping-boy, is accepted as synonym for all of the forms of knowledge, skill and attitudinal development which adults need to keep pace with accelerated life involvement and the enlarging concept of man's capabilities." Sohal further suggests that 'training' has the embodiment, requirements and characteristics of education. At no time should training be considered as less exciting or inferior to education. As a matter of fact, in hardly any other setting concerning the dissemination of knowledge leading to the adoption of newly evolved innovation by extension workers, are the principles and theories of education so intimately and thoroughly applicable as would be the case when any of the methods dealing with training are involved. The need for knowing fully well the process and theories of learning is much more pronounced for anyone connected with 'training' than for those utilising other approaches for disseminating knowledge or bringing about changes in behaviour. It must, however, be remembered that this comparison is of 'degree' and not of kind. It must not be inferred that knowledge of the learning process is of no consequence for the extension worker using methods other than training.

IMPORTANCE OF TRAINING

The per acre yields, or per milch animal milk production or egg laying per poultry layer is the lowest in India as compared to other countries. This is because there is a large gap in the latest technology known and the technology being used by the farmers, animal raisers and poultry keepers, etc. The same is true regarding Home Science, health and sanitation. Our resources are not being utilised properly because our

[1]T.S. Sohal, *Concept, Genesis and Philosophy of Extension Education.*

people in the villages are ignorant about many scientific innovations. The communication of the desired knowledge requires trained personnel, who have knowledge of the techniques, are interested in doing their job efficiently and know the ways of imparting this knowledge to the people who need it. To raise 60 quintals of paddy or wheat per hectare in place of 51 quintals per hectare requires the assistance of properly trained extension workers. These proper or appropriate training requires: (1) Relating the contents of the syllabus at the colleges or training centres to the needs of extension agents; (2) The teaching of manual skills; and (3) Teaching for developing desirable attitudes for working with villagers, kitchen gardeners or poultry keepers in the rural as well as urban areas.

In other words it can be said that the training needs to communicate: (1) What to extend, i.e., the knowledge of technical subject—how to grow crops scientifically, how to raise better animals, better birds, what crops to grow, what to feed animals, how to control pests and diseases, and (2) How to extend i.e., knowledge of extension education, including methods of extension, or communication, programme planning, administration in extension; rural sociology, rural social system, rural Organisation, Planned Social Change, etc.

Without such knowledge the extension worker cannot do his job effectively. Even if he has sound knowledge of a technical subject e.g., in crop-raising, and does not know how to communicate this knowledge effectively he cannot do his job properly. This is like knowing the mechanism of a motor car but not knowing how to drive it. Because of the lack of knowledge of extension methods, the extension service of the State Departments of Agriculture before 1952, could not do its job effectively. Before 1953 our country did not realise that there could be a subject like extension education. Graduate trained in Extension Education and Rural Sociology were available to the extension service after 1959 and this marks a turning point in India's extension service. The technology was there, the agricultural colleges existed in India since 1905, but they did not know "How to Extend". Because of the lack of this knowledge most of our technology remained in the files of plant breeders, entomologists and crop specialists. The gap between the research institutes and the farmers continued because of this missing link. The integration of the teaching, research and extension, and the training of the extension workers was responsible for the Green Revolution. The history of the development of Agriculture in the USA, Taiwan, Japan, Israel shows that it was because of trained extension personnel and in-service training of the extension workers that the gap between the technology known and the technology used by the farmers could be removed. So the earlier we are able to provide trained personnel who passed the technology and know the job of educating the farmers, the faster will be our rate of adoption and growth rate.

Need for training

It is felt that a young person entering a career will have to be trained for two or three professions in the span of their active lines of work. This is because many new developments will render much of today's knowledge obsolete.

Man's knowledge, like machines, can rapidly become obsolescent. "Training is a means to reduce the obsolescence among people and organisations in the face of relentless technological innovation."

The professional worker must keep abreast of the latest development in his field, otherwise he will soon be working far below his potential and capacities.

Training improves a person's skill, his power of intelligence and develops in him the desired attitudes and values required for his work. Training helps the new entrant to acquire occupational work-skills and the latest knowledge, makes him familiar with the objectives of the organisation to which he belongs and helps to make his potential contribution in promoting the goals of his organisation. Training also makes up for any deficiencies in the new recruits and maintains or boosts up the morale of the staff. It is conducive to cohesion in regard to methods of work and approach to problems.

Training has special significance in the field of agricultural development and in the context of community development extension since the very essence of these programmes is to train rural people to solve most of their problems individually or in groups. The success of the extension worker can be judged ultimately by the extent to which he has been able to make the village people self-reliant, in getting them to do things by themselves without relying on outside help.

Ensminger has stated that it is not enough to agree that all staff—administrators, specialists, village extension workers—should be trained in the methods of exten-, sion education. To be trained in extension for community development means, according to him, first to understand the philosophy and objectives of community development; second, to understand what is meant by extension; third, to know what can be expected from the correct use of extension; fourth, to know how to apply extension methods and finally to know how to evaluate the effectiveness of the extension methods used.

It has been pointed out that extension involves not only educating the rural people in determining their problems and methods of solving them, but also inspiring them towards positive action. It is, therefore, of the highest importance for this task that personnel of the right types are obtained who will take to their work with zeal and enthusiasm.

The role of the extension worker, discussed earlier, indicates clearly the need for a new kind of worker. This has been recognised by the planners and administrators of rural development programmes. This type of worker should be able to get on well with the common people, know their way of life, have sympathy with their hopes and aspirations and possess a genuine desire to help them. In contrast to the past, Government servants must approach the villager as a friend—one who wants to and will help the villager learn how to make decisions and achieve for himself and his family a better way of life.

TYPES OF TRAINING FOR EXTENSION WORKERS

The training of extension workers can be classified as follows:

(1) *Pre-service training:* i.e., the training the extension worker receives before joining the actual job. This includes his education at a High School or Higher Secondary School, a general college or professional college, namely: Agricultural University, Agricultural College, Veterinary College, College of Agricultural Engineer-

ing. Home Science college, Engineering college, Medical college from where the extension workers receive degrees of B. Sc./B. Sc., (Ag.), B.V. Sc., B.Sc. Agri. Engg., B. Tech/B.E. and the specific training as in case of a village level worker at the VLW Training Centre, for nurses at Nurses' Training Centre in Medical Science or Family Planning.

(2) *In-service training:* This is for improving the ability of the extension worker, or keeping him abreast of the latest knowledge, or giving him some special training in the new job he is required to do. This may be (a) Orienting the new worker after he joins the job, or orienting an old worker with the new job he is required to do; (b) Induction training; (c) Job training; (d) Short range courses; (e) Periodical meetings and conferences, seminars, workshops, etc.

(a) Orientation of new entrants: The worker when he joins the job needs to be oriented to the organisational set up where he has to work, the philosophy behind the organisation, the code of conduct e.g., the extension and C.D. worker have to have training in the correct approach to the farmer, his relationship, the ways of doing things, facilities he will get, reports he is to submit, broad principles of extension work, etc. For this job, there are some orientation and study centres.

(b) Induction training: Some institutions have been designed where extension workers can be given the knowledge of the working and organisation of community development and extension service, his place of work and his place in the work-team. The orientation centres do this job.

(c) Short-range courses: The Directorate of Extension in the Ministry of Food and Agriculture and Community Development through the State Agriculture and Veterinary Departments and Agricultural Colleges and Universities organises 45 days training at Agricultural and Veterinary Colleges. About 35 AEOs are deputed for such training and are paid Rs. 75 per month in addition to their pay and travelling allowance, etc. They are given training in technical subjects like latest varieties and cultural practices, plant protection, use of fertilisers, horticulture and extension methods. Similar training is given to Veterinary Extension Officers, also.

(d) Job training: If the extension workers are required to do some special job like soil conservation or land scaping, they may be deputed to get this special training being given at some specially designed centres. In soil conservation it may be at Dehradun Forest Institute in U.P., or at Kota in Rajasthan, etc.

(e) Periodical meetings and conferences: Agricultural Universities, now organise such training in collaboration with State Agricultural and Veterinary Departments, for Extension Officers, working at District Level or above. *Rabi* and *kharif* meetings are held to work out the Package of Practices for various districts for the coming crop seasons. At such meetings the research staff and the subject-matter specialists of the University or colleges are also invited. There may be some special workshops on information and communication, viz., Soybean Conference, Minor Irrigation and Water use, etc. These are held to refresh the extension workers. Similar courses of about three months are organised for village level workers at VLW training centres, and also for other extension personnel.

Training process

Lynton and Pareek divided the process of training into three phases: Pre-training,

Training and Post-training.

In case of pre-service and induction trainings, no previous experience is needed for the trainee as he is a fresher, and hence he usually accepts whatever he is offered as his need. But in case of in-service training, the participant may feel the need for more skill in a particular job so as to qualify for it, or to understand particular things or events, so as to continue to grow as a person. Here the participant's motivation and point of view will determine his focus of attention and learning. Sometimes the general reputation of the course, and the institution running it, the ways people are selected for it, and its cost, all play a part in the personal calculation that each prospective participant makes for himself before he is even sent for training.

Training phase: In addition to his work experience, the in-service training participant brings to the programme his expectations and explores in the training situation the subjects that interest him. The training institution's basic task is to provide the necessary opportunities to solve the job problems and meet his expectations. Having explored, the participant tries out some new behaviour. If the participant finds the new behaviour useful, he incorporates the new item into his habitual behaviour in the training situation. If he does not find it useful, he discards it or tries an alternative one. This intricate selection goes on continuously and more or less consciously.

After the training phase, the in-service trainee goes back to his work. He goes prepared with some anticipations of the encounters he will face. When he actually arrives he finds a changed situation and there begins a process of adjustment. For instance the newly learned skills undergo modification to fit in with the work situation. The participant may find his organisation encouraging and helping him to use his training and also offering him the additional support of continuing contact with the training institutions. At worst the colleagues, the organisation, the family members, will let the returning participant know they resented his absence and the extra burden it puts on those who stayed behind, that his holiday is now over, and that he better get back to work to make up for lost time. In that case, contact with the training institutions is broken off. Thus the preparation of the trainee prior to coming to the training institution and his behaviour after the actual training in his own organisation should also be considered for effective training.

Principles of extension training

Some of the basic principles of training are briefly discussed below:

(1) Motivation is basic to good training. A good trainer must start his work by creating a feeling of need or want in the trainee since the actual willingness and desire to learn come from within the person. Basic needs, wants, desires, motives, incentives or urges have been classified broadly in four ways:

   (i) the desire for security—economic, social, psychological and spiritual security.

   (ii) the desire for new experience—adventure, new interests, new ideas, new friends and new ways of doing things.

   (iii) the desire for affection and response—companionship, gregariousness and social mindedness; the need for a feeling of belonging.

   (iv) the desire for recognition—status, prestige, achievement and being looked upto. These are all powerful motivating forces for learning.

(2) Good training requires specific and clearly defined objectives. The different

aspects of the training objectives, namely the persons to be trained, the behavioural changes to be developed in them, the content or subject-matter to which the behaviour is related and the real situation in which the changes are to take place must be clearly spelled out in the training objectives.

(3) Good training must accomplish certain kinds of educational changes in relation to the subject matter learned. These may be changes in knowledge, or things known; changes in skills or ability to do new things, including mental skills and manual or physical skills; and changes in attitudes or feelings for or against things and issues, points of view etc., including changes in interest, and changes in understanding.

(4) Good training requires effective learning situations which include five major elements, viz., Teacher, Learner, Subject-matter, Teaching Aids and Facilities or Environment.

(5) Good training should provide effective learning experiences to the trainees.

(6) Good training requires usually a combination of training techniques. Training should involve appropriate activities engaging the maximum number of senses and a combination of techniques such as oral, visual, audio-visual and doing things.

(7) Training should be challenging and satisfying. To be challenging, subject-matter must be presented in the form of problems for which the trainees should be encouraged to find solutions. Appropriate and timely recognition should be given to the trainees' achievements. Fear and ridicule have no place in the training process and their use in a training programme is usually an adverse reflection on the ability of the trainer.

(8) Good training requires careful evaluation of results.

Nature of training

The nature of training depends upon the training needs of extension work.

Training needs can be determined by finding out the difference between what is being done now and what ought to be done in near future. The gap gives clues to the kind and amount of training needed.

The training needs may be those of an individual or of a group; needed immediately or sometime in the future; call for formal or informal activities; and the organisation can meet its needs by itself or meet through outside resources.

There are different ways of determining the training needs. Each may meet a specific situation and they can be used singly or in combination. Some methods of ascertaining training needs are:

(i) Analysis of jobs performed by extension personnel;
(ii) Analysis of equipment used in the job;
(iii) Analysis of problems faced by the workers;
(iv) Analysis of behaviour of the workers;
(v) Analysis of organisation; and
(vi) Appraisal of performance of the personnel.

Problems and prospects of training

It has been clearly understood that the main objective of a training programme is to bring about a desirable change in the trainee. According to R.L. Ebel, this change if it is important must make an observable difference in the behaviour, i.e., under some circumstances, a person who has more of training must behave differently from a person who has less of it, or not had it at all.

Thus the main problem is the problem of making training effective. That sometimes it is not due to the following sub-problems:

(1) What is taught to trainees, is often not relevant to their work or situation.
(2) The trainers do not know the techniques of transferring their knowledge to trainees.
(3) Lack of clear concept about training and wrong attitudes of the trainers and trainees.
(4) Lack of proper motivation and incentives.
(5) Reasonable methods of assessing effectiveness of training are absent.
(6) Problems in recruiting the right kind of trainers and trainees.
(7) Disparities of socio-psycho-economic status of trainees in a group.
(8) Information overloading, i.e., too much information in too short a time.
(9) Training processes do not correspond to the operations and timings.
(10) Lack of training about utilisation of available resources and inputs. No linking of training to the available inputs.
(11) Lack of communication and feedback in the post-training phase.
(12) Lack of media support and non-coordination among agencies to support an integrated training programme.
(13) Non-availability of resource persons and clashes between their timings and training schedules.
(14) Rare pre- post surveys of training effectiveness by the institutions.
(15) Non-utilisation of available research findings in shaping an effective, need-based and useful training programme.

In a research review on training A.N. Shukla made a critical review of the researches conducted in the field of "Training of Extension Personnel". His observations are given below:

(1) Very little interest has been shown by the extension research workers in this field. This necessitates that more research should be planned and conducted successfully.
(2) Sporadic attempts have been made to conduct researches on training of extension personnel. A sufficient number of comprehensive and in-depth studies should be taken up seriously.
(3) Most of the researches are based on opinion surveys. Also, most of the studies have made use of research instruments like questionnaires or schedules. The author feels that some sophisticated psychological research instruments like scales and tests should be utilised to collect empirical data.
(4) Some operational researches should be conducted to ascertain the effectiveness and adequacy of training of extension personnel.
(5) The following aspects should attract the attention of the research workers in extension education.
    (a) Working-efficiency/effectiveness of training centres in the light of the new Agricultural Universities especially when the Green Revolution has set in throughout the country.
    (b) Contents of training programme for each category of extension personnel.
    (c) Training needs.
    (d) Training methods.

    (e) Selection of trainees.

    (f) Establishment of performance standards for each category of extension personnel.

    (g) Effectiveness of training programmes in terms of behavioural changes.

(6) Coordinated research programmes should be initiated to evolve a somewhat universal pattern throughout the country.

TRAINING OF VILLAGERS AND PROFESSIONALS IN TECHNICAL THINGS

This covers the training of farmers, farmers' sons, auxiliary courses for poultry keepers, dairymen, kitchen gardeners and fruit preservation etc., for village people as well as urban people.

(1) Training of the farmers

Besides the National Demonstrations, Maximisation Demonstrations and other activities of the extension workers in the villages, there is a regular Farmers Training Programme in all Agricultural Universities. There are training centres for young farmers. In some States they also arrange short courses for the farmers. The training includes crop-raising, animal feeding and management, plant protection. For such training, the following points should be considered.

(a) Time of holding the training. It should be at the convenience of the farmers, i.e., when they are comparatively free from the rush of agricultural operations. This will differ according to the seasons and climate, for example in M.P., U.P., Punjab, and Haryana the months from January to March for *kharif* crop training and August to September for *rabi* crop are more suitable for courses in general agriculture.

(b) Duration of course. For farmers who are engaged in farming, a one week course is sufficient. On some special topics, such as, use of irrigation facilities and water management, operating some implements, plant protection, etc., it may be two or three days' duration.

(c) Venue of course. Besides physical facilities, the appropriate environment under which the course is to be conducted, i.e., where the farmers can see the actual crop, method demonstrations, operations with some machines and implements, or some treatments, such as the application of fertilisers, use of plant protection methods, etc. is to be given due consideration.

(d) Production-cum-demonstration camps and discussion groups of the farmers. These should be arranged in the villages because the farmers cannot afford to remain away from their farms and homes. The duration should be of 1-2 days only, and the trainees or participants should be from the same village or groups of nearby villages, so that the farmers can walk back to their home the same evening. This will provide technical knowledge to the farmers right in their villages, and the topics can be related to their local problems. This can be organised before each main crop season.

(2) Training for farmers' sons

In each State there are two or three Farmers' Sons Training Centres. In Madhya Pradesh there are four such training centres at Rewa (Kuthalia Farm), Gwalior, Raipur, and Jabalpur. The last two were established in July, 1970 and 1971. The procedure for such training is:

(1) The applicant who wants to receive training should himself be a farmer and should not be interested in service. His age should be 16-32 years. He should be able to understand simple Hindi and should be able to write and read it.

(2) He is given free boarding and lodging and second class railway or bus fare both ways.

(3) The duration of the course is five weeks, and four such courses are run in a year: (a) 16th Jan. to end of February; (b) 17th April to 31st May; (c) August 1st to 14th September; (d) 17th November to 31st Dec. The last dates for receipt of applications are: 31st December, 1st March, 1st July and 1st October for each course respectively.

The application is to be submitted to the Principal, Young Farmers Training Centre with details of land possessed, area under crops, number of wells, etc. The Young Farmers Association of India, New Delhi runs some of these centres.

Punjab Agricultural University runs a school for farmers' sons. Haryana also has a similar training school for farmers' sons. These can very well be utilised for farmers training also.

The efforts made in the past by various departments/agencies in this sphere are summarised below:

Ministry of Agriculture and Irrigation

The Rural Youth Programmes of the Ministry of Agriculture are being implemented by the Directorate of Extension, People's Action for Development India, Indian Council of Agricultural Research and Department of Rural Development.

Directorate of Extension (Department of Agriculture)

The Directorate of Extension have taken up the following programmes for farm youth:

Pilot young farmers clubs around extension training centres

With the start of the Community Development Programme in India, the Directorate of Extension took up the responsibility of training the Gram Sewaks (village level workers) in rural youth activities, so that after training they could organise these programmes in the Development Blocks. In order to provide them project oriented training in this aspect, ten pilot young farmers' clubs were organised in selected villages in each of the Development Blocks attached to the Extension Training Centres. The staff and trainees of the Extension Training Centres organise training for the club members in leadership development, organisational aspects, skill development in the field of agriculture, and project activities. After training, a regular follow-up is done to provide continuing education and guidance.

There are separate clubs for boys and girls. The membership varies with the age group of 15 to 25 years. The members of the clubs have taken up economic projects relating to crop production, grain storage, horticulture animal husbandry, home science and fisheries etc. Recreational activities are also taken up to sustain the interest of club members. There are individual as well as group projects and are guided by voluntary leaders and extension workers, so that the participants can acquire necessary skills and knowledge relating to that work. In addition, it also helps the members to earn while they learn through the project work.

Training-cum-demonstration camps of one to two days duration are organised before each cropping season in the villages where the Young Farmers Clubs have been formed, with a view to training the club members in the recommended Package of Practices for the crops so that they can adopt them. In addition, short duration institutional courses on leadership development and project activities are also organised at the extension training centres in which youth leaders are being trained.

Training of young farmers in districts

A massive programme of Farmers' Training and Education have been taken up in one hundred selected districts, with a view to training the farm family, i.e., farmer, farm women and farm youth in modern farming technology. The young farmers, within the age of 20 to 30 years, participate in programmes like demonstration-cum-training camps, short duration training courses and discussion groups. Special courses of three months duration were previously organised for young farmers, but later on they were discontinued as the courses became of longer duration. It is now planned to organise short duration courses of a specialised nature and to follow it up regularly through discussion groups.

Training of young farmers through voluntary organisations

National Level Farmers Voluntary Organisations are being encouraged to take up training programme for the benefit of young farmers by organising short duration training courses, seminars and exchange visits. Financial assistance is being provided to the Six National Level Organisations by the Directorate of Extension to enable them to undertake programmes relating to agricultural production. These organisations have branches at the State and District level and they work through them.

One of these organisations is the Young Farmers' Association of India which has set up Young Farmers' Training Centres at Rakhra and Vishakhapatnam to provide institutional training facilities in various disciplines of Agriculture and Animal Husbandry. They have also been organising youth activities in selected areas and are operating a Young Farmers' Exchange Programme.

International Farm Youth Exchange Programme with the USA

The Directorate of Extension has taken up this programme in collaboration with the National 4-H Club Foundation of the USA with a view to providing an opportunity to promising farm boys and girls to visit the USA to study modern methods of agricultural production, the rural youth programme and leadership development. So far 291 Indian farm youth have visited the USA and in exchange, 150 farm youth from USA visited India. The returned Indian I.F.Y.E.s have utilised their experience in improving their own farming and organising demonstrations on their farms to provide training and education to other young farmers in their locality.

International Young Farmers Exchange Programmes with countries other than the USA

Considering the utility of the International Farm Youth Exchange Programme with the USA it was decided to extend these programmes to cover other countries so that our young farmers could take advantage of the developments taking place in those countries. Similarly, it is proposed to invite the young farmers from the developing countries to visit India so that the experience gained by us could be shared with those countries. So far Sri Lanka has agreed to participate in this programme. The programme with other countries is being processed through our Embassies abroad.

Exchange of farmers within the country

The scheme of exchange of farmers within the country is being implemented through the National Level Farmers Voluntary Organisations. Under this scheme young farmers from one area being encouraged to visit other areas where considerable progress in the field of agriculture and animal husbandry has been made, and to see for themselves how the young farmers have taken up such programmes. The farmers voluntary organisations are being given financial assistance to take up this programme.

Regional rural youth staff and leaders training workshop

In order to provide training in Rural Youth Development to the trainers of the Extension Training/Farmers' Training Centres and Voluntary Youth Leaders, a National workshop in collaboration with FAO was organised earlier. Based on this experience Regional workshops are now being organised every year to meet this objective.

People's action for development in India (PADI) (Dept. of agriculture)

The people's action for development in India receives aid from FAO and other donor countries to provide assistance to voluntary organisations and training institutions for taking up programme for rural youth development and young farmers training. Some of the projects which were financed under this programme, are: (a) Kitchen Garden Competition among Rural Youth Clubs around selected Extension Training Centres: (b) Development of Village Youth Clubs in District Agra (U.P) and Udaipur (Rajasthan): (c) Poultry Development Programme through youth clubs in selected villages near Narendrapur (West Bengal); and (d) Establishment of young Farmers Training Centres at Vishakhapatnam (A.P.) and Rakhra (Punjab).

ROLE OF INDIAN COUNCIL OF AGRICULTURAL RESEARCH (ICAR) IN TRAINING

ICAR is an apex body involved in training at various levels. It has 31 research institutes and helps 22 Agricultural Universities functioning in the country. Some of these Institutes and Universities have taken up research studies on the Rural Youth Development Programme while others have taken up rural youth field projects in selected villages. In addition ICAR has established Krishi Vigyan Kendras.

Krishi Vigyan Kendra (Farm Science Centres)

In pursuance of the recommendations of the Education Commission (1964-66) to establish institutions for providing vocational education in agriculture at the pre- and post-matriculate level, the Indian Council of Agricultural Research has started a scheme to establish Krishi Vigyan Kendras (Farm Science Centres) in the country. The National Commission on Agriculture and the Planning Commission have strongly recommended its implementation.

To work out the details for the establishment of the Krishi Vigyan Kendras, a committee under the chairmanship of Dr. Mohan Sinha Mehta was constituted by the I.C.A.R. in the year 1973. The main objectives of the Krishi Vigyan Kendras are as follows:

(1) The Kendras will impart learning through work experience and hence will be concerned with technical literacy, the acquisition of which does not necessarily require as a precondition the ability to read and write.

(2) The Kendras will impart training only to those extension workers who are already employed, or to practising farmers and fishermen. In other words, the Kendras will cater the needs of those who are already employed or those who wish to be self-employed.

(3) There will be no uniform syllabus for the Kendras. The syllabus and programmes of each Kendra will be tailored according to the felt needs, natural resources and the potential for agricultural growth in that particular area.

Training programmes

The in-service courses envisaged at a Krishi Vigyan Kendra will be mostly of short duration (1-3 months) and only field level extension staff like village level workers will be trained at the Kendras. Courses in the Krishi Vigyan Kendras will be tailored to the needs of the areas served and will be for both men and women. The following types of courses might be provided; cultivation of local crops, application of package of practices; farm planning and plant protection; care and feeding of animals; poultry keeping; tubewell operation, irrigation and water control; nutrition, cooking and hygiene; food processing and cooking, marketing of agricultural products, catching and marketing of fish, etc.

The success of these Kendras will be ensured if the programme is made as flexible as possible, both in vertical and horizontal dimensions and is attuned specifically to the needs of the area of its location. The keynote of these Kendras should be to involve the local community in skills according to the stages of development in agriculture and the density of population, as a to enable it to improve the economic conditions for the better living standards of its members.

Women play an important role in agricultural production, particularly in post-harvest operations. Therefore, women's training programmes to increase their efficiency in agricultural operations, and to improve family living are also important. Since Krishi Vigyan Kendras will be an innovative institution, developing training programmes to suit the expanding needs of agricultural development, they will function as autonomous units insofar as their academic programmes and internal administration are concerned. The training programmes should mostly have need-based courses of a few week duration, a few months or even of a longer duration of one or two years. These may be part-time and full-time educational courses. Some of them could be correspondence courses. There could be detailed courses of sufficiently long duration, even one or two years. Evaluation will be a built-in component of the programmes, to review and improve the courses according to the needs of the region, clientele and the general development programmes.

Organisation aspects

In the staffing pattern, emphasis will be on recruiting a core staff, well-experienced and specialised persons. Some of expert craft-teachers may be hired for short periods, whenever required for specific courses. At the Krishi Vigyan Kendras, some of the progressive farmers may serve as very practical teachers.

An advisory committee on Krishi Vigyan Kendras was constituted by the council with a view to developing operational criteria and guidelines for the establishment of the Krishi Vigyan Kendras, and for screening the proposals which were received by the Council from different parts of the country. It was pointed out by the Committee that in view of the importance of such a scheme as the Krishi Vigyan Kendra, every Taluka in the country should ultimately have one Krishi Vigyan Kendra. It has been decided that the agencies which could be entrusted with the responsibility of running the Krishi Vigyan Kendras would be:

(a) Agricultural Universities and I.C.A.R. Institutes.
(b) Voluntary organisations with a good record of serving the rural communities, especially backward area, tribal areas or hilly areas etc.
(c) Institutes of Science and Technology who wish to organise agro-based industries; and
(d) State Government Agencies, if the above Institutions or Agencies are not available.

It was insisted that after the Kendra has been identified and approved by the I.C.A.R., a detailed survey should be made of the areas in which the centres will function. This detailed survey would serve as bench-marker and also will provide background information for formulating different kinds of training programmes based on the felt needs of the farming communities. This survey, as a matter of fact, should be done by the staff who are likely to be involved in the Krishi Vigyan Kendra Programme, either directly or indirectly. This will provide occasion to the staff members to understand the farmers problems in detail, not necessarily through the collected data alone but also through their own observations based on the interaction with the farmers.

The budget provision will be around Rs. 10 lakhs for the Fifth Five Year Plan period. The stress will be more on a humble beginning with quality training for the farmers, rather than a heavy investment in the establishment of the Kendras. Regarding the jurisdiction of the Krishi Vigyan Kendra for training the local farmers, it was felt that it should not be very large. A large area would mean varied types to training programmes involving more and more staff resulting in a large institutions which may follow in the footsteps of the traditional institutions.

In 1976-77, 18 Krishi Vigyan Kendras were established, this means that not all the States and the Union Territories has been covered. The initial effort is to cover each of the States and Union Territories in the first phase, and more such centres can be started after having established these first ones successfully. This scheme is of vital importance, for it is intended to provide problematic and field-oriented training which can have direct bearing on the agricultural and allied production.

As it has been explained, the training envisaged in the Krishi Vigyan Kendra Programme will be problem- and field-oriented, with due follow-up measures. This will have direct bearing in raising agricultural production. The programme further intends to cover the backward areas, weaker sections and tribes and the hill farmers on a priority basis. This class of farmers deserves our immediate attention.

Staff development programme

The teachers of the Krishi Vigyan Kendras will be initially given 4-5 months training in the Trainers' Training Centres established by the I.C.A.R. in its specialised institutions. Besides, the Krishi Vigyan Kendra will also have in-service training in Institutional Management at the Central Staff College for Agriculture for about a week or so. Based on the felt-needs, higher training will be arranged for the Krishi Vigyan Kendra staff. In fact, staff development will be a continuous process for keeping them abreast of the latest agricultural innovations, and doing an effective job of training the farmers.

Trainers' training centres (TTCs)

Since the Krishi Vigyan Kendras are going to be innovative institutions for imparting practical and skill-oriented to the farmers and fishermen, the I.C.A.R. has decided to establish seven Trainers' Training Centres in different parts of the country to provide specialised training to the teachers of the Krishi Vigyan Kendras as also to other in-service staff and teachers who are involved in vocational agriculture in different institutions. The main objectives of the Trainers' Training Centres are as follows:

(a) To impart training to the teachers of the Krishi Vigyan Kendras both in agricultural technology as well as in pedagogy with a view to improve their subject-matter background in agriculture, home economics and the skills necessary for the teaching—learning processes and techniques.

(b) To train the teachers who are, or likely to be, engaged in teaching or work-experience in agriculture and home economics in high schools and vocational courses at the plus 2 level under the new pattern of education of 10 plus 2 plus 3.;

(c) To train trainers of the Gram Sevika/Gram Sewak Extension Training Centres of the Region, specially in the latest Agriculture and Home Economics technologies so that their training programmes at the Extension Centres can be enriched;

(d) To organise vocational training programmes in agriculture and home economics, as and when required, for the teachers and social workers of the voluntary organisations who are committed to rural development; and

(e) To organise and conduct other short or long-term vocational courses for teachers/trainers as and when required by the Government and agricultural and home science institutions.

Organisation aspects

Initially seven Trainers' Training Centres were established at:

(1) Chettali (Coorg) in Horticulture, as an integral part of the Indian Institute of Horticultural Research, Bangalore;

(2) Hyatnagar, Hyderabad in Dryland Farming, with the All India Coordinated Research Project on Dryland Agriculture;

(3) Karnal, National Dairy Research Institute in Dairying;

(4) Dhauli (Bhubaneshwar) in Fisheries, under the Central Inland Fisheries Research Institute, Barrackpore (West Bengal);

(5) Bhopal in Agricultural Engineering, with the Central Institute of Agricultural Engineering;

(6) Indore (Madhya Pradesh) for the women teachers in-service staff; and

(7) One in the North Eastern Hilly Region areas for women teachers as well as in-service women staff of the State Departments. As a part of the plan with each Trainers' Training Centre, a Krishi Vigyan Kendra will also be established to serve as a training laboratory for the Trainers' Training Centre's trainees.

The Trainer's Training Centre will have a core staff of 5-6 specialists headed by a Chief Training Organiser. Wherever necessary, training organisers and training associates/assistants will also be provided. In addition, guest/specialists/visiting specialists will be invited for a specified period of time, depending upon the duration of the training courses.

It may be stressed that the Krishi Vigyan Kendras and Trainers' Training Centres are both innovative and institutions for practical training for the farmers and in-service personnel and hence more investment will be required. The staff of the Trainers' Training Centre will be provided short and long-term training depending upon their needs in their respective fields.

Department of rural development

The Department of Rural Development took up the Rural Youth Programme with the inception of the Community Development Programme in the country. The Rural Youth Clubs organised under this programme are known as 'Yuvak Mandals' and are open to both rural boys and girls within the age group of 15-30 years. There are about 5,000 Blocks in the country, and the average number of Yuvak Mandals in each Block is reported to be about 20. The basic objective of these Clubs is to provide a training ground for the youth club members to become better farmers, better homemakers, better citizens and better leaders. For this purpose, they take up economic, social, cultural and recreational projects. Their activities aim, on the one hand at developing civic sense and civic responsibility and on the other provide channels for dissemination of new knowledge and essential skills and techniques in agriculture and the allied fields. The project activities include agriculture, horticulture, dairying, poultry, pisciculture, piggery, home management, spinning, tailoring, embroidery and food preservation etc.

The village level worker helps in organising these clubs and provides necessary leadership in helping the club to take up project activities. The subject-matter extension officers in the Block provides technical guidance for organising the various programmes.

In order to strengthen these clubs, the Department of Rural Development is providing financial support to 2,500 selected Yuvak Mandals in the 500 Blocks. The clubs will also be federated at the Block level and suitable grants will be provided to meet their expenses. The office bearers of the Yuvak Mandals are also imparted training in organisational aspects and project activities. The training is organised at selected Extension Training Centres for a duration of five days.

Ministry of education and social welfare

Department of education—youth services wing

The Department of Education has set up a youth services wing to look after the development of youth programme in the country. The following programmes have been taken up by them:

Nehru Yuvak Kendras

The programme visualised the establishment of youth centres called Nehru Yuvak Kendras—one in each district, by the end of Fifth Plan period. The scheme was initiated in the year 1972, and so far, 255 centres have been established. These centres are primarily designed to provide a forum for the non-student youth, particularly in rural areas, with a view to giving them the opportunities to participate in the development process. The main activities visualised are:

(a) Non-formal education including functional literacy and education in agriculture, health, family life and community living;

(b) Opportunities for self-employment through appropriate training in productive skills and assistance in setting up small scale industries and other enterprises;

(c) Social service including cleanliness campaigns, vaccination, inoculation and other health services;

(d) Cultural activities like participation in the performing arts including community singing and theatre; and

(e) Promotion of sports and games particularly those which have the possibility of mass participation.

It is proposed to set up a network of youth services in the villages which will be the focal point for developmental and recreational activities. The programme is being guided from the district level by the youth coordinator supported by a professional coach for organising sports and games etc. The scheme is fully financed by the Central Government, and the State Governments are closely associated with the implementation, programme and activities. In order to provide proper coordination at various levels, organising committees have been formed at the National, State and District levels.

National service scheme

The National Service Scheme was launched in 1969 and at present it is being implemented in almost all the universities in India. It provides for utilisation of leisure time of the students in various items of social work and national development activities. As a part of the constructive involvement, largely of student youth during their vacation period, certain large scale camping programmes are also being organised under the NSS, in the course of which some aspects of rural youth are being covered. The major programmes taken so far are Youth Against Famine in 1973 and Youth for Afforestation and Tree Plantation in 1974-75. Similar programmes are proposed to be taken up in the future also. Special emphasis is also being laid on a literacy campaign. Each university has a National Service Scheme Coordinator to arrange programmes and special campaigns.

Department of social welfare

The Department of Social Welfare has taken up rural youth programmes as far as it relates to pre-vocational training programme for school drop-outs in the age group of 10-15 years. pre-vocational training centres have been established with a view to provide training in the mechanical engineering trades, besides general education to children who are not able to continue their education at Middle school level due to social and economic reasons.

Ministry of Labour

The Ministry of Labour has taken up a scheme for providing craftsmanship training to rural youth in various fields, including agro-industries, at their vocational training Centres. The scheme is meant for rural youth of the 15-25 age group.

Constraints on development of rural youth programme

There is a lack of a clear-cut national policy regarding rural youth development programmes, particularly in relation to the agricultural sector. The programme needs to be coordinated, guided and channelled properly at all levels so that the benefits could percolate to the farm youth. Since these programmes mostly relates to agriculture, the Ministry of Agriculture should go in a big way to take up farm youth development work, of course, in close partnership with other sister ministries and voluntary organisations.

There is inadequate staff for implementing the farm youth programme. At village level, the village level worker hardly gets time for youth work. At the Block level in some States, there is one extension officer for social education in the panchayat to look after the rural youth programme. He is generally entrusted with many other jobs and the real objective of the programme remains unrealised. In many States, this post has been abolished. Besides, in some States, there are no special officers at district and State levels to ensure proper implementation of the rural youth programme.

Youth development does not form a regular part of agricultural extension Education. What is being done in the name of rural youth at many places are cultural type of activities which neither sustain the interest of the youth, or of the parents, as it has no scope for economic or professional advancement on a long-term basis.

The agricultural extension worker has poor knowledge or experience to provide the type of service and support necessary to enable the farm youth to assume the role of an enlightened farmer, in due course of time. The job chart of the agricultural extension worker does not include providing service to this important section of the farm family.

There is no financial provision in the Development Block's budget to cater the education and training requirements of farm youth. As a result, this dynamic sector of the farming population, which could become an effective instrument for dissemination of modern technology remains unexploited by the extension machinery. The mass of idle manpower leads to unproductive and sometimes even destructive actions as energetic youth, by nature, cannot keep quiet.

The agricultural and veterinary institutions have so far neither offered attractive programmes to the rural youth to sustain their interest in rural areas nor have they suggested action plans to build up their knowledge and skill to take up farming as a profitable and interesting enterprise.

A number of educational type of programmes launched for rural youth by different organisations (official and non-official) are not designed according to the needs of specific age groups. Such education can be beneficial only if their state of physical and mental development is taken into consideration.

The voluntary organisations/institutions engaged in rural youth service are not self-sufficient. They have not developed enough so as to be able to render free service to farm youth. Apart from due encouragement from Government, they need to become popular amongst youth and build goodwill and confidence by working among the rural masses.

Mobilisation of rural youth in agricultural production and other development programmes

Some of the rural youth go for higher education, and after graduation return to their villages to take up farming as their occupation. Among these, some are agricultural graduates, and their services could be utilised to act as demonstrator farmers for the area and provide consultancy services to other young farmers. The nationalised banks are coming forward in a big way to give financial help to such agricultural graduates to purchase agricultural machinery, etc., and to settle on the farm. Such young farmers can provide custom-hire service to other small farmers and consultancy services to other farmers in matters relating to modern agriculture.

The remaining educated rural youth in the villages could be trained to act as voluntary leaders to provide guidance and leadership to other young people in taking up various development activities. They could also function as conveners of Radio/T.V. discussion groups and help people in discussing and understanding the programmes relayed by Radio/Television.

The rural youth can be mobilised for participation in the community programmes relating to agricultural production and rural development. While initiating such programmes, care has to be taken to provide proper incentives to the participants. Secondly the programme should be of interest to rural youth and its duration should not be too long, otherwise they will not have a sustained interest. The jobs which are of a challenging nature would attract a larger number of youth as compared to those which are labour-oriented. Some of the agricultural development programmes which could be of interest to them are listed below:

(a) Mass spraying, dusting and control of crop diseases and pests including baiting against rats;

(b) Afforestation, raising of community orchards, nurseries, etc.

(c) Maintenance, repair and cleaning of irrigation channels, village ponds including fish tanks, drinking water wells and village roads, etc.

(d) Maintenance and decoration of community buildings like panchayat ghar, village school, temple, etc.

It would thus be observed that rural youth, if organised properly and provided adequate training, supervision and incentives, could undertake a number of programmes not only for their individual benefit but also for the development of the community as a whole. The programme could also help in developing necessary skills and leadership qualities among the rural youth to become progressive farmers and help in agricultural production and rural development programmes.

Workshop wings

To train carpenters and blacksmiths there are 23 workshops in the country run by the Ministry of Community Development. These are at: (1) Rajendra Nagar (Hyderabad, A. P.), (2) Samalkot (A. P.), (3) Jorhat (Assam), (4) Muzaffarpur (Bihar), (5) Junagarh (Gujarat), (6) Mashobra (H. P.), (7) Kottarakara (Kerala), (8) Antri (M. P.), (9) Obedullaganj (M. P.), (10) Nowgong (M. P.), (11) Powerkhera (M. P.), (12) Manjri (Maharashtra), (13) Shindhewahi (Maharashtra), (14) Kullapatti (Tamil Nadu), (15) Kudgi (Mysore), (16) Bolangir (Orissa), (17) Nabha (Punjab), (18) Nilokheri (Hissar), (19) Bakshi ka Talab (Lucknow, U.P.), (20) Ghazipur (U. P.), (21) Fulia (Bengal), (22) Burdwan (Bengal).

Khadi gram udyog vidyalayas

Such training centres are being run to help the weavers. These are located at: (1) Gandhi Niketan Ashram, Kallupati (2) Wardha, (3) Sadakat Ashram, Patna, (4) Durwani Nagar, Bangalore (5) Himayat Nagar, Hyderabad, (6) Nilokheri, Haryana.

Auxiliary courses

Courses in Poultry Keeping, Livestock Management, Fruit Preservation, Kitchen Gardening, Home Management, Use of Soybean in Human Diet and the recipes from it, etc., are being organised by the Agricultural Universities and some Agricultural Colleges. Some such universities are organising flower, fruit and vegetable shows each year and encourage urban people to take advantage of such facilities. Some special courses for military personnel, retired persons etc., are also organised.

DEVELOPING COURSE SYLLABUS, COURSE OBJECTIVES AND LESSON PLANS

For any training programme—pre-service, in-service or training the farmers, etc., we need to develop the course syllabus, course objectives and lesson plans. This chapter will discuss how to develop these.

A. Course syllabus

Meaning of the term: The term course syllabus means organising the contents and amount of instruction in a subject designed to achieve specific objectives. This is the beginning point for training in a subject. The teacher/trainer should prepare such a course of study for his students/trainees. On the basis of this course of study, he should conduct various teaching activities. This indicates, what the trainees or students need to learn in order to be able to become good extension workers or teachers in the subject. The course of study should be in line with the framework of the syllabus and therefore it can also be said that it is an expanded and applied syllabus including all units to be taught in a subject to achieve specific objectives; the amount of time to be given to each unit and when it is to be taught. Thus it serves as a guide to what the teacher will need to teach his students. While listing the various jobs in the course of study, they should be broken up into meaningful units, based on jobs, seasons, sequence, priority, etc.

The course of study should be reviewed, revised and kept up-to-date. With the change of things, adoption of technology, coming in contact with outside world and improvement in conditions of living the social values, the level of understanding of the people are also changing. This also necessitates a change in the course of study in extension education, the rural social System and in all such subjects. The course of study helps the teacher to plan in advance and base his teaching on sound objectives.

Course of study embodies: (1) Teaching objectives, (2) Approximate time assignment, (3) selected content, and (4) means and methods to be used in teaching.

Factors for consideration in planning a course of study

(1) The aim or purpose of the course to be offered,
(2) The characteristics and needs of the students,
(3) The educative environment of the trainees.
(4) The sources of information available, and
(5) The requirements or demands of vocation, profession or field of work or other uses to which learning is to be put.

Illustration

Syllabus for Course No. AEX 305—Training of Extension Workers:
AEX 305—Training for Extension Workers: *Trimester II, Cr. Hrs. 3.*
Teacher : Dr. O.P. Dahama
Place :   Class Room No ... if theory
                Place of Practical. . . . . .Laboratory/village
                Day......Date........ and time from......to......
                Course Objectives : 1. .... 2. .... 3. ....
References : (1) *Extension and Rural Welfare*, by Dr. O.P. Dahama, Ram Prasad & Sons, Agra, 1971 Edi. Part III.
        (2) *Teaching Agriculture in India*, A. U. Patel & R.P. Singh, Ram Prasad & Sons, Agra.
        (3) *Improvement of Teaching and Student Evaluation*, C.V. Roderick, Orissa Univ. of Agri. and Technology.

Instructions regarding examinations and tests

The teacher may give instructions as follows;
(1) Each student will be tested on the content of the course, as related to the stated objectives in each unit of instruction and on the course objectives.
(2) There will be a ten minutes quiz once each week.
(3) There will be a 30 minutes' quiz on each major unit of instruction during the course. A paper may be substituted for one or more of these 30 minutes quizzes.
(4) The Final Examination will be comprehensive i.e., covering the entire course and will be for 2-3 hrs ... on Feb.,........ at 10.30 a.m. in Room No ...

Other instructions may be

(1) Each student is expected to read the assignment in preparation for each days' lesson. The teacher will assume that students come prepared for lectures, discussions or any other method of instruction that might be used, so that they can discuss the topic intelligently.

(2) Each student is responsible for his attendence and for quizzes missed. Except under certain circumstances quizzes will not be repeated.

(3) Students will be graded as: (1) Above 70 per cent marks—A, 55-70 per cent —B, 45-55—C, 35-45—D, Below it—F.

Steps in selecting course content

(1) List all major areas to be included in the course.

(2) Break each area or unit into its logical component or parts of subject-matter.

(3) Estimate how long it will take to teach each area of subject-matter.

(4) Add up all the time, you have indicated it will take to teach the subject-matter (include tests planned).

(5) Check the number of days available to teach (eliminate holidays, etc.).

(6) Reconcile item No. 3 and 4. Eliminate the items or subject-matter of least importance to get subject-matter within time available for teaching.

(7) Calendarise what you have left on the subject to be taught (when to teach ... days. . . . . time . . . . .).

(8) Where practical; plan the place of visit and make arrangements for transport, what to be shown, resource person, farmer, VLW etc., material: like fertilisers, seed, implements, tools, plant protection equipment, etc.

B. Developing course objectives

The objectives may be: (1) Objectives based on the needs of the individual student; (2) objectives and interests of the total class as a group: (3) objectives of the class as citizens of a community or as future extension workers or as farmers, administrators, teachers, etc.

For teacher the objective is a combination of the three. In some cases we have to start with the individual needs and interests of our learners.

Characteristics of good teaching objectives[1]

(1) Objectives should be stated in terms of life activities outside the college/training centre.

(2) Each objective should represent a change in behaviour to be brought about in the learner.

(3) Objectives should be clear and definite and stated in sufficient detail to serve as a basis of selection of subject-matter.

(4) Objectives should be attainable, with the time and facilities that may be used.

(5) Each objective should be relatively important and significant to the learner.

(6) Each objective when reached, should contribute to attaining the larger objectives or aims of the course.

(7) The smaller objectives should be derived from the larger objectives.

(8) The teacher should know when he has reached the objective i.e., it should be possible to evaluate the attainment of the objective.

(9) Each teaching objective should definitely imply a corresponding learner's goal (learners must have objectives too).

[1]Hammonds, Carsie referred in *Improvement of Teaching and Student Evaluation*, C.V. Roderick, University of Agra, p. 25.

(10) Objectives should belong to a particular course, so that anyone concerned may know what the objectives of the course are.

Considerations for deciding objectives

For deciding worthwhile objectives the teacher should consider:
(1) The present level of the students,
(2) Their ability to learn,
(3) Their motivation to learn,
(4) The amount of time to be devoted to the subject,
(5) The resources to be used,
(6) The opportunity for experience or practice by the learners, and
(7) His proficiency in teaching.

C. Preparing lesson plans

Meaning of lesson plan: It is the outline of activities that the teacher will follow in order to create an effective learning situation. To be more specific, "lesson plan is a plan for teaching a job or unit which may take one or more periods to cover." The lesson plan should include what to teach, how the teacher and learner will be active, when to teach and how long to teach a topic.

Difference between lesson plan and lecture notes: Many people are confused between lesson plan and lecture notes. A lecture note is merely a store of information. The lesson plan, includes how to teach it. The lecture note does not indicate the activities of the teacher and the learners.

Importance of lesson plans: Lesson plans help in:
(1) Clarifying and adopting definite objectives,
(2) Considering the local situation in the community,
(3) Developing confidence,
(4) Presenting the material in the logical sequence,
(5) Effective use of class room time,
(6) Developing better study interest,
(7) Organising the teaching materials and references well in advance,
(8) Gain respect of students and the institute, and
(9) Help to evaluate.

Essentials of a teaching plan

(1) *Identifying lesson plan headings:* This should be (a) Class, (b) Subject or enterprise, (c) Topic or lesson unit or teaching area, (d) Best season for teaching if it is a crop demonstration, (e) Number of periods allotted, and (f) Method of teaching, etc

(2) *Teachers' objectives:* It should be not merely "Importance of conducting result demonstration" but "Developing in the students/trainees, the understanding of the steps, considerations and activities involved in conducting a result demonstration in wheat/paddy crop. The teacher must be clear regarding the aim of teaching a particular topic. The aims of teaching specific topics might include: (a) developing knowledge; (b) developing skill of doing the work; (c) developing clear grasp or understanding of significant characters and relations; (d) developing interest in possessing knowledge and skills; (e) developing the ability to apply the specific knowledge or skill, and

(f) developing the favourable attitudes for an idea, job or a person.

(3) *Previous background of the learner:* If the teacher takes into consideration the formal or informal experience of the learners, this will help him in motivating the learners and in relating new experiences with the previous familiar experiences.

(4) *Material, tools and equipment:* Here the teacher will note all the teaching aids, equipments and materials that will be used by him in creating an effective learning situation for teaching particular topic.

(5) *Introduction:* The introduction of a lesson plan must help the learner to develop a favourable mental set-up or right frame of mind. It should be short, concise and should have, (a) Link, (b) Motivation, and (c) Purview or overview.

(a) *Link:* During this sub-step the teacher relates the new topic with the topic previously covered. In case the topic is new, the teacher can relate it with the previous experience the learner might have had in the society or in the field. The teacher should try to find out what the learners know about the topic to be discussed. The link can be established by:

(1) Giving suggestions which stir the imagination of the learners regarding experiences in home, farm, village, etc.

(2) Narrating an appropriate study or story.

(3) Recapitulating the important points of previous lessons related to the new material.

(b) *Motivation:* During this sub-step the teacher should convince the learner by telling him briefly when, how and where the new subject-matter will be useful to him in satisfying his immediate and long-term needs. In this way the teacher will be able to develop interest in the learners and secure and retain their attention on the topic. The teacher should clarify the aim of the coming topic, that is how it will be useful to the learners in doing their job as extension workers, administrators in extension and how the farmers could be motivated and helped to raise their standard of living, etc.

(c) *Purview or overview:* In this step the teacher will give the salient features of the new topic without giving details. This step helps the learners to organise subject-matter as it develops.

(6) *Presentation:* This will vary according to the age and abilities of the learners. The presentation of new subject-matter must never degenerate into the mechanical handing out of information. The learners must be made active in actual exploration of the new subject-matter. The teacher must create such situations in which the learners, can actually explore new subject-matter. Varieties of teaching methods must be used in which the learners may have chances to use more senses. Select methods according to the time and facilities available. The teacher may provide the learner with one or more of the following learning experiences:

(a) Lecture, description, narration or exposition by teacher, selected students or by resource person or guest speaker.

(b) Study of books or other references suggested by teacher.

(c) Conducting observations through field trips or study tours.

(d) Using specimens and other audio-visual aids, or visuals like flannelgraph, flash cards, philip charts, overhead projector, slides, etc., in the class room.

(e) Demonstration of skill by the teacher or the selected students or resource person.

   (f) Conducting practical work by the students in the laboratory, workshop or field/village.

   (g) Conducting group methods like: Role playing, dramatisation panel discussion, etc., in the class room.

   (7) *Application:* Under it the teacher will indicate how the learner will be provided with the opportunity to apply the new subject-matter. This can be done by encouraging the students to conduct individual and group projects on their own responsibility in a real life situation in the village, on a cooperative farmers holding, or on a farm, etc. The teacher should help the students to overcome their weaknesses and difficulties. This will give satisfaction to the learners when they are able to use the knowledge under field conditions. This is the success of teaching.

   (8) *Summary.*

   (9) *Evaluation:* Here the teacher will evaluate the achievements of the teaching process in relation to the educational objectives fixed by him at the beginning. He will also diagnose the success or failure of the students which will help in assigning the marks. Evaluation should be done in a way that it provides incentive to the learners.

   (10) *References:* The teacher should give a list of references appropriate to the topic and to the standard of the learner. The Chapters or pages should be indicated. It will be better if the learners are introduced to the sections of the library where such materials may be found.

CHAPTER 47

TRAINING AND VISIT SYSTEM (T & V)

Earlier extension efforts with some variations mostly concentrated in agricultural development work utilising block extension machinery with provision of more VLWs, Extension Officers and/or subject-matter specialists as per need of the programme. By and large the National Extension Service pattern which envisaged multi-purpose VLWs and BDO as a coordinator remained in vague. However, various constrains were experienced in this system as listed below:*

a) Lack of a single line of command;
b) Dilution of efforts by assigning multi-purpose role to field extension workers:
c) Excessively large areas of operation for VLW,
d) Lack of regular training programmes for updating knowledge of extension workers;
e) Lack of communication noteworks and support from research; and
f) Duplication of services by various agencies involved in the development, activities.

To overcome the above problems a new approach and strategy in extension and transfer of farm technology was adopted in the year 1974, when the Training and Visit System (T & V) was introduced in Rajasthan Canal area in Rajasthan and Chambal Command area in Madhya Pradesh. The system has since been extended to 13 States and 4 more are in pipe-line. This system will be further extended in the remaining states of the country by 1985. The main thrust of the T & V is on systematic time-bound programme of training based on intensive field visits by the extension workers under close supervision. The working objectives of the system are as follows:—

Objectives

a) Coordinating research, training and extension activities effectively;
b) To make research more effective by catering to the local needs and situation;
c) To evolve an intensive training programme on a systematic basis for extension

*Sharma, B.B. (1983). Models of Extension and Communication with Farmers. International Workshop on Communication and Cooperation for Rural/Agricultural Development among Developing Countries, Seoul: Korea.

workers and farmers and to ensure effective supervision and technical support to VEWs/ADOs.

The above objectives are to be achieved by:

a) Reorganisation of extension in a manner so that the VEW is able to meet the farmer with needed frequency and on find dates;

b) The visit is to be used for identifying the problems and to solve them;

c) In order to allow the VEW to work intensively his area of operation is reduced considerably;

d) Single line of command from government agencies responsible for agricultural development to the VEW is established;

e) The extension personnel are expected to devote their time exclusively to professional agricultural extension and are not assigned any regulatory and administrative work;

f) Extension Personnel do not have any direct responsibility for arranging the supply of inputs; and

g) The effective linkage between extension and research is established through subject-matter specialists in such areas as agronomy, plant protection, soil chemistry and water management, etc.

Basic assumptions

T & V system is based on the assumption that it is rather impossible to maintain regular contact with most of the farmers directly, which is neither necessary nor desirable. Hence, selected messages have to be focussed mainly on selected contact farmers, who will assist in spreading the new practices to most farmers in their area very quickly. It is assumed that the contact farmers must be willing to try-out practices recommended by the extension workers and be prepared to have other farmers visit their fields. The advice to contact farmers will thus diffuse and spread to other farmers, through the well-knit communication system in the rural area and through the process of dissemination and diffusion.

Methodology and approach in T & V

The fundamental approach in T & V is a systematic and problem-oriented programme of *training* of the VEWs, combined with frequent and well planned *visits* by him to the farmers' fields. The methodology adopted provides efficient mechanism for transfer of know-how from the research scientists/subject-matter-specialists to the farmers. The step I, —'Training'—ensures transfer of know-how from the research scientists/SMSs to the field level extension agents and step II, 'Visits' ensures transfer of know-how from the extension agent to the contact farmers and down to the other farmers in turn.

Frequent (weekly or fortnightly) one day training session for fields level extension agents covering three or four most important recommendations for the next one or two weeks of the crop season—mostly problem-oriented are an integral part of T & V system. Hence, a continuous training input is available 'before' and 'after' the 'visits' of the extension agents with the farmers. The training is so designed that both the trainers and trainees know and prepare themselves well in advance. The research specialists also train the subject-matter-specialists, who are trainers of extension agents, either in the monthly and/or seasonal workshops organised at research stations and/or a specified place, with participation and involvement of resource persons drawn from various agencies, working hand-in-glove for common cause of development. This training develops better understanding amongst extension agents about the technological components, which are received in digestible doses and enhances their self-confidence, that results in further convincing the farmer and/or target beneficiaries. Once this cyclic process starts it becomes 'reinforcing' and 'self-propelling' type.

The above approach systematically links extension with research and ensures proper coordination as well as two-way communication processes between the two. Moreover, the methodology also ensures working relationships between the extension and input supplying/credit agencies as a result of inflow of recommendations of package of practices for various crop-production-activities. This maintains consistency with the availability of inputs and supplies with that of recommendations that flow from the research stations.

Monitoring and evaluation

The T & V system has an inbuilt mechanism for monitoring and continuous evaluation of the performance and finally the impact on the target beneficiaries. At the National Level the Directorate of Extension under the Ministry of Agriculture monitors the extension activities and at the State level special monitoring and evaluation cells have been specially created for this purpose. The main indicators for monitoring are:

a) the number and frequency of visits of VEW to the contact farmers;
b) the regularity and quality of fortnightly training and monthly workshops;
c) the extent to which the recommendations (impact points) made by VEW are adopted or not adopted; and
d) the yields obtained by the farmers in the project area.

The evaluation studies are conducted before (ex-ante), during (concurrent) and after (ex-post) stages of implementation of the extension activities/project. However, the monitoring data collected in each of these three stages for each season is used along with evaluation data which is collected at the end of the season. The whole evaluation exercise revolves round the fixing and measuring the objectives set by the concerned agencies. An appropriate representative sample is drawn at two stages viz., (a) dividing district level farmers group and then (b) selecting suitable sample from these groups within the categories of contact and non-contact farmers. This is followed by administering pre-structured, pre-tested and an integrated questionnaire consisting of basic set of questions, both for early and repetitive studies. However, the assessment of impact is also judged by crop-cutting experiments and the overall methodology is quite conducive in isolating the effect of T & V system.

Organisational structure

Basic assumption in providing additional and appropriate staff under T & V system is the need and number of farm families in the village, block, district and state. As a standard practice, it is expected that an Agricultural Extension Officer (AEO) guides, trains and supervises about six to eight Village Extension Workers (VEWs). Six to eight AEOs are, in turn, guided and supervised by a Sub-Divisional Extension Officer (SDEO). The SDEOs are supported by a team of Subject-Matter Specialists (SMSs). Four to eight SDEOs are supervisied by a District Extension Officer (DEO) who is also supported by SMSs. Depending on the number of districts, the DEO is supervised either directly by extension headquarters or by an immediate supervisor. The objective is to ensure that each level of service has a span of control narrow enough to afford close personal guidance and supervision of the level immediately below. The following chart illustrates the arrangement and organisational pattern in one of the States in India.*

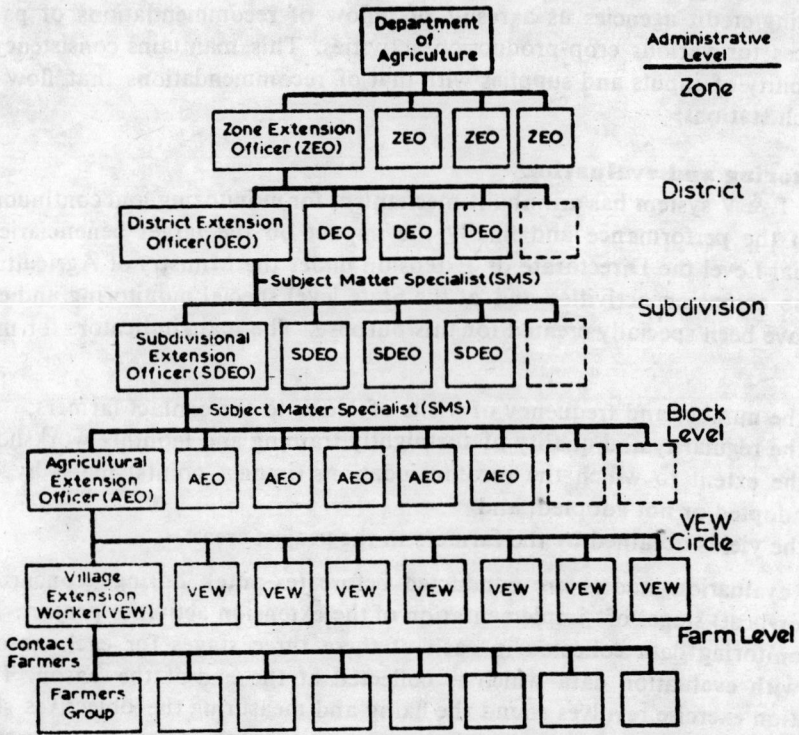

In a study Ray *et al.* (1979) reported that T & V system resulted in (a) increasing the cultivated area under High Yielding Varieties Programme, (b) dissemination of new knowledge of farming for increasing the cropping intensity, (c) increasing employment of family labour, (d) raising marginal value of productivity of all inputs; and (e) accelerating the extent of adoption of recommended practices. According to them, there was more impact of this system on the small holdings as compared to large ones. Thus T & V system has a considerable positive impact on the farming economy. (Ind. Jr. of Economics 1979, ISAE Bombay).

*Benor, D. and J.Q. Harrison (1977). Agricultural Extension, The Training and Visit System, World Bank, Washington, USA.

ABBREVIATIONS AND TITLES OF DEVELOPMENT PROGRAMMES IN INDIA

S. No.	Code	Title
1.	D.P.A.P.	Drought Prone Areas Programme
2.	S.F.D.A.	Small Farmers Development Agency
3.	C.A.D.	Command Area Development
4.	C.D.D.	Cattle and Dairy Development
5.	S.D.	Sheep Development
6.	P.D.	Poultry Development
7.	Pig.D.	Piggery Development
8.	I.A.D.P.	Intensive Agricultural District Programme
9.	I.A.A.P.	Intensive Agricultural Area Programme
10.	H.Y.V.P.	High Yielding Varieties Programme
11.	Pul.D.	Pulse Development
12.	I.O.D.P.	Intensive Oil Seed Development Programme
13.	I.C.D.P.	Intensive Cotton Development Programme
14.	I.J./M.P.	Intensive Jute/Mesta Programme
15.	T.D.P.	Tobacco Development Programme
16.	I.T.D.	Integrated Tribal Development
17.	I.D.A.D.	Integrated Dryland Agricultural Development
18.	C.B.	Cooperative Banks
19.	M.F.A.L.	Marginal Farmers and Agricultural Labour Programme
20.	T.A.D.	Tribal Area Development
21.	H.A.D.	Hill Area Development Programme
22.	W.V.D.P.	Whole Village Development Programme
23.	F.T.C.	Farmers Training Centre
24.	K.V.K.	Krishi Vigyan Kendra (ICAR)
25.	A.U.	Agricultural Universities
26.	T.T.C.	Trainers' Training Centre (ICAR)
27.	I.R.D.P.	Integrated Rural Development Programme.

Statement showing the States and Districts covered by various programmes in India

State and Districts   *Programmes covered*

ANDHRA PRADESH
1. Shrikakulam — 2, 12, 14, 16, 18, 20
2. Vishakhapatnam — 2, 4, 5, 6, 7, 12, 14, 19
3. East Godavari — 2, 15, 16
4. West Godavari — 3, 8, 10, 15, 18, 23
5. Krishna — 2, 3, 4, 7, 11, 13, 15, 18
6. Guntur — 2, 3, 10, 13, 15, 18, 23
7. Ongole — 2, 3, 7, 1
8. Nellore — 2, 3, 15, 18
9. Chittoor — 1, 5, 10, 12, 23
10. Cuddapah — 1, 3, 5, 6, 12
11. Anantpur — 1, 3, 5, 12, 18
12. Kurnool — 1, 3, 5, 6, 10, 12, 13, 15, 16, 17, 18, 23
13. Mahbubnagar — 1, 5, 12, 16, 18, 27
14. Hyderabad — 2, 4, 6, 10, 12, 17, 18, 23, 24, 25, 26
15. Medak — 2, 12, 18
16. Nisamabad — 2, 3, 4, 18
17. Adilabad — 2, 3, 16, 18
18. Karimnagar — 2, 3, 10, 12, 15, 18, 23
19. Warangal — 2, 6, 11, 18
20. Khammam — 2, 3, 15, 18
21. Nalgonda — 1, 2, 3, 4, 10, 12, 18, 19, 23
22. Prakasam — 1, 3, 13, 15
23. Bellary — 3, 13
24. Bhongir — 18
25. Kakinada — 18
26. Rajahmundary — 18
27. Ramachandra-puram — 18
28. Amlapuram — 18
29. Vijayawada — 18
30. Vijainagaram — 18

ASSAM
1. Goelpara — 2, 6, 7, 14, 18
2. Kamrup — 2, 4, 6, 7, 18, 19, 27
3. Darrang — 2, 16, 19
4. Nowgong — 2, 4, 7, 14, 18
5. Sibsagar — 16, 18
6. Lakhimpur — 16
7. Mikkir Hills — 2, 7, 19
8. North Cachar Hills — 20
9. Cachar — 8, 10, 18, 23
10. Mizo —
11. Gauhati — 10, 23
12. Jorhat — 10, 23, 26
13. Dibrugarh — 16

BIHAR
1. West Champaran — 2, 10, 12, 23
2. East Champaran — 3, 10, 12
3. Gopalganj — 18
4. Sitamarhi — 2
5. Madhubani — 2
6. Saharsa — 3, 8
7. Purnea — 6, 7, 8, 10, 11, 12, 14, 18, 23
8. Darbhanga — 2, 3, 10, 23
9. Muzaffarpur — 11, 18, 22
10. Saran — 2
11. Siwan — 18
12. Vaishali — 3
13. Samastipur — 2, 18, 26
14. Katihar — 2
15. Monghyr — 1, 2, 6, 12, 18
16. Bhagalpur — 2, 11, 18
17. Santhal — 2, 10, 12, 16, 23
18. Begusarai — 2, 18
19. Patna — 4, 6, 7
20. Nalanda — 2
21. Nawadah — 1, 2, 12, 18
22. Gaya — 3, 4, 12
23. Bhojpur — 8
24. Rohtas — 1, 8, 12, 16, 19, 27
25. Aurangabad — 3
26. Palamau — 1, 11, 12, 16, 17
27. Hazaribagh — 2, 12, 15, 18
28. Ceiridih — 2, 16, 18

29.	Dhanbad	2, 6, 12, 16, 18
30.	Ranchi	2, 4, 6, 7, 10, 12, 16, 18, 19, 20, 23, 24
31.	Singhbhum	2, 7, 12, 16, 18, 20
32.	Shahabad	3, 4, 6, 8, 23
33.	Arrah-Buxar	10, 11, 18
34.	Bettiah	18
35.	Bihar-Barh-Fatwa	18

GUJARAT

1.	Jamnagar	1, 2, 5, 10, 12, 18, 23
2.	Rajkot	1, 5, 12, 17, 18
3.	Surendranagar	1, 13, 18
4.	Bhavnagar	1, 3, 12, 18
5.	Amreli	1, 3, 5, 12, 17, 18
6.	Junagadh	6, 10, 12, 18, 23
7.	Kutch	1, 5, 18, 27
8.	Banaskantha	1, 11, 12, 18
9.	Sabarkantha	2, 4, 12, 15, 16, 18
10.	Mahsana	1, 10, 12, 15, 18, 23
11.	Gandhinagar	10, 18
12.	Ahmedabad	1, 4, 18, 24, 26
13.	Kaira	3, 10, 15, 18, 23
14.	Panch Mahals	1, 3, 11, 15, 16, 18
15.	Vadedara	2, 4, 15, 16, 18, 19
16.	Bharuch	2, 3, 16
17.	Surat	2, 3, 4, 6, 8, 16, 18
18.	Valsad	2, 16, 19
19.	The Dangs	16
20.	Baroda	3, 13
21.	Bulsar	8, 10, 18, 23

HARYANA

1.	Ambala	2, 6, 7, 10, 18, 19, 23
2.	Karnal	4, 8, 10, 18, 23, 24, 25
3.	Rohtak	1, 3, 4, 10, 18, 23
4.	Gurgaon	2, 3, 4, 5, 6, 7, 10, 12, 18, 23
5.	Mohindragarh	1, 3, 5, 12, 17, 18
6.	Hissar	2, 3, 5, 6, 10, 11, 12, 13, 17, 18, 23, 26, 27
7.	Jind	18
8.	Bhiwani	1, 11, 18, 19
9.	Brayne (Rewari)	18

10.	Kurukshetra	18
11.	Sirsa	18
12.	Sonepat	18

HIMACHAL PRADESH

1.	Chambla	16
2.	Kangara	18, 21, 27
3.	Mandi	10, 21, 23
4.	Kulu	21
5.	Lahaul & Spiti	16
6.	Bilaspur	
7.	Simla	2, 6, 26
8.	Sirmaur	2, 4, 5
9.	Kinnaur	18
10.	Mahasu	21
11.	Solan	2, 19
12.	Jogindra	18

JAMMU & KASHMIR

1.	Anantnag	2, 5, 6, 8, 18, 27
2.	Srinagar	21
3.	Baramula	2, 18, 19
4.	Ladakh	2
5.	Doda	1, 5
6.	Udhampur	1, 5
7.	Jammu	2, 3, 4, 6, 8, 10, 17, 18, 23
8.	Kathua	2, 3
9.	Rajauri	2, 19
10.	Punch	2, 19
11.	Bahujot	3

KERALA

1.	Cannanore	2, 6, 7, 10, 16, 19, 23, 27
2.	Kozhikode	18
3.	Malappuram	18
4.	Palghat	3, 8, 10, 18, 23
5.	Trichur	2, 3, 4, 10, 18, 23
6.	Ernakulam	18, 25
7.	Kottayam	18
8.	Alleppey	8, 18
9.	Quilon	2, 4, 6, 7, 18, 19
10.	Trivandrum	2, 10, 23
11.	Idukki	18
12.	Mannuthy	26

KARNATAKA

1.	Bangalore	4, 7, 10, 12, 15, 17, 18, 23, 24, 26
2.	Tumkur	1, 2, 4, 6, 10, 11, 12, 15, 18, 19, 23, 27
3.	Chitradurga	1, 5, 12, 15, 18
4.	Kolar	1, 4, 5, 18
5.	Bellang	1, 2, 3, 12, 13, 17, 18
6.	Mysore	3, 4, 5, 7, 11, 15, 18
7.	South Kanara	18
8.	Coorg	4, 7, 10, 18, 23, 24, 25
9.	Hassan	2, 4, 15, 18
10.	Shimoga	2, 10, 15, 18, 23
11.	Chikmagalur	1, 18
12.	Mawdha	4, 5, 7, 15, 18
13.	Belgaum	1, 3, 5, 10, 12, 18, 23
14.	Bijapur	1, 3, 5, 6, 12, 17, 18, 19
15.	North Kanara	2, 18
16.	Dharwar	1, 5, 6, 12, 13, 15, 18
17.	Gulbarga	1, 2, 11, 12, 18, 19
18.	Bidar	2, 5, 18
19.	Raichur	1, 3, 9, 10, 12, 13, 18, 23
20.	Karwar	12

MADHYA PRADESH

1.	Morena	2, 9, 11, 12, 16
2.	Bhind	3, 11, 12, 18
3.	Gwalior	10, 23
4.	Datia	2, 10
5.	Shivpuri	10, 16
6.	Guna	10
7.	Tikamgarh	2, 10
8.	Chhatarpur	2, 9
9.	Panna	2, 10
10.	Satna	2
11.	Rewa	17
12.	Shahdol	1, 2, 16
13.	Sidhi	1, 16
14.	Mandsaur	2, 9, 11, 12
15.	Ratlam	2, 4
16.	Ujjain	4, 8
17.	Jhabua	1, 5, 16
18.	Dhar	1, 4, 5, 9, 12, 16

19.	Indore	4, 10, 17, 23, 24, 25
20.	Dewas	4
21.	Khargone	1, 11, 12, 13, 16
22.	Khandwa(West Nimar)	12, 16
	(East Nimar)	16
23.	Shajapur	2, 10
24.	Rajgarh	2, 10
25.	Vidisha	3, 10
26.	Sehore	4, 10
27.	Raisen	4, 6, 11, 19
28.	Hoshangabad	3, 4, 9, 10, 11, 16, 23
29.	Betul	1, 5, 16, 18
30.	Sagar	2, 11, 12, 19
31.	Damoh	10
32.	Jabalpur	2, 7, 10, 11, 23, 29
33.	Narsimhapur	11
34.	Mandla	12, 16
35.	Chhindwara	2, 11, 12, 16
36.	Seoni	3, 16
37.	Balaghat	3, 9, 16, 18
38.	Surguja	2, 12, 16
39.	Bilaspur	2, 3, 6, 9, 11, 16
40.	Raigarh	12, 16
41.	Durg	2, 6, 7, 9, 16, 19
42.	Raipur	8, 10, 11, 16, 23
43.	Bastar	16, 18, 20, 27
44.	Rajanand Gaon	2, 16
45.	Barwani	18

MAHARASHTRA

1.	Greater Bombay	6, 18
2.	Thana	2, 4, 6, 7, 10, 16, 23, 24
3.	Kolaba	2, 10, 23
4.	Ratnagiri	2, 6, 12, 19
	Dapoli („)	26
5.	Nasik	1, 4, 5, 6, 7, 16
6.	Kihulia	2, 4, 16
7.	Jalgaon	3, 4, 10, 12, 23
8.	Ahmednagar	1, 3, 5, 16
	Rahuri („)	26
9.	Poona	1, 3, 4, 5, 11 16
10.	Satara	1, 2, 5, 12, 19
11.	Sangli	1, 5, 12, 15

12.	Sholapur	1, 5, 10, 12, 17, 23	7.	Dhenkankal	2, 12
13.	Kolhapur	2, 10, 15, 23	8.	Bandhkbendmas	2
14.	Aurangabad	10, 11, 12, 23	9.	Bolangir	2
15.	Parbhani	3, 6, 19, 26	10.	Kalahandi	1, 12
16.	Bhir	2	11.	Ganjam	2, 10, 11, 16, 20, 23
17.	Nanded	2, 3	12.	Puri	2, 4(M), 6, 12, 14, 15, 22, 27
18.	Osmanabad	2, 11, 12	13.	Koraput	7, 12, 16, 20
19.	Buldhana	2, 10, 12, 13, 23	14.	Phulbani	1, 12, 16, 20
20.	Akola	2, 10, 17, 23, 26	15.	Bargarh	12
21.	Amravati	3, 6, 10, 13, 16, 23	16.	Behrampur	12, 15
22.	Yeotmal	16	17.	Khurda	9, 12
23.	Wardha	27	18.	Attargarh	12
24.	Nagpur	11, 12	19.	Kendrapuda	12
25.	Bhandara	4, 12	20.	Jagpur	12
26.	Chandrapur	2, 10, 12, 13, 16, 23, 27	21.	Bhadrak	12
27.	Jayakwadi	2	22.	Beripoda	12
			23.	Angul	12
			24.	Bhubaneswar	10, 23, 24, 25, 26

MANIPUR
1. Manipur North — 2, 6, 7, 16, 19
2. Manipur West — 2, 6, 7, 16, 19, 21
3. Manipur South — 2, 6, 7, 16, 19
4. Manipur Central — 2, 6, 7, 16, 19
5. Manipur East — 2, 6, 7, 16, 19

MEGHALAYA
1. United Khasi & Jaintea hills — 2, 4, 6, 7, 10, 19, 23
2. Garo Hills — 2, 7, 19, 27

NAGALAND
1. Kohima — 2, 4(M), 7, 19
2. Mokokchung — 2, 7, 19
3. Tuensang — 2, 7, 19
4. Ghaspani — 10, 23, 24, 25

ORISSA
1. Sambalpur — 2, 3, 6, 8, 10, 12, 16, 23
2. Sundargarh — 16
3. Keonjhar — 2, 3, 7, 12, 16, 19, 20
4. Mayurbhanj — 12, 16, 17, 22
5. Balasore — 10, 12, 14, 16, 22, 23,
6. Cuttack — 2, 3, 4(M), 6, 11, 12, 14, 19

PUNJAB
1. Gurdaspur — 9, 10, 23
2. Amritsar — 2, 4, 5, 7, 10, 12, 23
3. Ferozepur — 2, 5, 9, 12, 13
4. Ludhiana — 4, 8, 10, 12, 19, 23, 26
5. Jullundur — 2, 4, 5, 6, 10, 19, 23
6. Kapurthala — 2, 19
7. Hoshiarpur — 2, 7, 10, 19, 23, 27
8. Ropar — 2, 19
9. Patiala — 4, 6, 7, 10, 12, 23
10. Sangrur — 2, 4, 5, 9, 12
11. Bhatinda — 10, 11, 12, 13, 23
12. Faridkot — 9, 12, 13

RAJASTHAN
1. Ganganagar — 3, 11, 12, 13
2. Bikaner — 1, 3, 5
3. Churu — 1, 5, 11, 13
4. Jhunjhunu — 1
5. Alwar — 2, 4, 5, 7, 11, 12
6. Bharatpur — 2, 4, 5, 7, 10, 11, 12, 23
7. Sawai Madhopur — 4, 12
8. Jaipur — 4, 11, 23

9. Sikar — 24,
10. Ajmer — 1, 2, 4, 5, 6, 12, 19
11. Tonk — 4
12. Jaisalmer — 1, 3, 5, 12
13. Jodhpur — 1, 5, 17
14. Nagaur — 1, 5, 11, 12
15. Pali — 1, 5, 12
16. Barmer — 1, 5
17. Jalore — 1, 5
18. Sirohi
19. Bhilwara — 2, 12, 19
20. Udaipur — 1, 2, 6, 10, 16, 17, 23, 26
21. Chittorgarh — 3, 16, 17
22. Dungarpur — 1, 5, 10, 16
23. Banswara — 1, 5, 16, 27
24. Bundi — 3
25. Kota — 3, 10, 11, 23
26. Jhalawar

TAMIL NADU
1. Madras
2. Chingleput — 2, 12
3. North Arcot — 2, 7, 10, 12 19, 23
4. South Arcot — 2, 6, 7, 10, 12, 23
5. Dharmpuri — 1, 12, 15, 27
6. Salem — 2, 4, 6, 12, 19
7. Coimbatore — 2, 3, 4, 10, 12, 13, 23, 26
8. Nilgiris — 2, 21
9. Madurai — 2, 3, 4, 6, 7, 10, 12, 23
10. Tiruchirapalli — 2, 3, 4
11. Thanjavur — 2, 3, 4, 8, 10, 11, 12
12. Ramanatha-puram — 1, 12
13. Thirunelveli — 2, 3, 10, 11, 12, 13, 22, 23
14. Kanyakumari — 2
15. Pudukottai — 2, 12
16. Tiruchi — 10, 12, 17, 23
17. Kovilpatti — 17
18. Thanjavur — 11, 23

UTTAR PRADESH
1. Uttarkashi — 12
2. Chamoli — 12
3. Tehri Garhwal — 12, 21, 27
4. Garhwal — 2
5. Pithoragarh — 12
6. Nainital — 10, 12, 23, "(Pantnagar) — 26
7. Bijnor — 12
8. Moradabad — 2, 6, 12
9. Badaun — 2, 7, 12
10. Rampur — 12
11. Bareilly — 2, 11, 12
12. Pilibhit — 2, 19
13. Shajahanpur — 2
14. Dehradun — 12
15. Sharanpur — 10, 12, 15, 23
16. Muzaffarnagar — 4
17. Meerut — 2, 4, 5, 11, 12
18. Almora — 12, 21
19. Bulandshahar — 12
20. Aligarh — 6
21. Mathura — 2, 6, 7, 19
22. Agra — 10, 11, 12, 17, 23
23. Etah — 3, 12
24. Manipuri — 2, 3
25. Farukkabad — 2, 3, 12
26. Etawah — 3, 10, 12, 23
27. Kanpur — 3, 4, 10, 12, 23, 26
28. Fatehpur — 2, 4, 12
29. Allahabad — 1, 2, 3, 5, 6, 11, 12
30. Jhansi — 11, 12
31. Jalaun — 1, 12
32. Hamirpur — 1, 5, 11, 12
33. Banda — 1, 12
34. Kheri — 2, 12
35. Sitapur — 2, 12, 14
36. Hardoi — 2, 12, 19
37. Unnao — 2
38. Lucknow — 3, 4, 6, 10, 11, 23
39. Rai Bareli — 2, 3, 4, 10, 12, 23
40. Behraich — 2, 14
41. Gonda — 2
42. Barabanki — 12

43. Faizabad   3, 10, 11, 23, 26,
44. Sultanpur   2, 3, 24
45. Pratapgarh   2, 3, 4, 7, 10, 23
46. Basti   2
47. Gorakhpur   2, 3, 6, 11, 12
48. Deoria   3, 12
49. Azamgarh   3, 10, 12, 23
50. Jaunpur   2, 3, 5
51. Ballia   2, 19
52. Ghazipur   2, 3, 10, 23
53. Varanasi   1, 2, 3, 5, 6, 11, 12
54. Mirzapur   1, 5, 6, 12, 17, 22, 27
55. Lalitpur   12, 17
56. Pauri Garwal   12, 21
57. Barabanki   3
58. Lakhimpur   3, 14

WEST BENGAL

1. Darjeeling   2, 4, 6, 7, 19
2. Jalpaiguri   2
3. Cooch Behar   2, 10, 14, 15, 23
4. West Kinajpur   2, 14
5. Malda   2, 7, 14
6. Murshidabad   2, 3, 4, 10, 11, 14, 23
7. Nadia   2, 4, 11, 19
   "(Mohanpur)   26
8. 24 Parganas   2, 10, 14, 23
9. Howrah   2, 3, 19
10. Hooghly   2, 3, 4, 7, 14
11. Burdwan   3, 8, 10, 14, 23
12. Bankura   1, 3, 6, 7, 10, 19, 23,
                    27
13. Midnapore   1, 3, 10, 23, 24

14. Purulia   1, 6, 10
15. Birhun   3, 10, 23

TRIPURA

1. West Tripura   2, 7, 10, 16, 19, 23
2. North Tripura   2, 7, 10, 16, 19
3. South Tripura   2, 7, 10, 16, 19

ARUNACHAL PRADESH

1. Kamenga   2, 7
2. Subanasiri   2, 7
3. Siang   2, 7, 10, 23
4. Lohit   2, 7
5. Tirap   2, 7

GOA, DAMAN & DIU

1. Goa   2, 4, 6, 7, 10, 19, 23
2. Daman   2, 4, 6, 7, 19
3. Diu   2, 4, 6, 7, 19

PONDICHERRY

1. Pondicherry   2, 4, 10, 19, 23, 24
2. Karikal   2, 19
3. Mahe   2, 19
4. Yanam   2, 19

DELHI

1. Delhi   4, 5, 6, 7, 19, 23

MIZORAM

1. Aizawal   4, 5, 6, 7, 24
2. Lunclei   4, 5, 6, 7
3. Chhimtui pau   4, 5, 6, 7

LIST OF RESEARCH INSTITUTES UNDER ICAR

A. Agriculture

1. Indian Agricultural Research Institute, New Delhi-110012.
2. Central Arid Zone Research Institute, Jodhpur (Rajasthan).
3. Cotton Technological Research Laboratory, Adenwala Road, Matunga, Bombay-400019.
4. Central Institute of Cotton Research, Taluka Seed Multiplication Farm, Panjre Parsai, Nagpur, Maharashtra.
5. Indian Grassland & Fodder Research Institute, Jhansi (U.P.).
6. Jute Agricultural Research Institute Nilganj, P.O. Barrackpore (W. B.).
7. Indian Institute of Horticultural Research, 255, Upper Palace Orchards, Bangalore-560006.
8. Jute Technological Research Laboratory, T-12, Regent Park, Calcutta-40 (W. B.).
9. Indian Lac Research Institute, P. O. Namkum, Ranchi (Bihar).
10. Central Plantation Crops Research Institute, Post Kudlu, Kasargod-4 (Kerala).
11. Central Potato Research Institute, Simla-1 (H.P.).
12. Central Rice Research Institute, Cuttack-253006.
13. Central Soil Salinity Research Institute, Karnal (Haryana)-132001

14. Indian Institute of Sugarcane Research, Rai Bareli Road, P. O. Dilkhusha Lucknow-226002 (U. P.)
15. Sugarcane Breeding Institute, Lawley Road, Coimbatore-641007 (Tamil Nadu).
16. Central Tobacco Research Institute, Rajahmundry-1 (A. P.).
17. Central Tuber Crops Research Institute, Sreekariyam, Trivandrum-895017 (Kerala).
18. Central Institute of Agricultural Engineering, Nabi Bagh, Bhopal (Madhya Pradesh).
19. Central Soil & Water Conservation Research & Training Institute, 218, Kaulagarh Road, Dehradun (U. P.).
20. Vivekananda Parvatiya Krishi Anusandhan Shala, Almora, (U. P.).
21. National Bureau of Soil Survey and Land Use Planning, Nagpur.
22. National Bureau of Plant Genetic Resources, IARI Campus, New Delhi.
23. Central Agricultural Research Institute for Andaman and Nicobar Group of Islands, Port Blair.
24. ICAR Research Complex for North-Eastern Region, Amrit Bhawan, Labha Shillong-4, Meghalaya.

B. Animal Sciences

25. Indian Veterinary Research Institute, Izatnagar (U.P.).

26. National Dairy Research Institute, Karnal (Haryana).

27. Central Inland Fisheries Research Institute, P.O. Barrackpore, Distt. 24 Parganas (West Bengal).

28. Central Marine Fisheries Research Institute, Gopala Prabhu Road, P. Box No. 1912, Cochin-682018, (Kerala).

29. Central Institute of Fisheries Education, Kakon Camp, Ja: Prakash Road, Bombay 400061.

30. Central Institute of Fisheries Technology, Willingdon Island, Cochin-682003 (Kerala).

31. Central Sheep & Wool Research Institute, Avikanagar, Malpura, (Rajasthan).

32. Central Avian Research Institute, IVRI Campus, Izatnagar (U.P.).

33. Central Goat Research Institute Makhdoom via Farah, Mathura (U.P.).

C. Statistics

34. Indian Agricultural Statistics Research Institute, Library Avenue, New Delhi 110012.

D. Management

35. National Academy of Agricultural Research Management, Rajendranagar, Hyderabad 500030.

LIST OF UNDERGRADUATE/POSTGRADUATE AGRICULTURAL COLLEGES/INSTITUTES IN INDIA (INCLUDING AGRICULTURAL UNIVERSITIES)

* 1. Assam Agricultural University, Jorhat (Assam).

* 2. Andhra Pradesh Agricultural University, Rajendranagar, Hyderabad, Agricultural College, Bapatla (Andhra Pradesh).

* 3. College of Agriculture, Rajendranagar (A.P.).

* 4. S.V. Agricultural College, Tirupati (A.P.).

* 5. Rajendra Agricultural University, Patna (Bihar), Agricultural College and Agricultural Research Institute, Sabour, P.O. Bhagalpur (Bihar).

* 6. Birsa Agricultural University, Agricultural College, Kanke, Ranchi (Bihar).

* 7. Tirhut College of Agriculture, P.O. Dholi, Distt. Muzaffarpur (Bihar).

* 8. Gujarat Agricultural University, B.A. College of Agriculture, Anand (Gujarat).

* 9. N.M. College of Agriculture, Navsari (Gujarat).

* 10. College of Agriculture, Junagadh (Gujarat).

* 11. Kerala Agricultural University, Mannuthy, Agricultural College, Vellayani, Trivandrum (Kerala).

* 12. Jawaharlal Nehru Krishi Viswa Vidyalaya, College of Agriculture, Jabalpur (M.P.).

* 13. College of Agriculture, Gwalior (M.P.).

* 14. R.A.K. Agricultural College, Sehore (M.P.).

* 15. College of Agriculture, Rewa (M.P.)

* 16. College of Agriculture, Indore, (M.P.).

* 17. College of Agriculture, Raipur (M.P.).

* 18. Tamil Nadu Agricultural University, College of Agriculture, Coimbatore, (T.N.).

* 19. Annamalai University, Annamalainagar (T.N.).

* 20. Agricultural College, P.O. Vouvalthottam, Distt. Madurai (T.N.).

* 21. Mahatma Phule Krishi Vidyapeeth, Rahuri, College of Agriculture, Poona (Maharashtra).

* 22. Punjab Rao Krishi Vidyapeeth, Akola (Maharashtra).

* 23. College of Agriculture, Dhulia (M.S.).

* 24. College of Agriculture, Kolhapur-4 (Maharashtra).

* 25. College of Agriculture, Nagpur (Maharashtra).

26. Sri Shivaji Agricultural College, Amaravati (Maharashtra).

* 27. Marathwada Agricultural University, College of Agriculture, Parbhani (Maharashtra).

28. Anand Niketan College of Agriculture Anandwan, Warora, Distt. Chanda (Maharashtra).

* 29. Konkan Krishi Vidyapeeth, College of Agriculture, Dapoli, Distt. Ratnagiri (Maharashtra).

30. University of Agricultural Science, Agricultural College, Hebbal, Bangalore (Karnataka).

* 31. College of Agriculture & Research Institute, Krishinagar, Dharwar.

* 32. Orissa University of Agriculture and Technology, College of Agriculture, Bhubaneswar-3 (Orissa).

* 33. Punjab Agricultural University, College of Agriculture, Ludhiana.

* 34. Khalsa College, Amritsar (Punjab).

* 35. College of Agriculture, Haryana Agricultural University, Hissar (Haryana).

36. College of Agriculture, Kaul, Karnal (Haryana).

* 37. Sukhadia University, Udaipur, College of Agriculture, Udaipur (Rajasthan).

* 38. S.K.N. College of Agriculture, Udaipur University, Jobner (Rajasthan).

39. Dayanand College, Ajmer, (Rajasthan).

40. G.V. College of Agriculture, Sangaria (Rajasthan).

41. Allahabad Agricultural University, Allahabad (U.P.)

* 42. C.S. Azad University of Agriculture and Technology, Kanpur (U.P.).

* 43. Banaras Hindu University, College of Agriculture, Varanasi (U.P.).

* 44. R.B.S. College, Agra (U.P.).

* 45. J.V. College, Baraut, Meerut (U.P.).

* 46. Amar Singh Jat College, Lakhaoti, Bulandshahar (U.P.).

47. Janta Agricultural Degree College, Ajitmal (Etawah) U.P.

* 48. R.M P.P.V. Degree College, Gurukul Narsan (Saharanpur) (Uttar Pradesh).

* 49. Shri Durgajee Degree College, Chandesar, Azamgarh (U.P.).

50. Ch. Chhotu Ram Degree College, Muzaffarnagar (U.P.)

51. Kissan Degree College, Simbhaoli (Meerut).

52. Gochar Agricultural College, Rampur, Manhyaran Distt. Saharanpur (U.P.).

* 53. G.B. Pant University of Agricultural Sciences and Technology, College of Agriculture, Pantnagar (U.P.).

54. Janta College, Bakewar (Etawah) (U.P.).

55. R.S.M. Degree College, Dhampur Bijnor (U.P.).

56. B.N.V. College, Rath, Hamirpur (U.P.).

* 57. Baba Raghawa Das Degree College, Deoria (U.P.).

* 58. Kulbhaskar Ashram Degree College, Allahabad (U.P.).

59. Tilak Dhari College, Jaunpur (U.P.).

60. Narain Degree College,
    Shikohabad (U.P.).

61. K.V. Degree College,
    Machhra (Meerut), U.P.

62. National Degree College,
    Barhal Ganj, Gorakhpur (U.P.).

* 63. Udai Pratap College, Varanasi
    (Uttar Pradesh).

64. Degree College,
    Ghazipur, Gorakhpur (U.P.).

* 65. Town Degree College,
    Ballia (U.P.).

66. R.K. Degree College,
    Shamli, Distt. Muzaffarnagar
    (U.P.).

67. Government Agricultural College,
    Sepore (J & K).

* 68. Himachal Pradesh Krishi Viswa
    Vidyalaya, College of Agriculture,
    Palampur (H.P.).

* 69. College of Agriculture,
    Solan (H.P.)

* 70. Bidhan Chandra Krishi Viswa
    Vidyalaya. Haringhatta,
    Nadia (W.B.).

71. Palli Siksha Sadan,
    Vishwa Bharati Santiniketan,
    Distt. Birbhum (West Bengal).

72. Narendra Dev University of Agri-
    culture and Technology,
    Faizabad (U.P.)

73. Sher-e-Kashmir Jammu and
    Khshmir University of Agricultural
    Sciences and Technology,
    Shalimar, Srinagar 190001 (J & K).

74. Indian Agricultural Research
    New Delhi.

75. College of Agriculture,
    University of Calcutta,
    Calcutta-19

76. Indian Veterinary Research Insti-
    tute, Izatnagar, (U.P.).

*College offering both undergraduate and postgraduate courses.

BIBLIOGRAPHY

BOOKS

Agricultural Production Team (Ford Foundation) (1959), *Report on India's Food Crisis and Steps to Meet it*, Ministry of Food and Agriculture and Community Development, New Delhi.

Allahabad Agricultural Research Institute (1956), *Experiment in Extension—The Gaon Sathi*, Oxford Press, London.

Allport, G.W. (1937), *Personality: A Psychological Interpretation*, Henry Halt and Co., New York.

Bacon, E.I. (1959), *Extension for Extension Workers*, Government Press, Trivandrum.

Batton, T.R. (1962), *Training for Community Development*, Oxford University Press, London.

Beal, G.M. and J.B. Bohlen (1955), *How Farm People Accept New Ideas*, Iowa.

Berfard (1958), *Rural Sociology*, McGraw-Hill Company, New York.

Bernhardt (1953), *Practical Psychology*, McGraw-Hill and Co., Inc., New York.

Berlo, David K. (1960), *The Process of Communication*, Holt Rinehart and Winston Inc., New York.

Berlo, David K. (1960). *An Introduction to Theory and Practice—The Goal of Interpersonal Communication*, Holt Rinehart and Winston Inc., New York.

Bhatnagar O.P. (1974) "Constraints to the Differential Acceptance of the Components of New Agricultural Technology", in *Transfer of Technology: Systems and Constraints*, U.P. Society of Extension Education, Kanpur.

Biddle, W.W. (1953), *Cultivation of Cammunity Leadership*, Harper, New York.

Boon, E.J. and C.M. Ferquson, *Changing Dimension in Agriculture and Home Economics: Impact on Cooperative Extension Administration*.

Broom, L. and P. Selznik (1955), *Sociology*, Row Peterson and Co., New York.

Bryson, L. (1957), *Communication of Ideas*, Harper, New York.

Clark Robert, C. (1959), *Administration in Extension*, University of Wisconsin, New York.

Clark Robert, C. (1965), "Extension Education as a Profession", *Ind. Jour. of Ext. Edn.*, New Delhi.

Cooley, C.H. (1966), *Social Organization*, Gleorco, Free Press, Illinois, U.S.A.

Dahama, O.P. (1973), *Extension and Rural Welfare*, Ram Prasad and Sons., Agra.

Dale Edger (1964), *Audio-Visual Methods in Teaching*, Holt Rinehart and Winston, New York.

Desai, A.R. (1973), *Rural Sociology*, Indian Society of Agricultural Economics, Bombay.

Devdas, R.D. (1958), *Teaching Home Science*, All India Council for Adult Education, New Delhi.

Devdas, R.D. (1958), *Meaning of Home Science*, Home Science College, Coimbatore.

Devdas, R.D. (1958), *Text Book of Home Science*, ICAR, New Delhi.

Dewey, John (1961), *Democracy and Education*, The Macmillan Co., New Delhi.

Dey, S.K. (1959) *Extension Work in U.S.A. and Japan*, Ministry of Community Development and Cooperation, New Delhi.

Dey, S.K. (1959), *Problem of Problems*, Ministry of Community Development and Cooperation, New Delhi.

Directorate of Extension (1961), *Extension Education in Community Development*, Ministry of Food and Agriculture, Government of India, New Delhi.

Donald et al., (1964), *A New Psychology for Leadership*, McGraw-Hill Book Company New York.

Dubey, S.C. (1953), *India's Changing Villages*, Routledge and Kegan Paul, London.

Dubey, S.C. (1967), "Communication, Innovation and Planned Change in India" in D. Lerner and Wilbur Schranm (Eds) *Communication and Change in Developing Countries*, East-West Centre Press, Honolulu.

oright, D.F. (1955), *Audio-Visual Handbook for India*, Audio-Visual Aid Council, National Christian Council of India, Decan Press, Madras.

Edger, J. Boone, *A Research Approach to Programme Development in Cooperative Extension*.

Edwards, A.L. (1957), *Methods of Attitudes Scale Construction*, Appleton Century Crofts Inc., New York.

Ensminger, D. (1957), *A Guide to Community Development*, Ministry of Community Development and Cooperation, Government of India.

Food and Agriculture Organization (1976), *Training for Agriculture and Rural Development*, F.A.O., United Nations, Rome.

Ghurye, G.S. (1956), *Caste and Class in India*, Popular Book Depot, Bombay.

Gillin and Gillin, *Cultural Sociology*.

Gordon Thomas (1955), *Group Centered Leadership*, Houghton Miffin Boston, U.S.A.

Government of India (1961), *Extension Education in Community Development*, Directorate of Extension, New Delhi,

Government of India (1964), *The Planning Process*, Planning Commission, New Delhi.

Government of India (1955), *Kurukshetra*, Ministry of Community Development and Cooperation, New Delhi.

Government of India (1976), *Fifth Five Year Plan*, Planning Commission, Yojana Bhavan, New Delhi.

Guilford, J.P. (1965), *General Psychology*, Affiliated East-West Pvt. Ltd., New Delhi.

Guthrie E.R. and F.F. Powers (1950), *Educational Psychology*, The Ronald Press Co., New York.

Honigman, J. J. (1954), *Culture and Personality*, Harper and Brothers, New York.

Haas, Kenneth, B. and H.Q. Packer, *Preparation and Use of Audio-Visual Aids*, Prentice Hall of India (Pvt.) Ltd., New Delhi.

Indian Council of Agricultural Research (1960), *Report of the Second Joint Indo-American Team on Agricultural Education: Research and Extension*, ICAR, New Delhi.

Kelsey, L.D. and C.D. Hearne, (1963), *Cooperative Extension Work*, Cornell University Press, New York.

Kinder, J.S. (1950), *Audio-Visual Materials and Techniques*, American Books, New York.

Knowles, M.S. (1951), *Informal Audult Education*, Associated Press, New York.

Krishnamachari, V.T. (1955), *Community Development in India*, Publication Division, Delhi.

Lady Irwin College (1972), *Studies of the Rural Community*, Lady Irwin College, New Delhi.

Laired, D.A. *Techniques of Building Personal Leadership*, McGraw-Hill Book Co., New York.

Leagans, J.P. (1961), *India's Experience with Training in Extension Education for Community Development*, Cornell University, Ithaca, New York.

Lindstorm, D.E. (1963), *Rural Social Change*, University of Illinois, U.S.A.

Lionberger, H. (1960), *Adoption of New Ideas and Practices*, Iowa.

Lippit, R.J. Watson & B. Westley (1958), *The Dynamics of Planned Change*, New York.

Loomis, Chals P. & Beegle J. Allen (1950), "Rural Social System", *A Text Book in Rural Sociology*, Prentice Hall, New York.

Luther, Gulick (Edn.) (1937), *Papers on the Science of Administration*, Institute of Public Administration, New York.

Lynton P. Rolf and Udai Pareek (1967), *Training for Development*, Richard D. Irwin Inc. and Dorsey Press, Home Wood, Illinois.

MacIver. R.M. and C.H. Page (1949), *Society*, Rinehart and Co., New York.

Margaret Mead, *Cultural Patterns and Technical Change*.

Maslow, A.H. (1954), *Motivation and Personality*, Harper and Row, New York.

Mayer, A. et al., *Pilot Project: India*, University of California Press, New York.

Mamoria, C.B., *Social Problems and Social Disorganization*.

Marton, R.K., *Social Theory and Social Structure*, The Free Press Glencoe, Illinois, U.S.A.

Ministry of Community Development, *Woman's Role in Community Development*, Publication Division, New Delhi.

Ministry of Community Development, *Child Welfare and Community Development*, Publication Division, New Delhi.

Mosher, A.T. (1958), *Varieties of Extension Education*, Cornell University, Ithaca, New York, U.S.A.

Mukherjee, B. (1961), *Community Development in India*, Orient Longmans Pvt. Ltd., Calcutta.

Murray, G. Ross (1955), *Community Organization: Theory and Principles*, Harper, New York.

Nair, K. (1962), *Blossoms in the Dust*, Gerald Duck worth and Co., London.

Narayan, J.P., *Socialism, Sarvodaya and Democracy*, New Asia Publishing House, New Delhi.

Nelson, Ramsey and Verner (1960), *Community Structure and Change*, Macmillan & Co., London.

Ogburn, W.F. and Nimkoff (1960), *Handbook of Sociology*.

Ogburn, W.F., *On Cultural and Social Change—Selected Papers*

Penders, J.M.A. (1956), *Methods and Programme Planning in Rural Extension*, International Agricultural Study Centre, Wegeningen.

Pollard, L.B. (1939), *Adult Education for Home Making*, John Wiley, New York.

Pool, I.S. and W. Sharamone (1973), *Handbook of Communication*, Rand Mcnally College, Pub. Col. Chicago.

Pififfner, J.M. and E.P. Sherwood (1968), *Administrative Organization*, Prentice Hall of India Pvt. Ltd., New Delhi.

Publication Division (1979), *India: A Reference Manual*, Publication Division, Ministry of Information and Broadcasting, Government of India, New Delhi.

Ralf, M.S. *Individual Behaviour and Group Achievements*, Oxford University Press, New York.

Randhawa, M.S. (1979), *History of Indian Council of Agricultural Research*, ICAR, New Delhi.

Rogers Everett, M. (1960), *Social Change in Rural Society*, Appleton Century Crofts Inc., New York.

Rogers, Everett, M. (1971), *Communication of Innovations*, Collier-Macmillan (Ltd.), New York.

Rogers, E.M. and L. Svenning (1969), *Modernisation Among Peasants—I, The Impact of Communication*, Holt, Rinehart and Winston Inc., New York.

Roy, P. and F.C. Eliegel (1968), *Agricultural Innovations Among Indian Farmers*, NICD, Hyderabad.

Ruch, F., *Psychology and Life*, Scott Forsman and Co., Chicago, U.S.A.

Rudramoorthy, B. (1964), *Extension in Planned Social Change*, Allied Publishers, Pvt. Ltd., Bombay.

Sahay, B.N. (1969), *Dynamics of Leadership*, Bookhive Publishers, East Patel Nagar, New Delhi.

Senders, H.C. (Edn.) (1966), *The Cooperative Extension Service*, Prentice Hall, New Jersey.

Sandhu, A.S. (1972) *Communication Process and Media*, Punjab Agricultural University, Ludhiana.

Schramm, Wilbur (Edn.) (1955), *The Process and Effects of Mass Communication*, University of Illinois, U.S.A.

Sehramm, Wilbur (1973), *Men, Messages and Media: A Look at Human Communication*, Harper & Row, New York.

Sharma, M.P. (1976), *Public Administration in Theory and Practice*, Kitab Mahal, Allahabad.

Shukla, L.R. (1957), *Elements of Educational Psychology*, Nand Kishore Brothers, Varanasi.

Singh, K.N., C.S.S. Rao and B.N. Sahay (Eds.) (1970), *Research in Extension Education for Accelerating Development Process*, Indian Society of Extension Education, IARI, New Delhi.

Skinner, Charles, E. (Ed.) (1945), *Educational Psychology*, Prentice Hall Inc., New York.

Smith, Alfred, G. (1966), *Communication and Culture*, Holt Rinehart and Winston, New York.

Somasundram, T. (1967), *Audio-Visual Aids*, GTC Rajendranagar, Hyderabad.

Somasundram T. and W.L. Prawl (1968), *Audio-visuals: Their Role in Agriculture*, APAV, Hyderabad.

Spicer, E.H. (Ed.) (1952), *Human Problems in Technological Change*, Russel Sage Foundation, New York.

Srinivas, M.N. (1966), *Indian Villages*, Asia Publishing House, Bombay.

Taylor C. Carl (1956), *A Critical Analysis of India's Community Development Programme*.

Tead, (1935), *Art of Leadership*, McGraw-Hill Book Co., New York.

Terman, L.M. and C.C. Miles (1936), *Sex and Personality*, McGraw-Hill Book Co. Inc., New York.

Thayer, Lee (1968), *Communication and Communication System*, Homewood, Richard D. Irwin, Illinois.

Thayer Lee (Ed.) (1967), *Communication—Concepts and Prospectives*, Macmillan and Co., London.

UNESCO (1975), *Learning to be The World of Education Today and Tomorrow*, UNESCO Place D. Fontenoy, Paris.

UNESCO (1977), *Communication and Rural Development*, by Juan E. Diaz Bordenave UNESCO 7 Place D. Fontenoy, Paris.

U.S. Department of Agriculture, *Evaluation in Extension*, Federal Extension Service, Division of Extension Service Research & Training, U.S.A., Washington D.C.

Wilson, M.C. and G. Gallup (1958), *Extension Teaching Methods*, Federal Extension Service, U.S.D.A., Washington D.C.

Willoughby, F.W., *Principles of Public Administration*.

Wilson Woodrow, *Study of Public Administration*.

Williams, H. Jr. (1956), *The Organization Man*, Simon and Schuster Inc., New York.

JOURNALS

Behavioural Sciences Centre, *Indian Behavioural Sciences Abstract*, B.Sc., 32 Subhash Marg, Delhi-6.

Indian Adult Education Association, *Indian Journal of Adult Education*, IAEA, 17-B Indraprastha Marg, New Delhi.

Indian Institute of Public Administration, *Indian Journal of Public Administration*, IIPA, New Delhi.

Indian Institute of Mass Communication, *Communicator*, IIMC, D-13, NDSE Part-II, New Delhi.

Indian Psychological Association, *Indian Journal of Psychology*.

Indian Society of Extension Education, *Indian Journal of Extension Education*, Division of Agricultural Extension, IARI, New Delhi.

National Institute of Community Development, *Behavioural Sciences and Community Development*, NICD, Hyderabad.

U.P. Society of Extension Education & Rural Development, *Journal of Rural Extension*, UNSEE & RD, Kanpur.

REPORTS

Report of Administrative Reforms Commission (1969), Ministry of Home Affairs, New Delhi.

Report of All India Seminar on Cooperative Education and Training (1957), All India Cooperative Union, New Delhi.

Report of the Committee on Panchayat Raj Institutions (1978), Ministry of Agriculture and Irrigation, Government of India, New Delhi.

Report of the Royal Commission on Agriculture (1931), Government of India.

AUTHOR INDEX

Babu, V.K., 228
Beal George, 225
Berlo, David, 332, 354, 366
Bernard, L.L., 208
Bhatnagar, O.P., 22, 80, 84
Binet Alfred, 125
Bogardus, E.S., 220
Bohlen Joe, 225
Brayne, F.L., 39
Brunner, E.D., 516
Brown, E.J., 86, 119, 121

Clark, R.C., 31

Dahama, O.P., 20, 22, 80
Deekens, A., 86
Desai, A.R., 208
Deutschmann, 359
Dey, S.K., 45
Dorothy D. Scott, 97
Dubey, S.C., 212, 259, 306, 393

Earl Moncur, 24
Elliot, G.M., 291, 296
Ensminger, D., 20, 22, 101, 212, 402, 593, 687
Foster, G.M., 204

Gandhi, M.K., 41, 45
Gardner John, 83
Gibbert, F. 207
Goel, R.B. 324
Gray, J.D. 86
Green J.W., 75, 526
Guilford, J.P., 33, 135
Gullick, L., 636, 639, 641
Gumesta, A.K. 325

Halayya, M., 33

Hall Milton, 684
Hamilton Sir Daniel, 40
Hatch Spencer, 40
Hearne, C.C., 21, 99, 489, 490, 495
Halsey, G.D., 673

Jalihal, K.A., 80, 496

Kelsey, L.D., 21, 489, 490, 495
Kroeber, A.L., 217, 222

Lawrence, J.R., 485
Leagans, J.P., 4, 19, 23, 197, 351, 348, 553, 554, 568, 567, 593
Lewis Jones, 19
Lundberg, G.A., 208
Lynton, R.P. 684, 688

Margret Read, 547
Mathews, 23
Mayer Albert, 42
McDougall, 129
Merril, 291, 296
Mildered Horton, 22
Milward, 641
Mishra, K.P., 80
Mosher, A.T., 43, 495, 522
Mounder, A.H., 86, 495
Mueller, A.D. 515
Mukerjee, B., 588
Murray, G.R., 549
Munn, Norman, 119, 121, 229

Narayan, J.P., 273-274, 592
Nelson, L., 230
Newman, 25, 36

Pareek, U., 672, 684, 688

Parwar, A.K., 303, 324
Pfiffner, J.M., 636
Prasad, C., 32, 370
Presthus, R.B., 636

Rafiq, Q.A., 326
Rambhai, B., 43
Rao, V.K.R.V. 624
Ray, 712
Read, Hadley, 400
Reddy, S.V., 148, 336
Roger, E.M., 357, 358
Rudramurthy, B., 22
Roy, P. 612

Sahaya, B.N., 336
Sehramm, W., 347, 355, 366, 369
Schulze, W., 641
Sen, B.R., 592
Sen, L.K., 612
Sharma, D.K., 260
Sharma, M.P., 641, 647, 649
Shearer, M.N., 86
Sherwood, B P., 636
Shoemaker, 357
Shukla, A.N., 19, 22, 684
Simon, 636
Singh, K.N., 31, 148
Singh, M.P., 102, 655
Singh, S.N., 227, 332

Singh, Y.P., 228
Sinha, P.R.R., 19
Smith, T. Lynn, 207, 212, 230, 232
Sohal, T.S., 19, 685
Sorokin, P.A., 230-231

Tagore, Rabindranath, 39, 82
Tawney, 31
Taylor, C., 100, 212, 497, 550, 551, 586, 592, 593
Terman, L.M., 125
Thayer, Lee, 353, 370, 372, 375
Tiwari, P.S., 303
Tiwari, S.K., 304
Thorndike, 119-120
Thurstone, 121

Venugopal, K.A., 515

Watson, J.B., 197
Webster, 31
Wechsler, D., 119
White, L.D., 636
Wilkening, E.A., 317

Yadav, J.P., 336, 377
Yang, H.P.E., 512

Zimmerman, C., 230-231

SUBJECT INDEX

Agricultural Extension, 6, 96
Attention, 185

Basic wishes, 173-174, 198
Behaviour, 4
   Component, 3
Bhoodan, 273

Campaigns, 466
Club, 60-62
Communication
   General, 204, 293, 325, 343, 347, 613, 653
   Definition, 347
   Process, 349
   Elements, 349, 565
   Models, 350-352
   Function, 353
   Channels, 357-361, 563, 565
   Feedback, 364
   Credibility, 364
   Planning, 379
   Problems, 389, 564
   Aproaches, 398
   Media, 598
Competition, 293
Conferences, 463
Conflict, 293
Consensus, 296
Culture, 216-222
Cultural factors, 595

Demonstration, 406-412
Disorganisation
   Family, 291
   Social, 295
   Individual, 297
   Community, 300
Development, 546
Drama, 456

DRDA, 625

Education
   Definition, 3, 5
   Need, 4
   Types, 5-6
   Non-formal, 7-18
   Formal, 27
   Aims, 189
   General, 284, 304, 343, 402
   Technical, 286
   Rural, 286
Exhibitions, 426
Extension Education
   Concepts, 6, 19, 28
   Definition, 21, 560
   Philosophy, 21
   Principles, 23
   Discipline, 27-30, 33
   Aims, 30
   Profession, 31
   Relationships, 33
   History, 38-79
   Role, 95, 102
   Aspects, 96-99
   Objectives, 99, 593
   Characteristics, 102
   Process, 594
   Form, 594
   Home Science, 6, 97-99
Extension Worker
   Role, 81, 88, 603
   Qualities, 90
   Communicator, 92
   Training, 665

Festivals, 260-262
Flash cards, 423
Flip chart, 422

Functional literacy, 15

Gramdan, 274
Group, 327-331, 400, 518, 597
Group dynamics, 168, 188, 190, 331

INSAT, 484
ISAC, 483
ISRO, 483

Krishi Vigyan Kendra 695

Leadership
  Principle, 188
  Effective, 189
  Characteristics, 193
  General, 331-338
  Development, 580, 615
  Training, 580
Learning
  By doing, 25, 101
  Definition, 150
  Objectives, 3, 5
  Processes, 9
  Experience, 150, 161, 505
  Laws, 151
  Principles, 151
  Theories, 163
  Factors affecting, 163, 172
  Types, 165
  Transfer, 167
  Problems, 204

Marriage, 262-266
Meetings, 461
Morale, 664

National Agri. Res. Project, 629
National Agri. Ext. Project, 630
National Service Scheme, 700
Need, 558, 559, 561

Perception, 185, 204
Personality, 193
Planned change, 310, 214

Planning Commission, 531
Problem solving, 169
Projection, 427
Puppets, 455

Radio, 451, 481
Ratings, 662, 670
Recording, 443
Role, 292
Rural Art, 266-270
Rural Psychology, 193
Rural Sociology, 107

Satellite, 483
  ISRO, 483
  Aryabhata, 483
  Bhaskara, 483
  Rohini, 483
  SITE, 484
  STEP, 485
  INSAT, 845
Satus, 292
Subject-matter Specialists
  Role, 84-85
  Training needs, 85
  Problems, 86-88

Talks, 457
Teacher
  Definition, 161
  Role, 80-81
  Attributes, 82
  Profile, 162
Teaching
  Definition, 151
  Types, 153
  Principles, 158
  Plan, 160
Teaching objectives, 705
Thinking, 187
Tours, 465
Training & visit, 709

Value system, 598